Hood's Texas Brigade
in the Civil War

Hood's Texas Brigade in the Civil War

Edward B. Williams

McFarland & Company, Inc., Publishers
Jefferson, North Carolina, and London

Frontispiece: Gen. John Bell Hood, C.S.A.,
Third Texas Brigade Commander (Library of Congress)

All maps are provided by Colonel Harold B. Simpson; permission for use was granted
by Texian Press, Waco, Texas. All photographs are from Historical Research Center, Texas
Heritage Museum, Hill College, Hillsboro, Texas, unless otherwise noted.

LIBRARY OF CONGRESS CATALOGUING-IN-PUBLICATION DATA

Williams, Edward B.
Hood's Texas Brigade in the Civil War / Edward B. Williams.
p.   cm.
Includes bibliographical references and index.

ISBN 978-0-7864-6860-7
softcover : acid free paper ∞

1. Confederate States of America. Army. Texas Brigade.
2. Texas — History — Civil War, 1861–1865 — Regimental histories.
3. United States — History — Civil War, 1861–1865 — Regimental histories.
4. United States — History — Civil War, 1861–1865 — Campaigns.
5. Hood, John Bell, 1831–1879.   I. Title.
E580.4.T4W55 2012   973.7'464 — dc23   2012022822

BRITISH LIBRARY CATALOGUING DATA ARE AVAILABLE

On the cover: *inset* General John B. Hood (Library of Congress);
monument to Hood's Texas Brigade on Capital Grounds, Austin,
erected March 1910 (Texas Collection, Baylor University, Waco);
background 2012 Shutterstock

Manufactured in the United States of America

*McFarland & Company, Inc., Publishers
Box 611, Jefferson, North Carolina 28640
www.mcfarlandpub.com*

Respectfully dedicated to the memory of
the members of Hood's Texas Brigade who served honorably
and suffered greatly in its ranks, 1861–1865,
and to all American combat soldiers of this nation's wars
who have endured the unimaginable hardships of campaigning in the field
and witnessed the unspeakable horrors of a field of battle.

"I rely upon those we have in all tight places, and fear I have to call upon them too often … with a few more such regiments as Hood now has, as an example of daring and bravery, I could feel much more confident of the campaign."
— Gen. Robert E. Lee in a letter to Confederate senator
Louis T. Wigfall requesting more Texas regiments, 1862

Table of Contents

Acknowledgments

I research and write as an independent scholar. Before embarking on this scholarly voyage, I sought the opinions of several individuals that I knew would be sufficiently interested in the topic to help me in deciding whether to cast off or remain moored safely dockside.

One was a former president of the Texas State Historical Association and, at that time, a member and chair of the history faculty of Southwest Texas State University, since redesignated Texas State University. Dr. James Pohl expressed the thought that it was time, probably, for a reprise. He doubted, however, that I would find anything new to add to the brigade's history. In the latter he was incorrect, depending upon what he meant precisely by new. I did find considerable material not included in Col. Harold Simpson's bibliography, it being the most recent on the subject. This was not due to a lack of diligence on the colonel's part; some of it was in private hands at the time of his extensive research, and some was not yet published. While some of the new material could be classified as more of the same, there was some that did add to the history. My appreciation for Dr. Pohl's having taken the time to respond and give encouragement.

Also queried was Dr. B. D. Patterson, then director, Simpson Confederate Research Center, Hill College, Hillsboro, Texas. Dr. Patterson expressed excitement about such a work and thought it would be "an asset to Confederate literature." Dr. Patterson has since retired and to him I extend my thanks for his kind comments and encouragement.

Dr. Grady McWhiney, now deceased, was Lyndon B. Johnson Professor of American History, Texas Christian University, Fort Worth, Texas. Dr. McWhiney was one of the nation's leading Civil War scholars. I had the opportunity on one occasion to meet Dr. McWhiney when I was among a throng of attendees and he was a guest speaker at the annual Civil War symposiums sponsored by Hill College, Hillsboro, Texas, in years past. Later, Dr. McWhiney's reply to a query letter was, "Your proposal to write a new history of Hood's Texas Brigade seems most worthwhile, especially since none has been written since Colonel Harold Simpson's study some twenty-five or more years ago." That observation has now been stretched to some forty years. My thanks for Dr. McWhiney's supportive remarks and my regrets that he is not alive to see the task completed.

Until one sits down to acknowledge the contributions of those individuals and entities helpful, if not absolutely essential, in accomplishing the research, writing, and eventual publication of a work such as this, one has no real idea of the extent and complexity of the processes that have been involved. Thus, the following:

First and foremost, my thanks to my wife and best friend of forty-eight years, Judith

Ann Fisher Williams, a seasoned veteran of twenty-nine years in the "education wars," for her support and companionship on our research trips that took us far afield from our Texas home. I savor the memories of it all. Thanks to her, also, for taking on the otherwise thankless task of indexing.

My thanks to Dr. Lynda Crist, editor-in-chief of the Jefferson Davis Papers project at Rice University, Houston, Texas. Dr. Crist, with whom I became acquainted as a member of the Houston Civil War Roundtable, was most generous in allowing me access to any pertinent materials included in the Davis project's considerable collection.

My thanks to the Texas Heritage Museum located at Hill Junior College, Hillsboro, Texas. That institution is the evolutionary successor of Col. Simpson's Confederate Research Center. Special thanks to Ms. Anita Tufts, archivist and librarian at the Historical Research Center, located within the museum. Ms. Tufts was instrumental in making the reproduction and acquisition of the photographs and maps that appear in this book possible, and she was very pleasant and helpful in the process.

Thanks to Dr. Earl Elam, Historian and Editor of the Hill Junior College Press located at the Texas Heritage Museum, for taking some time talking with me regarding some copyright issues.

My thanks to Laura Cole of Davis Brothers Printing Company, Waco, Texas, for her help in gaining permission for the use of some quotations and maps contained in Col. Simpson's *Hood's Texas Brigade: Lee's Grenadier Guard*. Davis Brothers Printing Company is the parent company of the Texian Press, copyright holder of that now out-of-print work.

My thanks to Amie Oliver, Tiff Sowell, and Geoff Hunt, archivists at the Texas Collection, located in the Carroll Library, Baylor University, Waco, Texas. Their collective help in examining the Frank Chilton Collection, materials relating largely to brigade reunions following the Civil War, housed there is very much appreciated. Thanks, also, to Kathy Hinton, administrative coordinator of the Texas Collection.

The eminent Civil War historian Emory Thomas noted in the preface to his 1995 biography of Robert E. Lee that in his first meeting with his graduate mentor, Frank E. Vandiver, Douglas S. Freeman was elevated to the status of god in his world as an aspiring Civil War historian. Let me here declare Freeman to be my intellectual god as well in writing this narrative of a unit of the Army of Northern Virginia. His four volume biography of Robert E. Lee and his three volume study in the command of the Army of Northern Virginia, *Lee's Lieutenants*, were invaluable references in establishing the historical thread of this history. My thanks to and admiration for that long-departed but forever eloquent historian.

Others from whom reference was sought and to whom acknowledgment is due include those soldiers, of both high and lowly rank, that wrote full-fledged memoirs of their military experiences during that great conflict. Some were members of Hood's Texas Brigade while others were not but, nonetheless, were vitally involved in one way or another when telling the brigade's story. Reference to the bibliography will provide the citation of their works. They include, Walter H. Taylor, James Longstreet, G. Moxley Sorrell, Edward Porter Alexander, John Bell Hood, Mrs. Clinton Winkler, Joseph B. Polley, William A. Fletcher, Val C. Giles, John Stevens, D. U. Barziza, John C. West, M. V. Smith, Nicholas Pomoroy, George T. Todd, D. H. Hamilton, O. T. Hanks and William D. Pritchard, to acknowledge the most prominent. And to the letter-writers and diary-keepers whose materials were always interesting but not always pertinent, acknowledgment is tendered.

The starting point for my research was the Confederate Research Center, Hill College,

Hillsboro, Texas. Established by the late Col. Harold Simpson, it contained, among many other things, many of the research materials he gathered while writing his four volume brigade history. I spent several weeks there and my thanks to Mrs. Peggy Fox, now long-retired, for her help in identifying and obtaining materials that I was to later put to use. I might add here acknowledgment of Col. Simpson's works. Although I avoided his brigade history, by and large, for fear of mere duplication of effort, I used extensively his *Compendium* when seeking information on individual soldiers that served in the brigade.

There were a number of repositories that yielded up new materials not listed in Col. Simpson's bibliographies. They include the Garnett Andrews Papers, Southern Historical Collection, University of North Carolina, Chapel Hill; B. M Aycock's *A Sketch—The Lone Star Guards*, Fredericksburg National Battlefield Park, Fredericksburg, Virginia; the Robert L. Brake Collection, U. S. Army Military History Institute, Carlisle Barracks, Pennsylvania; the Cobb-Hunter Family Papers, Southern Historical Collection, University of North Carolina, Chapel Hill, North Carolina; the A. A. Congleton letters, Antietam National Battlefield Park, Sharpsburg, Maryland; the Robert G. Holloway diary, Museum of the Confederacy, Richmond, Virginia; the Howard Family Papers, Southern Historical Collection, University of North Carolina, Chapel Hill, North Carolina; the Moses Warren Kenyon Papers, Perkins Library, Duke University, Durham, North Carolina; and the W. S. Shockley Papers, Perkins Library, Duke University, Durham, North Carolina. In 1996, Judith N. McArthur and Orville V. Barton's edited work, *A Gentleman and an Officer: A Military and Social History of James B. Griffin's Civil War*, was published by Oxford University Press. It added some interesting additional information about the brigade while Hampton's Legion was a member of the organization. John M. Priest's 1994 edited work, *Stephen Elliott Welch of the Hampton Legion*, was published by the Burd Street Press and also provided information about that unit while part of the brigade.

I would like to single out the Antietam National Battlefield Park for particular thanks. It was from their archives that were obtained some new materials that, in my opinion, add considerably to the purpose of this book. In particular, the typescript of W. D. H. Pritchard's Co. I, 1st Texas, series of newspaper articles based on an unpublished manuscript strikes to the core purpose of this book. In his introduction to the newspaper articles, Pritchard states that most of the articles to follow would be from the perspective of "the war as seen and felt from the 'Ranks.'" Continuing, he noted that "to the average reader there is much of interest in the every-day life of the camp, in the lonely vigils of the picket and the bitter reflections of such life, the tiresome march with its fatigues and provocations and even the horrors of the battlefield." Pritchard was wounded first at Sharpsburg and then later at Spotsylvania Court House on May 12, 1864. Alas, the latter injury resulted in his being retired for disability, nothing further being heard from him on the subject beyond that point in his postwar manuscript-cum-newspaper series. According to a cover letter accompanying the material, a typescript was provided to that archive by Pritchard's granddaughter, Mrs. Janice M. Hassig, in 1983. My thanks to her for pursuing the matter.

Other places visited or corresponded with and to the staffs of which I would like to extend acknowledgment include the Center for American History, University of Texas, Austin, Texas; the Fondren Library, Rice University, Houston, Texas; the Southern Historical Collection, University of North Carolina, Chapel Hill, North Carolina; the South Caroliniana Library, University of South Carolina, Columbia, South Carolina; the Perkins Library, Duke University, Durham, North Carolina; the Huntington Library, San Marino, California; the Library of Congress and the National Archives, Washington, D. C.; the U.

S. Army Military History Institute, Carlisle, Pennsylvania; the Museum of the Confederacy, Richmond, Virginia; the battlefield archives held at Sharpsburg, Maryland; Fredericksburg, Virginia; Gettysburg, Pennsylvania; and Chickamauga, Georgia. The unvarying courtesy and helpfulness of the staffs of those respective institutions has come to be expected routinely. My sincere thanks to them all.

Preface

The wisdom of the ages advises that war is an omnipresence and a very bad business to be engaged in. Plato predicted that only the dead have seen the end of it. William T. Sherman defined it as hell. Given the panorama of violence presented over the course of human history, they were prescient in their prediction and description.

Only those who have experienced combat and have endured the realities of life in the field will ever fully understand the dubious distinction of having had those experiences. William D. H. Pritchard, formerly of Co. I, 1st Texas, in a series of newspaper articles written some thirty-five years after the war, wanted to "enter into details" of soldier-life where "history had not had time to do so." Pritchard wanted to tell of some of the "cold, hard facts" about the everyday life of the private soldier, "the sickening horrors of the soldier as he stumbles over his first dead man in the maddening rush to the front.... The fevered excitement incident to the order to 'Forward'; ...How wildly the heart beats, how the hot blood courses madly through the veins, ... how the heart yearns for the comforts of home and a mother's love or ... the conflicting emotions of hope and fear 'that harrow up the very soul.' Nor indeed can they explain that heroic courage, that patriotic devotion that prompt men to throw themselves into the breach and die for their country's honor.... All this must be had from those who have felt them."[1] It may be concluded that war is inevitable, it is hellish and full understanding thereof requires personal experience.

In the American experience of war extending all the way back to the 1700s, none was more inevitable, hellish and incommunicably horrible than the internecine war of 1861–1865. Called variously the American Civil War, the War Between the States, the War for Southern Independence and the War of the Rebellion, it still holds the record for the most war-related deaths in our national history. Recent research indicates that the total number of deaths suffered during the Civil War more closely approximates 750,000, some 130,000 more than the previously accepted figure of 620,000.[2] As Sherman had predicted beforehand, disease claimed the largest proportion of the staggering number.

It still holds the record for the single bloodiest day in our entire military history, approximately 23,000 casualties suffered collectively on September 17, 1862, at Sharpsburg, Maryland. On that day, in Miller's Cornfield, the 1st Texas Infantry Regiment, Hood's Texas Brigade, suffered the highest casualty rate of any regiment during the course of the war, Gray or Blue. Like Sharpsburg, all the big engagements of that war were, quite literally, slaughter pens, with staggering casualty figures resulting.

In the earliest phases of the war, before the lengthy casualty lists began to appear in the newspapers regularly, there was a rush to the colors by patriotic innocents seeking glory and adventure. And, as always, but too late, they were very soon disabused of any such illusions. They came to learn that such foolish notions are entertained only by the uninitiated. By and large, most veterans with actual field and combat experience, then as now, did not want to remember or to discuss that "incommunicable experience" of their earlier life until, much later, as nostalgia took over. J. M. Polk who served in Co. I, 4th Texas, in a frankly-told post-war memoir, observed, ruefully, in recounting the slaughter at Sharpsburg (Antietam) that he "could not help but think how different [that] was from the way it was pictured out to us in war speeches at the commencement."[3]

Hood's Texas Brigade was present in most of the big battles fought in the East and several in the West where they were serving on detached duty in the fall of 1863 and winter of 1864 — the Seven Days, Second Manassas (Second Bull Run), Sharpsburg (Antietam), Fredericksburg, Gettysburg, Chickamauga, Chattanooga, Knoxville, the Wilderness, Spotsylvania Court House, Cold Harbor, the siege of Richmond and Petersburg, Appomattox — with the exceptions of First Manassas (First Bull Run) and Chancellorsville. In the case of the former, only a few Texas companies had arrived in Virginia at that time and were not present and engaged. In the latter, the brigade, along with other units of Longstreet's Corps, were on detached duty in the vicinity of Suffolk, Virginia, south of Richmond.

They were engaged in a war with a nation that had been in business for a considerable period of time. It was an experienced political entity vastly superior in every way, militarily and logistically — more men, better equipment, endless supplies and transportation — to support them from both domestic and foreign sources. The "Lost Cause" was just that pretty much from the beginning.

From their nineteenth century perspective and from the perspective of the society in which they lived, most believed, initially, that they were fighting under the banner of state rights, for the independence of their nation, just as their ancestors had done in the revolutionary eighteenth century. As the war progressed, one encounters often the soldier's comment that it was "a rich man's war and a poor's man's fight." Although it took time and experience, they were not without the perception about the true nature of the war they were fighting before it was all over.

There had been a great deal of opposition to secession — individual, political and economic — throughout the South up to the time when President Lincoln called for 75,000 volunteers to suppress the developing rebellion. Though many still viewed secession as unwise and continued to think so while marching, literally and figuratively, in the Confederate ranks, that one act by President Lincoln served to unite the South for the purpose of opposing the invasion of Southern soil. What followed is what the late, preeminent scholar and Virginian, Douglas Southall Freeman, referred to as that "mad, criminal war."

This story is arranged chronologically. The historical context is constructed from a broad range of recognized primary and secondary sources. The documentation was conducted in a scholarly and meticulous manner. The overall writing style is narrative and anecdotal. The emphasis is on the three Texas regiments that comprised three-fourths of the four regiment brigade. They were the only units to serve in the brigade throughout the course of the war. The 18th Georgia served from the fall of 1861 until the reorganization following the Maryland campaign in the fall of 1862. The infantry companies of Hampton's South Carolina Legion served for only a few months during the summer and fall of 1862. The 3rd Arkansas did not join the brigade's ranks until the fall of 1862. The main reason for the Texas emphasis is explicable; there is much more material in the form of letters, memoirs and books left behind by the Texans than by their brigade comrades representing Georgia, South Carolina and Arkansas. The story of their daring and bravery follows.

Introduction:
"An example of daring and bravery"

This is a chronicle of "daring and bravery," as exhibited by a brigade of volunteer Confederate infantry serving in General James Longstreet's Corps and General Robert E. Lee's Army of Northern Virginia during the American Civil War, 1861–1865. In an army that included many other infantry brigades, the Texas Brigade was considered a premier military unit, perhaps *the* premier unit in that remarkable army. The dean of Texas Brigade biographers, the late Colonel Harold B. Simpson, called them Lee's "Grenadier Guard." Theirs is a story of overwhelming difficulties surmounted in achieving military prominence.

During the course of the war there were eight men that commanded the brigade at one time or another. However, it was John Bell Hood's name with which the brigade was inextricably linked and that the men of the brigade revered most.[2] Hood was a Kentuckian by birth but a Texan by choice. An 1853 graduate of the United States Military Academy at West Point, New York, he was serving with the 2nd U.S. Cavalry Regiment on the Texas frontier when civil strife broke out in 1861. It was under Hood's aggressive command in the earlier phases of the war, particularly at Gaines Mill, Virginia, on June 27, 1862, that the brigade did some of its best fighting and under the most deadly of circumstances. The brigade prided itself on the fact that all of its men were volunteers. John Bell Hood understood volunteer troops better than most of his counterparts. The men responded well to Hood's leadership style and Hood's Texas Brigade it became and Hood's Texas Brigade it has remained.

Of the many military units furnished by the Lone Star State to the Confederate States of America, only three regiments, the 1st, 4th and 5th Texas Volunteer Infantry Regiments, served in Virginia with the Army of Northern Virginia. In the thirty-two infantry companies that ultimately comprised the three Texas infantry regiments, an estimated 4,000 men served during the course of the war.[3] The last company to be recruited, Company "M," 1st Texas, did not reach Virginia until August 1862.

In the inevitable confusion created by the flood of volunteer companies arriving in Richmond in the first months of the war, there was not sufficient time to give thought to organizational matters beyond getting the units to the front as quickly as possible. Military convention called for volunteer infantry brigades to be comprised of four regiments usually and preferably from the same state. However, in an atmosphere of undue haste, this convention was often disregarded. In the case of the Texas Brigade, during the first year of its service there were included within its ranks units representing states far removed from the state of Texas — the 18th Georgia Infantry and the eight infantry companies of Hampton's South Carolina Legion. When those units left the brigade in the aftermath of the Maryland campaign of 1862, they were replaced by the 3rd Arkansas Infantry Regiment.

"To narrate the exploits of Hood's Texas Brigade from 1862 until Appomattox would be to write the history of the campaigns of the Army of Northern Virginia."[4] The brigade participated in all of them save First Manassas and Chancellorsville, at which time in the latter case, it was on detached duty as a part of Gen. James Longstreet's Corps in southern Virginia and North Carolina. That absence was more than compensated for by the brigade's participation in the most fiercely contested battle of the war fought in the West, that at Chickamauga in northwest Georgia in September 1863. Beginning with their first real engagement at Eltham's Landing, Virginia, on May 7, 1862, during the retreat from the Yorktown line at the beginning of the Peninsula campaign, theirs was to be a record written in terms of blood, valor and endurance.

In the years following the war, wounds, both physical and emotional, healed gradually. In an effort to keep the memory of the brigade, its service and sacrifices alive, "Hood's Texas Brigade Association was formed May 24, 1872, and had its first meeting at Hutchin's House, Houston, Texas."[5] Annual reunions were held from that year forward until 1933, excepting the war years, 1898 and 1918. "Altogether sixty regularly scheduled annual reunions were held.... Reunions took place in twenty-eight different Texas cities and towns. Bryan, the last home of Hood's Texas Brigade Association, hosted more reunions than any other Texas community.... The date selected for the annual affairs was June 27. This was the date of the brigade's first great victory of the war, the breakthrough of Fitz John Porter's line at Gaines Mill in 1862."[6]

At the 1907 reunion held at Navasota, Texas, a movement was begun to erect a monument to perpetuate the memory of the brigade. Within three years, funds had been raised and at the 1910 reunion, held in Austin, the monument was dedicated and unveiled. "The monument is forty-four feet high, thirty-five feet of which is the granite shaft and the other nine feet being the statue of a private soldier of the brigade in bronze.... Chiseled on the faces of the shaft are quotations from Confederate President Jefferson Davis, Gen. Robert E. Lee, Gen. Stephen D. Lee, Gen. Hood, Gen. Albert Sidney Johnston, Gen. Stonewall Jackson and others."[7] The monument is sited on the Texas State Capitol grounds.

A few years later, former Confederate Postmaster General Judge John H. Reagan addressed a letter to the association in which he stated: "I would rather have been able to say that I had been a worthy member of Hood's Texas Brigade than to have enjoyed all the honors which have been conferred upon me. I doubt if there has ever been a brigade, or other military organization in the history of the world, that equaled it in the heroic valor and self-sacrificing conduct of its members, and in the brilliancy of its services."[8]

> "We led the charge on many a field,
> Were first in many a fray
> And turned the bloody battle tide,
> On many a gloomy day."[9]

CHAPTER 1

"You have treated me most shamefully"[1]: Texas Leaves the Federal Union

Alighting from his ambulance in front of the Read House in San Antonio on the afternoon of February 16, 1861, the passenger was immediately surrounded by a group of rough-looking men wearing red insignias on their clothing. Glancing around, he saw Mrs. Caroline Darrow, the wife of a friend, hurrying across the square toward him.

"Who are these men?" he asked as she approached.

"They are McCulloch's," she answered. "General Twiggs surrendered everything to the state this morning and we are all prisoners of war."

His characteristic poise lost momentarily, tears brimmed in his eyes and his lips trembled. "Has it come so soon to this?" he said.[2]

The emotionally-stricken man was Lt. Col. Robert E. Lee of the 2nd U.S. Cavalry Regiment arriving from Fort Mason. He was in San Antonio under orders to report to General of the Army Winfield Scott in Washington, D.C. A 1829 graduate of the United States Military Academy, Lt. Col. Lee had thirty-two years of exemplary service behind him. His rank belied his achievements and ability. He had languished over the years upon a becalmed sea of promotion.

Lt. Col. Lee reached the nation's capital in a time of national crisis. In a charged atmosphere of impending disaster brought on by the escalating Southern secession movement, Lt. Col. Lee met with various governmental officials, all very interested in saving his services in the cause of the Union should civil war erupt. Gen. Scott, too old to take the field personally and with President Lincoln's approval, offered him command of the U.S. armies that would be raised to maintain the Union.

Ultimately, as had been feared, Lt. Col. Lee declined the appointment. In an agony of conscience and in deference to his native state's secession stand he withdrew from further consideration. This was not unexpected by Gen. Scott for he knew that, although opposed to secession, Lee was first of all a Virginian.

"Lee," said Gen. Scott, "you have made the worst mistake of your life."[3]

* * *

It was a crisis brought on by a complex of political and social issues and one that had been brewing for decades. Going back to the beginnings of the Republic, one major issue still unresolved, even after the chaotic experience under the Articles of Confederation in the 1780s, involved the question of superior political power, the Federal government or the state governments. Also unresolved, the issue of black, African slavery, recognized in the

Federal Constitution and practiced in the Southern agricultural states. The Northern, pre-dominantly industrial-type states, harbored vehement and active anti-slavery elements styling themselves Abolitionists. Their agitation was particularly bothersome to the Southern plan-tation-owning class, with fortunes tied to a slave labor-based economy. Politically, the spread of slavery to newly-forming western states and its effect upon the composition of the U.S. Congress would have shifted the balance of political power to the South. Passions flared and blood was shed in such diverse places as "Bleeding Kansas," where pro and anti-slavery elements clashed, and on the floor of the U.S. House of Representatives, where a Southern congressman caned a Northern counterpart into insensibility over a perceived insult relating to the issue.

The climax occurred when, in the presidential election of 1860, Abraham Lincoln of Illi-nois, the candidate of the relatively new anti-slavery, strong Federal government, Republican Party was elected sixteenth president of the United States. Less than two months later, South Carolina, a major slave-owning state and long in the forefront of the federal-state power issue, declared herself seceded from the Federal Union on December 20, 1860. Other Southern states soon followed suit and the genie was out of the bottle! The grim specter of disunion and civil war loomed on the horizon. It was widely thought that President Lincoln had no intention of standing idly by while the hard-won Federal Union slipped quietly into oblivion.

In rapid succession, other slave-owning Southern states called conventions to consider the question of whether to continue in or withdraw from the Union. Within a matter of a few months, eleven Southern states had left the Union and formed the Confederate States of America.

In Texas there was much excitement and anticipation abroad in the aftermath of Mr. Lincoln's election and the imminent secession of South Carolina. In early December 1860, it was rumored that "Captain John R. Baylor, well-known throughout the state, was organ-izing a company of one thousand men for a buffalo hunt. As Captain Baylor's secession sen-timents were well known, this was believed to be a mere pretense. [His real design was thought to be to] seize the [federal] arsenal in San Antonio, in time to prevent any resistance on the part of the United States, should Texas go out of the Union."[4]

At that time, San Antonio was the headquarters of the military Department of Texas and the main base of supply for U.S. troops stationed in the state. The U.S. troops in Texas were there to defend the western frontier, mainly against Indian depredations. The consid-erable military stores maintained in San Antonio as well as elsewhere in the state would be a valuable addition to the scanty arsenal of the then-forming Southern nation

In late January 1861, as events accelerated, an election was held to select delegates to a state convention that would consider the question of Texas' secession from the federal Union. The Secession Convention first met in Austin on January 28, with the session extending through February 4. In a flurry of activity, the convention drafted a declaration of causes for secession, repealed the 1845 Ordinance of Annexation to the United States, drafted a secession ordinance and appointed a Committee of Public of Safety to represent the con-vention during any periods of recess. On February 4, when the convention voted on the secession issue, the galleries were full.[5]

Oran M. Roberts was the presiding officer and, even though everyone knew that Gov-ernor Sam Houston opposed secession and highly disapproved of the proceedings, Roberts scrupulously observed protocol and invited the governor to attend. Roberts saw to it that Houston was seated in a place of honor. He could have done nothing less without gravely insulting the state's greatest man, for Houston was, after all, still governor and a hero in

Texas' struggle for independence from Mexico in the revolution of 1836. Houston was not happy with developments and throughout the proceedings "sat with his arms folded across his chest staring straight ahead, unmoved by the significance of the events unfolding before him."[6]

It was a tumultuous affair from beginning to end. During the proceedings, Thomas Jefferson Chambers, a political foe of Houston, arose to speak in support of secession and, taking the opportunity to deride the governor, loudly proclaimed him a traitor for his anti-secession stand. When James W. Throckmorton, a Collin County lawyer, arose to cast his vote against secession, he stated dramatically, "Mr. President, in view of the responsibility, in the presence of God and my country, and unawed by the wild spirit of revolution, I vote, 'No.' As he sat down, pandemonium broke loose in the halls of the Texas House. When order was restored, Throckmorton again rose from his seat and fired a final verbal volley at the secessionists. In a clear, steady voice, he said, "Mr. President, when the rabble hiss, well may patriots tremble."[7]

Throckmorton's bravado was to no avail, however, and the convention voted overwhelmingly for secession, 166 to 8. Following the voting, the meeting was thrown into an uproar as "a boisterous demonstration began and an impromptu procession formed and snaked its way down the aisles. Many of the demonstrators were female spectators from the galleries and lobby who joined the wild march through the House chamber. The spirit of celebration permeated the entire hall as Attorney General George M. Flournoy assumed the lead position carrying a huge Lone Star flag. Gradually the demonstration subsided, but an overwhelming sentiment favoring secession had been registered."[8] Well might the revelers have reconsidered their behavior that day when four years thence the South lay in devastation and ruin.

As a last act before adjourning, the convention decreed that a statewide referendum be held on February 23 in order to allow the citizens of Texas to participate in the process and record their vote for or against secession. The Committee of Public Safety created by the convention and chaired by a Tyler attorney, John C. Robertson, assumed authority during the period of the convention's recess. The committee appointed Ben McCulloch to command state forces around San Antonio, his brother, Henry McCulloch, commander of federal forts on the northwestern frontier expected soon to be surrendered by U.S. forces, and John S. "Rip" Ford commander at Brownsville on the Rio Grande.

In the meantime, delegates from the six already seceded states — South Carolina, Mississippi, Florida, Georgia, Louisiana and Alabama — began meetings in Montgomery, Alabama. On February 8, 1861, a constitution was adopted and the next day Jefferson Davis of Mississippi was chosen as the president of the Confederate States of America. In his inaugural address, delivered on February 18, President Davis alluded to the fact that the new government was "born of a peaceful appeal to the ballot box." However, as William C. Davis has noted, "[n]ot one of the states there represented had decided on secession by a popular referendum. Rather their withdrawal from the Union and their presence in Montgomery now had been decided by just 854 men in the several state secession conventions — 157 of whom had voted against secession — and all of them had been selected by their legislatures. Without the ballot box ever being used by the population at large, the destiny of [nine] million had been decided by 697."[9] Texas and four other states, not yet seceded, had no voice in the proceedings at all.

* * *

Militarily, Texas was designated as the Eighth Military District but was more commonly referred to as the Department of Texas. In 1861, the department was manned by a force amounting to about 15 percent of the total forces mustered by the regular U.S. Army. The units comprising this force were widely deployed among the forts and camps along the western frontier of Texas. The last troop return before the outbreak of hostilities showed that the "department had 165 officers ... and 2,558 enlisted men.... However, there were only eighty- seven officers and 2,097 enlisted men actually present at the time."[10]

Headquarters of the military Department of Texas was San Antonio, a city with a long history dating back to the Spanish empire in North America. If it was in any way similar to the present-day city, it was a city with a certain charm, a place where cultures met and melded. In 1861, it was where the most dramatic act of the Texas secession crisis was acted out. The village centered around Alamo Plaza where the architecture was "all Mexican," windowless cabins, mud-plastered, roofs of river grass. The main thoroughfare, Commerce Street, was lined by American-style houses. However, "[i]n the outskirts of the town [were] many good residences recently erected by Americans. They [were] mostly of the creamy limestone, which [was to be] found in abundance nearby."[11] It was in a suburb such as that that the Federal commander of the Department of Texas maintained his personal quarters.

Maj. Gen. David Emanual Twiggs, the departmental commander, was an old and sick man in 1860. He was a Southerner, a native of Richmond County, Georgia, born there in 1790. Gen. Twiggs was seventy years of age in 1860 and had served in the United States Army since the War of 1812, during which he had been directly commissioned. He had remained in the army and had served in the Seminole Wars and in campaigns against the Plains Indians. In the Mexican War he had served under both Zachary Taylor and Winfield Scott. In both instances, he had distinguished himself.

Gen. Twiggs was known throughout the army for his rough-and-ready nature. Gruff in appearance, he was both "disagreeable and unprepossessing." In the ranks, where such qualities are usually admired, he was known as "the Horse" and "the Bengal Tiger." He was a great favorite among the troops, "who admired him ... for his brusquerie and coarseness of manner, and a singular habit ... of swearing most vehemently and flying into a passion on the most trifling occasions."[12] In January 1861, he had only recently returned to active service from a leave of absence for health reasons. The leave was of a year's duration, a lengthy period and indicative of the seriousness of his health problems.

During Gen. Twiggs' leave of absence from his Texas command, his relief was Lt. Col. Robert E. Lee, 2nd U.S. Cavalry. As mentioned before, Lt. Col. Lee was a particular favorite of Gen Winfield Scott, his admiration justly earned in the campaign to Mexico City as an engineer officer on Scott's staff. Gen. Twiggs was well acquainted with Lt. Col. Lee and Lee with him. With regard to Lee's appointment in his stead, Gen. Twiggs exhibited a professional jealousy typical in all organizations generally and in military organizations particularly. He was once heard to comment that "General Scott fully believes that God Almighty had to spit on his hands to make Bob Lee."[13]

It was on December 13, 1860, that Gen. Twiggs resumed departmental command. Lt. Col. Lee returned to 2nd Cavalry headquarters at Fort Mason a few days later. On December 20, South Carolina seceded from the Union.

Gen. Twiggs did not have to be prescient to know what was coming. Being a Southerner by birth and outspoken about any action he might be forced into against secessionist elements, he came under a great deal of pressure and criticism before, during and after the Texas secession crisis. Other Southerners in the same military situation were likewise in agonies of indecision; they were subject to conflicting loyalties to the United States Army on the one hand and to their native states on the other.

Twiggs had even delayed reporting back to Texas after his medical leave expired hoping that the secession of the South would occur before he resumed command, thereby taking the matter out of his hands. However, since he was no longer officially ill, any further delay might have forced his retirement; there were no retirement pensions awarded in that day. Anxiously, he wrote to Gen. Scott, "saying that he expected Texas to secede with other Southern states and asking Scott's advice should this occur."[14] He also indicated that he would never order his troops to fire on American citizens and would have no choice but to go with the South should his native Georgia secede.

To all of this Gen. Scott offered no helpful advice, replying that Twiggs should use his own judgment. In the weeks ahead, Twiggs requested instructions repeatedly. He also requested to be relieved of the command. Finally, on January 28, the War Department issued orders for his relief by Col. Carlos A. Waite, 1st U.S. Infantry, then stationed at Camp Verde, Texas. There were delays and the orders were not carried out until February 19 by which time Gen. Twiggs' fate had already been sealed. Throughout, Gen. Twiggs did not receive from the government any timely reply to his entreaties nor did he know of his relief until a period of time after the fact.

During the February 4–March 2 recess of the Secession Convention, the Committee of Public Safety, acting in the convention's stead, appointed three commissioners to negotiate with Gen. Twiggs on the surrender of U.S. property to the state of Texas. It was hoped that a bloodless conclusion could be reached. The commissioners appointed were Samuel A. Maverick, Philip N. Luckett and Thomas J. Devine.

The first meeting between Gen. Twiggs and the commissioners occurred on February 8, in what was described as an "amicable" atmosphere. As expected, the commissioners were demanding all "public property," meaning military stores, be surrendered to the state immediately. Twiggs informed them that he had no intention of doing so before March 2. He was, no doubt, playing for time in hopes that he would receive instructions from Gen. Scott as to his course of action. He did say unequivocally that he would never agree to any settlement in which his troops were required to surrender their weapons, an unthinkable act to a professional soldier.

To this the commissioners were not receptive. "Before they departed, Twiggs treated them to a brief lecture on the inadvisability of separation.... After musing over this interview, the commissioners later in the day sent a note to Twiggs' office, asking him to put in writing that he would surrender Federal property on March 2. Twiggs [did not fall into that trap and] replied through his adjutant that he would put nothing in writing. In fact, he was appointing his own commission to negotiate with the Texans, designating for this purpose Major David H. Vinton, Major Sackfield Maclin and Captain R. H. K. Whitely."[15] Gen. Twiggs was acting shrewdly in recognizing his disadvantage in negotiating solely with three adversaries.

Gen. Twigg's appointed military commissioners met first on February 9 to consider a request by the state commissioners for a meeting at noon the following day. Since they had not at that time received any instructions from Gen. Twiggs on how to proceed, they declined meeting the next day but suggested a meeting on February 11. By that time they hoped to be more prepared to deal with the situation. Twiggs' reluctance to surrender immediately, his refusal to talk with them directly and a rumor abroad that Col. Waite, a staunch Union man, would be relieving Gen. Twiggs, alarmed the commissioners. "They immediately contacted ... Chairman Robertson ... of the Committee of Public Safety, to inform him that they believed that Twiggs was about to draw more men into San Antonio to resist Texas forces. They [told him that they had] ... summoned Ben McCulloch to the field, instructing him to assemble his cavalry and come immediately to San Antonio."[16]

Although now somewhat forgotten, at that time Ben McCulloch ranked right up there with such legends as Sam Houston, William Barrett Travis, Davy Crockett and Jim Bowie, all of whom resided in the pantheon of Texas' heroes. As a matter of fact, when a youngster, McCulloch's family was neighbors to Davy Crockett back in Tennessee. Crockett's sons were his daily companions. In 1836, McCulloch had followed Crockett to Texas in the cause of Texas independence and, had it not been for a case of the measles delaying his journey to San Antonio, he would have arrived in time to achieve martyrdom along with the other defenders of the Alamo. However, after recovering, he went on to participate as a member of Sam Houston's rag-tag army in the Texan's victory over Gen. Santa Anna's Mexicans at San Jacinto. His subsequent career was somewhat varied but he was always ready to serve Texas and answered whenever she called.

Meanwhile, the meeting of the commissions scheduled for February 11, convened. At this meeting, the state commissioners placed heavy demands upon the Federal garrison's military stores. They were particularly interested in "arms of every description, military stores, including quartermaster's, commissary, and medical stores and public moneys, and everything else under the control of the general in command."[17] The military commissioners replied the next day and essentially agreed to the terms provided that the troops would be allowed to remain armed along with "requisite ammunition, clothing, and camp and garrison equipage, quartermaster's stores, subsistence, medical and hospital stores, and such means of transportation of every kind as may be necessary for an efficient and orderly movement of the troops from Texas."[18] Gen. Twiggs' plan was for the troops to march out overland to various locations in adjacent states.

After consultation for several days, on February 14, the Texas commissioners rejected the proposal relating to the movements or position of the troops and insisted that they be evacuated by sea from several points on the Texas Gulf Coast. They were taking no chances that the Federal troops might concentrate for a resistance. On the other hand, they did accept the troops retaining their arms provided they "[march] to the coast ... in detachments of not more than 200, each detachment to be at least three (3) days march apart."[19] However, upon arriving at embarkation points, the troop detachments would be expected to surrender their transportation means as well as any artillery they may have had with them.

The next day, February 15, the military commissioners responded stating that they could not agree to the stipulations regarding evacuation of the troop by sea because "[t]he commander of the department, whoever he may be ... has exclusive authority in such cases."[20] Further, they announced that Gen. Twiggs had been relieved officially of the command by Col. Waite and were expecting him in San Antonio at any time. In the meantime, Gen. Twiggs remained in command awaiting Col. Waite's arrival.

Washington had finally answered but "not in the way Twiggs most wanted.... There were still no implementing instructions. Instead, plans were set afoot to start evacuation by sea of the artillery companies ... especially ... two light (field) batteries."[21]

Gen. Twiggs was in for yet more stress on his nervous system. The next day, "[p]rompted by the breakdown in negotiations and the appointment of Waite, a pronounced Northern sympathizer, [McCulloch's] ... buffalo hunters ... moved into San Antonio, seized the arsenal and gave Twiggs six hours to surrender all his forces."[22] McCulloch's force consisted of a collection of ordinary citizens answering the state's call to arms and also a contingent of members of the Knights of the Golden Circle. The Knights were a shadowy group "whose members were sworn to [support secession]. This society had been started a year or more prior to the Presidential election [of 1860] ... [and were actually] ... insignificant, but from the fact of its perfect organization and secrecy it was a powerful instrument in the hands of the conspirators, inasmuch as there was not even a party organization to oppose them; they made bold to say that they would force secession with arms if the people refused it at the ballot box."[23]

On the evening of February 15, McCulloch's men had begun filtering into San Antonio and disbursed onto rooftops and in alleyways around the central plaza. They were all well-armed and numbered maybe as many as 1,000 men. Later on, the main column marched into town, perhaps three hundred strong. Lt. Col. Lee's friend, Mrs. Caroline Darrow, observed their entry. Looking out upon the plaza through the dark night, she saw horsemen, variously mounted in columns of two, some men on foot, all preceded by the Lone Star banner of Texas. It was cold outside and the armed throng was variously dressed, ranging from coats and shawls to shirt sleeves. In the atmosphere of intense excitement, coffee, refreshments and warm clothing were distributed among the arrivals. Union sympathizers were present as well, and, they being well-drilled and well-armed, "a conflict seemed inevitable. The arsenal building had been opened and was swarming with [McCulloch's] Rangers."[24] The city verged on violence urged on by the strong emotions of the time.

Lt. Col. William Hoffman had only assumed command of the 8th U.S. Infantry Regiment in San Antonio on February 11. He now had under his command only two companies of infantry immediately available for defense, perhaps 160 men or so. When informed of the impending threat of Maj. McCulloch's force, he inquired of Gen. Twiggs under what circumstances he should order his troops to use ball cartridges. Gen. Twiggs, still hoping to avoid a hostile confrontation and the shedding of blood replied, "[U]nder no circumstances, and added that he would not be the first to shed blood."[25]

Maj. Larkin Smith, also of the 8th U.S. Infantry Regiment, by chance, encountered Ben McCulloch in the street and asked him what he intended to do. McCulloch replied he had the advantage and would take possession of all "public property." He went on to assure Maj. Smith that his men would not be molested if they did not interfere. Later, Maj. Smith heard it rumored that his men's arms were going to be demanded. Seeking out McCulloch once more, he asked if he had heard correctly that his men would not be molested. McCulloch's reply was, "Yes." Smith gave fair warning that they would consider their persons very much molested if their arms were interfered with. McCulloch said that would be a matter for the state commissioners to determine.[26]

Later that morning, Gen. Twiggs arrived at his headquarters escorted by an armed guard from McCulloch's detachment. They marched him into the Grand Plaza where Col. McCulloch and his men were assembled. J. K. P. Blackburn was a bystander and overheard their brief conversation. The two men, observing the conventions of the times, exchanged greetings. Then Gen. Twiggs said,

> "Ben McCulloch, you have treated me most shamefully, ruining my reputation as a military man and I am now too old to re-establish it." [To which] McCulloch answer[ed], "I am serving my State, the State of Texas, sir." General Twiggs replied, that if an old woman with a broomstick had come to him and having authority from the State of Texas demanded his surrender, he would have yielded without a word of protest. "But you, Sir, without papers, without any notice have assembled a mob and forced me to terms. "General Twiggs in his humiliation wept like a child."[27]

The negotiations were continued inside with the state commissioners in attendance. Later that afternoon, after considering his options, which were few, Gen Twiggs agreed to surrender Federal property in San Antonio. Further disagreement occurred "on what to do about light artillery batteries, the exit route Federal troops would take from the state, and whether all Federal troops would be allowed to retain their weapons. In principle, Twiggs viewed the light batteries as being to artillerists what small arms were to infantry. He was willing to compromise, however, by accepting the commissioner's demand that the men leave via the coast rather than march overland. But he stubbornly refused to surrender the light batteries or the small arms."[28] This was where matters stood at the end of the day.

The following day, Saturday, February 17, because Col. Waite was expected to arrive at any time and that it was apparent that Twiggs would not budge on the arms issue, the state commissioners agreed to the terms. On Monday, February 19, Waite arrived in San Antonio and assumed command. He wanted to immediately rescind the surrender but changed his mind when he realized he had only 160 men with whom to oppose over 1,000 under McCulloch. The rest of the Federal force in Texas was scattered as small post contingents. It would have been fruitless to resist under the circumstances. Some troop evacuations began immediately with the two infantry companies in San Antonio moving out first.

There was considerable anti-secession sentiment among the citizenry of San Antonio. A large crowd gathered to bid the departing troops farewell, "and when the two companies ... marched out with colors flying and band playing the national airs and the old bullet-riddled and war-stained banner of the 8th Regiment floating in the breeze, there was a profound sensation amongst the people — strong men wept and hung their heads in shame.... The people cheered the troops all along the streets and many followed them to ... where they encamped."[29] According to the writer, after the troops had left, the city "settled down into a sullen gloom." Several days later, Washington's Birthday was celebrated and "the Union and the American flag was cheered throughout."[30]

* * *

San Antonio was still in a state of shock over Gen. Twigg's surrender, when on February 23, the state referendum on secession was held statewide. As in other towns and villages throughout Texas, crowds of voters had gathered to cast their ballots on the secession issue. Working their way through the crowd, women eagerly distributed the yellow ballots, on which were printed, simply, "For Secession" or "Against Secession." Proponents of both sides of the issue preyed upon the ignorant and non-committed who received instructions on how to vote and what to vote for. Even "[c]arteros from New Mexico, who were in town with their wagon trains, were bought by the secessionists, and some were known to have voted several times."[31] The final tally was overwhelmingly for secession, 46,129 to 14,697.[32] Texas had cast her lot with the Confederate States of America.

The old warrior Sam Houston took a dim view of the election outcome. Deposed as governor because of his unrelenting anti-secession stand and, on his way home, Houston fictionally shared the road for a time with John W. Thomason's equally fictitious Methodist minister, Praxiteles Swan. According to Elder Swan, he was on his way to Houston to enroll as chaplain of the 5th Texas Regiment and found the old general in great form. They talked for forty miles. One passage stuck with the elder for the rest of his life and probably came to mind frequently in the unhappy times following Appomattox four years thence:

> All the young men are going to this war, Elder, and you, who are old enough to know better, are going with them. And old Sam Houston tells you, Elder, that it is madness.... You rush on destruction! And you who live will see your substance wasted, your women and children homeless, your very social order destroyed. Elder, the day will come — and you will see it — oh, a chaplain seldom gets hurt — you'll see people draw the nails from

those cotton sheds out there to fasten planks above their heads against the elements! You'll see gentlefolk working with their hands where your Negroes work now — only a damned sight harder. Remember, in those days, that old Sam warned ye and you would not hear."[33]

Although Houston would not live to see the outcome, the fictional prediction proved to be prophetic in reality.

The value of federal property surrendered was substantial. *Harper's Weekly* placed the amount at $1,900,000.[34] By the end of March about 1,300 troops had been evacuated by sea. About 1,200 were still in the state when, on April 12, South Carolina forces fired on the U.S.-held Fort Sumter in Charleston Harbor. A message was immediately sent out from Montgomery, Alabama, the newly established capital of the Confederate States of America, declaring the existence of a state of war "and that all U.S. troops remaining should be made prisoners of war.... [It would not be until] ... February 1863, after almost two years of privation, [that] the last nine non-commissioned officers and 269 men were returned to Federal control at New Orleans."[35]

* * *

As to the *dramatis personae* of this tale: fate was not kind to Gen. Twiggs. After negotiating the surrender, ill and weary, Twiggs returned to his home in New Orleans. He was welcomed there as a hero. On March 1, 1861, after nearly fifty years of faithful service, he was cashiered from the United States Army by order of President Buchanan. It was a sad ending for an old soldier. Having no other choices readily at hand, he had accepted appointment as a major general in the Confederate States Army and assumed command of the Department of Louisiana. By October 1861, it was obvious that his health precluded his performing the required duties. Eventually, he returned to his home in Georgia where he died in July 1862, a broken and bitter man.

Ben McCulloch did not survive Gen. Twiggs. He was commissioned a brigadier general in the Confederate Army in May 1861. In August of that same year, along with Gen. Sterling Price, he participated in the Confederate victory at Wilson's Creek, Missouri. In March 1862, at the battle of Pea Ridge, Arkansas, Gen. McCulloch had ridden forward to reconnoiter an enemy position. Shortly thereafter, his staff heard a volley of at least twenty-five rifles. When his body was discovered, he was "lying full length on his back with a bullet hole in his right breast."[36] Gen. McCulloch's body was returned to Texas where it was interred in the State Cemetery at Austin.

Lt. Col. Robert E. Lee, after the painful experience of resigning his U.S. commission, offered his services to his beloved Virginia. Over the next year, he served in several staff and field capacities where he experienced varying degrees of success and failure. In June 1862, he assumed command of the force that would shortly thereafter become the Army of Northern Virginia.

Within that army there served throughout the war a brigade of infantry Gen. Lee described as "always ready" and "my Texans." That unit, in the spring of 1861, was beginning to assume an embryonic form.

CHAPTER 2

"*We were in earnest, terribly so*"[1]: On to Richmond, Texas Style

In 1861, the United States had a small standing army. The newly-formed Confederate States of America had, other than scattered militia units, none. Both had to turn to their respective states to furnish the numbers necessary to wage what promised to be war on a large scale. As Confederate Texas was caught up in the excitement of the times, rumors were rampant. One rumor had it that all troops raised in Texas would be retained there for the state's own defense. Were it not for the efforts of one man that likely would have been the case. If so, there never would have been a Hood's Texas Brigade in the Army of Northern Virginia.

The man most responsible for getting Texas represented on the Virginia front was neither a soldier nor a career politician; he was a newspaper editor. His name was John Marshall, a native Virginian and editor of the Austin *State Gazette*. What enabled him to wield such influence was the fact that he was a personal friend of the newly anointed Confederate president, Jefferson Davis of Mississippi.

Marshall was born in Charlotte County, Virginia, circa 1825. As a young man he moved to Jackson, Mississippi, where he entered the newspaper business and edited the *Mississippian*. It was during this period that he became friends with the influential planter and politician Jefferson Davis. In 1854, he moved to Austin, Texas, where he purchased the *State Gazette*. He was an ardent secessionist and, as a newspaper editor, influential. It was at Texas governor Clark's request that Marshall traveled to Richmond to plead Texas' case for representation on what promised to be the war's principal front. He was successful in his quest and three regiments were authorized for Virginia service.

As early as March 1861, the Confederate Congress, sitting in the prospective nation's chosen capital, Montgomery, Alabama, authorized up to 100,000 volunteers to be raised for service. Between April and July, three troop levies totaling 10,000 men were made on Texas. In the initial flush of widespread enthusiasm for the war, this posed no problem other than that of organizing large numbers effectively. In the grass roots towns and villages of East, Central and South Texas, as in other states, much the same process occurred beginning with the raising of local companies. Upon achieving varying degrees of organization, the next steps ignited a trajectory that led eventually to the expected main battle front, some 1,800 miles removed in far-off Virginia. Following are some typical examples of what transpired in the isolated, frontier-like towns and villages of Texas and Arkansas as they gathered together and sent away to war their fathers, brothers and sons to fight, suffer and die in their perceived cause of Southern independence.

* * *

Setting out from Waco, Texas, on July 22, 1861, the destination of the Lone Star Guards, Co. E, 4th Texas, was Richmond, Virginia. In his diary, Oscar Downs wrote of never forgetting the scene that morning as he bade farewell to friends and loved ones. Whether wife or sweetheart he does not say, but as he "pressed *her* tender hand in one long affectionate perhaps eternal farewell ... he felt an electric thrill" course through his veins.[2] Accompanied by the Waco Brass Band the send-off lasted down the road for several days before the band and last minute hangers-on bade a final farewell and turned back toward Waco.

Less than four years later, of a company numbering 126 officers and men that had departed Waco on that hot July day, only sixteen, many of them replacements, were in the company's ranks that surrendered and were paroled at Appomattox Court House. The rest had either been killed, disabled, captured, or, a few, had deserted. Downs? After being ill in a Richmond hospital, he was appointed acting first sergeant on February 7, 1862. Less than two months later, on March 20, he procured a substitute and returned to Waco, no reason given.[3]

In Houston County, Texas, William D. Pritchard enlisted as a private in the Crockett Southrons, Co. I, 1st Texas. The organization took several months and centered around "Captain Curry, two or three boys a fife, a tin drum ... a small flag and a few meager reports from the front."[4] Daily parades with the small band playing patriotic Southern airs soon helped fill the ranks. Saturdays brought forth speeches, war songs sung by the local girls and general enthusiasm for the Southern cause. When the would-be soldiers were uniformed, at the expense of the local community, the company felt ready to venture forth.

The date of their departure was set for July 17, 1861, just four days before the first great battle of the war was fought at Manassas, Virginia. In a ceremony reenacted repeatedly in the communities of both North and South, the company formed "in double ranks in front of [Crockett's] Hall's Hotel.... [F]rom the hands of Miss Sarah Jane Morgan ... [they received] a beautiful [C]onfederate flag, the gift of the ladies of Crockett. [Capt. J. H. Watters] ... [in] a gallant and characteristic speech, accepted the banner.... [Then], amid the cheers of the assembled citizens [they] bade a long farewell to [their] many friends and took up the line of march that would lead, eventually, to the fields of battle where glory would be theirs."[5]

In Livingston, Polk County, Texas, John W. Stevens enlisted in the Polk County Flying Artillery, Co. K, 5th Texas.[6] Remembering the "excitement that prevailed throughout the South," in the aftermath of Mr. Lincoln's election, he remembered also the events leading up to the company's departure for the front. Even amid the enthusiasm of the time, patriotic ardor was not without its limits. There was a decided cooling when the captain announced one day, from the eminence of a big white oak stump, "See here boys, while we are wasting precious time in idleness, our country needs us in the enemy's front, where there is work to be done."[7] Stating his intention to leave for Virginia in a few days, he invited any willing to die for their country's cause to step forward. While playing at soldiering is one thing, real soldiering, with its separation from loved ones, the physical hardships of living and campaigning in the field, and the chance of serious injury or death is quite another matter.

The company's reaction resembled a "thermometer drop[ping] in a blue norther" or a "strutting peacock collapsing." "You just ought to have been there to see how all that sputtering braggadocio blood and thunder patriotism oozed out of my brave command ... and to hear the frivolous excuses made for not coming.... Some were not willing to go to Virginia to fight, but if any of Lincoln's yankees put his foot on Texas soil they'd jes' show then what cold steel was mad of."[8] Finally, one man stepped forward, then Stevens and eventually more, a total of ten in all expressed a willingness to go to Virginia. That number was a far cry from the one hundred men, seldom achieved, that comprised an infantry company on paper.

When departure day arrived, the whole community gathered to see them off. A big dinner was served of "barbecue hog and beef." As the time to depart drew nearer the atmosphere became heavier and even the company commander appeared to be carrying a heavy load. Some thirty-five years after the fact, to Stevens it seemed as only the day before. A short service was conducted by the Methodist minister and the "whole assembly was bathed in tears." Reality had begun to set in already. Embracing their loved ones, "probably the last forever," they mounted and rode away. As Stevens reached the last bend in the road, he "turned [h]is head and took a last look at [his] dear wife with her infant in her arms and [their] oldest of three years standing by her side."[9]

In Arkansas, the same "carnival atmosphere" filled the air — barbecues, picnics, dances — as companies destined for eventual service in the Texas Brigade's ranks prepared to depart. The Hot Springs Hornets, Co. F, 3rd Arkansas, "were drilling and marching daily before the admiring eyes of the local belles. Each evening they were feted with dining and dancing in the town and at neighboring farms."[10] At Monticello, Arkansas, Capt. Thomas Whittington's Co. C, 3rd Arkansas, received a flag "of pure silk ... hand sewn by the ladies of the town and its scarlet and white fields waved over he assembled crowd.... [The] mayor ... after a few appropriate remarks from the Court House steps presented the flag to Capt. Whittington who responded with the promise that its glory would never fade nor its honor be tarnished.' ... [T]he alternately weeping and cheering throng watched their gallant heroes swing into the road for ... Virginia."[11]

A year later, in Trinity County, Texas, the last Texas company to join the Texas Brigade began to form up. As with their predecessors, the Sumter Light Infantry, Co. M, 1st Texas, "drilled on the public square during the day and attended balls and entertainments ... at night." The afternoon of May 5, 1862, saw their departure. In a moment of excusable bravado, D. H. Hamilton promised the girls that he would "never dance again until independence of the Confederate government was declared." In retrospect, he noted, ruefully, that he never danced again.

"The boys spent the forenoon ... visiting and bidding goodbye to their girls. They all made the girls great promises about how they would whip the Yankees when they got to Virginia.... Then marching "out of town in double file to the tune 'Dixie' played by two 'fiddlers,' [t]he 'Kids" in line were yelling lustily, fully believing that they constituted the main part of the army."[12]

These same cheering, enthusiastic youths died in their hundreds in hospitals, in the field and in battle over the next four years. They died of disease, often stemming from unsanitary field living conditions, the control of which there was little understanding in that benighted health era; typhoid, measles, pneumonia, dysentery, from exposure and because of inadequate or non-existent diet and of indescribably horrible wounds suffered in battle. Those that did survive the war, returned to their states and homes to find them economically and politically wounded as well. They had learned up-front and personally what the eminent Civil War historian, Bruce Catton, noted nearly a century later, that truly, the Civil War was "romantic only if viewed from a considerable distance."

The first eight companies that were raised and destined for service in Virginia were designated the 1st Texas Battalion. Those companies, anxious to reach the front and in the organizational turmoil of the time, simply straggled to Virginia on their own and individually during the late spring and summer of 1861. Three more companies that would later join to form the 1st Texas Infantry Regiment and twenty more companies that would comprise the 4th and 5th Texas did not go directly to Virginia upon initial local organization.

As things became better organized, a more orderly process for getting troops to the front evolved. For one thing, Confederate Secretary of War Leroy Pope Walker suggested to Texas Governor Clark that several "camps of instruction" be designated for purposes of rendezvous, mustering-in and training. Accordingly, Camp Clark on the San Marcos River in Central Texas and Camp Van Dorn at Harrisburg, near Houston, were setup for that purpose. Some companies mustered at Camp Clark but all rendezvoused eventually at Camp Van Dorn for some minimum of training and transportation to Virginia.

At that time, Houston was a growing commercial and rail center. It was named after the hero of the Texas Revolution, General Sam Houston. Harrisburg lay nearby and phoenix-like, it had risen, literally, from its own ashes. It had been burned to the ground by Mexican Gen. Santa Anna's army on its way to San Jacinto and defeat at the hands of Gen. Houston's rag-tag army in April 1836. Camp Van Dorn was named in honor of Brig. Gen. Earl Van Dorn, then commander of the Confederate Department of Texas. "Once in camp, the companies which had traveled all the way from Henderson County in the north, Bexar County in the west, Goliad County in the south and numerous counties in between, settled down to the serious business of soldiering."[13]

Bruce Catton has noted that Civil War soldiers, North and South, were unsophisticated by twentieth century standards. These young, bored store clerks and farm and ranch hands were prime candidates for the glory each of them felt sure awaited them. It did not take long, once they had signed on the dotted line, for their illusions to evaporate into hard reality. As it always does, the reality of army life removed any illusions of it being a romantic adventure. In the beginning they enlisted because "they thought army life was going to be fun, and usually it took quite a few weeks in camp to disabuse him of this strange notion. Right at the start, soldiering had an almost idyllic quality; if this quality faded rapidly, the memory remained through all the rest of life."[14] The Texas soldiers fit this mold perfectly.

Some older, cooler heads could see the problems looming. For one, Chaplain Nicholas Davis, accompanying the 4th Texas, was disappointed with the choice of the training camp-site at Harrisburg. He described it as "a low miasmatic, unhealthy region, [where] many men ... contracted disease, from which they never recovered."[15] And this was before they were within 1,500 miles of the Virginia front. Alas, this was to be the case in every encampment during the course of a very long war — disease taking more lives than those lost in combat. The personal health disadvantages of Camp Van Dorn were far outweighed by the military advantage of readily available rail and waterborne transportation.

Oscar Downs' company, the Lone Star Guards, Co. E, 4th Texas, from McLennan County, arrived by rail in camp at 2:00 A.M., on July 28, 1861. According to Downs, he and his fellow volunteers had not had anything to eat for the last thirty hours. This would become a common occurrence over the next four years. It would be due not only to shortages occasioned by wartime conditions but to a poorly led, inefficient Confederate Commissary Department.

As the first Sunday dawned, grim reality dawned as well. Downs remembered, wistfully, the preceding Sunday when he "was at home with all who [were] near and dear to me on earth.... But now what a difference, I am seated in a low pine valley with no one to cheer, no one to amuse and nothing beautiful to gaze upon save the bright silvery moon which calls up so many reminiscences."[16]

Campbell Wood of the Waverly Confederates, Co. D, 5th Texas, and his comrades were from Walker County. They arrived at Camp Van Dorn to begin training during the hot Texas months of July and August. Their labors were rewarded somewhat by the attention paid them by the local versions of the fairer sex. "The ladies from Houston visited the camp every day and between drill hours we enjoyed the society of the pretty girls who brought well filled hampers and there was a general picnic every day."[17]

For most, the training at Camp Van Dorn was brief, only several weeks, beginning in late July and continuing to mid–August at which time the companies began to depart for the Virginia front. Not all had been unrelieved training, however. Passes were freely distributed to visit the local attractions in nearby Houston and Galveston. Both were accessible from Harrisburg by rail or, if necessary, by foot. Although mostly treated as heroes of their young nation's struggle for independence, here they began to learn some of the realities of soldier life far away from home and caring friends. They had to learn to deal with some of the more avaricious citizens and the types that follow armies, called sutlers, offering goods for sale, usually at greatly inflated prices.

In his diary, Oscar Downs recorded some of his experiences in that realm. Price gouging is not a recent phenomenon. He records that "a Houston 'Dutchman' who has been sending little articles out here, such as peaches, eggs, etc, etc, sent a load out today. His prices were so very exorbitant that the boys, becoming enraged at his rascality, pitched into the wagon simultaneously and took everything the old fellow had."[18] Perhaps, feeling guilty about the affair, Downs wrote the man a note telling him to come out to the camp "acting the gentleman" and he would be paid for his goods.

Nor could the soldiers avoid committing acts that they would not normally have committed at home. On a trip into Houston, one of Downs' companions stole a turkey. On returning to camp he was questioned by Capt. Ryan, the company commander, as to where he had acquired the bird. His reply was that "the turkey was trying to bite him and he did not intend to be imposed upon."[19] Presumably, he was allowed to keep the errant bird and, probably, later shared the bounty with his captain, among others. Foraging for food from any source available was a practice discouraged by the army high command. Nonetheless, hungry soldiers were frequently reduced to that or facing the stark reality of starvation. The members of the Texas Brigade were practical men and expert foragers from the beginning.

Of the 1st Texas Battalion that went to Virginia independently in the late spring and early summer, 1861, eight of the companies followed pretty much the same route. That route led overland to Shreveport, Louisiana, thence by boat down the Red and Mississippi rivers to New Orleans. One company, the Woodville Rifles, Co. F, 1st Texas, went by way of Sabine Pass and Brashear City, Louisiana, to New Orleans. In New Orleans, during May and June, seven of the companies were mustered into Confederate service for the "duration of the war." The period of enlistment was a part of the price paid for being allowed to go to Virginia. Additionally, they had to agree that Confederate authorities would be allowed to select their regimental officers. The Reagan Guards, Co. G, 1st Texas, was mustered in at Palestine, Texas, on June 23, 1861.

The three companies that made their way to Virginia later in the summer and fall went by way of Alexandria, Louisiana, then by various rail routes to Virginia. Of these three companies, one was mustered into Confederate service at New Orleans and the other two were mustered in after reaching Richmond. The twelfth and last company, the Sumter Light Infantry, Co. M, 1st Texas, was mustered in on May 5, 1862, at Sumter, Texas, before their departure.

For the twenty companies that came to comprise the 4th and 5th Texas, the road from Camp Van Dorn at Harrisburg, Texas, to Richmond, Virginia, proved to be one of the toughest movements that they made during the entire course of the war. With only several weeks of company drill under their belts, the orders came down from on high for the units to proceed to Richmond, posthaste. The plan adopted was for groups of five companies, temporarily designated as battalions, to proceed with intervals of several days separating departures. This scheme was devised so as not to overly burden the already rickety rail system. The odyssey began on August 16, 1861, with the departure of the first group of five companies. On that date, the first battalion of five companies boarded the cars, as passenger trains were then called, at Harrisburg for Houston. At Houston they boarded another train bound for Beaumont, ninety miles to the east.

Campbell Wood of the Waverly Confederates, Co. D, 5th Texas, remembered the ride to Beaumont as a "fearful' and "horrible" experience. According to Wood, they were loaded on open flat cars with improvised seats constructed of pine planks. Of course, as might be expected, it was raining "incessantly," and "the road had never been ballasted. Much of it was underwater, and frequently mud and water would be spattered over the entire car from the sloshing of the cross-ties in the loose mud under the car wheels."[20]

To add to the general chaos, many of the wet, mud-bespattered men were drunk and shooting at the numerous alligators that were foolish enough to reveal their presence in the ditches lining either side of the roadbed. Wood marveled at the fact that no one was killed during the process. In an age long before animal rights had become an issue, he did not take into account the host of riddled alligators left in their wake.

From Beaumont, the next segment of the journey was by steamer across Sabine Lake to Niblett's Bluff on the Sabine River. At Niblett's, Gen. Van Dorn, already held in low esteem by the troops because of his non-appearance at the camp bearing his name, had arranged wagon transportation which approved to be inadequate and unsuitable. In fairness, this was not totally Van Dorn's fault but more the result of the blustering incompetence of the wagon contractor. The immediate destination was New Iberia, Louisiana. According to Chaplain Davis, 4th Texas, the first companies arriving at Niblett's found awaiting them only seven wagons served by "indifferent teams."

At this point, the men were fairly well equipped by their local sponsors for field service. The transportation being inadequate, they were forced to leave much behind with only a vague sense of hope that it would ever be forwarded to them as promised. Ahead lay some 135 miles of swamp, inhabited largely by snakes and alligators, many of which in the ensuing weeks were to give their lives in attempting to contest the Texans' passage. Swarming over all were clouds of blood-thirsty mosquitoes and no chemical repellents then available to stave off their constant, maddening mass attacks.

Basil Brashear of the Company Invincibles, Co. F, 5th Texas, would have been in the second group of five companies making the trek. During their passage, he remembered it "raining nearly all the time and we had to wade through water from six inches to four or five feet deep.... After walking until we became tired and disgusted, we came to a little rise in the land, just barely out of the water, so we concluded to stay right there until daylight. Sleep did you say[?] [N]ot much. There were a thousand mosquitoes to every inch. We had to take off some of our clothing to fight mosquitoes with them to keep them from eating us up."[21] Fifty years later, Brashear thought it was a pretty tough start for young boys but not too bad when compared with what came later.

For Dulcimus et Ultimus Barziza of the Robertson Five-Shooters, Co. C, 4th Texas, the trip from Camp Van Dorn to Virginia "was in some respects the bitterest experience of the war."[22] The trip took twenty-seven days including wading through 135 miles of swamp. Even while enduring these terrible hardships the Texans remained cheerful. Chaplain Davis, 4th Texas, recalled a common spectacle of seeing weary men wearing only their long-tailed shirts trudging along carrying their other wet clothing and still possessing adequate spirit to be singing "Dixie."

M. V. Smith, a musician with the Knights of Guadalupe County, Co. D, 4th Texas, said it took his group eleven days to make the march from Niblett's to Lafayette, Louisiana. The whole way "was through water and mud from ankle to waist deep."[23] At least one man, J. J. Sweeny of the Bayou City Guards, Co. A, 5th Texas, and former editor of the Houston *Telegraph*, drowned while trying to swim a creek near New Iberia.[24] There were probably, though unheralded, others that suffered a similar fate.

The exhausting and mosquito-ridden march ended at New Iberia where the troops were loaded on steamers for Brashear City and thence New Orleans by rail. In New Orleans, some large cotton sheds were assigned as camping grounds. At this point it fell to the responsibility of the officer in charge to arrange transportation to Richmond by whatever means available through the military commander of the Confederate Department of Louisiana. In this case, the commander was none other than the ever-irascible and now Confederate general David E. Twiggs.

Capt. Robert M. Powell of the Waverly Confederates, Co. D, 5th Texas, drew the duty for his group and experienced firsthand the frustration of dealing with that crusty soldier in particular and army red tape in general. Ushered into the general's presence, Powell found him suffering from the gout with a bandaged foot resting on a chair. Accidently, Powell had the misfortune to stumble into the chair. The old general was given "such intense pain that he swore fiercely and refused to give the transportation until it suited his convenience."[25]

Undeterred by this petty vindictiveness, Powell marched the men to a train the next morning determined to leave with or without the general's permission. Gen. Twiggs had gotten wind of the plan and ordered that the doors of the cars be locked. Thereupon, Capt. Powell displayed a determination that would, in the latter days of the war, put him in command of the battered and depleted Texas Brigade. Knowing that there were qualified locomotive engineers in his command, he took over the locomotive and ordered his men to enter the coaches via the windows. At this point the conductor gave in to superior numbers and agreed to run the train under Powell's orders. He telegraphed "ahead for a clear track [and] that a 'wildcat' train loaded with 'wild Texans' was on the track."[26] Later, learning of a bottleneck ahead at Knoxville, Powell had the train rerouted down through Georgia and the Carolinas and on to Richmond by that route.

From New Orleans, the route to Richmond was, generally, via Jackson, Mississippi, Grand Junction, Chattanooga and Knoxville, Tennessee, Bristol and Lynchburg, Virginia. According to Chaplain Davis, 4th Texas, the journey was "slow and tedious" with the countryside giving the appearance of a vast armed camp as the South girded for war. Being the first Texas troops passing through some areas, they were viewed with great interest. Campbell Wood, Waverly Confederates, Co. D, 5th Texas, said that "[i]mmense throngs of people gathered at each station to see the 'wild Texans' and seemed greatly astonished to find them like other people."[27]

J. M. Smither, Waverly Confederates, Co. D, 5th Texas, said that they were "a perfect curiosity" along the way. People flocked to see them first hand. At one stop, for instance, they were treated to a meal prepared by the local ladies. On their best behavior, they somewhat surprised their hosts. One lady was heard to comment to another, "Why ain't they quiet! I expected to hear them yelling all the time and they are good looking, too! I expected to see them with their hair down to their heels and yellow as an Indian! They are a little sunburnt but that makes them look manly and shows where they came from."[28]

All in all, it seems this portion of the journey went fairly well. In the process they had traveled on eight or nine different rail lines utilizing every type of rail car available. Where connections were made with other rail lines and where differing track gauges were involved, this necessitated the unloading of all their gear and making their way on foot with gear in hand to the connecting station, which may have been located on the other side of town.

Anyway, they had experienced the many perils of the road and then some and survived, at least most of them. For a trip that now takes several hours by air, they were in transit for about four weeks, not to mention the great discomforts and lack of conveniences now taken for granted to which they were subjected. At Richmond, what awaited them was further training and integration into the forming Confederate States Army.

"The young men who were arriving in Richmond from all over the South to be trained ... ranged from the sons of wealthy Charleston aristocrats to Mississippi planters, bringing trunks and body servants, to the gaily-dressed Louisiana Zouaves, many of whom had just lately emerged from New Orleans jails."[29] This was the sort of mix into which was added the human ingredients that would presently become the Texas Brigade.

Most of the Texas soldiers were at best small town boys and in 1861 Richmond was a developed and growing enterprise. Growing up around seven hills gave rise to comparisons with Rome. As always in similar situations, "[Richmond] was being overrun by soldiers, adventurers, speculators, gamblers, prostitutes and every other type of person who gravitates in wartime to the place 'where the action is.' Richmond, shortly before, had been a small, somewhat sleepy town just under 38,000 inhabitants of whom, 11,699 were slaves and 2,576 were free blacks. In a few months its population would be twice as big and far more heterogeneous."[30] By 1864, the population had more than tripled to 128,000 by some estimates.

The 1st Texas Battalion that had straggled to Virginia earlier in the summer had, upon their arrival in Richmond, encamped as instructed west of the city in an area known as the Fair Grounds. It was there that they entered into the enterprise of further learning the soldier's trade. They there were introduced to cadets of the Virginia Military Institute (V.M.I.) brought forth from Lexington, Virginia, in the Shenandoah Valley to help in turning the recruits into proficient soldiers. The encampment became "Camp Lee and was the scene of feverish drilling, marching and countermarching. [Here they fell under the command of the South Carolina-born Texas politician become Confederate colonel, Louis T. Wigfall.] Ladies drove out in their carriages to this area well beyond the city limits bearing cakes and sweetmeats for the toiling young men."[31]

The weapons carried by the recruits at this stage of the game were not of any standard issue. It is important that armies be armed with the same standard infantry weapon in order that supplying them with ammunition is efficient. O. T. Hanks of the Texas Invincibles, Co. K, 1st Texas, remembered the rustic nature of their arms in the beginning as "consisting of almost every conceivable kind of gun that could be [collected] in the country." There were double-barreled shotguns, squirrel rifles, some Colt repeating rifles, Mississippi rifles and old army muskets, to illustrate the variety. Other non-standard accouterments included butcher knives as bayonets. Attachment of impromptu bayonets to respective firearms was thanks to "Uncle Rance Horn who was an [i]ngenious workman."[32]

There is no account of any specific weapons training activities. At that time, prior to receiving standardized weapons, it is likely that there was nothing of a formal nature beyond instruction in the nine steps from loading to firing an infantry weapon. The weapons issued, eventually, to the Texans were Enfield muskets of English manufacture. They were obtained through the efforts of Confederate purchasing agents sent abroad for that purpose. They were one of the finest infantry weapons then available. In the hands of expert, experienced marksmen, they were a deadly weapon even at great distances. Most of the frontier-raised Texas boys had considerable experience with firearms.

Uniforms were never standardized as in modern armies. Essentially, the way it worked was that at first local communities or wealthy local leaders took it upon themselves to provide uniforms for their companies or regiments. Val Giles, Tom Green Rifles, Co. B, 4th Texas, said that eventually, once the Confederate Quartermaster Department became what passed for functional, the uniforms issued assumed a universally gray color. Later, after rough field service had faded them, the uniforms were butternut in color, the inhabitants therein being referred to by their opposite numbers as "butternuts." Describing his company as a "motley looking set," their uniforms were of about four different shades of gray. Even so, he voiced the sentiments of young men throughout the South then donning those suits of varied hues, "Oh, were we fine!"[33]

Some militia companies, such as Houston's Bayou City Guards, Co. A, 5th Texas, that had existed before the war were handsomely uniformed. As a result, and more likely when ten companies were joined to form a regiment, there were ten different kinds of uniform displayed. Later, once uniform contracts had been executed by the government with private contractors, the situation improved somewhat, but it was never consistently good or efficient. During campaigns it was not uncommon for soldiers in the field to be reduced to rags and be without shoes. One source of supply for scantily-clad Confederates were the well-dressed and splendidly equipped corpses of their Union counterparts dotting the countryside following an engagement. Although such looting of corpses was frowned upon in the early stages of the war, it became more and more common as the war wore on, as deprivations increased and as death became a daily fact of life.

According to W. D. Pritchard, Co. I, 1st Texas, while training in Richmond the men were learning, also, some of the many vices associated with soldier life: poker, chuck-a-luck and the like. He attributed that mainly to idleness and an abundance of copper cents dispensed as change by the local merchants which the men, not being accustomed to the coin, did not consider as being of much value and squandered them accordingly.[34]

The highlight of their Richmond sojourn was the presentation, by President Davis, of a large, satin Lone Star flag, a gift from Mrs. Davis and Mrs. Wigfall. The flag was purportedly made from the women's wedding dresses. In his presentation speech, Mr. Davis lauded the Texans stating that while troops from other states had reputations yet to gain, the Texans had a reputation but to maintain. Col. Wigfall, in his acceptance speech, pledged the honor of Texas and her sons "that the flag would never trail in the dust in retreat." Alas, that pledge was broken at Sharpsburg, Maryland, the following year where the flag "was found wrapped around the body of the last of sixteen men to have carried [it] on that bloody day of battle," and it fell into Union hands.[35]

For one reason or another, as the impending clash at First Manassas neared in mid–July 1861, the men of the 1st Texas Battalion remained in their Richmond camp drilling and otherwise whiling their time away. Then, on July 21, 1861, even as the first great battle raged to the north along the banks of Bull Run Creek, they were loaded hastily with not much time for preparation onto trains bound for the locale of conflict. Their Richmond training days were over.

George T. Todd of the Marion Rifles, Co. A, 1st Texas, remembered being rushed to a train made up of boxcars. He estimated that about 1,300 men were loaded on board. In a pouring rain that had been going on all day, the troop train chugged forth drawn by one steam engine and pushed by another, a double-header. At about 9:00 P.M., while speeding through the gloom, the train was plunged into a washed-out culvert. Ruefully, Todd noted that "first blood was shed here and 40 young men were killed and crippled and half a dozen cars crushed into kindling wood. While not on the battle field, our loss was as great as it might have been in the battle."[36]

Although they were too late to take part in the action of July 21, they were observers of the debris-strewn field in the aftermath. They saw the yet to be removed dead in their various forms of mutilation, the wounded in their agonies, dead and mangled horses, smashed wagons and artillery pieces — a gallery of shocking sights for inexperienced troops.

Following the clash, the two armies recoiled, the Union Army occupying the defenses surrounding Washington and the Confederates arrayed along the south bank of the Potomac River opposite. The eight companies, as the nucleus of the future Texas Brigade, took up their assigned post near Manassas Junction. Their encampment was named Camp Wigfall. Co. I, 1st Texas, was the ninth company of the regiment and arrived in Richmond only shortly after the first eight companies had been dispatched to Manassas. They remained in Richmond where they trained for several weeks. Shortly, they were joined by Co. K, 1st Texas. Later on in the summer, both companies joined their Texas brethren at their Manassas encampment, where the eleventh company, Co. L, eventually arrived also. The composition of the eleven company 1st Texas Infantry was then set until the twelfth company, Co. M, joined the regiment the following summer.

The training being conducted was described by Pritchard as a process of changing "an armed mob into a disciplined army." Illustrative of the depth of the problem faced by those burdened with the conversion task are some of the company regulations contained in the July 20, 1861, general orders of Co. D, 18th Georgia. That regiment would, a short time later after a change of position down river, join the three Texas regiments in forming the first Texas Brigade:

> The Chiefs of Squads must see that the men wash their hands & faces daily; that they comb their heads & beards...; If any man shall be so negligent of his person as to become offensively filthy, or infested with vermin, he shall be ordered ... to apply remedy immediately, & on failure to do so, or for a second offense, he shall be taken to the spring by a squad of men ... & publicly ducked....
>
> The men must not play with their bayonets by thrusting them at one another, nor must they snap their muskets except when on duty, & then only in obedience to the proper command from a superior.[37]

The first duty of a soldier, it was taught, was to obey all orders. This proved to be a hard concept to instill in "the proud spirits of those men born to the freedom of the prairie and each a chieftain upon his native heather."[38] Later, in the fall, the 1st Texas was moved from their Manassas position to one further down river around Dumfries, Virginia.

In the meantime, the first of the Van Dorn contingent began arriving in Richmond on September 12, with the other groups arriving every few days following. The assigned encampment for these troops was southeast of the city on the banks of the James River in the Rocketts neighborhood. John W. Stevens, Co. K, 5th Texas, said their encampment was called

Camp Winder. He described it as consisting of some "500 or more temporary buildings, 100 × 20 or 25 feet in regular order, on streets or open ways running at right angles with each other 25 or thirty feet wide. Into these buildings we were assigned, as many as could conveniently occupy each building. Our blankets were our bedding; our cooking was done in the streets or open ways in camp kettles or skillets issued to us by messes. We were formed into messes, usually five men to the mess."[39] Messes were formed for the purpose of drawing rations, when they were available, and for preparing meals for that group.

While at Rocketts the troops were formally organized into the 4th and 5th Texas Infantry regiments, the date being September 30, 1861. As per the agreement made by John Marshall with the Confederate government, they were allowed to elect their company officers and non-commissioned officers but the selection of the regimental officers, colonels, lieutenant colonels, majors and staffs was to be by the Confederate government.

In early October, the encampment was moved to a more favorable location about four miles east of Richmond. The Confederate government designated the site Camp Bragg, but to the boys from Texas it was always known as Camp Texas. As the green soldiers were issued implements of war, Stevens, Co. K, 5th Texas, noted that it began to dawn upon them that "war was not a school child's picnic, nor an excursion for pleasure.... [M]any began to understand that war meant fight, and fight meant kill, and that killing was a reality, to be sure enough dead; so dead that you would hardly ever return to Texas again.... All rushed in upon the mind like an avalanche, and in many, very many, cases completely overshadowed every sentiment of honor and patriotism — a sentiment so necessary in the heart of the volunteer citizen soldier."[40] Stevens claimed that the result, acute homesickness, was the worst foe that the armies, South and North, had to contend with. The only remedy was to keep the troops distracted with strict military duty, fatigue, reveille, drill, roll calls, dress parades, tattoo, and the like. Although unlikely, he says that anxiety kindled by homesickness killed more men on either side than any other cause.

With all of the brigade elements from Texas, though separated, in Virginia, the stage was set for their further training and introduction to active campaigning. Training continued but beyond that for the time-being, according to musician M. V. Smith, Co. D, 4th Texas, "they had nothing to do but drill and have the measles for several weeks."[41] On November 4, the two regiments received orders to prepare to move north to the Potomac line.

The issue that interested the soldiers most during this interval was who their regimental officers would be. "It was said that the lives of solders were too precious and the interests of freedom too dear, to permit incompetent men to have places in the army as officers."[42] Nor were the troops from Texas willing to accept officers for long that were not to their liking. As things turned out, they were to enjoy some of the best leadership then available in the Virginia army.

CHAPTER 3

"It is astonishing how such a splendid spirit was so long maintained"[1]: An Anatomy of the Brigade

The war fever that engulfed the South in the spring and summer of 1861 was not tempered by any prescience such as that exhibited by William T. Sherman. As a West Point graduate and superintendent of Louisiana's state military academy, news of South Carolina's secession from the Federal Union appalled him. Speaking to one of his young, Southern-born faculty members, he observed, "You people speak so lightly of war. You don't know what you are talking about. War is a terrible thing. I know you are a brave, fighting people, but for every day of actual fighting, there are months of marching, exposure and suffering. More men will die in war from sickness than are killed in battle. At best war is a frightful loss of life and property, and worse still is the demoralization of the people."[2]

Superintendent Sherman knew of what he spoke. Having been educated in the military arts, he, though not serving in active combat during the Mexican War, had heard the tales of those who had served in the campaigns south of the border. He knew that "war is hell," and, later, in applying that principle in his own campaigns as a leading Union general, he would play a key role in finally bringing the terrible tragedy to a conclusion.

Nonetheless, in the states of the forming Confederacy, men and boys rushed to the colors with enthusiasm and abandon, nowhere more so than in Texas. By the end of the war, four years thence, the survivors bore little resemblance to the men in the ranks of the companies that had marched away anticipating high adventure and military glory. Indeed, few of the men that filled the original ranks could be found there by April 1865.

Military organization is for the purpose of ordering and disciplining soldier life. Getting troops, many times in large numbers, to points where needed and, once there, maneuvering them in battle, is not an easy or simple task to accomplish. To help in facilitating that task, the basic military building block in Civil War-era armies was the "company." Companies were raised locally, often by prominent local leaders. Local companies contained men who knew each other as neighbors, as friends and as relatives. Ten companies were joined eventually to form regiments. When that happened their local company names gave way to military etiquette and were replaced by militarily conventional alphabetical designations, A through K. J was not used because of its similarity to and possible confusion with I. Uncharacteristically, the 1st Texas with its twelve companies included Companies L and M, the only regiment in the Army of Northern Virginia to have that distinction. All thirty-two

Texas companies were composed of volunteers. Even after the Confederate government began to conscript in early 1862, the company complements of the Texas Brigade remained volunteers.[3] As battle casualties and deaths from wounds and disease mounted, recruiting officers and men were sent back to Texas from time to time to fill the resulting gaps in the ranks. Their recruiting efforts were never effective enough to keep pace with death that, in its varied forms, stalked the ranks.

In the military scheme of things, an infantry company consisted of from sixty-four to 100 privates augmented by twelve or so commissioned and non-commissioned officers. It was the usual practice in Confederate companies for the men in the ranks to elect their commissioned and non-commissioned officers, a demonstrated bravery under fire and common sense being important qualities for the aspiring to possess. A captain commanded an infantry company although in the heat of battle with the wounding or death of officers, anyone available might be called upon to keep things together right down to the lowliest private in the ranks.

In the initial zeal and enthusiasm for the war, it was not uncommon for companies to muster full complements of officers and men. As the war dragged on, however, and battle losses and disease exacted their tolls, company numbers dwindled to the point that in the end at Appomattox in April 1865, most companies could muster only a handful of men.

Typical of all the companies throughout the forming brigade, in Harrison County, Texas, one such took shape styling itself the Marshall Guards. This was to be the common practice in the early months of the war, companies adopting names signifying towns or locales from whence the company originated. Other Texas companies adopted names signifying their fierceness, such as the Robertson Five Shooters, or their devotion to the Southern cause, such as the Dixie Blues. Once integrated into the Confederate Army, these colorful names gave way to the alphabetical company designations.

The Marshall Guards, Co. E, 1st Texas, like the eleven other companies that would come to make up the 1st Texas Infantry Regiment were fearful of missing the action to come and lost little time in setting out for Virginia, the likely scene of the coming clash of arms. The company departed Marshall, Texas, on May 28, 1861, numbering four commissioned officers, eight non-commissioned officers and fifty-five privates. Commanding was Capt. Frederick S. Bass, a graduate of the Virginia Military Institute and former president of Marshall College.[4] In New Orleans on the way to Virginia, the company was officially mustered into Confederate service for twelve months as of June 6, 1861.

Not with the company at the time but catching up later in Virginia to enlist were the four Perry brothers, Eugene, Howard, George and Clinton.[5] Of the four, only one, George Perry, survived the war. All four brothers were casualties in the battle of Sharpsburg in September 1862. Howard and Clinton were killed and the other two wounded. Eugene survived Gettysburg and Chickamauga only to be killed in the Wilderness in May 1864. The Perry family paid the last full but unheralded measure of devotion in a time before military decorations came into usage as recognition of valiant service.

Nor did the rest of the company fare much better. In the twenty-eight engagements in which it was involved, it suffered fifteen killed, forty wounded, nine missing or prisoners of war, an overall casualty rate of 53 percent including eight who died of disease. Of the 118 men who served in the company during the war, only eleven men were left standing to surrender at Appomattox in April 1865.[6]

From nearby Tyler County, when the Texas Ordinance of Secession was signed on February 1, 1861, among the signers was Philip A. Work. By the time the convention reconvened on March 2, 1861, Work was not among the returning delegates. He had resigned in the interim, intent upon raising an infantry company for field service in the cause of the Confederacy. Work's successor to the convention was friend and colleague Samuel A. Willson of Woodville. At age twenty-six, Willson was the only native-born Texan to the convention. Later, he joined his friend Work in military service as first lieutenant of an infantry company titled the Woodville Rifles, Co. F, 1st Texas. In 1862, Capt. Work was promoted to the lieutenant colonelcy of the 1st Texas and Lt. Willson became the captain of Co. F. The company was mustered into Confederate service for twelve months at New Orleans on May 28, 1861. Of the 103 names that appear on the muster rolls of the Woodville Rifles, thirty-two were killed, thirty-six wounded, some multiple times, and fourteen died of disease. This amounts to a total of eighty-two killed or wounded for a casualty rate of 79.6 percent. Only seven men were present for parole at Appomattox.[7]

In Navarro, Ellis, Freestone, Hill and Limestone counties, William Melton recruited a company designated as the Navarro Rifles, Co. I, 4th Texas. Most of the recruits were from Navarro County. Not long after the company's organization, Melton stepped down as captain pleading old age. His elected successor as captain of the company was Clinton M. Winkler. By the end of the war, Winkler had risen to the lieutenant colonelcy of the 4th Texas. The company was mustered into Confederate service on July 17, 1861, at Corsicana for the duration of the war. The original company consisted of four officers, nine non-commissioned officers and eighty-eight privates, a total of 101 men. During the course of the war, records indicate that thirteen were killed, some having suffered wounds in engagements prior to their deaths, forty-eight were wounded, many of them two or three times, and thirty-one died in hospitals of wounds or disease, mostly of disease. Eighteen men were present for the surrender at Appomattox.[8]

In southeast Texas, William A. Fletcher's introduction to military life came shortly after news of Fort Sumter reached Beaumont, Texas, in April 1861. Fletcher reported that he, "was on the roof of a two story house putting on the finishing course of shingles," when a friend came by and informed him of the fact. In order to enlist, Fletcher went to Houston, some ninety miles to the west of Beaumont. He traveled part of the way by railroad flatcar and the remainder by pumping a handcar.[9]

Arriving in Houston, and finding no enlistment opportunities presently available, he went on to Galveston where he found the situation to be the same. He then traveled north up Galveston Bay by steamboat to Liberty, Texas, in search of a company to attach himself to. There he learned of a company being raised locally and, although the local boys were favored, he was able to talk his way in. The company was launched as the "Company Invincibles," and became Co. F, 5th Texas.

The original captain of the company, King Bryan, rose to the lieutenant colonelcy of the 5th Texas during the course of the war.[10] Of the original complement of four officers, nine non-commissioned officers and ninety-one privates, the company suffered casualties of twelve killed, forty-nine wounded, many more than once and thirty-five dead of wounds or disease.[11]

William Fletcher was wounded and captured at Second Manassas and wounded again at Chickamauga. The latter wound rendered him unfit for further infantry duty and he transferred to the 8th Texas Cavalry, famous as Terry's Texas Rangers, for the duration of the war.[12] After the war, Fletcher's book, *Rebel Private Front and Rear*, became a minor classic of the period.

* * *

After the initial trials of organizing and getting from Texas to Virginia, the 1st Texas

Regiment enjoyed effective and fairly stable leadership for the duration of the war. The original colonel was Louis T. Wigfall. He was succeeded by Alex T. Rainey and then Frederick S. Bass. The original lieutenant colonel was Hugh McLeod, West Point Class of 1835.[13] A native New Yorker and active in the military affairs of Texas in the 1830s and 1840s, he was at one time adjutant general of the state. An experienced officer, his promise was never realized for he died at Dumfries, Virginia, of pneumonia on January 2, 1862.[14] He was eulogized as "one of [Texas'] most devoted and distinguished sons and [of] the army of the Confederacy a gallant soldier."[15]

Frederick Bass, with the 1st Texas except during the short period he commanded the brigade in 1864–1865, was much esteemed by the troops. Pvt. James H. Hendricks, Co. E, 1st Texas, said that Bass was very popular and that the "regiment made up $700 ... to purchase a fine horse for [him] as a slight testimonial of their regard for him."[16] Considering that privates, if they were paid at all, received eleven dollars per month and officers and non-commissioned officers received not that much more, this gift represented a great deal of admiration.[17]

In the 4th Texas Infantry Regiment, the original colonel, Robert T. P. Allen, resigned the post in September 1861 and was succeeded by Col. John B. Hood. When Hood left the 4th Texas to assume brigade command, he was succeeded by Lt. Col. John Marshall. The troops were not pleased as Robert V. Foster, Co. C, 4th Texas noted: " The men of this regiment have not half the confidence in him as a colonel as they had in Hood. He took us out a day or two ago to drill, and an awful out he made of it."[18] This should have come as no surprise to anyone for John Marshall was not a soldier; as mentioned earlier, he was a newspaper man in his former life.

Because of the public nature of his career, quite a bit is known about him. A young friend remembered him as being about five feet seven inches tall, fair complexioned, an eye like an eagle's and always dressed in black. He was said to have never missed, summer or winter, an early morning plunge into the river, presumably the Colorado, which flows through Austin. He quickly, unusually so, became the state's Democratic Party leader, suggesting a certain degree of dynamism and charisma.

As a political leader and newspaper editor, he on occasion found himself embroiled in controversy, sometimes, in those days, with the potential for lethal consequences. One such incident involved a certain Dr. Phillips, another prominent Austin citizen. They had a street fight, the reason for which has long been forgotten, in which Marshall

Col. John Marshall, 4th Texas, killed at Gaines' Mill, June 27, 1862.

showed "gallantry and chivalry." "With his pistol pointed in the air, he received the first two shots from Dr. Phillips, while he ... tipped his hat to a woman who was passing, possibly in range, and waited until she passed to safety."[19] Further shots were exchanged and, failing to do injury, the combatants resorted to hurling rocks at each other. The fight was finally broken up before any serious injuries resulted.

Col. Marshall was militarily inept in some technical ways, but he was willing in all others. This was illustrated when on a march, probably during the retreat from the Potomac line in March 1862, an unbridged stream brought the column to a halt. Riding to the front, Col. Marshall asked the reason for the halt. When asked how they were going to cross the stream, Marshall questioned their willingness to face death in battle but unwillingness to get wet wading a stream. Then, from the depths of the ranks someone shouted, "Colonel, suppose you get down and lead us across, and see how you like it yourself." Unhesitatingly, Marshall dismounted and wading into the stream up to his waist, he ordered, "Follow me." Raising a cheer, the troops waded through.[20]

In the Texas Brigade leadership meant leading from up front and sharing hardships. Col. Marshall was willing to do that and might have developed into an effective field commander given time, but, alas, this was not to be. He fell early on, shot through the forehead, out front on horseback leading his regiment into battle on the afternoon of June 27, 1862, at a place called Gaines' Mill on the Virginia Peninsula.

Col. Marshall's successors in command of the 4th Texas included John P. Bane and John C. G. Key and Clinton M. Winkler. Lieutenant colonel, or second-in-command, was Bradfute Warwick. Born in Richmond, Virginia, on November 24, 1839, he was a graduate of the University of Virginia and the Medical College of New York, the former at age seventeen, the latter at age eighteen, which might illustrate the state of medical education at the time. Not being decided if he wished to pursue a career in medicine, he roamed Europe and parts of the Middle East where he experienced some exciting adventures, including serving on the staff of the Italian liberator, Garibaldi. The fact that he was not a Texan did not sit well with some at first, but his performance at Eltham's Landing, the brigade's first real action, in May 1862, removed most doubts. His promise was not to be realized for he, too, fell mortally wounded at Gaines' Mill, only moments after Col. Marshall.[21]

A big favorite in the 4th Texas was Maj. William H. "Howdy" Martin. Originally captain of the Sandy Point Mounted Rifles, Co. K, 4th Texas, he was promoted major April 29, 1864.

Maj. William H. "Howdy" Martin, 4th Texas

Born in Twiggs County, Georgia, in 1822, he had moved first to Alabama and then to Texas in 1850. While in Alabama, he had studied law and was admitted to the bar. In Texas, he was elected to the state senate in 1853 and again in 1855. He was a colorful character and had been given the nickname "Howdy" because of his habit of waving and shouting a greeting rather than rendering the military salute expected. He was brave to a fault. A member of his company remembered that at Gaines' Mill he led the company forward, a pistol in each hand. "As his company raced down the rise toward Boatswain's Creek ... [he] launched into a regular Fourth of July oration to inspire his men. 'Remember your wives and children ... [r]emember your home and firesides ... [r]emember your,'" he started to say when a shell burst a few feet away enveloping him in smoke and dirt and, "subsequent proceedings interested him not." It was one of the few times he was ever observed at a loss for words.[22]

Val C. Giles, Co. B, 4th Texas, remembered on the march into Pennsylvania in June 1863, stepping out of ranks and waiting for Co. K to come by. Eventually, here they came, Capt. "Howdy" Martin out front with his saber slung across his shoulder. "Captain," [Giles] said, 'I have fallen back for reinforcements. I want you to help me capture the state of Pennsylvania.' 'All right, sonny, show me the keystone and we'll smash her into smithereens. Fall in line.' ' So, arm in arm, a Captain and a Fourth Sergeant invaded the United States.'"[23] Giles went on to observe that such a man they all could love and approach. After, Appomattox, Maj. Martin did not consider his service completed until he had gotten a large group of brigade members safely home to Texas, experiencing much difficulty in the process. Such was the leadership in the 4th Texas Regiment.

The 5th Texas Infantry Regiment was organized near Richmond, Virginia, September 30, 1861. It was first commanded by Col. James J. Archer, followed first by Jerome B. Robertson and then Robert M. Powell. Resigning his commission in the regular U.S. Army, Archer had reported to Virginia governor Letcher, who proposed to appoint him colonel of the 55th Virginia. On reporting to the secretary of war, Archer found that command had already been given to Col. Frank Mallory of Virginia. Later on that same day, President Davis appointed Archer to command the ten companies of Texans who were without field officers or organization. Thus, Archer began his association with the 5th Texas which was to last until his promotion to brigadier general in June 1862, and reassignment to command a Tennessee brigade.[24]

At first, Archer did not set well with the men of the 5th Texas. For one thing, he was not a Texan, he was a Marylander. Tacitus Clay, Co. I, 5th Texas, said of Col. Archer that he, "may possibly be a very efficient man if in the command of Regulars, but ... he is not of the right type to control or give satisfaction to Texas volunteers and the dissatisfaction in and out of the ranks is very general ... and there is a movement on foot with our captains ... to have him supplanted by our Captain R[obertson] [being] placed in command."[25]

Watson Dugat Williams, Co. F, 5th Texas, had heard of Col. Archer before his taking command and thought him "good, competent and brave." However, the 5th Texas Regiment generally opposed his appointment because "he [was] from a state too far North and too near Yankeedom for Texas to trust as their commanding officer.... The men all know that Texans are claimed as the best soldiers in the Army and they think the position of colonel is too high for a Marylander to hold over Texans."[26]

While the Texans disdained Archer generally, his feeling toward them was otherwise, albeit not publicly displayed. To his brother, he confided that he had "a most excellent regiment [with] ... officers ... almost all intelligent gentlemen [and] [t]he men if they were well would be all that I ask for."[27] Several weeks later he said that he was "on the best possible terms with all [his] people ... and [had] become warmly attached to Texas and Texans."[28] By January 23, 1862, he was writing that "[t]he officers of my regiment all say they want to keep me for their colonel but think I would make the best brigadier — and so it is with the officers."[29]

The first part of May 1862, Brig. Gen. W. H. C. Whiting, then the Texas Brigade's divisional commander, offered Archer command of a three regiment brigade which Archer declined on the grounds that he "would rather command [his] own regiment ... than take without rank or staff the command of a brigade of regiments which [he] knew nothing about and which might fail him in battle — The Texans will always stand by me."[30] And finally, a few days after the fight at Eltham's Landing, "[m]y regiment is perfectly game — our little fight has strengthened and perfected the confidence which has always existed between us. — The regiment is trying to find a fine horse to present to me."[31] Who knows how the relationship would have progressed had Archer remained with the Texas Brigade? Instead, he was placed in command of Hatton's Tennessee brigade upon Hatton's death leading the brigade in action near Fair Oaks Station, May 31, 1862.

Archer's successor, Jerome B. Robertson, came in for his share of criticism as well while in command of the 5th Texas. Later, when Robertson was appointed to command the brigade, Rufus Felder, Co. E, 5th Texas, said that some of the men in Robertson's company "condemn [him] for leaving ... but [that] most of them [were] very willing to get rid of him as he thought more of enjoyment and promotion than he did of his company. [The] government certainly must be scarce of military men to appoint him Col. [H]e [could not] drill a company much less take care of it. We were very much disappointed in him."[32] That opinion was to change as Col. Robertson proved his mettle.

By the time the Seven Days battles had been conducted, unit cohesion had improved. According to Nicholas Pomeroy, Co. A, 5th Texas, violating the usual military protocols, the officers were becoming friendly and there was much fraternization going on between the officers and men. Given the fact that they messed (took meals) and lived together, faced the same dangers and hardships, it was inevitable. Pomoroy became fast friends with "Capt. Farmer, and Lieutenant Fuller, the latter could spin a good yarn, and oftentimes I spent part of the night by the camp-fire listening to him. The former (Captain Fuller) was my best friend in the army, being always kind and true."[33]

Val C. Giles, although a member of Co. B, 4th Texas, remembered as one of his favorite officers Capt. J. D. Roberdeau of Co. B, 5th Texas. A Virginian by birth,

Val Giles, Co. B, 4th Texas (The Dolph Briscoe Center for American History, University of Texas at Austin).

Capt. Roberdeau had gone to Texas in 1858. Giles remembered first speaking to Capt. Roberdeau while on picket duty near Dumfries, Virginia, on a cold day in December 1861. Brushing snow off a fallen pine tree, Giles looked out over the wide Potomac and the snow-covered hills and the white tents occupied by Federal troops on the Maryland shore. Roberdeau, in charge of the picket detail, came along on an inspection tour. Sitting down next to Giles, he remarked on how tired he was in climbing over hills and tramping through deep snow. It was the beginning of a fifty year friendship.

Giles remembered Roberdeau as a disciplinarian and a natural-born soldier that the men at first disdained noting that "the Texans of that old brigade were hard to control. They had led a free independent life at home and didn't take readily to discipline and it took such men as Capt. Roberdeau to convince them that discipline and obedience to orders was their duty.... [He] was fair and just to his men and he was untiring in behalf of their comfort. He demanded of the commissary and quartermaster all that was due his company, and he generally got it."[34]

Col. Archer, while commanding the regiment, offered Roberdeau the position of brigade commissary but he declined preferring to remain with his company. Archer's comment was, "Lieutenant, I admire your spirit, but [damn] your judgment." Roberdeau said he often, while on the march, thought of the commissary's berth in a comfortable ambulance. Wounded at Second Manassas, Capt. Roberdeau lost twenty-six of forty-five men he led into that fray. The day after, because his mother lived nearby, Gen. Hood suggested he visit her on furlough. That evening, Gen. Lee began the army's march into Maryland, and "to the astonishment of all ... Roberdeau joined [them] and assumed command of his company. His devotion to the cause for which [they] were fighting would not permit him to remain quiet at his old home."[35] Wounded again at Sharpsburg a few days later, he was then captured at Gettysburg and imprisoned at Johnson's Island, Ohio, until exchanged the following year. Returning to his company, he was with it throughout the remainder of the war and surrendered at Appomattox.

Another favorite in the 5th Texas was Capt. I. N. M. "Ike" Turner, Co. K. At age twenty-two, he was the youngest company commander in the Texas Brigade.[36] At Sharpsburg, when all the 5th Texas' field grade officers fell, Turner as senior captain present took command of the regiment. He was killed on the Nansemond River near Suffolk, Virginia, in April 1863, and was much lamented. Gen. Hood, in a letter to Gen. Lee, mentioned that he had lost some of his best soldiers, including Capt. Turner, "the leader of [his] sharpshooters ... [a] more noble and brave soldier has not fallen during this war."[37] J. A. Howard, Co. B, 5th Texas, wrote home of Turner's death, reporting that he "was shot through the body and [feared] mortally wounded. His death will be a great loss to us and he is generally allowed to be the best officer in the brigade, and was, I believe, the bravest man I ever knew."[38] James E. Cobb, Co. F, 5th Texas, reported that Turner's death cast gloom over the whole brigade. Generous, brave, of excellent judgment, "in his death we have suffered almost irreparable loss."[39]

The three Texas regiments, although comprising the largest contingent during the war, were not the sole components of Hood's Texas Brigade. Over the course of the war units from other states were assigned to the brigade as the Confederate high command deemed necessary. These units served with a distinction that added to the military luster of the brigade.

The first unit from another state to be added was the 18th Georgia Infantry Regiment in November 1861. It fought with the brigade during the terrible summer campaign of 1862 and into Maryland in the early fall culminating in the blood-letting at Sharpsburg, September 17, 1862. Following Sharpsburg, there was a general reorganization of the Army of Northern Virginia more along state lines and the 18th Georgia was reassigned to Cobb's Georgia Brigade.

The Texans were sorry to see the "goobers" go; they had affectionately dubbed them the 3rd Texas, a title that the Georgians accepted as a high compliment. The 18th Georgia that served with the Texas Brigade from fall 1861 until November 1862 was organized from seven counties in various parts of the state.[40] The ten companies comprising the regiment arrived in Richmond August 8, 1861. The next day or thereabouts, the appointments of Col. Wofford, Lt. Col. S. Z. Ruff and Maj. Jefferson Johnson were made.

Of Col. Wofford, a sketch will be given later relative to his brief tenure as brigade commander. The second-in-command, Lt. Col. Ruff, was born in 1837 and was a graduate of the Georgia Military Institute. He was wounded in action at Second Manassas and was described as, "commanding in appearance, a fine tactician and a strict disciplinarian."[41] Major Johnson, in his early thirties, resigned March 29, 1862, due to disability from chronic hepatitis and dysentary.[42]

During the winter of 1861–1862, a brigade newspaper, *The Spirit of '61*," was published. The admiration of the Georgians for their leadership is illustrated in the December 25, 1861, edition. Acknowledging their good fortune in their camp location, the editorialist was complimentary of their officers, saying, "I must boast of our officers who have the power to move us at a moment's warning if they choose but I am glad to know that we have none who care to treat us thus but on the other hand it seems to be the chief desire of all both field and company officers to render us comfortable as circumstances will admit. This is owing all together to the energy of said officers that we are now blest with such pleasant cabins and also for the rich viands wherein we may feast during the Christmas days for which I for one extend to them my sincerest thanks and well wishes."[43]

W. D. Pritchard, Co. I, 1st Texas, paid high praise to his Georgia comrades: "[A]mid the many perilous scores of our early campaigns, they were ever with us, where the shot fell thickest, where death's frightful carnival was highest, the gallant Col. [Wofford] with his noble men could be found; they shrank from no duty, quailed at no danger. When the battle raged the hottest, when the hope seemed most forlorn, we could look to the right and always find 'Georgia....' No truer, nobler or braver men ever fixed a bayonet or tore a cartridge."[44] When the regiment surrendered at Appomattox, it mustered one officer and fifty-two men.[45]

Also serving briefly with the brigade were the eight infantry companies of Hampton's South Carolina Legion. Raised by the wealthy South Carolina planter Wade Hampton III, the Legion combined all three elements of the combat arms: infantry, artillery and cavalry. After Hampton was wounded at First Manassas, Col. Martin W. Gary assumed command and remained thus for most of the war. "The Hampton Legion, South Carolina Volunteers was organized June 12, 1861, with an Infantry Battalion of eight companies, A through H, a Cavalry Battalion of four companies, A through D, and an Artillery Battalion of two companies, A and B."[46] The eight infantry companies served with the Texas Brigade from the time following the battle of Seven Pines, May 31–June 1, 1862, until mid–November 1862, a period of about five and a half months. Those few months included the Seven Days, Second Manassas, Boonesboro and Sharpsburg.[47] Of the units serving in the Texas Brigade, the Hampton Legion served for the shortest period of time.

Attached in support of Hood's Texas Brigade beginning in the fall of 1862 was the

Rowan North Carolina Artillery. This battery of six guns entered active service on May 3, 1861. Captain James Reilly, a non-commissioned veteran artillerist of the U.S. Army, assumed command of the battery soon thereafter. Known to the Texans as Reilly's Battery, they were comforted and sometimes amused during the heat of battle to see and hear the loud and usually profane orders shouted by the short, stout, red-faced Irishman as he led his unit into action. Reilly's Battery was assigned elsewhere after the Gettysburg campaign.

The final unit to join the brigade hailed from Arkansas, one of Texas' neighbor states. The companies comprising the 3rd Arkansas Infantry Regiment joined Hood's Texas Brigade as the 18th Georgia and Hampton's South Carolina Legion left in November 1862. Commanded by Col. Van H. Manning, the 3rd Arkansas had been in Virginia since July 1861, serving in other commands. The nucleus of the original regiment was formed by two companies raised by Dr. W. H. Tebbs and Manning, a lawyer. The other eight companies were raised by Albert Rust, a former U.S. congressman and a Confederate congressman.

The companies straggled to Lynchburg, Virginia, where they were joined to form a regiment on July 5, 1861. Rust was elected colonel; Seth M. Barton, U.S. Military Academy, Class of 1849, lieutenant colonel; and Manning, major. Prior to joining the Texas Brigade, the regiment took part in Gen. Robert E. Lee's ill-fated western Virginia campaign in 1861, Gen. T. J. Jackson's winter campaign, 1861–1862, and served briefly in North Carolina in the spring of 1862. Returning to Virginia, the regiment was only lightly engaged during the Seven Days battles. Missing action at Second Manassas altogether, it was engaged at Sharpsburg suffering heavy casualties.

By this time, Col. Rust had been promoted brigadier general and transferred west. Maj. Manning became colonel and commanded until wounded and captured at the Wilderness in May 1864. He remained a prisoner of war at Ft. Delaware until paroled in July 1865.

With the addition of the 3rd Arkansas, Hood's Texas Brigade assumed its final form. Until the end of the war, the brigade would be the 1st, 4th, 5th Texas and 3rd Arkansas Infantry regiments. On their combat horizon at that time loomed Fredericksburg, Suffolk, Gettysburg, Chickamauga, Chattanooga, Knoxville, the Wilderness, Spotsylvania Court House, Cold Harbor, Petersburg and Appomattox. It was a long, bloody road yet to be traveled.

* * *

As in any army, leadership was a critical factor in getting Confederate armies moving in the right direction. Numbering 303, there was one group of men that played a role of great importance in the Confederacy's quest for effective leadership. It was this group that was responsible for bringing a degree of order to the generally chaotic organizational situation. "These singular men were the graduates of the U.S. Military Academy who used their training and skill to organize and lead the Confederate Army against the flag they had previously served."[48] President Davis himself was a West Point graduate, Class of 1828.

Within the regiments comprising the Texas Brigade at the beginning of the war and later there were West Pointers lending their expertise in leadership positions. Gen. John Bell Hood, under whose name the brigade was to be immortalized, was a West Pointer, Class of 1853. Other regimental officers, also graduates of West Point, were Hugh McLeod, Class of 1835, and Paul J. Quattlebaum, Class of 1857.[49] Since Quattlebaum departed early on and McLeod died in the winter of 1860–1861, Texas Brigade exposure to West Point leadership was mostly from the brigade level and higher.

Nonetheless, "[i]n assessing the contributions made by the West Pointers to the Southern cause, it may be said that they were the ones who provided the glue to hold the Confederate Army together — who gave it cohesion, order and a degree of professionalism. Without their leadership there would have been utter chaos."[50] Truth be known, there was utter chaos anyway but perhaps less so thanks to their presence.

During the course of the war, the Texas Brigade was led by eight different men of whom only three served in a truly full-time capacity.[51] The first commander was Brig. Gen. Louis Trezevant Wigfall, a South Carolinian by birth become a Texas politician by profession. He was flamboyant, being present in Charleston, South Carolina, during the siege of Fort Sumter, and acting as a go-between for the Southern commander, Gen. P. G. T. Beauregard, and the Federal fort's commander, Maj. Robert Anderson. It was rumored that prior to the battle of First Manassas in seeking intelligence of Federal intentions, "he made a trip to Washington, shaving off his whiskers and going through the city as a coal driver."[52]

On October 21, 1861, Wigfall was promoted brigadier general. Later, he assumed command of the 1st, 4th, and 5th Texas reg-

Col. Van H. Manning, 3rd Arkansas

iments and the 18th Georgia Regiment all encamped on the Potomac River near Dumfries, Virginia. Thus, the birth of the Texas Brigade as a unit. There were mixed emotions in the ranks about the first commander of the brigade as a military leader.

Joe Polley, Co. F, 4th Texas, and after the war a brigade biographer, saw Wigfall as a "brilliantly astute politician" but given to "hallucinations." Polley agreed with former Texas Governor Sam Houston's sobriquet describing Wigfall as "Wiggletail." Wigfall was a drinker and Polley speculated about whether the state of his leader's condition was "due to constitutional nervousness or that produced by the apple-jack and kindred liquid refreshments of which he was said to be so fond.... He sees a Yankee in every shadow ... [and takes] alarm and orders the long roll sounded by the drummer he keeps close at hand for just such emergencies."[53] Wigfall's tendency to overreact became so bad eventually that then Cols. Hood, 4th Texas, and Archer, 5th Texas, simply ignored the frequent alarms initiated by the agitated Wigfall.

Robert Gaston, Co. H, 1st Texas, later elected 3rd Lieutenant and killed at Sharpsburg, thought Wigfall an efficient commander but with one great fault: "He loves whiskey too well ... [and] has been drunk several times since we came here." He also complained that no one was allowed to leave camp without a pass from Wigfall and that "he [had] cursed so many of the boys about asking him for a pass that [they were] all getting afraid of him."[54] James Hendrick, Co. E, 1st Texas, whose fate it would be to die of wounds suffered in the Wilderness May 6, 1864, expressed the same general dissatisfaction because Wigfall "[k]ept them too close ... [and drank] a great deal ... [becoming] so drunk that he could hardly stand up."[55]

Providentially, the Texas Legislature, meeting in November 1861, elected Wigfall to the Confederate Senate, as was the practice at that time. So, on February 20, 1862, Wigfall resigned his command and traveled to Richmond to assume his political duties. The brigade showed little, if any, remorse at his departure.

As senior brigade colonel, James J. Archer, 5th Texas, succeeded Wigfall in command. Although he served in the position for only a short interim period, he was a qualified military leader. A Princeton graduate and a law school graduate of the University of Maryland, Archer served in the regular U.S. Army during the Mexican War. In recognition of gallantry in action at Chapultepec in the era before military decorations came into widespread usage, he was brevetted major, a brevet being an honorary promotion. He left the army in 1848 for the practice of law only to reenter the regular army again in 1855 as a captain in the 9th U.S. Infantry. He entered the service of the Confederacy in 1861 as colonel of the 5th Texas.[56]

On March 8, 1862, the same day that the army, then called the Army of the Potomac, began its strategic withdrawal from the Potomac line to that of the Rappahannock, Col. John B. Hood, 4th Texas, was promoted brigadier general. Effective March 12, 1862, Hood became brigade commander, relieving Col. Archer.

Col. Louis T. Wigfall, C.S.A., First Texas Brigade Commander (Library of Congress)

Although Hood was to serve as brigade commander for only six months, during that period the West Pointer captured the troops' admiration and respect. At the time of his appointment, Hood was thirty years of age and was a native of Bath County, Kentucky. Appointed to the U.S. Military Academy in 1849, his graduating class in 1853 included Union generals-to-be Phil Sheridan, James B. McPherson and John Schofield.[57]

His first assignment following graduation was a posting to the 4th U.S. Infantry in California. In 1855, he was reassigned to the newly-formed 2nd U.S. Cavalry, his relief in the 4th Infantry being Lt. Phil Sheridan. The 2nd U.S. Cavalry was an elite unit, its officer corps being a who's who of leading Civil War commanders; its commander was Col. Albert Sidney Johnston, its second in command, Lt. Col. Robert E. Lee. Also serving in the regiment, among others, were Majs. George H. Thomas and William J. Hardee. It was here that Hood became closely attached to Lee as they conversed often on long rides through the Texas countryside.

In November 1860, Hood was ordered to report to West Point as chief of cavalry. Seeing that war was looming, Hood requested to be relieved from the order, much to the astonishment of the adjutant general of the army, Samuel Cooper, who remarked, "Mr. Hood, you surprise me. This is a post and position sought by every soldier."[58] From this point, Hood's path took him to Montgomery, Richmond and into the service of his Texas mentor, Col. Robert E. Lee, then in command of Virginia's state troops.

Hood, unlike most other military men of the time, was practical. After a few false starts, he came to realize that it was unrealistic to apply regular army discipline to volunteer troops. His relations with his troops can be described as down-to-earth. William H. Lessing, Co. B, 4th Texas, not then even fifteen years of age at the time of the Seven Days battles, remembered an incident that illustrates this well. He was assigned guard duty at Hood's temporary headquarters near a place called Pine Island. The hours assigned were 4:00 to 6:00 A.M., not a good time for vigilance to be expected in any soldier, regardless of circumstances, especially in one so young and fatigued. He remembered that at about daybreak he had fallen asleep while standing upright. He, vaguely aware of Gen. Hood's passage, was brought rudely to full consciousness by a thunderous order to present arms. Questioned as to his company and the importance of alertness while on guard duty, he could only reply, "Yes, General, but I was so tired and hungry I forgot and just then a big tear stole down my cheek, which the General doubtless saw."[59] Summoning the corporal of the guard, Hood ordered the boy relieved of his duty. Ordered to follow his colonel, he feared the worst. Taken to Hood's tent, it being filled with "the pleasant aroma of a wholesome breakfast," he was then ordered to sit down and have some breakfast. Stories like that spread through military organizations like wildfire, as no doubt this one did, very quickly.

By the time of the Maryland campaign only a few months later, Hood had won the brigade's allegiance. Nicholas Davis, the chaplain of the 4th Texas, remembered that on the march into Maryland in September 1862, Gen. Hood had been placed in arrest by a fellow but senior brigade commander, Shanks Evans, within the division over a minor disagreement. Banished to the rear of the marching column, he was forced to eat dust, which was the military practice of that time.

News of Hood's arrest spread quickly. "Nearing Boonesboro Gap and hearing ahead the sounds of battle, Gen. Lee was approached by Capt. Ed Cunningham, Co. F, 4th Texas, and asked that Gen. Hood be released and returned to command. The men "were not willing to go into an engagement without him, and many had positively declared that they would stack arms on Gen. E[vans] before he should lead them.... " Gen. Lee knew Hood's value as a combat leader and ordered his release from arrest. "As [Hood] rode to the front he was cheered long and loud by each regiment of the division."[60]

In October 1862, Hood was promoted to major general and given divisional command in Longstreet's Corps. The following summer, while leading the division, which included the Texas Brigade, into battle on the second day at Gettysburg, Gen. Hood received a shrapnel wound from an artillery burst that shattered his left arm and left it useless for the remainder of his life.

When Longstreet's Corps was ordered to Georgia on detached duty to Gen. Bragg's Army of Tennessee in September 1863, Gen. Hood, still not recovered from the Gettysburg wound, accompanied the division anyway. Upon arrival at Ringgold, Georgia, the division was almost immediately plunged into battle, the name of which became known as Chickamauga.

In the aftermath of the first day's fighting on September 19, 1863, J. M. Polk, Co. I,

4th Texas, remembered that he was reading some personal letters when he heard behind him a horse approaching. Turning around, he found himself face to face with Gen. Hood. "Well," [Hood] said, " you didn't get hurt?"

> "No, sir," I replied.
> "How did your regiment come out?" he asked.
> "We lost a great many men," I answered, " but I don't know how many."
> "Well, I am sorry to hear it," he replied and rode off.

Polk characterized Hood as "a social, kind hearted man but a little impulsive at times. He would walk up to me and [shake] hands with me and talk to me, but never knew my name. He was different from most of the old army officers. He recognized the fact that most of the men in the Confederate army were good, respectable citizens at home, and that it was public spirit and sense of duty that caused them to be there. Gen. Hood could get order out of confusion on a battlefield in less time and apparently with less trouble than any man I ever saw."[61]

Firmly established by this time and according to Joe Polley, 4th Texas, "[a] mutual confidence and love existed between ... Hood and the Texas Brigade.... Each trusted the other — Hood that the brigade would accomplish all asked of it — the Texas Brigade, that he would make no demand on it beyond its power. It was this feeling between them that prompted the brigade to adopt and cling to the title of 'Hood's' Texas Brigade."[62]

On the second day of the Chickamauga fight, September 20, 1863, George Todd, Co. A, 1st Texas remembered that "[h]ere it was that I tried to get on both sides of a tree at the same time, as 'minies' were zipping from both directions. Here also Gen. Hood rode up and took the flag of the 4th Texas (his old regiment) to rally them under this rear fire, when he himself was again wounded, [this time losing a leg to amputation]. His old troops caught him as he reeled off his horse. This scribe saw this and believes a bullet from our own men struck him."[63] The limb lost was his right leg, amputated below the hip.

Col. Jerome B. Robertson, Fifth Texas Brigade Commander

Once recovered and promoted lieutenant general in February 1864, Hood was appointed a corps command in the Army of Tennessee. At this point the fortunes of Hood and the Texas Brigade diverged and never again would he command them upon a field of battle.

Hood's immediate successor as brigade commander on an interim basis was Col. William T. Wofford of the 18th Georgia. When the Georgia regiment was transferred to another brigade in November 1862, Col. Wofford's tenure was cut short. He was a native of Habersham County, Georgia, born there June 28, 1824. He was educated locally, studied law, was admitted to the bar and practiced in Caswell, Georgia. He served as a captain of volunteers in the Mexican War and later in the state legislature. As a member of the Georgia Secession Convention, he voted against secession. Service following his brief tenure in command of the Texas Brigade was with Cobb's Georgia Legion.[64]

Wofford's successor was Col. Jerome Bonaparte Robertson of the 5th Texas. Born in Woodford County, Kentucky, March 14, 1815, he was reduced to penury by the death of his father. Beginning at age eight, he served as a hatter's apprentice for a period of about ten years, most of it spent in St. Louis, a center for the hat trade.

St. Louis gave Robertson opportunities and expanded his personal horizons. By age eighteen, he had saved enough money to buy back the last three years of his apprenticeship. Inexplicably, somewhere along the way he had developed an ambition to become a physician. Returning to Kentucky in 1833, he was fortunate enough to fall under the mentorship of Dr. W. W. Harris of Owensboro. With Dr. Harris' help, he attended medical school at Transylvania College, graduating in 1835.

In 1836, Robertson, along with other Kentuckians, heeded the call from revolution-embroiled Texas for help in its struggle with Mexico. Although he arrived too late to participate in the final triumph at San Jacinto in April 1836, he remained in the service of the newly-formed Republic of Texas into 1837. When the army was disbanded, Robertson cast his lot totally with Texas, settling eventually in Washington County and taking up the practice of medicine. For the next forty-one years, he maintained a home there, practicing medicine but mainly farming. He took part in military campaigns against the Mexicans and Indians. He held a number of public elective and appointive posts, including both houses of the state legislature. He was a rabid secessionist and served on the secession convention.

Upon Texas' secession, Robertson raised an infantry company in Washington County for service in Virginia. The company, locally the Texas Aids, eventually saw service as Co. I, 5th Texas. On October 10, 1861, Captain Robertson was promoted lieutenant colonel of the regiment bypassing the rank of major. On June 2, 1862, he was promoted colonel. While leading the 5th Texas, Robertson received wounds at Gaines' Mill, Second Manassas and Gettysburg.

Upon Gen. Hood's promotion to divisional command in October 1862, and following Col. Wofford's transfer to Cobb's Georgia Brigade in the following month, Col. Robertson became Texas Brigade commander. This was soon followed by promotion to brigadier general. He was in command of the brigade at Fredericksburg, Suffolk, Gettysburg, Chickamauga and during the eastern Tennessee campaign.[65] To devotees and detractors alike, Gen. Robertson was known as "Aunt Pollie." As is always the fate of those in positions of leadership, there were detractors, but to most the sobriquet was one of affection, not of derision. It may be apocryphal, but some sources say Gen. Hood coined the title remarking that Gen. Robertson reminded him of his Aunt Pollie. According to Joe Polley, Gen. Robertson did exhibit "democratic ways and a certain fussiness over trifles."[66]

Polley remembered an incident that occurred near Richmond that contrasts the leadership styles of Gen. Hood and Gen. Robertson. On a march that featured mud and snow, at the end the troops had plans that included alcohol. The column had dwindled steadily to the point where Col. Robertson, peering back into the obscuring mist and snow, exclaimed, "Where the blankety-blank is the Texas Brigade?" The practical Gen. Hood counseled, "Let 'em go, General — let 'em go; they deserve a little indulgence, and you'll get them back in time for the next battle."[67]

Gen. Robertson's twin qualities of valor and concern for his men were recognized. B. I. Franklin, Co. I, 5th Texas, ill in Richmond while the brigade was in Pennsylvania, rejoined at Hagerstown, Maryland, on July 9, 1863. He found the weather very warm and the march south exhausting. In his weakened condition, he noted that "Gen'l Robertson kindly loaned me a horse ... and I have not marched but very little so far."[68] Later that fall, following the battle of Chickamauga, Franklin noted that "Gen'l Robertson was to be seen on all occasions in front of his brigade leading them on and exposing himself to every danger. Man never acted more gallantly. He had two horse shot under him but escaped unhurt himself."[69] This was the sort of leadership that the men of the Texas Brigade expected of its commanders.

Courage and kindness notwithstanding, Gen. Robertson's tenure as Texas Brigade commander was cut short when he ran afoul of the corps commander, Lt. Gen. James Longstreet, during the brigade's stay in eastern Tennessee during the winter of 1863–1864. Gen. Robertson was imprudent enough to let it be known publicly that he was not in agreement with Gen. Longstreet's leadership specifically and the campaign generally. Court-martial charges quickly followed.[70] The eventual outcome was a reprimand issued to Gen. Robertson. He was relieved of his command and reassigned to the Trans-Mississippi Department. His successor was Gen. John Gregg.

Gen. Gregg was a native of Lawrence County, Alabama, having been born there September 28, 1828. He was educated at LaGrange College and afterwards studied law. He emigrated to Texas in 1852 and in the years leading up to the war, he served as a district judge, a member of the Secession Convention and in the provisional Confederate Congress.

Resigning from Congress, he returned to Texas where he organized an infantry regiment to be duly designated as the 7th Texas. Elected its colonel, he and the regiment were surrendered at Ft. Donelson, Tennessee, in February 1862. After he was exchanged, Col. Gregg was promoted brigadier general and assigned to Gen. Hood's Division. Wounded at Chickamauga, upon his recovery and in the aftermath of the Robertson affair, he was assigned command of the Texas Brigade.[71] It was under Gen. Gregg's command that the brigade returned to Virginia and the Army of Northern Virginia in April 1864.

Gen. Gregg did not possess the charisma of Hood or outwardly exhibit the kindness and concern of Gen. Robertson. He has been described as exhibiting "an austerity of manner and a positiveness of utterance that at first didn't set well with the free and easy Texans."[72] However, he led the brigade ably during the Overland Campaign in Virginia that began in May 1864, thereby establishing his reputation and the troops' respect.

Alexander C. Jones, 3rd Arkansas, counted Gen. Gregg among his friends and categorized him as belonging "to that class of younger general officer whose ability and courage were rapidly developed during the closing scenes of the conflict."[73] Jones credited Gen. Gregg's efforts in defending a section of the Richmond line in the face of overwhelming enemy superiority in numbers as saving that city from capture several months prior to the actual fact.

On October 7, 1864, while leading the brigade in an attack on the Darbytown Road, Gen Gregg was struck down. Gen. Gregg's death marked the only time during the course of the war that a Texas Brigade commander was killed in action. He was the last general officer to fill the post.[74]

Gen. Gregg's successor was Col. Frederick S. Bass of the 1st Texas. Born in Brunswick County, Virginia, in June 1829, he was a graduate of the Virginia Military Institute, Class of 1851. Migrating to Texas during the years prior to the war, he first served as instructor of military tactics at Marshall College in the city of that same name. At the time the war commenced, he was president of the institution.

While many of the companies raised in Texas were poorly prepared for what awaited them at the front, the Marshall Guards, Co. E, 1st Texas, under the command of Capt. Bass, were an exception to the rule. His V. M. I. background had worked to the company's advantage. On the same day that the 1st Texas was decimated in Miller's cornfield at Sharpsburg, Capt. Bass was promoted to the rank of major. A year and a half later, January 5, 1864, he was promoted lieutenant colonel and colonel July 15, 1864. Although wounded himself on the Darbytown Road, as senior colonel present, he assumed brigade command on October 7, 1864.[75]

In February 1865, Col. Robert M. Powell, 5th Texas, returned to the brigade following his severe wounding at Gettysburg, capture, and imprisonment on Johnston's Island, Ohio. Being senior to Col. Bass, the brigade passed to him. Col. Powell was born in Montgomery County, Alabama, in 1826, and moved to Texas in 1849. A lawyer by profession, he served in the state legislature prior to the war.

Originally, Powell served as captain of the Waverly Confederates, Co. D, 5th Texas. He was promoted major August 22, 1862, lieutenant colonel August 30, 1862, and colonel November 1, 1862, a meteoric rise and testimony to the heavy losses suffered by the regiment in the summer campaign of that year. Col. Powell commanded the brigade for the remainder of the war and was at its head for the surrender at Appomattox.[76]

As companies joined to form regiments and regiments, usually four, joined to form brigades, so brigades joined to form divisions. During the period encompassing the withdrawal from the Potomac line in March 1862, until Gen. Hood was assigned divisional command in July 1862, the division in which the Texas Brigade served was commanded by Gen. William H.C. Whiting.

A Mississippian by birth, Gen. Whiting was born in Biloxi March 22, 1824. He graduated from the U.S. Military Academy, Class of 1845. While at West Point, Cadet Whiting attained the highest grades ever made at the institution to that time. After graduation, he served in the Engineer Corps and entered Confederate service in that capacity. After the Seven Days battles, he was transferred to Wilmington, North Carolina, to construct what became Ft. Fisher at the mouth of the Cape Fear River.[77]

Relieving Gen. Whiting, first as temporary divisional commander, was Gen. Hood. It was not until after Sharpsburg that Gen. Hood's promotion to major general was made permanent. Hood remained in divisional command, although severely wounded at Gettysburg and Chickamauga. He vacated the post upon assignment to the Army of Tennessee.

The last divisional commander succeeding Gen. Hood was Maj. Gen. Charles W. Field. Gen. Field was born in Woodford County, Kentucky, April 6, 1828. He graduated from the U.S. Military Academy, Class of 1849. Resigning his commission in May 1861, he first served as colonel of the 6th Virginia Cavalry. He later transferred to the infantry and was present at the Seven Days, Cedar Mountain and Second Manassas. At the latter place, he was so severely wounded that he was out of action until promoted major general and assigned divisional command effective February 12, 1864. He was the last man to serve in that divisional capacity.[78]

Divisions, usually three or four in number, were joined to form corps. Corps were not officially established until the reorganization in the fall of 1862. Briefly, in the spring of 1862, the Texas Brigade served in a diversionary capacity under Maj. Gen. "Stonewall" Jackson. A little later, on paper at least, the brigade was placed under Maj. Gen. D.H. Hill's command in North Carolina. That never happened and somewhere along about the time of Second Manassas, the brigade passed under the command of Gen. James Longstreet of First Corps fame. Here it would stay for the remainder of the war.

A South Carolinian by birth, January 8, 1821, Gen. Longstreet grew up in Georgia. He graduated from the U.S. Military Academy, Class of 1842, where one of his best friends was Cadet Ulysses S. Grant, Class of 1843. He served in several Indian campaigns and was breveted for bravery in the Mexican War. At the beginning of the war, he held the rank of major in the U.S. Army and was serving as a paymaster.[79]

Gen. Longstreet was a stubborn fighter and was referred to by Gen. Lee at Sharpsburg as his "old warhorse." At Chickamauga, he won the sobriquet "Bull-of-the-Woods," where the troops under his command, including the Texas Brigade, broke the Union line and forced that army's retreat back upon Chattanooga. Longstreet was a fighter and it was Longstreet's Corps that Hood's Texans belonged to for the remainder of the war. John M. Smither, 5th Texas, said of Longstreet and Hood that "they [will] fight at the drop of a hat and drop it themselves."[80]

* * *

Save for a few days in May 1862, and during detached service in the winter and spring of 1863 and fall and winter of 1863–1864, the Texas Brigade served in the Army of Northern Virginia under the command of Gen. Robert E. Lee of Virginia. Gen. Lee's military resume was impeccable, second in his class at the U.S. Military Academy, Class of 1829, an outstanding career in the Engineer Corps, breveted service in the Mexican War on Gen. Winfield Scott's staff, superintendent of his alma mater and lieutenant colonel of the 2nd U.S. Cavalry Regiment at the time of his resignation and the tendering of his services to his native state.

Although some studies subsequent to the war concluded that he blundered at times, particularly at Gettysburg, his record of victories against a numerically and logistically superior enemy is daunting. Gen. Edward Porter Alexander, chief of artillery, Longstreet's Corps, remembered a conversation he had with Col. Joseph P. Ives serving on President Davis' staff several weeks after Gen. Lee's appointment to army command. There was some concern in the army about Gen. Lee's aggressiveness, or lack thereof. Most of his career to that time had been in a staff capacity. His resort to the shovel to entrench rather than to the musket as the Union Army approached Richmond had the men in the ranks referring to him as "Granny" Lee and the "king of spades." Alexander remembered asking Ives about Lee's audacity, a much-needed characteristic for any commander about to face a vastly superior force. Reining-in his horse, Ives' earnestly replied, "Alexander, if there is one man in either army, Confederate or Federal head and shoulders above every other in *audacity*, it is Gen. Lee! His name might be Audacity. He will take most desperate chances and take them quicker than any other general in this country, North or South, and you will live to see it, too."[81]

Alexander did live to see it although at a loss as to how, at that time, Ives or the president could have divined such depths of Lee's abilities. He went on to reflect, "No one could meet Lee and fail to be impressed with his dignity of character, his intellectual power, and his calm self-reliance; but all those qualities might be recognized without deducing from them also, the existence of such phenomenal audacity, except by an inspiration of genius."[82]

It did not take long for Gen. Lee to establish his reputation — audacity indeed! The men of the Texas Brigade came to worship the gray man on the gray horse, as did everyone else in the Army of Northern Virginia, for that matter. On the way to Sharpsburg, John W. Stevens, Co. K, 5th Texas, had an unexpected opportunity to observe Gen. Lee and Gen. Hood close up. He remembered, "What a privilege to be near [Lee's] person, to look at and study his form and the expression of his countenance, to catch an occasional word as it falls from his lips.... As he is dictating to his adjutant general his orders for the movement into Maryland, Gen. Hood also nearby with his sadly smiling countenance, speaking to the Texas boys in the ranks, assuring them of his confidence in them as soldiers and how proud he is of them."[83]

The men of the Texas Brigade worshiped the men and followed them faithfully and beyond.

With good leadership, generally, what of the men who filled the ranks? Glimpses can be had and conclusions drawn. In the winter of 1861–1862, six months or so prior to its brief affiliation with the brigade, Hampton's Legion occupied a portion of the Potomac line adjacent to that held by the Texans.

William A. Kenyon, Co. A, Hampton's Legion, was in frequent contact with the Texas scouts thrown out to harass the enemy. Noting that the scouts only numbered ten, their numbers were magnified by the enemy to thousands because "they were very shy of the Texans."[84] Robert H. Gaston, Co. H, 1st Texas, wrote his parents from Richmond in July 1861, that the "Texians have a great reputation here as fighters. The people here look upon a Texian ranger (as they call all Texians) as a person who don't care for anything. They say that they had as soon fight devils at once as Texians. We will have enough to do, if we get into a fight, to sustain our reputation."[85]

A copy of Frank Leslie's *Pictorial Paper* displayed an artist's conception of the Texans in which they were portrayed as being "half wolf, half hyena and man." This, no doubt, delighted the Texans and conformed much to the image they had of themselves as legatees of the Alamo, San Jacinto and the wars against the Indians.

The privates in the ranks of Hood's brigade were young and more often than not, no doubt, unmarried. "Median age for the 304 privates in Hood's brigade whose ages were listed on muster rolls was [twenty-four] years."[86] Capt. A. C. Jones, Co. G, 3rd Arkansas, characterized the young men in his command as stalwart and vigorous. Going on, he further described them as intelligent, and, "with a few exceptions ... well educated in English — at least sufficient for business purposes." He admitted that their schools were not first class, "a good academy was located in the township, and every family had access to a school of some sort.... Newspapers were freely circulated among our people, and the men were well-informed as to current events.... Our company became G. This regiment was about a fair sample of similar organizations throughout the Confederate army."[87]

According to Bell I. Wiley, Confederate soldiers almost universally displayed "a streak of individuality and of irresponsibility that made him a trial to officers during periods of inactivity."[88] Indeed most Confederate soldiers were highly independent and jealous of what they perceived to be their personal prerogatives. The Confederate armies, all of them, were pretty poorly disciplined in camp and on the march. Straggling was endemic. Perhaps as much attributable to lack of proper commissary and quartermaster support as for any desire to defy authority, straggling on the march was a serious problem for the leadership at all levels. James I. Robertson goes so far as to say that Civil War troops "were the worst soldiers and the best fighters that America has ever produced."[89] It was a demonstrated fact that if they could be brought to battle in sufficient numbers they would fight fiercely, thereby considerably increasing their chances of victory.

Gen. Hood remembered that on the diversionary march from Staunton in the Shenandoah Valley to Richmond in late June 1862 he had become a straggler himself and had come upon a group of stragglers gathered around a rail fence fire. Regaling the group about Comanche hunting in West Texas was Bill Calhoun, whom Gen. Hood recognized as the wag of Co. B, 4th Texas. Stifling his impulse to laugh, Hood rode into the circle of light cast by the roaring fire. Knowing that Calhoun recognized him immediately, Hood put on his sternest face and ordered Calhoun to "join your regiment, sir. I don't know why you are loitering here, so far behind your command." Shouldering his rifle and stalking off into the dark, Calhoun gave Hood a hard look replying, " Yes, and what you don't know Gen. Hood would make a mighty damned big book."

Later, Gen. Hood caught up with the plodding soldier and in striking up a conversation found him to be "one of the brightest and best informed young men in the army."[90] He had handled the situation well and in return Calhoun, insubordinate to the end, served faithfully, suffering wounds at Second Manassas and Sharpsburg in the service of the brigade. John W. Stevens , Co. K, 5th Texas, in his reminiscences, agreed that they "were the brightest types of the citizen soldiery. The Southern as a soldier met every responsibility that was laid upon him."[91]

The only significant recognition that a Confederate soldier in the ranks might expect to receive for acts of bravery and generosity was the respect and admiration of his comrades. There was no provision in the Confederate army for decorations or field promotion for distinguished acts of valor. To be recounted at greater length in a later chapter, at Sharpsburg, Nicholas Pomeroy, Co. A, 5th Texas, saved a wounded officer from almost certain death on the battlefield. Receiving the thanks of the wounded officer, he then continued on to his post. In later wars, such bravery would be highly decorated. Pomeroy, not expecting any recognition, was satisfied to feel self-gratification.

Randolph H. McKim served as an aide-de-camp in the Army of Northern Virginia, and years later served as rector of the Church of the Epiphany in Washington, D.C. In reminiscing about his experiences in that remarkable army, he thought that one of the things that most strongly identified that army was the independence of the individual soldier. Although a stricter discipline, he thought was lacking, it was made up for by the strong individuality of the units. Such units, he thought, were hard to demoralize.[92]

D. H. Hamilton, Co. M, 1st Texas, thought that the men in the ranks knew the spirit of the army better than its leadership often did. He thought that he and his comrades "always had the most implicit confidence in their ability to whip the enemy whenever and wherever we met them on equal terms, even when outnumbered, if the odds were not too great. This confidence was inspired and justified by what was done in every battle until we were literally overpowered with numbers and exhausted. When I look back upon the trials and hardships of the campaigns, the scant food, clothing and equipment that we had, and the comparatively little protection from rain, cold, and snow, to which we were all unaccustomed, it is astonishing how such a splendid spirit was so long maintained."[93]

The Texas Brigade was a part of an army led by a man epitomizing audacity, a corps commanded by a warhorse, and bull-of-the-woods, a first brigade, then divisional commander, who would fight at the drop of a hat, regimental and company officers who led out front exhibiting extremes of bravery, and mainly, young men filling the ranks of frontier backgrounds that were rough and ready and spoiling for a fight. This is a military recipe containing all of the ingredients essential in establishing a premier fighting unit. After a brief period of trial and error, the leadership got it right for that time and that place in history. The result was not a spit and polish outfit; however, it came to be recognized as an outstanding and famous fighting one.

CHAPTER 4

"Those Texians are number one men"[1]: From the Potomac to the Peninsula, July 1861–June 1862

The American Civil War erupted as shot and shell showered down upon the Federally-defended fort named Sumter in the harbor of Charleston, South Carolina, on April 12, 1861. It ended for the Texas Brigade three days short of four years hence with the surrender of the Army of Northern Virginia at Appomattox Court House, Virginia, on April 9, 1865. The brigade's war encompassed approximately 1,458 days. If one will but consider, very few of those days were spent engaged in actual battle with an armed foe.

The seemingly endless days intervening between "the interesting episodes" of battle were spent in bivouacs, camps, winter quarters or on the march. They were what, in John W. Thomason's *Lone Star Preacher*, the fictional Methodist minister and captain, 5th Texas Regiment, the Rev. Praxiteles Swan, referred to as "bad, dull business."[2] They were days lived with illness, death cloaked in many forms, physical and emotional exhaustion, personal discomfort, dispiriting homesickness and, probably worst of all, unrelieved boredom.

If the men of the Texas Brigade had not already become aware of the foregoing facts after their first few months of Confederate service, their experiences of the coming years would leave them fully informed. Nonetheless, it was not the "bad, dull days" they endured but rather their performance in the few days in which they were engaged in battle, "the interesting episodes," that won them their place in Texas history, specifically, and in American military history, generally.

* * *

While the contending armies, following the Confederate victory at Manassas (Bull Run) in July 1861, prepared for the next round of fighting, the first year of the war slipped slowly by as the Blue and Gray armies remained encamped, training and contemplating their war-waging futures. Around the first part of October 1861, the eleven companies comprising the 1st Texas Regiment broke camp and made their first long march as a unit. Weighed down with weapons and equipment, the move was from Camp Wigfall near Manassas Junction to the vicinity of Dumfries, a town located near the south bank of the Potomac River below Washington. Nearby, an artillery battery had been established overlooking the Potomac for the purpose of interdicting the flow of Federal traffic on the river. Upon the Texans' arrival, the defense of the battery, composed of three heavy guns, was assigned to their keeping. A little later, another battery of four guns was established at Cockpit's Point about three miles farther upstream and in concert with the other batteries "all the [Federal] traffic on the river was virtually stopped."[3]

A typical experience was Co. E,'s 1st Texas. Their move to Dumfries began early in the morning to the lively strains of "Dixie," a tune sure to arouse patriotic spirits and emotionally blunt the hardships of a heavily-laden march. The Rev. W. C. Collins recalled, "We all felt light-hearted, strong and happy and though we had our knapsacks all on our backs, with rifles, muskets etc, we felt equal to the task of carrying it to the place of our next encampment; but not so with all; many throw away their blankets and much of their clothing. Poor fellows! I don't know what those of them will do who haven't money, and are too honest to steal." They were two days on the march to reach their new campsite. At least for the time being, the Reverend Collins said that the "health of the boys is good with a few exceptions.... Our fare is very good, considering the inconveniences of market etc. We are pleasantly situated and are supplied with the best of water."[4]

A few weeks later, in Richmond, on November 4, 1861, the 4th and 5th Texas received orders to shed any of their excess baggage for deposit at the Texas Depot. This depot was a brigade storage location shared by all and situated on the corner of Main and Seventh streets in Richmond. A few days later, they were marched into Richmond where they boarded the cars of the Richmond, Fredericksburg and Potomac line, their ultimate destination being Dumfries.

Upon arrival at Brook's Station above Fredericksburg, they remained bivouacked until November 12. Then, acting upon an urgent request from Gen. Wigfall at Dumfries for support against an expected attack, they made their first forced march for Dumfries — after dark and in the rain. Eighteen hours later, their exhausting, rain-soaked slog was revealed to have been in response to a false alarm. This was the first of many false alarms responded to by the men while under the command of the nervous, alcohol-prone Louis T. Wigfall.

On the same march, Mark J. Smither, Co. D, 5th Texas, related that "[w]hen we came up here we made a forced march of 28 miles from nine o'clock in the night until day light and the boys were very noisy and uproarious at the prospect of a fight and were singing and yelling as they pushed on ... the inhabitants on the road knowing that we were coming and hearing so much noise. We could see [whole] families taking to the woods in every direction." He thought that the perception that the populace had at that time early in the war about the nature of the Texans was incorrect. "They thought we were a set of desperadoes that would kill a man if he looked hard at them, a band of lawless adventurers who respected neither God nor man."[5] The Texans, no doubt, took great pleasure in observing the civilians' opinion of them and did nothing to refute their fierce reputation

Rain-soaked marches meant rain-swollen streams. On that march from the vicinity of Fredericksburg to Dumfries all the streams were out of their banks. At one flooded crossing point, Miles V. Smith's, Co. D, 4th Texas, was trying to avoid a soaking by walking one at a time across a foot log. It was a time-consuming process. When Col. Hood saw what was going on he rode up and ordered, "O, boys, pitch in, pitch in, and come across, it's not more than ankle deep." When they "pitched in" they found the water to be up to about their middle. One of the thus duped fellows yelled out, "Colonel, if you call this only ankle deep, what in the H[ell] would you call waist deep?"[6] Smiling, the wise and wily Col. Hood turned his horse and rode away.

By the time the brigade elements had combined at Dumfries, the harsh northern Virginia winter was beginning to set in. In that era, Civil War armies could not maneuver effectively during the characteristically wet, cold winter weather months. This was due,

"Wigfall Mess," Co. L, 1st Texas at Dumphries, Virginia, 1861–1862 (Museum of the Confederacy, Richmond, Virginia).

mainly, to the tendency of the many unsurfaced roads winding their way through the campaign theaters to become potential quagmires as rain and snow cascaded down during the inclement winter months. The tramping feet of passing armies, often numbering in the thousands, with their accompanying animal-drawn wagons and artillery pieces transformed such roads into impassable morasses. Armies bogged down and were often reduced to immobility. So it was that, prior to the advent of widespread, hard-surfaced roads, armies went into encampments known as winter quarters. The winter respite, occasionally interrupted by attempts at minor campaigning, lasted until the following spring. Then, as the weather conditions improved and the budding trees and wild flowers heralded the coming of spring, the arousing armies gathered their instruments of war and prepared to go forth and meet the enemy.

Thus it was, that as winter in Virginia deepened, the three Texas regiments, united in the Dumfries area and thence brigaded with the 18th Georgia, began preparations for going into their first winter quarters. In their assigned position the brigade comprised the extreme right flank of the Confederate Army lining the Potomac River opposite and below Washington, D.C. In their position, the brigade's primary duty was to support the artillery batteries interdicting the river and to repel any attempted crossing of the river by the Federal forces arrayed along the opposite bank. Gazing across the river, Robert Gaston, Co. H, 1st Texas, noted "a large United States flag hoisted over there." And he clearly heard their drums.[7]

Taking advantage of the terrain, access afforded to water and natural building materials, the regiments went about laying out their winter homes. M. V. Smith's, Co. D, 4th Texas, wisely chose a site with an east-west ridge to the north as protection from the wintry blasts regularly sweeping down from the north. (In Texas, they were and are called blue northers.) It was up to the troops to procure the materials available in the neighborhood for the construction of their winter homes, Typically, their cabins were constructed of slim pine poles, often including mud-chinked pole chimneys. Occasionally, although expressly forbidden, building materials were procured from the private property of the citizens populating the area.

Co. I, 1st Texas' "winter quarters [were] some little distance back from the river but sufficiently near to protect the batteries. [They] were assigned quarters with a street of about 80 feet between companies and told to build as [they] pleased."[8] The weather during their sojourn at Dumfries was frequently cold, with alternating periods of rain or snow. The cabins erected varied greatly in architectural design. The only regimental restriction was that they be erected in a straight line. That task completed, Co. I settled in with officially little to do but attend roll call three times daily and perform picket duty on the river front every twelfth night.

Deeming his winter quarters "quite comfortable," Joe Polley's Co. F, 4th Texas, quarters were constructed, generally, to house individual messes. Mess halls in the modern sense of buildings seldom existed to serve the troops, except perhaps those on garrison duty. In the field messes were usually comprised of 5–10 men organized to draw rations and thence prepare them for meals in the rough.

In Polley's mess, "the responsibility for constructing the cabin ... was impartially and judiciously distributed among its members."[9] In the case of Polley's cabin, the space required for a six-member mess was underestimated and the two individuals involved in planning were banished to a tent for the rest of the winter for their miscalculation.

In, Co. A, 5th Texas, Nicholas Pomoroy thought their cabins were very comfortable and that supplies were plentiful, but, "the winter was cold with sleet and snow, which many of our boys from Southern Texas saw now for the first time, and this, added to the strict watch we had to keep night and day along the riverbank, told heavily on some of the tenderly reared youths of our company. Many got sick from exposure and were sent to the rear and very few of them returned."[10] The deadliest enemy of the soldiers of the Civil War was disease in its many forms.

This was true particularly during the early phases of the war before the fittest had survived. They lived in the day before the nature of bacteria and viruses were known and before inoculation against disease was available. Although the importance of sanitary conditions was recognized, it was not practiced effectively. Young, inexperienced men, unaccustomed and not acclimated to life in the field and to living in close quarters with large numbers of other people were easy prey for disease of all kinds.

Company E, 4th Texas "was particularly hard hit during this first fall and winter in Virginia. Six men died "who fell victim to typhoid fever on February 1, 1862.... Fifty-two men were hospitalized during this period of time. This was 50% of the assigned company strength. Once a soldier had fallen victim to one disease, he was usually left in such a weakened condition that he was easy prey for the other diseases bred by the unsanitary conditions that were prevalent."[11] When the spring campaign season began and the army fell back to the Rappahannock line, Pomoroy, Co. A, 5th Texas, said that about one-third of his company had been placed *hors de combat* by disease of various kinds — typhoid, typhus, pneumonia, hepatitis, diarrhea and all of the childhood diseases.

In the experience of the 1st Texas at its several encampments along the Potomac in the first year of the war, it was the measles, a viral disease of varying severity but always highly communicable, that felled many. It could be and was in that day often fatal. Characterized by high fever and red spots on the skin, those infected were removed to hospitals, when possible. There were no hospitals readily available to the 1st Texas, so some of those not infected were detailed as nurses. Membership in the Confederate Army required versatility. Needless to say, such details were scrupulously avoided by the more nimble-minded not anxious to place themselves in harm's way.

While not to be found in any official training curriculum in any age, there is an unwritten rule for all soldiers that must be observed: "Thou shalt not volunteer for anything!" W. D. Pritchard, Co. I, 1st Texas, learned the importance of that unwritten rule the hard way. He remembered, regretfully, being detailed for nursing duty as a result of his own lapse. 2nd Sgt. Jon H. Foster, who himself would survive wounds at Gaines' Mill in 1862 only to be killed at Chickamauga in 1863, was cautioning the men to be careful in the presence of measles when Pritchard's mouth took over and he remarked:

"[Damn] the measles, I had them when I was a boy."
To which the sergeant replied,
"You are the man I am looking for; I want you for a nurse in the hospital."

Although he survived the detail, Pritchard remembered the next six weeks as "miserable" in that "wretched place."[12]

Living in the rough, enduring very primitive conditions, being irregularly paid, poorly fed and supplied, and beset by episodes of violence and epidemic diseases, one can but wonder at their will to endure.

In military encampments of all types, camp security is always a matter of the utmost importance. In such circumstances, attacks by the enemy coming as a surprise was unforgivable. Thus, providing security by mounting standing guards was the way to avoid surprise attacks and was organized on a rotating basis. During that time on the banks of the Potomac, an amusing incident involving guard duty and illustrating the difficult task faced by those trying to turn the Texans and Georgians into soldiers is told by William H. Pritchard, Co. I, 1st Texas. According to Pritchard, "old man, Ebin Andrews" of his company was on guard duty one night when the "grand rounds" were made. Grand rounds were tours of the picket line made by the upper level army brass, in this case, Gen. Joseph E. Johnston, Gen. P. G. T. Beauregard, Gen. Wigfall and their various staffs. The purpose of such rounds was to impress upon the soldiers the importance that the brass placed upon the guard's duty being properly discharged. As they approached "old man Ebin's" post, the elderly sentinel properly challenged them. When they identified themselves as "the Grand Rounds," he expressed his disappointment, military courtesy notwithstanding, saying "'Oh! H—l. I thought it was the relief.'" Gen. Beauregard took Ebin's weapon and then scolded him saying, "I have your gun; you are a fine soldier to give your gun to a man. Don't you know when the relief comes around and finds you without a gun, you will be shot? What are you going to do?" The old man was paralyzed for a moment but quickly recovered. He hastily drew from his pocket an old brass barrel pistol which he shoved full in the General's face, saying, "'Give me my gun or I will blow H—l out of you.'"[13] Hastily, Gen. Beauregard returned the weapon and continued on his rounds. He was, perhaps, less prone in the future to weapons inspection when minimally-trained, volunteer troops were involved.

As the men settled in for their long winter's night, thoughts of home were often on their minds. In a letter home one soldier speculated that "if the young ladies want good and available husbands — just tell them to wait until the soldier boys return. We all have learned to cook, wash and sew — and hereafter, in case the cook should get sick, we could assume the onus of the Kitchen.[14] Writing home in January 1862, Robert V. Foster, Co. C, 4th Texas, described the time as "dull and monotonous." Living roughly in the field, his situation made it difficult to write regularly, having only knapsacks, boards and the like to write on. Once winter set in, it was too cold to venture away from the fire in the cabins and too crowded in the small spaces to find room to write. He described this as "only a few of the inconveniences, to which we are faced." Other accounts to the contrary, Foster said they had nothing to read except an occasional newspaper, usually weeks old by the time it was acquired. Earlier, he had tried to buy a volume of Shakespeare in Richmond but found it too heavy for carrying in a knapsack, a fact he continued to lament. As to local sources, "[t]here is nothing in this little Dumfries, that a person wants, except a few cooking utensils, a little sugar and coffee, tobacco, molasses ... all of which are sold for about three prices."[15] It should not have made any difference to most, he added, as they had not been paid for the last two months.

In a letter to the Marshall, Texas, *Republican*, "J. M. T." Co. E, 1st Texas, observed that "[c]amp life will either kill us or make men of us.... Military life is hard — a bitter enemy of ease, luxury or a debouched palate; but we embrace the difference with pleasure, and would endure any and everything rather than submit to Lincoln [tyranny] or affiliate with Federal despotism."[16] The men of the Texas Brigade were learning the hard facts of soldier life in the field.

However, not all was unrelieved camp boredom and inactivity. There were always opportunities for verbal contact with the enemy across the expanse of the Potomac separating the belligerents. Such was usually in the nature of posturing and taunts, but it sometimes resulted in small actions. Although then not yet affiliated with the Texas Brigade, Hampton's South Carolina Legion was encamped nearby. Sometime early in the fall of 1861, Col. Hampton secured the services of some eight frontier-experienced Texas scouts for the purpose of watching his front. The scouts, described as "fine and brave as ever lived and armed with Mississippi rifles, ... were quartered in a house on the north edge of Colchester on a bluff overlooking the Occoquan."[17] By January 1862, the Texans had proved to be active and annoying to their Federal counterparts, so much so in fact, that a plan was hatched by the Federals to attack and capture or kill their tormentors.

The Federal units involved, as it was later learned, were detachments of the 37th New York Infantry and the 1st New Jersey Cavalry.[18] Later, it was passed around that during the attack in which the Texans were outnumbered, one of them had the presence of mind to shout for his comrades to hold out because Col. Hampton was on his way with a relief force. Reputedly, the Federals heard this and broke off their attack.

At that stage of the war, all was youthful enthusiasm and excitement over anything and everything that happened. The real tests would come soon enough. Minor though this action was compared to those of later vintage, it marked the beginning of the Texas Brigade legend in the Army of Northern Virginia. Lt. Col. Griffin, Hampton Legion, paid the Texas scouts high praise. "Those Texians are number one men, and their conduct on that occasion was as gallant and brave as anything that has occurred in this war."[19] In Special Order Number 29, Brig Gen. Whiting, commanding the division, noted the incident stating that "[s]uch conduct deserves praise and invites emulation, and is worthy of the success of the men who, many years ago, gallantly defended their cause at the Alamo and San Jacinto."[20]

As winter began to give way to spring and the active campaigning season neared, army commander Gen. Joseph E. Johnston decided that the Potomac line was indefensible; there was too much territory to defend and too few men to defend it. The order was given that the army would retreat south to the line of the Rappahannock River. In order to not alert the enemy of the move, camps and fortifications were to be left intact. This retrograde movement would be, for the Texas Brigade, the first of many marches as a complete unit over the course of the next four years. But, before relating of some of the hardships experienced during the movement, specifically, a word about some of the hard realities of all Civil War-era marches generally.

All Civil War–era marches shared common characteristics. They were frequently long. Depending upon the season, they were either hot and dusty or they were cold, wet and mud-laden. Often they were at night in order to be in line of battle in the early morning hours for engagements that might last for several days. And, they were exhausting — always. On those marches, one authority has noted that "Southern troops were seldom orderly.... Lee's men moved 'at a slow dragging pace' and were 'evidently not good marchers naturally.' Particularly in the early years of the war Southern soldiers found victory nearly as demoralizing as defeat, and after a battle 'many would coolly walk off home, under the impression that they had performed their share."[21]

March discipline was but one of the things that the citizen soldiers of the South had no experience in dealing with. Gen. Jackson did have experience and his unit's march routine was normally fifty minutes of hard marching (his soldiers referred to themselves as foot cavalry) with ten minute rest breaks every hour. As the war progressed and experience was gained, that routine, or something similar, evolved throughout the army. Of course, in circumstances where haste was required, normal routines were ignored and forced marches became the order of the day.

Marching columns, usually four wide, particularly when the entire army was on the same roads, could stretch out for miles. As a result, at the commencement of a march and following rest periods, the strung-out units were not always notified in a timely fashion of the resumption of the march. The result was an accordion effect with the army being distributed unevenly and farther apart than necessary had all units started at the same time. Lagging units were forced to speed up in order to catch up. Some of the extreme fatigue experienced was unnecessary had marches by all units commenced simultaneously.

Units were not always rotated in the march order. The result in hot, dusty weather was the rear elements having to eat the dust raised in billowing clouds by the preceding units with but little respite. Dust mixed with sweat transformed visages into ghostly apparitions. Water usually was not available in sufficient quantity to quench the thirst torturing the thousands of dust-clogged throats. In cold, wet weather, the rear elements had to struggle through seas of mud, each step adding to their burden, created by the passage of thousands of feet preceding them. All of it was exhausting; they were hot or cold, dusty or drenched to the skin, routinely hungry because the rickety commissary wagons, drawn by poorly fed, equally exhausted animals, with their limited fare, could not keep up. They were often in rags and barefoot because of a dearth of quartermaster supplies. Nonetheless, many found the hard marches preferable to the unrelieved boredom of camp life. At least they were on their way somewhere even though they all knew that that somewhere might mark the site of their extinction.

Preparations for marches were elaborate. Well-experienced in the process, W. D. Pritchard, Co. I, 1st Texas, said that the first sure sign that a change of venue was in the offing was the order being passed down to cook rations for multiple days and be ready to march at a moment's notice. Another sure signal that a march was coming was the issuance by the commissaries of hardtack and bacon, which were rations for campaigning with little preparations necessary for consumption.

Once these orders came down, the camps became beehives of activity with the messes collecting wood for cooking fires and gathering water. Out came the cooking implements with each individual in the mess performing his assigned task, frying the bacon, mixing the ingredients for making biscuits. If they were lucky, they would have time to finish the task without wasting any of their always short rations. If not, they would have to pack in whatever ingenious way they could come up with — pockets, cartridge boxes, bayonet tips — in order to preserve their half-cooked fare.

Then, the order to be prepared to march at a certain time came down and might be, and frequently was, in the middle of the night. At this point, the men would wander from mess to mess inquiring of all they met, "Where are we going?" only to be told that they didn't know either. Then, with all in readiness, the order to fall in was heard as "[c]ompanies form into regiments, which in turn form into brigades, and they into divisions, and take their places in line.... Fully rested and flushed with [their] recent victories, [they] went forth to conquer."[22]

The retrograde movement to the Rappahannock line commenced on March 8, 1862, each company being allowed half a wagon for transport of the company's property. Everything else had to be carried by the men or abandoned. Simultaneous with the move, Col. Hood was promoted to brigadier general. Effective March 12, he was relieved of command of the 4th Texas and given command of the four regiment Texas Brigade.

Among the various marching units, Co. I, 1st Texas, marched to Brook's Station on the Fredericksburg and Aquia Creek Railroad at which point it boarded the cars for Fredericksburg.[23] For less fortunate companies that had to tramp the entire distance, the march was made even more difficult due to inclement weather. Robert Gaston's, Co. H, 1st Texas, marched to Fredericksburg "through mud nearly knee deep all the way and through water sometimes waist deep. The weather was [very] cold and [the company] had [to] lie out three weeks [altogether] without their tents."[24]

Hood's reputation as a leader continued to build, even though Gaston said that "some of us" preferred John H. Reagan, a Texan and the Confederate States postmaster general. On the march to Fredericksburg, some of the units "came to a creek about waist deep and very wide. They halted for Gen. Hood to come up to see what he would do. When he came up he dismounted and gave his horse to some of his staff and plunged into it, telling the boys to follow him. They went through without hesitation."[25] That was the kind of leadership, sharing the troops' difficulties, that the frontier-types most respected and responded to.

In a letter to the folks at home, John F. McKee, Co. K, 5th Texas, wrote that "we have had hard times for the last two weeks. We have marched ... [many miles], laid out three days and nights without even blankets. It snowed and rained on us every day and night."[26] Such travails were only the beginning; three more years of campaigning that included hundreds of miles to be marched were awaiting them just over the horizon.

There were few men hardy enough to make all the marches strictly on their own. Usually, and if available, a few wagons were set aside to provide temporary transportation for the lame or infirm. A. A. Congleton, Co. I, 1st Texas, was able to make the march most of the way under his own steam but eventually had to be placed on a wagon to complete the trip. Setting out early and heavily laden they marched quick-time until midnight when they camped for the first night.[27] The woods were quickly lighted up by campfires as they prepared their late dinner of bread and pork broiled on a stick. After a brief sleep in the open, the drums signaled the call to rise to begin the second day's tramp. The weather was so cold that stoppers froze in the mouths of their canteens and had to be thawed before a drink of water could be had. The second day went well but the third day it commenced raining and poured until late in the afternoon. Congleton said that their individual loads were heavy, consisting of haversack, canteen, cartridge box, heavy rifle and knapsack stuffed to capacity with the toiler's clothes. "I tell you that mud and such a [load] was hard [getting] along. You could see them giving out [spread] on the road[side] all the time." He made it until close to Fredericksburg. There they stopped while the leadership went ahead to pick a camp-ground. Then, still in an exhausted state, he had to stand guard that night after the hard day's march. Becoming ill, he said "the next day I had to go on the wagon."[28] Upon arriving at Fredericksburg, according to Robert Gaston, they, for what must have been about the only time during the war, were introduced into "very good quarters (houses having been built for the purpose) and we get plenty to eat & of course we are doing finely."[29]

It was a report of a force of 5,000 Yankees at Stafford Court House, north of Fredericksburg, that once more put the brigade in the ranks and retracing its route into the night. Issued three days rations of crackers and pork off they quick-timed at midnight, continuing, according to Congleton, until 10:00 in the morning. When within a few miles of their destination, intelligence reached them that the Federal force had withdrawn. Ordered to stay in position, that night it began to rain. After a sodden night, the next morning they started back from whence they had come. "The road was so slick that we could [hardly] stand up. So after plowing in the mud and clay all day we got to camp.... [W]orn out and about fatigued to death, out of the [1st] Texas Regiment, there were not more [than] 200 got into camp in order. All the rest [gave] out on the road.[30] He reported, also, that some were drunk in town.

In the meantime, the mantle of command of the Federal army had passed from Gen. Irving McDowell to Gen. George B. McClellan. Appointed by President Lincoln, effective November 1, 1861, as general in chief of the Armies of the United States, the confident 1846 West Point graduate had declared, "I can do it all." Along with the new commander came a new strategy for a winning campaign in the East.

The strategy proposed by Gen. McClellan entailed withdrawing the bulk his army from the Manassas front where it had lain licking its wounds following the Manassas (Bull Run) debacle, transporting it by water down the Chesapeake Bay and landing it in the environs of Fortress Monroe, the Federally-held fort overlooking Hampton Roads at the tip of the Virginia Peninsula. Stretching westward from the fort, the Peninsula was formed by the James River to the left, and the York River to the right. At the far end of this tactically-beckoning highway, a scant ninety miles away, lay the jewel in the Confederate crown, Richmond, its capital city and symbol of the candidate nation's perceived sovereignty. With the army's flanks anchored firmly on the two rivers, both would be secured by the gun-studded vessels of the U.S. Navy prowling those river's waters. With flanks thus secured, the strategy was for the Army of the Potomac, over 100,000 men strong, to sweep up the Peninsula and capture the Confederate capital.

Although there were simpler alternatives favored by President Lincoln, he was willing to give his new commander the benefit of the doubt. And, it was not a bad plan. It would have worked had it not been for the usual unforeseen and overlooked factors. For one thing, Federal intelligence information was inaccurate and Confederate numbers were vastly over-estimated. The result was an exaggerated caution exhibited by the Federal commander. What the tactical situation called for was a rapid, bold advance against an outnumbered foe. Alas for the Federal cause, it did not happen that way.

While overestimating their opponent's numbers, Gen. McClellan and his planning staff underestimated the physical reality of the tactical stage upon which their performance was to be acted out. A flat map of the area, of which there was a dearth, was one thing but the physical realities of the region were quite another. The Peninsula was certainly more difficult than anticipated. There were almost impenetrable stretches of pine forests. The roads, that were poor to begin with, became bottomless morasses when deluged by seasonally drenching rains. The climate during the campaigning season was hot, humid and insect-ridden. It was enervating and a rich breeding ground for the rise of disease that could and did ravage the ranks of the armies struggling within its sweat-drenched grip.

By the time the Federal Army began its advance in the spring, Confederate forces, then under Gen. John B. Magruder, guarding the lower Peninsula had been considerably augmented as Gen. Johnston moved from his Rappahannock line down the peninsula to York-town. Some of the Texas Brigade soldiers had not yet recovered fully from the rigors of their recent march to the area. Several days prior to the move down the peninsula to Yorktown, Congleton, Co. I, 1st Texas, reported himself as "alive but considerably unwell." "My back is in such a condition that I am unfit for any use. It appears that my [kidneys] are rotten or in the worst sort of a condition. I can [get] nothing that will do them any good, and in addition to that I have the Rheumatism in my knees and feet, or some other [damned] disease. So I am in an awful condition but I hope to [get] over them all. If I don't I am played out."[31] Thousands of others suffered in some similar manner but, alas, there were no medical means readily available there to help them deal with their conditions. And about that time, when matters could not possibly get worse, they got worse. A night march was ordered.

The Texas Brigade marched from Fredericksburg on April 8, 1862, after less than a month in residence there. Tramping to Milford Station, it took the cars to Ashland Station on the Fredericksburg line north of Richmond. There it again took up the march leading to Yorktown, one which Hood described as presenting the worst weather he had ever experienced on a march."[32] They arrived at Yorktown on April 15, 1862, "footsore and tired."

For the next several weeks they remained in that area around Yorktown acting as scouts and sharpshooters. Reputedly, their position "occupied the same ground as that of the rebel army during the revolutionary struggle."[33] Also, reputedly, the Texans joined in with other soldiers in the area in seeking souvenirs that reduced a stone monument on the site to rubble.

While there the noncommissioned officers and privates of the 4th Texas presented Gen. Hood with a horse as an expression of their esteem. In the presentation speech, Sgt. J. M. Bookman, Co. G, 4th Texas, killed at Chickamauga in 1863, praised Hood, saying, "Sir, we recognize the soldier and the gentleman. In you, we have found a leader whom we are proud to follow, a commander whom it is a pleasure to obey.... In a word ... you stand by us, and we will stand by you."[34] Hood, springing into the saddle, expressed his gratitude and steadfastness in their behalf.

About the first of May 1862, Gen. McClellan, a very cautious commander, at last set his vast, well-equipped army, about 100,000 strong, in motion up the Peninsula toward Richmond. As he would do frequently throughout the course of the war, an equally cautious Gen. Joseph E. Johnston concluded that his position was indefensible. In this situation he was probably correct in his assessment given the vulnerability of his flanks resting on two rivers and subject to the those big naval guns. Orders were issued for the army's retreat to begin on May 3, 1862. The Texas Brigade was assigned the position of honor — they would serve as the rear guard of the army.

Using siege tactics at times, Gen. McClellan's forces advanced with the Confederate forces falling back slowly before them. Yorktown fell on May 4, and a sharp action on May

5, resulted in a Confederate withdrawal from Williamsburg. The Texas Brigade was directed to proceed to the vicinity of Eltham's Landing, located on the banks of the York River. Gen. Johnston believed that Gen. McClellan might attempt to land a flanking force in an effort to cut off the Confederate retreat. Eltham's Landing appeared to be the most likely point for such a landing.

On May 6, 1862, the Texas Brigade was at the landing and on May 7 engaged the expected Federal landing force. What had evolved was a lively, aggressive action in which the Federals, with losses, were forced back to their landing craft. In the brief fray, Gen. Hood's career came close to ending right there. He owed his life to John Deal, Co. A, 4th Texas, who, disobeying orders not to cap his weapon until ordered, dropped a Federal corporal who had drawn a bead on Gen. Hood. Company B, 4th Texas was credited with killing three enemy soldiers, fully six hundred yards [away] with Enfield rifles "the first we ever saw killed in battle" according to W. D. Pritchard (Co. I, 1st Texas).[35] The action at Eltham's Landing was revered as the first that the Texas Brigade was involved in as a complete unit.

However, all of this exceeded Gen. Johnston's instructions to Gen. Hood to "feel the enemy" and determine their intentions. Strict obedience to orders is a hallmark of military discipline. Gen. Johnston was not pleased with Hood's apparent disobedience of those orders. Summoned to army headquarters Gen. Hood was asked to repeat the orders he had received. When he had done so, Gen. Johnston asked if his actions were the Texan's idea of "feeling the enemy and falling back. What would you have done had my orders been charge and drive them back?" Confident in the aftermath of his success, Hood replied: "I suppose, General, they would have driven them into the river, and tried to swim out and capture the gunboats." With a smile, Gen. Johnston replied: "Teach your Texans that the first duty of a soldier is literally to obey orders."[36]

Remembering that following their first real fight it took a little while to get reorganized and resume the retreat toward Richmond, W. D. Pritchard, Co. I, 1st Texas, said that in camp, after a short march "it was ... the events of the day brought out in their strongest light. Every man was the hero of the occasion. Each told what he did and saw — most marvelous tales of hair-breadth escapes, close calls and acts of personal prowess."[37] In retrospect, it was a minor action and in no way comparable to the big battles yet to come.

It was a sodden retreat that dragged on as heavy rains continued. The roads were blocked frequently by the wagons and artillery, and the mud was simply terrible. To keep things from bogging down totally, Gen. Whiting ranged the column urging the men forward. "Close up, men, close up,' said he. 'Don't mind a little mud!' 'Do you call this a little mud?' said one of the men. 'S'pose you get down stranger and try it. I'll hold your horse.' 'Do you know who you are talking to? I'm Gen. Whiting.' 'General be [damned]! Don't you reckon I know a general from a long-tongued courier?' said the man and stepped into the dark.'"[38] It took a great deal of patience and discretion to command men such as these. On that occasion Gen.Whiting chose discretion and wordlessly rode on.

Describing the march in terms of mud, M. V. Smith, Co. D, 4th Texas, lamented, "O! the mud, the mud we had to trudge through from shoe mouth to knee deep, and sometimes march half the night when it was so dark we couldn't see our file leader, and would have to hold onto one another to keep from getting separated. Nevertheless, the almost insupportable fatigue and hardships we had to endure, the boys would be sounding the mud and water like sailors sound the sea. All up and down the line they would be hallowing: 'Ankle deep, knee deep, thigh deep etc.'"[39]

In Co. I, 1st Texas, on the same sodden march, one soldier was loudly venting his feelings against the Yankees whose fault it was for their being in that uncomfortable situation. Their chaplain, passing on horseback, overheard the deprecations and reminded the man of the biblical injunction that vengeance was the Lord's to wreak. Undeterred, the soldier replied "All right Parson, I believe I am an instrument in the hands to punish those d — n Yankees and you bet I am going to give them h — l."[40]

Co. H's 1st Texas, march was "frequently … all day without anything to eat, & never … more than three crackers (hardtack) a day." Otherwise, about the only thing they got on the march was a flour ration. This they tried to cook on their bayonets over open fires. Alas! it was noted "they would not give us time to cook it in that way."[41] Co. A, 5th Texas, had much the same experience "constantly on the move, … very little rest, and owing to the difficulty of following us up with supplies, we had to live on very scanty rations."[42]

When the exhausted, hungry but still defiant army reached the outskirts of Richmond, it took up defensive positions to meet the expected Federal onslaught. The Texas Brigade's position was part of the army's left flank across the Chickahominy Creek, swollen beyond its banks by the heavy rains. Making the best of the situation, one Texan noted the transition from mud to water was "rather agreeable." The Federal army, three infantry corps with supporting units and numbering about 105,000 men, soon followed and, within sight and sound, respectively, of the steeples and bells of Richmond's churches, strung out its line and began siege operations.

There soon followed, from May 31 to June 1, 1862, the battle of Seven Pines (Fair Oaks). In the course of that fight, Confederate commander Gen. Joseph E. Johnston was seriously wounded. On the spot, Gen. Robert E. Lee was appointed in his stead by Confederate president Jefferson Davis, both being on the field at the time. From that day forward plans were being formulated to relieve the pressure on Richmond and deal the Federal Army a staggering blow.

Further complicating military matters for Gen. Lee and his planning staff was the presence of a considerable Federal command in their rear threatening from a position only several days march to the north. Located in the vicinity of Fredericksburg, it was then under the command of Gen. Irving McDowell, the losing contender at the battle of First Manassas (Bull Run). Estimated as numbering between 30,000 and 40,000, its purpose was threefold: to protect the Federal capital

William H. Gaston, Co. H, 1st Texas

from assault, to go to the aid of Federal forces fighting Gen. "Stonewall" Jackson's Army of the Valley in the Shenandoah, if needed, or to reinforce Gen. McClellan's army if similarly needed. From the beginning, Gen. McClellan fully expected that this force would join his "badly outnumbered" army, ultimately, and participate in the capture of Richmond.

For the next several weeks, as the two armies took each other's measure and remained quiescent, Gen. Lee developed plans to drive the Federals back. Gen. McClellan, reacting to the inaccurate intelligence information about the enemy's superior strength, failed to use his superior manpower to crush his opponent. This gave Gen. Lee and his staff the time necessary to fully assess the situation and to formulate a bold counteroffensive that they thought had a reasonable chance of success.

Providing signally important intelligence, a Confederate reconnaissance in the form of Gen. J. E. B. Stuart's flamboyant cavalry command rode completely around McClellan's army, and in the process, discovered the hoped-for chink in the Federal armor. The hard-riding cavalrymen noted that the Federal right flank northeast of Richmond consisting of Gen. Fitz-John Porter's V Corps, was separated from the rest of the army by the flood-prone and thence swift-flowing Chickahominy River. It was apparent that if a quickly-executed and crushing attack could be delivered to that isolated flank, it might be rolled up and destroyed before a retreat could be accomplished or reinforcements reached the scene. Adding significantly to the possibilities was a dearth of adequate bridges spanning the Chickahominy in the rear of the V Corps' position. Pinned against the river with further retreat not possible, the V Corps might be destroyed in detail and the rest of the Federal Army put to flight.

As an additional bonus, this attack would pose a grave threat to the Federal jugular, its base of supply located to the rear of the V Corps line. It was located on the York River Railroad at White House Landing on the Pamunkey River. According to Gen. Porter, he and his commander, Gen. McClellan, were aware of the potential danger posed by this separated disposition. Factoring in the presence of Gen. McDowell's command only a few days' march away from the right flank position, the situation seemed risky but manageable. And, history has lavishly recorded the achievements of the successful military risk-takers.

Gen. Lee, recognizing an opportunity when he saw one, began to devise a plan that would launch an attack in that quarter. A cornerstone of the plan was to fix McDowell's army in place, thereby keeping it from moving down to reinforce the Federal right flank. The method chosen to achieve that end was a ruse, that is, a diversion that would appear to Federal intelligence observers to pose a threat to the Federal capital. That end was to be achieved by sending troops from the already thinly-stretched Richmond front to join Gen. Jackson's victorious army in the Valley. Federal intelligence would almost surely interpret such a move as preliminary to moving that combined force against the national capital. In turn, that would require the movement of McDowell's command in defense of that city. The Confederate intelligence calculations proved to be correct.

For the troops chosen to participate in the diversion it meant exhausting forced marches, uncomfortable train rides, short rations, little rest and no information as to where they were bound and why. Once the feint was made and it was determined that McDowell's army remained in place, Gen. Jackson was to force march his entire command from the Valley. Arriving in a timely manner, that force would join with the forces on the scene and fall upon the right flank held by Gen. Porter's Corps. The surprise attack would turn that flank and, in the process, roll up the Federal line before any reinforcements could arrive on the scene. Whiting's Division was chosen as the diversionary force, that division including

Hood's Texans. So, it came to pass that on June 11, Whiting's Division, with great display, banners flying and drums beating, marched through the streets of Richmond. Boarding trains, they set out by way of Lynchburg for the Shenandoah Valley. There, as was proclaimed loudly and publicly by officers high in rank, they would join Jackson in an "'... on to Washington [effort].'"[43]

The alert, listening ears of Federal spies and sympathizers were quick to pick up the information and to pass it on to the authorities in Washington, D.C. Ultimately, the ruse proved to be successful and Gen. McDowell's army was kept in place. This was over the repeated protests of Gen. McClellan, who, still thinking his army vastly outnumbered, was frantically requesting reinforcements of his Washington masters.

As was frequently the case when Civil War-era armies were moved over longer distances, part was on foot and part was by rail. The South did not have an extensive rail system and what it did have was in poor condition. Recounting several incidents during the diversionary movement to the Valley, William A. Fletcher, Co. F, 5th Texas, said their train experienced a decoupling from the engine. The troop-laden flatcars gathered speed at an alarming rate on a downhill slope. Eventually, the engine was able to slow the cars speed but only after the troops had been placed in a temporary state of terror. Changing to boxcars in Lynchburg, they were soon crowded within as well as without with troops. Continuing on, a tunnel was encountered, in which there appeared to be little vertical clearance. Fletcher said the troops riding on top of the cars "had to be down and flatten out, but the feeling of insecurity was felt in entering for there appeared but little room between the roof and top of the tunnel. There were reported two men crippled and one of them with a broken leg."[44]

The day after reaching the Valley destination of Staunton, Co. I, 1st Texas, was, "surprised to see wagon trains and long lines of men filing down the mountain sides, and met for the first time Jackson's men." They also got their first look at "Mighty Stonewall," who informed them that we "were upon the eve of very important events. And those of us who kept up would always be glad of it, and those who failed to be there would regret it."[45]

According to William Powell, Co. D, 5th Texas, they remained in Staunton for a few days before beginning the return leg. Taking up the line of march they made twenty-three exhausting miles, ending the first day "pretty much all broken down." The next day, he was ill and taking medicine but, resolutely, stuck it out. They made twelve miles by 10:00 A.M. They reboarded the cars and "proceeded to Gordonsville by rail then to Louisa Court House then to Bumpas where [they] camped for several days."[46]

Recalling the return trip, W. D. Pritchard, Co. I, 1st Texas, said that at one point, they halted at a small station to await cars: "The train proved to be one of the empty flatcars without any seats. Orders were given to get aboard and as Pritchard was trying to climb on the cars that were rather high, someone behind him said: 'Do you want to get on that car, sergeant?' and before he could answer, felt himself taken by the nape of the neck and bosom of the breeches and lifted bodaciously on the car. When sufficiently recovered to look around, he saw Gen. Hood walking off smiling."[47]

On June 26, after the two-week diversionary round-trip and as the combined force approached the point of their assigned attack position, Gen. Lee launched his offensive. Thus began the round of fighting that became known as the Seven Days battles — Mechanicsville, Gaines Mill, White Oak Swamp, Savage Station, Glendale Farm, Malvern Hill. With the fate of the capital city in doubt and within sight and sound of the battles, the citizens of Richmond anxiously awaited the outcome of the hard-fought campaign.

CHAPTER 5

"*Soldiers indeed*"[1]:
The 4th Texas and 18th Georgia at
Gaines' Mill, Virginia, June 27, 1862

In order for the Confederate attack on the Federal V Corps' front to be successful, steady nerves were required of the Southern commanders. Most of the defending force in front of Richmond, estimated at 80,000–90,000 men and consisting of the divisions of Longstreet, Huger, A. P. Hill and Holmes and supporting artillery and cavalry units, would have to be repositioned stealthily to the left in preparation for the attack. This would leave a numerically inferior force, Gen. Magruder's command, including Huger's and Holmes' divisions, confronting the superior Federal force before them. That force included the corps commanded by Gens. Sumner (II Corps), Heintzelman (III Corps), Keyes (IV Corps) and Franklin (VI Corps). With the various supporting units, the total Federal manpower came to about 105,000 men. If the Federals detected the shift, the game would be up.

The key to the success of the attack was Gen. Jackson's now-renowned Valley army. Including Whiting's diversionary division, that force was moving from the Valley and into position on the Confederate left. Their attack position was to be the right and rear of Gen. Porter's line in the vicinity of Mechanicsville. The plan called for Jackson's force to deliver a crushing blow to the exposed right flank of the V Corps. That position was also the extreme right flank of Gen. McClellan's besieging army.

Meanwhile, responding to orders to report immediately, the North Carolinian and divisional commander in Gen. Jackson's command, Gen. Daniel Harvey Hill, mounted his horse and rode rapidly toward Confederate army headquarters, then located on the Mechanicsville Road several miles northeast of Richmond. The date was Monday, June 23, 1862. Approaching headquarters, Gen. Hill noticed leaning on the fence enclosing the yard an officer, dusty, travel-worn and, obviously, very weary. As he was dismounting, the disheveled figure straightened up. Only then did Gen. Hill recognize him to be his brother-in-law, his divisional commander and the hero of the recently completed Valley campaign, Gen. Thomas J. Jackson, he having ridden ahead of his approaching Valley army. After exchanging greetings, they entered army headquarters, anxious to know more of the coming operation and their respective parts in it.

Received by the ever-courteous Gen. Lee, they were joined shortly thereafter by divisional commanders Gens. James Longstreet and Ambrose P. Hill. Closing the door, Gen. Lee informed the four of the planned attack and that their respective commands had been

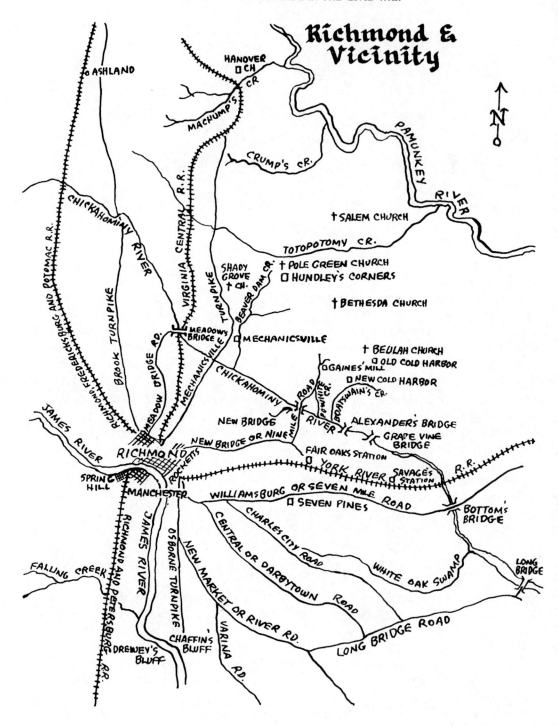

Richmond and vicinity

selected to participate in delivering the blow. He informed them that he believed Gen. McClellan regularly read the Richmond newspapers and had fallen for the diversionary ruse performed by Gen. Whiting's division. Then, retiring from the room, Gen. Lee left to attend to other matters. As was his habit, he entrusted the arrangement of details, subject to his final approval, to those who would have to carry them out.

When Gen Lee returned, the plan was discussed and finalized. A key element was the projected time that Gen. Jackson thought that he could have his troops in their attack positions. As it developed, the order of battle had Jackson at and marching from Ashland Station on the Richmond, Fredericksburg and Potomac Railroad, about twelve miles north of Richmond on June 25, and encamping for the night west of the Central Railroad. At 3:00 A.M., June 26, he was to advance his force rapidly, fall heavily upon and turn Porter's right flank anchored on Beaver Dam Creek northwest of Mechanicsville. The sounds created by that event would be the signal for A. P. Hill's command to cross the Chickahominy at Meadow Bridge and move upon the Federal position around Mechanicsville. This, opening the Mechanicsville Bridge, would allow Longstreet's command to cross and support A. P. Hill's advance. A bridgehead established, D. H. Hill's command would cross after Longstreet and proceed to the support of Jackson. The four commands would then sweep down the north side of the Chickahominy toward the York River Railroad, Jackson on the left and in advance, Longstreet nearest the river and in the rear. On the other side of the river, the Confederate right under Magruder was to hold his position observing the Federal line opposite. If there was a retreat, they were to follow. Stuart's cavalry would screen Jackson's left.[2] With the plan's formalization, the meeting broke up. Mounting Little Sorrell, it was a travel-worn Jackson that wearily set out to rejoin his army even then on the march toward Richmond from the west.

Alas, the best laid plans—Jackson's hard-marching foot cavalry, fresh from their exhausting but wildly successful Valley campaign, was late in reaching Ashland. With the Texas Brigade in the van, they had been "delayed by the excessive heat, lack of water and halting to repair bridges destroyed by the federals."[3] Also threatening the efficacy of the plan, it was learned later that a Confederate deserter had informed his captors that Jackson was in the vicinity and would take part in an attack. As a result, Federal cavalry screens became more active, doing everything they could to slow down any Confederate advance, from burning bridges to felling trees across roads. Jackson's force did not reach the designated point until the night of June 25.

Marching before dawn on June 26, the Texas Brigade once again in the

Joseph B. Polley, Co. F, 4th Texas.

van of Whiting's Division, they continued to experience delays occasioned by the harassing activities of the Federal cavalry. Moving down the Ashcake Road they crossed the Central Railroad about 10:00 A.M., with skirmishers deployed. The dust raised by this large infantry force was seen by Federal observers within their lines and generally assumed to be Jackson's force from the Valley. However, there was no great concern exhibited because the Federal position behind Mechanicsville was very strong and there was, hovering above, McDowell's force.

One of the deployed skirmishers that day, Joe Polley, Co. F, 4th Texas, described the experience as "the hardest days' work I ever did." Skirmishers were a thin screen of soldiers thrown out ahead of the main line of advance at intervals of about ten feet. Their function was to determine the position of the enemy while the main body followed slowly at a distance awaiting developments. Polley described their advance with skirmishers formed in a well-dressed line, on that day with an interval of about twenty feet separating them. The line of advance was through a "wilderness of pine timber and matted undergrowth." At about 11:00 A.M., he joined the others in driving away an outpost of the 8th Illinois Cavalry. In their haste to vacate the scene, the Blue cavalrymen left behind their cooking utensils and provisions. Polley's share of the unexpected bounty was a ham and a cup of well-cooked rice. Having to move on quickly, he was unable to transport the still hot rice. So, Polley did what any experienced Confederate soldier would do under the circumstances; he sat down and quickly ate it all, "not wasting a grain."

Having allayed, temporarily, the Confederate soldier's frequent and most demanding companion, hunger, Polley noticed some mounted men nearby. His curiosity and the Confederate soldier's tendency to informality getting the better of him, he sauntered over toward them. "[A] particularly seedy, sleepy-looking old fellow, whose uniform and cap were very dirty, and who bestrode a regular Rosinante of a horse" attracted his attention. He was about to make some impertinent remark about cavalry soldiers "when an officer, all bespangled with lace, came up in a gallop and, saluting, addressed my man as Gen. Jackson." Reconsidering his impertinent remark, Polley withdrew since no one "offered to introduce us to each other, and as we were both bashful, we lost the best chance of our lives to become acquainted."[4]

By 3:00 P.M., Totopotomoy Creek was reached, the bridge spanning ablaze, set by retreating Federal cavalry. Reilly's battery was brought up to disperse the cavalry still lingering in the area across the creek. W. R Hamby, Co. B, 4th Texas, noticed an old Virginia farmer sitting on a fence by the roadside, his Negroes cutting wheat in the field behind him. Cheering the troops on, he waved his hat, saying, "Hurry on boys; the Yankees have just gone flying over the creek." At this point, Reilly's battery moved in behind the old man and pulled down a fence, running their pieces into his field where they quickly unlimbered and went into battery. At the opening of fire, the old man was greatly startled, falling backward from his perch. "My God! A battle here on my plantation!" Shouting to his Negroes to get to the woods, he led the way.[5] With the Federal cavalry driven off, the Texas Brigade moved on bivouacking that night near Hundley's Corner. All ranks were curious about the heavy musketry and cannonading that they had heard from afar all afternoon and into the evening in the general direction of their destination, Mechanicsville.

Although soldiers trudging wearily along in the ranks of Civil War-era armies seldom had any accurate knowledge of a plan of battle, they did know that the sounds of musketry and cannonading reaching their ears from the direction of their movement could portend no good for their personal safety. Even so, everyone wanted to be in the brigade's first big fight, if for no other reason than to not appear cowardly in the eyes of their comrades. In Civil War armies, a battle no-show risked the disdain of his comrades regardless of the reason, legitimate or otherwise. M. V. Smith, Co. D, 4th Texas, had been sick with the flux for two or three weeks. However, when those in the sick camp well enough to fill gaps in the ranks were mustered prior to the battle, Smith fell in for duty only to be dismissed as being too sick to be of much use. Next day, as the sounds of battle rolled over the countryside, Smith was distraught. Seeking solitude so as not to be seen by his fellow patients, he "began to cry like [he] had lost all. [H]e thought the war was being ended right then and [he] would never receive [his] share of the fame."[6] It soon became apparent to him that ample opportunities still lay ahead.

John Stevens, Co. K, 5th Texas, while bedding down for that night of June 26–27, 1862, must have mirrored the thoughts that were running through the minds of all present. On his blanket, the stars looking down upon the scene, his thoughts were of "the dear wife and little ones at home ... blithely unaware of the danger their loved one was to be in upon the morrow. Finally, as most discover in dire circumstances, with a faith that only is brought out under severest trials, [he] committed [his] soul and all to [his] heavenly father, [and] dropped [off] to sleep (sweet rest) and slept as soundly as an infant upon its mother's arm."[7]

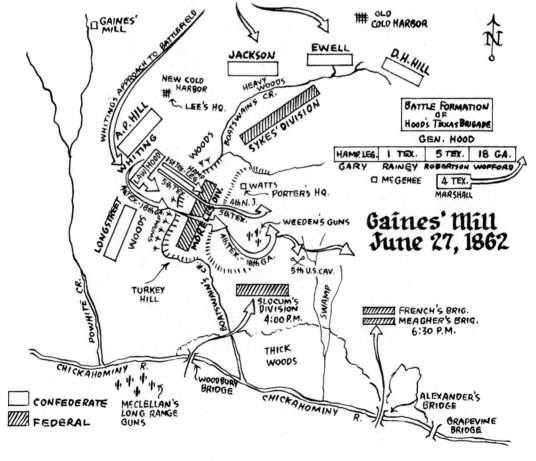

Gaines' Mill, June 27, 1862

The troops at Hundley's Corner were astir early on the morning of June 27, 1862, eager for news of the battle, the sounds of which they had heard the day before. The facts that emerged revealed that Gen. A. P. Hill's troops were in their assigned position early on the morning of June 26, anxiously awaiting the sounds of Jackson's attack to their left. As the sun advanced steadily, morning turned to afternoon and still no sound of Jackson's past-due attack. By 3:00 P.M., unable to contain himself further, the characteristically impatient A. P. Hill launched his attack, Jackson or no Jackson. The first of what were to be known as the Seven Days battles erupted in shot and shell.

A lightly-held Federal position was pushed back through Mechanicsville with the retreating troops taking up a prepared position along the north bank of Beaver Dam Creek. Meanwhile, Longstreet's and D. H. Hill's commands crossed at the Mechanicsville Bridge. According to Gen. A. P. Hill, the Federal line behind Beaver Dam Creek was naturally a strong one but further strengthened "by rifle pits and earthen epaulements for guns."[8] Hill's spirited attacks resulted in heavy casualties to his ranks and by 9:00 P.M. the battle had trailed off with the Federal position defiantly intact.

During the respite occasioned by the night and under the cover of darkness, the Federals abandoned their position for an even stronger one also prepared in advance. Their retreat was about six miles across a rough countryside covered with thick forest stands and broken by gullies, ravines and hills. They took up the prepared position behind a boggy area known locally as Boatswain's Swamp. The swamp was formed along the course of Powhite Creek, it tracing a torpid path to the point where it emptied into the Chickahominy. It was a position sited by Gen. Porter himself. A masterpiece of defensive engineering, it proved to be the most formidable Federal position the Texas Brigade was to be confronted with during the course of the war.

The next morning, June 27, Jackson's tardy command began crossing Beaver Dam Creek above Mechanicsville. Following up, they joined the other three commands arrayed before the new Federal position. From a defensive standpoint, it appeared impregnable, defended by the V Corps divisions of Gens. Morell, Sykes, McCall and their artillery support units. Semicircular in shape, its flanks were protected by the Chickahominy on the Federal left and a swamp on the right. The entrenchments followed the line of the bluff forming the east bank of Powhite Creek. The line was composed of three layered and heavily fortified trenches, each paralleling the others up the steep side of the creek bank. On a plateau in rear and above were numerous well-placed Federal artillery positions. In examining the position, Gen. Lee noted that in addition to the daunting entrenchments, the "approach ... was over an open plain, about a quarter of a mile wide, commanded by this triple line of fire and [enfiladed] by the heavy batteries south of the Chickahominy.... The woods on the farther side of the swamp were occupied by sharpshooters, and trees had been felled to increase the difficulty of its passage and detain our advancing columns under the fire of infantry massed on the slopes of the opposite hills and of the batteries on their crests."[9]

Pushing ahead intent upon cutting the York River Railroad and thereby the Federal line of retreat and supply, A. P. Hill's troops encountered and attacked the new Federal V Corps line about 2:00 P.M. There, the fight was joined as other Confederate units came up during the course of the afternoon assuming a concave-shaped position in conformity to the Federal position opposite. Jackson's late-arriving command formed eventually on the left, D. H. Hill's Division occupying the extreme left flank. A. P. Hill's command held a center position, through which Whiting's Division was to pass later in the afternoon as it renewed Hill's stalled attack on the Federal center. Longstreet's command occupied the right with his flank resting on the Chickahominy. Across the Chickahominy, on the southern side the other units of the Federal army stood ready to provide reinforcements and artillery support as needed, and it was later required.

The fight raged fiercely for several hours with heavy Confederate casualties being inflicted upon A. P. Hill's command. The stoutly defended Federal position seemed impregnable and, eventually, it was recognized that "[t]hese brave men had done all that any soldiers could do. Directing their men to lie down, the fight was continued and help awaited."[10] At this time, the tactical situation did not bode well for the Confederates. The attack that had been directed at the point where Morrell's Division across Powhite Creek adjoined that of Sykes' Division had failed. There were heavy casualties inflicted upon the Confederate ranks.

At about 3:00 P.M., upon arriving on the field, Gen. Whiting was instructed by Gen. Jackson to form his division into line of battle and advance through the woods toward the sounds of battle. Struggling through the dense forest and swamp, the overly-exerted command arrived behind the front at about 4:00 P.M. Here Whiting was met by aides from various commands all frantically seeking support for their respective units. Shortly thereafter, he was met by Gen. Lee who directed him ahead and a little to the right. Gen. Whiting was distressed to see men were leaving the field in every direction and in great disorder.

Even before arriving within sight of the enemy's lines, the Texas Brigade began to come under Federal artillery fire. D. U. Barziza, Co. C, 4th Texas, said that "[s]hells [were] bursting above, around, before and behind us scattering their blazing fragments and sulphurous contents reminding us that we are now in the tide of battle. Moving slowly along, now well within the range of the batteries, a poor fellow's head is smashed right by me, and his brains scattered on his comrades near him.... Gen. Lee meets us, and hurries us on as if the fate of mankind depended upon our coming."[11] As the advance hastened through the smoke-cloaked environment, the situation became even more dire as volleys of musketry were added to the deadly symphony of battle.

When within a few miles of the front, Joe Polley, Co. F, 4th Texas, said they began to see the signs indicating the severity of the fight "in the persons of wounded men, these increasing in numbers as we went nearer and nearer to the firing line. When close in rear of A.P. Hill's command, we ... saw individual stragglers by the score.... Still further on, the signs of battle, and of failure and perhaps defeat, become more numerous, and more than one of the boys expressed the opinion that we had come too late to do any good."[12] The position that the Texans took was "opposite the high point of the ridge south of the little creek upon which the Federals had massed ... twenty pieces of heavy field artillery — the center of the Texas Brigade exactly opposite these guns — the First Texas, Fifth Texas, Hampton's Legion and all but two companies of the Eighteenth Georgia, in the forest where lay the swamps and morasses, the Fourth Texas in reserve on the right of the Eighteenth Georgia."[13]

D. U. Barziza, Co. C, 4th Texas

At about the same time the division reached the front, from his place in the ranks, Granville Crozier, Co. B, 4th Texas, recognized Gen. Hood as he rode away at a gallop from a group of officers and out into an opening in the heavy woods on the right. Crozier knew what to expect next.The conference he observed included Gens. Lee, Whiting and Hood. William R. Hamby, Co. B, 4th Texas, was near enough to hear parts of the leader's conversation. Gen. Lee told the others that the efforts to break the enemy's line in front had been unsuccessful and it was of the utmost importance to do so, to which Gen. Hood replied: "We will do it." As Gen. Lee turned his horse to ride away, he lifted his hat and said: " May God be with you!"[14] Dismounting, Hood called for "his old 4th Texas," and they sprang to their feet, anxious to follow him wherever he should bid them go.

Such moments of extreme peril required the summoning up of all the individual reserves of courage and fortitude that one possessed. Granville Crozier, Co. B, 4th Texas, who was to receive an abdominal wound that day and another a month later at Second Manassas (Bull Run), was among those present. After the war he admitted years later to not naturally being a soldier and instinctively "shrinking from the hideous details of war.... Those noisy death-dealing missiles disgusted me, and I had a perfect abhorrence for the carelessness with which the Yankees handled their guns when we were approaching them."[15] We know now that Crozier's fears were shared, to varying degrees, by all present but, like Crozier, most were able to maintain self-control and not disgrace themselves in the eyes of their comrades.

William R. Hamby, Co. B, 4th Texas

Ranks became confused in the advance through the rough countryside. Waiting for the order to move forward, Joe Polley, Co. F, 4th Texas, found himself kneeling near Lt. Barziza, Co. C, 4th Texas. Polley admitted to trembling and heart palpitations. He noticed comrades beginning to fall to his right and to his left. He could not help but wonder in what part of his body he must inevitably be hit. Too soon, he was struck in the middle of his forehead. Backward he tumbled to the ground unconscious. "In the instant between blow and unconsciousness ... [he] had time to think that it was death." Gradually regaining consciousness, Polley's first reaction was to feel for the expected hole in his forehead. The next thing he remembered was Barziza's saying, "They would have got you that time, Polley, if your head hadn't been so hard."[16] Polley was dazed and bleeding as well as unamused and lucky. He had been hit by a wood splinter when a solid shot had struck a nearby tree. He would live to fight another day.

Enemy fire is not the only hazard on a battlefield. Friendly fire accidents accounted for some Civil War-era casualties. Leonidas Holliday, Co. E, 5th Texas, said that Bob

Pearson "was killed before we made the charge, by someone in the rear from a Ga. regiment."[17] Loaded weapons in the hands of an excited, frightened and semi-disciplined multitude are hazardous to all those present in the neighborhood.

In the meantime, Gen. Hood, having discovered a field to the right with an open view all the way to the Federal position some 800 yards distant, moved the 4th Texas by its right flank across the rear of Gen. Evander Law's brigade — the other brigade of Whiting's division — into that field. Almost immediately they began to come under Federal artillery fire as Gen. Hood dressed the ranks in preparation for the advance. Hood's plan was to move upon the enemy works quickly without pausing to fire and reload until he ordered them to do so. They would take the initial volleys and the resultant casualties. Then they would overwhelm the Federal lines using the threat of the bayonet before they were able to reload. Placing himself on foot at the head of the regiment, upon his command, they began to move forward at a rapid pace. The field of advance sloped upward slightly to a crest before plunging down into the ravine through which Powhite Creek meandered.

Joe Polley's company, Co. F, 4th Texas, moved through troops from the prior attacks now taking advantage of what safety there was afforded by the crest. Some of these troops implored the Texans to take cover because the Federal position could not be taken. Ignoring the pleas "[a]t the crest of the hill leading down into the swampy area, Hood shouted rapidly the orders: 'Fix bayonets! Make ready! Aim! Fire! Charge!'" Polley said that "the timber between us and the enemy hid them from our view, but we pulled triggers, nevertheless, and rushed down the hill into and across the branch and at the Yankees in the first [line] of breastworks."[18] The breastworks were fronted by abatis, which was outwardly angled, sharp-pointed timber manned by Berdan's Sharpshooter regiment, a lethal mix.

During the initial rush, Granville Crozier, Co. B, 4th Texas, saw a "rider less horse [dash] through our lines with his lower jaw shot off. There was a cry from a screeching voice: 'Close up that gap!' [He] looked and saw a mounted officer bareheaded and with blood streaming down his face. He pitched forward on the neck of his horse for an instant, then fell to the ground."[19] Since Col. John Marshall was the only officer mounted and it was later determined that he fell at the beginning of the charge, Crozier had probably just witnessed the death of the regimental commander.

Val Giles, Co. B, 4th Texas, ran down the slope leading to the swampy bottom passing through a peach orchard, across the stream and then over the Federal breastworks. To his right he saw Lt.

Lt. Col. Bradfute Warwick, 4th Texas, killed at Gaines' Mill, June 27, 1862

Col. Warwick and Lt. W. C. Walsh, the former carrying a Confederate banner and, above the tumult, heard to be shouting, "Come on." While moving up the hill and over the lines of breastworks, heavy casualties were suffered; Giles estimated over 200. At the crest of the hill, Giles saw both Lt. Col. Warwick and Lt. Walsh go down at which time he said there was not a single regimental field officer left standing. Warwick's wound proved to be mortal and Walsh's permanently disabling. Giles did not make it past the crest, himself falling victim to Federal canister. As he lay there in pain, those coming up behind him swept past, shouting, swearing, struggling for the crest.

Giles was still in great peril as the ground was swept by hails of Federal fire. A passing soldier, seeing his dilemma, grabbed him unceremoniously by the collar and dragged him to what little safety there was available behind a nearby tree. The rough treatment was painful, and, although it saved his life, Giles cursed his benefactor roundly. The samaritan made no comment in reply and continued on up the hill. Giles did not know him nor did he ever see him again.

Within a few minutes, a panic-stricken soldier came running past from the direction of the front. When a volley of canister passed nearby tearing limbs from trees and plowing up the ground, the soldier sought shelter in the same space occupied by Giles, landing squarely on his back. Giles, in great pain, struggled to get him off but to no avail. Swearing and shouting did not help any as the man, in his great fright, did not seem to hear his imprecations. Giles, looking around in desperation saw W. H. Hamman, 4th Texas commissary sergeant, pistol in hand hurrying by. Calling him by name, he was elated to see his cry had been heard. Hamman took in Giles' situation immediately. Grabbing the fear-crazed soldier by the head, he threw him backward shouting as he did so, "Where is your gun, you damned coward? Go to your regiment." Later, Hamman told Giles, "I came very near shooting that arrant coward at Gaines' Mill for when I told him to go to his regiment, he fairly flew to the rear."[20]

Over on the left of the brigade line, Robert Campbell, Co. A, 5th Texas, said that his unit was ready for battle and that "we pitched down the bank, jumping over felled trees. Gen. Hood led the 4th Texas (his old regt) .... Down the hill we went yelling like madmen with men falling at every step. We reached the ravine and plunged in, and in drawing my foot, from the mud and water, I lost a shoe — but now was no time to tarry."[21] He had to walk gingerly for the rest of that day because it wasn't until the next that he was able to replace the shoe.

The 18th Georgia was taking its share of punishment. Its ranks were being decimated as artillery rounds plowed great gaps through them. Major John C. Griffis and Lt. A. H. Patton, regimental adjutant, could be heard over the noise of battle encouraging the men to "Close up, dress right or left." Lt. L. A. McCullock of Co. C was killed, mangled by an artillery round. He was succeeded by Lt. J. B. Silman who fell only a few steps further on. Lieut. John Grant, commanding Co. H, was wounded, the command devolving upon 1st Sergt. W. M. Cotton. The story was much the same in the other companies of the hard-pressed regiment.

In crossing the bottoms, their line became disordered and once across the Georgians found themselves briefly under cover of the hill beyond. Soldiers from other commands were also there in a state of leaderless confusion. Before them all, the regimental flag of the 18th Georgia was planted. After a brief consultation among the officers present, the command "Forward" was given and the amalgamated mass moved once more up the hill.[22]

Even in the midst of such carnage and confusion, a grim sort of humor could be found.

Over to the left, advancing with Co. I, 1st Texas, W. D. Pritchard said that he witnessed a race that attracted a great deal of attention. The race was between a Federal six pound shot and a badly frightened rabbit. The shot, bounding across the field nearly spent, was paralleled by the rabbit, flushed from the woods by all the noise and activity. The contest gained the interest of the men who immediately began placing bets on the perceived winner, those on the rabbit predominating. As they approached, the infantry line opened up and let them pass, the rabbit the presumed winner. One of the men thought to stop the shot and put his foot out in the effort. He found, no doubt to his surprise, that even slowly moving shot could be injurious when he suffered a dislocated ankle.

Pritchard said that a dog had attached itself to the attack and was hit by an enemy missile. At about the same time one of the soldiers was hit and the men could not decide among themselves who "hollered the loudest, man or dog."[23]

About this time, according to Granville Crozier, Co. B, 4th Texas, the whole Confederate line from right, Longstreet, to left, Jackson, Ewell and D. H. Hill, swept forward in one grand charge and sent McClellan and his army skedaddling away toward his gunboats. But [Crozier] was 'not in it.' A Minie ball had struck the hammer of Val Giles' gun and, glancing, had entered [his] diaphragm just below the belt and [he was] quietly reclining on the side of the hill, awaiting further orders."[24]

Having faced fierce assaults all afternoon, the Federal line began to crumble as the Texas Brigade, willing to take the severe punishment, overran them. Chaplain Davis, 4th Texas, said that when the first line of defense at the foot of the hill broke that it "pressed ... upon the second entrenchment, which was so masked by their retreating ... comrades as to protect us from their fire until we had gained near half the distance to the second position. And by the time they were unmasked, seeing Southern steel advancing at rapid strides, they joined their frightened friends & made for the third line composed of U.S. infantry drawn up on the crest of the hill. The advantage gained at this point was also improved & soon the three lines were mixed in glorious confusion & hastening for shelter towards the heavy batteries of 16 guns on the hill to the rear."[25]

To Joe Polley, Co. F, 4th Texas, all was tumult and confusion. The three Federal lines, collapsing back on each other, fled like " a flock of sheep." Reaching the crest of the hill and looking over to the left through the thick smoky haze of the battlefield in the direction of the rest of the brigade's line of advance, they saw, dimly, large bodies of troops. These troops were so far behind the front then occupied by the 4th Texas that they were thought to be the other elements of the Texas Brigade. However, they were actually Federal troops falling back but at a slower pace than those fleeing before the onslaught of the 4th Texas and 18th Georgia. Not a shot was fired at them at that time.

A road meandered behind the crest and just across from the 4th Texas' position was a lot enclosed by a rail fence. In the center of the lot stood a log stable and behind it was to be seen an armed Federal soldier. One of the first to spot him was John M. Stringfield, Co. A, 4th Texas, who climbed the fence and ran forward hoping to make a capture. Ordinarily mild-mannered, Lt. Lemuel Hughes, Co. F, 4th Texas, urged him on, shouting, "Go it Stringfield, go it! Kill him, god damn him, kill him." Stringfield needed no urging but was brought up short when confronted by the muzzle of a loaded musket. Had it not been for the quick action of Simon Wolf, Co. F, 4th Texas, who shot the Federal soldier dead, Stringfield would have become a casualty himself.[26] As it was, Stringfield was to survive until permanently disabled by a wound received the following summer at Gettysburg. Pvt. Wolf lasted only until September when he received a mortal wound at Sharpsburg (Antietam).[27]

Robert Campbell, Co. A, 5th Texas, said that upon overrunning the Federal lines they sat down for a few moments to rest. Lt. J. E. Clute, sitting nearby, remarked, " 'Boys, they have put a hole through my coat.' Just then the order to advance once more was given. As Clute rose, '...he gave a groan- and fell back dead — hit by a piece of shell.'" "Some of the men removed the native New Yorker's watch and valuables to be sent later to his mother and sisters of Buffalo, New York.[28]

Having overrun the three Federal lines and gained the height on the far side of the stream, the brigade came under heavy fire from the batteries located to their left and in rear of the main Federal lines. Seeing the urgent necessity of taking the guns, Gen. Hood took time to reform his casualty-riven ranks before moving upon the position. In the advance, Lt. Barziza, Co. C, 4th Texas, said he and his comrades found themselves about 300 yards from the batteries and in a sort of lane formed by a fence on one side and a barn on the other. Stopping to catch their breath, they could plainly see ahead the Federal gunners working their pieces. "[D]own they would drive the horrid grape — a long, blazing flame issued from the pieces, and then crushing through fence and barn shattering rails and weatherboarding, came the terrible missiles with merciless fury."

When within seventy feet of the batteries they were engulfed in the smoke created by the firing of the batteries. They "could see nothing but the red blaze of the ... cannon, and hear nothing but its roar and the hurtling and whizzing of the missiles."[29] In this already deadly and precarious environment another threat arose; the very ground they stood on began to shake and shudder as word was passed down the line — "Cavalry!"

The attacking Federal cavalry column was composed of a battalion of the 5th U.S. Cavalry, under the overall command of Gen. Philip St. George Cook. One of his sons-in-law was in the Confederate States Army, the flamboyant Gen. J. E. B. Stuart. Exhibiting the kind of discipline necessary for infantry to repel cavalry charges, the Texans "held their fire until the enemy were within good range and then poured in a deadly volley that broke their front, brought down their leader [Maj. Whiting, captain of Hood's company on the Texas frontier, stunned but otherwise unharmed], and so discomfited them that they changed their direction and endeavored to make their escape, but before they succeeded in doing so scores of their saddles were emptied and many a crippled steed left hobbling across the field.... At this moment the scene was indescribable. Cavalrymen, artillery limbers and caissons and infantry all rushed away in one wild sea of confusion running for dear life."[30] In the aftermath, Gen. Porter and others were very critical of the ill-timed, uncoordinated and unsuccessful cavalry charge. Nevertheless, the Federal line had been broken prior to the cavalry incursion. The charge did not result in but only added to the confusion of the retreat.

In the midst of the chaos, some of the Federal gunners stood to their guns valiantly. Members of the 18th Georgia rushed the batteries in their front. One gunner was shot down in the act of ramming down a cartridge, another while adjusting a friction primer. Lt. Elvis Laws, Co. D, 18th Georgia, with four men, rushed a piece and prevented its being fired by gunning down the entire crew serving it. John D. Foster, Co. F, 18th Georgia, bore the unit flag and when "he reached the battery, he mounted one of the pieces and waved his flag in triumph."[31] In all, fourteen of the Federal guns fell into the hands of the Texans and Georgians.

Numerous Federal prisoners were taken, including Gen. John Reynolds, a close friend of Gen. D. H. Hill in the old army. Theirs was an unhappy reunion, Gen. Reynolds lamenting the fact that they were fighting each other. Declining a loan of Confederate money from his old friend, Gen. Reynolds departed for a Confederate prisoner-of-war camp, only to be later exchanged and, still later, killed by a Confederate sharpshooter in the opening phases of the Gettysburg fight. Two complete regiments, the 4th New Jersey and the 11th Pennsylvania Reserves found themselves engulfed by unidentifiable troops in the confusion of the smoke-shrouded battlefield. An officer was sent forward to ascertain the truth. "He soon came back, pointing to the bullet-holes through his clothes as evidence that they were rebels."[32] Indeed, it was the 5th Texas, and realizing their dire predicament, both Federal regiments felt compelled to surrender.

In the absence of Col. Robertson, 5th Texas, who had been wounded, both Col. Simpson, 4th New Jersey, and Col. Gallagher, 11th Pennsylvania Reserves, surrendered their swords to [Maj.] John Upton of the 5th Texas. Upton, laying down the frying pan he carried into battle in lieu of a sword, held the tendered blades awkwardly in his arms. Distracted by a commotion in the surrendered regiment's ranks, Upton sprung upon a log to better see, the surrendered sabers protruding at disarrayed angles from under his arms.

The commotion was caused as "Big John" Farris, Co. C, 5th Texas, was attempting to keep some Union prisoners from melting away into the nearby woods. Perceiving the problem Upton shouted: "You John Farris! What in the h[ell] and d[amn] are you trying to do now?" To which Farris replied: "I'm trying to keep the d[amn] fellows from escaping." "Let them go, you infernal fool," was Upton's reply. "We'd rather fight them a d[amn] sight than to feed them."[33] The colorful Upton had a month more to live. He was killed at Second Manassas on August 30,1862.

To Arthur Edy, Co. A, 5th Texas, the capture of Federal prisoners in some instances bordered on the ridiculous. An unnamed bugler of the 5th Texas went to a branch to fill his canteen. "[H]e met with twenty-five Yankees huddled up as if in fright; he told them to throw down their guns or else he would blow his horn and the Texans would kill every one of them; so out they march in double file commanded by Mr. Bugler."[34]

Robert Campbell, Co. A, 5th Texas, still missing the shoe lost in crossing Boatswain's Swamp, was detailed to guard prisoners. He gave his last chew of tobacco to one of the P.O.W.s and found them very talkative. One asked him when he thought the war would end, to which Campbell replied, "When you think you have a bigger job on hand than you can manage." The prisoner replied, "You will then fight till your heads are gray."[35] Another prisoner admitted to Campbell that he was glad to be captured.

Once begun, the Federal retreat was pell-mell and unit cohesion pretty much evaporated. The battlefield was heavily shrouded in smoke and, the battle not having opened until mid-afternoon, nightfall came on quickly. As a result, both Federal officers and men became badly disoriented as they groped their way in the darkness trying to find the way to the Chickahominy bridges somewhere to the rear. The Confederates were in about the same shape as they attempted to regroup.

Any battle leaves in its wake a landscape dominated by scenes of total death, destruction and waste. Chaplain Davis, 4th Texas, said of the Gaines' Mill battlefield, "Thousands were left lying on the field and scattered through the woods, weltering in their blood, while hundreds more were left dead upon the soil.... Night has hung its dark curtains around and over the arena.... All is quiet as the grave, only when disturbed by busy trains of ambulances and the heart-rending groans of the ten thousand sufferers, comingling their voices in piteous discord on every hand.... But low, deep murmurs rose upon the gloom of night, which lent to the surrounding scene the darkest shade to which earthborn sufferers are heir in their brief stay in a world of sin and woe."[36]

Soldiers often returned to the field of action seeking to learn the fate of missing comrades. O.T. Hanks, Co. K, 1st Texas, visited the battlefield afterwards on such a mission and was witness to some of the horrors of the place: "[W]hile loitering about I noticed the top of a man's skull hanging by the hair to a limb some [eight] or [nine] feet from the ground."[37] He supposed that an exploding artillery round had cast the fragment there.

Gen. Hood spent most of the night on the battlefield seeing to the needs of his wounded and the burial of the dead. At one point as he "rode over the field, about 2 o'clock in the morning, [he heard] a voice in the distance ... calling [him] by [his] surname in tones of deep distress." It turned out to be an old friend from Texas days and the 2nd U.S. Cavalry. Sending him immediate aid, Gen. Hood visited him later on the field where their friendship was renewed. Gen. Hood had him sent to a hospital, where later he and Gen. Fitz Hugh Lee, also formerly of the 2nd U.S. Cavalry, visited both he and Capt. Whiting during their captivity at Libby Prison in Richmond.[38]

Robert Campbell, Co. A, 5th Texas, and the Federal prisoners he was guarding marched to the rear as night fell over the battlefield. Once the prisoners were delivered it was too late and he was too weary to return to his company. After feasting on abandoned Federal provisions, he spread his blanket on the ground and fell into a deep, deep slumber.

The next morning in returning to the brigade he passed over the ground of the previous day's fight. "[W]hat a sight greeted our eyes.... On every side lay the victims of Death — three Confederates to one Yank.... [Caissons], rifles of every patent, muskets, belts, knapsacks, cartridge boxes, ammunition, haversacks, and all the necessaries of war, lay scattered about as the Yanks had thrown them when we drove them from their works."[39]

William R. Hamby, Co. B, 4th Texas, said that "gentle breezes of that night in June were whispering requiems for the brave spirits who had fought their last battle when our regiment was re-formed in line about nine o'clock by Gen. Hood, who counted only seventy-two present; but others reported during the night who had been separated from us in darkness in the latter part of the battle."[40]

Although other Confederate units were later to claim the distinction, Gens. Jackson, Whiting and Hood credited the 4th Texas with the crucial breaking of the Federal line at Gaines' Mill. Although it was a distinction cherished by the 4th Texas, it was purchased at a high price. Said M. V. Smith, Co. D, 4th Texas, of his regiment while paying tribute to the other regiments in the brigade, the "famous charge at Gaines' Mill had placed forty-five per cent of the Fourth Texas 'hors de combat,' who were weltering in their blood, on the ground over which they had traveled. Three of the lieutenants of the company to which I belonged ... were killed outright, the captain was wounded, many of whom died in the hospital afterward."[41]

In inspecting the field after the attack, Gen. Lee was very complimentary. Gen. Jackson said of the 4th Texas specifically and of the Texas Brigade, generally, "The men who carried this position were soldiers, indeed."[42] Gen. Longstreet added his approbation, saying of the attack, "No battle-field can boast of more gallantry and devotion."[43] Justifiably proud of their role, the men of the Texas Brigade surviving the war scheduled the majority of their post-war reunions around the June 27 anniversary of the fight at Gaines' Mill.

Following the conclusion of the other battles of the Seven Days in early July, the Texas Brigade, having been only lightly engaged, remained in camp on the Mechanicsville Road about three miles north of Richmond for a well-deserved rest until August 8, 1862. The men of the brigade remembered that respite fondly. Having erected tents and "made things comfortable," they received "plenty of rations" and military duty was reduced to being present for roll-calls. Passes to Richmond were theirs but for the asking. "[T]he man who was seen with the 'Lone Star' on his cap ... was looked upon with special favour by the people of that city."[44] When that encampment was broken up, the line of march was taken up that led to the Second Manassas (Bull Run).

Back home in Texas, news of the victory was not received for some weeks. Then, while paying tribute to the Texas Brigade's part, a requiem was sounded for John Marshall, the fallen colonel of the 4th Texas. "Upon the altar of this country's liberties has he fallen.... Another Texas patriot is gone. Texians let his memory be sacred!"[45] Nearly three more casualty-strewn years of war lay still ahead.

CHAPTER 6

"*The 5th Texas regiment was a flame of terror*"[1]: The 5th Texas at Second Manassas, Virginia, August 29–30, 1862

The unexpected and near fatal catastrophe suffered by the Federal Army of the Potomac at Gaines' Mill on June 27 resulted in a serious threat being posed to that army's base of supply located at White House Landing on the Pamunkey River. Declaring a "change of base," Gen. McClellan was forced to establish a new base across the Peninsula at Harrison's Landing on the James River. In the process of abandoning the White House base it was necessary that many tons of supplies be put to the torch. The night skies above the landing were aglow as a result of the conflagration. Huge smoke plumes could be seen rising to the heavens during the day. Much of what was not destroyed fell into the hands of the advancing Confederates.

In quick succession, with the off-balance Army of the Potomac reeling backward toward its new base, were fought the remaining battles of the Seven Days campaign — Savage Station on June 29, Frayser's Farm or Glendale on June 30 and Malvern Hill on July 1. The fight at Malvern Hill, another excellent defensive position selected by Gen. Fitz John Porter, was brutal. The frontal attacks launched against that line resulted in a slaughter inflicted by massed Federal artillery and U.S. Navy gunboats in rear on James River. Gen. D. H. Hill referred to it afterwards as "not war but murder." In these battles, the Texas Brigade was not heavily engaged.

The next day, July 2, much to the surprise of not only the Confederates but also to the men in the ranks of the Federal army, the formidable position was ordered abandoned. In a downpour, the retreat continued for some six miles on downriver. It was a rain-soaked Army of the Potomac that took position in the sodden landscape encircling the new supply base fronting on the James River at Harrison's Landing.

The days following proved to be somewhat of a respite for the two armies in their respective encampments. There they licked their considerable wounds while preparing for the next round of fighting. For the time being, the Federal army remained quiescent within its positions, showing no predisposition for further offensive operations. Gen. Lee, ever mindful of the threat posed by the Army of Virginia to his other flank and to the capital began the withdrawal of the Army of Northern Virginia from in front of Harrison's Landing. Taking up a position in front of Richmond with the bulk of his army would allow him to deal more effectively with threats to either or both flanks. Several divisions and the cavalry, brigades in rotation, were left to keep an eye on and report of any signs of renewed activity on the part of the Army of the Potomac.

As the Peninsula campaign was being waged, Mr. Lincoln's administration had struggled to come to grips with the twin problems posed by Gen. McClellan's incessant requests for reinforcements and the perceived needs for the proper defense of the nation's capital on the banks of the Potomac. Gen. McDowell's army, now dubbed the Army of Virginia, was not sent to McClellan's aid nor had it been required to fall back to protect the capital. It had grown in numbers as several scattered commands, mainly from the Valley, had been added. Stigmatized by his earlier defeat at First Manassas, the administration now had the respite necessary to consider his replacement. As the various candidates were considered there eventually emerged as first choice a general junior to all. Having achieved some degree of success in the Western theater, and success was what the Federal chief executive was looking for, Gen. John Pope, a Kentuckian and West Pointer of the star-studded class of 1842, was President Lincoln's choice. He assumed command on June 27, at the same time the battle at Gaines' Mill was raging to the south along the banks of the Chickahominy.

It was a double-edged game that was being played, the Confederates, by their diversionary ruse, trying to keep that army in place. President Lincoln and his advisers' idea was that this army's location and composed of the commands of McDowell, Fremont and Banks, the latter two the defeated at the hands of Jackson in the Valley earlier, about 38,500 men, would be used to threaten Gen. Lee's left flank and rear while interposed between the enemy and the nation's capital. Perhaps, this would draw off some of the strength being directed toward McClellan's army in front.[2] Of course, Gen. McClellan expected the entire force to come to his support. Had demonstrations by that army toward Gordonsville and Charlottesville been made it would certainly have had the effect the Federal authorities hoped for. The fact that it did not happen as quickly as the president would have liked was because the force had been widely scattered and poorly organized initially.

By July 12, it was reported that units of Pope's army had crossed the Rappahannock and occupied Culpeper Courthouse a short distance beyond. This move gave them control of the northern reaches of the Orange and Alexandria Railroad, a key logistical factor for campaigning in that area. A short distance south of Culpeper, along that rail line lay Gordonsville. That junction city was also astride the railroad, it passing through roughly on a north-south course while the Virginia Central Railroad passed through roughly east-west. If Gordonsville fell into Federal hands that would cut also the only direct line of rail communication that existed between Richmond and the Shenandoah Valley. The strategically-important Valley served not only as the breadbasket of the Confederacy but as a direct line of march into or out of Union territory north of the Potomac.

So, on July 13, Gen. Lee ordered Gen. Jackson with his and Gen. Richard S. Ewell's Divisions northward to deal with the threat. It was at this point that Gen. Whiting's Division was returned to Gen. Longstreet's command. Arriving at Gordonsville Jackson found he had little intelligence information available to him regarding the exact locations and strengths of his prospective opponents. So, while most of Stuart's cavalry was occupied in keeping an eye on Harrison's Landing, some scattered elements were gathered and dispatched toward Fredericksburg to see for themselves where the Federal strength was located and report their findings to Gen. Jackson.

In the meantime, the newly-installed, confident Gen. Pope set about, unwittingly, through a series of injudicious acts directed toward the civilian populace and some bombastic public pronouncements, to set himself up for the destruction predicted by the gods as retribution for arrogant behavior. When news of all this reached him, the usually courteous Gen. Lee took umbrage referring to Pope as a "miscreant" and expressing the need for his "suppression."

Back on the James, on July 22, Confederate observers keeping watch over McClellan's army, still hunkered down around Harrison's Landing, were concerned when they began to notice increasing activity in the Federal camps. Not at all sure of what this meant, Gen. Lee did know it would develop slowly due to his knowledge of the cautious habits thus far exhibited by Gen. McClellan. So, Gen. Lee, the audacious gambler, decided that Jackson would be reinforced with an additional 18,000 troops, or thereabouts, thus enabling him to deal effectively with Pope should an opportunity arise. The choice of leadership for the expeditionary force to be sent to Jackson was narrowed to the sometimes impetuous but always aggressive Gen. A. P. Hill. Hill and his troops began entraining for Gordonsville on the afternoon of July 27.

Then, on August 5, elements of McClellan's army fell into ranks, shouldered arms and began an advance up the James once more headed toward the Confederate capital. A Confederate force, advanced to block the move, found the Federals drawn up once again in the exact same defensive position held so successfully and devastatingly a month earlier at Malvern Hill. Scattered skirmishes flared, while over the arrayed hosts a sense of impending battle hung. Night fell and an uneasy quiet prevailed. As dawn broke the next morning and the Confederates steeled themselves for another blood-letting ordeal, they were astounded to find themselves confronted by — no one! Under cover of darkness, the Federals had slipped away and were once again safely ensconced within the lines surrounding Harrison's Landing.

In light of these revealing developments it was evident that McClellan was not going to renew the campaign. So, even more emboldened, Gen. Lee issued Gen. Jackson discretionary orders to act as he saw fit against Pope based on his on-site observations. Should reinforcements be required as that campaign developed, Gen. Hood was advised of a move to Hanover, just north of Richmond. There a junction of the Richmond, Fredericksburg and Potomac Railroad and the Virginia Central occurred. That move would provide security for the Virginia Central Railroad and put Hood within marching distance of Jackson along the line of that vital rail route.

In the meantime, the Texas Brigade remained encamped near Richmond but ready to answer swiftly when called upon. During that time, a command change occurred. Gen. Whiting was given a thirty day disability leave. In his stead, Gen. Hood, the senior officer, was appointed as division commander of the small, two brigade unit. Due to uncertainty as to the length of Gen. Whiting's leave, Hood served as both his brigade's as well as the division's commander. As it turned out, Gen. Whiting never returned. It was at Sharpsburg that Col. Wofford, 18th Georgia, assumed command of the Texas Brigade and Gen. Hood of the division, solely.

* * *

About August 8, according to Joe Polley, Co. F, 4th Texas, camp was broken and the next phase of the campaign of 1862 got underway. It would last until December, four months thence. By this time sufficient experience had been gained so that the troops carried only that which they knew to be the essentials. Even so, the essentials weighed in at about thirty-six pounds. "A gun weighed about ten pounds, the cartridge box, cap box, bayonet, and the belts and straps to which these hung, another ten, and the roll of blanket and tent, or oil cloth, still another ten. Add to these the weight of the haversack, in which not only provisions but underclothing and many other necessities were carried, and the total or a fair estimate, was never less than thirty-six pounds, and often went a little beyond forty. A canteen full of water weighed at least three pounds.[3] However, as time passed and experience was gained they learned to travel ever lighter.

Nicholas Pomoroy's Co. A, 5th Texas regiment had shed its tents and extra camp equipage before making the march from Richmond down to Yorktown earlier in the year. From that time onward "we went in light marching order." "Every soldier carried, in addition to his blanket, a small tent cloth, and two of these put together formed a shelter for two persons to sleep under, and keep out the rain." Their beds consisted of the soft tops of the pine trees and dry leaves. "We never removed our clothing except to change, or wash our under garments." The latter could be accomplished only if the stay was for several days, and, of course, if there was an available stream in the vicinity.[4]

For three days the heavy-laden northward march was leisurely. However, the troops and the commissary trains became separated and rations that had been issued for one day were required to serve for three and, in some cases, even longer.

On August 11 it was learned that Jackson had crossed the Rappahannock and engaged in battle with Pope at a place called Cedar Run, near the mountain of the same name, on the 9th. He had not only defeated the Federals but inflicted upon them a heavy loss. Following his victory, Jackson had fallen back across the Rapidan to await the arrival of reinforcements, those taking the form of Longstreet's command. Unsupported, Jackson was in some peril and haste became of the greatest urgency, the fact of which he informed his approaching reinforcements.

Their pace was quickened, the march forced, fifty minutes of marching, ten minutes of rest each hour with the march continuing on into the night. The weather was described as "intensely hot" with many cases of sunstroke occurring. "Oh, the remembrance of that long, weary tramp!" said W. D. Pritchard, Co. I, 1st Texas, long afterwards. "It comes like some hideous nightmare and today we can feel again that anxious waiting for old Collins' bugle to sound 'halt' and we can almost hear the vehement 'D — n that bugle!' as he calls to 'fall in.'"[5]

In the Texas Brigade "Old Collins" was Daniel Collins, the leader of the 4th Texas' military brass band. Of the three regimental bands, Collins' was recognized from the beginning as the best of the lot. Chaplain Davis, 4th Texas, said that there was nothing better to call forth the soldier resident in every man than martial music played by a well-trained band: "When the men are weary and exhausted, its soft notes on the night air, drive away the thoughts of fatiguing marches, and quietly lull the soldier to rest. And the bugle's blast at reveille reminds him, as he is aroused from slumber, that he is a soldier; and to his guardianship has been committed the weal of a great nation, as well as the peaceful enjoyment of his own little home." When not supplying martial music, the band members rendered service as guards for personal equipment shed by the troops before going into line of battle. They also served as stretcher bearers and nurses in getting the wounded from the field to regimental hospitals set up to the rear.[6]

On August 14, it was confirmed that Fitz John Porter's V Corps had left Harrison's Landing via waterborne transportation. The withdrawal of the V Corps could only mean that it was being sent to join Pope. That added weight would tilt considerably the preponderance of force in favor of Pope over both Jackson and Longstreet. However, if Pope could be struck a decisive blow before Porter's reinforcements arrived a good result might be achieved.

Early on the morning of August 15, Gen. Lee went to Gordonsville to review the sit-

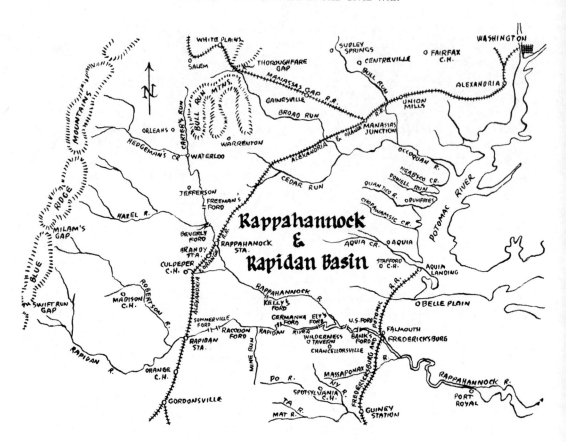

Rappahannock and Rapidan Basin

uation. Arriving there in the afternoon, a conference was held with, by then, the reunited Jackson and Longstreet. In anticipation, several days prior on August 12, Jackson had instructed his chief topographer, Jedediah Hotchkiss, to make as many maps as he could of the country stretching from Gordonsville to the Potomac. Using his time efficiently, Hotchkiss turned out some excellent maps. A close scrutiny of the maps revealed an interesting tactical situation promising success if quick action accompanied by stealthy troop movements could be accomplished..

North of Gordonsville and meandering down from a generally northwesterly direction flowed two rivers, the Rapidan, the nearer, and the Rappahannock, the farther. The Orange and Alexandria Railroad spanned both with stations located on the banks of each. To the east a short distance, about halfway to Fredericksburg, the Rapidan converged with the Rappahannock. From that juncture the comingled waters continued on as the Rappahannock, eventually emptying into the brackish waters of the Chesapeake Bay beyond.

The significance of these topographical features coupled with intelligence available seemed to present a military opportunity simply too good to be true. The relative positions of the Orange and Alexandria Railroad and the east-southeasterly flowing rivers formed a rough triangle, or, ignoring the railroad, from where the two rivers merged a "V." It had been discovered that Pope had his entire force encamped between the two rivers, fronting on the north bank of the Rapidan and backing on the south bank of the Rappahannock.

For the moment, Pope did not seem to be aware of his precarious situation. Potentially, he was trapped between two rivers, his only routes of escape the bridges and fords over and through the Rappahannock to his rear. If Gen. Stuart's hard-riding cavalry could destroy the bridges, only the fords would remain. Fords could, and often did, disappear quickly as a result of locally heavy rains or from rains far-removed upstream. Quick action was required before Pope came to the realization of his precarious position. Due to problems, mostly logistical, and the necessity of concentrating Stuart's cavalry for the Rappahannock bridges raid, August 18, was designated for crossing the Rapidan and going after Pope.

It did not happen. The participation of Stuart's cavalry was critical and due to the scattered condition of that command, invaluable time was lost as it strove to get into respective positions. On the day set for the operation to commence, Confederate lookouts on Clark's Mountain, a prominent landmark east of Rapidan Station, reported the entire Federal army retiring to and crossing over the Rappahannock as quickly as their blue-clad legs could carry them. Later analysis revealed several events that had alerted the Federal commander of his impending doom.

The most telling factor had been the capture of Gen. Stuart's adjutant, Maj. Fitzhugh, near Verdiersville. A search of his person had provided his captors with a document showing Confederate troop dispositions in the area. This document found its way to Gen. Pope, who, considering other intelligence reports, realized suddenly the danger his army was in. He promptly ordered a withdrawal. Philosophically resigned to the disruption of his plan, Gen. Lee ordered his army to follow. The advance began at 4:00 A.M., August 20.

The advance was begun by the Army of Northern Virginia arranged as two wings, the left commanded by Gen. Jackson, the right by Gen. Longstreet. A portion of the cavalry under Fitz Lee was to screen the right flank where there was potential danger from the direction of Fredericksburg. Accompanying Gen. Jackson, Gen. Stuart, smarting from the loss of his famous plumed hat captured by Yankee cavalry during a brief skirmish several days earlier, led the rest. Once over the Rapidan, the infantry column, 50,000 strong plus a few thousand more in the cavalry plus artillery units were to make for Culpeper Courthouse on their way to the Rappahannock crossings a short distance beyond. By the end of the day, August 20, Longstreet's troops were on the Rappahannock around Kelly's Ford and Jackson was nearby around Brandy Station.

By then the Federal army was fully across and ensconced behind the Rappahannock. The available fords were heavily defended with the terrain favoring the defenders, the north bank being higher, generally, than the south. For the next few days there was skirmishing, some of it sharply conducted as the Army of Northern Virginia maneuvered up the south bank of the river in a sidling fashion, seeking an opening whereby the river barrier could be breached. This portion of the campaign was managed rather well by Pope as he parried the Confederate thrusts skillfully.

Seeing each move to cross the river checkmated, Gen. Lee knew that this could go on indefinitely. He knew also that the further up the river he went, the further behind fell the thinly defended but highly valued Confederate capital. Gen. Stuart, always thinking aggressively, proposed to the army commander a raid be made on the Federal line of supply, in this case, trailing up the line of the Orange and Alexandria Railroad. Gen. Lee not only liked the plan, he approved the expedition, the objective point to be Catlett's Station. Not only would this disrupt the flow of supplies reaching the Federal rear, it might create panic and disorder in the enemy ranks, the most attractive of traits when exhibited by a military opponent.

Stuart received news of the approval of his plan while skirmishing with the enemy around Freeman's Ford, a few miles north of Rapphannock Station. By nightfall, August 22, he and most of his mounted command moved upriver. Crossing the river at Waterloo Bridge, they were bound for Catlett's bent upon creating panic and spreading destruction in the Federal rear.

Meanwhile, Gen. Jackson continued to sidle upriver and probe for opportunities followed by Longstreet's command engaging in the same tactics. Whiting's Division, Hood in command, comprised of the Texas Brigade and Evander Law's Brigade of Alabamians and Mississippians were in the van of the latter. Coming to the aid of Jackson's command attempting a river crossing contested by a Federal force that had crossed over to the south bank, they moved in on his right with Law on his left. "With line of battle thus formed the 'Forward' was given; the line of the enemy was instantly broken and driven headlong into the river. Pouring a dreadful fire into their crowds of confused and broken lines, as they were huddling together to cross, many were shot in the back, and others drowned by the crushing crowd which pressed for the other shore. It was the work of but a few minutes, yet about [300] of their killed and wounded were left upon the ground and in the river."[7] Chaplain Davis, 4th Texas, said Hood's losses were ten men all from the 5th Texas.

The pursuit continued across the river and that night was spent on the farther shore. It rained all night long, drenching all present and turning the ground into a quagmire. The river became swollen and the commissary wagons were unable to cross. Robert G. Holloway, Co. B, or I, 4th Texas, said they were "ordered to the woods to sleep, ... nothing to eat. Rested very badly all night."[8]

Next day, August 23, nearby cornfields yielded up green corn and resulted in the so-called "roasting ears fight." That hand-to-hand brawl with some of Gen. Franz Sigel's equally hungry blue-clad boys on the other end of the corn rows resulted in some bloody noses and skinned knuckles but no fatalities. Following the fight, the belligerents returned to their former positions. John W. Stevens, Co. K, 5th Texas, said that the "mud in the field was half leg deep, if we set down it was in the mud, to stand up was terrible." When night fell Stevens and two comrades were placed on picket, according to him, "in thirty or forty steps of the enemy's line, in high corn." In later years in thinking of his experiences he remembered that night as "the terriblest night I ever spent, we could not sit down or lie down without being in the mud, but we did sit down in the mud.... We were so close to the enemy that we could hear their feet pop in the mud as they moved around in line. We could hear, all night, the low rumbling sound of their voices in suppressed tones as they conversed. Occasionally we could hear them pull a roasting ear and slip the shuck from it and eat it raw from the cob."[9] Between the lines, a "Dutchman" with a broken thigh cried out all night for water which only added to the gloomy night. Next morning the Confederates brought the injured man within their lines after the Federals had withdrawn.

Finally, when the commissary wagons came on the scene, William D. Pritchard, Co. I, 1st Texas, said that they were issued rations of flour. Some of the boys had gotten a sheep and with the part he received, Pritchard said he cut it up and "with water and a little salt proceeded to prepare supper. We had fairly commenced to prepare our evening meal, when orders came to fall in at once. All was bustle and confusion. We gathered up our half-cooked meat and stuffed into our haversacks the dough now ready for the skillet, and fell in."[10] Chaplain Davis (4th Texas) said that supper "was in every imaginable shape and condition, except one — ready to eat." As to the soldiers attitude, he said, "whether they said any bad words at such a disappointment, it is not my business to tell, nor yours to guess. Some objected and others complained ... the boys wet, hungry, and with a long night's march ahead ... they charged it to the account of profit and loss and moved off."[11] Pritchard, carrying his skillet, ate its half-cooked contents as he marched along.

Meanwhile, upon reaching Catlett's Station, Gen. Stuart's expedition very nearly bagged the miscreant himself. Having left his headquarters tent to visit some of his unit commanders, Pope left behind his uniform coat and dispatch book. Stuart swept them up with considerable relish, no doubt considering them just recompense for the loss of his hat and cloak a few days earlier. He captured also several staff members, one of whom was the Federal Army's quartermaster, a particularly loquacious type. Attempts to burn the railroad bridge at Catlett's failed because of the rain. The need for haste precluded chopping it down although chips did fly for awhile until it was seen that it could not be done, at least in a timely fashion. Gen. Stuart withdrew,

John W. Stevens, Co. K, 5th Texas

captured intelligence firmly in hand, returning his rain-soaked command to within the lines of the Army of Northern Virginia still along the south bank of the Rappahannock River.

From the unexpected cornucopia of information provided by Gen. Stuart, Gen. Lee found out that Pope's army actually numbered about 45,000 men and that the advance elements of McClellan's Peninsula army, that is Gen. Porter's V Corps, had not yet reached the front. Once that junction occurred, the Army of Northern Virginia would be hopelessly outnumbered. This important intelligence coup by Gen. Stuart set the stage for all that followed.

Gen. Lee considered the options available to him — remain in his present place, advance, or retreat. Standing still or retreating were never options favored by Gen. Lee. Recognizing the importance of delaying the union of Pope and the V Corps moving up from its landing point near Fredericksburg, he decided that by continuing upriver with Pope following to block the fords would result in that desirable effect. He summoned Gen. Jackson to his headquarters tent.

According to Douglas S. Freeman, that meeting, which took place at the village of Jeffersonton was "one of the most important Lee ever held."[12] The overall gist of their conversation was that Jackson would, by forced marches, get in rear of Pope via Thoroughfare Gap in the Bull Run Mountains and cut his line of communications and supply on the Orange and Alexandria Railroad. Freeman said Jackson became very excited at the prospect. Jackson's three divisions — Taliaferro's, Ewell's and A.P. Hill's — would march early on August 25. The crossing of the Rapphannock was to be around Waterloo Bridge, later changed to Hinson's Mills. Stuart's cavalry, back from its Catlett's triumph was made ready to support Jackson's march.

Jackson marched on the morning of August 25, having been relieved of his positions opposite Warrenton Spring Ford the evening prior by Longstreet's command. Pope's troops, with their right extended upriver for some distance, exchanged fire with the new arrivals. The plan was no sooner put into operation than unexpected activity on the part of the enemy was detected. But, uncertainty as to what it meant led Gen. Lee to decide upon the necessity of reuniting his forces. But not in the form of a retreat — Longstreet would follow Jackson's looping line of march up the river. Passing through the villages of Orleans and Salem they were bound, like Jackson, through the Bull Run Mountains at Thoroughfare Gap and around the Federal right flank.

The march of Gen. Longstreet's Corps, with Gen. Lee in attendance, began on the afternoon of August 26. By then Jackson and his foot cavalry were already more than a day ahead. The march was necessarily harsh. The rains of several days prior notwithstanding, it was hot, dry and there was little water to be had for drinking. Gen. Pope, realizing that he was outflanked decided to "abandon the line of the Rappahannock and communications with Fredericksburg, and concentrate [his] whole force in the direction of Warrenton and Gainesville, to cover the Warrenton Pike, and still to confront the enemy rapidly marching to [his] right."[13] From this point on and for the remainder of the Manassas campaign, inexplicably, Gen. Pope lost accurate track of where his adversary was located at any one time and to where he might be bound next. That omission was to prove disastrous for his army and ruinous to his career.

Around Salem a courier arrived with a message from Gen. Jackson for Gen. Lee informing him that his "foot cavalry," marching at their prodigious best and supported by Gen. Stuart's cavalry, had fallen upon the Federal supply line at Bristoe Station on the line of the Orange and Alexandria Railroad. And, there was more. Gen. Jackson had sent his crusty old brigade commander, Gen. Isaac Trimball, with several regiments supported by Stuart's cavalry, on to Manassas Junction, which had likewise fallen. Mountains of Federal supplies were thus rendered the legitimate and much-needed property of the thin-ribbed Army of Northern Virginia. There had followed a day of rest, with plenty to eat and drink courtesy of the U.S. Army, which was thoroughly enjoyed by the weary raiders. With no way to transport the captured supplies, that is, what was left after the savaging by Jackson's and Stuart's famished soldiery, the remainder was put to the torch.

Afterward, Jackson retreated toward Centreville assuming that Gen. Pope would follow and with the plan that further retreat, if necessary, would be through Aldie Gap to the west. After several brushes with the enemy, Jackson took to the woods, concealing his entire corps in the vicinity of Groveton to await Longstreet's arrival on the scene. Jackson was now just where Gen. Lee wanted him, in a hidden position in rear of Pope's army, on his line of supply and communication and intervening between that army and the Federal capital.

The march of Longstreet's Corps continued albeit at a slower pace for the remainder of the day; there was no indication that Jackson required their immediate support. The route taken by Gen. Longstreet's Corps in coming to Gen. Jackson's aid was a Confederate favorite and used on many occasions, a wide flanking, forced march. After crossing the Rappahannock they moved westward passing through Salem and moving on toward Thoroughfare Gap in the Bull Run Mountains. Late in the afternoon, carried by the wind, there came the faint, distant rumble of artillery and the rattle of musketry. It could only be Jackson under attack.

Upon approach, it was discovered that the pass was held by a Federal force, Rickett's Division, McDowell's Corps, and an engagement ensued. The Texas Brigade, being further back in the column of march, was ordered to skirt the pass to the left and cross on over the mountains at that point. About halfway through the maneuver, orders came to about face and return to the road as the Federal force defending had been put to flight. "It was night and the climbing of that mountain side, over rocks and through the stubborn laurel bushes was pretty tough. All having passed through the gap, we camped for the remainder of the night on the field where we found dead men lying around everywhere,"[14] recalled W. D. Pitchard, Co. I, 1st Texas. Exhausted, they slept immediately and soundly.

Later, in the darkness blanketing the scene, someone accidently kicked over a feed barrel that had been used by some cavalrymen earlier in the day to feed their mounts. The barrel went bounding down the hill, the noise accentuated by the stillness of the night. The racket spooked one of the brigade's favorite pack animals, dubbed the "old gray mare," and, loaded with pots, pans and other noise-producing items, she bounded into the midst of the sleeping brigade. Someone shouted, "Look out!" and the race was on, a fence being destroyed in the troops' headlong rush down the hill. Finally, once everyone became fully awake, the race slowed and stopped. Laughing at their heedless stampede, they made their way back to their hastily abandoned bivouac. The incident became the basis for a favorite brigade song that included the line, "The old gray mare came tearing out o' the wilderness."[15]

Dawn, August 29, with only a few hours of sleep, the column set out once more. In the van was Hood's Division, the van of that composed of Texas marksmen acting as skirmishers and commanded by the daring Lt. Col. John Upton, 5th Texas. Gen. Hood's instructions to Upton were to push forward resolutely regardless of any opposition or losses. Gen. Jackson was beset and needed immediate support. Gen. Hood said that Upton's force performed its assigned duty in a manner "which is entitled to the admiration of every soldier.... The gallant Upton was, indeed, pre-eminent in his sphere as an outpost officer."[16]

As hot, dusty and exhausting as that day's forced march was, the troops took the time to view their surroundings and some recorded later their memories of the lovely countryside. As Longstreet moved forward, a cavalry column was spotted that, after a few moments of uncertainty, proved to be a column of Stuart's cavalry come from Jackson's front. Advised of Jackson's location, Stuart was dispatched by Gen. Lee to protect the right flank of Longstreet's column. When Longstreet's Corps reached the vicinity of Gainesville on the Warrenton-Centreville Turnpike, the boom of artillery could be heard in the left distance and was increasing in intensity. Gen. Lee quickened the pace; Jackson could be seriously imperiled.

Lt. Col. John C. Upton, 5th Texas, killed at Second Manassas, August 30, 1862.

As the Texas Brigade turned left onto the turnpike, a grizzled figure in nondescript clothing with an old army kepi pulled down over his eyes rode out to greet Gen. Hood. Gen. Jackson had been watching the column's approach and was glad, undoubtedly, of its arrival and even gladder to see the aggressive Hood at its head. As word filtered through Jackson's line that Longstreet was on the scene, a mighty cheer was raised. Once again the Army of Northern Virginia had concentrated and been made whole on the day of battle.

If the condition of the 18th Georgia upon arriving upon the field is any indicator of the condition of the command as a whole, it is remarkable that they were able to fight at all. According to Chaplain Doll of the 18th Georgia, "[s]ufficient provisions could seldom be commanded. Only *seven* days' rations were drawn out of thirty-one; and repeatedly while in the act of cooking them, orders came to march. Many were without coats, blankets or shoes. With some concealed object of grandeur before them, these soldiers, good, brave, obedient, patient, press on further by night than by day, crossing meadows, wading rivers, climbing hills, stumbling over rocky roads, often jaded, sleepy, sick, and in more than one instance staining with blood the stones that had bruised and cut their feet."[17] Not much should have been expected of troops operating under such conditions but they always seemed to answer the call and usually came through.

While his headquarters was being set up, Hood began deploying his troops in line of battle across the Warrenton Pike and at a near ninety-degree angle with Jackson's troop disposition. Subsequently, they learned of the last few days' course of events as Jackson rampaged behind the Federal lines wreaking destruction and confusion at Bristoe and Manassas Junction. It was from his hidden woodland vantage point that Jackson had been able to observe the comings and goings of Federal units in search of his whereabouts.

Thanks to a dispatch captured by Stuart's troopers, Gen. Jackson learned of Pope's plans to concentrate first around Manassas Junction later changed to Centreville and of the Federal troops' positions and lines of march to reach that locale. Seeing advantage in attacking in the knowledge that Longstreet was on the way and that the attack would in some way impede the concentration plans, he set upon a passing Federal column the evening prior. That column turned out to be the division of Gen. Rufus King, McDowell's Corps, on the move from Warrenton to Centreville. This was the source of the sounds of battle heard by Longstreet's ranks the day before. The battle was fought at Brawner's Farm near Groveton and is referred to interchangeably. The Southerners were in command of the field when the smoke cleared but at a high cost in officers and men. In the Federal ranks, the Iron Brigade got its name as a result of its performance and heavy losses suffered that day.

Jackson's position subsequent was well-chosen. The main line conformed to the excavated bed of an unfinished railroad. It was a ready-made defensive position, with Gregg's brigade anchoring the left, Baylor's the right and the other units of the command strung out between. It was adjacent to the field where an earlier contest had been decided in favor of the Confederacy, First Manassas (Bull Run). "Overall Jackson's defensive position was approximately two miles in length, supported by 40 guns, and with both flanks secured by Stuart's cavalry."[18]

When Pope received, in a rather roundabout way, King's report of the Groveton fight, he jumped to the conclusion that Jackson had been caught retreating in an attempt to escape. Pope thought that he had Jackson trapped between elements of McDowell's Corps, King's Division at the scene, and Ricketts' Division at Thoroughfare Gap. So, later, when he gave the order to attack Jackson's position in the railroad cut, he was confident in the outcome. He simply did not know that King and Ricketts were both in retreat upon Manassas Junction and Bristoe Station, respectively, and that the road from Thoroughfare Gap was open for Longstreet, who was, in fact, on the way, and about to be in a position to strike the Federal left like an avalanche.

When, during the night of August 28–29, Pope learned finally of King's and Ricketts' retreat, he was forced to improvise using units that just happened to be on the scene. "As far as Pope's knowledge went, he was all set to achieve his goal of erasing Jackson, who was, he thought struggling desperately to escape the net. Longstreet must still be west of the Bull Run Mountains."[19]

The second big battle on the plain of Manassas began on the morning of August 29, when Federal forces, including units of McDowell's Corps with Sigel's Corps in reserve, attacked Gen. Jackson's formidable line. Later in the day, when Longstreet arrived on the field and his command was deployed, Law's Brigade was sited on the north side of the Warrenton Turnpike and Hood's Brigade was on the south side. As they arrived over time, arrayed beyond to form the right flank of the army were the other units of Longstreet's command, Kemper, D. R. Jones and on the far right, R. H. Anderson. As it formed, the Texas Brigade position was along a strip of timber that extended on for some distance to the right. The right flank of the Texas Brigade was held by the 5th Texas, then to its left in order, Hampton's Legion, 18th Georgia, 4th Texas and the 1st Texas, the latter's left on the pike.

Across the Pike on Law's left there was a large open field intervening between Longstreet's and Jackson's lines of battle. Into that gap was deployed the Washington Artillery

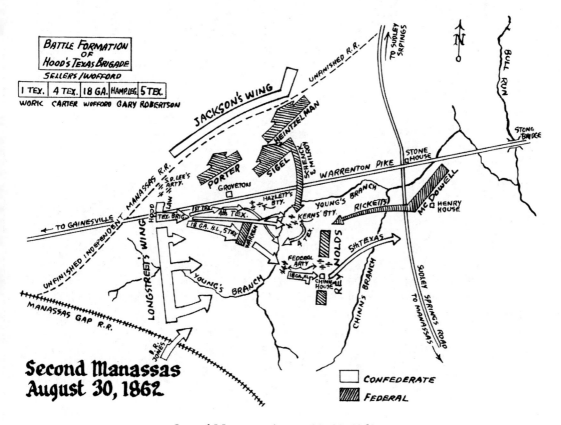

Second Manassas, August 29–30, 1862

of New Orleans and other artillery units. By midday, Gen. Longstreet's Corps was in line of battle and ready for action. As a result of the misunderstanding Gen. Pope had of Confederate troop dispositions, the Army of Virginia largely ignored their considerable presence.

In Longstreet's ranks, John K. Stevens, Co. K, 5th Texas, said that after being moved into position only skirmishing occurred in their front at first but that in Jackson's sector the fighting was quite heavy at times. His observation, exhibiting a degree of pride in the eccentric Jackson, was that he "was never happy, if there were any yankees around, unless he was pegging away at them — he seemed to think they were made to be shot at."[20]

On the other end of the Texas Brigade position, W. D. Pritchard's Co. I, 1st Texas lay in line of battle awaiting orders listening to the sounds of battle on their left as Jackson fought hard to maintain his position in the face of the heavy Federal attack. By then, their battle-trained ears could "tell even at that distance the varied progress of the fight. The 'hip! hip! hurrah!' of the Yanks told when they had gained some ground and the stirring Rebel yell told when our boys got it on them. Soon it became evident that Stonewall had the best of the fight, as the yell increased in volume and seemed to be moving off."[21] Soon thereafter, an artillery round passed through their ranks, "cutting off both legs of one man in the front rank close to the body and completely carrying away the head of a man in the rear rank, scattering his skull and brains over those of us that were near him."[22] As if it afforded any more protection, Pritchard and his comrades sought shelter behind a nearby tree only to be called back into ranks by their company commander.

Between 3:00 and 6:00 P.M. the Federal ranks were launched in a series of bloody frontal assaults against Jackson's troops in the railroad cut. Confederate ammunition ran low and, in some instances, was exhausted. Defense by the bayonet, rocks and anything else that came to hand was the only thing that saved the day on that front.

Along about sundown from Longstreet's front, a reconnaissance in force was advanced. As it turned out, a Federal advance commenced at about the same time. Gen. Law's Brigade advanced on the north side of the turnpike and Gen. Hood's Brigade advanced on the south side. The regiment of direction for the Texas Brigade was the 1st Texas with its left on the turnpike, then the 4th Texas, 18th Georgia, Hampton Legion and 5th Texas arrayed out to the right. Lt. Col. P.A. Work, 1st Texas, said that after having laid in line of battle near the enemy for most of the day Friday, August 29, they moved forward when the order to advance was given.

Moving into the open field in their front, the enemy opened on them with artillery. Pressing on toward some farther woods, the enemy's artillery barrage stopped as they approached close on. Moving into and through the woods, two companies on the 1st Texas' left emerged into an open field beyond where they became engaged with the 79th New York. Firing broke out until someone in the Federal ranks raised the cry of "Friends." In the gathering gloom and the confusion created by the false cry, the 79th New York made good its escape.

Before they left, however, things got pretty nasty with hand-to-hand fighting occurring. George T. Todd, Co. A, 1st Texas, who described Col. Work as a "very small man physically," said that his colonel "got into a rough and tumble fight with a big Yank, and marched him to the rear."[23] W. D. Pritchard, Co. I, 1st Texas, said that Col. Work was clubbed over the head by a Federal soldier "knocking him down, but ... that he recovered to a sitting position and shot his man before he could get away."[24]

Continuing to advance following their clash with the New Yorkers, the 1st Texas soon established contact with the 4th Texas and 18th Georgia. Together they moved on beyond a small stream and onto a ridge where they stopped to rest. Later, in his after-action report, Col. Work reported that T. R. Oldham and J. M. Steinsipher, both of Co. H, 1st Texas, were killed during that time "while lying down at their place in ranks in front of the enemy by a discharge of grape-shot which remained in the tin case unexploded."[25] The former, thirty years of age, the latter twenty-one, had been recruited in Texas only five months earlier.

In its advance, the 18th Georgia encountered elements of the 17th, 24th and 44th New York Regiments. According to Col. Wofford, his regiment captured the colors of the 24th and an aggregate of fifty-three prisoners of war from the 17th, 24th and 44th, respectively The 24th's colors were not relinquished without a fight. The color bearer refused to surrender them to T. H. Northcutt, Co. A, 18th Georgia, even after being shot by the 18th's adjutant, Patton. Finally, it took both Northcutt and J. J. O'Neill, Co. A, 18th Georgia, to wrest them from his grip.[26] O'Neill said the flag was sent back to Georgia where it was displayed at Milledgeville, then that state's capitol. When Sherman's troops on their way to the sea passed through there in the fall of 1864, the much-traveled flag passed back into Federal hands.[27]

Over on the right, the 5th Texas formed a line of battle with Companies A and B thrown forward as skirmishers. Going forward, R. H. Leonard, Co. F, 5th Texas, said they passed through woods and open fields before being halted at the edge of a narrow strip of woods awaiting further orders. Over to the left they could hear heavy skirmishing by the 18th Georgia and Hampton Legion nearby and farther away the 1st and 4th Texas. About that time the command to advance was given and the whole brigade moved forward. Leonard said as they moved forward enthusiastically, from a field on their right there arose the "wildest shout and unearthly yell" he had ever heard. The field was fenced and "in the field were several head of cattle and a herd of swine, which, being frightened by the noise, flew in the utmost confusion — the cattle bawling, the hogs squealing, as they ran to and fro, trying to find a place to exit."[28] The louder the livestock bawled and squealed, the louder the young men and boys in the ranks yelled in accompaniment.

As twilight gave way to evening and darkness began to fall, it was discovered that the advance had taken the Texas Brigade beyond the enemy's lines. In the darkness, it became apparent that they were surrounded at some places, Federal officers giving orders to Confederate troops and the like. Gen. Hood reported to army headquarters that his troops were in a dangerously vulnerable position and requested permission to withdraw to a more defensible line. He reported also that the Federal position ahead was an exceedingly strong one. Gen. Lee granted Hood permission to withdraw. By then, the night having fallen like a dark blanket over the battlefield, the withdrawal was made stealthily and without major incident.

Waiting is one of the worst parts of a combat soldier's life. Knowing that coming events might very well spell the end of one's life or a frightful maiming does not make for contentment in the ranks. Among others, John Stevens, Co. K, 5th Texas, remembered that night and said that, "we lay there on our arms, catching a few snitches of sleep.... While awake our minds are engaged in contemplating the serious work of the morrow that we well know will surely come. Some of our boys seem to be careless and indifferent regarding it, others look and speak in serious tones, and seem to have forebodings that they will be killed."[29] For what remained of the night, the troops waited, wondering what the dawn would bring.

As the sun rose on August 30, 1862, it promised to be another hot summer day in more ways than one. An uneasy quiet pervaded the battlefield. As both armies bestirred themselves and were observed from the opposite lines, each perceived, inexplicably, the possibility that the other was withdrawing. According to Gen. Longstreet, there was apprehension that "Pope was going to get away from us, and Pope was afraid that we were going to get away from him."[30]

Federal troops captured the night before and thence paroled were returned to their own lines that morning. Some of them reported to their superiors that their recent captors were retreating. Apparently, the withdrawal of the Texas Brigade the evening before along with the reports of the paroled soldiers convinced Gen. Pope that the Army of Northern Virginia was abandoning the field, an opinion he communicated prematurely to his superiors in Washington. In his postwar memoir, Gen. Hood thought that the result of the midnight necessity of moving R. H. Anderson's late-arriving division from where they had mistakenly bivouacked in his front caused Gen. Pope's mistaken perception. Warned of his peril, Anderson "promptly aroused his men and just after daybreak [August 30th] marched to the rear of my line of battle. The pike was dry, and his division, as it moved back, left a cloud of dust in its wake, which circumstance, [Hood] ... thought, induced General Pope to send his celebrated dispatch to Washington to the effect that General Lee was in full retreat."[31] It proved to be a perception that spelled disaster. Gen. Longstreet was there and he was there with his entire corps primed for a fight.

There was an artillery duel early on but it trailed off. William R. Hamby, Co. B, 4th Texas, observed that skirmishing occurred all morning and into the afternoon. His company suffered some casualties from the musketry and came under artillery fire from Federal batteries located on a hill about a half a mile to their front. The artillery fire into the woods that concealed the Confederate troops was random. Hamby described the artillery fire as "annoying," mainly, but it did add greatly to the tension: "[A]s the shells came shrieking through the tree tops over our heads, they seemed to say, 'Where are you? Where are you?' and when they burst there is no question but what they plainly said, 'Found you.'"[32]

Later in the morning, the sound of moving artillery trains accompanied by clouds of rising dust behind the Federal lines signaled the arrival of more troops, Heintzelman and Porter's from the Peninsula as it turned out, and indicated that no retreat was being contemplated from that quarter. Indeed, troops seemed to be massing on the Federal right opposite Jackson's already badly battered and hard-marched ranks. Hope began to rise in the Confederate ranks. They knew from experience that they were in a good defensive position. If their resolve and ammunition held out they saw a great opportunity to decimate a massed Federal advance as had been done to them two months earlier at Malvern Hill. In the meantime, as the sun climbed ever higher heating the scene, in their positions the troops sweated, the summer insects buzzed and light breezes whispered through the pines. They all waited for the fury they knew all too well was coming.

About mid-afternoon a massive Federal attack commenced, falling first on Jackson's right adjacent to Longstreet's position. The lines were so close at one time that the ammunition-starved Confederates once again resorted to rocks and whatever else was available to hurl their attackers back. The attack was short-lived as the emphasis shifted over to Jackson's left, that flanking portion being manned by A. P. Hill's stalwarts who had borne the brunt of the attack the day before. In the meantime, Longstreet's skillfully concealed position on their exposed left flank was being largely ignored by the Federals, they thinking Longstreet to be in the process of retreat because of Hood's withdrawal the evening prior and the dust raised by R. H. Anderson's repositioning division.

The attack on the railroad cut position ebbed and flowed but with increasing intensity. Finally, and uncharacteristically, Jackson was compelled by the weight of Federal numbers to request reinforcements, which Gen. Lee ordered. From his vantage point on the line, Gen. Longstreet could see plainly the exposed left flank of the advancing blue-clad ranks and of its vulnerability to an enfilading artillery fire if delivered from his lines.

From his position, Granville Crozier, Co. B, 4th Texas, observed, as had others, that the Federal advance did not seem to be aware of Longstreet's considerable presence "although we remained in line of battle nearly all day.... Fighting was going on all morning on the Confederate left and center, and it was two o'clock or later in the afternoon before we were ordered to charge."[33] Included in the anxiously awaiting artillery units for the order to open was Capt. James Reilly and his Rowan Battery.

When given the order to commence firing, the massed batteries opened with a deafening crash. The surprise of being attacked from that quarter and the weight of the barrage yielded results rather quickly as the Federal left shuddered and slowed. At about the same time, Jackson signaled that he no longer required reinforcements as the Federal attack on his front began to fade. Gen. Lee's military sense registered the scene before him; now was the critical moment to strike Pope in flank and from ahead. Gen. Longstreet had seen also the same opportunity and was already preparing to move forward when the order to do so reached him. The Confederate lines sensed that the advantage had shifted suddenly to them and that a victory was in the air. On command, Longstreet's Corps swept forward in its entirety with the Texas Brigade on its feet and in advance.

As in the previous day's disposition, the 1st Texas was designated the regiment of direction with its left resting on the Warrenton Turnpike, then 4th Texas, 18th Georgia, Hampton's Legion and 5th Texas arrayed beyond. The attack began between 4:00 and 4:30 P.M. M. V. Smith, Co. D, 4th Texas, said his company had lain somberly in line of battle all day listening to the battle raging over to their left. "I have never seen a man who could explain the feelings of a fellow under such circumstances. The rolicksome, noisy boys who were ever ready for any prank, became calm and serene and a deathlike hush took possession of the whole brigade.... We arose from our recumbent position, shook ourselves as it were, moved out through the wooded eminence."[34]

Their line of advance was through a series of rolling, wooded hills over which the retreating Federals fell back. After some initial confusion as to the position of the 4th Texas to the right, the 1st Texas moved forward where it came under fire from a Federal battery which limbered up as the Texans closed in upon it. Moving up the turnpike at a rapid gait, the battery wheeled off and into an orchard located on a knoll overlooking the Texans' advance where it unlimbered and resumed its harassing fire. Moving from hollow to hollow and inclining to its right, the 1st Texas finally reestablished contact with the 4th Texas.

Advancing with the 4th Texas, Granville Crozier, Co. B, described the scene spread before him as "a magnificent sight" with "the Confederates marching for several hundred yards across a plain in straight line and as calm as if on drill."[35] Wounded two months earlier at Gaines' Mill, Crozier said he was beginning to feel confident, like he was going to make it through this one unscathed. Then, his left arm became numb suddenly. Hopes dashed, he looked down but was relieved somewhat to find the arm still in place. He made for the rear and any convenient field hospital he could find. On the way, coming under fire, he paused to take cover under some big guns left behind by the retreating Federals. The battery horses were lying down, most of them probably dead, felled by Confederate infantry fire. Nearby a Federal officer was sprawled under an ammunition box. When some of the horses began kicking, the Federal officer raised up and, resting on his elbow looked directly at Crozier. Crozier said he returned the stare and was "just going to ask him if he didn't wish this 'cruel war was over' when he saw his command falling back."[36] Asking one of his company officers what the retreat was all about, he was told they had whipped the Yankees and were just falling back to rest in the shade for a few minutes.Actually, they were compelled to fall back, but only momentarily, when they had come under enfilade fire from their left flank. Crozier made it to the aid station and ultimately survived his second wounding.

William R. Hamby, Co. B, 4th Texas, said that the right of his regiment encountered and overran a Federal battery of four guns while farther to their right the 5th Texas, 18th Georgia and Hampton's Legion were slugging it out with the ordered ranks of the 5th New York Zouaves. Hamby thought it ironic that the captured battery was manned by some of the same troops that they had fought at Gaines' Mill in late June. On both occasions the battery was manned by Pennsylvanians under the command of Capt. Mark Kerns. Although wounded at Gaines' Mill, then-Lt. Kerns had been able to avoid capture. He was not to be so fortunate on this day. His battery was decimated by the infantry fire delivered by the 4th Texas. Now alone, he continued heroically to man the guns, loading and firing until struck down himself. Hamby said, "When we reached the gun beside which he fell, with his life blood fast ebbing away, he said: 'I promised to drive you back, or die under my guns, and I have kept my word.'"[37]

Col. Wofford's 18th Georgia with Hampton's Legion and the 5th Texas to his right and the 4th and 1st Texas on his left advanced very quickly. The regiment encountered units of the just arrived Federal V Corps in the form of the 5th and 10th New York. They had been moved forward in support of a battery of artillery, Lt. Charles E. Hazlett's Battery D, 5th U.S.

On that side of the line and from the perspective of the Federal ranks as the Confederate attack began, it seemed that "the Rebel skirmish line suddenly rose up and started forward.... Rank after rank of Southern troops emerged from the cover of a wood line, and came sweeping across the fields like a vast, gray wave, flecked with glinting steel and crowned with blood-red battle flags."[38] The Federal regiments broke, pursued by Wofford's men as well as Hampton's Legion and the 5th Texas. Nearly all the Federals were either killed or captured. The 18th Georgia captured the colors of the 10th New York thereby adding to their capture of the day before. Overrunning a battery, the 18th's color bearer mounted one of the guns waving the regimental flag in triumph for all to see. Moving on to attack a second battery, the color bearer, Sgt. Weems, was shot down soon followed by two more, Sgts. McMurry and Jones.[39] The act of color-bearing in Civil War combat was to invite serious or fatal injury but, nonetheless, was a sought after honor to perform.

Lt. Col. Gary, Hampton's Legion, reported advancing about 4:00 P.M. They had moved only a short distance when their skirmishers in advance came into contact with the 5th New York Zouaves. After receiving a volley from the New Yorkers, the South Carolinians returned fire killing, wounding and capturing a number of them

On down the line and manning the brigade's right flank, the 5th Texas spearheaded the advance of the Texas Brigade. Across the line, Federal brigade commander Col. Governeur K. Warren, uncertain of and seeking information about what was on his front, had sent six companies of his 10th New York forward as skirmishers. Light skirmishing went on for several hours. It was about 4:00 P.M. when, much to the surprise of the Federal line, the concealed Confederate skirmishers rose up out of the ground and began to move forward. From the concealment of the wood line behind their skirmish line followed the rest of Longstreet's Corps, 30,000 strong.

The 5th Texas broke a line of skirmishers from the 10th New York which then fell back in confusion and panic on the 5th New York. The 5th New York Zouaves were easily recognizable by their unusual apparel. Their gaudy uniforms were composed of short blue jackets trimmed in yellow, baggy red trousers gathered below the knee, white leggings and red caps with long yellow tassels.

At this time, the 5th New York's former regimental commander, Col. Warren, had been elevated to brigade command. The regiment itself was commanded by Capt. Cleveland Winslow. Reporting later of the battle, Col. Warren said the 10th New York was routed and in falling back made it difficult for the 5th to fire in a timely fashion. Even though some of the 10th New York's skirmishers were still out front, a ragged volley was managed upon the rapidly advancing Texans, South Carolinians, and Georgians. The hasty volley was high, most of the balls whining harmlessly above the heads of their intended targets. Even so, many of the .58 caliber missiles did find a mark, the recipients thereof crashing to the ground either dead or wounded.

After permitting any surviving comrades to pass through their ranks, the Zouaves reformed presenting a solid front to face the onrushing Confederate avalanche. Capt. W. T. Hill, 5th Texas, who would be one of the few left standing at Appomattox and the 5th Texas' last commander, said as the Texans, Georgians and South Carolinians emerged from the timber with the Federal skirmishers fleeing before them, the Texans' bloodlust was up and they were "yelling their loudest." Here they came face to face with the Zouaves who "stood in perfect alignment as if on dress parade."[40]

At this point and for a few minutes, the antagonists exchanged volleys, both sides suffering heavy casualties. Then, raising a blood-curdling rebel yell, the 5th Texas launched a fierce attack striking the Zouaves "square in front" causing them to wheel and run. A new recruit in the 5th New York's line of battle was a fifteen year old named William H. Platt. Later he was to relate that "[w]e fired three volleys at them when the rebels charged us.... We broke and run [;] they shot us down by hundreds."[41] Even in the heat of battle, John Stevens, Co. K, 5th Texas, described admiringly the gaudily attired Federal infantrymen as "one of the finest looking bodies of men I ever saw, not one of them under six feet in height ... their uniforms ... a sort of cross between a night gown and a bloomer rig, except it was red in color with red head dress with a tassel hanging down about a foot from the crown. From the point we struck them, it was about 300 or 400 yards to [Young's] Run creek; of all the running I ever saw in a battle that was the swiftest."[42] Not all the Zouaves were panicked. Among many others, "G," Company 1st Sgt. William McDowell, although wounded severely in the body, kept his place "glaring defiantly at the advancing enemy until killed by a bullet in the forehead."[43]

Hard in pursuit and "rebel yelling" at the top of their lungs, Stevens, Co. K, 5th Texas, said that many of the Zouaves were shot in the back of the head, turning complete somersaults in the process of crashing to the ground. Corporal Theodore Hart, Co. A, 5th New York, received a horrendous face wound, the bullet "ripping through his head and exiting from his neck. Both sides of [his] jaw were broken, his palate destroyed and most of his teeth shattered. One tooth was propelled upward and passed out of his right eye."[44] As if that was not bad enough, afterwards, Hart was to lie wounded on the bare ground four or five nights, two of them in a drenching rain with little to eat before he was removed finally from the battlefield. It was during this phase of the attack that the 5th Texas' lieutenant colonel, the valiant and colorful John Upton, was killed.

As it is with all organizations, military and otherwise, there were many devoted soldiers in the Texas Brigade. One such soldier was Sidney V. Patrick, Co. E, 5th Texas. Remembered by comrades as a good and true man and a dependable soldier, even in the tumult and chaos of battle he was observed to not be excitable and seldom showed any emotion. During the pursuit of the 5th New York, that regiment had to ford Young's Branch, their baggy Zouave pants becoming water-logged in the process. Hot on their trail, the 5th Texans were shouting, cursing and shooting at them. One of the Zouaves, for some unknown reason, seemed to be receiving more than his share of attention, getting several bullet holes in his baggy pants as a result. Unharmed, as he scampered up a hill each step yielded a jet of water from the various bullet holes ventilating his trousers. One of Patrick's comrades said that it was, indeed, a funny sight but that most of the men were too scared to see the humor at the time. Not so with the usually stolid Patrick. " [H]e was laughing fit to kill himself.... In the hottest part of the work .... he was evidently thinking of that zouave and his waterworks, for he was grinning and apparently enjoying the memory of it. After ... we had halted for a breathing spell, the first words he said were: 'Say, did you see that Yankee?'"[45]

Col. Robertson, 5th Texas, reported that the Zouaves' precipitous retreat left "the field-strewn with their dead and wounded. Such was the impetuosity of the charge and the unerring aim of my men that very few, if any, of that regiment reached the hill beyond."[46] Young's Creek ran red with Zouave blood and was clogged with the bodies of their dead and wounded.

Inexplicably, Col. Robertson noted that the right flank of the 5th Texas regiment had moved far ahead of the advance and disappeared over the ridges in their front. Shortly thereafter he received word of Lt. Col. Upton's death. It was this tragic occurrence that had resulted in the uncontrolled, unordered advance.

Although the 5th New York suffered horrible losses, the 5th Texas did not escape unscathed, suffering heavy casualties in the rapid advance. Col. Robertson, noting the decimated state of his regiment with some companies totally devoid of officers, considered ordering a retreat in order to regroup. However, due to the heavy cost paid in getting to where they were and the aggressive state of mind of the survivors, he decided to advance those under his immediate command to a defile some 300 yard ahead and toward the Chinn House ridge. On the way they came under heavy artillery fire and upon taking shelter in the defile, they stopped for a breather. When shortly thereafter they emerged from the defile and moved on, Col. Robertson himself fell wounded near the Chinn House. Even so, the blood-lusting 5th Texas plunged ahead recklessly in hot pursuit of the fleeing enemy, never mind the rest of the brigade and the lack of flanking support.

Following close in the wake of the attack, division commander Hood noted a field "where lay the dead and dying zouaves in their gay uniforms, amid the tall green grass, presented indeed a singular appearance, as I passed down the slope and across the creek."[47] Over to the left, glancing back upon the field to their rear, soldiers of the 4th Texas saw "evidence of what the Fifth Texas had done in the ghastly, horrifying spectacle that met our eyes as, while lying in the branch, we looked at the hill-side then in our rear, nearly an acre of which that regiment had covered with killed and wounded Zouaves, the variegated colors of whose gaudy uniforms gave the scene, when looked at from a distance, the appearance of a Texas hill-side when carpeted in the spring by wild flowers of many hues and tints."[48]

As darkness approached, Jackson's battered command joined in the pursuit of the surprised, panic-stricken and demoralized Army of Virginia. In their rapid advance, the Confederate ranks became hopelessly confused. Rain threatened, eventually sweeping through and drenching the area. Outflanked and routed, Pope's army fled across Bull Run Creek.

Once again and on the same field where Southern arms had proclaimed victory a year earlier, the Army of Northern Virginia had carried the day in an impressive fashion.

Gen. Pope's army was defeated soundly and forced to fall back on the defenses of Washington, D.C. Of the Federal debacle, Rufus K. Felder, Co. E, 5th Texas, thought that had "there been a Joshua to stay the setting sun, we might have made captives of almost the entire army."[49] That was, indeed, one possibility. As one would expect, shortly, Gen. Pope was relieved of his command and banished to the western frontier. There, having failed to keep the unruly Rebs in check, he spent the remainder of the war and beyond attempting to keep the unruly Sioux in check. The Lincoln administration, viewing a bleak leadership landscape, resorted to the expedient of reinstating the overly cautious and vanquished author of the Peninsula debacle. Gen. George B. McClellan was returned to the command of the Army of the Potomac.

With the blood-red sun sinking below the horizon, John W. Stevens' Co. K, 5th Texas, gathered to assess its losses. In that company alone, a roll call revealed two-thirds of its number missing. Later, in his official report of the 5th Texas' action, Col. Robertson named seven color bearers shot down, the eighth, W. G. W. Farthing, Co. D, 5th Texas, bearing the flag for the remainder of the fight. Although unscathed in this fight, Farthing's reprieve was only temporary. He would be wounded and taken prisoner at Gettysburg the following summer. After his exchange, his left leg was amputed probably as a result of the Gettysburg wound. Eventually, he was discharged for obvious medical reasons.[50] Three companies were left devoid of any commissioned officers at all. So many officers had fallen, including Col. Robertson, that command of the regiment had been taken up by Capt. Ike Turner, Co. K, 5th Texas. Foremost among the officers killed, the much lamented Lt. Col. John C. Upton. One account had Upton, while crossing a stream, probably Young's, being "shot through the head and [falling] dead into the water."[51]

A war correspondent visited Hood's divisional hospital following Second Manassas and reported on what he saw there. The casualties, including William Fletcher, Co. F, 5th Texas, "were lying upon the ground awaiting their turn with patience, some dead, some dying, but the great majority with only painful wounds in the extremities. The operating tables ... were slimy with blood ... and as fast as one patient was removed another took his place to be anesthetized by the merciful chloroform and undergo the necessary surgical treatment. The men all appeared to bear their wounds cheerfully, and it was only now and then when the knife cut deep that a smothered groan revealed the sharp pang of pain.... A distinguishing feature of all field hospitals at such times, according to one veteran surgeon, was 'that ineffable smell of gore.'"[52]

That night, while participating in the gristly search of the day's battlefield for the company's missing men, Stevens, Co. K, 5th Texas, came upon a wounded Federal with two broken legs. The Federal begged him for water. In response to the plea, Stevens gave him his own full canteen. In return the Federal gave Stevens his haversack that was filled with three days rations. Among the rations was included some ground coffee, sugar and a small coffee boiler. The delighted Stevens said he went down to a nearby stream where, kindling a fire, he brewed the coffee and drank down the entire boiler full. And, "Oh, how I enjoyed it; the first sure enough coffee I had drank in many long weeks."[53] There, on the battlefield, cluttered with debris of battle and scores of the ghostly dead and painfully wounded of both sides, he stretched out on the ground where he slept soundly and unvexed until the next morning.

M. V. Smith's Co. D, 4th Texas, lay upon the battlefield that night where any possibility of a much needed rest was impossible because of "the dismal moans, and heart-rending screams of the wounded and dying." A detail was organized to recover the nearby wounded of both sides.[54]

The next day, Nicholas Pomeroy, Co. A, 5th Texas, was witness to what he described as a "pathetic incident." Detailed to bury two of his company who had died of their wounds during the night, Pomeroy and a comrade struggled to dig a double grave in hard ground with worn-out tools and with even more worn out bodies as a result of the exertions of recent months. A shallow trough completed, they gently laid the bodies side-by-side in the grave. Blankets were placed over them and then they were covered with the excavated soil.

Just as they were completing their sad task, a young Virginia cavalryman rode up inquiring for the 5th Texas. Pomeroy identified himself as a member of that regiment. Introducing himself, the cavalryman stated his mission as being to locate his brother who had gone to Texas the previous year and, according to his most recent information, joined the 5th Texas. Recognizing the name, Pomeroy pointed to the result of their recent labors. He identified the cavalryman's brother as one of the two men just buried. The cavalryman's shock and grief were a sad sight to witness.[55]

That same day, citizens from Richmond and elsewhere came out. The news of the fight between the 5th Texas and the 5th New York Zouaves had already spread. Most of the curious citizenry were seeking the field where the 5th Texas had wreaked such havoc on the 5th New York and its sister regiment.

With the evacuation of the last of the wounded, Pomeroy and his comrades were able to get a night's sleep and even a few rations which they cooked as best they could. The next day, September 3, they hastened to rejoin their regiment.

Though it seems impossible to exceed the slaughter that attended Second Manassas, in a little over two weeks an even more dreadful and trying time awaited all of them across the Potomac in the lush, green countryside that was Maryland.

CHAPTER 7

"They fought bravely, and unflinchingly faced a terrible hail of bullets and artillery"[1]: The 1st Texas at Sharpsburg, Maryland, September 16–17, 1862

The Southern victory at Second Manassas had been a close-run affair. Even as the fight was in progress, reinforcements from McClellan's Peninsula army were arriving on the field and into the area generally. Had they been better coordinated, the battle could have gone the other way. The heavy rains that swept through the entire area on August 31 further added to the Federal gloom.

The chase was on but slowed considerably by the rain-swollen conditions as the roads turned into quagmires. On September 1, the rain stopped for a time. Later, in the afternoon, Gen. Jackson's troops approached the mansion of Chantilly and found it to be occupied. Jackson ordered an attack by A. P. Hill. The Federals, including the troops of Hooker's, McDowell's, Reno's and Kearny's divisions, fought hard and, in the midst of a severe thunderstorm, drove the attackers back. At the head of his division, the remarkable Gen. Philip Kearney was killed, his body later returned by his former friends in the "old army" to the Federal lines. But then, as night fell, the Federal line gave way and fell back. Confederate cavalry followed up and found the trailing elements to be moving into the formidable Washington works surrounding the capital. Gen. Lee recognized both the futility of investing the unassailable bastion with an insufficient number of troops and the need for his half-starved and ragged army to rest and recover. What next?

Considering the points of the compass and the existing conditions, only one point was both logical and promising: north, across the Potomac, the untouched and bountiful farmlands of Maryland and Pennsylvania beckoning beyond. With the enemy capital clearly visible across the river, the Army of Northern Virginia took up the march, moving northwestward along the south bank. On that march they passed through Leesburg on a night bathed in moonlight. All of the ladies of the town and their female relatives had turned out to cheer them on. Stevens, Co. K, 5th Texas, thought he had never seen so many women in such a short time in his life. They covered the sidewalks and front yards and were in every door and window. They all seemed to be waving white handkerchiefs and some young mothers went so far as to wave their babies at them.

Breaking ranks, they camped there that night. The next morning, September 4, the army forded the Potomac, and, now wet in addition to weary, set foot on enemy territory for the first time in the course of hostilities. At that point, Stevens estimated the river to be about 500 yards across, shallow and swift-flowing. The scene was memorable, the men filling the river, yelling, singing to the accompaniment of eight to twelve regimental bands, "drums beating, horns a'tootin and fifes screaming out such tunes as 'Dixie,' 'My Maryland,' 'The Girl I Left Behind Me' and even 'Yankee Doodle.'" Stevens confessed that he did not feel jolly and did not share the euphoria because, as he put it, he realized the "serious side of the situation."[2] The experiences of the past several months left no doubts in anyone's mind who had survived them that the face of battle that they were bound to encounter soon was terrible beyond words.

At the same time, another Texan, A. N. Erskine, Co. D, 4th Texas, admired the landscape and "wished for the pencil of a [Raphael] ... to repeat the beautiful scene." The men he saw crossing the river he described as "ragged, dirty, sun-browned and careworn and tired ... picking their way over the rough and rock bottom of the river."[3] He did not express any felt emotions but if he harbored any fears for his future, they were justified. Wounded at Gaines' Mill in June, he was killed at Sharpsburg a week later.

Some weeks thereafter, in a letter to his sister, Rufus Felder, Co. E, 5th Texas, told of the hard march into Maryland in which it was "hard ... to keep up at times." Hot weather, hard roads, dust forced him to ride half a day in an ambulance. Somewhat restored, he was able to continue. In Maryland, he observed the country to be "beautiful & fruit plentiful." However, any thoughts of Southern sympathy and recruiting in that border state area he thought hopeless. "There are some trusted men there, but the majority are Union."[4]

By September 7, the army had reached Frederick. Its arrival aroused much curiosity and some consternation as the streets were lined with the citizenry. In marching past, Hanks, Co. K, 1st Texas, overheard a small boy ask if the passing troops were Texicans. When assured they were, he remarked, "Oh, Mama, they look just like our folks." Another commented on the passing of a "bonny blue flag," which Hanks said was, in reality, the Lone Star flag presented to the regiment by Mrs. Wigfall.[5] Soon, the main body of the army left its lines of march, took to the surrounding fields and encamped along the banks of the Monocacy River.

Erskine observed the remains of the Baltimore and Ohio Railroad bridge lying in ruins in the riverbed since the day before. He lamented the destruction, describing the structure formerly as "beautiful and splendid ... composed almost entirely of iron; it must have cost several hundred thousand dollars."[6] What a waste! he must have thought.

While encamped on the river, Gen. Hood ordered the entire brigade into the water, clothes and all, to wash away the accumulated grime of the last several months. Stevens, Co. K, 5th Texas, waded in, noting that they had not been out of their clothes for at least a month. During that time they had experienced dust, rain and slept on the ground at night or whenever they had the chance. The marching column stirred up a choking dust cloud so dense that one could not see a hundred yards ahead. By that time, most of the men possessed only remnants of clothing, an old piece of a hat or cap and many were barefoot.[7] When they emerged from their combination bath and laundry, they stood in the sun and dried out, the grime, probably, relocated on their persons rather than removed.

During the brief time around Frederick, Erskine had an opportunity to go into town, which he estimated to be populated by about 10,000–12,000 people. The only evidence he saw of human habitation, under the circumstances, was the occasional "lady's face ... seen peering from the upper story window of the houses, viewing our ragged, bare-footed and mottled soldiers with amazement." Because pro–Union storekeepers closed their stores, he was unsuccessful in his efforts to buy some coffee and sugar. He was successful, however, in getting some "fine fruit" which he described as "very cheap." He judged the political sentiments there to be "pretty nearly equally divided between Union and Secession; both parties are afraid to make any profession of their sentiments and very prudently remain quiet."[8]

Leaving Frederick twenty-four hours later, the army moved west on the Washington Pike, a roadway that Stevens described as "the finest road I ever saw, 60 feet wide finely macadamized, up and down hill, across the valleys and even where the little streams cross the road there is a nice little trough for water to run in. Imagine a nicely paved road 60 feet wide and as smooth as the best paved sidewalk." Their planned route of march led on to Boonesboro and Hagerstown beyond. The column consisted of two wagon trains moving along side by side in the center of the road with four ranks of infantry on either side of the wagons for the protection of the train. Straggling, or falling behind, was bad on the march with perhaps as many as one-third or more of the entire army left exhausted in its wake.[9]

Now situated in Maryland, the problem of supply, recognized before the undertaking began, had to be solved before the Army of Northern Virginia could continue on to Pennsylvania, a source of even greater bounty. Federal garrisons at Harper's Ferry and nearby Martinsburg in the Shenandoah Valley were astride the most direct supply route leading into Virginia. Their threat could not be ignored and had to be dealt with swiftly.

Again, Gen. Jackson's Corps, known for its aggressiveness and the rapid marching ability of the foot cavalry, was chosen for the difficult and vital work. With three of his own divisions, Ewell's, A. P. Hill's, and his own former division now commanded by Gen. John R. Jones, and three of Longstreet's — McLaw's, R. H. Anderson's and John G. Walker's — the attack forces were organized into three columns. Dividing the divided, the three columns would close upon the Federal garrisons from three different directions. The movement got under way on September 10.

With Jackson's multi-columned mission underway, Gen. Longstreet's remaining command, the divisions of Hood, David R. Jones and D. H. Hill of Jackson's Corps, the commanding general in attendance, proceeded on toward Boonesboro. D. H. Hill's division followed along in the corps' wake. Gen. Stuart's cavalry division provided screens for all the columns and in the process gathered up many stragglers. This part of the movement began also on September 10, with the army to reconcentrate around Boonesboro or Hagerstown once all the objectives had been accomplished. Once reconcentrated, the army would move on into Pennsylvania.

The advance was continued along the route of the National Road. It's hard-packed, gravel-strewn surface exacted a heavy toll on those in the ranks devoid of footwear, and they left bloody imprints in the dust. Even so, high spirits predominated as Longstreet's command passed through some truly beautiful countryside. Moving in a northwesterly direction, the column crossed first through the low passes of the Catoctin Mountains. Ahead could be seen looming in the distance the line of South Mountain, it appearing to block the line of march. Fast marching brought the column to the foot of the range and then up and through Turner's Gap. Several miles beyond lay Boonesboro, where it was thought the army could encamp while awaiting the return of the scattered elements.

Sometime during the day, intelligence was received which seemed to indicate a Federal column moving upon Hagerstown from the direction of Chambersburg, Pennsylvania. If this proved to be correct, such a column could play havoc with the commanding general's plans. As a reconnaissance in force was indicated, on September 11, Longstreet's column girded up once more, taking to the road in route-step fashion bound for Hagerstown.

D. H. Hill's trailing division came up to hold Boonesboro while awaiting developments. The command was now divided into five columns — three down around Harper's Ferry, D. H. Hill at Boonesboro, Longstreet swinging toward Hagerstown. The cavalry division was likewise scattered over the landscape in support of the infantry operations. Meanwhile, Gen. Pope had been relieved of command in favor of Gen. McClellan, who, at the head of an army 90,000 strong, was in pursuit intent upon revenge for the army's debacle suffered at Second Manassas.

Upon reaching Hagerstown, there were no Federal troops to be found. In the face of some hostility exhibited by the citizenry, the countryside thereabout was scoured for supplies. When that failed to provide much bounty, it became even more apparent that an unimpeded supply route back to Virginia was essential. While Longstreet's troops enjoyed several days' respite, word from Harper's Ferry was anxiously awaited in order that the next act could be ushered onstage.

On September 12, there was still no direct word from Jackson although rumor had it that the Federal garrison at Martinsburg had fallen back on Harper's Ferry. Also, Gen. Stuart reported that Gen. McClellan's army, inexplicably, had advanced upon and occupied Frederick. This information was received with puzzlement on the part of the commanding general, he having become accustomed to his opponent's more languid ways. At this point he was unaware that a copy of his General Order 191 outlining his army's dispositions and plans had fallen into the enemy's hands. One thing he did know: Gen. McClellan was acting in an uncharacteristic fashion given past experience. If this continued, a threat to Jackson's rear was developing. The next day, September 13, brought no word from Harper's Ferry.

Later on September 13, further intelligence from Gen. Stuart was received saying that not only was McClellan moving but that he was moving with resolution and dispatch. Once he reached the vicinity of South Mountain with its multiple passes, a real danger to the Army of Northern Virginia's safety would be posed. Considering his alternatives, Gen. Lee reasoned that he really had only one. He directed D. H. Hill and his command at Boonesboro to take positions to defend the passes against the onrushing Federal army. It was vital that the defense of the passes be staunch until such time as the Harper's Ferry operations could be concluded and the victors returned to the army's protective folds.

Later, at South Mountain, what D. H. Hill saw from atop Turner's Gap did not give him any confidence in his ability to deal with the onrushing blue tide. Gazing eastward, what he saw he described as "marching columns extend[ing] back as far as the eye could see in the distance; but many of the troops had already arrived and were in double lines of battle, and those advancing were taking up positions as fast as they arrived. It was a grand and glorious spectacle, and it was impossible to look at it without admiration."[10] Considering his responsibility, Gen. Hill must have swallowed hard as he looked down upon what he described as a "tremendous army" the likes of which he had never before seen and was never likely to see again. It was a "tremendous army," indeed, composed of six army corps including seventeen infantry divisions.

At about the same time, Gen. Longstreet received orders to prepare his command to countermarch on Boonesboro in support of Hill's precarious position. A small garrison was left in Hagerstown while the remainder took up the march on the morning of September 14. After sending dispatches warning Jackson's command of its vulnerability, Gen. Lee joined Longstreet's march. The distance was not great, about thirteen miles. The nearer they approached, the more distinctly echoed the sounds of a battle in progress — the rattle of musketry and the boom of artillery. D. H. Hill was up to his neck in Federals, all of whom were attempting valiantly to pour over Turner's Gap and spill into the Pleasant Valley beyond.

No sooner had the sound of battle wafted down to Longstreet's marching column than word was received from Hill urgently requesting support. The pace was quickened and about mid-afternoon, with Gen. Lee observing from the roadside, the Texas Brigade portion of the column came swinging by. Seeing the commanding general observing their progress, from the ranks arose the cry, "Give us Hood." As mentioned before, their former brigade commander was in arrest, the result of a prior confrontation with a more senior brigadier. The trouble stemmed from the capture of some Federal ambulances at Manassas, after which both general officers claimed the right to their retention. Hood, being the junior of the two and refusing an order to surrender the ambulances, found himself in arrest. As such, he had been exiled to bring up the rear, simultaneously eating and being coated with a thick layer of dust raised by the column's passage.

Responding to their outcry, Gen. Lee raised his hat while assuring them, "You shall have him, gentlemen." Summoning the dust-laden Hood to his side, Gen. Lee awaited as his prodigy rode up and dismounted. With his usual and great dignity, Gen. Lee said to his valued lieutenant, "General, here I am just upon the eve of entering into battle, and with one of my best officers under arrest. If you will merely say that you regret this occurrence, I will release you and restore you to the command of your division." To this Gen. Hood, exhibiting admirable integrity, took exception, replying, "I am unable to do so, since I cannot admit or see the justness of General Evans' demand for the ambulances my men have captured. Had I been ordered to turn them over for the general use of the Army, I would cheerfully have acquiesced." Gen. Lee needed the man and again asked for a statement of apology. Again, as his sense of honor required, Hood respectfully declined. Seeing the fruitlessness of pursuing the matter further and with the roar of battle increasing in the background, Gen. Lee said, "Well, I will suspend your arrest till the impending battle is decided."[11] Afterwards, it was Gen. Evans who, for various reasons, remained in trouble with his superiors. As a result, nothing further came of the incident. In a thinly disguised "thumbing of his nose," in his postwar memoir, Hood said that "in lieu of being summoned to a Court Martial, I was shortly afterwards promoted to the rank of Major General with the command of two additional brigades."[12]

In the meantime, Hill was in a tight spot. He had been fighting a vastly superior force on South Mountain and in its passes since that morning. By the time Longstreet began to move up the mountainside in support that afternoon, Hill's left was on the verge of being overwhelmed. Pressing his troops in support, Hood's Brigade reached the summit of Boonesboro Gap where shortly it was "ordered to fix bayonets, and when the enemy came within a hundred yards, to fire and charge."[13] Polley's Co. F, 4th Texas, with the rebel yell echoing above the scene, charged sending the Federals in their front pell mell back down the mountainside. Years later, John Stevens, Co. K, 5th Texas, recalled that they were "maneuvered and moved from one point to another on the mountain up and down, all the evening under fire from both artillery and small arms, sometimes in full view of the charges and counter-charges made at different parts along the line of battle, but as my memory now reaches back, I am inclined to think that so far as results to either side it was not much of a battle."[14]

Meanwhile, Gen. Longstreet, reappraising the situation, realized that, at best, their forces could only slow down the Federal hordes at their front. Having secured the South Mountain passes, the entire situation had suddenly shifted in favor of Gen. McClellan's army. When Longstreet, accompanied by Hood and D. H. Hill arrived at headquarters to report, they unanimously expressed their opinions that a retreat was required.

Shortly following, word reached Gen. Lee that troops of Gen. William Franklin's Federal VI Corps had overrun Crampton's Gap, south of Turner's, and was in the rear of McLaws' division astride Maryland Heights just across the river from Harper's Ferry. What had gotten into McClellan? If the Federals continued their push they would be able to reach Sharpsburg and the Potomac ford at Botler's first. Then the Army of Northern Virginia, devoid of roughly half its strength, would be trapped with the Potomac in rear and confronted by a vastly superior enemy in front. The war could be over the next day!

Shortly, a courier arrived at army headquarters with a message from Gen. Jackson, suggesting that possibly Harper's Ferry might well fall the very next morning. Taking Gen. Jackson at his laconic word, Gen. Lee did a quick about face. Since Harper's Ferry was only seventeen miles from Sharpsburg, Jackson's victorious "foot cavalry" would be in reasonable marching distance of that point once the Federal garrison had been disposed of. With that in mind, the main army would concentrate at Sharpsburg. Gen. McLaws' division was ordered to get to that same point by whatever route necessary.

Marching early on the morning of September 15, the main body of the army soon passed over the middle bridge of the three spanning a creek that, just east of the sleepy village of Sharpsburg, Maryland, made its meandering way to the Potomac a short distance beyond. The obscure creek's name was the Antietam.

As various units of the Army of Northern Virginia crossed the creek and tramped a short distance beyond, they entered the eastern outskirts of the village. There, they crossed the Hagerstown Pike, a road connecting Hagerstown to the north with Harper's Ferry to the south. Reaching that point they were about-faced and deployed briefly to face their pursuers. They did not have long to wait; early in the afternoon blue-clad columns were observed to be moving in great numbers approaching the Antietam bridges. The clouds of dust they raised and the number of banners, uncased and displayed, sparkling brightly in the early autumn sunlight, indicated that the whole Army of the Potomac was arriving on the scene. Once that army finally concentrated, it comprised six army corps, perhaps as many as 90,000 men.

Little time elapsed before their artillery unlimbered and began to throw shells randomly but in the general direction of their Confederate adversary. Temporarily commanding the Texas Brigade, Col. Wofford, 18th Georgia, reported that their movement up the Pike attracted Federal long-range artillery attention, wounding one lieutenant and one soldier of the 4th Texas.[15]

As in all battles, a major determinant in the course of the action is the nature of the surrounding topography. Plenty of cover was available in the form of rail and rock fences, limestone outcroppings and woods. Essentially, the Confederate line of battle faced east, eventually arrayed along the Hagerstown Pike and centered on the village with the coils of the Potomac only a short distance away to the rear. The Federal line faced west, Antietam Creek to their front. The Hagerstown Pike, passing north and south through the village, bisected the battlefield. North, up the Pike, not too far beyond the limits of the village, lay farmland, some of which was owned by a man named Miller. It was wooded and known as the North Woods. On Miller's property, south of the farm buildings, was a large field under cultivation — tall, tasseled corn stalks, thickly planted, impenetrable — Miller's cornfield bordering on the east side of the Pike.

Around the Miller farm itself, the road was straddled on the east and southeast by woodlands, after that day called the East Woods. South, down the Pike, about halfway between Miller's and Sharpsburg and on the west side, was a small, single-story, whitewashed church. Because the congregation practiced immersion as part of its ritual when inducting new Christian soldiers into its ranks, it was known thereabout as the Dunker or Dunkard Church. Extending up and down the Pike and surrounding the church were woods — the West Woods.

Just across the pike from the Dunker Church, the Smoketown Road led off toward the northeast. Once the army was deployed, Hood's divisional position was in that general area. Col. Law described his Alabama brigade's position, saying, "The right of my brigade rested at Saint Mumma's Church (Dunker Chapel), and the line extended along the turnpike in the edge of a wood [West Wood] which bordered it on the southwest."[16] The Texas Brigade position abutted Law's southern flank, extending south down the west side of the Pike in the direction of Sharpsburg. They remained quiescent there in the woods for the remainder of September 15 and until late September 16.

As the armies were in the process of arraying themselves opposite one another, things began to look up for the Army of Northern Virginia. Late in the morning of September 15, a courier had arrived from Harper's Ferry bearing a message from Gen. Jackson. Dated 8:00 A.M., that same day, Jackson announced the surrender of the Federal garrison manning Harper's Ferry. Gen. Lee ordered, first by courier to Jackson, that he come up as soon as possible, and, second, that the good news be passed on to the troops. It produced laudable results, reviving sagging morale in the ranks.

At Harper's Ferry, leaving one of the six divisions with him, A. P. Hill's, to parole the prisoners and tidy up, Jackson put the other five divisions on a staggered march toward Sharpsburg. In the meantime, until Jackson's command arrived on the scene, Gen. Lee was confronted by the entire weight of the Army of the Potomac with only Longstreet's command, bereft of its Harper's Ferry contingent, and the division of D. H. Hill. Later that evening, Gen. Stuart rode up from Harper's Ferry with more detailed news of what had transpired at that place. He reported, also, that Jackson's troops had taken to the road for Sharpsburg.

As dawn broke on September 16, Gen. Lee's partial force at Sharpsburg, additionally depleted by straggling, numbered, perhaps, 18,000 men at most. It was a force vastly inferior to its Federal, six corps counterpart. Even so, the commanding general expressed confidence in the knowledge that, at least to that point, Gen. McClellan had yet to order an offensive fight. Later in the afternoon, Gen. Jackson and Gen. John G. Walker with several divisions in tow — Jackson's own and Ewell's, both under Gen. John R. Jones, Lawton's and Walker's — rode up to army headquarters from Harper's Ferry. After brief congratulatory greetings, Gen. Lee sent Gen. Jackson to assume command from Hood on the left, taking his own division, commanded by Jones, with him and also, Lawton's. Walker's Division, including Walker's Brigade commanded by Col. Van H. Manning, 3rd Arkansas, and Ransom's Brigade, commanded by Gen. Robert Ransom, Jr., were deployed to extend Longstreet's right and watch for any Federal moves to cross the lower fords and bridges over the Antietam.

During the afternoon, Jones' Division was deployed adjacent to and north of Law's left along the pike. The accompanying artillery units were deployed, some to the left where on Nicodemus Hill they joined Gen. Stuart's horse batteries. The artillery batteries on Nicodemus Hill were in an excellent enfilade position for any Federal troops advancing southward down the Pike from the direction of Miller's farm.

Below those positions centered around the Dunker Church and comprising the army's left flank, D. H. Hill's Division was sited to the right and somewhat in advance of Jackson's line and facing east. The main part of Hill's line was in a road worn down to a level below the surface of the surrounding ground by the passing of countless wagon traffic over the years. Known as the Sunken Road, it would, after the impending clash be known thence as the Bloody Lane. That portion of the line extended on down to near the Boonesboro Road, the route by which the army had arrived at Sharpsburg the day prior. The remainder of Longstreet's command, Walker's Division and Toomb's Georgia Brigade of David R. Jones' Division, occupied the bluffs overlooking the southernmost of the three Antietam bridges, known locally as the Rohrbach Bridge. All commands were thinly stretched due to the absent stragglers and the anxiously awaited arrival of the divisions of Gens. McLaws, Anderson and A. P. Hill on their way from Harper's Ferry.

On September 16, with the exception of those detailed to the skirmish line, the fatigued and hungry Confederates rested in the fields and surrounding woods. Later in the day, Gen. Joseph Hooker's Federal I Corps crossed the Antietam and took up positions north of the Confederate left flank. The Federal artillery was active all morning but in a desultory fashion. The Confederates deigned to reply with any vigor due mainly to a shortage of ordinance rather than to any timidity in the face of overwhelming numbers.

At one point and in sight of the 1st Texas, Gen. Longstreet rode up, and dismounting, took charge of an artillery piece. He "lengthened fuses, elevated, aimed and fired it several times in an effort to reach the Federals."[17] Only at the urgent insistence of his staff did he finally desist as counter-battery fire began to burst all around them. A little later, Hooker's divisions moved forward to pick a fight. About sundown, as their artillery support quickened and the sound of musketry and general tumult reached straining headquarters' ears, the opening round began with Gen. McClellan and staff looking on. The attack fell squarely upon Hood's Division with the Texas Brigade in the thick of it.

Col. Law first reported that enemy skirmishers had moved into the East Woods. The skirmish line was checked there by his own skirmishers assisted by the Texas skirmish line thrown out in advance of their main line of battle. Then, Gen. Hood ordered Col. Law to advance his entire brigade in support, which he did, his Alabamians, Mississippians and North Carolinians spilling over the fences lining both sides of the Smoketown Road. The Texas Brigade was ordered in and, moving over the same fences, crossed behind Law's command then across the Smoketown Road and into the clover fields beyond. Their advance continued as far as the southeastern limit of farmer Miller's cornfield with Hampton's Legion on the left, and the 18th Georgia, 1st Texas, 4th Texas and 5th Texas arrayed to the right and adjoining Law's left. The Texans came under heavy artillery fire from their front and left wounding a dozen men of the 4th Texas. Rather peevishly, Col. Wofford said that their position had been betrayed by "the firing of a half dozen shots from a little battery of ours on the left of the brigade, which hastily beat a retreat as soon as their guns opened on us."[18]

On the right, the 5th Texas, commanded by Capt. Ike Turner, Co. K, due to the wounding of Col. Robertson and others of the staff at Second Manassas, moved into the East Woods, driving back Federal skirmishers. The regiment skirmished until relieved at about 8:00 P.M. and then fell back into the woods behind the Dunker Church. Other brigade skirmishers, led by Capt. "Howdy" Martin, Co. K, 4th Texas, performed some hot work. In the process, the enemy's skirmish line was driven back to the far side of the East Woods as darkness fell over the battlefield. Lt. Col. Ruff's 18th Georgia advanced to the southern edge of the cornfield where it remained until midnight without ever firing a round.[19] Had it not been for night blanketing the field, the big battle might have been fought on that day. However, darkness quieted things down and the lines were defined for the remainder of the night as well as for the morrow. The respective positions were about where they had been when it all started. Later, under the cover of darkness, Gen. Mansfield's Federal XII Corps, the divisions of Alpheus Williams and George Greene with artillery units, crossed the Antietam and moved into position on Hooker's left. Gen. Edwin Sumner's Federal II Corps was readied to cross the Antietam as needed. The Confederates knew of their arrival and what it boded for the morrow.

As quiet and a degree of calm returned, Gen. Hood called at army headquarters to request that his command be relieved from the line in order to rest and cook a meal. Said Hood, they had not had anything substantial to eat in three days — substantial being a euphemism for ears of green corn and a half-ration of beef. Since troops were in such short supply and the aggressive menace so close, all Gen. Lee could do was refer Hood on to Jackson out there in command of the left. Gen. Jackson, having witnessed Hood's division in action, knew of their value in a standup fight which daybreak promised to bring. Wanting them in some degree of fighting trim, Jackson agreed to pull them back, replacing them with two brigades, Lawton's and Trimble's, from Ewell's Division. As if it were necessary, a pledge was extracted from Gen Hood that he would return his command immediately to the front when called upon to do so.

So, later that night the switch was made. With the acrid stench of expended gunpowder burning their nostrils, stomachs growling in protest from lack of sustenance for three days and the cries of the wounded at their back echoing in their ears, Hood's men moved into the woods just vacated behind the Dunker Church. The movement was cloaked by the darkness and the rain that had begun to blanket the area further adding to the gloom and discomfort already present on that dreadful and foreboding field.

Too soon dawn began to lighten the eastern horizon heralding a new day, the last for many of those present. The rain had abated and the battered Confederate ranks numbered maybe 25,000, all arms included. With the three divisions thought to be still at Harper's Ferry or, at best, on the way, there were no reserves immediately available. A short distance north up the Hagerstown Pike, after a night spent in a barn on the Poffenberger farm, a somewhat refreshed Federal I Corps commander, Gen. Joseph Hooker, peered southward down the Pike. Through the early morning mist and fog that shrouded the area he could just make out the outlines of the white-washed Dunker Church. That, said he, would be the designated object of his Corps' impending attack.

Meanwhile, things began to look up a bit down south as news arrived that contact had been established with advanced units of the divisions of McLaws and R. H. Anderson. They had marched all night to reach their destination. Their ranks were exhausted and sleep-deprived but they would be available for duty when the time came.

It was not too long before the rattle of musketry and the boom of Federal artillery reverberated all along the northern end of the line. They were answered by Confederate musketry and counter-battery fire. Then, between 6 and 7:00 A.M., there issued forth from the depths of the North Woods, Gen. Hooker's "right division, under Doubleday led by the choice brigade under [Gen. John] Gibbon."[20] Deployed across the Hagerstown Pike and supported by Rickett's and Meade's division, Doubleday fell heavily upon Jackson's thinly stretched position. Rickett's Division descended on the area around the East Woods. From the Confederate left, Gen. Stuart's artillery sited on Nicodemas Hill opened on the advancing Blue ranks. Stuart's efforts were supported by the batteries of Col. Stephen Lee that had been unlimbered in the field across the road opposite the little white church. The

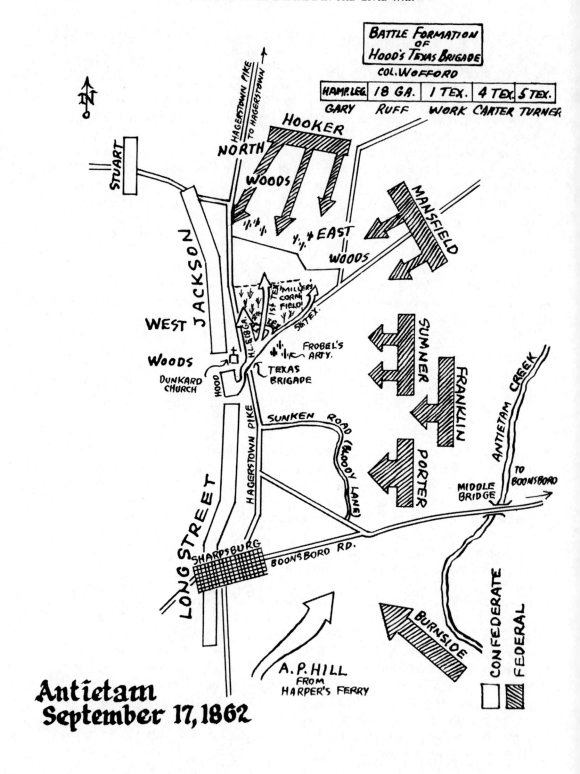

Antietam
September 17, 1862

Sharpsburg, Maryland, September 16–17, 1862

artillery duel between the two lines increased steadily in intensity, reaching a crescendo, later described as "artillery hell." In the melee that followed, Lawton, then in command of Jackson's Division, his own brigade, Trimble's and Hay's, all of Ewell's Division, were driven steadily backward. A great gap appeared in the Confederate line, the left end of the gap being shored up by Early's Brigade, the right by the brigades of Ripley, Colquitt and McRae, of D. H. Hill's command. Things looked grim for the Confederates unless that line could be restored.

Faced with massive numbers, Gen. Lawton called in the markers pledged by Gen. Hood the evening prior. A courier arrived with the message for Hood, "Gen. Lawton sends his compliments, with the request that you come, at once, to his support."[21] The Texans had been finally issued some meat and flour just before daylight, the first they had received in three days. Cooking fires were lighted and ration preparations begun. By now accustomed to innovative techniques, they used anything that came to hand to prepare their meager ration, "an old scrap of oil cloth or one corner of [their] blankets as bread trays." Stevens' Co. K, 5th Texas knew that "we must work in a hurry or go into battle with very empty craws."[22] Receiving only a little bacon and flour, Polk, Co. I, 4th Texas, was doing his best to "wet up the flour without grease" and, using his ramrod as a spit, to cook it over an open fire. An artillery shell landed nearby rendering that effort fruitless and, for good measure, breaking the leg of a man nearby.[23]

The smoke from the cooking fires had attracted the Federal attention. Enemy artillery missiles began to shred the trees overhead as errant musketry whirred through the surrounding air. The call to arms resounded through Hood's camp. As the troops, grumbling about their interrupted respite and trying to figure out what to do with their half-cooked rations, moved forward to the sound of the guns, the Federal attack continued in their direction.

As the Texas and Alabama brigades moved forward, Gen. Lee received word of the Federal breakthrough and was trying to decide upon reinforcements from his non-existent reserve. Even though it meant weakening the right and inviting attack, he had no choice but to move some units from that quarter to shore up the opposite flank. So, other units, G. T. Anderson's and J. G. Walker's brigades, not immediately threatened, were hurried to the left piecemeal. Gen. Lee was, by force of circumstances, concentrating most of his strength on the left while hoping for the best at the center and on the right.

Arriving on the line, Col. Law's Brigade passed through a gap in a fence around the Dunker Church and crossed the Pike into the fields beyond. On the way they encountered the shattered remnants of their last evening's relief column and a litter carrying Gen. Lawton's wounded form to the rear. Finding much noise and confusion on the smoke-enshrouded field, Law formed his brigade on the right side of the Smoketown Road. Soon, Wofford's Texans joined them across the road on their left. The Texans' alignment at that point was as it had been the previous evening: the 5th Texas adjoining Law's left, then the 4th Texas, 1st Texas, 18th Georgia and Hampton Legion stretched on toward the left and the pike. Together, they moved forward astride the Smoketown Road stepping over the dead and wounded left from the last evening and earlier that morning. Ahead, through the smoky haze of the battlefield, Blue ranks were glimpsed extending from the East Woods around to the cornfield and on the west side of the Pike.

Ahead, Lt. Col. Gary's Hampton Legion caught sight of the enemy in the distance. They were formed on the southern edge of Miller's cornfield and the Carolinians engaged them immediately.[24] Lt. Col. B. F. Carter's 4th Texas, although in rear of some of Law's regiments, the 18th Georgia and the Legion, saw much the same thing. Upon entering the field across from the Smoketown Road, Carter noted that "the fire upon us became severe, and, owing to our troops being in front of us and the dense smoke pervading, we were unable to return fire.[25]

As the Texas Brigade advanced toward the cornfield, the left flank units were the first to closely encounter the enemy positioned across the Pike and in front of the cornfield. Hood, upon seeing the enemy's positions, recognized the danger of a flank attack on his left from across the Pike. At that time, he ordered the 4th Texas to move double-quick across to the brigade's left flank. There, it was to take up a position along the east side of the Pike and move toward the cornfield along the line of the rail fence that lined the road. During the advance they were to engage the Federals across the Pike. The 5th Texas was ordered to Law's right flank to protect that quarter.

Once the 4th Texas reached its assigned position, the advance began. In Co. I, 4th Texas, J. M. Polk "didn't [even] take time to [re]load his gun, for there were plenty of loaded guns lying on the ground by the side of the dead and wounded men.[26] Another member of the regiment described their position as "the hottest place I ever saw on this earth or want to see hereafter. There were shot, shells and Minie balls sweeping the face of the earth, legs, arms and other parts of human bodies were flying in the air like straw in a whirlwind."[27]

As the 4th Texas was moving across the rear, the 1st Texas, Hampton Legion and 18th Georgia ran headlong into what appeared through the haze to be a large body of Federal infantry. Those troops, it was later learned, were the 2nd and 6th Wisconsin regiments of Gibbon's "Black Hat" Brigade, recently dubbed the "Iron Brigade." Others included Phelps' New York Brigade. The advance of Hampton's Legion, the 18th Georgia and 1st Texas forced the two Wisconsin regiments and Phelps' Brigade to retreat through the cornfield, fighting over their shoulders as they did so.

Col. Martin W. Gary, Hampton's Carolina Legion

Across the Pike was the rest of the "Black Hats," the troops from whom Hood feared a flanking attack, 7th Wisconsin, 19th Indiana plus Gen. Marsena R. Patrick's four regiment New York Brigade. They were supported in their position by Campbell's Battery "B," 4th U.S., that had advanced from the cover of the North Woods. That battery was sited on the west side of the Pike opposite Miller's cornfield. Lt. Col. B. F. Carter, 4th Texas, could see that the Federal position in the cornfield was on the crest of a slight hill. Across the Pike, the Federals were in a ravine running down toward the Potomac.[28]

Clambering over those sections of rail fencing still standing on either side of the Pike, the retreating Badgers took up position behind Campbell's Battery. Once reunited with their fellows, they and their

New York comrades poured an enfilading musketry into the Texans' exposed left flank. Unseen by Wofford's and Law's men beyond the northern limits of the cornfield and positioned in a slight swale awaited Gen. Meade's Division of Pennsylvania Reserves with their supporting artillery. Meade, as he saw the troops in his front falling back through the cornfield, ordered his troops to move forward.

At this point, Texas Brigade alignment had been lost. Carter's 4th Texas, upon arriving at its assigned position along the Pike, saw that the 1st Texas was receiving heavy enfilading fire from the Federal infantry and artillery across the Pike. So were the Hampton Legion and 18th Georgia. Lt. Col. Ruff watched helplessly as Campbell's Battery "poured a round or two of grape into [his] ranks with terrible effect."[29]

In the melee, the Hampton Legion's Lt. Col. Gary counted four of the Legion's color bearers shot down during the advance upon the cornfield, Maj. Dingle being the last. Having taken up the fallen colors, Dingle admonished the Legionnaires to "follow your colors." The troops responded to the major's valiant leadership example and the advance carried forward through a hail of gunfire to the southeast corner and then beyond into the fury that was the cornfield. Within fifty yards of the enemy line and holding the colors aloft, Maj. Dingle was shot dead. Seizing the fallen colors himself, Lt. Col. Gary then passed them on to a volunteer bearer, Marion Walton, Co. B, who was somehow able to survive and bear them for the remainder of the fight.[30]

In the ranks of Co. H, Hampton Legion, Stephen Welch saw the flags go down but did not attempt to pick them up. Going forward, he found his rifle would not fire. Randomly picking up another from the field, he found that it would not fire either. A third worked and after firing several rounds, Welch found himself on the ground and slowly regaining his senses. Examining himself, he found his right eye to be already swollen shut, an ear full of blood and a pool of his blood forming by his side. He had been struck by an artillery shell fragment. Game still, he picked himself up and "fired every shot [he had] at the U.S. flags [he saw to the front] and as fast as [they were] raised they fell again." Moving to within fifty or sixty yards of the Federal line across the Pike, Welch saw "men fall so fast and thick [that] in about one hour's time our whole division was almost annihilated." Eventually, making his way from the battlefield, he found a field hospital where he able to get his head wound dressed.[31]

Both the Hampton Legion and 18th Georgia tended to oblique to their left in response to the heavy firing traversing the Pike. The result of the 4th Texas' position facing west across the Pike and the left oblique movement of the Legion and the 18th Georgia was to form an arc, the front of which faced from about west to northwest. At the same time the 1st Texas continued on toward the north into the corn, each step further exposing their uncovered flanks.

In the advance of the 1st Texas into the cornfield, Lt. Col. Work was in regimental command as a result of Col. A. T. Rainey's wounding at Gaines' Mill earlier. Work directed the fire of his men toward the Federal units in their front in the cornfield and across the Pike to their left. The result was that the enemy's line "broke and fled and the artillery, presumably Campbell's, was limbered up and started to the rear when the whole fire of [his] regiment was concentrated upon the artillerists and horses, knocking over men and horses with such effect that the artillery was abandoned."[32] They would return, however.

During the advance, in the ranks of Co. K, 1st Texas, O. T. Hanks saw that the heavy fire was "cutting us down almost like grain before a cradle." Then, in what must have been an oddly focused moment under the deadly circumstances, he noticed at about thirty yards' distance a Federal soldier on his knees peeping through an opening between some rails. Drawing a bead, Hanks thought to himself, "If we whip I am going to see if I killed you." In the confusion and murk of battle, infantrymen seldom knew afterwards if they had killed anyone but were always wondering if they had. Just as Hanks fired, the marksman became the mark as "a bullet passed, struck me in the left side, close up under the arm, coming out under the shoulder blade near my backbone." He was able to make it to safety but in the process had another close call when he received a bullet hole through his hat brim.[33] Carried to a field hospital in the rear, Hanks never was able to determine the effect of his marksmanship because that part of the field eventually fell back into Federal hands where it remained for the duration of the fight.

Lt. Col. Phillip A. Work, 1st Texas

Raising the rebel yell, which, according to Maj. Rufus Dawes, 6th Wisconsin, was originated by Hood's Texas Brigade and "was heard on this occasion in all its terror," the Texans pushed ahead through the tall corn.[34] The 1st Texas approached the northern edge of the field far in advance of their diverted comrades and, with both flanks in the air. Here they ran head on into Meade's Pennsylvanians. These troops, having just moved forward, were lying down along a fence line with their rifles resting on the rails that they had heaped up to form breastworks. When, through the smoke and haze, they caught sight of the approaching Texans' legs, they opened fire. The Texans were receiving artillery fire also from batteries behind the Pennsylvanians as well as from some resumed fire from across the Pike.

Lt. Col. Work sent word to the brigade commander, Col. Wofford, that unless he could be reinforced by his left, he would have to withdraw. Work had but a handful of men left and was in danger of losing even them if he lingered much longer. Potential death filled the surrounding air as Work conferred with the regiment's acting major, Matt Dale, as whether to stand or retreat. The sounds of combat were so deafening that Dale had to place his mouth close to Work's ear and shout to be heard. Just as their conference concluded, still standing breast to breast in the corn, Work felt Dale straighten up suddenly, stiffen and then fall straight back. Stricken by a musket ball, he was dead before he hit the ground.[35] Retreat was an obvious necessity if there were to be any survivors at all. Grudgingly, the remaining troops began to move back through the bloodied cornfield. Stepping and stumbling over the bodies of fallen friend and foe alike, they paused frequently to deliver fire upon their tormentors close upon their heels.

During their withdrawal, Acting Major John R. Woodward, 1st Texas, looking for a rallying point, noticed that the regimental flags were nowhere to be seen. Above the tumult, he found himself shouting, "The flags, the flags. Where are the flags?"[36] Concluding that all the flag bearers had been shot down, he made his way through shot and shell back into the cornfield seeking the lost colors. There he encountered only a wall of advancing Blue. Turning, he fled, escaping unharmed but without the flags.

The beloved colors were lost and it was too late to recover them. During the fight, Lt. Col. Work saw that the flags were receiving their usual share of unwanted attention. Through the haze and confusion of battle, Work saw four known color bearers and least four more he did not know shot down.[37] He was devastated but viewed the loss as such that "no blame ... should attach to the men or officers, all of whom fought heroically and well. There was no such conduct upon their part as abandoning or deserting their colors. They fought bravely and unflinchingly faced a terrible hail of bullets and artillery." Even so, to Work, the loss of the regimental colors would, "remain always a matter of sore and deep regret."[38] They had special meaning to the men of the 1st Texas; they were the colors presented to them by Mrs. Wigfall, the one made from her wedding dress.

By that time Work said he had only seventeen men of the 226 with whom he had begun the lethal journey. Fleeing before the oncoming Federal juggernaut, they were fired upon, the bullets "striking the ground raised puffs of dirt, just as in the beginning a shower's large drops of rain does on a dusty road."[39] Miraculously, none were hit, however, Capt. Woodward's canteen was shot through and Lt. Col. Work's saber scabbard was struck, causing him to fall, a most inopportune time to do so. In their wake and across the line, nineteen year old Pvt. John Rankin, Co. A, 27th Indiana, watched the Gray ranks receding in their front. In a memoir written long after the war, he marveled at the fact that he and his comrades were "the first Union troops to have ever seen the backs of Hood's famous Texans."[40]

Reaching the safety of a fence line and a little sunken road, they found many stragglers there, leaderless and taking advantage of the safety afforded by the cover. Taking them in hand, Work and Woodward soon had them firing upon the advancing Federal line, which they helped successfully repulse. Then, resuming their retreat they soon came upon Gen. Hood who conducted them to the woods in rear of the Dunker Church where they joined the sparse remnants of Hood's decimated division. There they replenished ammunition, moved forward behind the church and waited.

The 4th Texas was caught in much the same dilemma So, Lt. Col. Carter wheeled his regiment to the left and posted them "along the fence on either side of the turnpike, and replied as best [they] could to the tremendous fire of the enemy."[41] The regiment remained under heavy fire in that position until the Hampton Legion, 18th Georgia and 1st Texas, what was left of them, were able to back out of the cornfield and move back over the field of their former advance. What must have seemed like ages was actually only measured in minutes. The 4th Texas worked its way down the pike, then, taking position on the west side until ordered to the rear to replenish ammunition with the rest of the brigade.

Capt. Turner's 5th Texas, separated from their brigade and with Law's Brigade in the East Woods, came to the aid of Douglass' and Walker's Brigades, some of the same troops that had relieved them the evening prior. In Co. K, John Stevens noted that those Georgians, Alabamians and North Carolinians had been cut to pieces with at least half their number stretched upon the ground. The 5th Texas and Law's troops moved forward, raising the shrill, piercing rebel yell as they drove ahead, forcing the Federals in their front to retire. About then, Stevens received a wound that placed him flat on his back on the ground.

Within the span of a few minutes, while still prone, he received a second wound that rendered him, momentarily, unconscious.

Upon regaining consciousness, he looked around dazedly and dimly realized that he was out there alone as the fight see-sawed back and forth. Not wishing to become a prisoner-of-war, he found he was able to regain his feet. He must have been still under heavy fire as he began to painfully make his way to the rear. There he knew a field hospital was located in an old barn about 700 yards or so back in the woods. It was only 8:00 A.M. Stevens reached the hospital but his ordeal did not end there. Examined by Dr. R. J. Breckinridge, the regimental surgeon, he was advised that if he felt able "to walk to try to cross the Potomac River, three miles distant at Shepardstown. So, on [he] moved, weak and faint from loss of blood and the pain [he] was suffering. Just at sundown that evening [he] got into the town, on the south side of the river."

At Shepardstown, he met the regimental quartermaster, Maj. Littlefield, "who gave [him] three army biscuits — more than [he] had to eat in three days previously. [He] thought it was the sweetest morsel of bread [he] had ever tasted. A bed was provided for [him] and [he] remained until the morning of the 19th."[42] It was after a few days' rest that he felt recovered sufficiently to return to his command. Unable to get an official release, he left of his own accord, rejoining the brigade in the vicinity of Martinsburg.

In Co. A, 5th Texas, Nicholas Pomoroy said they withstood three counterattacks, the intervals between characterized by a few minutes of unearthly silence. Finally, bereft of ammunition and reduced to scavenging the bodies of the dead and wounded for replenishment, the 5th Texas was forced to fall back toward their morning's departure point at the Dunker Church. By that time, Pomoroy estimated his regiment had suffered at least 60 percent casualties.

In the retreat, Pomoroy said that shot and shell were raining down around them. He was about halfway to the safety of the West Woods when, over the tumult, he heard his name being called. Pausing to look around, he saw it was Lt. Henry Boyd of Co. C, 5th Texas, lying on the ground with a leg wound and unable to make it to safety on his own. In that situation, he was vulnerable to further wounding or death. Succumbing to Boyd's pleas for assistance, Pomoroy hoisted him onto his back and began his perilous journey to safety:

> I moved as quickly as I could. I met another man of my regiment. He was lying on his back with his blanket roll under his head reading his pocket testament and seemed resigned to die at any moment.... Ahead I saw that the 5th Texas had now disappeared into the woods at the end of the field, and I was about 300 yards in their rear.... A shell struck the ground near us, throwing the earth on us, and at the same time the force of the wind of it threw me on my knees. My wounded comrade at the same time begged me not to abandon him, and I did not, I reached the edge of the woods and as I now moved down in safety on the other side I heard loud cheering, it was Jackson's Division coming to the rescue.[43]

Pomoroy was met by the assistant regimental surgeon, Dr. John [J.] Roberts, who held his exhausted body upright while his assistants removed Boyd's body from his shoulder. While accepting the profuse thanks of Boyd, Pomoroy noticed that his wound was a shattering one to a thigh. He learned later that following the inevitable amputation, Boyd had died. In the age before the presentation of decorations for heroic behavior in battle, Pomoroy had to settle for the self-satisfaction of a comrade's life saved even though it proved in the end to have been in vain.

In the heat of battle, the 5th Texas had ended up on the right flank of Law's Brigade, far removed from their brigade comrades. In conjunction with the Alabama Brigade they were able to push the Federals back into the East Woods in their front and beyond. Theirs was a short-lived triumph because Federal reinforcements appeared ahead and in great numbers. It was Gen. Mansfield's two division XII Corps, he having only arrived from a staff job to take command a few days prior. While deploying his inexperienced troops, he was struck in the chest by a musket round. The wound proved to be mortal, ending any hopes he might have harbored for military distinction. XII Corps command then devolved upon division commander Gen. Williams for the remainder of the fight.

When the XII Corps had entered the fight, Gen. Hooker, having received a severe foot wound, Gen. Doubleday assumed command. The I Corps, badly disorganized and having suffered severe casualties, was withdrawn to its initial position around the Poffenberger farm. Then, moving forward, "Mansfield's Corps [had] smashed an opening between Hood's Division and D. H. Hill's Division on the Texans' right."[44] It was by then about 9:00 A.M. and Hood's Division had withdrawn to the vicinity of the Dunker Church. At about 10:00 A.M. they were relieved by McLaw's division, it having arrived finally from Harper's Ferry only a short time before. The division remained in a holding position in that area for the rest of the day after replenishing ammunition and regrouping. Having been thoroughly mauled, the division was not recommitted to battle that day.

When asked by a fellow officer the whereabouts of his division, Gen. Hood's grim reply was, "Dead on the field." Later, Gen. Hood said they had faced at least two Federal corps while his command numbered, perhaps, 2,000 muskets at most. Nonetheless, they were able, inexplicably — sheer courage and force of will — to push them back through the woods and Miller's cornfield and force them to abandon some artillery that had been hammering from positions on the left. Describing the combat as deadly, Hood said they fought to the last round and that the, "First Texas Regiment had lost, in the corn-field, fully two-thirds of its number, and whole ranks of brave men, whose deeds were unrecorded save in the hearts of loved ones at home were mowed down in heaps."[45]

In his after action report, Lt. Col. Work reported that out of 226 1st Texas men that he had led forward that morning "170 are known to have been killed and wounded, besides 12 others who are missing, and doubtless, also killed or wounded."[46] Nine regimental color bearers had gone down and the regimental colors had been lost in the confusion. Of the 226 1st Texans, 186 were either killed or wounded, a casualty rate of 82.3 percent, the highest percentage loss suffered by any regiment, North or South, during the course of the war

Gen. Lee now turned his attention to D. H. Hill's imperiled position at the center of his stretched line as a Federal attack was seen to be imminent. Riding to that part of the field, Gen. Lee joined Hill as he surveyed the situation on his front. Riding down the line, they offered words of encouragement to the troops arrayed along their main line in the sunken country lane.

There, they were joined by Gen. Longstreet. Gens. Lee and Longstreet dismounted while Hill remained astride his mount. To this Longstreet took exception: "If you insist on riding up there and drawing fire ... give us a little interval so that we may not be in line of fire when they open upon us."[47] The oft-times irascible Hill ignored the entreaty and remained mounted, scouring the battlefield with his binoculars. It was not long before a puff of smoke appeared in the enemy lines opposite signaling the fact that they had been spotted and had attracted Federal artillery interest. In a matter of seconds, a solid shot came screaming through the air taking off cleanly the forelegs of Hill's mount. Hill managed to dismount as the stricken animal tried to stay upright on its suddenly foreshortened legs.

Beginning at about 10:30 A.M., two divisions of Gen. Sumner's II Federal Corps, Gens W. H. French and Israel B. Richardson's, began their assault upon Hill's position. Three times in heavy numbers they attacked Hill's line and three times they were hurled back with the help of some artillery that Hill had been able to bring into action. Just when it looked as if the fight was over, an order was misunderstood and one of Hill's brigade commanders began to withdraw. This unexpected turn of events resulted in the entire line being forced to fall back toward the vicinity south of the Dunker Church. There were no reserves available to stem the Federal advance. Refusing to give in, Gen. Hill found additional artillery support and put it to work with a vengeance. Himself leading a small band of soldiers against the onrushing Federal attack, they were able to stop the advance.

With no further reserves available and evidence of an attack building on his right, Gen. Lee ordered Gens. Jackson and Stuart to launch a diversionary attack on their now quiescent front. The objective of the attack was to turn the Federal right, then extending tenuously to the banks of the Potomac. As that was being organized, Gen. Lee was called away as an attack on his far right began to heat up. The withdrawal of units from that quarter to other imperiled points during the course of the morning's fight had left the entire defense of the right to the division of Gen. David R. Jones. The position fronted on the Antietam, it crossed at that point by the Lower or Rohrbach Bridge.

Several Federal attacks had been launched earlier that day by troops of Gen. Ambrose Burnside's IX Corps. They had been channeled toward the bridge, ignoring the relatively easy crossings afforded by adjacent and shallow fords. They had been repulsed by Toombs' Georgia Brigade, they in their elevated position in some low ridges overlooking the bridge. However, later in the afternoon, Burnside's troops, in large numbers, were seen once again massing for an attack. Toombs could not hold out much longer against such overwhelming numbers. Now, all eyes became even more focused upon the road leading south toward Harpers Ferry. Their only hope in stemming the about-to-be unleashed Blue tide seemed to be the eventual arrival of Gen. A. P. Hill's Light Division. It was known to be marching hard toward Sharpsburg somewhere down the length of that road.

Even the stoic Gen. Lee, after shoring up the center as best he could, rode to the south end of his line to observe developments in hopes of catching sight of a dust cloud heralding the arrival of the awaited column. As mid-afternoon approached, the left was quiescent as Gen. Jackson tried to put together Lee's ordered counterstroke. The center was stable temporarily although thinly defended by the survivors of the earlier attacks, including one battery manned by Gen. Longstreet and his staff. Had Gen. McClellan not lapsed into his overly-cautious ways, he could have easily overrun the position with the troops that he had not committed to battle.

Finally, Gen. Jackson reported from the left that his ordered attack was impracticable in the face of overwhelming Federal artillery superiority. Explicitly confident in his subordinate's military judgment, no further thought of an attack in that quarter was considered. The Southern ranks were decimated. Ammunition of all kinds was either expended or in very short supply. The only readily available supply was that that could be taken from the bodies of the fallen, both dead and wounded.

While the arrival of A. P. Hill was anxiously awaited, Gen. Burnside, under discretionary orders, decided the time was right to again move forward with his IX Corps. It looked like the war was about to be over, when in the distance, a body of troops, battle flags dimly flashing in the sunlight, were observed advancing toward the front. Were they gray or blue-clad, starred and striped or starred and barred?

Gen. Lee asked a passing artillery officer with a telescope prominently displayed, "What troops are those?" Placing the glass to his eye and seeking out the distant column, the officer studied the image intently. Lowering the telescope, the officer answered, "They are flying the United States flag. Not those, those," Gen. Lee indicated, pointing to another nearby column and their displayed allegiance. Once more the officer peered through the scope intently before announcing, "They are flying the Virginia and Confederate flags."[48] It was, at last, A. P Hill at the head of his Light Division, and not a second too soon.

Shortly thereafter, Hill and his dust-laden staff rode on the scene. The general commanding was so relieved and happy "to see Hill and to have the promise of more troops that [he] forgot his usually controlled emotions and embraced 'Little Powell.'"[49] The Light Division had marched seventeen miles in seven hours, a rate of about 2.5 miles per hour; not bad for a frazzled column. The main body, about 3,000 strong, was not far behind their commander.

Hill's troops wasted little time in forming line of battle. Taken in flank, Gen. Burnside's forces melted away recrossing the Antietam and seeking shelter on the far side. Although the Federal cannonading continued into the evening, the unnerving arrival of Hill's Division spilled the wind from the Blue sails and the battle was over. On the field at midnight, a major asked Gen. Hill if he had known Gen. Burnside in the old army. "'Ought to,' Hill snorted. 'He owes me eight thousand dollars.' Burnside had borrowed that sum several years earlier from his West Point chum, and the debt remained unpaid."[50]

Seldom in military history had so few fought so many with the few prevailing. It rivaled Agincourt in its unlikelihood. In his report of the battle, Gen. Longstreet observed, " [B]efore it was entirely dark the 100,000 men that had been threatening our destruction for twelve hours had melted away into a few stragglers."[51] The bloodiest single day in American military history was over and it was time once again to bury the dead and care for the thousands of wounded.

"The battle ground at Sharpsburg during the two day fighting was littered with dead and wounded," remembered D. H. Hamilton, Co. M, 1st Texas. A number of those belonged to Co. M: "Lieutenant Thomas Sanford, Josh Boon, James Story ... Vondry Wi[s]by and Jeff Bowman."[52] Although the 1st Texas suffered the most horrendous losses of all in the Army of Northern Virginia, the other Texas, Georgia and South Carolina regiments suffered heavy losses as well.

In Co. I, 4st Texas, J. M. Polk listed a number of men — Milt Garner, "a little fellow named Paul" — that he went into the fight with and never saw again. He could remember that, "out of over

D. H. Hamilton, Co. M, 1st Texas

one hundred, after we came out of that fight [all that was left of our company was] Captain Winkler, Lieutenant Mills and eight men."[53]

Lamenting their losses, John Stevens, Co. K, 5th Texas, thought that a battle that resulted in such staggering losses did not look like a battle to him and his comrades: "The captain of my company and his entire command, cook and eat out of one skillet—five men—just five. One company is entirely annihilated, not one man left in it.O, what sad letters we have to write home to the bereaved loved ones in Texas."[54] (For total figures of Texas Brigade losses, see Appendix B.)

As the sun was rising the next morning, September 18, Federal sharpshooters began to ply their deadly trade. Masses of Federal artillery were observed moved into place on the farther banks of the Antietam. All of this seemed to suggest that "Little Mac" was still in hopes of Gen. Lee's having a mental lapse and repeating the blunder and subsequent massacre at Malvern Hill in July just passed. As a matter of fact, the entire Federal line had been extended and strengthened to the point of invincibility.

About midmorning, Nicholas Pomoroy, Co. A, 5th Texas, said that Gen. Lee ordered one of his bigger guns to fire into the Federal line, to which there was no response. Pomoroy thought that it was the only artillery shot fired that day.[55] About mid-afternoon, Gen. Lee ordered that the army prepare for a withdrawal across the Potomac and back into less hostile territory under the cover of the coming darkness.

L.A. Daffan, Co. G, 4th Texas, remembered that later in the day, maybe 6:00 or 7:00 P.M., the Army of Northern Virginia began to quietly abandon the field and move toward the Potomac River fords in its rear. Along the line of march down to the river, Daffan saw what he described as a "horrible sight": "We passed an old school house, or an old church, where our wounded had been carried that day and the day before to have their wounds dressed and their limbs amputated. There was a dim light burning in the church and the doctors were at work. At each window was a pile of legs and arms nearly as high as the sill. The men were being placed in ambulances and carried to Richmond."[56] An agonizingly painful trip in horse-drawn wagons over rough roads it would be for those that survived. Scenes such as this and even worse were repeated throughout the course of the war.

Word gets around quickly in a rumor-prone army. Several days after the fight, in passing the 6th North Carolina, one 1st Texan indiscreetly asked of his Tarheel brethren, "Halloa, fellers! Have you a good supply of tar on your heels this morning?" "Yes," answered one of that troop, "and it's a real pity you'uns didn't come over and borrow a little the other day; it mout have saved that flag o' your'n."[57]

While the rank-and-file might banter about lightly, it was not in the nature of the higher command to do the same. Gen. Longstreet could be described as temperamentally less than effusive on most occasions. However, after the great battle at Sharpsburg he was liberal in heaping praise upon his command, reporting that every man, officers and enlisted, should be singled out for recognition. He pointed out that "[i]n one month these troops had marched over 200 miles, upon little more than half rations, and fought nine battles and skirmishes, killed, wounded, and captured nearly as many men as we had in our ranks, besides taking arms and other munitions of war in large quantities."[58]

Among the officers singled out for special praise were included the names of Gen. Hood and Col. Wofford, Gen. Longstreet estimated the Army of Northern Virginia to have numbered about 61,000 before divided up at Frederick.[59] Gen. Lee estimated his force engaged at Sharpsburg to number about 37,000. He was heard to comment that his army had been "ruined by straggling," and thought that there were as many as 20,000 men thus lost to his ranks That is not an insignificant number of men missing from their places in the ranks under that circumstance. It merits further comment.

* * *

Any reading of Texas Brigade literature will reveal regularly either personal or observed experiences with straggling. Marches were conducted at all hours of the day and night and in all kind of weather. Confederate soldiers were frequently ill-clothed and ill-shod, if at all. Due to the primitive state of transportation in that age, subsistence ranged from some to none. They were usually tired, hungry and on their way to, what they viewed as very possibly maiming or death.

Some Southern solders harbored the idea that the war they had joined was a defensive one. Taking the offense and moving outside the boundaries of the Confederate States was not what they had signed up to do. Many stragglers had simply dropped out in Virginia when the Army had crossed into Maryland. Most were gathered up by provost marshal troops and later returned to their units after the army recrossed the Potomac. Others came back on their own but only after the army returned to Virginia's shores.

It was sort of a game they played and proved a largely unsolvable problem throughout the course of the war. A good example of what the leadership had to deal with in curbing straggling was Bill Fuller, Co. I, 4th Texas. Described by J. M. Polk of the same company, he was an old man and one whom their captain, Clinton Winkler, in his wisdom, never tried to control. Typically, Fuller was always present for the fights but "was never very particular about keeping up on a march or staying in camp." Fuller frequently pestered Gen. Hood for the use of his horse. His avowed purpose was to go into town to "pick up stragglers."

On the withdrawal from Maryland, the company was taking a march break alongside the road when Fuller strolled up. This time he was in possession of a supply of whiskey, probably somewhat depleted, that he had obtained along the way. No doubt under the influence, he began regaling passing units of artillery and supply much to the delight of the rest of the company. About that time, along came Gen. Hood, staff in tow. Jumping up and rendering the general a salute, the following exchange occurred:

> "Early camps tonight, General Hood, and plenty of meat and bread," [says Fuller]. "Sir, replied General Hood, we will stop about a mile and a half from here." "If it's all the same with you General,' said Bill, "Leave out the 'about' and tell us how far it is, for we are awful hungry and tired." [Fuller's comrades egged him on but the usually patient Capt. Winkler had heard enough and turning to his lounging company, he said], "You confounded fellows, I am trying to quiet the man and you all are encouraging him. I'll have the last one of you arrested if you don't let him alone. Fuller, if you don't dry up I will have you put in the guard house as soon as we stop, [to which the irrepressible senior replied, getting in the last word], "All right, Captain, ... I am either on guard or under guard all the time, and it's all the same to me, sir."[60]

That was the sort of attitude that sometimes had to be dealt with and, with the exception of several periods of notable improvement, Southern soldiers continued to straggle for the remainder of the war. As a matter of fact, Bill Fuller was later granted a furlough to Texas, one from which he never returned to the front, the ultimate straggler now become a deserter.[61]

Pomoroy, probably like most of the Texas soldiers, took a philosophical view of straggling. After recrossing the Potomac following Sharpsburg, he noted that "[i]n a short time all our stragglers came up, many of them in pitiful condition — some without shoes — footsore and lame. We had some habitual stragglers in all our regiments, but the majority of those poor fellows could not help it, and were good soldiers."[62]

Stragglers were taking a big chance for Gen. Lee's orders were that any such stragglers captured by the provost marshal troops bringing up the rear were to be summarily shot. It sounds harsh, but it was a rule adhered to by necessity and was practiced in most of the world's armies. If the Army of Northern Virginia, consistently inferior in numbers to the Army of the Potomac, could not be brought into the presence of the enemy with its ranks reasonably intact, it could not possibly hope to prevail. The Confederate armies, all of them, were pretty poorly disciplined in camp and on the march and straggling was endemic. Recall what James I. Robertson had to say about Civil War troops: "the worst soldiers and the best fighters that America has ever produced."[63] It was a demonstrated fact that if they could be brought to battle in sufficient numbers they would fight fiercely, thereby considerably increasing their chances of victory. That did not happen at Sharpsburg, Maryland. But, the pages of history are replete with such "ifs."

CHAPTER 8

"As ... invited guests ... to witness that grand ... panorama of splendid murder"[1]: Fredericksburg, Virginia, December 13, 1862

As dawn broke on the morning of September 19, 1862, the last units of the Army of Northern Virginia splashed across the Potomac at Boteler's Ford, clambering wetly onto the relative safety of the Virginia shore. Moving away from the river, the army encamped to rest momentarily from its recent Sharpsburg rigors. Left to guard the ford against pursuing Federals was the reserve artillery of the army, some forty-four guns in all, under the command of Gen. William Nelson Pendleton. He was allocated, however, only 300 infantrymen in support of his guns.

At about mid-morning the first of the Federals arrived on the scene. With them were some long-range artillery pieces which were put into immediate action supported by infantry sharpshooters. Later in the day, the Federals were able to get some men across and these came very close to capturing the majority of the Southern artillery. In the end, A. P. Hill was sent back with part of his command and they successfully drove the Federals, with great loss, back across the river. What had appeared at first to be a great disaster with the loss of the entire reserve artillery, proved to be something less with the loss of only four artillery pieces. Not good, but not fatal either.

On September 20, the army shouldered arms once more and withdrew, first to the vicinity of Martinsburg and thence to Winchester. In the days and weeks that followed the Sharpsburg fight after recrossing the Potomac and encamping eventually near Winchester, Virginia, Val Giles, Co. B, 4th Texas, remembered fondly "drifting slowly up the Shenandoah Valley, taking it leisurely, bathing in the pearly pools and resting after our long summer campaign. Autumn was coming on, and the soft, mellow haze of Indian Summer hung over the sleepy valley."[2] Similarly, Joe Polley, Co. F, 4th Texas, described the weeks following the devastating battle as a period welcomed by the badly battered troops. Except for guard, duties necessary for preserving camp cleanliness and order and an occasional drill, the troops were allowed to rest. Being in the bread-basket of the Confederacy and with several unobstructed routes to Richmond, the Commissary and Quartermaster Departments were able to replenish the army with badly needed rations and clothing. A member of the 5th Texas, in a letter to the Houston *Tri-Weekly Telegraph,* described the boys as being "in fine condition having entirely recovered from the fatigues of the Maryland campaign." Supplied with "good, warm clothes" he said the stories of their "excessive suffering" were "greatly exaggerated."[3] However, it was not over yet and such were the exceptions rather than the rule.

During that time, the newly promoted brigadier general, Jerome B. Robertson, appointed to command the Texas Brigade, attentive to the spiritual as well as the physical needs of his command, issued an order outlawing all gambling in the brigade. There were various penalties threatened to all ranks choosing to ignore the order. Given the frequent boredom of camp life, one can but doubt that the order had any effect upon the boys' behavior with respect to gambling.

As all of this was going on, nearly a month and a half elapsed since the Sharpsburg fight. While clothing and arms were resupplied footwear remained a major shortage. Here, according to Joe Polley, Co. F, 4th Texas "came to the army the mails withheld from it since its departure from Richmond."[4] Although nothing ever came of it, it was during this period also that Gen. Lee made "[a] vigorous effort ... to strengthen the Texas units, which had now become [his] favorite shock-troops." In a letter to Sen. Louis T. Wigfall, Lee praised the Texans, saying, "I rely upon those we have in all tight places, and fear I have to call upon them too often ... with a few more such regiments as Hood now has, as an example of daring and bravery, I would feel much more confident of the campaign."[5]

During this time, John Stevens, Co. K, 5th Texas, noted that it had been two months since he and his comrades had had the opportunity to change clothes. In the interim they had slept on the ground, on the sweaty marches been coated with dust or weighed down with mud, waded creeks and rivers from ankle to neck deep with no chance to cleanse themselves afterward from "the unavoidable accumulation of filth," the brief dip in the Monocacy during the march through Maryland, notwithstanding. As a result, among other unpleasant things, he said that "every man from the colonel of the regiment, and even our general officers ... were covered with what [he] called the 'Confederate bug.'"

The bug was described as being about the size of a "grain of wheat." "It is said he has legs — how many I do not know, as I never tried to find out. I know he has a mouth and he understands how to use it.... His favorite morsel is a good fat rebel. His usual haunts are about the seams of the clothing .... He's there in force and the force is continually augmenting. He is never idle.... [H]e will eat the skin off and gnaw into the flesh.... They seem to be indigenous to army life.... You might, if possible destroy every one on you every morning, and before night, you would be full again." And, they did not confine themselves to the gray ranks; the boys in blue were seen to be doing their fair share of scratching, too.

While encamped near Winchester, Stevens remembered that Gen. Robertson, after an evening dress parade, addressed the assembled troops of the 5th Texas. Among other things, he stressed the importance of personal cleanliness in controlling the troublesome bugs. During the course of the admonition, the ranks noticed that "he was busy with first one hand and then the other scratching himself on the shoulder, on the arm, then around the waistband of his pants, and then his hips, then quickly the other hand went to the shoulder and under his arm." The amused troops could barely contain themselves when someone called out, "Say, general, what makes you scratch so?" Seeing the humor, the kindly Robertson joined in the laughter and dismissed the regiment. Stevens said the fact was "[w]e could not avoid the bug, he was everywhere.... He could wear the gray or the blue, he was at home in both armies, was loyal to both flags."[6] Yet another source of great and unremitting discomfort for the men of both armies.

During that period Gen. Lee harbored some hopes of resuming the Maryland campaign. However, as the terrible state of disorganization that the army was in became more evident, that plan had to be foregone as organizational matters were attended to. Up to that time the largest military unit provided by law was the division, even though the amalgam of divisions prior and commanded by Jackson and Longstreet, respectively, were, in effect, corps. It was a stroke of luck that the two senior major generals were competent, aggressive commanders. Even so, there had been command and control problems and an obvious need for a change. All of this was addressed on September 18, 1862, when President Davis signed into law an act providing the organization of the existing divisions into corps. The end result was the official establishment of two army corps, one, the First, to be commanded by Longstreet, the other, the Second, to be commanded by Jackson. The new positions carried with them not only great responsibility but also the exalted rank of lieutenant general.

Reorganization and promotions, to replace the many vacancies left as a result of the Sharpsburg blood-letting, rippled their way on down through the ranks. Among those promoted to major general was John B. Hood. His theretofore two brigade division (Hood's and Law's) now became four with the addition of Gen. George "Tige" Anderson's Georgia Brigade and Toombs' Georgia Brigade commanded by Col. Henry L. Benning. Hood's Brigade was now to be commanded by Gen. J. B. Robertson, formerly colonel, 5th Texas. Detached from its ranks were the valiant 18th Georgia and the Hampton's South Carolina Legion infantrymen. In their stead, the 3rd Arkansas, commanded by Col. Van. H. Manning, filled out the ranks. The 3rd Arkansas later joined the Texas Brigade in front of Fredericksburg.

While all of this was going on, nearly a month and a half had elapsed since the Sharpsburg fight. Gen. McClellan's army, much to Mr. Lincoln's chagrin and except for the affair of September 19, had not bestirred itself to renew the contest. Gen. McClellan was not going to "change his stripes." Eventually, on October 26, the Army of the Potomac appeared at the Potomac fords east of the Blue Ridge and began to cross, exact destination unknown.

In anticipation of the two most obvious possibilities, the Army of Northern Virginia was divided once more. Jackson's Corps was left in the vicinity of Winchester to check any advance up the Shenandoah Valley. With the commanding general in attendance, Longstreet's Corps was dispatched over the Blue Ridge to Culpeper County to meet any advance on the eastern side of the mountains. Gen. Stuart's cavalry, after a punitive raid into Federal territory as far north as Chambersburg, Pennsylvania, several weeks earlier, screened the passes.

Almost simultaneous with the Blue appearance on the Potomac, Longstreet's Corps began breaking camp and taking up the march toward Culpeper Courthouse. By November 7, they were in position behind the Robertson River, near Culpeper.While there, Gen. Robertson wrote to the editor of the Houston *Tri-Weekly Telegram*. This was intended for the information of the newspaper's readers who would thus know that the brigade was comfortably, if uncharacteristically, clothed and shod. There was noted, however, a shortage of blankets. In praise of his brigade, Gen. Robertson wrote, "I wish I had time ... to write... at length on the trials, hardships and achievements of our gallant comrades. Braver and truer hearts never beat in human bosoms, steadier nerves never governed human muscles. Whether it has been towards the cannon's mouth from which was pouring showers of shot and shell, and in one case, iron slugs by the thousands or [through] the hailstorm of bullets, their cry has been onward!"[7]

As October passed into early November, the Federal army continued moving in force east of the Blue Ridge. With several plans of action in mind, depending upon the Federals' movements, Gen. Lee waited. Then, inexplicably, on November 9, a report was received that the Federal advance had ground to a halt. It was not until the next day that intelligence revealed the reason for the halt; Gen. McClellan had been relieved of his command on

November 5. Effective November 9, the command of the Army of the Potomac had passed to Maj. Gen. Ambrose E. Burnside, a close personal friend and supporter of the deposed McClellan. Joe Polley, Co. F, 4th Texas observed later that "Burnside was far more successful in fixing a fashion in which to wear whiskers than in conducting the operations of a large army."[8] The general's elaborate hair style led to the term "sideburns," while his brief command of the Army of the Potomac added to the meaning of the word "fiasco."

For the next week, the intentions of the new commander were uncertain although an advance on Culpeper seemed the most logical. Actually, Burnside's elaborate plan was to move the army quickly to Fredericksburg for a crossing of the Rappahannock at that point and a rapid advance upon Richmond. The plan was approved by President Lincoln, with the advice to move quickly or it could not succeed. General Lee, with his usual military acumen, expected from the time of the appointment for him to move on that place. On November 17, with the arrival of Gen. Edward Sumner's Right Grand Division at Falmouth opposite Fredericksburg, all doubt was removed. The remainder of the Federal army took post in succeeding days. Several days earlier, Gen. Lee had placed some small units of his army in motion toward Fredericksburg.

Under the pseudonym Wanderer, a Texas Brigade soldier described the march from Culpeper to Fredericksburg and beyond. Leaving the Culpeper camp, there followed three days of severe marching in "wind, cold rain and other disagreeable weather." On the march, they met many civilians, citizens of Fredericksburg and thereabout, fleeing the scene of what they correctly perceived to be the site of the next great clash of armies. Noting that "[m]en — no matter how strongly constituted, can stand up under severe privations always," Wanderer expressed what turned out to be the incorrect opinion that the armies would go immediately into winter quarters to await the next spring campaign season. Made also was the rueful observation of what only a few months of hard and violent campaigning had wrought. "We look around us in vain for the faces which smiled manly kindness on us then. We listened in vain for the soft, merry tones that once lent poetry to the asperities of war and smoothed down the rugged front of inevitable destiny for the gentle touch of human affection! Ah! They are buried now! From Eltham's Landing to the historic Sharpsburg, you may see their whitening bones, and lingering the ruins that war has made." Nonetheless "[t]hose who remain are hardened, strong and unfearing — true soldiers,"[9] he concluded.

During the march, the Texas Brigade bivouacked on the site of the battle fought at Cedar Mountain a few months earlier. While there they drilled on the very ground where Gen. Winder was killed leading the Stonewall Brigade, according to John Stevens, Co. K, 5th Texas. When they stopped drilling to take a rest, he and his comrades would see who could pick up the most spent musket rounds without moving out of place. His recollection was that, "I often picked up as many as thirty or forty, possibly more." He found it hard to realize that "two lines of fellow-humans of the same country, speaking the same language, professing the same holy religion, can stand and hurl these death missiles at each other by the ton — all for the sake of our peculiar views on an instrument called a constitution."[10]

On November 19, Longstreet's Corps occupied the ridges west of the city. The rest, Gen. Jackson's Corps in the Valley, were to follow eventually as the military picture came into better focus. Gen. Lee, with his headquarters, arrived behind the city on November 20.

Arrayed along the right bank of the river, Fredericksburg was a town of great historic charm. It was also a manufactory for Confederate war materiels. On November 21, a Federal deputation under a flag of truce appeared on the riverbank opposite. In a letter from Gen.

Sumner, it was demanded that the city of Fredericksburg be surrendered. If not, the missive read, an artillery bombardment by Federal long-range artillery would begin the next day at 9:00 A.M. According to John Stevens, Co. K, 5th Texas, the Federal commander did not know of Gen. Lee's presence, thinking they had stolen a march on the Army of Northern Virginia. Meeting with the town's mayor, Gen. Lee reviewed the demands. Wanting to spare the town and its citizens as much grief as was militarily possible, he stated that the Army of Northern Virginia would not occupy the town nor would it use any of the manufactories. However, neither would he sanction the occupation of the town by the Federal forces.

These terms were forwarded to Gen. Sumner who must have been startled to see, according to Stevens, the endorsement signed by Gen. Lee, saying, "I am in command here; come on."[11] However, later in the evening word came back that the terms were accepted. There would be no shelling the next morning. However, there were no guarantees beyond that. Under those circumstances, it was apparent that the evacuation of the town by its citizens must begin as soon as possible.

Under those unnerving conditions and in a driving snowstorm, with great suffering by young and old alike, the evacuation of the citizens of Fredericksburg began that evening, continuing into the next day. Eventually, some crept back into town and reoccupied their homes. That danger was much preferable to trying to live in the wintry countryside behind the city. Later, some probably wished that they had stayed in the woods once they were exposed to the terrors of the great battle of December 13, raging all around them.

The citizens of Fredericksburg met with many acts of kindness during their otherwise unpleasant stay within the Army of Northern Virginia's lines. The 3rd Arkansas, in particular, tried to assist by building shelters to shield them from the severe winter conditions and foraging food for the children. In return "[t]he women of Fredericksburg reciprocated by collecting bits of red, white and blue cloth which they stitched into a new battle flag."[12]

Unknown to Gen. Lee at the time, Gen. Burnside's plan to cross the river quickly and outflank the Army of Northern Virginia hinged on bridging pontoons being present at Fredericksburg prior to the Army of the Potomac's arrival there. It was planned that the bridges would be thrown across the Rappahannock which the Federal army could then quickly cross. Once across, the Army of the Potomac would be between the Army of Northern Virginia and the Confederate capitol at Richmond. Alas for Burnside's plan, through a series of blunders the pontoons were not there on time. They did not arrive until November 25, too late for their effective use. As a result, several days were lost as the Blue host, in great numbers, occupied Falmouth and the Stafford Heights across the river from Fredericksburg.

When it became apparent that Gen. Burnside was not going to mount an immediate attack, Gen. Lee gave Gen. Jackson discretionary orders to leave the Valley and advance to Culpeper. There he would pose a threat to the Federal flank across the Rappahannock and discourage Gen. Burnside from any unexpected movements. Jackson's Corps was on the march to Culpeper on November 23. By November 27, with the Federal army remaining quiescent and the worsening road conditions threatening troop movements, Gen. Lee ordered Gen. Jackson to bring his entire command to Fredericksburg. "Old Jack" arrived at Gen. Lee's headquarters at Hamilton's Crossing late on the evening of November 29, the foot cavalry not far behind, many struggling barefooted in the snow and ice.

Preparations continued for the battle inevitably to follow. The line the Southerners occupied was formidable. The main sector of the line behind Fredericksburg, occupied by

Gen. Longstreet's Corps, was a long, low ridge, known locally as Marye's Heights. It was separated from the town by a large open field, diagonally bisected by a ditch. Trained upon the field from the vantage of Marye's Heights was the Corps artillery. At the foot of the Heights was a sunken road, buttressed by low stone walls on either side. That imposing defensive position was occupied by the infantry units of Gen. T. R. R. Cobb's Georgia Legion and one North Carolina regiment. To the right of Marye's Heights was Lee's Hill, so-called because there was located the commanding general's headquarters. It was higher and somewhat farther back from the town and studded with Confederate artillery. The remainder of the line, a low line of hills stretching on down roughly parallel to and back from the river behind the line of the Richmond, Fredericksburg and Potomac railroad to the vicinity of Hamilton's Crossing, was occupied by Jackson's Corps. The terrain in front of the Confederate line there was, essentially, a level plain.

By December 10, the Army of Northern Virginia numbered about 78,000 men in round figures and the Army of the Potomac, maybe 110,000. On that same night, as rumor had it, a Southern woman on the Falmouth side of the river beckoned Confederate pickets on the opposite bank advising them that the Federal army had been issued rations and ordered them cooked. Soldiers of that era knew that such orders presaged movement. Then, in the early hours of the next day, December 11, signal guns fired two rounds from the Confederate position atop Marye's Heights. It was the agreed upon signal that the Army of the Potomac appeared about to force a Rappahannock crossing.

The alarm had been raised by Confederate pickets of Gen. William Barksdale's Mississippi Brigade occupying the buildings of Fredericksburg overlooking the river. Through the darkness and the haze arising from the river's surface, Federal combat engineers were seen to be launching their pontoons, the first step in the deployment of a portable military bridge. As the engineers came under fire from the Mississippians, Federal artillery opened on the city wreaking considerable damage in the process. The barrage battered but failed to dislodge the Mississippians from their positions overlooking the river and the ever-lengthening portable bridges.

In the end, there were three pontoon structures thrown across the river. Two were opposite the city and one below. The latter was in front of the position held by Hood's Division and consequently, the Texas Brigade.

William A. Fletcher, Co. F, 5th Texas, recovered sufficiently from his wound suffered at Second Manassas, reported for duty at that time and was immediately pressed into a dangerous assignment. He ran into Capt. "Ike" Turner, Co. K, 5th Texas, in command of an outpost and who thought that the enemy might be attempting to bridge the river in his front. However, his view of the river was obscured by the presence of a house on the riverbank. He asked Fletcher if he thought he could work his way into a position from which he could obtain the required intelligence. The country was flat and open and several attempts earlier by others had failed when they had been observed and brought under fire from the opposite bank. Noting some "small timber growth" at one point on the river, he thought it probably indicated a drain or slough and told Capt. Turner that he thought he could get a view of the river at that point.

Fletcher worked his way across and eventually even reached the back of the interposing house. Going inside, he found it to be deserted and a scene of great destruction, the result of Federal artillery attention. Based on its construction, its location on the riverbank and its contents, Fletcher assumed that its former occupants were wealthy. (Although Fletcher does not name the mansion specifically, it was Mansfield, the Barnard house.) Seeking the upper floor, he found a place for observation, there being many holes in the walls, secure from enemy discovery. What he saw was just as Capt. Turner suspected: "about three hundred yards below the house he observed the point of the laying in of the pontoon bridge, and [a] second bank at that point had allowed the material for the pontoon to be placed there at night and they could put it in unobserved by our lines during the day."[13]

Making his way back, he reported his intelligence to Capt. Turner and, being the curious type, said he would like permission to go back to further observe the bridge construction in progress. "Sure, go ahead," said the captain but it seems a very dangerous venture just to satisfy one's personal curiosity. So, back he went, this time situating himself on top of a haystack not far from the house of his recent visit. There he said he "remained comfortable, sitting and lying, and sure did enjoy several hours of sight-seeing. The men [Federals] looked at me considerably at first, but I was apparently unnoticed by the bridge gang, although the boys on the riverbank who were in line seemed to be interested."[14] As night began to fall, the Federals began to cross their now completed bridge and Fletcher thought it high time for him to get back to the safety of his own lines. Sliding down from his perch, he ran across the open space, coming under considerable musket fire as the Federal ranks debouched along the riverbank in his rear. Achieving the safety of his own lines, he could but wonder at his own foolhardiness.

Meanwhile, the two upper bridges lengthened across the river's surface thanks to the Federal engineers' valiant efforts. Barksdale's men kept them under a heavy fire of accurate musketry greatly reducing their ranks, many of them being toppled into the river's icy folds. Consequently, they were forced to withdraw. The Federal artillery barrage continued to rain down destruction on the city. To the south, the Texans left their positions for a better view of the scene. It was only the beginning of the reduction of a large part of that fair city to rubble.

After throwing their allotted rounds, the Federal artillery fire slackened and finally ceased altogether. An eerie silence followed, but only for a short time. As the bridge builders ventured forth once more, they were immediately taken under fire by the determined Mississippians from their now rubble-strewn positions. Around noon, Gen. Barksdale received discretionary orders to withdraw to the strong Confederate position strung out along the crest of Marye's Heights behind and commanding the city from the west.

Before the withdrawal began, around 1:00 P.M., Federal troops in numbers were seen to rush down the farther hills to the riverbank where they boarded waiting small boats. If they could not use the pontoon bridges, maybe the boats would work. Coming under the lingering Mississippians' musketry, blue-coated figures in numbers were seen to topple from their boats, easy prey for the Southern riflemen's marksmanship. However, they were persistent and courageous and it was not long before a beachhead had been established. Others followed and it was apparent to Gen. Barksdale that it was time to exercise his discretion. By early evening, the last of his men had stolen away through the deserted streets of the city, crossed the plain separating it from Marye's Heights and entered the Confederate position located there. In the meantime, the two upper bridges had been completed.

The next day, December 12, dawned with haze covering the river bottoms. The big guns of the Federal artillery on Stafford Heights shelled the Confederate positions to no great effect. The Confederate batteries were silent, largely because there were no guns in their inventory capable of reaching the Federal positions. Around noon and under the direct scrutiny of Gens. Lee and Stuart, the Federal forces were seen to be moving in great numbers across the spans of the lower pontoon bridge. While observing the movement, Gen. Lee stopped in front of the Texas Brigade position and studied the scene along the river with his field glasses. Nicholas Pomeroy, Co. A, 5th Texas, said some of the men asked one of Lee's staff officers for a look through the binoculars. Gen. Lee overheard the request and said he had no objection to their having a look. Pomeroy said he "seemed to be in very good spirits that day."[15] As he returned to his headquarters, Gen. Lee was convinced by what he had seen that a major attack was going to be made on his right flank at Hamilton's Crossing, probably the next day.

Also riding with the group were Gens. Jackson and Hood whose conversation casually turned to the future. Gen. Jackson asked Hood if he expected to survive the war. Hood replied that he did, however, in a "badly shattered" physical condition. Hood asked what Gen. Jackson's expectations were, to which the latter replied that he did not expect to survive. To this he added that "he could not say that he desired to do so."[16] In view of what eventually happened to them, both exhibited a remarkable prescience in their views.

The night of December 12–13 was miserably cold, as were the pickets on duty and everyone else, for that matter. When dawn broke the scene as viewed from the Confederate positions was obscured by a thick fog. Then, as the Southern ranks cooked their meager rations, there reached their ears the distance-muffled sounds of drum rolls, shouted commands and the occasional sound of military band music. Eyeing each other knowingly, the soldiers finished their rations, gathered their weapons and moved toward their positions on the line. The entire Army of Northern Virginia stood concentrated, ready and in a most favorable defensive position.

By about 10:00 A.M. the thick fog began to slowly dissipate. Across the narrow valley, the steeples of Fredericksburg penetrated the haze and the shadowy outlines of Stafford Heights began to take shape. As the sun peeked through and the fog continued to dissipate, there was displayed to wondering Southern eyes a scene of military might and grandeur that brought gasps to many lips. Thousands of blue-ranked men and artillery arrayed in line of battle stretched from Fredericksburg to the lower pontoon crossing. It was at the lower crossing, as Gen. Lee had supposed, that the first Federal attack of the day was developed. It was at this time, while viewing from above the grand scene unfolding below, that he made his oft-quoted comment to Gen. Longstreet about war being so terrible that it precluded any fondness for it.

Dressing their lines, battle flags flashing in the crisp, cold sunlight, they moved forward as if on parade. They had moved forward only several hundred yards when the artillery of A.P. Hill's division boomed forth. The Federal ranks were raked twice and then fell back in confusion, leaving in their wake clusters of blue-clad figures, well-defined on the snow-covered field. There was no elation in the Southern lines at the repulse; they knew that they would be back. Meanwhile, at about 11:00 A.M., on the Confederate left Gen. Longstreet loosened his batteries on his front to create a diversion in favor of his comrades on the right.

Among the interested onlookers, John Stevens, Co. K, 5th Texas, watched as the attack fell upon the Confederate line to his right. He remarked that it was the only battle he ever had the opportunity to observe without being engaged in it. He described what he saw as "the grandest sight that ever human eyes beheld to see these two lines of humanity moving against each other."[17] He remembered this years later and might not have been so enthralled had he been in the line of fire.

Awaiting in their assigned position while the battle raged to their right and to their left was Val Giles Co. B, 4th Texas. There, he said "we stood ... in the center, silent and anxious, seeing it all except where clouds of smoke enveloped the combatants, shutting them out from our view.... The Battle of Fredericksburg, as viewed from the hill where we stood, was as grand a battle-scene as mortal man ever witnessed," although "[t]he suspense of waiting, expecting orders every minute, is a severe strain on the nerves of a soldier, worse than going into the battle." Those orders never came and Giles said that "[a]t no time during the war was my old Regiment so sorely tried."[18]

With the Federal advance stalled on the Confederate right, what would be their next move? The answer came soon; at about 11:30 A.M., there issued forth from the hidden recesses of Fredericksburg a river of blue, quickly forming itself into rank upon rank of a mighty host, its figures appearing in miniature to the on-looking Confederate defenders. Surging forward in militarily precise ranks, their point of advance was directly toward the most formidable part of the opposing line, the rock wall-lined sunken road backed up by the steepest part of Marye's artillery-studded Heights. What followed was a slaughter of immense proportions. The fire of the skillfully posted batteries on Marye's Heights raked the advancing Blue line. The survivors of that first blast scurried quickly to cover afforded by the diagonal ditch traversing the field.

At about 1:00 P.M., the scene of action shifted once more to the Confederate right. From Stafford Heights issued forth a terrible barrage of Federal artillery fire, soon followed by a massed attack against Jackson's position. This was a major assault with the intent of turning the Confederate right flank. It was met first by Southern artillery fire that cut bloody swaths in the Blue ranks. As the attack moved closer to the Southern positions the cause was taken up by the infantry posted there as volley after volley of musketry erupted leveling the advancing lines of Blue and wreathing the countryside in gun smoke. Yet on they came, relentlessly, as if drawn toward a vortex, a woodland neck near the center of the Confederate right. They had found a weak spot in the line.

As it turned out, the point to which the Federal attack gravitated was undefended, a defensive vacuum. That section of the line was the responsibility of Gen. A.P. Hill's Light Division. The area was marshy and Gen. Hill, when establishing his position, had considered it to be impassable, therefore, unnecessary to occupy.

From the heights to the north, peering through field glasses, anxious eyes could see that the advancing Blue tide had, indeed, penetrated the Confederate defense line. The fighting was so fierce, at such close quarters and so wreathed in clouds of smoke that the observers could not tell what was happening. On the left another attack was moving once again toward Marye's Heights only to be met with the same fate as its predecessor. All of this was punctuated by the supporting fire from the heavy-weight Federal artillery across the river and on the elevation of Stafford Heights. Reports from the right were sketchy but indicated penetrations in two places in the Confederate line, one around Deep Run and the other further south and over the line of the Richmond, Fredericksburg and Potomac railroad.

Then to the straining ears on the Heights came the familiar, chilling strains of the rebel yell. Seen running from the trees were the Blue hosts with men dressed in butternut in close pursuit. Observing all of this, John Stevens, Co. F, 5th Texas, had great respect for the "boys in blue" as fighters but maintained that "if you get him where you can charge him and 'yell,' he'll run or bust."[19] It proved to be true on this occasion. It was observed from afar also that the Confederate officers had a difficult time in halting the pursuit before it became endangered by the superior Federal artillery across the river. Reluctantly, the pursuers gave up the chase and returned to the restored line.

As it was learned later, the Federal attack had fallen on that section of the Light Division's line where the brigades of Gen. Lane and Gen. Archer adjoined. Behind them was posted the South Carolina Brigade of Gen. Maxey Gregg. Although the Federals made a serious penetration of the line, they were pushed back with losses both suffered and inflicted. Gen. Gregg was mortally wounded in the fray but the front had been restored in that quarter. A little to the left of this position, astride Deep Run, Hood's Division was involved but not the Texas Brigade. Val Giles, Co. B, 4th Texas said that "he was in the line of battle from the beginning to the end and never fired a shot."[20]

Gen. Hood did throw forward the 57th and the 54th North Carolina Regiments of Law's Brigade from his position on the right bank of Deep Run. These regiments were successful in driving the Federals back to the line of the railroad. Their officers had difficulty in stopping them and returning them to their line. Joe Polley, Co. F, 4th Texas, said that 54th North Carolina was made up of young men under twenty and old men "dressed in homespun, and presenting a very unsoldierly appearance." They made up for it by their courage and grit. On their return and while passing the Texas Brigade, one old fellow was heard to exclaim to all within hearing distance, "Durn ole Hood, anyhow! He jess didn't have no bus'ness't all ter stop us when we'uns was uh whippin' them ar durn blue-bellies ter h —- an' back, an' eff we'uns hadder bin you Texikins, he'd never o' did it."[21] With that kind of spirit and the 4th Alabama in support, this line was held until the Federals withdrew back across the river several days later.

It was then about 3:00 P.M., and to the north, the advance against Marye's Heights was taken up for a third time. In the sunken road, Gen. Cobb had been wounded mortally and the line had been reinforced by Kershaw's South Carolina Brigade and two more regiments from Cooke's North Carolina Brigade. Filing into the sunken position behind the protection of the stone wall, there was not enough room for each rifleman to have a place on the line. Standing sometimes six deep, those in the rear loaded weapons and passed them to the front where they were directed with great effect into the ranked Blue lines. The third attack was showing some signs of perhaps succeeding through sheer weight of numbers. Gen. Lee expressed concern to Gen. Longstreet to which the latter replied, "General ... if you put every man now on the other side of the Potomac on that field to approach me over the same line, and give me plenty of ammunition, I will kill them all before they reach my line. Look to your right; you are in some danger there, but not on my line."[22]

A fourth attack was mounted and Longstreet, true to his word, hurled them back. Not a man got anywhere near the sunken road. Attack followed attack until everyone lost count. The Confederate position was invulnerable and, quite literally, a death trap. At about 3:30 P.M. there was a lull; the battle on the right was over with the Confederates standing firmly in the lines held at the battle's opening. Even though dusk was coming on rapidly, Gen. Burnside continued the attacks in the desperate hope that numbers would prevail. It was a forlorn hope and only added to the already ghastly butcher's bill. By 7:00 P.M. it was all over. One man got to within thirty yards of the wall before being shot dead but the majority did not get within 100 yards. It was murderous on that field.

On the right, Gen. Jackson briefly tried a counterattack but the superior Federal artillery across the river was too much to bear. To attempt more would have resulted in a slaughter similar to that suffered by the Federals on the left. So, darkness fell and to add to the eeriness of the scene, the rarely observed *aurora borealis* danced across the skies as if to punctuate the drama and tragedy enacted on that field that terrible day. The Southern leadership fully expected that Gen. Burnside would renew the fight on the morrow. In this opinion, only Gen. Hood demurred.

During the night details were put to work further strengthening the already formidable positions. As Gen. Lee surveyed his line, dawn began to break on the following morning, December 14. He was satisfied with what he saw. Remnants of the prior day's attacks were seen to blanket the field while observed crouching in the diagonal ditch in front of Marye's Heights were living survivors in some numbers. They gave no indication of hostile intent. Other signs convinced him that there would be no further action in that sector. Expecting that any further attack would go against Jackson's front, he shifted some of his artillery to Jackson's end of the line.

The day before, after the enemy repulse on the right, William Fletcher, Co. F, 5th Texas, was sent forward to reconnoiter. Passing through the main Confederate line behind the railroad grade he reached the picket line beyond which he could see the "enemy's dead in great numbers." He returned to his company for the night but the next morning, December 14, they were sent forward to relieve those on the main line of battle. As it was to be discovered in front of Marye's Heights, during the night nearly all the Federal dead had been stripped of their clothing.

According to Fletcher, the Federals had withdrawn across the river at that time and he and his comrades were allowed to "sight-see" in front of their position: "As the dead bodies were all nearly naked and lying mostly on their backs, there was exposed to view a surprisingly large number of them who were so diseased, one would think: Why weren't you fellows all in the hospital; or were you run into our protected front to put an end to your miserable condition?... I think I saw the youngest boy laying beside what we took to be his father, that I ever saw, either dead or alive, on [a] battlefield."[23]

While some were in front of their line sight-seeing, others took the time afforded to break out the cards. Soldiers had to take their leisure as it became available. In Joe Polley's Co. F, 4th Texas, four or five of his company had spread a blanket on the ground and a poker game was quickly in progress. One Bill Smith was apparently in possession of a fine hand and had just raised the stakes when a Federal artillery shell passed close overhead. It knocked a limb off a tree, a piece of it striking Smith in the chest, sending him and his winning hand head-over-heels backward. Stunned, Smith thought the missile was the malevolent handiwork of one of his card-playing companions. Jumping to his feet and glaring menacingly about he said, " D — d if I can't whip the cowardly whelp who threw that chunk! Now's his time to cheep, if he's got any sand in his craw." It took quite a bit of time and talk to convince the angry man that "the person responsible for his loss was on the other side of the Rappahannock, fully two miles away."[24]

Later, Gen. Lee visited the line accompanied by Gens. Jackson and Hood. On the far right they had a very good view of the opposing line. The Federals were observed in great numbers; Hood estimated them to be 50,000. One telling thing Gen. Hood did notice was that there were no colors displayed. He saw that as a clear sign that no further action was being contemplated by those across the river.

John Stevens, Co. K, 5th Texas and his comrades got a chance for a close-up look at the "Mighty Stonewall" that morning — and in a new, full-dress uniform. He said the vaunted warrior "stopped in about forty feet ... and sat there on his horse with the side of his face to us for 15 or 20 minutes. The boys began to figure out that it was Jackson, another said 'Stonewall h–ll! Who ever saw old Stonewall dressed up?' This dispute among the men as to whether it was Old Jack or not became so animated and the tone so elevated that the famous soldier could hear the dispute.... Finally, the old general ... turned his face around square to our front for some moments and looked at the boys with a smile to settle all disputes."[25] The Texans raised a yell in tribute to which Stonewall responded by raising a hand in recognition and "laughing heartily" at having confirmed their suspicions. The new uniform? It was a present from the fun-loving Gen. Stuart who had a difficult time in persuading the homespun Jackson to don it on that occasion.

The day passed with the Federals gathering up their dead and wounded. The only signs of continuing belligerence were skirmishers exchanging fire and an occasional artillery round being thrown toward Confederate lines. Confederate commanders were puzzled at the Union inactivity given their numbers and the dreadful showing of December 13.

It was not until later that day that a Federal flag of truce came forward requesting time to bury the dead and recover the wounded, to which Gen. Lee assented. By that time the wounded had been lying on that blood-soaked, frozen ground without succor for two days. There were few that had survived and a closer look was even more sickening as the numerous dead were already in varying degrees of grotesque decomposition. Later, when casualties had been totted up, it was estimated that of the some 12,000 Federal casualties, fully 9,000 fell in front of Marye's Heights and the Sunken Road. The Confederate loss in that sector, less than 1,700.

The morning of December 16, came with a heavy fog blanketing the area. Nothing of the Federal positions could be seen. Once again, Gen. Lee, accompanied by Gen. Jackson, went to the far right where they expected an attack might develop to have a look. To their chagrin and somewhat to their embarrassment, it was discovered that under the cover of the prior night's darkness and gale-like winds, the Federal line had been withdrawn back across the river, pontoon bridges and all. The Federal army was safely beyond the choppy waters of the Rappahannock River.

Also on the morning of December 16, Lt. A. C. Jones, Co. G, 3rd Arkansas, was ordered to advance to the vicinity of the Barnard house and establish a picket line. Having accomplished his mission and discovering the enemy withdrawn across the river, he went on a sight-seeing expedition of his own. He described it as "the most remarkable and unique of all my experiences as a Confederate soldier." Scattered over a large area,

> There was something of almost everything that belongs to the equipment of an army. There were a few dead bodies left unburied, a few small arms, a quantity of ammunition, several pieces of artillery dismounted, many broken wagons, ambulances, and a great quantity of camp kettles, which were much wanted in our army; but the most conspicuous article scattered all over the place was hardtack, which is the staple food of an army in an active campaign. A great many boxes were unbroken, others were half used, until the ground seemed to have been sown with bread, most of it trampled underfoot and spoiled.[26]

In the aftermath of Fredericksburg, Gen. Hood came under criticism by his corps commander. Prior to the attack of December 13, Gen. Longstreet had visited Hood's position on the Confederate right. Pointing out the likelihood of any attack in that quarter falling upon Jackson's front, he instructed Hood to take advantage of any exposed Federal right flank that might present itself. He gave the same instructions to Gen. Pickett whose division held the line to the left of Hood's. When the attack, as anticipated by Gen. Longstreet, did come to pass "Pickett rode to Hood and urged that the opportunity anticipated was at hand, but Hood failed to see it in time for effective work."[27] In his memoir, Gen. Longstreet referred to Gen. Hood's "failure to meet his orders." The incident was reported in his official account, however, Longstreet said that since Hood was in such high favor at the time, it did not seem "prudent" to pursue the matter further. It would appear that Gen. Hood, as at South Mountain, felt very secure in his position and was, at times, loath to execute orders in contravention of his own view of the situation. That view, given the general's subsequent history of command, proved to be flawed frequently, valor and devotion to his cause, notwithstanding.

The Fredericksburg campaign was over, little having been accomplished by either side other than a boost in Confederate morale and the decimation of the Blue ranks. The Texas Brigade, for once, had come through relatively unscathed. Although Federal casualties had been high, Gen. Lee knew they could be readily replaced. It would be only a matter of time before the re-ranked Army of the Potomac would once again be advancing upon his front in even greater numbers. Nothing had changed substantially. The war would continue unabated and would become increasingly violent.

CHAPTER 9

"O, my, ain't we in it?
We just swim in bacon"[1]:
Campaigners and Commissaries
on the Nansemond, Spring 1863

George T. Todd, Co. A, 1st Texas thought it could not get much better, at least under the existing circumstances of a great civil war being in progress and him being in the middle of it. He said they "had a fine time" in the winter of 1862–1863. In the aftermath of the great battle at Fredericksburg, he and his company, indeed the whole army, were on picket duty along the south bank of the Rappahannock River below that devastated city. The picket line extended as far down the stream as Port Royal. Even though not sanctioned officially, an almost truce-like atmosphere existed along the picket lines at times. Sailboats were fashioned to ply the waters of the river laden with coffee if bound for the southern shore and tobacco if bound for the northern. Newspapers were another item of cargo. The benign belligerents chatted and even swam across for more personal fraternizations. The officers knew of these forbidden practices but usually chose to ignore them unless circumstances dictated otherwise. Chivalry counted and sometimes "the truce was declared 'off,' and the rifle spoke along the lines."[2]

Going into their second winter quarters, they began erecting shelters and mud-caulking them to stem the wintry blast. John Stevens, Co. K, 5th Texas, said they then filled them to a depth of ten inches or so with leaves for bedding. Over the leaves they placed blankets, with the remainder of their blankets being used for cover. One end of the cabin was left open and it was there that a fire would be built. The heat was reflected off the covering of the house resulting in what was described as a warm and comfortable place. An open fire near a bed of dry leaves seems counterintuitive.

Given their rigors of the past eight months, for the time being, their situation was an idyll. Stevens said that when not engaged "in camp duty we [sit] around our fires, talk and gossip and discuss the various fights, and the prospects of an early ending of the war, reading the daily papers and writing letters home. Some of the boys, forgetting their early moral training at home, are off in a big game of poker and Confederate money is piled up in regular gambling style, others are visiting friends in other messes, companies or regiment and passing the time off very pleasantly, considering the circumstances with which we are surrounded."[3]

While in winter quarters, military camp routine returned except that afternoon drill was seldom conducted. In the evenings dress parade was held at which time various bits of information and orders were read to the troops by the adjutant, he being the organization's paper-pusher. On one such occasion, an announcement was read detailing the offense of being absent without leave committed by an unnamed brigade member. The punishment for the offense was set to be a flogging. In this case, thirty-nine lashes were to be administered to the AWOL's bare back. The general attitude was that a flogging was not appropriate for one of their comrades. He should receive some severe form of punishment for the misdeed but, he, having always been a good soldier, a public whipping was not appropriate.

After the formation had been dismissed, the men wasted no time in expressing their determination that no such whipping would be allowed. In the face of this universal disapproval, the matter was ended and nothing more was heard of it. It was speculated that the punishment was never intended to take place and that it was

George T. Todd, Co. A, 1st Texas

meant as a warning more than anything else. Nonetheless, this is a good example that, once united on an issue, the citizen soldiers could force the leadership to reconsider their positions.[4] The Texas soldiers had a strong sense of justice and felt that the punishment should be commensurate with the crime. In this case, the leaders probably recognized this and chose to just let the matter drop.

In an age where religion played an important role in most people's lives, chaplains were often in demand. John Stevens, Co. K, 5th Texas, also doubled as a minister since the 5th Texas had no regular chaplain. To meet the troops' religious needs prayer meetings and the like were held. Stevens said he was often asked by other units to minister to their spiritual needs. He said there were others "in the brigade who would sometimes preach for us."[5]

While in winter quarters on the Rappahannock, more attention was paid to amusements than had been done the prior winter spent along the Potomac. Some were arranged and some were impromptu. The men contributed their labor to erect single-story log theaters where performances by Collins' 4th Texas band and plays performed by brigade members relieved the monotony of the long, cold winter evenings being spent far from home and family. General Hood was in attendance frequently and on at least one occasion Gen. Lee was a member of the audience."[6]

There were other amusements that erupted spontaneously as youthful exuberance boiled over in reaction to dull, grim surroundings. No account of the history of the Army of Northern Virginia would be complete without mention of the great snowball fight waged in the winter of 1862-1863 along the banks of the Rappahannock. On that occasion, a snowball fight developed that grew to such proportions that it was remembered long afterwards by veterans in much the same way that battles with the Federals were remembered.

Describing the event in detail, Val Giles, Co. B, 4th Texas, said that it all began with companies ranging themselves against each other and eventually spread to include other regiments, brigades and finally divisions. It was as "rough as modern football" and culminated with one grand battle involving more than 6,000 soldiers. Across the river, the Federals, aroused by the hue and cry, lined the riverbank and covered the hills to observe their military adversary's winter fun.

Owing to the overzealousness of some participants who secreted rocks and other hard objects in their snowballs, there were serious injuries resulting. Because of this, General Longstreet issued orders prohibiting further snowball fights. In their usual insubordinate fashion the Texans continued snowball fighting anyway. However, it was never again on the grand scale of that memorable battle fought along the banks of the Rappahannock that cold day in early January 1863.[7]

Sometimes, after the afternoon dress parades and inspections, the military brass bands would play popular airs of the day and sometimes a musical competition would develop. From the Blue side of the river might swell the thundering strains of the "Star-Spangled Banner" and the jaunty rhythms of "Yankee Doodle." These might be answered from the Gray side of the river with the likes of the "Bonnie Blue Flag" and "Dixie." However, once one side took up the popular and nostalgic strains of "Home Sweet Home" they were quickly joined by all the bands and voices of the other side. For a brief moment both sides of the river were reunited in their collective yearnings for an end to the dreadful war and a return to their homes.

Then, in mid–February 1863, any plans that the men of Hood's Brigade had for continuing their idyll were unexpectedly dispelled.

Intelligence reports reaching the South indicated heavy Federal waterborne troop movements down the Potomac, destination unknown. Of several possibilities, it seemed highly probable that southeastern Virginia was the destination with Richmond and the various railroads leading to and from it as objectives. With a considerable Federal force already in place at Suffolk southeast of Richmond and some fifteen miles west of Norfolk, the Confederate government was jittery at the prospect.

In reality, the Federals were just as jittery as their Gray counterparts. Gen. John J. Peck, commanding at Suffolk, thought the James River only second following the Mississippi River in strategic importance to the Confederacy. When first ordered to Suffolk in September 1862, he found that city without any defenses whatsoever. In light of his opinion that it was only a matter of time before the Army of Northern Virginia retired to the James River line in preparation for the recapture of Norfolk and Portsmouth, he began hastily to fortify the city. Recovery of those ports by Confederate forces would serve to make them available to blockade-running vessels and as safe havens for Southern gunboats operating in the Chesapeake Bay. By April 1863, he had made the city militarily formidable.[8]

At the request of President Davis and with it being all quiet on the Rappahannock front, on February 15, Gen. Lee put Gen. George Pickett's Division on the march toward the capitol. As subsequent intelligence reports indicated Newport News as the immediate objective of the waterborne Federal troops, more troops in the form of Hood's Division were put on the march in the wake of Pickett's movement. A battalion of artillery accompanied the two divisions.

Winter was still in full swing and on the march, the two commands experienced terrible conditions. As recounted by A. B. Hood, Co. I, 5th Texas, it all began on the morning of February 17, when they were ordered to cook three days' rations, signaling a hard march and, perhaps, something worse in the offing. With the beginning of a heavy snowstorm looming menacingly overhead, the hard march commenced. Progress was slow because the brigade wagons and the artillery had started in advance thus transforming the roads over which they passed into a muddy morass. Within a half a day, the infantry drew up alongside the advance train, it having been brought to a standstill when every piece of artillery became bogged to the axles.

Snow had begun falling and was six inches deep and growing. Under these difficult conditions there were many stragglers. The march continued all day with only two stops to rest. During the halts the exhausted troops would throw themselves on the ground wherever they might find a promising spot. Hood said of it, "Ah God you cannot realize our sufferings.... Imagine you see us that night on a bleak hill-side preparing to [lie] down in a bed of snow [ten] inches deep. You would have doubtless exclaimed 'farewell troopers.'"[9]

At first light the next morning, the march continued. By midmorning the snow of the day before had been replaced by a freezing rain. The roads, made mush by the deluge, were worse even than that of the preceding day. There were rivers, brooks, creeks and rivulets to ford. Even so, they made fifteen miles before filing off the road to go into bivouac for the night. Hood said that at least a third of his division were stragglers and that, wet and muddy, they continued to arrive in camp throughout the course of that bleak night.

The third morning commenced as had the preceding two, early. Right at the beginning of the day's march, a creek 200 yards wide presented itself as an obstacle. On the far side, Gen. Robertson supervised the crossing, offering words of encouragement to the soaked and freezing men. As A. B. Hood passed, Gen. Robertson remarked to him: "This will do to go down in posterity and to tell your children of." Hood, at the moment, not sharing the general's interest in posterity's education, replied through blue and quivering lips: "D — n a man that wouldn't be a soldier and make eleven dollars a month."[10]

Arthur Edey, Co. A, 5th Texas, had been detached in February 1862 to serve as the agent of the Texas Depot in Richmond. A year later, he was back in ranks. He left his own description of the same march, recalling it as a "sliding and trudging" march to Richmond. According to his account, preparations began Monday night, February 16, with tents struck and all baggage packed into the wagons. Setting off on the following morning with blanket rolls made more burdensome having become water soaked, the march continued all day in weather that alternated between rain and snow. Going into bivouac that night, large fires were built and blankets and wet clothing held up to dry. When nightfall came, the exhausted troops lay their tired bodies down, rain falling on their prostrate and exposed forms.

Daylight the next morning found the weather rainy and in a very short time the troops were completely soaked again. Edey commented that he then knew what a heavily packed mule must feel like. Not given time to cook breakfast, the troops had to content themselves with raw, fat bacon and sea biscuits pulled soggily from their knapsacks. Even with such rough fare and dismal conditions, he portrayed them as munching away while "thinking of the glory of our cause, the girls we left behind us and the good times coming." Mercifully, little did they know that those good times lay decades in the future for most.

Because of the long march of the day prior, a halt for the night was called shortly past noon. Fires were kindled, what rations that were available were consumed and comfort sought by whatever means available as the rain continued to fall. Thursday morning saw an early start, with "no rain, no snow, but *Mud, Mud, Mud.*" The first part of the day's march was spent in trying to avoid mud holes and slush but when the only alternative was discovered to be ankle-deep mud, the men just plowed on through whatever the obstacle presenting itself. After what was described as a "troublesome and harrassing day," a bivouac was made only to find that there was "no butter, no anything but wet garments, longing stomachs and fat bacon to fill them." They were near Hanover Junction, about six miles from Richmond on the line of the Central Railroad.

On that night, recognizing the broken-down nature of many of the men, Gen. Hood issued an announcement that any men who felt they could not make the remainder of the march could take the cars. About two thousand men fell out and were placed in charge of Capt. J. J. McBride, Headquarters, 5th Texas. Capt. McBride was not well himself having been severely wounded at Second Manassas (Bull Run). This large number seeking a train ride exceeded Gen. Hood's estimate and it was found that there were not enough cars for all to ride. So, many were forced to walk anyway but were given three days to rejoin their regiments. Capt. McBride, "true to his charge," led the walkers and to everyone's surprise they reached their destination the next day. Of course, when they arrived they received the friendly jibes of their comrades about having to fall out. Capt. McBride, for his leadership qualities and fighting record—he was to be wounded in both legs at the Wilderness and retired as a result thereof—was "never forgotten by the boys."

When entering the outskirts of the capital, the men were formed in parade formation, each man being expected to put his best foot forward. The troops manning the defensive positions ringing Richmond rushed to the roadside to observe the veteran troops passing and to receive from them the usual insults, the fare of all rear echelon troops. Entering the city, the boys became even more vocal. Businessmen and government employees, some sporting stovepipe hats and wending their ways about on the day's business found themselves singled out for public attention. Some of the boys were yelling, "Come down out of that hat, I see your ears." Soon the others joined in the chorus much to the discomfiture of those gentlemen thus singled out. A "fine, fancy young man with a white shirt, black boots, gold chain, etc.," was standing on a corner and attracted the attention of the dirty and ragged troops. When drawing abreast, one of the boys shouted, "Here's your fancy Captain," immediately and visibly deflating the young dandy's haughty demeanor as he beat a hasty retreat.

Passing by the Spotswood Hotel and thence on to their designated campground some three miles south of the city, it had begun again "to snow, snow, snow, with a bitter cold wind." It was a truly wretched and uncomfortable time for the ill-equipped troops. All that night and through the next two days it continued to snow. Finally, on the third day, a Tuesday, the sun came out, "shining so pleasantly and shedding ... warm beams upon [the troops], driving away the cold snow from the ground that we soon forget our troubles and promised to make no complaints."[11]

On the march to Richmond, J. M. Polk, Co. I, 4th Texas, said snow was falling all the time and that some of the men, being barefooted, left blood in their tracks. They moved on through to a campsite south of Richmond . They were cold and hungry but in need of sleep more than anything else. When they were halted for the night, they bunked up three and four together for warmth.

The next morning at roll call two men, J. Q. Harris and S. B. Terrell, were missing. It wasn't until about ten o'clock in the day that they were discovered when somebody stepped on them; they were covered under ten inches of snow. When they were excavated they were still sound asleep.[12] Their survival was only temporary, however. Harris was killed in action on the second day at Gettysburg and Terrell died at Petersburg in June 1863, probably as a result of wounds to be suffered at Suffolk.

As it began to appear that even more Federal troops were heading in that direction, Gen. Longstreet was ordered south to take personal command of the developing operation there. His instructions were to hold the two divisions in readiness in the vicinity of Richmond. They were to bivouac near railroad transportation, ready to move in either direction as developments dictated. The Richmond government clerk and diarist John B. Jones recorded that on February 21, "Major-Gen. Hood's Division passed through the city today and crossed over the river."[13]

After the march from Fredericksburg to Richmond, Joe Polley, Co. F, 4th Texas, said that once they were situated in their new camps, the Texas Brigade welcomed the change. The Texas Depot was nearby and needed personal items could be retrieved readily from storage maintained there. Gen. Hood was liberal in granting passes which the men took advantage of, visiting Richmond and partaking of its recreational opportunities, some good and some probably not so good. Also, the proximity to the main supply depot for the army and the popularity of Gen. Hood assured the fulfilling of submitted requisitions, or as Polley put it, "the ragged were clothed and the barefooted shod."

One item not available was hats — but not for long. A novel scheme for securing same is credited to an unnamed but clever member of the 1st Texas. Near the Texas campsite a railroad bridge spanned a creek, the crossing requiring passing trains to slow. Men in need of hats, and many that did not need them but who did need a diversion, would form a line on one side of the tracks. Armed with tops cut out of young pine trees, as the train puffed slowly by, a cry was raised thereby attracting the attention of the train's occupants. Curiosity aroused, the unwary passengers would rush to the windows. Then as they stuck their heads out to see what the uproar was all about, the pine tops would be wielded. Off would tumble a cascade of hats — take your pick, boys. Complaints about the practice were dismissed laughingly by the authorities as just a practical joke by young and energetic soldiers. That is, until on one occasion the train carried a brigadier general, his staff and a congressional junket. The loss of hats by that humorless group brought the practice to an abrupt halt. Those still hatless had to seek their covers by other more legitimate but less humorous means.[14]

In a letter to his mother, James Hendricks, Co. E, 1st Texas, pinpointed their encampment as "six miles from Richmond South Side James River." They were to remain in that location for over a month and camp routine was quickly reasserted. Hendricks complained that they "had nothing to do but drill." With some men on furlough, some in hospital for various reasons and some not yet replaced in the aftermath of the last year's costly campaign, his company numbered only twenty men, sometimes being able to muster only six for drill. A company, on paper, was supposed to number about 100 men. With such grim facts displayed before them daily, the men had become reconciled to the fact that the war was far from over and would last at least until "President Lincoln's time is out." One good thing that helped in reinforcing any sagging morale was that they were "getting plenty to eat, such as it is, bacon, flour, and sugar." Hendricks added that there was plenty of snuff in Richmond and if he had the opportunity he would send some home.[15]

Circumstances were better in the officer corps, offering opportunities to socialize frequently. It was during this respite near the capital, that Gen. Hood met the Southern diarist, Mary Boykin Chesnut, and through her the Richmond belle, "Buck" Preston, of whom he became enamored. Gen. Hood had arranged and invited Mrs. Chesnut, "Buck" and others to a picnic at Drewry's Bluff down on the James River. However, just as the picnic party was about to get under way, news of a Federal thrust from the Rappahannock line toward Richmond reached Gen. Hood. Orders were for the Texas Brigade to move north immediately to Ashland to counter the threat. The party was off for the time being, so the disappointed picnickers decided to go and give their heroes a sendoff.

Sitting by the turnpike, Mrs. Chesnut said they had not seen the likes of this before. Hitherto "it was only regiments, marching spic and span in their fresh smart clothes, just from home on their way to the Army. Here, such rags and tags, nothing alike — most garments and arms had been taken from the enemy — and such shoes! 'Oh, our brave boys!' moaned Buck. They had tin pans and pots tied to their waists, bread or bacon stuck on the ends of their bayonets. Anything that could be spiked was bayoneted and held aloft."[16] Even in their state of destitution, Mrs. Chesnut said they did not utter a disrespectful word as they "laughed and shouted and cheered" as they passed her party.

As it turned out, they were responding to a false alarm. Nonetheless, it resulted in the Texas Brigade making a needless and difficult march back toward the Rappahannock that consumed some four days' time. Soon thereafter, Gen. Longstreet arrived on the scene and in keeping with the responsibility being placed with him, he was appointed to the position of commander of the Department of Virginia and North Carolina. This would be the first independent command exercised by the First Corps commander.

At this time, the importance of Eastern North Carolina as a commissariat, under the circumstance of having two infantry divisions in the area, attracted attention. It was an area lightly touched by the war thus far and rich in agricultural products. Gen. Longstreet's Commissary, Maj. Raphael J. Moses, surveyed the area with relish and reported that there were available also, in quantity, bacon and barreled fish. He went on to say that if his commissaries could be properly protected from the Federal threat posed by Suffolk, he would scour the area of the available commodities just waiting to be plucked from their respective vines, at government prices, of course.

In a letter to Gen. Lee, Gen. Longstreet pointed out that Maj. Moses' reported areas of "abundant supplies" all lay within the Federal lines in that area. His estimates of the Suffolk garrison and other troops within supporting distance was about 27,000. Doubting his ability to mount an operation against the Suffolk garrison with the troops he had on hand, he felt he needed at least another division to make it militarily sound. "If," he said "we can supply our army otherwise the expedition should not be made." However, "[i]f it is a case of necessity we should lose no time."[17]

The army commander felt otherwise, that his subordinate corps commander was being overly cautious and that he had sufficient troops to accomplish the contemplated operation. In a letter of reply to Gen. Longstreet, Gen. Lee expressed an interest in the prospective bounty from a different perspective: "I consider it of the first importance to draw from the invaded districts every pound of provision and forage we can. It will lighten the draught from other sections and give relief to our citizens."[18] On his part, Gen. Longstreet thought that his commander had sufficient troops to deal with any Federal threat, under its new commander, Gen. Joe Hooker, that might develop along the Rappahannock line. Under those circumstances, he thought the dispatch of the remaining two divisions of his corps would not hazard the Army of Northern Virginia. Yet, given their divergent opinions, both yearned for the agricultural bounty afforded in the area and for the succor it would offer their short-rationed troops. Both men, educated at West Point with its emphasis on Napoleonic strategy and tactics, were mindful of that military icon's attention to logistics and the dictum that " an army marches on its stomach."

Eventually, the desire to procure the goods overrode the military risks and the operation was put in motion. However, the requested reinforcements remained with the Army of Northern Virginia on the Rappahannock. Gen. Longstreet's command would operate to contain the Federals around Suffolk. The wagons for gathering the commissary bounty would have to come from the subarea designated Southern Virginia commanded by Gen. Samuel G. French.

Between Richmond and Suffolk, the Blackwater River meanders across the landscape in a generally northwest to southeast direction. At places it was lightly fortified to at least slow up any Federal thrust that might develop toward the Confederate capital. Beyond the Blackwater, the city of Suffolk is located on the south bank of the Nansemond River, that north-flowing stream following a convoluted course to eventually empty into the waters of Hampton Roads ten or so miles away. Entering from the west, a few miles north of Suffolk, is a tributary, the Western Branch. To the south and east of the city is located the vast Dismal Swamp, traversed in its northern reaches by the Petersburg and Norfolk and the Roanoke and Seaboard railroads. Both railroads passed on through Suffolk to their respective destinations.

While the commissary contingent with its array of wagons prepared to fan out over the land, Gen. Longstreet gathered his forces. Including some from other subarea commands, he crossed the Blackwater in early April driving in the Federal pickets and skirmishing with the Federal cavalry outpost. That force, according to John W. Stevens, Co. K, 5th Texas, was commanded by a Col. Spear, an old army friend of Gen. Hood. Apparently forewarned, Hood told his men that any troops under Spear's command would give them a good fight because their leader was of a nature to "charge a circular saw." In the interim, one of Hood's scouts fell into enemy hands and upon interrogation had the presence of mind to mislead his captors by greatly exaggerating the size of the Gray force. His Federal interrogators believing him, the scout was then released on parole and returned to his command with a personal message for Hood. "'...[D]— n [Hood's] long bowlegged heart, [Spear] wanted to meet him in a fair open field and he'd give him h —.'"[19] All of this was accompanied by a great deal of profanity, to which Hood responded with "hearty laughter." There was a second message of a more sociable tone in which Spear said he would like to meet Hood for a chat should an occasion arise.

The Federals fell back, and in his sector, the pursuit was led up front by Gen. Hood, sharpshooter's balls whizzing by in close proximity. On April 11, the Confederate force arrived in front of the fortress city of Suffolk with its various interlocking forts and batteries looking out menacingly at them. The city lies south of the Nansemond which makes an almost 180 degree bend along the point where the city adjoins its bank. Thus, almost the entire western approach to the city was not protected defensively by the river. The two Confederate divisions were deployed in a concave fashion that covered the entire western approach to the city from north to south. Gen. Pickett's Division occupied the southwestern quadrant with its right flank resting on the Dismal Swamp. Gen. Hood's Division occupied the northwestern quadrant, a portion of its ranks compelled topographically to occupy a line following the course of the Nansemond River. To cover the exposed left flank of Hood's Division, Gen. Longstreet had earthworks thrown up along the south bank of the Western Branch.[20] Gen. Peck divined the Confederate plan to be to "cut the Nansemond River some [six] miles or so below Suffolk, on our right flank, while another force was to be thrown against the Norfolk Railroad, on our left flank and rear, and thus surrounded [our] entire army and the city of Norfolk were to fall a rich and easy prize into the hands of the enemy."[21]

As the siege operations began and boredom increased, a humorous event occurred that gave both sets of combatants a brief moment's relief from the otherwise grim circumstance of war. At one point on the Confederate front there was a tall pine tree that stood out plainly from its surrounding fellows. It had been trimmed considerably, and near the top there was constructed a platform. Clearly, its original purpose was as a Federal observation post or, perhaps, a signal station. Now it was within Gen. Longstreet's lines. One young Confederate soldier, unable to contain his curiosity, shinnied up the trunk to the platform and was settling himself down to enjoy the view thus afforded him of the Union troops within their new lines just ahead. It did not take long for him to be discovered atop his perch. A Union artillerist, sighting his piece at the platform, soon sent a rifled round screaming toward its objective. A near miss, the shell burst too close for the young Confederate infantryman's comfort but youthful pride prevented him from a precipitous retreat. A second round helped him to overcome his reluctance and down he came "his legs, to the amusement of the men on both sides, soon [bringing] him to safe cover."

Not to be outdone, under the cover of darkness that night, he contrived a means of getting even with his blue-coated tormentors. Constructing a life-size mannequin complete with Confederate butternut clothing, he hauled him up to the platform. He then arranged him in a lifelike posture and secured him in place. He dubbed him, master of all he surveyed, "Julius Caesar."

Dawn soon followed and the vigilant Federal artillerists were aware shortly thereafter of their newest "target of opportunity." Unleashing a barrage, they were somewhat annoyed as the object of their attention sat with total indifference amid the fusillade bursting all around him. The Confederate onlookers were thoroughly enjoying the show, but finally, no longer able to contain themselves, called out for "three cheers for Julius Caesar." It did not take the Federals long to catch on to the fact that they had been had. Good-naturedly they joined in the cheers for Julius Caesar.[22] Although his identity is unknown, the prank-playing Confederate soldier could very well have been a member of Hood's Texas Brigade.

Meanwhile, and at the confluence of the Western Branch and the Nansemond, the latter is navigable and there were Federal gunboats operating in the area. At that point, known locally as Hill Point, stood the remnants of a small fort that had been constructed by Confederate forces in 1861, Fort Huger, or as it was sometimes called, Old Fort. On April 16, in order to interdict any Federal gunboats attempting to pass up the river, Gen. Longstreet had heavy artillery batteries occupy the tactically attractive Fort Huger. The battery was under the command of Capt. Robert M. Stribling, Fauquier Artillery. His orders were to fire upon any vessels attempting to pass the fort from either direction . To the west of the fort, two thirty-pounder Parrotts of the Alexandria Light Artillery, commanded by Capt. D. L. Smoot, were sited. The Federals were quick to respond to the threat.

On April 17, the fort came under fire from Federal gunboats and from an artillery emplacement across the river. Then, on the morning of April 19, the gunboats opened a cannonade, increasing in severity into the afternoon. It was probably during this time period that Capt. Ike Turner, 5th Texas, was mortally wounded by a Federal sharpshooter. Later in the afternoon, the firing abruptly ceased and a gunboat, the *Stepping Stones*, ran close to the shore. A force composed of several hundred troops from the 89th New York Infantry and the 8th Connecticut Infantry with some artillery were put ashore near the fort. Due to a mix-up in Confederate picketing responsibilities and because the riverbank was heavily wooded, their landing went undetected initially.

According to Capt. Stribling, the Federal landing force wasted no time in taking advantage of their surprise. "They double-quicked ... then faced to the front, discharged their pieces, and charged upon the fort.... They soon ... flanked the fort on either side and entered it through a swamp and over the parapets on the river side."[23] The beleaguered and overwhelmed captain and his men were then quickly marched out and boarded on the *Stepping Stones*. Five artillery pieces, two twenty-pounder Parrots and three twelve-pounder howitzers, nine officers and 120 enlisted men were captured.

Immediately following the action, the Federal troops were put to work "to place the captured guns in position to resist any attempt of the enemy to retake the Point."[24] That would mean they were turned around in their emplacements. Reinforcements arrived a little later and the night was spent in improving the defenses. A half-hearted Confederate attack at about 10:00 P.M. succeeded in driving in the Federal pickets but the lost ground was quickly recovered. At about noon the next day, covered by the gunboats, the troops were withdrawn back across the river. Under the circumstances, the Confederates could only look on in frustration. Gen. Longstreet termed the affair the "only occurrence of serious moment while we had our forces about Suffolk."[25] Of course, in the aftermath there were loud recriminations in the always contentious Confederate command ranks as to who was responsible for the fiasco. As a matter of fact, several duels came out of it but, fortuitously, no loss of life occurred in those affairs of honor.

Again, as every soldier, past and present, know, a primary rule of soldiering is "never volunteer for anything." Sometime during the almost two week period that Suffolk was under siege, J. M. Polk, Co. I, 4th Texas, volunteered to help man some rifle pits. Although he does not identify the time or location, it could have been around Ft. Huger in the aftermath of its capture by the Federal forces. Each pit accommodated ten to twelve men, each with a cache of 125 rounds of ammunition. He mentions the enemies breastworks as "barrels filled with sand on top of them, with just enough room between them for a musket, and when we could not see daylight between the barrels of sand that was the time to shoot."[26] He had a close call when a Federal sharpshooter drew a bead on him, the round striking the brim of his hat and taking off a small chunk of his right ear. Philosophically, he noted that a miss was as good as a mile.

Another close call was artillery-based. A shell appearing to be about the size of a "lamp post" exploded in their front. "A piece of it struck the back part of my hat brim and shaved the breast of my jacket — another close call. Another piece struck the ground about ten feet in front of the pit, digging a hole deep enough to bury a horse and rolling about two wagon loads of dirt in on us." All of this gave Polk a different perspective on volunteering: "I thought if I did what I was ordered to do after that, that would be enough."[27]

James Hendricks, Co. E, 1st Texas, had a chance to practice his skirmishing skills, of which he admitted, "I am not very fond of the business." He said that his company with two others from the 1st Texas, maybe fifty men in all (three companies should have numbered about 300 men) "advanced to within [200] yards of three heavy Yankee batteries across an open field. General Hood ordered the advance. It beat anything I ever saw. The Yankees seemed astonished. They got up on top of their batteries and looked at us with surprise."[28] Undoubtedly, the dauntless Hood and these men would have pressed the attack although the odds were totally against them. This attack was to feel out the enemy and it indicated in the end that fortress Suffolk was invulnerable to their numbers. So, even though the military operations achieved nothing of any tactical or strategic consequence some individuals were able to improve their otherwise deprived lot.

One of those was John W. Stevens, Co. K, 5th Texas, and his friends who got in some good foraging. They found a cache of what he said was 120,000 pounds of bacon. The owner had it under contract for the Federal army they found out. Searching further, they found another 100,000 pounds hidden under bushels of corn in a corn crib. "O, my, ain't we in it?" said Stevens. "We just swim in bacon. Big rations — and all the time we have an immense wagon train hauling out bacon, corn, wheat, flour and great droves of beeves."[29] He said that it was a big haul they were making and that it lasted about four weeks.

Isaac A. Howard, Co. B, 5th Texas, experienced the same momentary bounty. In a letter home from "Camp Suffolk," he implored his mother to never "let the thoughts that I am suffering for anything needful disturb you at all." He said that any impression "that I am always hungry" was false. Continuing he acknowledged that "it [was] true that for a while we were on very short allowances at Fredericksburg, but that was chiefly owing to the great size of our army and the consequent difficulty of supplying it properly with provisions." After leaving Fredericksburg he became a member of the "captain's mess" and "have always had a plenty and whenever we are in camp we live very well."[30]

Federal reinforcements arriving on the scene made it even more evident that an offensive was not practicable. It became even more so when on April 29, Gen. Longstreet received word that the Army of the Potomac was crossing the upper fords of the Rappahannock. His orders were to "return to General Lee with all speed." He replied that his "trains were at the front along the coast collecting supplies; that they would be hurried to our rear, and as soon as safe we would march."[31] Calls for his return were "frequent and urgent." However, whenever he inquired if he should abandon his trains, he received no reply. Left to his own discretion, he gathered his train before taking up the march north on May 4th. On that date, a two-day march commenced "to Petersburg, where they could entrain and move north by rail.[32]

The retreat began after darkness fell, recalled Stevens, Co. K, 5th Texas, the enemy not detecting the retrograde movement. The next day, Federal artillery shelled the woods where the Confederate lines had been the day before. By that time, according to Stevens, the command had recrossed the Blackwater and was well on its way to Petersburg. The Suffolk campaign was over.

On May 8, the Texas Brigade arrived in Richmond, encamping for several days at Frederick's Hall. In the interim, a great battle had been fought on the Rappahannock line and the improbable Confederate victory at Chancellorsville had been won. However, it had been won at a great price; the "Mighty Stonewall" had been severely wounded and his left arm had been amputated. He should have survived but complications set in, including pneumonia, and the great captain succumbed on May 10. His military genius would be sorely missed by the Army of Northern Virginia.

The great victory at Chancellorsville, the coming of spring with much improved weather and the chance to rest all helped to restore the spirits of the troops. According to M. V. Smith, Co. D, 4th Texas, the sick and wounded from prior months began to return and the entire "Army of Northern Virginia was buoyant with courage and determination. Their bosoms thrilled with confidence in their ability to accomplish almost anything."[33]

General Hood concluded that "[n]othing was achieved against the enemy on the expedition to Suffolk, at which point he possessed a safe place of refuge within his strong fortifications, protected by an impenetrable abatis."[34] However, the commissary train, its wagons groaning under their bountiful loads, bespoke success of another kind. Such bounty was, however, anomalous and of little immediate relief to the responsible command as it was fed into and eventually doled out through the ponderous Confederate Commissary system.

By the time Pickett's and Hood's Divisions returned to the Army of Northern Virginia, plans were being made for the next phase of the campaign of 1863. Ultimately, those plans would take the army north across the Potomac and into Maryland once more with the lush farmlands of southern Pennsylvania beckoning beyond.

CHAPTER 10

"[T]hese men were tried and seasoned soldiers ... yet they were not made of iron"[1]: The Pennsylvania Campaign, June–July 1863

In the aftermath of Chancellorsville, the Army of the Potomac had withdrawn back across the Rappahannock to lick its considerable wounds and rationalize its humiliation at the hands of a numerically inferior and physically divided enemy. "Fighting Joe" Hooker, the Union commander succeeding Gen. Burnside in the aftermath of the Fredricksburg debacle and now trying to come to terms with the aftermath of his own debacle, needed time to come up with another plan of action. In the meantime, on the south side of the river and once more back in the Fredericksburg defenses, Gen. Lee reorganized his army to compensate for the death of his most trusted and esteemed lieutenant, Jackson.

After consideration, a third corps was established. In the reshuffle, Gen. Longstreet remained as the First Corps commander. Gen. Richard S. Ewell, Jackson's trusted lieutenant, up and moving, albeit slowly and in a carriage after the loss of a leg at Groveton the summer before, was assigned command of the Second Corps. The new Third Corps command went to the combative Virginian, Gen. A. P. Hill. That done, Gen. Lee turned his attention to the military options available to him.

One option was to maintain the Rappahannock line in Virginia. Another possibility was to once again detach Gen. Longstreet's command, this time to join Gen. Braxton Bragg's Army of Tennessee. In the western theater an offensive might be mounted to break the line of the opposing Federal forces commanded by Gen. William Rosecrans in the vicinity of the rail center, Chattanooga. Ordered to Richmond, Gen. Lee traveled there by train and conferred with the president and his aides on May 14–17. After having considered the various options, an incursion into Northern territory was selected.

For one thing, after two years of war battle-ravaged northern Virginia could not support an army whereas the agriculturally-bountiful countryside of Maryland and Pennsylvania was a source of plentiful commissary. Secondarily, by thus threatening the Federal heartland, the campaign might serve to draw off some of Gen. Grant's troops even then engaged in strangling by assault and siege the strategically important Confederate garrison on the Mississippi River at Vicksburg, Mississippi. And, although increasingly a forlorn hope, a major military victory on Northern soil might bring the elusive foreign recognition of the Confederate States that diplomacy had theretofore failed to obtain.

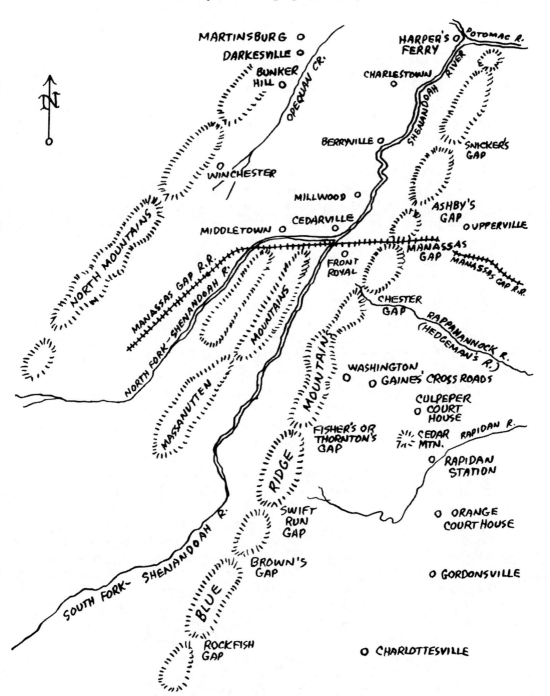

Shenandoah Valley

Shenandoah Valley

Back at his old headquarters at Hamilton's Crossing south of Fredericksburg on May 18, Gen. Lee began to put into motion a plan that would move the army from its positions across from Fredericksburg and by its left to concentrate around Culpeper Court House in preparation for the march north. From there the army would move into the Shenandoah Valley, the natural invasion route for the coming campaign. As early as May 11, Gen. Lee had begun to move Gen. Stuart's cavalry to Culpeper. From there as the army prepared for the campaign, the cavalry was to observe and report any movements the Federal army might put in motion in that direction that could pose a security threat to the coming campaign.

In early June, the newly appointed Second Corps commander, Gen. Ewell, and Gen. Longstreet were called to army headquarters where they were informed of the plan and received their marching orders for the coming movement. Ewell's Corps was given the responsibility to march into and clear the Valley of Federals, mainly Gen. Milroy's sizeable command at Winchester. Meanwhile, Longstreet's Corps was to move north on the eastern side of the Blue Ridge screening the mountain passes and awaiting further orders depending upon developments. A.P. Hill's new Third Corps would remain in its positions in the vicinity of Fredericksburg. There, Hill was to keep an eye on the Army of the Potomac, to report any observed movements from its Falmouth base and to, by whatever ruse available, give the enemy the impression that the entire Army of Northern Virginia remained on its front. When the Army of the Potomac was observed to be moving, Hill's Corps was to march into the Valley in the wake of the passage of Ewell's Corps. Once Hill's Corps had passed down the Valley, Longstreet's Corps would move through the Blue Ridge passes and take up the rear of the march north. At that point, Gen. Stuart's cavalry would take over where Longstreet's Corps had left off and screen the passes from Federal observation. The troop withdrawal from Fredericksburg was undertaken beginning on June 3. Within a few days, the army, less Hill's Corps, was encamped around Culpeper Court House.

It was during that time-frame that the fun-loving cavalry commander Gen. J. E. B. Stuart took advantage of the opportunity to display his celebrated troopers. On June 8, 1863, he scheduled a grand cavalry review. Gen. Lee, among others including the local gentry and their ladies, was invited to attend and had agreed to do so.[2] Gen. Hood and "some of his people" were among those invited to view the proceedings. Gen. Hood, no doubt with a twinkle in his eye, arrived on the field bringing with him *all* of his friends, in this case, his entire division. Somewhat taken aback by this unexpected mass arrival and given the command's reputation for sometimes rowdy behavior and rude remarks, they were nonetheless welcomed and allowed to stay although admonished to be on their best behavior.

Arranged in two lines, the five brigade cavalry ranks numbering 9,536 sabers, stretched out for three miles.[3] Their drawn and burnished blades and battle-worn regimental flags flashed in the early summer sunlight as they awaited eagerly their opportunity to display their skills. After an inspection of the troops by Gen. Lee, he and his staff took their places as the mounted troopers passed in review. Then, led by Gen. Stuart, the troopers cantered past in a full-fledged cavalry charge. Some of the cavalrymen left in their wake their hats, blown off by the wind in their wild charge. Lt. Col. W. W. Blackford, of Gen. Stuart's staff, said that before the owners could come back to retrieve their property "Hood's men ... [had] a race for them and [bore] them off in triumph."[4]

As a finale, the cavalry command mounted a charge against the guns of Stuart's horse artillery situated on a nearby hillock. Blackford noted that "[t]he effect was thrilling, even to us, while the ladies clasped their hands and sank into the arms, sometimes, of their escorts in a swoon, if the escorts were handy, but if not they did not."[5] Ruefully, he noted also that it was the last of their carefree ways for a long time to come. Soon enough the Army of Northern Virginia would once again be on the march north bound for Pennsylvania and its biggest fight of the war.

The next day, June 9, pickets reported Federal cavalry to be crossing the Rappahannock upriver via the fords at Beverley and Kelly's in some force. Gen. Lee sent urgent instructions to conceal his infantry's concentrated presence from prying Federal eyes at all costs. In the effort to preserve that security, there occurred on that day the greatest cavalry battle ever fought on North American soil, before or since. At Brandy Station, as many as 20,000 men were engaged in shooting and slashing at one another for the better part of the day. Charges and countercharges surged back and forth until late in the afternoon, when the Federal forces were finally forced to retreat back across the river. At the end of the day, Gen. Lee was relieved in thinking that the security of his plan had not been compromised.

On June 10, Ewell's Corps initiated the campaign as it stepped out on its route of march over the mountain passes of the Blue Ridge, principally Chester's Gap, and into the Shenandoah Valley beyond. Once having dealt with the Federals, which he had done by June 15, he was to march on Maryland and thence on into Pennsylvania. Gen. Longstreet's Corps followed on June 15 and by June 19 "McLaws' Division was posted in Ashby's Gap, Hood's at Snickers Gap, and Pickett supporting Hood's and guarding points between the two Gaps."[6]

As usual, weather, the bane of the poor infantryman, proved fickle. At Snickers Gap, newly arrived from a Texas judgeship, John C. West, Co. E, 4th Texas, experienced the "hardest storm of wind and rain" he ever had seen. To him, "[i]t seemed ... as if the cold and rain, like the two-edged sword of holy writ, penetrated to the very joints and marrow. [He] laid down but did not sleep a wink until about an hour before day, and woke up cold and stiff."[7] Some of the soldiers stayed up all night as the winds howled through the pass in a continuous effort to keep a fire blazing.

At first thinking that the atmosphere in the Gap was a dense fog, John Stevens, Co. K, 5th Texas, decided they were encamped in a rain cloud! Everything was wet as a result, blankets, ammunition; they could keep nothing dry. Later, detailed to deliver a message, he was sent down the west side of the mountain. He had to cross the Shenandoah at a ford, as a result of which he became soaking wet. Once having delivered his message, exhausted, he lay down in a clover patch where he slept the rest of the night. Admonishing posterity, he implored: "When you see ... poor old Confederate soldiers, all crippled up with rheumatism and suffering so many aches and pains, you will

John C. West, Co. E, 4th Texas

see ... that it is the result of suffering and hardships that ... [you] have no idea of. Treat them kindly, when they all pass away, you will never see their like again on earth."[8]

Several days later the columns took up the march that would lead them on down the Shenandoah Valley, across the Potomac, through Maryland and into southern Pennsylvania. That day was remembered as a bad day's march because of the number of men that fell from ranks the victims of sunstroke. "Under every shade tree men were lying senseless, overcome by the heat. Whether they ever recovered or not ... we could not wait to see."[9]

Meanwhile, back on the Rappahannock front, on June 14, Gen Hill reported that the Army of the Potomac seemed to be evacuating Stafford Heights across the river from Fredericksburg. On the evening of June 15, Gen. Lee received the welcome dispatch from Gen. Ewell of Gen. Milroy's defeat at Winchester and that the army's march into Pennsylvania was now unimpeded. With the way clear, Ewell's command could focus attention on gathering subsistence. On June 17, Gen. Lee broke up his headquarters camp at Culpeper and joined the march. The exact whereabouts and intentions of the Army of the Potomac was then unknown.

Gen. Lee's plan for Stuart's cavalry was the usual role expected of cavalry, that is, it served as the eyes of the army. However, that role notwithstanding, the ambitious and aggressive cavalry chief suggested to the commanding general a plan of his own. Stuart proposed that with the larger part of his command he would locate the Army of the Potomac, certainly moving toward the Potomac crossings, and disrupt its attempt to cross the river. Certainly in need of current intelligence as to his adversary's whereabouts, Gen. Lee approved the plan, as did Longstreet. Given somewhat discretionary options, Gen. Stuart was admonished in a dispatch dated June 22, that once it was established that Hooker had actually crossed the Potomac, the cavalry command was to return to the army's right flank post haste. Inexplicably, at the time, Stuart's command was not heard from for the next eight days, theirs a critical absence.

With the mission accomplished at Winchester, the advance units of Ewell's Corps began crossing the Potomac at Williamsport on June 15. Over a week later, on June 23, Longstreet received orders to proceed down the Valley and to cross over at Williamsport into Maryland. Marching at dawn on June 24, the First Corps' order of march was Pickett's Division, reserve artillery battalions, Hood's Division, and last, McLaws' Division. On June 25, the first two units of Longstreet's Corps crossed followed by Hood and McLaws on June 26.

There were somber thoughts by some Texans as the soldiers' Rubicon was contemplated. It was no light matter to venture into the enemy's home territory. Memories of Sharpsburg, less than a year removed, were still fresh in everybody's memory. D. U. Barzizas, Co. C, 4th Texas, thought was that "alas! it was the last to many a noble Southerner! ... Many a father ... will say 'it was *my* boy's last night in Virginia;' many a mother ... wife, sister and loved one ... will often recur to this night, the last of their loved one's rest on the soil of the Old Dominion."[10] Yet, being young mostly, their exuberance predominated the gloom. With their cartridge boxes and haversacks attached to their muskets and the muskets held high overhead, the shouting, laughing young soldiers waded the river and arrived, once more, on the Maryland shore dripping wet but confident in their army's future prospects.

Circumstances, notwithstanding, the younger members of the brigade were always looking for a laugh. In John Stevens' Co. K, 5th Texas, a newly promoted lieutenant, not wishing to soil his new gold-bespangled uniform, persuaded a private, for the consideration of five dollars, to carry him across on his back. Seeing a chance for some fun and profit, the private readily assented. Predictably, at midstream and about waist deep, the private suddenly lost his footing and under they went! "Everybody but the lieutenant was expecting it and of course [they] all yelled, the Rebel yells."[11]

Upon entering enemy territory, Gen. Lee issued Order Number 89 to the army that prohibited any disturbance of the property of private citizens. However, it did not specifically prohibit the soldiers purchasing stores. What would make that chance unlikely was the presence of provost marshal troops (military police) charged with confining troops to their own camp areas.

One day, while briefly bivouacked, M. V. Smith and another Co. D, 4th Texas, comrade, Jim Patterson, who would win later a Texas Gold Star for bravery and survive the war, had some money and harbored no qualms about bending rules. Knowing of the abundance of the land and confident that they could avoid the "provos," they set out to make some purchases. Their shopping plans were ended abruptly, however, when having gotten no more than a few hundred yards out of camp, they were picked up by "that everlasting, contemptible provo guard." They were taken to their headquarters and an explanation was demanded of them to which they explained their honorable intentions. For one reason or another, they were released upon their statement but ordered to report back the next day. Apparently, the provost marshal captain at his headquarters failed to take their names or they gave false ones in that day before military I.D.s came into usage, because, according to Smith, " [w]e haven't reported yet."[12]

In the process of learning his way around his new environment, John C. West, Co. E, 4th Texas, described the march to Gettysburg as "hot and dusty" most of the time with periods of heavy rain. He found himself "completely soaked" at times, if not with sweat then by rain. At one point in the march and at about ten o'clock at night a halt was called and camp "without fires" ordered due to the possible close proximity of the enemy. To West, it was a novel sight to see, or as he put it "to hear, 20,000 or 30,000 men rushing into the woods on the side of the road to secure a place to lie down." He compared their lying down on the "cold ground" to that of "tired hounds after a chase." Very wet and very weary, he "spent a few minutes listening to the hum of 10,000 tongues cursing the Yankees, talking of home and thinking of how pleasant it would be to take a bath and a toddy, and how sad my wife would feel if she knew all that I was undergoing." Listening to the random remarks in the darkness, he could not help but be amused: "Get off my hand," "Now you are on my foot," "For heaven's sake," (or something worse), "Keep your feet out of my face," "Oh, my back, you are right on top of me," "You weigh six hundred pounds,"etc, etc.[13] West's bed was so close to the road that he could stretch his arm out and his hand would become mired in mud.

Not long afterwards a ration of whiskey was made available. Reputedly, the whiskey was captured Federal stores and the ration was ordered by Gen. Hood. Anyway, the results were disastrous, at least temporarily. Many of the non-drinkers gave their rations to the less temperate, the result being about half the Texas Brigade becoming, in M. V. Smith's, Co. D, 4th Texas words, "how come you so?"

Col. Manning, 3rd Arkansas, thought it hazardous to have a drunken regiment while in enemy territory and thus ordered the sober ones to dunk the drunken ones in a creek in order to sober them up. There is no report on the outcome of that order. Anyway, it became a brigade legend that it was in four states in the course of one day, the state of Virginia, the state of Maryland, the state of Pennsylvania and the state of inebriation.

"[R]eaching the stone marker on the side of the turnpike that marked the boundary line between Pennsylvania and Maryland," Val Giles' Co. B, 4th Texas "waved [their] hats and gave a Rebel yell that was taken up by the soldiers in front and carried back for miles by those in the rear."[14] An observant Col. Powell, 5th Texas, noted that there was either an increase in the number of field officers or that the infantry was converting to cavalry. Somehow, "[t]he bare-footed and sore-footed had secured horses. Some horses bore three men."[15] They were very jolly that afternoon, he said. Encamping that night at Greencastle, the next day, June 27, Longstreet's Corps was at Chambersburg, Pennsylvania, where a welcome two day rest was ordered.[16]

On June 27, General Order 73 was issued governing the behavior of the army regarding the acquisition of private property and individual soldiers' expected behavior. Nothing was to be seized without payment or receipt for payment later by the Confederate government. One difficulty proved to be the rude manner in which soldiers acquired hats — hats again! Soldiers marching through the crowded streets of Chambersburg took to snatching hats from the heads of the onlookers. Efforts to return them to their rightful owners appear to have been futile.[17]

From his place in the ranks of Co. D, 5th Texas, Mark Smither guessed that Chambersburg was about the size of Houston and "the prettiest place [he] ever saw," as were the local girls! The troops took a great deal of abuse from the wayside onlookers as a result of their shabby, ragged appearance but by and large took it good-naturedly, marching silently onward. At the time, Smither had mixed emotions, feelings of exultation on the one hand and feeling very badly on the other. "[O]n every side ... as far as the eye could reach and seeing nothing but unfriendly looks from the whitehaired sirs down to the child.... We passed a crowd of people who enquired of me what troops were passing and on receiving the answer of 'Texas Brigade' one turned around to the rest and remarked, 'They are the ones that have killed so many of our soldiers.'"[18]

Of Pennsylvania and Pennsylvanians, James H. Hendricks, Co. E, 1st Texas, said "[It] is the finest country I have seen ... but ... [t]hey despise us.... Every lady and girl has a badge of red, white, and blue and some ladies have dresses made of red, white and blue." Observing that the army was grabbing "every horse that [could] be found" he noted also that "[o]ur army has behaved very well so far."[19] Passing on through town, the brigade then encamped and for the next several days enjoyed a well-deserved and needed rest.

Soldiers were detailed to perform various necessary duties while in bivouac. While near Chambersburg, J. M. Polk, Co. I, 4th Texas, was posted to guard a private residence "to keep the men from depredating on them." In return, he was invited to dinner by those whose property he was protecting and enjoyed "one of the finest meals [he] ever sat down to." His hostess had some ideas about ending "this cruel war:" "I just wish you men with your muskets could get them big fellows in a ring and stick your bayonets into them and make them fight it out. You could settle it in a few minutes."[20]

It was customary for foreign governments to send observers, usually military officers, to war zones in order for them to get ideas that might be useful to their respective armies at later dates. One such observer was Lt. Col. Arthur J. L. Fremantle of the British Coldstream Guards. He was fascinated with the soldiers of the Texas Brigade and with their colorful state history and reputation for frontier-brand ferocity. While the army was resting in Chambersburg he observed some Texas soldiers detailed to destroy some whiskey barrels in the town. He termed it a "pretty good trial for their discipline" when the only time they were allowed in town was to destroy "their beloved whiskey." "However, they did their duty like good soldiers," he said.[21]

In the meantime, Ewell's Corps, out front, had advanced as far north as Carlisle, Pennsylvania. Early's Division was as far east as York and Wrightsville on the Susquehenna River having passed through the little village of Gettysburg to get there. The eventual objective of the army was the state capital at Harrisburg and, if things went right, Baltimore and Washington City. Due to lack of information, Longstreet's and Hill's corps remained encamped around Chambersburg and Fayetteville. Once Stuart's cavalry reported back to the army with information as to the whereabouts of the Army of the Potomac, the remainder of the army was to move on Harrisburg. At the time, it was thought the Federal army remained south of the Potomac.

By June 28, there was no word yet from Gen. Stuart, the last dispatch having been received on June 25. With confidence in Stuart's past services and assuming all was well in his rear, Gen. Lee ordered Gen. Ewell to continue his advance on Harrisburg. To Longstreet and Hill, preparatory orders were issued for them to follow Ewell on June 29. Then, during the night, Longstreet's favorite spy and scout, one Harrison, arrived in the Confederate camp with the unwelcome news that the Federal army, seven corps in all, was not only across the Potomac but well into Maryland. And, oh, yes, Gen. Joe Hooker had been relieved of his command. His replacement was an old friend and comrade of Gen. Lee in the "old army," Gen. George G. Meade.

Not ever having had much confidence in the intelligence provided by the likes of Harrison, Gen. Lee found it even harder to believe that he had been failed by his bold and dependable cavalry chief. And now, if Harrison's report was true, which it was, the right flank of the army was not only open to attack but its communications with its base back in Virginia was in danger of being severed. As Lt. Col. G. Moxley Sorrell, Gen. Longstreet's chief of staff, has pointed out, "It was on this, the report of a single scout, in the absence of cavalry, that the army moved."[22]

Orders were dispatched north to Gen. Ewell to abandon his operations as previously ordered and to rejoin the main army post-haste.Longstreet and Hill were ordered to cancel their planned marches north. The army's concentration point was to be around Cashtown and Gettysburg. Hill's Corps would lead the way from Chambersburg followed by Longstreet. Ewell's scattered Corps would rejoin from the points of the compass ranging from northwest to northeast.

The day dawned dark and rainy on June 29, as Heth's Division, Hill's Corps, gathered up to begin its march east across the northern extension of South Mountain toward Gettysburg. Through Cashtown Gap the road led to Cashtown and, further on, Gettysburg. Rain mired the road and without the usually present cavalry screen, the advance was slow and cautious. The next day, June 30, the advance continued with two of Longstreet's divisions, McLaws and Hood, taking to the road. Pickett's Division was left in camp near Chambersburg to act as a rear guard in the absence of the customary cavalry. Law's Brigade, Hood's Division, and a battery of the reserve artillery were detached and posted at New Guilford southwest of Fayetteville and Greenwood. They were to act as pickets, the specter of hard-marching Blue hordes just beyond the first bend down that road on their mind.. The Texas Brigade marched as far as Fayetteville where they bivouacked for the night.

In the meanwhile, the new commander of the Army of the Potomac, was wasting no time in putting a plan together. Having learned of the Confederate presence in Chambersburg, Gen. Meade soon had his army on the move in that direction. Things were aligning for a collision of forces just over the hills.

Accompanying Longstreet's troops was the commanding general. Late in the day, June 30, he received word from Gen. Hill up ahead that one of his brigade commanders, Gen.

J. Johnston Pettigrew, Heth's Division, was in search of shoes for his many unshod infantry-men. A large supply was rumored to be stored in the Gettysburg area, and Pettigrew had advanced his troops to that locale. Riding ahead to reconnoiter, Gen. Pettigrew was just in time to observe a column of Federal cavalry pounding up the road from the direction of Emmittsburg to the south. "[S]ome of ... [Pettigrew's] officers reported that they had heard the roll of infantry drums beyond the town."[23] Without close support, Pettigrew had with-drawn a few miles toward Cashtown. Gen. Heth, his appetite whetted by the rumor of shoes, requested of Gen. Hill, "If there is no objection, General, I will take my division tomorrow and get those shoes." "None in the world," replied his red-shirted superior.[24]

The next day, a Wednesday, marked the first day of July 1863.

On that day, Gen. Lee rode with Gen. Longstreet toward Gettysburg. On the way, they met some columns of Ewell's Corps and a fourteen mile-long wagon train coming down a road from the direction of Carlisle. Longstreet's Corps was halted near Greenwood to allow the passage of Ewell's troops and their train as they took the road east toward Get-tysburg. A considerable delay ensued for Longstreet's column. As Gens. Lee and Longstreet, their staffs trailing, rode on ahead, they were puzzled by the unmistakable, deep-throated boom of artillery up ahead.

Impatient and increasingly annoyed by his cavalry chief's absence with the resultant lack of information about what was ahead, Gen. Lee left Gen. Longstreet to lead his corps forward and rode on to see for himself. At Cashtown, he found Gen. Hill as puzzled as he was as to what the cannonading meant. Gen. Heth's Division was out there seeking the elusive shoes but with orders not to engage the enemy until the rest of the army was up. Mounting, Gen. Hill rode ahead to see what he could find out. A little later, Gen. Lee fol-lowed.

When he reached the western outskirts of Gettysburg, Gen. Lee was troubled by the increasing volume of artillery fire but downright alarmed by the sound of musketry in volleys which meant infantry in numbers. Along the way he came upon the troops of William Dorsey Pender's Division, Hill's Corps, deployed across the Chambersburg Pike. Ahead, with the village of Gettysburg providing the background, the field of engagement occupied by the rest of Heth's Division and his Federal opponents was visible and wreathed heavily in the smoke of battle. Scanning the battle scene and the lay of the terrain in the vicinity, he recognized that this was no mere skirmish; a Federal force was there in numbers.

As the morning advanced, the battle intensified. It had all started when Heth's early morning advance came upon Federal cavalry dismounted and deployed afoot ready for a fight. Thinking to brush the improvised Blue line aside, Gen. Heth deployed two brigades. Ordered to take Gettysburg, they swept down upon the Federal line in force. The outnum-bered cavalrymen were putting up a good fight and holding their own, all the while anxiously looking over their shoulders for the infantry reinforcements that they knew to be on the way. Just about the time the dismounted cavalry line was showing signs of giving way, the first elements of Gen. John Reynolds' Federal I Corps arrived at the battle scene. Later, dur-ing the morning and early afternoon Gen. Oliver O. Howard's Federal XI Corps also took the field.

Deadly fighting occurred all along the line. As the Federal units continued to take the field, other units of Ewell's Corps began to arrive via roads that directly connected Carlisle and Gettysburg. Spilling out of the woods from the northwest, Ewell's men found themselves on the flank of the Blue line. The Federals adjusted to the threat and a tough fight ensued. Still not willing to commit his army to an all-out fight, Gen. Lee was inclined to delay until

Longstreet could be brought forward. His attitude was changed, however, as yet other units of Ewell's Corps began to arrive from the direction of York to the northeast and on the right flank of the Federal line of battle.

Gen. Lee's practiced eyes, taking in the scene, recognized the opportunity presented and ordered an all-out attack. The rebel yell-punctuated onslaught that followed struck like a tidal wave. It swept the Federal line from the field, sending the overwhelmed and dispirited survivors stumbling backwards in disorder through the streets of Gettysburg seeking defensive positions to occupy. Lying east of the village, Cemetery Ridge was a long, low elevation anchored on the north end adjacent to Gettysburg by Cemetery and Culp's hills. It then stretched southward behind and below the city and was culminated on the south end by two hills named, respectively, Little and Big Round Tops. The fleeing Blue troops began to establish defensive positions initially on Cemetery Hill and then gradually extended on down the entire length of Cemetery Ridge. Time was of the essence for the Gray army as from captured and loquacious members of the routed Federal I and XI Corps it was learned that the entire Army of the Potomac was not far behind.

An immediate attack was indicated before the visibly strengthening positions on Cemetery Hill became impregnable. Gen. Lee considered his options. A. P. Hill was ill that morning and his troops were somewhat disorganized and bloodied by the morning's fight. Longstreet's Corps was still strung along the Pike reaching all the way back to Chambersburg. That left only Ewell's troops as readily available to carry the fight forward.

The attack orders Gen. Lee sent to Gen. Ewell by a mounted courier were discretionary, as they usually were to his subordinates. "If practicable," Gen. Ewell was directed to push the then disorganized Blue crowd off Cemetery Hill while the time was ripe. Unfortunately for his cause, General Ewell, with discretionary orders, did not arise to that occasion. The enemy position opposite grew ever stronger and more impregnable as each hour passed.

At about this time, Gen. Longstreet joined Gen. Lee on Seminary Ridge, it being a long, low ridge running north to south just west of the town, facing and about equidistant from Cemetery Ridge across the gap of several miles separating them. Still somewhat uncertain about the military situation, Gen. Lee surveyed the field through his binoculars. Also surveying the field, it was at that time that Gen. Longstreet suggested an alternative plan. Why not have the entire army move by its right flank and interpose itself between the Army of the Potomac and the Federal capital? Once having achieved that rather formidable task, the army would assume a defensive position and force its Federal antagonist to attack, hoping for another Fredericksburg- like slaughter to ensue. Hearing him out, Gen. Lee was not moved and replied, "If the enemy is there [on Cemetery Ridge] we must attack him." To this, Longstreet replied rather peevishly, "If he is there, it will be because he is anxious that we should attack him — a good reason, in my judgement, for not doing so."[25] At that point, the subject was dropped, at least for the time being.

Late in the afternoon, things quieted down somewhat. Gen. Lee rode over toward his left to seek out Gen. Ewell and discuss with him the tactical situation and to determine why his suggested attack on the then thinly-defended Cemetery Hill position had not occurred. Once seated in an arbor behind a house commandeered as Ewell's headquarters, he learned from Gen. Ewell, attended by several of his divisional commanders, that although his initial attacks had succeeded that morning, it was in spite of some serious tactical blunders. Even more serious than the blunders, to Gen. Lee, was the irresolution and uncertainty displayed by Gen. Ewell in failing to attack in a situation loudly calling for one.

After extensive discussion, brushing the lost opportunity aside, Gen. Lee announced his decision to attack the next morning the lengthening positions observed to be developing on down the course of Cemetery Ridge. The sounds of that attack would be the signal for Ewell to demonstrate against the Federal positions on Cemetery and Culp's hills, the latter lying to the east and forming the hook of the developing Federal line slowly assuming the general shape of a fish hook. If the feint appeared to be moving the Federal position, an all-out attack was to be launched with vigor.

On July 1, when the Texas Brigade received its marching orders it immediately began to prepare. "Everybody was in a stir in camp, rolling up blankets and fly tents, gathering up cooking utensils, buckling on cartridge boxes, etc." Leaving their overnight campground, they were soon on the march toward Gettysburg. "Tramp, tramp, tramp, all day the boys were marching and, alas, it was the last march for many of the poor fellows." As was not uncommon in the ranks, Rod Meekins, Co. B, 1st Texas, had a premonition of death which proved to be all too true. At one moment, as they marched along, he was whistling gaily when suddenly he said to all of his comrades within hearing, "Boys, I have been through many hard fought battles, but if I get through this one to which we are going, I shall count myself the luckiest man in the world."[26] As a company color bearer, he was killed the next day in his brigade's assault on the Round Tops.

That evening, after a hard day's march under the hot July sun, the brigade bivouacked on the roadside near Cashtown, not bothering to stack arms in their close proximity to the enemy. "[R]ations of flour were issued. The hungry men immediately set to work to cook bread. They had scarcely prepared the raw dough when suddenly the long roll beat, and orderlies came rushing through with the familiar cry: 'Fall in! Fall in!'"[27] Within minutes they were off on the march.

On the march to his first fight as a soldier in the ranks of the Texas Brigade, John C. West, Co. E, 4th Texas, a "Texan in search of a fight," passed a field hospital in operation. There, the medical personnel were tending to the bountiful crop of wounded from the first day's encounter. The scenes he viewed, unnerving though they must have been, were the usual for those circumstances. However, at that time they were beyond his experience. He saw wounded soldiers "mangled and bruised in every possible way, some with their eyes shot out, some with their arms, or hands, or fingers, or feet or legs shot off, and all seeming to suffer a great deal."[28] Fortunately, for West's peace of mind, he did not realize that the worst was yet to come. A.C. Sims, Co. F, 1st Texas, a newcomer also, saw the "bloody shirts ... wending their way back to the old Virginia shores," and having never seen such before thought it, "no pleasing sight to behold."[29]

In the meantime, Pickett's Division remained at Chambersburg. Law's Brigade had been relieved of its picket duty and ordered up at 3:00 A.M. According to Gen. Longstreet, Law's troops "completed [the] march of twenty-eight miles in eleven hours, — the best marching done in either army to reach the field of Gettysburg."[30] All of these troops had experienced difficult and exhausting marches. As will be seen, they were then marched and counter-marched much of the day, July 2, not reaching their assigned attack positions until late in the afternoon. And, though exhausted, their assault was to be against what had developed over the last twenty-four hours into a very rough and well-defended position.

It was before dawn, Thursday, July 2, at army headquarters, that Gen. Longstreet once more renewed his argument for a turning movement of the enemy's left. Once more Gen. Lee listened intently but was unmoved in the end from his decision to assail the Cemetery Ridge positions. Later, A. P. Hill arrived and after serious discussion of the various options, it was decided that the attack would fall upon the Federal left now extended for much of the length of Cemetery Ridge to around the Round Tops. The designated assault troops would be of the yet-to-be-bloodied Longstreet's Corps, specifically, Hood's and McLaws' Divisions. Pickett's Division, although on the way from Chambersburg, would arrive too late to participate. Ewell would launch his diversionary attack on the Federal right upon hearing the increasing sounds of Longstreet's battle to the south. Adjoining Ewell's Corps on their southern flank, the divisions of Hill's Corps were to threaten attack and if an opportunity presented itself move forward with aggressive intent.

As the morning dawned, the recent arrivals reported to army headquarters. Gen. Hood reported, his troops not far behind. Shortly, Gen. McLaws reported. Sending for McLaws, Gen. Lee briefly outlined his plan. Referring to a map, he explained that he wanted to deploy McLaws' Division beyond the Federal left and across the Emmitsburg Road. Once the attack was signaled to begin, McLaws was to sweep up the road perpendicularly, rolling up the Federal flank before it. Shortly thereafter, Longstreet's Corps artillery under the command of Col. Edward Porter Alexander arrived on the field. Alexander was appointed to act as director of the artillery in the coming attack and began immediately to deploy his batteries.

As Gen. Longstreet was left with the task of deploying his troops, Gen. Lee took the opportunity to check once more the left end of his line. There he observed that the Federals on Cemetery Hill had taken advantage of the overnight respite allowed them to greatly strengthen and lengthen their positions. In the meantime, the beginning of Longstreet's attack was awaited as the signal for Ewell's demonstration to commence. As mid-morning arrived, only silence greeted the expectant listeners.

Returning to Seminary Ridge, Gen. Lee sought out his First Corps commander. He was somewhat dismayed to find that, even having route-marched over hill and dale from the Chambersburg Pike, Longstreet's troops were nowhere near to their assigned attack positions. At that point, Gen. Lee deviated from his usual practice of suggesting movements and directly ordered an attack and as soon as possible.

By noon, Lee found the troops being deployed but in a manner much slower than his orders had indicated. The one trait displayed by Gen. Longstreet that vexed Gen. Lee, and he mentioned it to others, was that his "old war horse" was "so slow." Lt. Col. Sorrell, Longstreet's chief of staff, commenting in his post-war memoir, observed that at Gettysburg there was indeed "apathy" in his chief's movements: "They lacked the fire and point of his usual bearing on the battlefield."[31] Fact of the matter was, the corps commander did not have any confidence that the developing attack would be successful, not a good state of mind for a commander directing a critical action.

While their corps commander might have been in a reluctant state of mind, his soldiers were not. In the ranks, Val Giles, Co. B, 4th Texas, noted some of their prior marching records and was critical of the excessive time it took for them to reach their attack positions. "[W]e covered twenty miles in less than five hours [at Second Manassas], and yet at Gettysburg we were ten hours going eight miles." It was not the fault of the rank and file that the deployment was slow. They were there — and ready."[32]

Led by an engineer officer on Lee's staff who had reconnoitered the ground and who had instructions to conceal the movement from watchful enemy eyes, Longstreet's troops moved to the right. During the deployment it became apparent that the Federal line was being extended southward and that it was only a matter of time before the Round Tops would be occupied. There was a further delay in the deployment occasioned by the need to detour by means of a difficult countermarch in order to avoid observation from a Federal

Signal Corps station whose busy semaphore flags could be seen wigging and wagging from the heights of Little Round Top.

By the time McLaws' Division arrived at its designated jumping off point for the attack, it was seen that the Federal line now extended farther down Cemetery Ridge and beyond that command's planned attack position. It now became necessary to extend the right farther to the south. To do so, Hood's Division was moved beyond McLaws' right so that the line of the enemy across the way was exceeded. Hood's Division became the extreme right of the Army of Northern Virginia on that second day of the battle at Gettysburg.

Gen. Hood, acting as any prudent commander should, sent out a group of Texas scouts to determine the exact location of the Federal left. The group included Sgt. Charles Kingsley and Wilson J. Barbee, Co. L, 1st Texas, John M. Pinckney, Co. G, 4th Texas, and James H. Dearing, Co. B, 4th Texas.[33] At about the same time, Gen. Law sent out scouts for the same purpose. Later, Law's scouts reported the Federal left to be in the air, that is, unsupported, and ripe for a turning attack. They had seen the exposed rear of the Army of the Potomac, its supply wagons and other equipment there for the apparent taking. Two Federal prisoners of war, captured by Law, when interrogated, confirmed this. Further, they said that "the other side of the mountain could be easily reached by a good farm road, along which they had just traveled, the distance being a little more than a mile."[34] Upon their return, Gen. Hood's scouts reported about the same information.

Law informed his division commander of this intelligence. Gen. Hood sent word to his corps commander that a turning movement would be much more fruitful in outcome and economical in lives than the advance ordered to take place up the Emmitsburg Road. Longstreet acknowledged Hood's intelligence but, having been unsuccessful in dissuading Lee from his planned course, ordered the attack to be made exactly as Gen. Lee had ordered it — up the Emmitsburg Road. Three times Gen. Hood made the request; three times Gen. Longstreet ordered the attack to be made as specified. Finally, under orders, Hood was bound to make the attack, which he did, but with an official protest. The next year, J. M. Polk, Co. I, 4th Texas, said he asked of the general, indirectly, why the attack was made as it was, to which Hood replied, "Well, that was one place I went into with a great deal of reluctance, and I told General Lee that I could put my division in there and would if I was ordered to do so, and lose a lot of my men and accomplish nothing."[35]

The Federal troops in left front before McLaws and occupying a peach orchard were of Gen. Daniel Sickles' III Federal Corps. Their right was supported by Hancock's II Corps, their left would be supported shortly by Sykes' V Corps, it arriving behind the ridge but not yet up on the line. Having received some information relayed by the Signal Corps station on Little Round Top, Gen. Meade sent the chief engineer of the Army of the Potomac, Gen. Gouverneur K. Warren, to observe the situation. What Warren saw from the vantage point of Little Round Top was "the enemy's line of battle, already formed and far outflanking our troops." He thought the discovery "was intensely thrilling and almost appalling."[36] On his own accord, Warren hurried units of Sykes' V Corps into the developing breach, a valiant decision that would lead eventually to his commanding that very corps in the later stages of the war.

The ground that Sykes' V Corps came to defend and over which Hood's Division was to advance was described as "very rugged, with no field for artillery, and very rough for advance of infantry."[37] A big part of the very rough, and in front of the Round Tops, about ten acres in extent, lay the locally-designated Devil's Den. It was a jumbled assortment of granite rocks of varying size that would be more in place in a Rocky Mountain setting than

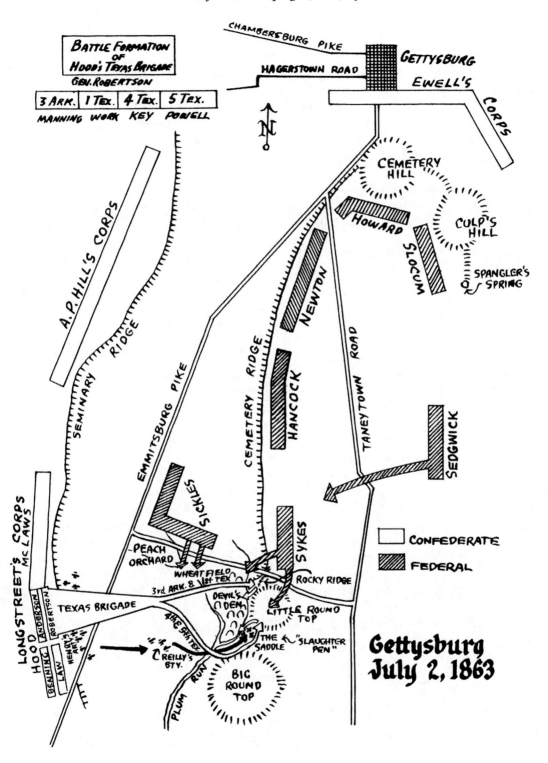

Gettysburg, Pennsylvania, July 2, 1863

in the state of Pennsylvania. Federal artillery batteries, supported by infantry and sharp-shooters, were moved there in support and the position was made to be formidable in a short time period.

At last, with the assault troops in place and preceded by an artillery barrage to develop the enemy's lines courtesy of Alexander's artillerists, at about 4:00 P.M., Gen. Law's Alabama Brigade moved forward on the extreme right of the Southern line. They were going into a tough fight after marching most of the preceding night and much of that day without suf-ficient rations or rest. The in echelon advance was joined by the Texas Brigade moving out on Law's left, then, finally, McLaws' Division further to their left. "The Artillery Battalion, composed of Reilly's, Latham's, Garden's, and Bachman's batteries, twenty guns in all, were disposed at advantageous points upon the ridge occupied by the line of infantry."[38]

The objective in front of Hood's Division was the Round Tops, the boulder-strewn Devil's Den intervening. Behind Devil's Den, Plum Run Valley, or the Valley of Death as it became known afterwards, separated the boulder-strewn area from the western slopes of the Round Tops. An insufficiency in numbers and stiff opposition on the right greeting them, it became quickly obvious that the advance could not adhere to the Emmitsburg Road. In order for the units of the division to maintain contact, the attack had to be veered right toward the hills. This opened up a gap between Hood and McLaws. However, if the hills could be overrun, then the movement would be able to sweep up the length of Cemetery Ridge driving the Federal line before it.

Commanding the Texas Brigade, Gen. J. B. Robertson said the division arrived at its assigned position only minutes before the advance began. The Texas Brigade formation was from the left adjoining McLaws' right and extending to the right, 3rd Arkansas (Manning), 1st Texas (Work), 4th Texas (Key) and 5th Texas (Powell). Beyond that extended Law's Ala-bama Brigade, the extreme right of the army. Behind and supporting the Texas Brigade were the other units of the division, Gen. George T. Anderson's Georgia Brigade, while Gen. Henry L. Benning's Georgia Brigade was in support of Law's Brigade.

Robertson's orders were to keep his right closed on Gen. Law's left and his left on the Emmitsburg Road. As the advance began, he saw that he could not fill that space. The only choice was to abandon the line of the road. The advance was then across the open fields fronting the Federal position. This brought them under a "a destructive fire of canister, grape, and shell from six pieces of their artillery on the mountain ... and the same number on a commanding hill but a short distance to the left of the mountain, and from the enemy's sharpshooters from behind the numerous rocks, fences, and houses in the field."[39]

Almost immediately, Gen. Hood, out front and mounted, received a severe wound to his left arm from "a spherical [case] shot which exploded some [20] or [30] feet above him — and immediately began falling from his horse — but was caught and eased down by his aides who instantly had dismounted."[40] At that point, command of the Division passed to Gen. Law, the next senior officer. Hood's wounding was witnessed by many and the news spread quickly. Lt. Col. Fremantle, the Coldstream Guardsman, said he heard that upon receiving the news of their general's wounding, "that his Texans [were] in despair."[41]

Passing to the right of the Devil's Den and upon reaching the base of Big Round Top, Law's Brigade moved to the right and in closing on him the Texas Brigade came under the fire of the main Federal line posted behind a stone fence and the many large boulders strewn across the field. Returning fire and driving the Federals before them, the 4th and 5th Texas continued to close on Law's left. At the same time, the 3rd Arkansas and 1st Texas were threatened by a Federal force on their left in a peach orchard. Benning's Brigade, crossing behind G. T. Anderson's Georgians and coming up to the left and deploying became entangled with the Texans. Attempts by their officers to untangle them under fire and in the midst of battle proved to be futile. The 15th Georgia fought the rest of the battle in the ranks of the 1st Texas.

The Texas Brigade, thus, had become split, a gap opening up as the 4th and 5th continued on to their right, the 1st Texas and 3rd Arkansas to the left. Gen. Robertson, attempting to reunite his troops, sent a message for the 4th and 5th Texas to move back to their left. The courier returned with the news that he could find only Alabama units on the right. The 4th and 5th Texas had disappeared; they were somewhere beyond in the middle of Law's Alabamians and engaged in the fight of their lives.

The 3rd Arkansas and 1st Texas came under heavy artillery fire. One of the murderously placed solid shot was seen to kill Capt. Allen of Co. H, 3rd Arkansas, and then "ricocheted, severed the right arm of the Orderly Sergeant, tore off the Third Sergeant's head, mangled a corporal's leg and shrieked off through the trees."[42] Col. Manning at the head of the 3rd Arkansas, in advancing, finding its left in the air and unsupported because of the gap opened with McLaws', was forced to face his companies on that flank toward the threat. He continued to move the regiment forward in that configuration forcing the enemy to slowly withdraw toward Little Round Top. Momentarily, he was forced to withdraw a little way to deal with another threat to his left. The arrival of the 11th and 59th Georgia regiments of Anderson's Brigade on the left took care of that problem. Not long afterward, Col. Manning suffered a concussion from a nearby artillery discharge and wounds to his head. Lt. Col. R. S. Taylor assumed command of the regiment for the remainder of the fight.

To the right of the 3rd Arkansas, A.C. Sims, in the ranks of Co. F, 1st Texas, upon reaching the assigned attack position, noticed an ordinance wagon, which to him meant "ammunition and guns." While waiting, a scant lunch was had though he found he had no appetite under the circumstances. The regimental bands attempted to play but gave off only a "plaintive sound without much music." It was a suspenseful time as they awaited orders to fall in. That came around 4:00 P.M. and as they moved forward, they first loaded their weapons and a little farther on were ordered to cap them. Capping was a simple operation and was delayed as long as possible in order to prevent accidental discharges and friendly fire injury. Emerging from the woods they crossed the Emmitsburg Road and entered the open fields beyond noting Reilly's battery set up just ahead.[43] Fifty-four pieces of Alexander's artillery opened soon thereafter and was answered by counter-battery fire from the Federal artillery opposite.

The 1st Texas fought its way to the Devil's Den in front of where Federal artillery was located. From there the battle surged back and forth. Courage abounded and Lt. Col. Work singled out W. J. Barbee, Co. L, for special praise. Barbee was assigned as a mounted courier for Gen. Hood and was one of the scouts sent out to find the enemy's line. Apparently, after completing that assignment and during the fighting on July 2, he rejoined his company. As a matter of fact, it seems that he always rejoined his company when a fight was imminent. He was not required to do that; he was a courier, officially. Someone in the line of battle remembered seeing him coming, "as fast as his little sorrel horse could run, and waving his hat as he came."[44] The horse was shot down but Barbee hit the ground running, taking his place in the line. At one point, wrote Lt. Col. Work, Barbee "mounted a rock upon the highest pinnacle of the hill [in the Devil's Den], and there, exposed to a raking, deadly fire from artillery and musketry, stood until he had fired twenty-five shots, when he received a Minie ball wound in the right thigh, and fell."[45] Although the valiant Barbee survived that wound, he was killed the next year when the brigade was in Tennessee. Later, for his valor at Gettysburg, Barbee was awarded a C.S.A. Medal of Honor.[46] In that fight, Col. Work noted also, some officers were seen to shed their swords in favor of muskets, and like Barbee, joined the ranks in the desperate fray.

Later in the evening, his left flank becoming exposed, Lt. Col. Work was forced to fall back. Leaving a few men with the regimental colors under the command of Capt. H.E. Moss, Co. D, 1st Texas, to cover the retreat, the remainder of the regiment withdrew to the cover of a stone fence about 100 yards in the rear. Others, seeing the colors remaining in place refused to withdraw. Later, the withdrawn troops led by Maj. F. S. Bass returned to the forward position.[47]

In the 4th Texas prior to their attack, J. M. Polk, Co. I, and his comrades gathered around Lt. Matt Beasley, partly to commiserate and partly to tease. Beasley had been ordered to take command of Co. H, for the coming fight. That company had the reputation of being a bad luck outfit. "They had never gone into a fight and [come] out with a captain or lieutenant." Eyeing the condemned gravely, they said "Good-bye; you are gone now," one adding, "I am sorry for you, but I can't help you any."[48] Beasley failed to live — or die — up to their expectations. He survived, the only captain of that company to ever come out of a fight intact.

The 4th and 5th Texas' line of attack, once entrapped within the confines of Law's Alabamians, carried them to the northwestern slope of Big Round Top and then beyond into Plum Run Valley and against Little Round Top. Polk, Co. I, 4th Texas, estimated the distance from their starting point to a rock fence at the foot of the hill (Round Top) to be 300 or 400 yards. Across the way they could see the Stars and Stripes afloat on the breeze. As they advanced, the Federal batteries opened, killing and wounding many. "No time for shining shoes," he said. In the excitement of the moment he did not remember crossing over a rock wall. On up the hill, he stepped behind a boulder to reload and behind glimpsed Reilly's battery at work "a solid blaze of fire in front of his battery." He saw Bill Smith fall nearby and later expressed doubt that his wife back home in Texas ever knew what happened to him. No graves registration personnel, no dog tags in those days and often the dead were buried hastily in mass graves. With no records kept usually, the internees thus vanished, were never to be seen again by those at home awaiting their return.

Reaching the top of the hill, the Federal batteries were found to be abandoned with only a few Federal dead remaining. J. Q. Harris was ahead of Polk, and, putting his hand on one of the tubes was surveying the scene even as the minies whizzed closely by. As Polk watched in horror, a shell burst near them and a piece of shrapnel went through Harris' chest leaving in its wake " a wound that Polk thought he could put his arm through." "[Harris'] face turned as white as cotton, and strange to say, he turned around and tried to walk in that condition, but fell over and was dead in less than five minutes."[49]

In the exposed ranks drawn up to begin the advance, John C. West, Co. E, 4th Texas, said they were under artillery fire for a half hour before moving forward. Noting that a good many soldiers around him were killed, he said one of them only a few feet away had his "head knocked off," an unnerving sight for any soldier, much less for one experiencing his first battle. His reaction was that he "felt as if [he] would never see [his children] again."[50]

Through the "fog of battle," D. U. Barziza, Co. C, 4th Texas, glimpsed Gen. Longstreet "sitting on his horse like an iron man with his spyglass to his eye," coolly watching the effects of his corps' artillery support. In the rain of Federal counter battery fire, "limbs of trees fell and crashed around him, yet he sat as unmoved as a statue." Said Barziza, "I really believe he loves the music of cannon-shot; if so, it is an affection that is not indulged in by his faithful soldiers."[51] As noted earlier, Longstreet's demeanor was what was expected of their leaders by the men of the Texas Brigade, and, for that matter, by the rest of the army.

Maj. John P. Bane, 4th Texas, assumed command of the regiment during the attack as his superiors were felled one by one. He described his regiment's advance as at the "double-quick." D. U. Barziza, Co. C, 4th Texas, thought it more a "wild, frantic and desperate run, yelling, screaming and shouting; over ditches, up and down hill, bursting through garden fences and shrubbery, occasionally dodging the head as a bullet whistled by the ear."[52] They encountered Federal skirmishers and came under artillery fire. They were successful in driving the Federal skirmish line back but then encountered the main line in "heavy, wooded ground, sheltering themselves behind rocks, from which, after a sharp contest, he was driven to the heights beyond, in our front and in close proximity of the mountain (Round Top)." It was here that Maj. Bane learned of the severe wounds received by Col. Key and Lt. Col. Carter and took command of the regiment. Val Giles, Co. B, 4th Texas, said that "order and discipline were gone and every fellow was his own general. Private soldiers gave commands as loud as the officers. Nobody paid any attention to either."[53]

After Second Manassas, J. J. Haynes, Co. B, 4th Texas, had been assigned to the Litter Corps (stretcher-bearers for the wounded). He did not want to leave his company, but out of his strong sense of duty, he accepted the assignment without complaint. At Gettysburg the Litter Corps was busy, to say the least, and "no man worked harder or exposed himself more recklessly than Haynes." At one point, while moving forward, a "bomb shell" struck soft earth just in front of him and, penetrating to some depth "exploded with a tremendous roaring crash under his feet." Witnesses nearby saw, "[m]an, litter, bandages, canteens of water, old clothes and all went up in a cloud of dust and smoke." Everyone thought him a goner for sure. But slowly, as the dust and smoke cleared, Haynes was seen to rise shakily to his feet. Then, "[d]rawing his sleeve across his dusty brow, he faced the enemy ... took off his old wool hat, waved it high over his head, and shouted at the top of his voice: 'Hurrah for hell! Damn you, shoot again.'"[54] General Robertson complimented him as being the "bravest man in Lee's Army."

With its ranks decimated, the 4th Texas was forced to fall back to the skirt of woods behind. There, according to Val Giles, Co. B, 4th Texas, Major Jefferson Rogers, 5th Texas, "mounted an old log near 'his boulder' and began a 4th of July speech" in which he was a little ahead of time since it was only July 2nd. Nobody was paying any attention to Rogers who, along with Capt. Cousins, 4th Alabama, were the only two men standing.[55] Joined by the 5th Texas and returning to the attack, it proved to be impossible to break the Federal line. Once more, with the support of the 44th and 48th Alabama, the Federal line was charged but like the others was repulsed. The Federal position was formidable "a mass of rock and boulders amid which a mountain goat would have reveled."[56] The attack in that sector had failed to carry the enemy positions.

Later, during that night a low stone barricade was thrown up for protection. Giles said that during that dreadful night at Gettysburg "[o]fficers were cross to the men, and the men were equally cross to the officers. It was the same way with our enemies. We could hear the Yankee officer on the crest of the ridge in front of us cursing the men by platoons, and the men telling him to go to a country not very far away from us just at that time."[57] To his left and sheltered behind a tree, he saw a soldier from the 3rd Arkansas loading and firing, all the time singing at the top of his lungs, "Now let the wide world wag as it will, I'll be gay and happy still."[58] There they remained until withdrawn late on July 3.[59]

Wounded "threw the thigh," as he put it, Jeremiah Caddell, Co. I, 4th Texas, was left behind when the regiment withdrew down the hill. Later, under cover of darkness, Federal soldiers came down to repossess their former positions and look for any rebel wounded to take into custody. Caddell, lying face down, did not move and thus avoided capture. Later, using his musket as a crutch he was able to make his way down the hill to his company. There he learned of others killed or wounded, including his company commander, Capt. Winkler, wounded in the thigh also.[60]

In the ranks of the 5th Texas, at the word "Forward," the troops moved forward at about 4:00 P.M. They quickly came under sharpshooter fire from the stone fence, presumably, the extension of the same one encountered by the 4th Texas advancing on their left. The 5th Texans drove the Blue riflemen from their position, they retreating up the hillside and taking up another position. The Texans took a few moments to rest and realign before jumping the stone fence and moving on. The Federals once more fled upon their approach taking a third position, this time on Little Round Top. Because of the rocky nature of the terrain, the 5th Texans were unable to dislodge the Federals from their strong position. In the saddle between the two hills, which came to be known as the Slaughter Pen, many casualties were suffered. Taking shelter behind the many boulders they were able to direct an effective fire upon their tormentors similarly sheltered by rocks further up the hillside.

Taking shelter behind a tree, Nicholas Pomeroy, Co. A, 5th Texas, said it was poor protection as "numberless bullets ... came pouring down with their wicked whizzing noise striking the rocks ... and some knocked off the bark quite close." Then, he "was struck by a bullet that glanced along [his] right side tearing the flesh and lacerating [his] ribs, and at the same instant one passed through the lower joint of [his] little finger of [his] right hand." The wound to his side, although not too serious, was very painful. Falling back down the hillside, he saw the flag of the 5th Texas on the ground, its bearer, T. W. Fitzgerald, nearby but severely wounded. As he watched, John Morris of Co. A, dashed forward from behind a rock, and although shot through the right arm, grabbed the flag with his left, and "amidst a [fusillade] of bullets rushed down the rocky hillside, and ... brought it out safely and left it with [the] regiment where it rallied at the foot of the hill."[61] Regimental flags were treasured items and the 5th Texas' colors were not going to suffer the same fate as those of the 1st Texas' colors at Sharpsburg.

In the middle of the fight, John Stevens, Co. K, 5th Texas, watched as two twin brothers, members of Co. C, and separated from their company, came up next to him and took up the fight. "In a moment [he saw] one of them shot down by [his] side. The other brother caught hold of him as he fell and gently laid him down on the ground, and as he did so he also received a death shot. This was a very affecting scene — those two boys were twin brothers, so much alike that you could hardly tell them apart. They were always together — where you saw one you saw the other. They had passed safely through all the previous battles unhurt — now they die together." Others came up and when it was over, Stevens said six bodies lay at his feet.

Feeling a saber slap on his back, he heard a command to throw down his weapon. Looking around, much to his surprise, he saw that "the woods behind [him] were full of Yankees" and that he and a goodly number of his comrades were surrounded by the men in blue. Marched up Round Top, they passed through the Federal line that they had so recently assaulted. He was chagrined to observe just how thinly the Federal line was spread. There was only one line of battle buttressed by an even thinner line of cavalry deployed fifty yards behind "to keep the infantry from breaking when we charged them." Five hundred yards behind them was a supply train of some 4,000 wagons he estimated. At that point, he realized how close they had come to victory. Said he, "Had Gen. Hood not been wounded and had we been properly led into this battle, we would have gone through this line like a deer in a walk, and right into their wagon train, as we had done so often before."[62] Ruefully, he noted, it was not to be. Instead, Stevens was to be confined at, first, Fort Delaware, Delaware, and then Point Lookout, Maryland, until exchanged in November 1864, another whole story in itself.

Meanwhile, on their right and further around the base of Little Round Top, the 15th Alabama was having its fight with Col. Joshua L. Chamberlain's 20th Maine. Fighting in the ranks of Co. F, 5th Texas, to William Fletcher, the hill became "well photographed" in his memory and he learned only sometime later "that the peak was called Round Top or 'Heights.'"[63]

Lt. Col. King Bryan, 5th Texas, seeking out his colonel for orders, found Col. Powell severely wounded. Mark Smither, Co. D, 5th Texas, was witness and said that the colonel was waving his saber and cheering the men on when "Lt Harper was shot down at his side and the Col caught him as he was staggering and helped him down and he had hardly got straight himself before he was struck in the left side the bullet passing out of his backbone."[64] In a rain of bullets, Smither ran to his colonel's side and lowered him to a place of safety behind a rock. Lt. Col. Bryan received a wound to his left arm and noting that his colonel's wound was severe, he feared that it was mortal.[65] His own wound began hemorrhaging and he was forced to leave the field or bleed to death. At that point command of the regiment devolved upon Major Rogers. He, responding to orders from "an unknown source," withdrew the regiment to the location of its second position during the attack on the side of Round Top.

From there another attack was launched only to be once more repulsed. Withdrawing "it was discovered for the first time that nearly two-thirds of [the] officers and men had been killed and wounded." Another attack was ordered in which the 5th Texas "advanced boldly over the ground strewn with the bodies of their dead and dying comrades to the base of what they knew to be an impregnable fortification."[66] Heroic intent and valiant actions notwithstanding, in danger of being flanked, the regiment was finally withdrawn once again to the side of Round Top. There, a rock breastwork was thrown up hastily to provide what protection was available.

Later, William Fletcher, Co. F, 5th Texas, said word was passed along the line to prepare to advance once again. Shocked and feeling a "cowardly horror" creeping over him, he felt it would be "the ending" of him, given what he had seen in the earlier attempts. Seeing no

Col. Robert M. Powell, 5th Texas, last commander of the Texas Brigade at Appomattox.

chance of success and feeling they had gotten a "good whipping" all along the line, he was weighing the respective merits of "disgrace or death." At about that time and adding to his anxiety, Confederate batteries opened to the rear and, firing low, he said were "doing fine work on our position." All was confusion in the gathering dark but finally word was gotten to the errant batteries to cease fire. The attack was canceled, much to Fletcher's relief and undoubtedly to that of all of his comrades as well.[67]

Left behind on Round Top, the severely wounded Col. Powell raised his head and surveyed the scene around him. The only live man he saw was Sgt. Ross who "leisurely approached the enemy's lines and taking his ramrod which had been left leaning against a rock, he walked deliberately to the rear." Powell could see bodies lying all around him as silence descended on the scene. As darkness came on, there was the sound of movement into the area. They were Federal soldiers come to gather up the wounded and make them prisoners of war.[68]

Capt. Tacitus Clay, Co. I, 5th Texas

Later, Maj. Rogers cited Capt. John S. Cleveland, Co. H, and Capt. Tacitus Clay, Co. I, for their handling of the right and left wings of the regiment, respectively. Also cited, the hardy band of regimental color bearers, they always in front and first to fall. T. W. Fitzgerald, Co. A, was badly wounded "far in front." Then, somewhat at variance with Nicholas Pomeroy's eyewitness account of Fitzgerald's heroism, J. A. Howard, Co. B, took the flag and was "almost instantly killed." Then Sgt. W. S. Evans, Co. F, took the colors up and "planted them defiantly in the face of the foe during the remainder of the fight."[69]

They had done their best and paid dearly in the effort. "It is very true that these men were tried and seasoned soldiers, with powers of endurance equal to any, yet they were not made of iron, and there is a limit to all human endeavor."[70]

As Hood's Division had moved forward and become engaged, the left of the Confederate line, Ewell's Corps, began its diversionary demonstration in the form of an artillery barrage. On Hood's left, McLaws' Division moved forward overrunning the heavily defended peach orchard. According to Gen. Longstreet's report of the action, the enemy occupying the position opposite the attack of McLaws' Division was "soon dislodged and driven back upon a commanding hill, which is so precipitous and rough as to render it difficult of ascent. Numerous stone fences about its base added greatly to its strength. The enemy, taking shelter behind these, held them, one after another, with great pertinacity."[71] The position proved to be too strong to be carried and both McLaws' and Hood's Divisions were forced to fall back and hold what they could as night fell.

At about 6:00 P.M., to the left of McLaws' Division, units of A.P. Hill's Corps, seeing an opportunity, moved out to cross the deadly 1400 yards that separated them from the Federal positions on Cemetery Ridge. Meeting heavy opposition, they nonetheless were able to make it to the slope of the ridge where they were turned back by a series of strong counterattacks. At about the same time, Gen. Ewell sent Gen. Edward Johnson's Division against Culp's Hill. The attack carried into the Federal lines and the fighting was fierce. At one time, Gen. Early's command was within spitting distance of the Federal artillery position on Cemetery Hill but was unable to carry it and forced to abandon the attack.

As the darkness deepened, an uneasy quiet pervaded the battlefield punctuated by the cries of the wounded yet uncollected on the field. Among the countless wounded was Gen. Hood. Gen. McLaws saw the loss of two of his brigade commanders, Gens. William Barksdale and Paul Semmes, both wounded mortally. Texas Brigade commander Gen. Robertson had received a leg wound which put him out of action temporarily. He was moved back from the front several hundred yards as Lt. Col. Work, 1st Texas, took command at the front. Late that evening "a terrific fire of artillery was concentrated against the hill, occupied by [the 1st Texas] and many were killed and wounded, some losing their heads, and others so horribly mutilated and mangled that their identity could scarcely be established."[72]

Under the cover provided by the night, the wounded were removed and captured artillery pieces withdrawn. At about 2:00 A.M., the 3rd Arkansas and 1st Texas were moved to their right and rejoined with the 4th and 5th Texas. A. C. Sims, Co. F, 1st Texas, was placed on picket duty there. For two hours he stood "between the two armies and listened to the cries and groans of the wounded and dying, and to their pleading for water. One man who lay just in front of [him implored], 'oh, pardner, bring me a drink of water, I'll assure you that no one will hurt you, My leg is shot off or I would come to you. I'll give you a dollar for a drink of water. I'll give you all the money I have for a drink of water."[73] Sims made no reply; he could not leave his post and he had no water to give anyway. Burial of the dead did not begin until the next day.

Even though the day's fight had not gone in favor of the Gray, some ground had been gained. Gen. Longstreet called it "the best three hours' fighting ever done by any troops on any battle-field."[74] As the third day of the great battle approached, Gen. Pickett's Division was now within marching distance of the front. And finally, Gen. Stuart's cavalry had returned and was on the left flank of the army. With the army still in high spirits, Gen. Lee determined to renew the fight. The depleted and exhausted Texas Brigade would only be a spectator to that day's events. They were to witness one of the most dramatic events to ever be played out on the continent of North America.

Friday, July 3, dawned clear and with the promise of it being a hot day. With the memories of yesterday's delays fresh in his mind and the knowledge of their military costs, Gen. Lee was at First Corps headquarters on the right at an early hour. Once again and based on overnight scouting reports, Gen. Longstreet renewed his appeal for a turning movement around the Federal left. All of this Gen. Lee heard with a patience somewhat renewed by several hours sleep. Then, having heard his stolid lieutenant out, he once again expressed his plan to attack the Federals where they were, now on Cemetery Ridge, and with the three divisions of Longstreet's Corps — Hood's, McLaws' and Pickett's. Longstreet remained unconvinced of the plan's chances of success and told his chief so: "General, I have been a soldier all my life. I have been with soldiers engaged in fights by couples, by squads, companies, regiments, divisions, and armies, and should know, as well as any one, what soldiers can do. It is my opinion that no fifteen thousand men ever arrayed for battle can take that position."[75] However, Lee was convinced that his plan would work and had confidence in his army's *elan* to accomplish the task. It had worked miracles before; why not now?

To Longstreet's arguments against using the exhausted and depleted divisions of McLaws and Hood, Gen. Lee gave in. They had been marched hard and fought bravely the day before Because Pickett's Division was fresh, the march from Chambersburg, notwithstanding, and had not been involved in the prior two days' fight, it was designated to be the spear point of the attack. To replace McLaws and Hood, Gen. Lee chose units from Gen. A. P. Hill's Corps — the divisions of Pettigrew and Trimble. Once again in support, Ewell's Corps was to renew the thus far unsuccessful attack on the north end of the Federal fishhook.

The basis for the plan being laid, Gens. Lee and Longstreet rode together to the launching point for the coming attack to study the tactical situation and the correct siting of the supporting artillery. In charge of the artillery was First Corps battalion commander, Col. Edward Porter Alexander, thought by some then and most all later to be the best artillerist in the Army of Northern Virginia. In advance of the infantry positions on Seminary Ridge, Col. Alexander skillfully placed the 172 pieces of artillery that he had at his disposal to support the coming infantry assault.[76] The attacking infantry units were quietly moved into their assigned places shielded from the watchful eyes across the way by the trees lining the Confederate positions on Seminary Ridge.

With all in readiness, Gens. Lee, Longstreet and Hill conferred in order to clear up last minute details. Designated by Gen. Lee, the point of attack on the center of the Federal line on Cemetery Ridge was a "little clump of trees" known thereabouts as Ziegler's Grove. Around the clump of trees were some wooden fences and low stone walls behind which Federal infantry was seen to be strongly ensconced. As an anticipatory quiet fell over the front, the stage was set for the advance of Pickett's Division and its supporting units from Hill's Corps.

Prior to the launching of the attack, a concentrated artillery barrage was to maul and demoralize the Blue defenders on Cemetery Hill and to suppress any counter-battery fire. The attacking columns, still hidden from view of the Federal lines, were to commence the advance once the barrage was lifted. Gen. Longstreet was in overall command of the assault. The signal for the commencement of the artillery barrage to be laid down by Col. Alexander's massed batteries was to be quick-firing of two cannon. Satisfied that the details were understood, Gen. Lee folded his map and the three parted to their respective sites to view the assault.

An eerie silence pervaded the field as if in anticipation of the carnage that surely must follow. From the front, first one cannon and then a second broke the stillness that had enshrouded the field. It was then 1:00 P.M., July 3, 1863, with the fate of two nations hanging in the balance.

The twin echoes resounding across the fields and hills had not had time to die out before the booming of the massed batteries of Col. Alexander's formation began to surge forth from one end of the artillery line to the other. The very earth itself shook and some told later of it being heard as far away as Philadelphia. William Fletcher, Co. F, 5th Texas, and his comrades from their vantage point on the Confederate right were in a position to watch the drama unfolding. To them there "was sure enough noise, from the roar of guns and bursting of shells, to have moved the Yanks when the Rebs charged, if they had been moveable; but they were like those in front of Hood — had a good thing and knew it."[77]

After two hours of bombardment, a lull in the counter battery firing by the Federal artillery prompted the calling forth of the assaulting column. Gen. Pickett asked of his Corps commander, "General, shall I advance?" To his friend with whom he had gone over the wall at Chapultepec Castle as members of the U.S. 8th Infantry Regiment fifteen years earlier during the Mexican War, the reluctant Longstreet could only nod his head in the affirmative. To which, the courtly Pickett, his perfumed hair in ringlets, saluted, saying, "I am going to move forward, sir."

The infantry tide swept forward, skirmishers deployed, clearing the fencing in their paths with ease. As the advance closed on the front marked by the low stone walls, Federal volley fire began. The Federal artillery was throwing grape into the closing ranks. For the first time, the Confederate ranks were halted and ordered to return fire. All was enshrouded in artillery and musketry smoke as well as confusion as the converging Confederate ranks became mixed in closing on the little clump of trees.

Of the thousands that had stepped off from Seminary Ridge only minutes before only hundreds were at and then over the wall as the massed Federal ranks closed in. There were no reinforcements to bolster and enlarge the small breach. The struggle continued hand to hand for a time, the Confederate numbers dwindling even more quickly. Finally, with any hopes of victory gone, those survivors not killed or captured began to pull back, painfully returning from whence they had come with such high hopes and which now seemed an eternity ago. To their rear and all along the victorious Federal line there issued forth from thousands of Blue throats the cry of "Fredericksburg, Fredericksburg, Fredericksburg!" A bitter score had been settled.

As the broken and bleeding returned, they passed through Col. Alexander's artillery line and sought out the safety of the tree-lined ridge beyond. Coming out to meet them and offer words of encouragement was Gen. Lee mounted astride Traveler and accompanied by Gen. Longstreet and some of his staff. Meeting a disconsolate Gen. Pickett attempting to rally his battered command, Gen. Lee told him to "place your division in rear of this hill, and be ready to repel the advance of the enemy should they follow up their advantage." Grief-stricken at the losses and defeat, Pickett could only reply, "General Lee, I have no division now." Gen. Lee tried to console him, taking personal responsibility for the failed attack: "Upon my shoulders rest the blame," he said.[78]

Although the Texas Brigade was not involved in the dramatic events of July 3, the 1st Texans did have the unique experience of a Federal cavalry charge. As they had ended the day before the brigade remained in those positions. The 1st Texas remained posted behind a stone fence to guard against Federal cavalry reported to be in the area. In was a demonstrated fact that cavalry was no match against infantry entrenched or arranged in squares. The frontal charge was generally an outmoded maneuver by the time of the Civil War. By then cavalry was used largely to gather intelligence, to protect the flanks of their armies and to hound relentlessly enemy troops broken and in retreat. Nonetheless, elements of Gen. Judson Kilpatrick's U.S. Cavalry Brigade led by Gen. Elon Farnsworth attempted a frontal assault against the front of the 1st Texas. W. T. White, Co. K, 1st Texas, said they were behind a three and a half foot stone fence and that the Federal cavalry made a direct frontal charge; it was devastated by the 1st Texas musketry, withdrew and charged a second time with the same results.[79]

The charges ended unsuccessfully and resulted in Gen. Farnsworth's death. George Todd, Co. A, 1st Texas, said they killed or wounded most all in the front of the charge but they did turn both flanks, some getting in their rear, capturing some teamsters and litter bearers.[80] W. T. White, said Gen. Farnsworth was shot from the saddle by a Co. L, soldier and when ordered to surrender, the general drew his revolver and shot himself in the head.[81] One of Todd's comrades, Bent Allen "jumped over the wall, and got Gen. Farnsworth's epaulets and spurs."[82] Undoubtedly, there were occasions when elements of the brigade encountered cavalry. However, there seems to have been only two noteworthy ones, the first at Gaines' Mill and the second at Gettysburg.

All day July 4, the two armies kept their respective positions while 1,500 miles away at Vicksburg, Mississippi, the Confederate garrison there surrendered to the besieging armies of Gen. U. S. Grant. Later that night, in a driving rain, the Army of Northern Virginia, with a train seventeen miles long transporting its wounded, began to take up the march that would return it to the soil of Virginia. The retreat was not closely pressed by the Army of the Potomac although there were harassing cavalry probes. Once across the Potomac, the Army of Northern Virginia, its life on the wane, would never again venture across that waterway in search of battle on enemy soil.

The march south became more leisurely with the Texas Brigade finally landing at Port Royal on the Rappahannock about twenty miles below Fredericksburg. It remained there for the next month and a half before being called forth once more. This time the call took it away from the ranks of the Army of Northern Virginia on a difficult assignment in an entirely different theater of the continuing war.

CHAPTER 11

"[T]he meanest, most unsatisfactory place I struck during the whole war"[1]: Operation "Westward Ho" to Chickamauga, September 1863

Even before the twin debacles at Gettysburg and Vicksburg in early July 1863, Confederate leaders were agreed that if the war was to be won, their armies would have to strike ever more boldly. Their only disagreement was where to strike the most effectively given their limited, dwindling manpower situation. While passing through Richmond with his corps following the conclusion of the Suffolk campaign, Gen. Longstreet paid a visit to James A. Seddon. The Confederate secretary of war listened politely as, in the course of their conversation, Longstreet suggested that his corps be sent to bolster Gen. Braxton Bragg's Army of Tennessee, even then in the process of losing the strategic rail center at Chattanooga in south central Tennessee.

At the time, Seddon dismissed Longstreet's proposal, mainly because, so Longstreet thought, he knew Lee would be opposed to any reduction of his army. When Longstreet rejoined Lee, he presented his plan to him. According to Longstreet, Lee was seriously impressed with the need for an offensive campaign but was opposed to dividing his own forces. So, that was that for the time being. Ultimately, the plan to raid into Pennsylvania was adopted. Pursued to its disastrous conclusion, a reconsideration of the earlier, shelved plan was brought forth once more.

Meanwhile, Confederate Gen. Braxton Bragg's Army of Tennessee and General William S. Rosecrans' Federal Army of the Cumberland were at loggerheads in central Tennessee. Following a bloody stalemate — 25,000 casualties — experienced at Murfreesboro (Stone's River), Tennessee, in late 1862 and early 1863, the respective armies had fallen back, eyeing each other warily from a respectful distance. Bragg, with about 43,000 troops, was behind the Duck River around Tullahoma, Tennessee. Rosecrans remained in the vicinity of Murfreesboro.

For six months the standoff around Tullahoma dragged on, Presidents Lincoln and Davis urging action by their respective commanders. Refusing to be hurried, it was not until June 24, 1863 — about the time the Army of Northern Virginia was marching into Pennsylvania — that Rosecrans felt sufficiently prepared to move forward into the Cumberland Plateau, the tactically difficult and logistically isolated terrain separating him from his opponent. The ultimate objective was to outmaneuver Bragg as bloodlessly as possible and capture and occupy the important rail hub at Chattanooga lying behind Tullahoma.

In conjunction, as early as March 1863, Gen. Ambrose Burnside, of Fredericksburg notoriety, with two divisions of the IX Federal Corps, was ordered to enter Kentucky and assume command of the Department of the Ohio. The movement's objectives were twofold: to interdict the railroad connections between Tennessee and Virginia and to liberate the pro–Union population of eastern Tennessee. Additionally, the region was a "fertile farming area." "East Tennessee's rich grain fields supplied not only wheat, corn and hay, but beef, pork, bacon, horses, and mules. It was a vital region for the armies of the Confederacy."[2] The campaign there centered on the occupation of Knoxville, thereby establishing a threat to Bragg's right flank. In response, Gen. Simon B. Buckner was ordered from Mobile to assume command of the Department of East Tennessee and organize for the defense of the area.

Rosecrans, in a series of deceptions and flanking movements, often described as brilliant, but not helped any by bad roads and bad weather in the form of torrential rains, on July 1, forced Bragg to retreat beyond the Tennessee River and into Chattanooga. The city, being too well fortified for a frontal assault, another stalemate developed. For the next month and a half the two armies, separated by the slowly flowing waters of the river, gathered strength and resolve for the next phase of their continuing struggle.

It was on August 16, that Rosecrans felt sufficiently ready to put the Army of the Cumberland in motion toward the crossings lying west of the city. It was a good move because Bragg was anticipating otherwise, that Rosecrans would move upon the city from the east. It made more tactical sense, Bragg reasoned, that moving from that direction the Army of the Cumberland would be in closer physical proximity with Burnside once that army began advancing from the direction of Knoxville. However, Rosecrans chose the western approaches because, among other reasons, he knew that that was not what Bragg would be expecting and, for another, the railroads then in operation in that quarter provided a better line of supply.

Of course, the presence of Gen. Burnside in East Tennessee complicated greatly the situation for Bragg. Should the Federals combine to take Chattanooga and its rail links, it would lay open the way to the heart of the South, to Atlanta. It was that tactical environment and in response to Bragg's continuing pleas for reinforcement, that led first to Gen. Simon B. Buckner's assignment to Knoxville to contest Burnside's efforts there and to Longstreet's detachment from the Army of Northern Virginia to reinforce Bragg's army.

Rosecrans' campaign plan proposed to cut Bragg's rail supply lines, mainly with Atlanta, and effectively squeeze the Confederate force between his army and that of Gen. Burnside moving down from Knoxville. In order to accomplish this, a strong feint was directed toward the river crossing points north of Chattanooga. The ruse proved successful and, Bragg falling for it, blundered further by failing to protect his other flank south of the city. Taking advantage, Rosecrans, on September 4, with the main body of his army, crossed the Tennessee River relatively unopposed around Bridgeport, Alabama. With Rosecrans' army over the river in strength and beyond his left flank, Bragg realized he had no alternative but to abandon the city and withdraw south in order to protect his line of supply leading to Atlanta. This he did by September 8, employing a little deception himself by feigning confusion and disorder in his ranks in hopes of luring his pursuers into an unfavorable disposition. These developments resulted in the recall of Buckner's troops from Knoxville to the aid of Bragg. Other reinforcements included the divisions of Gens. John C. Breckinridge and W. H. T. Walker and two brigades under the command of Gens. John Gregg and Evander McNair sent from Gen. Joseph E. Johnston's army in Mississippi. Altogether, these reinforcements numbered about 20,000 men. On September 6, Gen. Burnside occupied the abandoned city.

Further, relying on "planted intelligence" acquired from some Confederate deserters, Rosecrans now believed Bragg's army to be beaten and in full retreat. Rosecrans, in that state of mind and unsure of Bragg's exact whereabouts, followed in three widely-separated corps columns spread over a forty mile front, the objective to parallel and outflank the retreating Confederate column. The orders to the three corps commanders were for Gen. Thomas Crittenden's three division XXI Corps to keep an eye on and occupy Chattanooga, Gen. George Thomas' four division XIV Corps to cross the mountains twenty-five miles or so south of Chattanooga and move toward Trenton, Georgia, and Gen. Alexander McCook's three division XX Corps to cross the mountains some forty-six miles south of Chattanooga and occupy Alpine, Georgia. Gen. Gordon Granger's two division Reserve Corps hovered in the rear awaiting a call. Gen. David S. Stanley's Cavalry Corps covered the flanks of the advancing army.

On September 9, about the same time that Longstreet's Corps began its trek west from Virginia, the all-important railroad hub was occupied by units of Crittenden's Corps without opposition. By mid–September, Bragg's army was not in retreat, but rather, concentrated about twenty-five miles or so south of Chattanooga around the village of Lafayette, Georgia.

Following the losses at Gettysburg and Vicksburg during the first four days of July 1863, and Bragg's retreat into north Georgia in September, the Confederate leadership was forced to revisit strategic issues. Once again, Longstreet approached Secretary of War Seddon, this time by letter in which he resurrected his original plan to reinforce Bragg. Several days later, the subject came up when Longstreet was discussing the matter with Gen. Lee. At the time, "[Lee] inquired if [he] was willing to go West and take charge there."[3] Longstreet readily assented his willingness to go but only provided he be allowed time to gain the confidence of the troops that might fall under his command and that should he succeed in routing the enemy, means for an aggressive follow-up would be available. Ultimately, Longstreet's proposal was approved by President Davis. "The transportation was ordered [about September 6] by the [Q]uartermaster's [D]epartment at Richmond."[4]

Longstreet's Corps began the move about September 9. As they arrived in Richmond, they were welcomed as heroes. They drew new uniforms from the Quartermaster Department, a rare event in the armies of the Confederacy. It was the donning of those new garments that would lead to a serious and unintended consequence in the coming events in Georgia. While in Richmond, some men of Hood's Division sought out their chief where he was still recovering from his Gettysburg wound and loudly insisted he accompany them on their next adventure. The aggressive Hood could not resist such an invitation.

Due to the recent and severe losses that the corps had suffered at Gettysburg, organizational changes were considered necessary. At Gen. Longstreet's suggestion, Gen. Lee detached Pickett's decimated division to duty in the Richmond defenses. After other detachments and additions, it was the divisions of Hood and McLaws, with the addition of Micah Jenkins' South Carolina Brigade, that made the journey. The corps artillery was commanded by Col. Edward Porter Alexander. Although estimates vary as to numbers, there were probably about 15,000 troops that took part in the big move.

Then, as if things were not complicated enough, on September 9, Burnside captured a 2,000 man Confederate garrison from Buckner's command left behind to defend the Cumberland Gap and the railroad traversing it. That loss severed the shortest direct rail link between Richmond and Chattanooga afforded by the Virginia and Tennessee Railroad by way of Bristol, Virginia, and Knoxville, Tennessee. The only rail routes left open were circuitous: Richmond, Petersburg, Wilmington or Charlotte, North Carolina, to Augusta, Georgia, and then by a single track through Atlanta to Catoosa Station, Ringgold and Chattanooga. What Gen. Longstreet had calculated would be a two day direct trip had now become a nine day, 900 mile one, that is, if everything worked out as planned.

Security was poor. "Every man in the ranks knew where they were going, the Northern papers were already printing stories of Longstreet's detachment for service in Tennessee."[5] An even more vexing problem was the state of Southern railroads which was not good in late 1863. The manpower demands of the war and shortages of materials had resulted in a dilapidated rail system. Southern lines were often of differing track gauges and did not connect with one another directly. Passengers traveling on more than one line frequently found it necessary to disembark with their belongings and make their way across town to the depot of the connecting line.

For the troops the journey was difficult — the trains were crowded, the weather was unseasonably hot. Seats were few and most of the men were crowded into and onto a variety of rolling stock — boxcars, flatcars, and even coal and stock cars. As Lt. Col. Moxley Sorrell, Longstreet's chief of staff, noted, "Never before were so many troops moved over such worn-out railways, none first-class from the beginning. Never before were such crazy cars ... all and every sort wobbling on the jumping strap iron used for hauling good soldiers."[6]

However, the troops being, by and large, young and exuberant, according to the few accounts of the movement that are available they viewed the whole affair as one big parade. The diarist Mary Boykin Chesnut caught a glimpse of the troops as they passed the station in Kingsville, South Carolina. "God bless the gallant fellows," "No one drunk, no rude remarks." She thought it a strange sight. "What seemed miles of platform cars, and soldiers rolled in their blankets packed in regular order, they looked like swathed mummies.... All these fine fellows going to kill or be killed, but why?... Poor children!" she mused.[7]

Of the few accounts, the experience of Kershaw's South Carolina Brigade on the trip must have been typical and is worth recounting at some length:

> Long trains of box cars had been ordered up from Richmond and the troops were loaded by one company being put inside and next on top, so one-half of the corps made the long ... journey on the top of the box cars. The cars on all railroads in which troops were transported were little more than skeleton cars; the weather being warm, the troops cut all but the frame work loose with knives and axes. They furthermore wished to see outside and witness the fine country and delightful scenery that lay along the route; nor could those inside bear the idea of being shut up in a box car while their comrades on top were cheering and yelling themselves hoarse at the waving handkerchiefs and flags in the hands of the pretty women and the hats thrown in the air by the old men and boys along the roadside as the trains sped through the towns, villages, and hamlets of the Carolinas and Georgia....
>
> The news of [their] coming had preceded [them], and at every station and road crossing the people of the surrounding country, without regard to sex or age, crowded to see [them] pass, and gave [them] their blessings and God speed as [they] swept by with lightning speed.... At the towns which [they] were forced to stop for a short time great tables were stretched, filled with the bounties of the land, while the fairest and the best women on earth stood by and ministered to every wish or want.[8]

O. T. Hanks, Co. K, 1st Texas, observed that the crowds were almost exclusively women; the only males to be seen were old men or wounded soldiers, arms in slings or hopping around on crutches or home on furlough. From the crowds would be cast various items.

They included hand–made articles of clothing, bouquets of flowers and written addresses. The latter were placed in small, split sticks so as to add heft. These would give anyone who was interested someone to write to and from whom to receive words of encouragement.[9]

All things considered, it went fairly well. There were only several untoward incidents that occurred along the way. One falls into the "boys will be boys" category and involved the Texans. It seems that during a twenty-four hour layover in Wilmington, North Carolina, a group of Texans paid the inevitable visit to Paddy's Hollow, a disreputable section of town. Becoming "boisterous, obnoxious and abusive," they set upon the city's elderly-ranked "night police" force sent to corral them. In the melee that ensued, the "roughed up nocturnal guardians limped a hasty retreat carrying their wounded with them and left the waterfront to the Lone Star victors. No arrests were made or charges filed."[10]

It was Benning's Brigade of Hood's Division that was the first to reach Atlanta on September 12. However, as they were compelled to linger there to draw rations and obtain shoes, it was the Texas Brigade that was first to arrive at what was to be the scene of the impending fight at Chickamauga. "Actually, only three of the brigades from Lee's army (Robertson's, Bennings, Law's) arrived in time to participate in the first full day of battle, September 19. Two more brigades, Kershaw's and Humphrey's, made their appearance on the 20th, the final day of action. The remaining four infantry brigades of Jenkins, Wofford, Bryan and Anderson and Alexander's artillery did not arrive until long after."[11] The newly arrived brigades were assigned to the division of Gen. Bushrod Johnson, Buckner's Corps. Gen. Longstreet and his staff did not arrive at the front until the middle of the night just a few hours prior to the last day of the battle.

Rosecrans' pursuit was hampered by poor roads and steep mountain ridges that were interspersed by deep, forbidding valleys called coves. Numerically, Rosecrans' army was inferior with approximately 57,000 total compared to Bragg's approximately 71,000. At that moment he did not fully comprehend that his piecemeal army was vulnerable, imperiled and about to come under attack. Bragg's army was arrayed north and south between Lafayette and Graysville, Tennessee, along the east side of Chickamauga Creek. The Army of Tennessee was composed of the mixed commands of Polk, Walker, Hindman, Buckner, and D. H. Hill, the latter only recently promoted lieutenant general and dispatched west from the defenses of Richmond. The right, or northern, flank of the army was screened by Gen. Nathan Bedford Forrest's cavalry while the left, or southern, flank was screened by Gen. Joe Wheeler's cavalry.

It was at that critical moment on September 10 that Gen. Bragg, knowing of Rosecrans' widely separated condition, ordered an attack. Gen. Hindman's Division, Polk's Corps and Gen. Cleburne's Division, Hill's Corps, were to move against the isolated division of Gen. James S. Negley, Gen. Thomas' XIV Corps, positioned west of Lafayette in a valley known locally as McLemore's Cove. However, things went awry when Hindman and Cleburne, disenchanted with Bragg's leadership and he with theirs, failed to carry out the attack. Several days later, on September 13, a second attack by Polk's and Walker's Corps was ordered by Bragg to be made against some units of Gen. Crittenden's XXI Corps by then located around Lee and Gordon's Mill. For similar reasons, that attack failed, also. It seemed the Army of Tennessee was verging on disintegration.

Bragg's personality played a large part in the misadventures. He had replaced Gen. P. G. T. Beauregard in command of the Army of Tennessee in June 1862. He was a difficult individual, described as "possessed of an irascible temper and was naturally disputatious." He did not get along very well with anyone. By the time Longstreet's troops reached the scene he had been in command long enough, fourteen months or so, for his subordinates to hate him thoroughly. That attitude had been transmitted readily on down to the ranks.

As a result of the bungled Southern attacks, Gen. Rosecrans was granted a reprieve and the opportunity to recoil his army from harm's way. Beating a hasty retreat and without opposition, the Army of the Cumberland, all three corps, was reconcentrating by late on September 17, around Lee and Gordon's Mill, on the west side of the Chickamauga and about halfway between Chattanooga and Lafayette. Across the Chickamauga, frustrated by his subordinates' failure to attack and his adversary's resultant escape, Gen. Bragg decided upon an all-or-nothing attack to be launched on the morning of September 18 against Gen. Crittenden's XXI Corps then forming the left, or northern, flank of the developing Federal position.

On that morning, Bragg began by moving Gen. Bushrod Johnson's Provisional Division, four brigades of infantry that would come to include Robertson's soon-to-arrive Texas Brigade, and three batteries of artillery northwestward from Lafayette seeking to flank the Federal left. Screened by the cavalry of Gen. Nathan Bedford Forrest, Johnson's Division moved up the east side of Chickamauga Creek toward a crossing point at Reed's Bridge, located southeast of Chattanooga. The plan of attack was to cross the Chickamauga, flank the Federal left, then, turning south, move toward Lee and Gordon's Mill, rolling up the position and blocking the line of retreat for Rosecrans' entire army via Rossville leading back to Chattanooga.[12] In support, other units of the army were to cross the Chickamauga upstream, that is, further south, Walker's corps at Alexander's Bridge, Buckner's Corps at Tedford's Ford and Polk's Corps at Lee and Gordon's Mill. D. H. Hill's Corps was to cover the army's left. Across the way, Gen. Rosecrans was moving quickly to reinforce his left and defend the roads comprising his line of supply and, if necessary, retreat leading back to Chattanooga.

The march of Johnson's Division north beginning on the morning of September 18 had already been underway for some time when Hood and the first elements of Longstreet's Corps arrived at Ringgold Station, a few miles southeast of Reed's Bridge.[13] The train had scarcely come to a halt when its travel-weary soldier-passengers began to disembark, musket barrels glinting in the afternoon sun, field accouterments clattering noisily at their sides. Too impatient to wait for unloading ramps to be put in place, Hood had his horse jumped from the train. Mounting Jeff Davis, a warhorse his superstitious troops thought made him bulletproof, Hood received a "rousing welcome" from the 8th Texas Cavalry, known as Terry's Rangers, as they happened to pass nearby. This was the first time the Texas Brigade had met other Texas troops in the field and "as many of them were personally known ... salutations were exchanged by the lifting of hats and the waving of handkerchiefs."[14] Spurring Jeff Davis northward, he rode hard to join Johnson's column. The orders awaiting at Ringgold from Gen. Bragg were for him to join and take command of Johnson's column.

Gen. Hood caught up with Johnson's column about 3:00 P.M., the Texas Brigade a little later. With Gen. Bragg's orders in hand, Hood assumed command. As frequently happened, by the time the attack began it was too late in the day to expect great results. The advance was held up for several hours by stiff resistance at Reed's Bridge by the Federal cavalry units of Cols. Robert Minty and John Wilder and also at the crossing points to the south. The Texas Brigade, once across the bridge, aligned with 3rd Arkansas on the left, 1st, 4th, 5th Texas, in that order, to the right, and awaited the order to move forward.

In the ranks of Co. E, 4th Texas, John C. West, still whole and with the Gettysburg experience under his belt, while awaiting the order to move forward had the opportunity

to observe the effect the presence of two hostile armies had on some of the civilians populating the area. He saw men, women and children attempting to move to their rear and out
of harm's way. "One poor woman was overloaded with coverlets, tin pans and other utensils,
with a child on each side and two or three bawling behind. She fell down two or three
times, but scrambled on for life while muskets sputtered in the surrounding hills."[15]

When they moved forward finally, the day turned out to be only preliminary—skirmishing with light casualties suffered. Hood's command drove away the defenders at Reed's
Bridge and then advanced forward a short distance to the site of a place called Jay's Sawmill.
Turning by his left flank, from there he advanced southward toward Alexander's Bridge to
link up with the other Confederate units crossing in that area. All the while the movement
was being harassed by Federal cavalry.

It is not surprising to hear one member of Co. A, 5th Texas, saying that the Texas
Brigade, on September 18, did not exchange any shots with the enemy.[16] Notwithstanding,
J. M. Polk, Co. I, 4th Texas, said that they "ran into some Federal cavalry and knocked
some of them off their horses."[17] Probably the most important thing that occurred to the
men in the ranks was that some new Federal cavalry hats were acquired by some lucky Texans.

That night the Texans bivouacked in deep woods just east of a site known thereabouts
as the Viniard House on the Lafayette-Chattanooga Road. While the troops were setting
up their bivouac, Gen. Hood rode in search of army headquarters to report and receive further orders for the morrow. There he met some of the officers of the Army of Tennessee for
the first time and was stunned by their demoralization and defeatism. It was something he
had not encountered in the Army of Northern Virginia. Even his old friend Gen. John C.
Breckinridge of Kentucky, a former vice president of the United States, was less than optimistic about their chances. Hood "found [him] ... seated by the root of a tree, with a heavy
slouch hat upon his head. When ... [Hood] ... stated that [they] would rout the enemy the
following day, [Breckinridge] sprang to his feet, exclaiming, 'My dear Hood, I am delighted
to hear you say so. You give me renewed hope; [adding] God grant it may be so.'"[18]

Across the ill-defined line, Gen. Rosecrans' command could be heard preparing for
the morrow, axes felling trees, logs being arranged as breastworks.

"The sun at Chickamauga rose blood red on the morning of September 19."[19] What
was an approximately six mile front was where the battle of the next two days would be
fought. The field of battle lay within the confines of an elongated area that was defined by
the northward-flowing branches of the Chickamauga River to the east and the spurs of the
massive rock formation known as Missionary Ridge to the west. That ridge, breached by
two passes behind the battlefield, McFarland's and Rossville, afforded the only routes of
retreat for the Federal army, should they be needed, back to the safety of the Chattanooga
defenses. Beyond Missionary Ridge, farther west, lay Lookout Mountain, its heights overlooking the city of Chattanooga. The field of the coming action was bisected by a road running south from Chattanooga through the Rossville Gap in Missionary Ridge thence to
Rossville, Lee and Gordon's Mill, Lafayette and beyond The countryside at that time was
heavily wooded with very thick underbrush. It was a rough terrain that made it difficult for
troops to maneuver in, for command and control and for artillery. There was a scattering
of farms with their usual small buildings, fields and pastures over which the battle would
inevitably spill.

Commenting on the terrain, Val Giles, Co. B, 4th Texas, said that the "underbrush
and muscadine vines were so thick and interwoven that it was almost impossible to get

through," and that, as a result, the "lines were broken and irregular." The effect on military formations for the individual soldier was that "he [was] in big luck if he [could] keep in touch with his file leader and hear the commands of his officers." He added that, "[s]oldiers in pictures who stand up in unbroken lines and fire by platoons don't represent the soldiers who fought the Battle of Chickamauga.... [A]s Chickamauga was a battle in the wilderness, such battle formation was an utter impossibility."[20]

During the night of September 18–19, both armies altered their positions, somewhat. West of the Chickamauga, Forrest's cavalry still screened the Confederate right at Reed's Bridge. To Forrest's left were arranged Walker's Corps, Polk's Corps, Longstreet's Corps under Hood's command in Longstreet's absence and Buckner's Corps. Remaining east of the river and forming the Confederate left were D. H. Hill's Corps, Hindman's Division of Polk's Corps, and Breckinridge's Division of D. H. Hill's Corps. Gen. Joe Wheeler's cavalry screened the left flank.

The first full day of battle got under way on the north end of the line as planned. Bragg's plan of attack was directed toward what he thought to be the northernmost flank of the Federal line defended by Crittenden's XXI Federal Corps around Lee and Gordon's Mill. However, during the night and early morning, Gen. George Thomas' XIV Federal Corps had been moved to extend the line even farther northward. Gen. Granger's Reserve Corps was located farther north around Rossville. McCook's XX Corps held the Federal right around McLemore's Cove.

It was Gen. Thomas who opened the ball and seeking out the Confederate lines sent a Federal reconnoitering force, Gen. J. M. Brannan's Division, eastward where it ran into elements of Gen. Forrest's cavalry dismounted in the vicinity of Reed's Bridge. Forrest was driven back but reinforcements allowed him to regain the lost ground. The battle built in the tangled woodland west of the Chickamauga as each side threw its forces into the fray. Bragg ordered his left wing divisions across to the west side of the Chickamauga as the fighting spread southward eventually embroiling the whole line during the course of the day. All units comprising the Federal XIV, XX and XXI Corps were engaged. On the Confederate side only the divisions of Breckinridge and Hindman on the south end of the line were not involved.

Theretofore, in the ranks of the Texas Brigade, after bivouacking the night of the 18th-19th, J. M. Polk's, Co."I, 4th Texas, on "Saturday morning, [September, 19], ... continued [their] march, and about 3 o'clock in the afternoon ... were near the center of the Federal's line of battle."[21] Joe Polley, Co. F, 4th Texas, does not mention the march but said the boys were up early that morning, "munching hard tack and nibbling at the rancid bacon issued ... at Atlanta."[22] At the time, they had no idea they were within close proximity of the Army of the Cumberland until Capt. "Howdy" Martin came down from "Aunt Polly's headquarters" confirming the coming fight.

About that time they heard a "terrible roar, the like of which [they] had never heard in [their] lives." What they were hearing was the opening of the attack from the Federal left. From that point the battle swelled as unit after unit from both sides was fed into the fight. To the anxious listeners to the south, the sound of battle seemed stationary. "The earth ... seemed to tremble with its concussions, the trees above ... to rock back and forth." Speculation about the source of the "terrible sound" ranged from a tornado, to a cattle stampede, to an earthquake, to "all the bands in the Yankee army ... playing 'Hell Broke Loose in Georgia.'" After a good laugh, it was decided that the sound was a battle in progress to the north of their position. As they later learned, the reason the noise seemed stationary was because of the different style of fighting practiced in the West. Western battle lines had either stand-up or lie-down musketry duels with no charges and counter-charges as was practiced in the East. On which 4th Texas wag Bill Calhoun commented, "Well, boys ... if we have to stand up or lie down in a straight line, and let the Yankees shoot at us as long as they want to, this old Texas Brigade is going to run like [hell]."[23]

About an hour later, the brigade was moved forward behind the front line, where they "were ordered to halt and lie down."[24] Hood's division alignment was Robertson's Texans on the left, Law's Brigade (Sheffield) in the center and Bennings' Georgians on the right. The Texas Brigade was aligned with the 3rd Arkansas on the left, and the 1st, 4th and 5th Texas, in that order, to the right.

J. M. Polk, Co. I, 4th Texas, knew they "would soon be ordered into the fight and that some ... would never come out." Walking up to Tobe Riggs, a cousin of his who he said had never missed a roll call or a fight, he saw him to be ill with a fever. "Tobe," he said," you ought not to go into this fight; the doctor will excuse you." "Oh, I'm all right," he said. Polk said no more.[25]

The forest was so dense that no one could tell much about what was going on. The troops were in place for some time and engaged in conversations when Gen. Hood rode through their ranks and was greeted by a cheer. At about the same time, a Federal solid shot landed in front of Joe Polley, Co. F, 4th Texas, and, ricocheting, passed so close that he felt the wind of its passage. Said he of the near miss, "It scared me, and, I am confident, my face turned white as a sheet."[26]

At about 2:00 P.M. Rosecrans' committed his right, crossing the Lafayette Road around the Viniard farm. The fighting became heavy as Bushrod Johnson's Division advanced and engaged the enemy. Around 3:00 P.M., the Texans were ordered forward. As they moved up they were met by troops falling back. While not running, neither were they "idling." One of the throng shouted to the Texans, "You fellers'll catch [hell] in thar ... them fellers out thar you ar goin' up agin ... [won't] ... run at the snap of a cap — they are Western fellers, an' they'll mighty quick give you a bellyful of fightin."[27]

Advancing under heavy musketry and artillery fire, they came upon a Confederate general officer unhorsed and shot through the neck. It was Gen. John Gregg, a brigade commander in Johnson's Division. He had ridden too far forward to reconnoiter and found himself confronted by the Federal skirmish line. Putting spurs to his mount, he had tried to escape but was fired upon, falling heavily to the ground severely wounded. The enemy skirmishers quickly relieved him of his saber and spurs. The advancing Texans reclaimed his body and his horse.[28] Taken to the rear, he survived his wound and was, later in the war, in command of the very Texas troops that had come to his aid.

For a time failing to locate visually their antagonists, the Texans then realized that the Federal line was in a ravine, lying down and fighting Indian-fashion from behind any obstacle handy. Beyond was a hill with a breastwork of fence rails thrown up. John C. West, Co. E, 4th Texas, moved forward waving his hat and firing as rapidly as he could reload. He was struck by a ball that shattered his bayonet, the pieces wounding him in the right hip. Feeling sick and spitting blood, he fell upon the body of a severely wounded Federal soldier who asked him to unbuckle his belt. In the midst of a battle and with difficulty West obliged the request. By the time the belt was unbuckled, the soldier was dead. With minies and canister flying about and throwing dirt on him, West was able to make his way to the rear. By daylight the next morning, he returned to his company bruised and sore but ready for duty.[29]

D. H. Hamilton's Co. M, 1st Texas, was deployed on a timbered ridge where they came under heavy artillery fire that afternoon. By that time "the Yankee batteries had about topped all the timber.... The shells had kept every man as busy as a Cranberry Merchant dodging their flying fragments. We could hear the singing noise of the shells and their frequent crashing in the timber above us."[30] Falling timber injured some. Finally, they were ordered forward still under heavy artillery fire. Coming up behind Johnson's Division, they found their Tennessee compatriots hard pressed in front of an old farm, the Viniard farm.

The Tennesseans had been hit so hard, observed J. M. Polk, Co. I, 4th Texas, that their line looked more like a picket line than a divisional line of battle. About 250 yards across the way around the old farm, the rail fences had been converted into a breastwork and the Federal soldiers were lying down behind it. As the advance continued, the Federals waved the Stars and Stripes at them in defiance. Then, when they were about 100 yards from the breastworks, the Federal line arose and delivered a devastating volley. Polk, said it seemed that the volley felled every third or fourth man. According to Hamilton, once the volley was delivered the Federal soldiers "ran like turkeys." Actually, many remained at their post fighting hand-to-hand with fixed bayonets and clubbed muskets before being forced to flee. Then, the Texans "[a]ll who were not killed or wounded raised the Rebel yell and took up the chase."[31] The fighting around the Viniard farm was brutal.

The 4th Texas got into a fight with some Federal troops who, routed from their position, took refuge behind a house. A fierce fight ensued in which Col. Bane was wounded seriously enough to have to leave the field. Capt. Robert H. Bassett, formerly of Co. G, 4th Texas, assumed command. It was only a short time thereafter that he received a bizarre, disabling wound. Val Giles, Co. B, 4th Texas, said a "bombshell struck in the fork of a big red oak tree about twenty feet from the ground and split it wide open. It came crashing down among the men, breaking limbs off the nearby trees, and crushing everything in its reach. A large limb from half of the falling tree struck Captain Bassett on the shoulder, injuring him so badly that he was never able to rejoin his regiment and subsequently died in Texas from the effects of that wound."[32]

Somewhere in the midst of all this confusion, Giles observed the aberrational behavior of one soldier, probably a member of Co. E, 4th Texas. What he saw was a "fellow shooting straight up in the air and praying lustily." "[W]hen Lieutenant Killingsworth remonstrated with him about it, he paid no attention to him whatever. Captain Joe Billingsley threatened to cut him down with his sword if he didn't shoot at the enemy, for the woods in front were full of them. He retorted to the Captain: 'You can kill me if you want to, but I am not going to appear before my God with the blood of my fellow man on my soul.'"[33] At the end of the day, both Lt. Killingsworth, promoted to captain only the day before, and Captain Billingsley lay dead on the field. The physically and morally upright-standing Christian came through unscathed.

In the ranks of Co. F, 5th Texas, William Fletcher moved forward until the command was given to lie down. Fletcher went to sleep immediately! Rudely awakened, a hail of enemy rounds was coming their way. Ordered forward, they fired as they went. Passing by a nearby house, probably the Viniard farmhouse, he was struck in the left foot by what turned out to be a minie ball. Making his way toward the rear with his wound beginning to "come to life" and cause him great pain, he sought momentary refuge from the enemy's heavy fire. The safety afforded by the handiest tree had already been claimed by a wounded Federal soldier and there was not room for two. Shoving the Federal aside Fletcher said, "The day is ours," in other words, "to the victor belongs the spoils." The wounded Federal could only groan in reply. As things began to get hotter, Fletcher hopped to the rear. Passing through his own lines, he told them, "We are giving them hell, boys." "He has been there, you bet," was one of the replies. As it turned out for Fletcher, his wound would disqualify him for further infantry duty.[34]

A member of Co. A, 5th Texas, said then they were ordered forward at about 3:00 P.M. After firing one or two rounds at the opposing line, the boys could not be held back and with a "Texas yell" they "drove them like dogs." Then they "heard a whoop, and saw the Yankees rushing upon us. We waited till they got within about a hundred yards of us when with a jump and a yell, we rushed upon them. We drove them into a field when a fresh line of battle coming on us, half the regiment stopped to shoot at them, while about 100 of us took after the running Yanks and also made for a battery that was pouring a heavy fire upon us."[35] At about that point the 5th Texan was struck down by a minie ball and had to leave the fight.

Julius Glazer, Co. D, 4th Texas, and his comrades came across a pocket of resistance being offered by a group of Federal soldiers around a log-constructed blacksmith shop. The place was somewhat concealed by the thick forest growth and the Texans were unable for a time to determine from whence came the deadly musketry. Glazer was first to spot the source of the fire and with ten or fifteen other Texans, they moved on the position. Going ahead and calling for the defenders to surrender, Glazer was answered by a fusillade, several shots of which flesh-wounded him. This would be his second wound; his first was received at Gaines' Mill a year earlier. He returned fire, dropping one of his opponents. While going through the time-consuming reloading procedure, he was attacked by two soldiers who came from the building to close quarters. Both bayoneted Glazer. Instead of falling, he continued to try and reload. The two Federals came at him again with leveled bayonets and in the melee, Glazer was able to disable one. At that time several more Federals came forward. Glazer fought the three until other Texans arrived at his side, shooting down two of them while the other escaped back to the relative safety of the log shop. The gallantly defended bastion was finally forced to surrender after losing about half its defenders. The lieutenant commanding was asked why they did not just shoot Glazer down rather than attacking him with the bayonet. The reply was that he was but a "mere boy," and "after he fired his one shot we thought it would be cowardly to shoot him. But if the fighting he did against two of our best men at first, and then against three, and that too, after he was four times wounded, is a sample of what you Texans are in the habit of doing, I am going to throw up my commission and return to peaceful pursuits."[36] Glazer survived his wounds, only to be wounded for a third time the following year in the Wilderness fight.

At about the same time, Joe Polley said that he was placed "hors-de-combat" for the next few days and that while the Federal soldiers from the western states were good at stand-up firefights they were unaccustomed to the Virginia-style charges: "[T]he Western men were about as easily forced out of the way of the Texas Brigade as had been the foes of that command in ... [Virginia]."[37]

Relieved by other troops, the Texans marched to the rear to prepare for more to come. J. M. Polk, Co. I, 4th Texas, observed dead and wounded Federals everywhere. Retracing his steps, he found his cousin Riggs with a leg broken at the knee. Lifting him up, he noticed his face was "white as cotton" from the pain. Noting other acquaintances, now dead, he helped Riggs to the rear and turned him over to the regimental surgeon. While returning to the company, he gave a wounded Indiana soldier water from his canteen and talked with him awhile. Later, he noted that the Kansas, Illinois and Indiana men that they had fought that day "could stand killing better than any men I ever saw."[38]

As the battle tapered in the late afternoon, both badly battered armies were about where they had started earlier. Gen. Bragg's plan to turn the Federal left had not succeeded and Gen. Rosecrans still commanded the roads leading to Chattanooga. During that night both sides worked feverishly to strengthen their respective positions. Polk and his comrades could hear their opponents across the way chopping down trees and building breastworks: "[W]e knew that we would have to get up next morning and take those breastworks, regardless of cost, and with that vast army in front of us, and they behind the breastworks, we knew that it was a serious matter."[39]

In the meantime, Longstreet and members of his staff had arrived at last at Catoosa Station at about 2:00 P.M. September 19, along with other troops. They waited there for several more hours for the arrival of their mounts. Due to an oversight or neglect, no one had been provided to guide them. So, they set out blindly to try and locate Bragg's headquarters through the darkening and unfamiliar countryside. The sounds of distant conflict were their only reference. As it worked out, their search consumed the better part of seven hours.

The night that overtook them was a bright moonlit one, but nonetheless, one filled with shadowy menace. After narrowly avoiding capture by Federal troops, they finally reached army headquarters. There they found that Bragg had already retired to a field ambulance. Arising and without any acknowledgment of pleasure in having Longstreet and his troops present, the ill-tempered North Carolinian plunged immediately into an explanation of his battle plans for the morrow. "[H]owever, "[i]n deference to Longstreet's rank, [he did] ... [divide] his forces in two. Lt. Gen. Leonidas Polk, the senior corps commander prior to Longstreet's arrival, took charge of the right wing, which contained some 20,000 men. Longstreet was assigned the left, five divisions of more than 22,000 infantrymen and attached artillery."[40] Bragg's orders, already issued to his subordinates, were that the battle was to open at daybreak, starting on the Confederate right and then moving on down the line division by division by the left. The objective was to roll up the Union left, forcing it back on its right, and thus exposing the Federal supply lines leading back to Chattanooga which were to be then cut.

The next day, Sunday, September 20, although it got off to a shaky start, proved ultimately to be a great one for Southern arms. However, when the fog-enshrouded dawn came and went with only the Sunday sounds of distant church bells greeting his ears, Gen. Bragg grew more and more restive. Finally, riding to the far right to see for himself what was delaying the ordered movement, he found his wing commander, Gen. Polk, reading the morning newspaper. Ordering the attack to begin immediately, it was not until about 9:30 A.M., several hours behind schedule, that the troops began to move forward.

When things did begin to move, the attack was taken up progressively from the right. The fighting on that end of the line was furious with neither side able to make any appreciable gains. At about 11:00 A.M., a lull in the battle occurred as Longstreet's wing on the Confederate left prepared to enter the fray. Gen. Longstreet was on the field at dawn. Finding his wing out of contact with Gen. Polk's right wing, Longstreet moved Hood's command forward to fill that space in the front. The new Texas Brigade position was now opposite a rude log cabin identifiable as the Brotherton house.

While other units were deployed in lines, Hood's five brigades were in columns, as a lance point at the end of a shaft. The point of Longstreet's attack was ordered westward toward the Union center where the Brotherton Road intersected the Lafayette Road and continued on as the Dyer Road to intersect with the Dry Valley Road beyond. It was a posi-

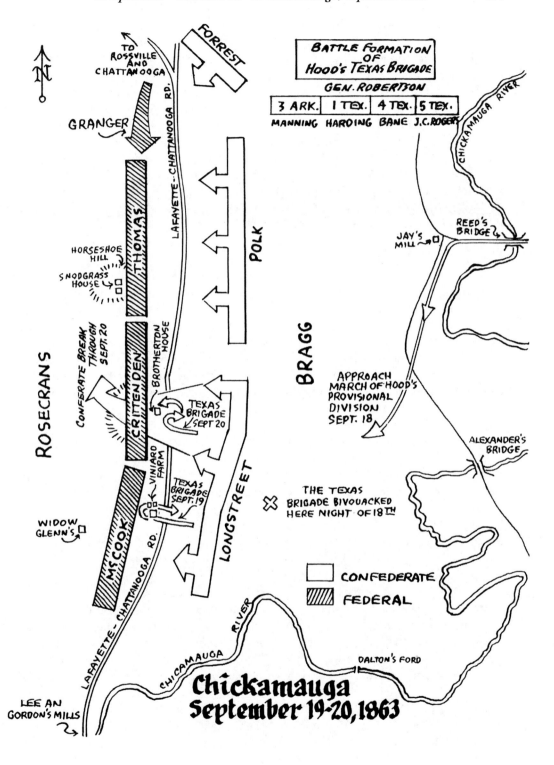

Chickamauga, Georgia, September 19–20, 1863

tion also made formidable during the night by hastily thrown up rail and log breastworks supported in rear by artillery positions. J. M. Polk, Co. I, 4th Texas, saw Gen. Longstreet and other officers riding the line that morning and "knew from this that we would soon have another big killing."[41]

As a result of Gen. Rosecrans' misunderstanding of the true location of some of his units, a serious blunder occurred in the Union positioning as a division-sized gap was opened up in the middle of the Federal line. Purely the result of luck, Bonaparte's favorite trait when exhibited by a subordinate, Gen. Longstreet launched his left wing, five division attack toward that very sector at that very moment. Moving forward, Longstreet reported that "Hood's column broke the enemy's line near the Brotherton house and made it wheel to the right."[42] Attempting to fill the gap, the Federal divisions of Gens. Philip H. Sheridan and J. C. Davis were shattered, and along with the entire right wing of the Federal army fell back in panic and confusion toward Chattanooga.

It is not clear which day Val Giles, Co. B, 4th Texas, is describing but it was most likely September 20 that a bizarre scene unfolded before his advancing company's eyes. Advancing through a "deep tangled jungle" the heat of the September day was described as "oppressive." Emerging from the woods on the east side of a clearing, they saw ahead on the other side of the clearing a Federal major "in full uniform dash[ing] out of the woods on the other side, holding his right arm high over his head, throwing his hand forward as if warning us back. He was mounted on a splendid bay horse, his trappings and bright uniform flashing in the sunshine of that hot September day. Someone cried out, 'Don't shoot!' but too late. Two or three muskets went off, then a whole volley. The officer dropped his hand, his horse plunged forward and fell in [a] little dry branch, throwing his rider heavily to the ground."[43] When the advance reached the scene, both rider and horse were found to be dead. Disdainfully, Giles observed one of the men stop to unbuckle the dead officer's pistol belt. Before he could take it off another passerby scooped the pistol from its holster. This performance brought laughter from the ranks as the first man, blind to his own avarice, "swore like a pirate and called the other rogue and thief." The strange behavior of the Federal officer and what he was trying to do mystified Giles for the remainder of his life.

In Co. I, 4th Texas, the command was, "Attention, forward, guide center, march." J. M. Polk, said that, with black humor, "Jack Massie took hold of me and said: 'You get by the side of me; when you fall I want that watch you have got on.' Bob Crawford said: 'I want his boots.'"[44] Within minutes, Polk was down with a severe head wound and Massie with a leg wound that necessitated amputation.

According to Gen. Longstreet "[a]t the early surging of his lines through the forest, General Hood came under the fire of this formidable array of artillery and infantry, and found his lines staggering under the galling missiles, and fast losing strength as the fire thickened."[45] From the Federal perspective, a young soldier of the 9th Indiana serving as a topographical engineer on the staff of Gen. William B. Hazen observed the Confederate assault. Writing of the incident years later, he said of the drama that unfolded before his eyes, "I saw the entire country in front swarming with Confederates; the very earth seemed moving toward us! They came on in thousands, and so rapidly that we had barely time to turn tail and gallop down the hill and away."[46] Soon, he had an opportunity to observe the effects of the Blue artillery on Gray ranks in action that day. It is possible that he was watching salvos fired that struck down men of the Texas Brigade.

Of the deadly cannonade, he saw masses of Confederate troops advancing out of the woods as the Federal artillery opened with grape and canister. For what seemed an eternity "nothing could be heard but the infernal din of their discharge and nothing seen through the smoke but a great ascension of dust from the smitten soil. When all was over, and the dust cloud had lifted, the spectacle was too dreadful to describe. The Confederates were still there — all of them, it seemed — some almost under the muzzles of the guns. But not a man of all these brave fellows was on his feet, and so thickly were all covered with dust that they looked as if they had been reclothed in yellow. 'We bury our dead,' said a gunner grimly."[47] The observer would become, in the years following the war, the acerbic and celebrated journalist and story-teller Ambrose Bierce.

In the midst of such destructive artillery fire, it was, ironically, a musket ball that devastated and affected the separation of Gen. Hood from his right leg. L. A. Daffan, Co. G, 4th Texas, was nearby and thought that the wound was inflicted by other

Lawrence A. Daffan, Co. G, 4th Texas

Confederate troops. "They mistook us on account of our neat, new standard uniform. They took us for Federals, as Bragg's army had never seen a well-uniformed Confederate regiment." Seeing him being carried away in a blanket, Daffan rushed up, pulling the blanket apart to see for himself. An officer angrily told Daffan, "Yes, it is General Hood; say nothing about it."[48]

Supporting Daffan's thoughts, in his report, Gen. Robertson expressed the opinion also that prior to Hood's wounding he thought that his command was being fired on mistakenly by other Confederate troops.[49] Capt. R. J. Harding, commanding the 1st Texas, reported a "very destructive fire from some regiment not known, but supposed to be friends, on our left and to the rear."[50] George T. Todd, Co. A, 1st Texas, further confirmed the suspicion when he said it was there that he "tried to get on both sides of a tree at the same time, as 'minies' were zipping from both directions."[51]

Onlookers thought that Hood had surely been killed outright and the news passed through the ranks quickly. Actually, Hood had been struck in the upper part of the right leg and fell from his horse into the arms of members of the Texas Brigade. His last command issued to his troops was "Go ahead, and keep ahead of everything."[52] Taken to a division hospital, the leg was amputated by Dr. T. G. Richardson, chief medical officer of the Army of Tennessee.[53] Gen. Evander Law assumed command of the division, thereafter, as he had earlier at Gettysburg in the aftermath of Hood's wounding on that field.

At the Brotherton house, point of the breakthrough, command of the 4th Texas fell to Maj. J. T. Hunter, 4th Texas, after the wounding of Lt. Col. Bane and Bane's successor, Capt. Robert H. Bassett, the day before. At that time, the regiment's left wing had forced some Federal gunners away from their section of two guns standing in a public road to the front. Beyond that position and behind a rail fence was a strong Federal line of battle. Deciding to advance and capture the two guns, Hunter ordered the regiment forward. The troops behind the fence opened on them with such a heavy fire that they were forced to fall back. Upon retiring, it was discovered that the regimental flag and its bearer, Ed Francis, were missing. Hunter, determined to recover the colors, returned to find Francis dead, his body fallen on the flag. Rolling his body over, Hunter returned with the flag under a heavy fire from the enemy line. He said later "Though they shot my blanket and haversack full of holes and several in the flag, I was not touched. I don't think anyone during the war had more shots fired at him individually than I had on [that] occasion. I have always felt that the prayers of some good Southern woman must have been heard in my behalf."[54]

In Co. B, 4th Texas, Val Giles saw that the smoke from the cannonade and the musketry hung low to the ground further adding to the confusion, there being no breeze to disperse it. They were ordered to "take obstacle," which meant every man for himself in seeking cover. Finding a vacant pine tree, he said, "Shells, grapeshot, canister, shrapnel and Minie balls were tearing through the air, while dirt, leaves, limbs, and bark were falling and flying all over and around us." Ahead, a huddle of Federal prisoners was ordered to the rear. Holding hands, two of them headed directly toward Giles' tree. When they got opposite, the Federal battery loosed another "wagonload of grapeshot" and one of the Federals was hit in the back. Giles said, "He was so close to me that I distinctly saw the dust rise from his shoulders where the grapeshot struck him. He fell forward on his knees, raised his hands in an attitude of prayer and exclaimed in a loud, strong voice, 'O Lord! I am done with the wicked world.'" His companion never stopped, never looked back. With two close friends dead nearby, the dead Federal at his feet and scores of wounded trying to make their way to the rear Giles said, "That was the meanest, most unsatisfactory place I struck during the whole war."[55]

With the Federal line broken and falling back in disorder, Longstreet ordered all his units forward. The Federals were driven from their positions and back upon the strong reserve position around the Widow Glenn's house, site of Gen. Rosecrans' field headquarters. After a "severe struggle" the Federals were forced to abandon that position as well. Unable to stem the retreating tide, Gens. Rosecrans, Crittenden and McCook were carried along with it all the way back into Chattanooga. Confederate General Bushrod Johnson described the breakthrough in almost rhapsodic terms as "unspeakably grand ... the glitter of arms, the onward dash of artillery and mounted men, the retreat of the foe, the shouts of the hosts of our army, the dust, the smoke, the noise of firearms — of whistling balls and grape-shot and bursting shell — made up a battle scene of unsurpassed grandeur."[56]

Gen. Longstreet called for the cavalry to pursue the retreating enemy and ordered them to take control of the gaps leading through the mountains to Chattanooga. Noting that the Federal left still held, Longstreet modified the overall battle plan and wheeled his wing to the right toward Snodgrass Hill. After the collapse of the Federal right, it was the panic-proof XIV Corps of Gen. George H. Thomas, along with fragments of some Federal right wing units, that valiantly defended the left of the line and comprised the sole remnants of the Army of the Cumberland remaining on the field. A great deal of the credit for the staving off of complete disaster must be given to Gen. Gordon Granger, commanding the Federal Reserve Corps east of Rossville. Sensing a crisis and ignoring his specific orders to protect the avenues of retreat, he brought his troops forward to Gen. Thomas' aid, a most valiant action. They saved Thomas' command from annihilation and the Army of the Cumberland from total disaster. Moving to a rise called Snodgrass Hill, they continued the fight.

Taking advantage of a lull, Gen. Longstreet rode the line to determine the situation and to reestablish contact with the Confederate right wing. He was lucky to escape death when he rode too close to the Federal lines and came under the fire of their sharpshooters. Unruffled by his close call, he returned to the safety of his own lines under the cover provided by heavy timber and thick underbrush. There he took time out to enjoy a lunch of "Nassau bacon and Georgia sweet potatoes." During the brief but nonetheless dangerous respite "a fragment of shell ... came tearing through the woods, passed through the book in the hands of a courier who sat on his horse hard by reading, and struck down [the] chief of ordnance, Colonel P. T. Manning."[57] Fearing the ordnance chief to be seriously wounded, the other lunchers sprang to his aid. Looking on, the observant Longstreet suggested that first they remove the portion of sweet potato that he was choking on. That done, Manning's breathing was restored to normal and his injury suffered from the shell fragment proved to be minor.

Shortly, Gen. Longstreet was summoned to Gen. Bragg to confer. There, Gen. Longstreet made several suggestions to the commanding general for the continuation of the battle. However, about all he got from Gen. Bragg was a soliloquy on how the right wing had failed to achieve its objectives and the lack of fighting spirit in that sector. Then he rode off without any instructions for Longstreet and his wing! Longstreet concluded that "[t]here was nothing for the left wing to do but work along as best it could."[58]

On the Confederate right, the battle seesawed back and forth as darkness approached. The Confederates were pushed back until several batteries of artillery were got into action. Late in the day Thomas' left was turned. This, according to Longstreet, convinced Gen. Thomas that the time had come to fall back on Rossville. Then "[l]ike magic the Union army melted away.... The dews of twilight hung heavy about the trees as if to hold down the voice of victory; but the two lines nearing as they advanced joined their continuous shouts in increasing volume, not as the burstings from the cannon's mouth, but in a tremendous swell of heroic harmony that seemed almost to lift from their roots the great trees of the forest.... [Then] the Confederate army made its bivouac on the ground it had gained in the first pronounced victory in the West, and one of the most stubbornly contested battles of the war."[59]

Nonetheless, his heroic and stubborn defense at Snodgrass Hill saved the Union Army of the Cumberland from total destruction and earned for Gen. Thomas, a native Virginian, the sobriquet, "Rock of Chickamauga."

As darkness fell, G. Moxley Sorrell, Longstreet's chief of staff, said that "there sprang up on that bloodstained battle-ground camp fires innumerable, and the wildest Confederate cheers and yells for victory that ever stirred the hearts of warriors — and such warriors as had that day borne the battle-flags forward. It was one of the greatest of the many Confederate successes."[60] The cheers and yells were heard by those Federals still in close enough proximity to be able to do so. Sgt. Ambrose Bierce, 9th Indiana, said, "It was the ugliest sound that any mortal ever heard — even a mortal exhausted and unnerved by two days of hard fighting, without sleep, without rest, and without hope."[61]

Even as the blood-curdling yells were reverberating across the battlefield, O. T. Hanks,

Co. K, 1st Texas, and some of his comrades were detailed to bury the dead. For no good reason other than curiosity, Val Giles, Co. B, 4th Texas, accompanied Lt. Wash Masterson back to the battle site the next morning. They found the site where the Federal major had been shot from his horse. The horse, greatly increased in size, was there but the body of the officer was gone. The place where he had "taken obstacle," was littered with dead, mostly in gray. The site of the artillery battery that had wreaked so much havoc on the ranks of the Texas Brigade was then a site of havoc itself. "Caissons and gun carriages lay in splinters, covered with fallen trees and limbs, and all around demolished batteries, along the crest of the ridge and fifty yards out in the field, the ground was covered with blue uniforms. Thirty-two dead and wounded horses lay in the rear of the place where the batteries had stood."[62] The plight of the wounded animals distressed Giles but he learned later a detail was sent over the battlefield to end their sufferings.

       Gen. Bragg did not realize the full extent of the victory until the next morning. Stopping by Longstreet's bivouac, he asked his lieutenant for his views on the army's next move. Longstreet suggested several possibilities, none of which Bragg chose to pursue. Instead, valuable time was wasted as over the next few days a march upon Chattanooga was taken up finally and siege positions on Missionary Ridge and the surrounding mountains were established. By that time the Army of the Cumberland had made the defenses of Chattanooga unassailable.

       Bragg was later criticized roundly by Longstreet, Nathan Bedford Forrest and others for failing to quickly follow-up on the victory won on the field of Chickamauga. But it was the man in the ranks that put the real face on it. Said Val Giles, Co. B, 4th Texas, the army was simply "fagged out." "Forty-eight hours of almost continuous fighting had worn the men out and they dropped down on the firing line, hungry and thirsty, and slept like logs.... There was not a regiment, battalion, or company on either side at Chickamauga but what had been heavily engaged, and tired nature could stand no more."[63] Ultimately, Gen. Bragg was removed from command, much to the delight of his disenchanted subordinates.

       At Chickamauga the Army of Tennessee gave Longstreet a new *nom de guerre*— they called him the "Bull of the Woods." Regardless of other faults, Longstreet was a consummate soldier and knew how to manage troops in battle and proved it on many a bloody field. He would have his abilities further tested as an independent field commander when, less than two months later, his corps moved into East Tennessee in November 1863.

CHAPTER 12

"We had been detached from home … family, Virginia and from Lee to go down to Tennessee"[1]: Chattanooga to Knoxville, September–December 1863

On the morning of Monday, September 21, following the collapse of the Army of the Cumberland, at least of its right wing, the day before, the right wing of the Confederate Army of Tennessee took up the march on Chattanooga. While the left wing waited to follow, it was occupied with caring for the wounded and burying the dead left on the field. It was not until the morning of September 22, that the Left Wing at last took to the roads. Gen. Bragg, initially unaware of the extent of his army's victory, had not pursued his advantage as promptly as tactics and his fractious subordinates demanded. Once in pursuit, Bragg had it in his mind that the Federal army would continue its precipitate retreat, falling back beyond Chattanooga on Nashville. Thus, the Army of Tennessee could expect to enter the city of Chattanooga unhindered but by crowds of grateful citizens thronging its flower-strewn line of march. Gen. Longstreet thought the strategy wrong and the commanding general more a "spirit eager for applause" seeking the praise "of the inhabitants of a city so recently abandoned to the enemy, and a parade through its streets with bands of music playing and flaunting banners … than [one willing to take up] the tedious march for fruition of our heavy labors."[2]

Bragg's praise-seeking would have to wait, however. Gen. Rosecrans, surprised but relieved by the failure of his victorious opponent to immediately follow up, decided to linger in the already fortified city. As they arrived at the city's outskirts an examination of the defenses revealed to the pursuing Confederates that it defied a direct assault. Col. Alexander, commanding the artillery brigade, said that "the approaches were generally level and open, exposing an assaulting column to long and heavy fire."[3] During their occupation of the city prior to Chickamauga, the Confederates had constructed some formidable defenses and upon this the Federals were working feverishly to strengthen and improve.

When Bragg realized that his task continued unabated and that the place was too strong to assault, he sought to invest the city by "stretch[ing] his army in a semicircle of six miles along the southeast front of Chattanooga, from the base of Lookout Mountain on his left, to his right resting on the Tennessee River, and ordered Alexander's batteries [at last arrived

185

on the field] to the top of the mountain, [Longstreet's] command, McLaws,' Hood's, and Walker's Divisions, occupying the left of his line of investment."[4] Below, the besieged city of Chattanooga lay spread along the left bank of the Tennessee River.

There, the Texas Brigade, with the other units of Longstreet's Corps and the Confederate Army of Tennessee, took up their positions anticipating a lengthy stay. Commanding the considerable heights overlooking the city, Bragg's plan was to use his artillery posted along the line and from the elevated position atop Lookout Mountain to pound the enemy positions below; and then to dislodge them with his infantry. It proved difficult enough to get the artillery up onto and sited on the rugged heights. It proved to be even more difficult to make it effective once the task was completed. "Alexander managed to drop an occasional shell or shot about the enemy's lines by lifting the trails of his guns, but the fire of other batteries was not effective."[5] The Federal artillerists below were more successful by elevating their guns. After a week of this, it became obvious that Bragg's tactic was not having the expected result. Both armies set about strengthening their respective positions and, for the time being, began settling into the monotony characteristic of a siege operation.

One proven way soldiers turned to to break the monotony of manning a siege line was to play poker. As usually happened when the opposing lines were stationary for any extended period of time, an informal truce took shape, at least between the men manning the opposing rifle pits if not by their officers. On one such occasion, some of the men of the Texas Brigade were lounging around on the ground playing poker in plain view of their opposite numbers, they little more than a hundred yards away. Not so with the Texans' South Carolina allies manning the continuation of the picket line to their left. While the Texans moved about freely, the South Carolinians were kept to their pits, unable to show themselves for fear of being shot down on sight. In the Blue ranks the South Carolinians were singled out often as the ones responsible for starting the whole bloody mess in the first place. As such, they were not allowed any of the dispensations sometimes enjoyed by those considered less culpable.

Joe Polley, Co. F, 4th Texas, tells of one adept South Carolina poker player who could not resist the temptation of a chance to enlarge his treasury at the expense of the 1st Texans. He was willing to the take the risks necessary to do so. One day before daylight, he removed the uniform coat that identified him as one of the most vile of the secessionist race and slipped over to the Texans' position for a hand or two. Becoming engrossed in the task at hand, he did not notice that dawn had gradually illuminated the scene. It was not long before one alert Yankee shouted out across the line, "Say, you Texas Johnnies! ain't that fellow playing cards, with his back to a sapling, one of them d — d South Carolina secessionists? Seems to me his breeches are newer'n they ought to be." The hosts were placed upon the horns of a dilemma; "hospitality demanded the protection of [the] guest — prudence, the observance of good faith toward the Yankees." The awkward pause that followed the angry query removed all doubt and the Yankee, raising his weapon to fire, shouted, "D — d him, I just know it is." However, the South Carolinian was too fast for him and scurried to the safety of a gulch before the round could be sent on its unerring way.[6]

Meanwhile, the Army of the Cumberland, its back to the Tennessee River with only pontoons available as a means of retreat and with a most tenuous line of supply, seemed to be settling in for a stay. Commissary and quartermaster — supply, or the lack thereof — is the key to understanding the events that transpired. There was no efficient line of continual supply and any army's daily demand is considerable.

Almost immediately, upon reentering the city, the Army of the Cumberland was dangerously short on supplies of all kinds. Both troops and army animals were soon on reduced rations. In the ensuing weeks, thousands of the animals, horses and mules, actually starved to death. Not enough remained functional to even move the artillery around. Ammunition was inadequate for any major effort and there were no quartermaster supplies available. Firewood was in short supply, having to be cut down upstream on the north side of the river and then floated down to the city.

Having few alternatives, Rosecrans sought to take the initiative by threatening the Confederate left that stretched from Lookout Mountain through the Lookout Valley on the west and northward to Raccoon Mountain overlooking the Tennessee River. To establish a supply line, a strong Federal force and supply point was established down that serpentine waterway at Bridgeport, Alabama, some twenty-six miles west and south of the city. Crossing the Tennessee River at that point, the Nashville and Chattanooga Railroad connected the Federal supply base at Nashville with Bridgeport. From Nashville down to Bridgeport, the rail line was under Federal control, Confederate cavalry raids notwithstanding.

Getting supplies from Bridgeport upriver to Chattanooga was the hard part. The Confederate occupation of positions overlooking the whole area made use of the railway, the roads and the Tennessee River impracticable. To make matters even worse for the Federals, on October 9, a contingent of Gen. Longstreet's sharpshooters established positions on the left bank of the river northwest of the city between Raccoon Mountain and Walden's Ridge. Their purpose was to interdict the Federal supply wagon traffic across the river from a distance of about 300 yards. Law's Alabama Brigade was deployed in the area in support of the sharpshooters. Their pickets extended along the river all the way back to the foot of Lookout Mountain, about five miles.

With few other choices available, over the next several weeks and with much effort the Federals fashioned a tortuous route over bad roads through the rough mountain country well north of the river. It was some sixty miles in length. The route led from Bridgeport north up the Sequatchie Valley thence south over Walden Ridge to the north side of the river opposite the city. Pontoons completed the tenuous route into the city. With the arrival of the rainy season, the trip sometimes took eight or more days. Because of these conditions, the amount and types of supply were severely restricted to mainly foodstuffs.

Gen. Rosecrans, because of his logistical situation, was seriously considering abandoning the city and advised his Washington masters of the possibility. That was one course of action that his superiors did not relish hearing about and could not allow to happen. That confession, in addition to the acceptance of responsibility required of his station for the debacle at Chickamauga, resulted in his removal from command of the Army of the Cumberland within a few short weeks. It was an ignominious end for one who, overtaken by the vagaries of fickle fortune, had performed so brilliantly up to that point.

The strategic importance of holding Chattanooga as a rail hub and gateway to the lower South was foremost in the thoughts of the Federal high command, including President Lincoln. As early as September 13, a week before the Chickamauga fight, Gen. Henry Halleck, the army's chief of staff, responding to calls for reinforcement by Gen. Rosecrans had begun dispatching to the theater units of Gen. Grant's Army of the Tennessee then unemployed and languishing around Vicksburg and Memphis following the Vicksburg triumph. Additionally, two veteran corps from the Army of the Potomac in Virginia, the XI and XII, were entrained for the Western front. By September 30, the first of the Virginia troops had arrived at Bridgeport after a circuitous trip that surpassed in miles those traveled by Longstreet's Corps on its journey west. By mid–October, all the troops were there. When, on October 20, Gen. Rosecrans' was relieved from command, he was replaced by the stalwart and deserving Gen. George H. Thomas, the recently anointed "Rock of Chickamauga."

Another change that occurred in the Federal camp was particularly significant. Gen. U. S. Grant was named commander of the newly created Military Department of the Mississippi. In his new capacity, he proceeded to Chattanooga to take charge of operations personally. Grant arrived in Chattanooga on October 23 to assume his new duties.

Soon following his arrival in the city after a difficult journey, Gen. Grant was informed of a promising plan proposed by the Army of the Cumberland's chief engineer, Gen. W. F. "Baldy" Smith, to relieve the city of its investment. When briefed, Gen. Grant liked the boldness of it, additional credence being lent, perhaps, by the fact that Gen. Smith was Grant's former and respected commandant of cadets at the military academy in the early 1840s. Their meeting in Chattanooga was the first since that earlier time.

Gen. Smith's plan called for a movement to capture a place called Brown's Ferry down river below the city, to capture or drive off Confederate forces in the area and then throw a pontoon bridge across at that point. If successful, a foreshortened route from Bridgeport to Chattanooga would greatly reduce the distance and improve the efficacy of the supply effort. Grant's stamp of approval set the plan in motion and, having confidence in Gen. Smith's abilities, placed him in charge of its execution.

On the night of October 26–27, Gen. Smith with about 1,800 men gathered along the fog-enshrouded river's bank and readied themselves for the night's work. Under the cover of darkness they cast off and, floating downstream in pontoon boats, they passed Confederate positions on and above the river undetected, undeterred. Arriving at Brown's Ferry, they took possession and wasted no time in throwing up defensive breastworks.

By daybreak, the tactical table had been turned and an effective supply line had been opened between Bridgeport and Chattanooga. It was dubbed the Cracker Line. When the news reached the city of the successful operation, it spread like wildfire through the army's camps. "The Cracker line is open. Full rations, boys! Three cheers for the Cracker line," was the soldier's cry.[7]

As all of this was developing, from their elevated positions surrounding Chattanooga, it was observed by the Confederates that Federal reinforcements were arriving in the area over time and in numbers. On the afternoon of October 27, Longstreet's signal party at Trenton, southwest of Lookout Mountain, reported a heavy enemy column moving from Bridgeport toward Chattanooga.[8] Gen. Bragg ignored the report. It was not until the Federal capture of Brown's Ferry that night that Bragg's attention became riveted. He was outflanked and recognized immediately that something had to be done about Brown's Ferry and the new Federal supply line if the Confederate investment of the city was to continue. On the face of it, there appeared to be little that could be done.

On the day following the Federal capture of Brown's Ferry, October 28, Gens. Bragg and Longstreet conferred atop Lookout Mountain. Their parlay was interrupted by a courier from the signal party at Trenton bringing the news that large Federal troop columns were being observed approaching from the west. After chiding the soldier for bringing exaggerated reports, one of his numerous pet peeves, the courier suggested: "General, if you will ride to a point on the west side of the mountain, I will show them to you."[9] With Longstreet accompanying, they went to the point suggested where they saw spread out far below them a grand scene highlighted by long, winding blue columns of infantry moving in from the west. The heads of the columns were seen to be establishing encampments in Lookout Valley below. The presence of this large force ended any hopes of recapturing Brown's Ferry and closing the Cracker Line. But, there were other possibilities, or so, in his memoirs, thought Gen. Longstreet.

According to Gen. Longstreet, he proposed to the commanding general an attack on the rear guard by a night action "merely to inflict such damage upon [them] as might be accomplished by a surprise."[10] After discussion, Bragg approved the plan, allocating Hood's Division, by then commanded by a Longstreet favorite, the South Carolinian General Micah Jenkins, and McLaws' Division to carry out the mission.

Leaving Gen. Longstreet to work out the details, Bragg rode, reputedly, to notify Jenkins and McLaws of their assignment. According to Longstreet, on the way to advise McLaws, Bragg decided that that division would not be needed to accomplish the mission. However, he failed to notify Gen. Longstreet of that key detail. According to Bragg, he authorized Longstreet to use his entire corps if he wished and even offered other troops, if needed. As a result, McLaws' Division did not participate and what transpired on the night of October 28–29 was a bungled attack by one brigade of 1,700 men against a Federal force numbering 12,000.[11]

Because of McLaws' absence, responsibility for the attack fell to Hood's Division solely. As fate would have it, that theretofore illustrious unit was in a state of leadership disarray. Temporarily commanded by Gen. Micah Jenkins, the division was the locus of internecine warfare among its leaders not much less brutal than that being fought on the division front. After Hood's wounding at Chickamauga, while in the heat of battle, command of the division had passed temporarily to Gen. Evander Law, the senior brigadier. Then, Jenkins' South Carolina Brigade had been transferred to Hood's Division at Longstreet's request following Chickamauga. The addition of that brigade brought Hampton's South Carolina Legion once again to Hood's Division, along with the 1st, 2nd, 5th and 6th South Carolina Infantry Regiments and the Palmetto Sharpshooters. At that point, command of the division had passed to Jenkins, temporarily, he being the senior brigadier by about three months. Nonetheless, this was much to the dismay of Gen. Law, who had a feeling of strong proprietorship. Nor was this "pleasing to the Texas regiments. They had been too long associated with Law's brigade, and too often under Law's command, not to know and have a high regard for his courage and ability, and to regard him as the logical successor of General Hood."[12] Jenkins, in their mind, was a newcomer and usurper of their command.

The controversy simmered, and in the end, the issue, as is often the case with difficult matters, was side-stepped and no permanent commander was designated. So, the egos of the two candidates, both young, fiery, competitive South Carolinians, were, as open wounds, left to fester over who should command. It was not a good leadership situation where a harmony of purpose among all concerned was required.

So it was, under a scudding moon, that the attack was launched at midnight. The terrain over which the advance proceeded consisted of a "half dozen high, parallel ridges, whose tops [were] open and level enough for a road-way, and whose thickly timbered sides slope at angles of forty-five degrees, into deep, lonely hollows."[13] Several of these steep-sided, narrow-topped ridges had to be crossed in order to get into position. Just before reaching the Brown's Ferry Road, with skirmishers deployed, Gen. Law was joined by Gen. Robertson and the Texas Brigade. Acting on orders from Gen. Jenkins, the 3rd Arkansas and 1st Texas were put in line with Law's troops, while "[the 4th Texas] was placed in reserve on the road to [the right], and the [5th Texas] was used to guard the bridge in ... rear [across Lookout Creek] and to watch the space intervening between [the] right and the river, which was at least half a mile."[14] Once the advance began, the 4th Texas was brought forward to form the extreme right of the advancing line. Val Giles, Co. B, 4th Texas, destined soon to become a prisoner of war, said that there "was not a man among us who knew where he was or what he was there for. I don't believe the officers knew," he added.[15]

Col. John Bratton, commanding Jenkins' Brigade, crossed Lookout Creek with orders to move to the left on the line of the Nashville and Chattanooga Railroad, winding its way through the area, and seeking out the enemy's rear guard. Gen. Benning's Brigade would follow Bratton across the creek and take up a position to Law's left. So, the advance proceeded with the Texans on the right, then strung out to the left, Law's Brigade, then Benning's Brigade, whose mission it was to cut the Brown's Ferry Road. Bratton's Brigade moved south across the rear on the line of the railroad thence down the Trenton road seeking to attack Gen. Geary's XII Corps rearguard division bivouacked around Wauhatchie Station.

Joe Polley's 4th Texas Regiment marched across the bridge guarded by the 5th Texas, and, moved toward Raccoon Mountain in the distance "climbing up and sliding down the steep sides of the intervening ridges, until brought to a halt on the moon-lit top of the highest, and formed in line on the right of an Alabama regiment."[16] Dropping to the ground to rest before beginning to scoop out rifle pits, they were unaware that at the foot of the slope in their front elements of the XI Corps from the main body of the enemy at Brown's Ferry were present. The commencement of the engagement on the left, probably Bratton, had brought the Blue giant, now below, to the scene. Drum rolls, shouted orders, general chaos erupted from the depths of the canyon as the 73rd Ohio, 33rd Massachusetts, 55th Ohio and the 136th New York regiments readied themselves for battle.[17] Above on the ridge, the 4th Texans became aware that they "stood upon the outermost edge of a human volcano, which might soon burst forth in all its fury, and overwhelm [them]."[18]

The 4th Texas formed the extreme right of the formation and, in this situation, its right flank was "in the air" all the way to the south bank of the Tennessee River a mile away. Scurrying up the steep slope in front, the Texas skirmishers reported what everyone already knew, the approach of the force from the darkened depths below. It was not long before their labored efforts could be clearly heard and the ball was opened. In the Federal ranks, Col. James Wood, Jr., commanding the 136th New York, said that as they struggled up the steep slope they were "under a brisk and constant fire," presumably from the 4th Texans.[19] Adding to the tension of the moment, like wildfire, a rumor passed from left to right through the Texas ranks that the Alabamians on the left had "abandoned the premises." Then, illuminated dimly by the fleeting moonbeams, in front "what seemed to [their] agitated minds a hundred thousand bright gun-barrels, revealed the near and dangerous presence of the hated foe."[20]

At that moment, it seems a collective decision was made as if by telepathy. The officers and men of the "gallant and hitherto invincible Fourth Texas stood not upon the order of their going ... in short, they disappeared bodily, stampeded ... and plunged recklessly into the ... shadowy depths behind them."[21] The triumphant Blue host, reaching the summit, which Col. Wood described as no more than six feet wide, loosened volleys that did no harm to the Texans but shattered the treetops through which they passed.

In the downhill plunge, through the gloom, Polley observed a soldier he knew only as Dennis career from obstacle to obstacle, ending up face down across a "ditch-like drain" at the foot of the slope. In the blackness of the moment, Bill Calhoun, the 4th Texas wag, came plunging down and, mistaking Dennis' dimly-perceived form for a log, planted his foot solidly on his back and bounded across the drain. Dennis howled in pain and protest, "For the Lord Almighty's sake, man, don't make a bridge of me!" Startled by the log's protest,

Bill could only reply, "Lie still, old fellow — lie still! The whole regiment has to cross yet, and you'll never have another such chance to serve your beloved country."[22] Polley did not record any further comments by the patriotic bridge.

Following up, the 136th New York found the ground over which the Texans had fled to be "strewn with rifles, swords, hats, caps, and haversacks."[23] M. V. Smith, Co. D, 4th Texas, said that once the flight was over and the troops were reunited in the ranks that the relating of experiences produced "a laughter so loud and so long that we didn't know but was heard by Rosecrans' Army in Chattanooga, three miles away."[24]

Overpowered and flanked, Gen. Law ordered a withdrawal of his troops to the hill from which the advance had begun and thence to the hollow behind. From there the retreat was over the bridge crossing Lookout Creek. The retreat was covered by skirmishers and the 1st Texas and part of the 5th Texas. Ignoring or unaware of the 4th Texas' mode of retreat, Gen. Law said the "movement was executed in a quiet and leisurely manner, the enemy in front making no effort to follow."[25] Similarly, Gen. Robertson, later in reporting one wounded, eight missing, described the retreat as "leisurely, in good order, without any confusion or excitement."[26]

In withdrawing, Law left Bratton's South Carolinians still engaged at Wauhatchie although he claimed later that he thought that they had disengaged already and withdrawn beyond the creek. With the aid of Benning's troops, Bratton was able to extricate his command and escape. They formed a rear guard allowing Benning to cross the creek, themselves being the last to cross. In his postwar memoir, Gen. Longstreet dismissed the affair by saying it was "an oversight of mine not to give definite orders for the troops to return to their camps before leaving them [prior to the launching of the operation]."[27]

Known as the battle of Wauhatchie or Raccoon Mountain or the Raccoon Races to the 4th Texans, it was ill-coordinated with Law's Brigade suffering only light casualties while Jenkins', under Col. John Bratton, bore the brunt and suffered the most casualties. Gen. Robertson and the Texas Brigade did not perform up to their usual level of excellence and came in for criticism as well. It was in the aftermath of all of this and despairing of being able to dislodge the Federals from Chattanooga that Bragg decided, upon President Davis' suggestion, to detach Longstreet's command for the ostensible purpose of dealing with Gen. Burnside's Army of the Ohio then holding Knoxville and various points intermediate.

The movement against Knoxville, which Longstreet thought deficient in the numbers of troops required and only serving to weaken Bragg's army, got underway on November 5. They were to pick up any other units scattered in the area and otherwise unattached. A request for maps, engineer, quartermaster, and commissary officers familiar with the area went unfulfilled, those items and individuals, unfortunately, being essential for the success of their mission.

Numbering about 20,000 men, including Gen. Joe Wheeler's cavalry loaned by Gen. Bragg — which Burnside's command thought erroneously to number about 15,000 — the operation lurched forward. General Grant's orders to Burnside were to hold East Tennessee at all costs, even at the sacrifice of "most of his army." The strategy that Burnside adopted as the Confederate advance moved forward was to fight skirmishes while avoiding major engagements. Withdrawing up the Tennessee River Valley with Longstreet in close pursuit, they would finally shelter within the defenses of Knoxville.

The first stage of the march on Knoxville was along the line of the Tennessee and Georgia Railroad northeast to Tyner's Station thence by rail to Sweetwater Station. At Sweetwater, where they remained for two days, supplies were supposed to be awaiting the arrival of the already short-rationed troops. And, indeed, there were rations there, however, they had been preempted for shipment to Bragg's army. Also learned there, the Federal troops in Knoxville numbered about 23,000. This was considerably more than the number originally estimated.

Although Burnside was helped by the enlistments of many loyalist Tennesseans and North Carolinians, his effective force was much less because his troops occupied widespread points. At the time, he was laboring under false intelligence information that Gen. Richard S. Ewell's Corps had been detached from the Army of Northern Virginia against him. Exhibiting due caution, he was watching both his flanks and was deployed accordingly.

Capt. Frank Potts, a Confederate assistant quartermaster officer, found the supply problem appalling. Noting Longstreet's Corps was numerically short of transportation "the condition of what we had was beyond all question the worst I ever saw; wagons frequently breaking down, mules just able in a large proportion of the cases to carry their harness, harness much worn, and many teams without collars or saddles."[28] One battery of Leyden's Artillery Battalion had to be left behind because of a lack of battery horses. Considering that a possible siege at Knoxville was in the offing, the loss of four artillery pieces was a matter of serious concern.

Maj. R. J. Moses, chief commissary of the corps, had his own dire problems in trying to feed the troops. At one point he had to forcibly commandeer a train whose engineer refused to proceed in order to get some flour rations from Sweetwater forward to the troops by the time they arrived at Loudon.[29] Foraging became the only recourse available to feed the army.

So, on short rations and in the midst of increasingly cold winter weather — with what winter clothing they owned back in storage in Virginia — the Virginia soldiers marched toward a bleak-looking future. Said Longstreet, "We found ourselves in a strange country, not as much as a day's rations on hand, with hardly enough land transportation for ordinary camp equipage."[30]

Pushing on over mud-laden roads, the infantry and artillery force crossed the Tennessee River on November 14–15 by way of a pontoon bridge thrown over to the north bank with great difficulty at Hough's Ferry, about two miles below Loudon. At Loudon the Tennessee and Georgia Railroad crossed the river, also. Joe Polley, Co. F, 4th Texas, said from that point the Texas Brigade "marched and countermarched, advanced, retreated, and halted, much as if a game of 'hide and seek' were being played between it and the enemy."[31] He further noted that lack of quartermaster supplies was becoming ever more of a problem for the troops, many of them being barefoot in increasingly frigid winter weather.

The Federal pickets at Loudon escaped capture and warned Gen. Burnside of the Confederate advance. As a result, the first contact with Burnside's force occurred the next morning as the last of the Gray troops were crossing over the pontoon bridge. The Federals formed in line but were driven back and then retired without further offering battle.

Following through the ridged countryside in what Col. Alexander described as a "sort of running skirmish" to Lenoir's Station, they found a Federal rear guard in "considerable force." It is at Lenoir's that the Holston and Little Tennessee rivers join to form the Tennessee River. As dark approached, in rain and on rough ground without knowledge of the topography, mistakes were made in deployment and the Federal force escaped during the night, leaving behind a part of its wagons. Some of the booty included in the wagons was picks and spades which proved to come in quite handy in the coming days. Even more important to the men in the ranks, the Federals had set themselves up there as if in winter quarters.

Even under the miserable circumstances John C. West, Co. E, 4th Texas, thought the countryside through which they were passing to be beautiful, as were the women — "very fair, black eyes, black hair, pretty teeth"- and could not understand why people had ever left such a place to go to other places, such as Texas, for instance. Of the overrun Federal camp, he said there were 500 or 600 cabins "nicer and more neatly arranged than most of the cabins on the prairies in Texas.... They are all laid off into streets, with the regularity and precision of a city, with fire places, mantel pieces, bunks and stools, and the scoundrels have taken nearly all the sash out of the windows in the neighborhood, as well as cooking and parlor stoves, omitting nothing which could contribute to their comfort or convenience."[32] He was fascinated by a captured medical wagon that he described as being as complete as "a drug store." His most valued find was some coffee thrown out on the ground which he carefully gathered up for future enjoyment. He was quick to note that one of the largest and most comfortable huts had been appropriated by the quartermaster, regimental, presumably.

Rumor quickly made the rounds that the vacated and ready-made site would serve as their quarters for the winter. Joe Polley, Co. F, 4th Texas, was overwhelmed by the prospect: "When I saw the neat, well-framed, and plastered huts, each of a size to cozily accommodate two men, and was led to believe that within one of them I was to find shelter from wintry blasts, and comfort and rest for my poor, hunger-gaunted *corpus*, my heart filled with gratitude to my adversaries, and had they come unarmed and with peaceful intent I would gladly have 'fallen upon their necks and wept.'"[33] Wasting no time, he and Lt. Park, that officer having less than a year to live, commandeered one of "the most elegant" and within no time had settled in front of a roaring fire, pipes lit, tales on the tips of their tongues. Alas, before a yarn could be spun the call to arms resounded throughout the area and, noting his natural aversion to fighting, Polley said he had "faced the enemy with far less of reluctance than [he] left that comfortable little hut.... We rushed from a paradise into a frozen inferno; from warmth into bitter, stinging cold; from cheering homelike firelight, into that of glittering and unsympathetic stars."[34] Standing in ranks for most of the remainder of the night awaiting the order to take up the line of march, Polley thought that at that time, "any part of the Texas coast [would be] preferable to [that] part of Tennessee." The march was taken up finally on two roads toward Campbell's Station. Jenkins' (Hood's) Division advanced on the right, McLaws' on the left, the two roads converging at Campbell's.

Campbell's Station is located just thirteen miles southwest of Knoxville. On November 16, a battle appeared imminent as Jenkins' Division arrived there about noon, McLaws' several hours later. There they found the Federals were drawn up in a strong position. McLaws was to assault frontally while Jenkins was sent on a flanking movement to the right as Alexander's artillery opened on the enemy position. Before Jenkins could get into position, the enemy was seen to withdraw rapidly to their rear. Col. Sorrell said it "was principally an artillery fight, in which the gallant Alexander was tormented by defective ammunition. It should have been a strong and decisive battle, but things went wrong with the infantry divisions and an effective co-operation was not secured."[35] In the meantime, the enemy force retired to the safety afforded by the defenses of Knoxville.

By November 17, Longstreet's command was encamped at Hazen's within sight and sound of Knoxville. Gen. Burnside's forces were withdrawn within the city's defensive confines. As Confederate reconnoitering parties prowled its periphery seeking likely places for attack, the defenders worked feverishly to improve and complete their works.

The next day, there was a sharp skirmish on the Kingston road between Kershaw's Carolinians and some dismounted Federal cavalry whose commander, Gen. William P. Sanders, was mortally wounded in the deadly fray.[36] Gen. Burnside needed time in order to complete the city's defenses and Sanders and his men provided it but at a high cost. It was in Sanders' honor that what turned out to be the city's key fort was redesignated as his namesake.

As the last of the Federal troops gave way and filtered back into the city's defenses, Gen. McLaws occupied the vacated positions, his line extending from the banks of the Holston River, upon whose northern bank the city lies, to a point beyond the northwest bastion, soon to renamed Fort Sanders. From rifle pits quickly established in advance, a game of constant sniping began with the Federal riflemen firing from the fort's parapet and embrasures. The siege was on and in earnest.

Knoxville towers 150 feet above the Holston, its eastern limit defined by First Creek to the east and Second Creek to the west. About a mile further down the Holston, Third Creek flows into the river from the north. The East Tennessee and Georgia Railroad becomes the East Tennessee and Virginia Railroad as it passes to the north of the city. Connecting with that road coming down from the north was the East Tennessee and Kentucky Railroad. The enemy was well-ensconced in defensive positions situated upon a series of heights encircling the city, each end of their semicircular and formidable line leading down to and abutting the river.

Much of the work on the defenses had been started by Buckner's Confederates prior to their being withdrawn to Chattanooga by Gen. Bragg several months earlier. When they left, there were two uncompleted forts, Ft. Sanders, or Ft. Loudon as it was known to the Confederates, on the northwest and Ft. Huntington Smith on Temperance Hill on the east side of the city. Supervised by engineering officer Capt. Orlando Poe, the two forts had been completed by Burnside's engineers, contrabands and citizens by the time the last elements of the Army of the Ohio staggered into the city's confines. The heights were connected by rifle pits and artillery redoubts. Other defenses along the line included loop-holed houses, abatis and chevaux de frise (sharpened stakes mounted at a forty-five degree angle). First and Second Creeks were dammed to create lakes at some points. There were skirmishers deployed about 1,000 yards in front.

Even greater heights on the south side of the river overlooked the city. They were fortified as, from west to east, Fts. Higley, Dickerson and Stanley. Crossing the river at the southeast corner of the city, a pontoon bridge connected the defenses. Several unsuccessful attempts were made to break the pontoon connection by floating timber rafts down the river. It was an important point because some supplies reached the city by way of the bridge. Capt. Poe countered with protective booms across the river that thwarted the attempts.

Gen. Longstreet did not have the troops necessary for a complete investment of the city. Much of the perimeter from the northwest clockwise around to the southeast lay unperturbed, subject only to the harassment of Wheeler's cavalry. What meager supplies that reached the city via the pontoon bridge were thanks to the efforts of the pro-union citizens of the French Broad River basin. Even so, there was not enough. The Federal garrison suffered much the same pangs of hunger and bone-chilling conditions as did their Southern counterparts across the line. In order to conserve forage for the army's animals, beeves were slaughtered and preserved in salt. Used up horses were slaughtered on the riverbank, their carcasses' rolled into the river. The Confederates, short on horseshoes, fished them out downstream and extracted their valuable hoofware.

On November 19, as President Lincoln was delivering his "little noted nor long remembered" address at Gettysburg, Pennsylvania, Longstreet's Confederates, without personal knowledge of the locale and without maps, continued to reconnoiter seeking a weak spot. Oddly enough, the only place that seemed to afford any chance of a successful assault was the bastioned, star-shaped earthwork emplacement, Fort Sanders. Col. Alexander evaluated the fort's vulnerability in terms of its being on "a hill which fell off to the north west so that a large force could be marched under cover and approach within 200 yards of the fort['s northwest face] without being exposed to view or to fire either from the fort, or the adjacent lines on either side, which [there] made an obtuse angle."[37] Other lines of advance were still under consideration as preparations for the attack, wherever it might fall, were in progress until November 24.

By November 20, Longstreet determined, for tactical reasons, to contest the Federals for control of the heights lying along the south bank of the Holston. That task was assigned to Robertson's Texans and Arkansans and Law's Alabamians. Several days later they were crossed over the river's frigid waters in flatboats. According to Joe Polley, Co. F, 4th Texas, they were there to "assist Wheeler's cavalry in preventing the escape of the enemy in that direction."[38] Occupying a hill known locally as Cherokee Heights, it appeared to be a promising site for an artillery emplacement overlooking Ft. Sanders. Surveying the site personally, Col. Alexander declared it to be too far for effective usage. The Confederates did not have enough artillery ordnance to play any speculative games.

It was there that the Texas Brigade remained during the course of the siege, under fire constantly from positions across the river and from the Federally-occupied heights, Forts Higley, Dickerson and Stanley to their east, on the same side of the river. Once over, they drove back the defenders and occupied the hilly area opposite the point where the enemy's line abutted the river on the farther shore. In the days to come, Polley, while showing disdain for the Federal troops at Chickamauga and in Virginia, said of Burnside's troops at Knoxville that they "not only stood well, but also shot well. The hardest and most stubbornly contested skirmish fighting I ever witnessed took place there, and our lines needed to be frequently reinforced."[39]

Discipline was necessarily lax because of the urgent necessity for foraging. Of course, when an army's ingenious inhabitants are suffering the pangs of hunger constantly and are poorly clad, many unshod, in severe winter weather conditions, no amount of discipline could restrain them. Wandering the neighborhood, John West, Co. E, 4th Texas, found the countryside pretty well denuded of commissary by the Federals who had gotten there first. They had taken everything "chickens, ducks, turkeys, hogs, etc. [He] succeeded in getting two or three canteens of buttermilk, and gave the old lady three or four pounds of wool which [he] had taken from the hides of slaughtered sheep."[40] He had skinned a sheep and was using the hide for a pallet to sleep on. If one were to survive all the hardships in their varied forms that the Texas Brigade encountered, one had to be always on the alert for any opportunity and be a jack of all trades. (In Texas, West had been a lawyer and a district attorney.)

An unfruitful attack was mounted on November 25 against the three hills in front. When Polley's Company "F," went forward, it was up a steep ridge and in full view of the enemy. Two of his more intrepid comrades, Jim Mayfield and Jack Sutherland, moved beyond the company front and, taking cover behind the trees, proceeded to practice their sharpshooting skills. It was not long before Mayfield received a wound to a leg and foot. Making his way to the rear using his rifle as a crutch, he asked his envious comrades, "What will you give me for my furlough, boys?" He had received a parlor wound in the parlance of that day that in World War II would be called a million dollar wound. Such were wounds not considered to be life-threatening but serious enough to send a man elsewhere to recuperate, hopefully to the comfort and safety of one's own home. Company "F" continued the fight and later, a litter bearer brought the unexpected news that Mayfield's wound had proved fatal after all. He had died of lockjaw in an age before tetanus injections routinely administered staved off such fatal bacterial onslaughts.[41] That foray pretty well ended the confrontations on the south side of the river.

Meanwhile, that same day, Longstreet received by telegram from Bragg the disturbing news that the besieged Federal garrison at Chattanooga had left their positions. In a forward movement, they had attacked and then threatened the strong Confederate positions glowering down upon them from atop Lookout Mountain and Missionary Ridge. Bragg urged Longstreet to immediate action in order to relieve the pressure on him.

On November 26–27, more telegrams arrived reporting of an engagement at Chattanooga. With no specifics, their numbers indicated that something important had, indeed, transpired. That something, it would be learned later, was the unlikely but spectacularly successful Federal assaults that had carried Missionary Ridge several days earlier. Bragg and the Army of Tennessee were forced back on Dalton, Georgia, a major reversal of fortunes for that command. Longstreet, urged on by the vague but disquieting news from Chattanooga, decided that an immediate attack on his front was needed in order to distract whatever might be the Federal intent in his rear. For that matter, because of a disruption in Federal telegraphic communications, neither did Burnside know of the events that had transpired at Chattanooga.

By that time, and after considerable mud-bespattering reconnaissance and earnest discussion among the principals, it was decided that the key to the city's defenses was, indeed, Ft. Sanders. Among those principals, and concurring, was the chief engineer of the Army of Tennessee, Gen. Danville Leadbetter, who had arrived with the reinforcements sent by Gen. Bragg from Chattanooga. These troops were detached from Gen. Simon B. Buckner's Division, Johnson's Tennesseans and Gracie's Alabamians. Leadbetter had been instructed by Bragg to hurry things up. Longstreet set the date of attack for November 28.

Located on the northwest corner of the city's defenses, Fort Sanders was of earthen construction. Like any effective fort of that day, it was surrounded by an infantry-confounding ditch of varying and unknown width and depth. Adding to its formidability, the fort was constructed on elevated ground, an uphill fight adding to the attacking force's fatigue. It was manned by troops of the IX Army Corps commanded by Gen. Edward Ferrero. By virtue of special orders issued by Gen. Burnside, even though outranked on all sides, Lt. Samuel N. Benjamin, 2nd U.S. Artillery "exercised supreme authority" in Ft. Sanders.[42]

On the appointed day it was a cold, befogged dawn that dimly illuminated the scene. As the time for the attack arrived, the countryside remained blanketed in a heavy covering of fog obscuring the enemy's works. Under the circumstances, Gen. McLaws urged that the attack be delayed. Under the cover provided by the fog, he proposed his line be advanced to drive back the enemy's skirmishers. Then, rifle pits to shelter his sharpshooters could be dug as close to the fort as possible. Those marksmen could keep Federal heads below the fort's parapet while the attacking force could draw closer to its objective. McLaws' proposal was approved by Longstreet, and the attack was reset for dawn the morning of November 29.

The attack was to be against the northwest angle of the fort's wall, to be preceded by a demoralizing artillery barrage. The artillery role, later downgraded much to the chagrin of Col. Alexander, was to be followed by a quickly executed infantry assault moving from its position, by then, close up on the fortress wall. Three of McLaws' brigades, Humphrey's Mississippians, Bryan's and Wofford's Georgians, with Kershaw's South Carolinians in reserve, were the main elements of the attack. One of Jenkins' brigades, Anderson's Georgians, was to attack the enemy's right and rear. The absence of Law's and Robertson's Brigades, shock troops theretofore, in this attack is notable and may have been Longstreet's way of conveying his continuing displeasure with their leadership. Following up McLaws' initial assault were to be the two brigades of Gen. Buckner's Division, Gracie's Alabamians and Johnson's Tennesseans.

In preparing for the assault, the question as to the width and depth of the surrounding ditch troubled McLaws and Jenkins. Longstreet told them not to concern themselves too much. He thought the ditch to be fairly shallow, maybe three feet on average. The width he estimated at five to six feet. What he did not say was that his estimates were based on his viewing from a distance a Federal soldier crossing the ditch at one point without any apparent difficulty. As a result, no scaling ladders or fascines were included in the plans for the attack. For that matter, there were no means or materials available for constructing them.[43]

While preparing for the attack, Jenkins ran into Gen. Gracie, who had been in Knoxville as a part of Gen. Buckner's defending force. Gracie told Jenkins that the ditch was four or five feet deep and, being clay, when wet the walls were very slippery.[44] Towering overhead, the fort's walls reached a height of about twelve feet. Jenkins voiced his concerns but was told, in effect, be positive! By now, the rumors making the rounds of a Confederate defeat at Chattanooga tended, also, to affect the troop's morale. Nonetheless, Longstreet determined to concentrate on the task at hand which was to take Ft. Sanders, and thus, Knoxville.

On the evening of November 28, the Confederate skirmishers were advanced to capture the Federal pickets and dig rifle pits, a daunting task under the circumstances. That was accomplished, according to Capt. Poe, Burnside's chief engineer "with such spirit as to indicate an important movement."[45] In the skirmishing a member of the 8th Michigan was captured and promptly yielded up all the information that anyone interested in capturing the work should ever wish to know. Gen. McLaws' and Jenkins' assault troops were brought forward to attack positions where, according to Col. Alexander "they lay upon their arms without fires and suffering greatly."[46] Once again, the tables were turned. Less than a year earlier, some of Fort Sanders' present military garrison had lay in a similar fashion before these same Confederate units entrenched on Marye's Heights at Fredericksburg, Virginia.

At about 6:30 A.M. the next day, three signal guns, fired in rapid succession, announced the attack. "Alexander watched the fuses of his shells spin through the sky like shooting stars until they exploded in midair."[47] A desultory barrage from Alexander's batteries followed as sharpshooters sought any head showing above the fort's parapets. Longstreet's instructions were that the advance was to move out quietly and once at the works it was to move forward with a shout, no firing, bayonets fixed. "Then in two columns, nine regiments of McLaws' veterans rushed forward. In rear of the left column was Anderson's Georgians of Hood's Division, Micah Jenkins' command, which was to attack the line to the left of McLaws' men."[48] Kershaw's Brigade was to attack to the right of the assaulting column once the fort had fallen. "The unassigned brigades of McLaws' and Jenkins' Divisions, together with the brigades of Bushrod Johnson and Gracie, were to be held in readiness to follow any success."[49] Sharpshooters were to keep up a constant fire upon the parapets and embrasures. While not as famous as Pickett's charge at Gettysburg, obscured by fog and bringing them no glory,

Col. Alexander said that "it illustrated as well as Pickett's or any other which was ever made, those qualities of Longstreet's infantry which made them at once an admiration and a delight to their comrades in the Artillery."[50]

The advancing troops chanted "a breathless 'hep-hep-hep' as they trotted [forward]."[51] Nearing the fog-enshrouded fort the advance was halted as the front ranks crashed noisily to the ground. They had been tripped up, literally, when they found their way to be obstructed by telegraph wire stretched about. When the Confederates controlled Knoxville and were constructing Ft. Loudon, a second growth of obscuring small pine trees on the west front had been cut down. This left a field of pine stumps in front averaging about eighteen inches in height. When the Federals took up occupation and after the Confederates began their investment the vulnerability of the northwest front of the fort became more and more apparent. Seeking any and all means to remedy the situation, Capt. Poe accepted the offer of the local railroad representative of "a lot of old telegraph wire" to be used as obstruction. "Its use as a net-work entanglement, by carrying it from stump to stump over the sector ... was so obvious that no time was lost in putting it in place."[52] Its rusty appearance, along with the foggy conditions on the morning of the attack, allowed it to blend in against the "pine litter" covering the ground.

It took the front companies a while to pick themselves up and reorganize. When the renewed attack reached the ditch. McLaws' men piled into its wet, slippery depths as the well-sited Federal artillery in the fort and from adjacent batteries opened with canister and began to sow its usual bloody havoc. From the walls of the fort shells were ignited and thrown by hand into the seething mass below. Following, Anderson's men entered the ditch and it became a jammed mass of men pinned in with no place they could go. The actual depth of the ditch proved to be more like ten to fifteen feet in places.

Approaching from the rear, Gen. Longstreet saw the attack to be proceeding, apparently as planned, with several colors appearing to be planted on the works. Drawing closer, he met some stragglers who said the wall could not be surmounted for a lack of ladders or some other means to pass over. The berm, a narrow shelf ordinarily found at the foot of fortress parapets that offered, unintentionally, a foothold for assaulting troops, had been shoveled away Adding to the difficulties posed by the wall, overnight, the enemy had poured buckets of water down the parapet's side making it slippery with ice. Cotton bales atop the parapet made the wall even higher.

A few scattered men were able somehow to clamber up the slippery side of the wall on the shoulders of their comrades only to be killed or captured once they reached the top. The battle flags "of the 13th and 17th Mississippi and the 16th Georgia [were planted] upon the parapet, but every man who rallied to them was either killed or captured, and the flags taken."[53] Lt. Munger, of the 9th Georgia, Anderson's Brigade, was able to enter the fort through an embrasure, and "finding himself alone emptied his revolver at the gunners and made his escape." The adjutant of the 16th Georgia, T. W. Cumming, entered the fort through an embrasure and "was captured inside, assuring his captors that they would all be his prisoners within a few minutes."[54] "A New York sergeant burst from one embrasure and dragged a Mississippi color sergeant back in with him, flag and all."[55] A Massachusetts major watched in horror as a sergeant of the 79th New York, wielding an axe, cleaved "open the skulls of three Southern boys before he took up his rifle again."[56] In Wofford's Brigade, Col. Ruff, 18th Georgia, earlier in the war of Hood's Texas Brigade, commanding the Brigade, and Col. Henry P. Thomas, 16th Georgia, were killed. Col. Kennon McElroy, 13th Mississippi, Humphrey's Brigade, was killed also. "Nowhere in the war was individual example more splendidly illustrated than on that fatal slope and in that bloody ditch," was Col. Alexander's observation from his artillery position.[57] The dead began to pile up in the face of the well-placed Federal artillery and the musketry from the walls of the fortress.

Across the river to the south, Joe Polley, and Co. F, 4th Texas, braving three inches of snow and bone-chilling winds, were on picket duty. From their elevated position they had a full view of what transpired. He said of Humphrey's Mississippi Brigade, misidentifying them as Barksdale's, that former commander fallen at Gettysburg, that their attack "if terrible while in progress, it was awful when, having been repulsed with great slaughter ... was forced to withdraw and leave hundreds of its wounded upon the field, too close to the fort to be carried off by their friends."[58] Their cries for help carried clearly across the river in the crisp winter air and many froze to death before the day was over.

As the casualties continued to mount it was obvious that the attack had little or no chance of succeeding. "Such of the assaulting forces as had not entered the ditch fell back, at first sullenly and slowly, but flesh and blood could not stand the storm of shot and shell that was poured upon them, and they soon broke in confused retreat."[59] Maj. Goggin, of McLaws' staff, was a West Point classmate, a friend of longstanding and one in whom Longstreet had a great deal of confidence. Riding from the front he advised Longstreet that to continue the attack was futile: "The enemy had so surrounded the fort with network of wire that it was impossible for the men to get in without axes, and that there was not an axe in the command."[60] Without hesitation, Gen. Longstreet had the recall sounded. Rather than brave the open space before the fort again, many men chose surrender to almost certain death. Gen. Jenkins asked permission for a second assault. Col. Alexander thought the attack could have succeeded with the support of his thirty pieces of artillery if no longer held back and hampered as it had been in the predawn assault.

Simultaneous with the debacle unfolding before him, Longstreet was handed a dispatch from President Davis dated November 27. Without giving any details, the dispatch advised him that Bragg had fallen back on Ringgold and Longstreet was to rejoin the Army of Tennessee as soon as possible. Longstreet must have been puzzled, to say the least, upon receiving confirmation of what had been suspected. Somehow or another Bragg had been forced from his strong, dominating position overlooking Chattanooga and was now in retreat. How could that possibly be? Defeat loomed on all sides as a temporary truce, offered by Gen. Burnside, was called in order to remove the dead and wounded from the field.

Across the river, a diversionary advance was ordered. Co. F, 4th Texas, thinking that their picket duty would exempt them from the attack, was quickly disabused of that thought when ordered to the skirmish line. Even after the exertion of running uphill they had to warm their hands over the campfires left ablaze by the former occupants before they were able to reload their weapons. Federal resistance stiffened as the advance came to a halt. Joe Polley came upon Capt. "Howdy" Martin of Co. K, 4th Texas. He described Martin's usual battle demeanor as never drawing saber or pistol, but "[rubbing] his hands together and [smiling] merrily as if it were the greatest fun imaginable. Not even when he came near me that day and said, his voice choking and the tears standing in his eyes, 'They have killed brother Henry, Joe,' did the movement of his hands cease or the smile disappear from his countenance."[61]

The temporary respite, courtesy of Gen. Burnside, was extended until dark and gave Longstreet time to contemplate his next move in light of the new information. He had about decided to abandon Knoxville and fall back on Bragg until he received further information. A telegram from Bragg advised that he and his command had fallen all the way back to Dalton, Georgia. He also advised that a large force under Gen. Sherman had been set in motion toward Knoxville. He expressed the desire that Longstreet fall back on Dalton but if unable to do so, he might have to move into Virginia.

A council of war was called to discuss possible courses of action. Ultimately, it was decided that it was impracticable to reach Bragg given the route through mountainous terrain that would have to be taken. By staying in East Tennessee, they could draw Sherman and the others off and away from Bragg and at least pose a threat which Gen. Grant could not ignore. This was the course that Gen. Longstreet favored and so, stay it was.

The troops, drawn back, remained in their pre-attack positions until December 3. In addition to Gen. Sherman, several other columns, including one from the Cumberland Gap under Gen. Foster, was also reported converging on the city from the north. Thus, out-numbered and unsupported logistically, there was nothing left but to depart the area. The movement toward Virginia began on the evening of December 3, as the command's wagon trains moved out accompanied by the Texas Brigade, Law's Alabamians and a battery of Alexander's artillery. Twenty-four hours later, on December 4, the remaining infantry col-umn followed but along the farther bank of the Holston River.

Public opinion quickly decided that Longstreet, with superior manpower, had suffered a major defeat. About 500 men manning Ft. Sanders, commanded by a lieutenant whose responsibility under ordinary circumstances would not exceed several artillery pieces, had soundly defeated Longstreet's veteran attacking force. Later, Longstreet admitted that he was demoralized at the time, but after reflecting on it, he decided the real culprit was Gen. McLaws, his childhood friend and West Point classmate, who had not supported him and the attack properly. Others came under the cloud of his criticism, including Gen. Jerome B. Robertson and, eventually, Evander Law, both already in hot water as a result of the Rac-coon Mountain affair a few weeks earlier. Later, the convergence of these matters would make the bleak winter in East Tennessee all the more grim.

As the march east began, the weather was very cold, the country sparsely populated and rough. The Texans felt that they had played an important part in defeating the Federal army at Chickamauga and that their efforts had not been appreciated by the Army of Ten-nessee, at least by Gen. Bragg. M. V. Smith, Co. D, 4th Texas observed, "We had been detached from home, and from family, from Virginia and from Lee to go down to Tennessee and to Bragg to assist him to repulse Rosecran's Army. We did the work. Helped hold them in Chattanooga a month and notwithstanding all this, we felt like orphans, and had been treated like orphans."[62] And so it was that Longstreet's veteran corps marched toward an uncertain future, for the time being, in the bleak, snow-covered fastness of East Tennessee.

CHAPTER 13

"Oh! Carry me back to ole Virginny"[1]: The Brigade's Tortuous Road Home, December 1863–April 1864

Gen. Longstreet's strategy, once the decision had been made to remain in East Tennessee, was to move around to the north of Knoxville and seek out the Federal column reported to be moving down from the Cumberland Gap to the northeast. On December 3, in preparation for the general retreat from Knoxville northeast up the Holston Valley, the Texas and Alabama brigades and the cavalry supporting them launched a diversionary attack against their adversary on the south bank of the Holston. That night, after forcing the enemy back, they crossed the river and marched around the west side of the city to join the rest of their corps gathering on the north side. They then led the column away from Knoxville.

Their mission completed and silence no longer required, Joe Polley, Co. F, 4th Texas, said they "gave expression to their feelings ... [and] made the woods ring and resound with loud and unchecked rejoicings .... [T]hey were on their way to rejoin 'Marse Robert's' army. Some enthusiastically broke into song, and the opening words of [an] old melody floated in musical cadence from [every man's lips] ... with music in his soul ... 'Oh carry me back to ole Virginny, to ole Virginny's shore.'"[2] Their rejoicings were tempered in the coming days and weeks, however, when it became apparent that their return to "ole Virginny's shores" would take a while longer than they expected.

On December 4, the corps columns were on the march up the line of the East Tennessee and Virginia Railroad accompanied by Robertson's Texas and Law's Alabama brigades supported by a battery of Alexander's artillery. The 3rd Arkansas was the first of the Texas Brigade to move out. The weather and attendant conditions were described as "sinking, bitter cold and the roads were a solid sheet of glazed ice. The animals slipped and fell and were too weak from hunger to rise. The half-starved, ragged men used levers and [pry] poles to put them back on their feet. As the animals died from starvation and falls, they were promptly divided and eaten."[3]

For the first and only time during the war, M. V. Smith, Co. D, 4th Texas, found himself shoeless. Because of that, he and four companions, similarly disadvantaged, decided to ignore regulations and the provost guard and to march at their leisure. He did note, as presumably did all the others, that during the course of the war though they might be short of commissary and quartermaster stores, they were always "well supplied with munitions of war." During this march they were pressed by Union cavalry whom they would confront if they drew too close.

On the march, the four noticed an abandoned house, most likely the property of Union sympathizers of which East Tennessee abounded. In addition to the shelter, Smith and his companions found two fat chickens. Smith was detailed to catch the unfortunate fowl and to cook them for supper. The others fanned out in search of more provender, returning later with a "huge bee gum, the enormous cavity of which was filled to overflowing with nice honey." It was a meal, even if of only two chickens and a few "moldy biscuits," to be remembered though meager for five men. Then, with stomachs a little less "pinched, drawn and shrunken ... by almost continual fasting," they "took themselves to the land of knownothingism."[4] Foraging, by necessity, was a way of life in the armies of the Confederacy.

Crossing to the south bank of the river at Strawberry Plains, they encamped there for a time. It was a march the Arkansans, in the lead, and their comrades would not soon forget. The next day, the remainder of the troops followed along the line of the Holston River. Blain's Crossroads was reached on December 5 and Rutledge on December 6, where a two day halt was called. Not encountering the Cumberland Gap force, it was the immediate need to find food for the short-rationed men and animals that became of prime importance. The march continued, reaching Bean's Station on December 8.

By December 9, Longstreet had established his command around Rogersville overlooking the Holston River and opposite a spur of the East Tennessee and Virginia Railroad just across the river. There were grist mills in the area available to provide at least a few day's rations for the troops. Several days later, it was learned that a pursuing Federal cavalry and infantry force commanded by Maj. Gen. John G. Parke was fifteen miles away at Bean's Station in the very rough country to the southwest. On December 14, hoping to bag the whole lot, and over the next several days, Gen. Longstreet moved against them only to be disappointed once more as the attacks were bungled. Joe Polley, Co. F, 4th Texas said the brigade came under some artillery fire but took no active part in the fight. The key to success was the closing of a mountain gap in rear of the enemy, thereby shutting the door on his retreat. According to the disappointed Longstreet, "...When I went up in the morning, looking for their doleful surrender, my men found only empty camp-kettles, mess-pans, tents, and a few abandoned guns, and twelve prisoners, while the Yankees were, no doubt sitting around their camp-fires enjoying the joke with the comrades they had rejoined."[5]

Gen. Micah Jenkins, still temporarily in command of Hood's Division, was ordered in pursuit. In organizing for the pursuit, Gens. Law's and Robertson's Brigades were slow in reporting. A brigade from McLaws' Division was ordered but was also tardy. Gen. McLaws' attributed the delay to the brigade not yet having received its bread ration. Kershaw's Brigade was sent instead. As a result, the contemplated attack did not occur. This time, fault for failing to pursue the retreating foe in a timely fashion was laid at the doorsteps of McLaws and Law. These two subordinates were losing ground fast in the estimation of their corps commander.

In the meantime, Gen. Foster's Cumberland Gap force passed to the south and reached Knoxville. On December 12, Gen. Foster, under orders from the War Department, relieved an exhausted Gen. Burnside of command of the department. Command changes occurred also in the Army of Tennessee. On December 2, Gen. Bragg was relieved of the command of the Army of Tennessee. Ordered by President Davis to Richmond, he took up his new duties as the Confederate Army's chief of staff. As noted by Douglas S. Freeman, ironically "after the President reluctantly had concluded that the man who lost Lookout Mountain and Missionary Ridge was not qualified to command one Army, he decided to give that unsuccessful officer command of all the Armies."[6]

He was replaced briefly by Gen. William Hardee, a corps commander in the Army of Tennessee who, declining permanent command, was replaced, in turn, by Gen. Joseph E. Johnston on December 16, 1863. Unsuccessful in stopping Gen. Sherman's advance on Atlanta, Johnston was relieved of the army's command in August 1864, by the now somewhat recovered and "becrutched" Gen. John B. Hood. In his attempt to cut Gen. Sherman's line of supply as the latter marched to the sea, Hood was ultimately and soundly defeated before Nashville in December 1864, by Federal forces commanded by Gen. George H. Thomas. With no one else qualified, Gen. Johnston was once more called forward to command the army. This time he remained in command of that troubled army until its surrender, much reduced in numbers, in North Carolina in May 1865.

With the weather deteriorating even further and the roads becoming impassable, Longstreet decided it was time to "give up the game of war for the time, seek some good place for shelter, and repair railroads and bridges, to open our way back towards Richmond."[7] On a somber note, he said, "...We found bleak winter again breaking upon us, away from our friends, and dependent upon our own efforts for food and clothing."[8] Under those adverse circumstances he praised the men for their "brave, steady, patient" attitude. "Occasionally they called pretty loudly for *parched corn*, but always in a bright, merry mood.... [All] were then so healthy and strong that we did not feel severely our really great hardships."[9]

John C. West, Co. E, 4th Texas, bore this out, remembering in retrospect, that they lived "part of that time ... on corn issued to us in the ear from the wagons — three or four ears per man per day; which we shelled, parched and ate ... and received nothing else. Parched corn, a pipe of good tobacco, clear water, was the menu for several days. There were barefooted men making bloody tracks on the snow."[10] Yet, even under those grim conditions he heard little complaint and saw no signs of revolt. In February 1864, West received his discharge from the army of the Confederate States of America. Exempt from service from the beginning due to his position as Confederate States district attorney, Western District of Texas, West, nevertheless, had felt the call to duty and had acquitted himself admirably.

By December 20, the corps was crossed to the south bank of the Holston River and by Christmas was encamped on the railroad around Morristown. Joe Polley, Co. F, 4th Texas, said they reached that place the afternoon of December 22 and "went into winter quarters on the top of a wooded hill, a mile north of the little town."[11] Not expecting that long-term winter quarters were likely, the huts were rudimentary. Without elaboration upon the source of sudden bounty, presumably a rare Confederate States Quartermaster delivery, Polley says there was a generous issue of tents, abundant wood, a plentiful supply of good water and a generous issue of rations. They still needed shoes and clothing. Gen. Longstreet described that season as "the severest winter of the war."

Shoes were an important item in an infantryman's limited wardrobe. D. H. Hamilton, Co. M, 1st Texas, said he had to tie the pieces of what he had left to his feet. At Gen. Longstreet's order, the men were encouraged to obtain available rawhide, cut it to the shape of one's foot and secure it to the foot with rawhide lacings. They were known as "Longstreet moccasins," and, without any inner lining, must have been little better than going barefoot. Nonetheless, Hamilton thought they were much better than nothing. Hamilton said there was no necessity to ever take them off, even at night since they were not in polite company. Once those moccasins were in place they stayed there until they wore out. By the time Hamilton and his comrades began their return trip to Virginia and the Army of Northern Virginia in early spring, 1864, their moccasins were used up and they tied pieces of any remaining tent cloth they might have to their feet.[12]

Later, in early January 1864, the railroad leading eventually to Richmond was opened and "a shipment of three thousand shoes from Gen. Lawton, quartermaster-general [arrived] ... and the soldiers life seemed passably pleasant."[13] Gen. Longstreet included in the category of those to receive the shoes only the infantrymen and the artillerymen, the cavalry being mounted and less in need than their land-based comrades.

In the meantime, a war of another kind was brewing, an internecine one, the most savage of the genre.

In the immediate aftermath of the Ft. Sanders debacle, Gen. Longstreet had said nothing regarding blame for the attack's failure. However, having had time to think things over and after the Bean's Station affair, Longstreet, in a burst of bad temper and judgment, relieved Gen. Lafayette McLaws, his childhood friend and West Point classmate, of his division's command. When Longstreet got around to specifying the charges there was no mention of the Bean's Station affair, but rather, all charges were based on McLaws' "failure to take precautions in the assault on Fort Loudon." Gen. Longstreet seems to have momentarily lost his grip in the face of the extremely difficult situation with which he found himself confronted with as an independent commander. Like all leaders, military and otherwise, he was learning that not only is leadership fraught with an endless array of problems, it is a lonely pinnacle with room for no more than one at the top.

The stalwart McLaws was not one to be scapegoated and did not suffer his fate lightly; he fought back. Citing many reasons why the "bullheaded" general commanding had singled him out, including his refusal to join a clique that had been formed against Bragg before and after Chickamauga. He demanded a court-martial and the return of his command. At the same time, other officers were exposed to Longstreet's wrath. Charges were brought against Gen. Robertson by Gen. Jenkins for some of his utterances overheard at Bean's Station. Longstreet sided with his protégé and agreed that Robertson's remarks were "prejudicial to good order and morale." Reputedly, Gen. Robertson had, on December 18, held a meeting with his regimental officers, telling them that there were only three days' rations on hand and that "he had no confidence in the campaign ... that our men were in no condition for campaigning ... that he was opposed to the movement."[14]

Another source, T. L. McCarty, Co. L, 1st Texas, said that Robertson was relieved for disobedience of orders: "One night Gen. Robertson received orders to move his command out at break of day [the] following morning. It was an awful cold night ... about [ten] degrees below zero & a strong north wind blowing. Gen. Roberston did not obey the order until about [nine] or [ten] oclock. He waited until the sun shine [came] out and warmed the ground so his men could stand it & not suffer so much. He was relieved of his command for it but he always had the love and respect of his men."[15] From what is known of the man, he was probably guilty of both charges; his men's welfare was his primary concern. Regardless of the reason, he was relieved and ordered to Bristol, Virginia, to await the disposition of his case.

In the meantime, Longstreet requested reassignment for himself and his command. He was thoroughly weary of Tennessee, a place that he once saw as his chance for higher command and responsibility. "Gone was the desire to direct an army of his own; gone, too, was the confidence in which he had come to Tennessee."[16] Charles Minor Blackford, a judge advocate on Longstreet's staff, voiced the concerns of others when he confided in a letter to his wife that he was "much afraid there is a want of energy in General Longstreet's management of a separate command."[17]

Nor was Gen. Longstreet getting any support from President Davis and the Adjutant General's office in his vendetta against McLaws, et al. They were skeptical of Longstreet's authority to relieve an officer and order him beyond the limits of the command. And, Gen. McLaws got his court-martial as requested. Ordered from his home in Georgia to which he had been banished to await orders, he arrived back on February 3. The court-martial was convened on February 12, Gen. Simon B. Buckner presiding as president of the court. The trial proceeded on into March with many interruptions. The final outcome, in order to get on with the war against the blue-clad enemy, was that Gen. McLaws was exonerated by President Davis and transferred to another department, his military reputation intact. The president saw him as too valuable to lose and, indeed, he was. For the remainder of the war he served under Gen. Joe Johnston and surrendered with him at Greensboro, North Carolina, in May 1865. Eventually, command of McLaws' Division passed to the South Carolinian Gen. Joseph B. Kershaw, the brave, dependable and then senior brigade commander in that division since the beginning of the war.

In the case of Gen. Robertson, charges were brought on January 26, 1864, but no court-martial was ever convened. Instead, he was suspended from command and, eventually, in June, he was ordered to Texas where he took command of his state's reserve forces for the remainder of the war. The charges against Gen. Robertson and his departure did not affect him in the esteem of the Texans and Arkansans that he commanded. According to Joe Polley, Co. F, 4th Texas, "...The Texas Brigade heartily approved of his course, and its survivors are yet grateful to him for the firm stand he took and for the interest and fatherly solicitude he always manifested in the well-being of his men.[18] Command of the Texas Brigade went to Gen. John Gregg, the same whose life had been saved by the Texans when they came across his prostrate form on the field of Chickamauga.

In the case of Evander Law, Longstreet's dissatisfaction stemmed from the affairs at Wauhatchie and Bean's Station, the rivalry with his protégé, Jenkins, notwithstanding. On December 19, Law tendered his resignation. While awaiting confirmation, he requested and was granted a leave of absence. Traveling to Richmond, it was rumored he was trying to get his brigade transferred, en masse, to its home state, Alabama . After intrigue worthy of that practiced within the Roman Empire, Gen. Law was returned to the com-

Gen. John Gregg, sixth commander of the Texas Brigade, killed on the Darbytown Road, October 7, 1864

mand of his brigade. He remained in command until wounded the next spring, his relations with his corps commander strained, to say the least. He deserved better; he was a fine soldier of proven valor. After recovering from his wound and at his own request, he left the Army of Northern Virginia and commanded a cavalry force under Gen. Joseph E. Johnston until the end of the war.

Longstreet's continuing and convoluted attempts to get his favorite and protégé, Micah Jenkins, in permanent command of Hood's Division were never successful. That responsibility was assigned directly by President Davis. The appointee was Gen. Charles W. Fields, a Kentuckian and West Point graduate, Class of 1849. Still not completely recovered from serious wounds suffered at Second Manassas, Fields took the command, nonetheless. Of the new commanders, Gens. Field and Gregg, Joe Polley, Co. F, 5th Texas, said that "the former did not win from the division the admiration and confidence it felt for and in General Hood, and that the latter failed to secure such a hold on the affection of the Texas Brigade as Robertson had gained, was due, perhaps, more to lack of opportunity than to any want of merit in either. In truth, the standard of excellence in a commander for whom they would 'do or die,' which had been adopted by the members of the Texas Brigade, was John B. Hood."[19] Difficult is the path for one who follows close in the wake of a successful and beloved leader.

A number of plans of campaign were considered in the latter part of the year and in the first months of 1864. Longstreet suggested that his corps be mounted. Once that was accomplished, his command would advance into Kentucky and seize the Louisville and Nashville Railroad. Control of that line would have the desired effect of forcing the Federal armies out of Tennessee. Their withdrawal would open the way for the occupation of the state by Gen. Johnston's Army of Tennessee. The disinterest of the government and its obvious inability to provide the animals necessary to mount the proposed offensive quickly consigned that plan to the dustbin of history.

Another plan advanced by Longstreet attracted enough attention to merit him a trip to Richmond to confer with the government and Gen. Lee. As in the first proposed plan, control of the Louisville and Nashville Railroad was central. In this proposal, Gen. Beauregard's infantry in and around Charleston, South Carolina, would be marched northward joining Longstreet's command at Abingdon, Virginia. From that place, the combined command would move on Louisville, Kentucky. Holding the railroad at that point, it was conjectured, would force the Federal armies out of Tennessee. Gen. Johnston's Army of Tennessee would follow them up in the wake of their retreat. This accomplished, the three armies would be combined for further operations. As with the first proposal, this plan did not succeed, ultimately, in attracting the support of the government. There were too many details that could not be worked out.

Of that time Col. Alexander said, "We spent the winter between Russellville and Greenville, living off the country, having occasional expeditions and alarms enough to destroy most of the comfort of winter quarters."[20] There were however, continuing shortages of quartermaster stores. "Tattered blankets, garments, and shoes (the latter going — many gone) opened ways, on all sides, for piercing winter blasts."[21] Gen. Longstreet had given his permission for the men to exchange shoes with Federal prisoners of war. This was with the admonition that it must be a swap that did not leave the prisoner barefoot. Col. Alexander said it was amusing to watch the men inspect prisoners for suitable swaps. Generally, it was all conducted in good humor. As one captured Federal soldier put it, "When a man is captured, his shoes are captured also."[22]

Winter had unleashed its total fury during the last few days of the year with temperatures near and below zero and lasting for several weeks. Gen. Longstreet described affairs as "bright and encouraging," which, in fact, they were not. He attributed this to the fact that "the disaffected [meaning McLaws, Law and Robertson] were away, and with them disappeared their influence."[23] If others felt that optimistic there was little or no mention of it. He said the soldier's life was "passably pleasant" except for the cavalrymen who "were looking at the enemy ... and the enemy was looking at them, frequently burning powder between the lines."[24]

Longstreet's chief of staff, G. Moxley Sorrel, notes in his memoir that President Lincoln and his army chief of staff, Gen. Henry Halleck, were intensely uneasy about the Confederate presence in East Tennessee: "The emphatic tone of many letters and orders from the Federal capitol was that they should, under any circumstances and apparently at any sacrifices, be driven out."[25] In its position, Longstreet's Corps was in striking distance of Kentucky via the Cumberland Gap and that spelled political trouble for the Lincoln administration.

Being a threat and being able to do anything about it were two different matters. The Federals did not know the true situation across the lines, that Longstreet did not have the means to invade Kentucky. So it was that, at the administration's urging Gen. Grant ordered Gen. Foster at Knoxville to mount an offensive against Longstreet's Corps to drive it at least "beyond Bull's Gap and Red Bridge." Those points are only a short distance northeast of Morristown up the line of the East Tennessee and Virginia Railroad. A formidable force, consisting of three Federal infantry corps and cavalry, began the campaign on January 14–15. The IX and XXIII Corps were ordered to Mossy Creek, the IV Corps to Strawberry Plains and the cavalry to Dandridge.[26]

By then, Longstreet's Corps' winter quarters around Morristown consisted of huts and a shoe factory that was turning out cowhide shoes, albeit of a very inferior quality. What domestic tranquility there was available was interrupted when it was learned that Foster's Federal force in numbers was advancing from the direction of Knoxville. Might as well face the enemy now and protect the winter quarters rather than retreat and have to face them later, Longstreet decided.

Gen. William T. Martin's cavalry, who had discovered the advance around Dandridge was already on the enemy's front. Jenkins' Division, including the Texas Brigade, Bushrod Johnson's Division and Alexander's Batteries were ordered to march in support of Gen. Martin's cavalry. Gen. McLaw's Division, commanded temporarily by Gen. Wofford and Gen. Ransom's Division, under Gen. Carr, were advanced on the Dandridge Road and held in reserve. Col. Sorrel said the weather was bitterly cold "the ground hard and sharp with ice, and not less than 2,000 of our little army were without shoes [and] their bleeding feet left marks at every step."[27]

By the time Gen. Longstreet reached the front, Gen. Martin's cavalry was hotly engaged with the enemy. Wishing to spare his infantry an exhausting march, if possible, he ordered Gen. Martin to take the enemy position, there being no Blue infantry presence observed. Successfully taking the position and there still being no enemy infantry in sight, Longstreet urged Martin to take the next position. To this urging Gen. Martin demurred, respectfully, saying he did not think it could be taken without infantry support. Acceding to Gen. Martin's assessment, Longstreet left him to engage the enemy's attention, while he with a small cavalry force attempted a turning movement on the enemy's left flank.

Reaching the point of attack under cover and unobserved, the Gray cavalrymen were dismounted and formed into a single line of battle. Stepping out, the cavalrymen-cum-infantry advanced. Longstreet observed that their advance took them near a farmhouse. "As our line marched, a chicken, dazed by the formidable appearance, crouched in the grass until it was kicked up, when it flew and tried to clear the line, but one of the troopers jumped up, knocked it down with the end of his gun, stooped, picked it up, put it in his haversack, and marched on without losing his place or step and without looking to his right or left, as though it was as proper and as much an every-day part of the exercise of war as shooting at the enemy."[28] Confederate soldiers, from hard experience, knew to never pass up an opportunity for obtaining something to eat. It might be a long time before the next opportunity presented itself.

Joined by Gen. Martin's main body, the objective ridge was taken. The infantry column arrived late in the afternoon and the enemy was forced back on Dandridge. The Federal command, due to various circumstances, was commanded alternately by, first, Foster, then by Gen. Parke, Gen. Phil Sheridan and, finally, by Gen. Gordon Granger. In the final analysis, Gen. Granger, not finding any advantage, led his troops back across the Holston toward Knoxville destroying his bridges behind him. Longstreet's Corps returned to its winter quarters. Gen. Martin's cavalry pursued the retreating column to the vicinity of Knoxville, scooping up some stragglers, equipment and a herd of 800 beef cattle. That few cattle did not go very far toward feeding an army numbering in the thousands.

In the vicinity of Morristown, Lt. Col. Sorrel said that there was an abundance of fuel in the form of "primeval forests of oak and hickory." There were made "some of the grandest campfires ever seen, but we froze in front while scorching in back, and vice versa.... At this time the roads were so bad as to be almost impassable; artillery and wagons would be drawn hub deep. The artillery horses, Leyden's especially, were in bad condition, very weak, and six or eight pairs would be hitched to a single gun or caisson."[29]

Sorrell observed the native populace with acuity, terming them "an interesting study." Allowing for their suffering during the war, and with some exceptions, he found the "general run of people [to be] hard in the extreme." "Apparently they were without pity or compassion — generosity and sympathy were strangers to them; but hatred and revenge made their homes in the breasts of these farmers." Divided politically, it was neighbor against neighbor. "Burnings, hangings, whippings were common — all acts of private vengeance and retaliation."[30] It was with people such as this, in addition to the weather and shortages of rations and clothing, that the soldiers of Longstreet's Corps had to contend for their forage.

Bearing Sorrell's observation out was William A. Fletcher, Co. F, 5th Texas, returned to his regiment in East Tennessee after treatment of his foot wound suffered at Chickamauga and pending his transfer to the 8th Texas Cavalry. As the army's presence rapidly diminished the countryside's bounty, foraging at a distance became increasingly necessary. That country was inhabited by "nearly all Union people," and "there was little mercy shown..., a fellow had to watch the jayhawkers or he would lose his scalp, and ... foraging was done by details of good number, as the jayhawkers were bad." Relating a comrade's experiences of trying to capture jayhawkers at night, on one occasion, Fletcher said, "They had surrounded a house of a noted one and burst open the door. They found him under a bed and with cocked guns pointing, the wife yelled out saying all the rough, abusive words at her command and that if they were going to shoot him, to take him from under the bed and out of the house, and to leave her no nasty mess to clean up."[31] Another realistic and grim aspect of an internecine war usually glossed over in more romanticized versions of Civil War history.

The weather improving somewhat, as did the roads, on February 10, Gen. Jenkins' Division was ordered to prepare to march once again, this time toward Strawberry Plains.

That place is maybe thirty miles or so northeast of Knoxville on the line of the East Tennessee and Virginia Railroad. When Gen. Grant learned of the advance, he ordered Gen. Foster to meet it and sent additional troops. Gen. Thomas personally took command. The orders to Thomas were to drive Longstreet "beyond the limits of the State of Tennessee." Federal cavalry from Cumberland Gap was ordered to gain the Confederate rear. Gen. Martin, advancing to meet the threat, was severely routed losing several guns and several hundred men as prisoners of war. Eventually, the Federal column was forced to retire back on Maryville, leaving Longstreet in command of the good foraging ground.

On February 14, Gen. Jenkins, still at Strawberry Plains with his division, was ordered by Gen. Longstreet to throw the pontoon bridge in his possession across the Holston in preparation for an advance on Knoxville. Other troops were ordered to concentrate at Strawberry Plains from various locations and to await Longstreet's arrival for further orders. However, before this could be further set in motion, Gen. Longstreet, on February 19, received orders from Richmond to send Gen. Martin and his cavalry to the support of Gen. Johnston at Dalton, Georgia. A previous request by Gen. Longstreet for 10,000 additional troops was denied as well; they just were not available. As a result, Gen. Longstreet, albeit for differing reasons, was forced to abandon his offensive just as his old friend, Gen. Grant, was forced to abandon his plans. Under the circumstances, Longstreet decided to withdraw his command to a safer locale where the foraging would be better. On February 22, the retreat was begun with Gen. Jenkins' division and the remaining cavalry providing cover. The march was to the vicinity of Bull's Gap where once again winter quarters were resumed between the Holston and Nolachucky rivers.

While still around Strawberry Plains, the troops were invited to reenlist for the duration of the war. "As it was to enlist or be conscripted, not a man declined,"[32] was the way Joe Polley, Co. F, 4th Texas put it. Arbitrary is another word that comes to mind and is the way of governments in times of war when manpower is uncertain but required.

Meanwhile, in a joint resolution of the Confederate Congress, approved February 17, 1864, the thanks of the Congress was extended to Longstreet, and the officers and men of his corps. The resolution noted "their patriotic services and brilliant achievements ... sharing as they have the arduous fatigues and privations of many campaigns in Virginia, Maryland, Pennsylvania, Georgia, and Tennessee, and participating in nearly every great battle fought in those states." Longstreet was singled out as "ever displaying great ability, skill, and prudence in command." The officers and men were praised as displaying "the most heroic bravery, fortitude, and energy, in every duty they have been called upon to perform."[33] Even though things had not gone well following the great victory at Chickamauga, the accolade was well-merited. The campaign was conducted under the most unfavorable of circumstances and the accolade, no doubt, had a salutary effect on the corps' morale.

In a letter home dated March 7, one perceptive officer, probably of Co. A, 4th Texas, noting a chimney going up on Gen. Gregg's tent, concluded that they were going to be in the area for a while. Awhile meant anything from a few weeks to a few months. It turned out to be a few weeks in this instance. Nonetheless, it was a signal, also, for the troops to put up at least semi-permanent living quarters. Any respite from field operations saw the return of military camp routine. Idle troops were considered to be the devil's workshop, and for some, it usually was true. "Have no idea what our movements are to be, our orders prescribe drill in the morning, dress parade in the evening. We are living on poor beef and flour made of sick wheat."[34] He said that the new divisional commander superseding Gen. Jenkins, Gen. Field, and the brigade commander, Gen. Gregg, superseding Gen. Robertson, were making favorable impressions with their subordinates.

Conditions varied on a day-by-day basis. While the Texas Brigade picketed "two mountain passes," the Texan letter-writer had time to visit the other units of the division. On March 13, he then found it "in good health and spirit and now tolerably well shod and clothed, the greatest need now being underclothing." By March 18, he noted that "[w]e are having pretty tight times here now in the way of rations. Usually we have bread and beef of the very poorest quality and deficient in quantity, but on yesterday for breakfast we had bread and a small bit of bacon; for dinner, bread and boiled rice, and for supper, bread alone, and the same this morning; so, if my letter is uninteresting, it is attributable to something else than over-eating."[35] In feeding and clothing an army numbering in the thousands, commissary and quartermaster supplies do disappear at an alarming rate, much to the dismay of those responsible, in this case, the harried commissary and quartermaster officers.

Even though the lack of logistical support bordered on disastrous at times, there were extenuating circumstances. While in East Tennessee, Nicholas Pomoroy, Co. A, 5th Texas, attributed their want of supply to interruption of rail service to their isolated locale and to the area having been scavenged by both armies. The lack of adequate commissary and quartermaster supplies "combined with the hardships of standing guard and picket duty ... out in the snow, sleet and wet slush of the rigorous winter season made it very trying on our soldiers."[36] Even in the face of these hardships, he said that "the spirit of our soldiers never faltered." Nonetheless, they did have to be innovative.

In hard times such as those being experienced, military executions were not uncommon, usually for desertion. On March 19, while picketing the gaps, a 4th Texas officer and his men noticed far below them some troops drawn up in a "hollow square." A "hollow square" had troops forming three sides of the square the fourth side occupied by the convicted. That formation was recognized for what it was and never portended a good thing. It was not long before a cloud of smoke was seen to form over the formation followed by the distance-delayed crash of a musket volley. "Some poor fellow, who thought more of his own comfort than his duty, was suddenly ushered into the presence of his maker. These military executions are fearful affairs, though necessary for the discipline of large armies and the success of our righteous cause. Who this was or what his offense, I have not the slightest idea."[37] A deserter, most likely, he speculated.

Although not official yet, the First Corps was on the way back to Gen. Lee's army. On March 28, according to the officer, probably Co. A, 4th Texas, Gregg's Division took up the march eastward from Bull's Gap to Greenville, Tennessee, reaching that place that same night. It was a rain-swept, mud-impeded trek at the end of which they bivouacked. There Lt. Marchant, Co. A, 4th Texas, received a letter and a box from Virginia, which indicates the mail service was still operating even in that remote location, the time from mailing to delivery unknown. The reading of the letter was delayed until later as the box was torn asunder by the hungry soldiers who perceived it contained food. It did. "That ham was fine, the biscuit excellent, and the cake could not have been beaten by any confectioner in Richmond, and all was a great treat for half-famished soldiers."[38]

The next morning the march continued "through a terrible snow storm, over the worst roads ... ever seen, and on the 1st [April] ... reached [Zollicoffer, Tenn] ... ten miles from the line of the Old Dominion."[39] The next morning, in a transformation, the weather is described as "spring-like" kindling hopes that the worst of winter was over. Speculation was rife as to the corps' destination, back to Virginia or a foray into Kentucky? Col. Key returned to the 4th Texas at Zollicoffer. He had been wounded at Gaines' Mill and promoted to the regimental command in July 1862. He was in poor health, however, and retired soon thereafter.

On April 7, Gen. Longstreet received official orders for his corps to return to the Army of Northern Virginia then holding the line of the Rapidan River. The return was to be by way of Charlottesville. On April 14, Co. A, 4th Texas, and presumably the rest of the Texas Brigade, moved down to the railroad where the baggage was sent off to Virginia. By April 28, they were at Cobham, Virginia, eighteen miles from Charlottesville. They were returned, at last, to "old Virginny's shore." Any hope for rest and recuperation was to be short-lived, however, as they were to learn once they rejoined Gen. Lee's army.

CHAPTER 14

"*Texas Brigade! The eyes of General Lee are upon you!*"[1]: The Wilderness, May 5–7, 1864

The weather was spring like, a sharp contrast with what they had experienced over the recent months in East Tennessee. It was April 29, 1864, and Longstreet's Corps, once more an integral part of the Army of Northern Virginia, was drawn up in its reduced numbers awaiting review by the army's commander, Gen. Robert E. Lee. After a brief encampment in the vicinity of Charlottesville, the corps had moved on to the area southwest of Gordonsville around Mechanicsville, Cobham Station on the Virginia Central Railroad. According to the artillerist, Col. E. P. Alexander, it was the first grand review to be held since the one held in the aftermath of Sharpsburg while the army was bivouacked in the Shenandoah Valley. As things were to turn out, it would also be its last.

The review, a welcome back as much as anything else, was held "in a cleared valley, with extensive pastures, in which [the] two divisions of infantry, & [Alexander's] guns could be massed."[2] Numbering only about 10,000 in the aftermath of its recent travails away from the Army of Northern Virginia, the troops were nonetheless anxious and enthusiastic to see and to please their beloved gray commander mounted on his familiar gray charger. "Guns were burnished and rubbed up, cartridge boxes and belts polished, and the brass buttons and buckles made to look as bright as new.... [C]lothes were patched and brushed up ... boots and shoes greased, the tattered and torn old hats were given here and there 'a lick and a promise,' and on the whole ... [they] presented not a bad-looking body of soldiers."[3]

By the time Col. Alexander got around to preparing his memoir in which this episode was recounted, forty years had passed. Even so, that earlier day stood out in his memory vividly. Thinking of that distant time, he had mused, as Gen. Lee, mounted upon Traveler, and his staff came upon the field of review "My bugle sounds a signal, & my battalion thunders out a salute, & the general reins up his horse, & bares his good gray head, & looks at us & we shout & cry & wave our battleflags & look at him again. For sudden as a wind, a wave of sentiment, such as can only come to large crowds in full sympathy, something alike what came a year later at Appomattox, seemed to sweep over the field. Each man seemed to feel the bond which held us all to Lee. There was no speaking, but the effect was that of a military sacrament, in which we pledged anew our lives.[4] Riding alongside Lee's aide, Col. Venable, Chaplain Boggs of South Carolina, asked, "Does not it make the General proud to see how these men love him?" Venable answered, "Not proud. It awes him."[5]

The next time that these troops and their gray commander were in each other's presence was a week later. At that time, dawn on the morning of May 6, the circumstances were such that Gen. Lee, according to Col. Alexander, was in "the most desperate strait he had ever known."[6]

A few weeks earlier, ominous signs of Federal activity were observed on the north bank of the Rapidan River. Across there, the Army of the Potomac had grown noticeably larger during recent months. Given the time of the year, it was obvious and anticipated that a major campaign effort was in the making. After a winter of relative inactivity, except for the abortive Mine Run affair, the Army of the Potomac was restive as seen by the observers of the Army of Northern Virginia from their positions on the opposite bank. In point of fact, the Federal army was a reorganized one. It had been thoroughly reequipped and was, in all respects, ready for field operations. Most significantly, the Federal command structure had been altered since the last clash of arms back in the winter.

The recent appointment of the successful campaigner from the West, now promoted lieutenant general, Ulysses S. Grant, as general in chief of all Federal armies in the field signaled that a new era had dawned for the Union cause. Gen. Grant's string of successful operations in the West beginning in 1862 were quite impressive — Forts Henry and Donelson, Shiloh, Vicksburg, and most recently, the breaking of the Confederate siege of Chattanooga. He was a man to be reckoned with. No one knew that better than Gen. James Longstreet, who had been a close friend in the "old army." Of Grant "an all-around soldier, seldom if ever surpassed; but the biggest part of him [is] his heart." was how Longstreet described him.[7]

Although Gen. Grant chose to take the field with the Army of the Potomac, command of that steadily improving body of men remained with Gen. George G. Meade, the commander since the victory at Gettysburg. Gen. Grant's instructions to Meade were, "Lee's army will be your objective point; wherever he goes, there will you go."[8] Gen. Sherman, commanding the Federal armies in North Georgia now around Dalton, received the same instructions: go for Joe Johnston's Army of Tennessee. Prisoner-of-war exchanges were ended; the armies of the South were to be worn down by unremitting attrition. President Lincoln thought that he might have found the man that could, as he put it, "face the arithmetic," that is, accept the inevitably heavy casualties that such a winning strategy would require.

The Army of the Potomac, estimates running anywhere from 100,000 up to 130,000 strong, was now reorganized into three corps, the II, V and VI, commanded by, respectively, Gens. Winfield Scott Hancock, G. K. Warren and John Sedgwick. A fourth corps, the IX, was under the direct command of Gen. Ambrose E. Burnside, returned to the Army of the Potomac after a respite following his successful defense of Knoxville. Originally in the Eastern army, the IX Corps had only recently returned from a year's service in the West. As the campaign began that much-traveled corps was being held in reserve at the Rappahannock railroad bridge, a unit unto itself and under the direct orders of Gen. Grant.

The Army of Northern Virginia braced for the fury it knew was to come. It was to be a war of attrition in which replaceable Federal troops in large numbers would be thrown against irreplaceable Confederate troops in lesser numbers. About 64,000 strong, "Lee's army lay west of the Rapidan, R. H. Anderson's Division facing Madison Court House; the Second (Ewell's) and Third (A. P. Hill's) Corps ... two divisions of the First (Longstreet's), and Alexander's artillery were at Mechanicsville [near Gordonsville]; Pickett's division of the First was south of the James."[9] The combative Lee told his chief of staff, Walter Taylor, "We have got to whip them; we must whip them, and it has already made me better to think of it."[10]

That had always been the primary task of the Army of Northern Virginia, one that had been achieved on many an unlikely field. But now the task was becoming ever harder as the supplies so necessary to successfully wage war were waning daily. The army had not increased significantly in numbers over the winter and commissary and quartermaster supplies were scant, even more so than usual. "A new pair of shoes or an overcoat was a luxury, and full rations would have astonished the stomachs of Lee's ragged Confederates." The commander of the Alabama Brigade, Gen. Evander Law, described the plight of all when he recalled one scantily clad Confederate soldier whose oft-patched trousers were finally shed. "Unable to buy, beg, or borrow another pair, he wore instead a pair of thin cotton drawers. By nursing these carefully he managed to get through the winter. Before the campaign opened ... a small lot of clothing was received."[11] He was the first to receive replacement clothing. Many were not so fortunate.

While awaiting the weather to brighten and the ground to dry out, Gen. Lee studied the intelligence reports that reached him from various sources. At a meeting with his corps and divisional commanders at the signal station on Clark's Mountain on May 2, he told them he expected the crossing of the Rapidan to occur at Germanna or Ely's Fords or both. Once again his military prescience proved accurate. Beginning several days later, that is precisely what happened.

After a period of heavy rains in which the roads leading south were unnavigable, by the evening and early morning hours of May 3–4, things had dried out enough, and, it was certain from reports of signalmen watching from the heights of Clark's Mountain, that the Army of the Potomac was on the march. The only question remaining was, whither to, precisely? The light of dawn provided the answer. The Army of the Potomac, in its thousands and with its trains, was marching to its left. As predicted, it was bound for the Rapidan fords, the four division V and three division VI Corps for Germanna and the four division II Corps for Ely's. The crossing of the Rapidan at those points posed a threat to the Confederate right held by Ewell's Corps.

The Army of Northern Virginia faced an army almost double its size. That number would grow even more when joined by Burnside's four division IX Corps once ordered forward from its position protecting the Orange and Alexandria Bridge over the Rappahannock. After the unopposed crossing of the Rapidan, where Gen. Grant had expected a fierce resistance, he sent Gen. Burnside the order to bring his corps to the front.

Avoiding battle, Gen. Grant's plan was to pass quickly through the practically impenetrable area of second growth forests and underbrush known thereabouts as the Wilderness. It was an area ten or twelve miles square, bounded north and east by the Rapidan and Rappahannock Rivers, and lying between Fredericksburg and Orange Court House. It was described by Joe Polley, Co. F, 4th Texas, as a "dark, damp, dense, miasma-breeding forest ... into which sunlight never penetrated, and the tangled undergrowth of swamplands and morasses, are remembrances that are yet vivid, and at which old soldiers yet shudder."[12]

Once gaining the roads beyond, the Federal plan called for getting between the Army of Northern Virginia and the Confederate capital at Richmond some seventy miles to the south. There, with its overwhelming advantage in numbers, the Army of the Potomac would bring its opposite number to battle and overwhelm it. Simultaneously, the Army of the James, composed of the XVIII and the XXIII Corps commanded by the political general Benjamin F. Butler, was to advance upon and capture Richmond by way of the peninsula. Anticipating the moves on his front, Gen. Lee alerted Gen. Ewell. As a matter of fact, Gen. Lee's plan was to bring on a battle in the thickness that was the Wilderness. In that jungle-like setting, the Blue's superior numbers in troops and artillery would be neutralized somewhat.

During the first day's advance, while the river crossing progressed quickly and without opposition, the advance units of the Army of the Potomac were held up in the Wilderness beyond the river to wait for its supply train to close up. Crossing below at Ely's Ford, Hancock's II Corps, bivouacked the night of May 4, around Chancellorsville. Crossing farther up at Germanna Ford, Warren's V Corps was at Old Wilderness Tavern with the cavalry divisions under Wilson and Gregg forward to Piney Branch Church and Parker's Store, respectively.[13] Sedgwick's VI Corps and Burnside's IX Corps were moving forward to cross the river.

At the command of Gen. Lee, in the meantime, Gen. Ewell committed his troops, the divisions of Rodes, Johnson and Early, to a parallel march east in the direction of the fords at about noon on May 4. Their line of march was along the Old Turnpike (also known as the Orange Court House Turnpike), that term dignifying what was in reality only a country dirt road. It led on a fairly straight-line course paralleling the Rapidan from Orange on the west to Fredericksburg to the east. By that evening, Ewell's Corps was at Locust Grove, within about three miles of Warren's V Federal Corps bivouac.

A. P. Hill's Corps, the divisions of Heth and Wilcox, the commanding general accompanying, swung out south of the Old Turnpike and parallel with Ewell along the line of the Orange Plank Road. As the term implies, it was a road covered with wooden planks in the day before asphalt and concrete became the standard materials for hard-surfacing roadways. Located two or three miles south of the Turnpike, that road zigged and zagged its erratic way eventually to Fredericksburg.

By that evening, Hill's Corps was within about three or four miles of Wilson's Federal cavalry division bivouac area. The remaining Third Corps division, that of Gen. R. H. Anderson, was far in the rear, left to guard the Virginia Central Railroad around Gordonsville until it was clear that no threat was posed to the vital rail link. Gen. J. E. B. Stuart's cavalry division was making its way to the scene from around Fredericksburg. Longstreet's Corps was at least a day's march away to the west in the vicinity of Gordonsville. The contending forces were converging, at right angles, for an inevitable clash of arms somewhere south of the Rapidan fords.

Gen. Lee dispatched orders to Longstreet for Gen. Field's Division to lead off Longstreet's Corps' march to join up with the rest of the army marching "to Richard's Shop ... southeast of Verdierville."[14] Receiving the orders about 1:00 P.M., May 4, the march was taken up at about 4:00 P.M. The route ordered to be taken by Field was some distance south of the line of the Orange Plank Road. Followed up by Kershaw's (McLaws') Division, Longstreet's Corps thus formed a third Gray column well to the west and rear of the other two advancing toward the vicinity of the Wilderness. Longstreet's Corps, short Pickett's Division still garrisoned at Richmond, bivouacked around Brock's Bridge late the night of May 4. Resuming the march the next day, twenty-eight miles later found them bivouacking at Richard's Shop the night of May 5–6. In his private notebook, Col. Winkler, 4th Texas, recorded that they started before daylight and "marched hard till late in P.M. passing ground of cavalry skirmishing; met Federal prisoners; camped."[15] They were within easy marching distance of the battlefield of that day and would, upon reaching the field, play a pivotal role in the continuing battle the next day.

To the east on the morning of May 5, the march of the respective armies was taken up again. Both armies had been engaged in the area before; a year earlier the great Battle of

Chancellorsville had been fought there. On this day the intelligence of both sides was imprecise as to whom was exactly where and as to what exactly was their immediate intent. Gen. Lee's orders to Gen. Ewell were to remain parallel and even with Hill's Corps to his south on the Orange Plank Road. He was to regulate his march in order to facilitate Longstreet's Corps, then on the march, catching up thereby concentrating the army for maximum effectiveness.

Gen. Lee was concerned about the gap, at some places two or three miles wide, that existed between his two parallel advancing corps occasioned by the separation and divergence of the Old Turnpike on the north and the Orange Plank Road on the south of the army's line of advance. It was all right for the moment but could not be ignored for long. Such a gap offered a weak point. If discovered by an alert enemy, a Federal wedge could be driven into it with the possibility of devastating results.

Somewhat in advance of Hill, Gen. Ewell thought it prudent to halt his column and form in line of battle. In the entangled fastness of the Wilderness, he wanted to be prepared for any unexpected attack. Requesting further orders, an aide was sent to find Gen. Lee for instructions. It was about the same time that the Federal army moving along the Germanna Plank Road up ahead was sighted moving across the intersection of the two roads. Simultaneously, the Blues sighted Ewell's Grays advancing from their right on the turnpike. The Federal hosts were of the V and VI Corps with the IX Corps still across the Rapidan but coming up. Reporting the Gray presence, the response from army headquarters was for Warren to attack what was thought by Gens. Grant and Meade to be only a division-size force. In reality, the troops seen dimly through the gloom and distance were Gen. R. S. Ewell's entire three division corps.

Thus, if one can picture the respective lines of march, as the various commands converged, the Confederates were, to borrow a tactical naval term, in a position to cross the Federal "T." Meanwhile, Gen. Hancock's II Federal Corps, breaking its overnight bivouac, had advanced from Chancellorsville to Todd's Tavern located farther south behind the Brock Road. That road continued south toward Spotsylvania Court House, to become the main thoroughfare to that point several days later.

As Ewell surveyed the scene before him, the distant Federals were seen to be forming in line and launching what appeared to be a demonstration against his leading elements. Remember, this was in thick woods and visibility was severely limited. Cautiously, Gen. Ewell advanced other troops in support. Their orders were to retire slowly if opposed. Once a battle was joined, it was impossible, usually, to halt its spread. In the meantime, artillery units, rendered largely useless in the thick woods, were withdrawn from the front.

It was the Federals who chose to embolden the demonstration. In launching a heavy attack, Gen. Grant, knowing something of his opponent's divided state, wanted to take advantage of the situation and perhaps destroy Lee's army before it could concentrate. And, he almost succeeded. Ewell's leading brigade, John Jones,' Johnson's Division, was shattered, its commander killed, as its remnants fell back in disarray. Their decimation and attendant panic threw their supports into confusion also as the survivors streamed through their ranks. In the meantime, farther to the rear, the division of Gen. Jubal Early, well-closed up, was moving forward to the sound of the guns.

Riding to the rear seeking to stem the tide posed by his fleeing troops, Ewell came first upon Gordon's Georgians, Early's Division. "General Gordon," piped Ewell excitedly, "the fate of the day depends on you." Surrounded by his troops, they hoping to hear a snatch of what was going on, and for their benefit, cutting a fine figure, Gordon replied, "These men will save it, sir."[16] Their counterattack, in conjunction with other units, stabilized the situation. The Federals were compelled to pull their entire line back. The fight raged on over the ground with heavy losses on both sides in both commissioned and enlisted ranks.

Simultaneously, to the south along the course of the Orange Plank Road, Hill's troops could hear the rising sound of battle in the distance through the heavily forested thickets to their left. Advancing and encountering the Federal cavalry pickets of Wilson's Division, Hill's troops drove them back. Early in the afternoon, they were confronted by a Blue line of battle arrayed along the Brock Road and perpendicular to the Plank Road upon which they were advancing. They were, as with Ewell, the troops of Warren's V Corps and Sedgwick's VI Corps soon to be joined by units of Gen. Hancock's II Corps that had been ordered to move to that position from Todd's Tavern earlier that morning. Skirmishers of both lines soon came in contact and the ball opened on that front.

At about 3:00 P.M., a Federal attack was mounted with vigor westward along the Orange Plank Road. It was turned momentarily by the Confederates but only after they had been forced to retreat to the vicinity of the Widow Tapp's farm located on the north side of the road. The heavy fighting fell upon the divisions of Gens. Heth and Wilcox. In recalling the desperate battle some years after the war, Gen. Law described it as "a desperate struggle between the infantry of the two armies, on a field whose physical aspects were as grim and forbidding as the struggle itself.... It was a field of close quarters ... for as night came on, in those tangled thickets ... the approach of the opposing lines could be discerned only by the noise of their passage through the underbrush or the flashing of their guns. The usually silent Wilderness had suddenly become alive with the angry flashing and heavy roar of the musketry, mingled with the yells of the combatants as they swayed to and fro in the gloomy thickets.[17] Col. Alexander said that "[t]here was never more desperate fighting."[18] It continued until about 8:00 P.M.

That night, as the fighting trailed off, Gen. Lee made the decision that the next day's primary objective would be to turn the enemy's left, anchored by Hancock's II Corps arrayed along the Brock Road. It was thought to be in the air. If not, then the secondary objective would be to envelop his right thereby severing the Federal line of supply from its base. Both objectives showed the possibility of favorable results, the former more so than the latter.

At about 8:00 P.M., Gen. Lee sent an urgent message to Gen. Longstreet, his command still on the march to the west, ordering him to make a night march in order to be on the field by the next morning. The additional weight of that formidable organization could make a big difference in the day's outcome.

During the night, divisional commanders Heth and Wilcox, Ewell's Corps, were extremely concerned about the condition of their front. Their men had fallen to the ground, completely exhausted by the exertions and dangers of the day. No defensive works were thrown up; they were simply not capable of the effort. Both generals felt the close presence of the enemy and were concerned that their troops should be aroused and repositioned. There were reports that nothing separated the two armies, not even a skirmish line.

Repeated trips by both to Gen. Lee's and Gen. Hill's headquarters to plead their case was rebuffed by the commanders. Hill, as was often the case, was very ill. Neither Lee nor Hill wanted to disturb the troops after the terrible rigors of their day. Gen. Hill assured Gen. Heth that "Longstreet will be up in a few hours. He will form in your front. I don't propose that you shall do any fighting tomorrow; the men have been marching and fighting all day and are tired. I don't wish them disturbed."[19] Still not satisfied and filled with "foreboding," Heth returned still later for the third time. This time Gen. Hill lost his

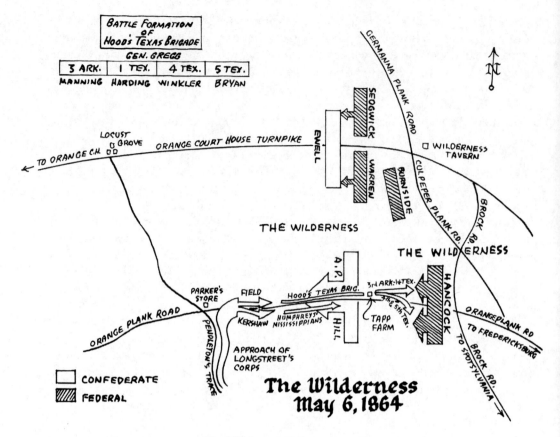

The Wilderness, May 5–7, 1864

temper: "Damn it, Heth ... I don't want to hear any more about it; the men shall not be disturbed."[20]

Actually, the seeming lack of proper concern was occasioned by the belief that, as voiced by Gen. Hill, the vanguard of Longstreet's Corps was expected to arrive on the scene at any moment. R.H. Anderson's detached division was expected, also. Even though some pioneer troops were brought forward to prepare defensive positions, the lines were so close that they could not work because of constantly being brought under fire. Meanwhile, nearby and exhibiting the foresight to prepare for the worst, Hancock's men in blue worked throughout the night fortifying in preparation for what the next day might bring.

The preliminary battles fought by Hill on the Orange Plank Road and by Ewell on the Old Turnpike on May 5 were distinct unto themselves. No connection between the two corps had been established. It was not until the morning of May 6 that the two corps were joined when elements of Wilcox's Division, Hill's Corps, joined with elements of Ewell's Corps. During the night, Burnside's IX Corps moved up in support of Hancock's II Corps and Longstreet and Anderson moved up to reinforce A. P. Hill.

As dawn began to illuminate the surroundings, around 5:00 A.M. on May 6, the Federals, hoping to gain the initiative, launched the first attack of the day all along the front. Warren and Sedgwick attacked Ewell and Hancock attacked Hill. The heavy and repeated attacks upon Ewell, his line well-fortified overnight, were repulsed. By late morning, the Federal troops, decimated, exhausted, and deficient four artillery pieces, were back behind their fortifications where they wisely chose to remain for the remainder of the day.

On Hill's front, it was a different story altogether. Wilcox' troops were the first to be struck and they, unprepared, were overwhelmed, broken and, panic-stricken, ran for the rear. Heth's were soon to follow. The commander's concerns of the night before were fully revealed as justified. This was something seldom experienced before, two battle-hardened veteran Confederate divisions fleeing a field! In his after action report, a diplomatic and understated Lee said the enemy advance had "created some confusion."[21] Anticipating the worst, Gen. Lee ordered the army's trains in rear at Parker's Store to be prepared to move quickly or, in other words, retreat.

Since Gen. Hill was incapacitated that day, any rallying to be done would have to be by Gen. Lee and his staff, personally. The army's headquarters was in the vicinity of the Widow Tapp's farm on the Orange Plank Road. The Federal ranks were advancing now down the road almost unopposed except by scattered bodies of Southern troops. A little to the north, a Federal column was seen to be advancing into the thinly defended area separating Hill's Corps from Ewell's Corps. Even though there were still Confederate troops in front, wounded and otherwise, if the day was not to be lost, drastic measures were called for.

Confederate troops to his front, notwithstanding, Col. Poague's batteries, Hill's Corps, located at the Widow Tapp's farm were ordered to open with grape and canister. The Federal avalanche was almost upon them. The tactical situation at that moment can only be described as grim in the extreme. Gen. Lee, astride Traveler, entered the Orange Plank Road in an attempt to stem the receding tide and was engulfed by some of the fleeing troops, they being of McGowan's South Carolina Brigade. "My God, General McGowan," he cried, "is this the splendid brigade of yours running like a flock of geese?" McGowan replied, "General … these men are not whipped. They only want a place to form, and they will fight as well as they ever did."[22] Meanwhile, looking back down the Orange Plank Road stretching out to the west, anxious eyes sought for any sign of Longstreet's or Anderson's commands.

It was at that moment, almost as if staged for maximum dramatic effect, that vaguely through the murkiness of the smoke-wreathed scene, the vanguard of Longstreet's Old First Corps was seen coming into view, "Old Pete," himself and his staff leading out front. Advancing at a double-quick pace and in four columns, in the van on the left side of the road was Gen. Field's (Hood's) Division, the Texas Brigade leading, 3rd Arkansas out front. On the right side of the road, Kershaw's (McLaws') Division, Barksdale's (Humphrey) Mississippi Brigade leading.[23] Gen. Law described their advance as "in perfect order, ranks well closed, and no stragglers, those splendid troops came on, regardless of the confusion on every side, pushing their steady way onward like a 'river in the sea' of confused and troubled human waves around them."[24] A mighty cheer went up for the veteran corps returned to the bosom of its natal army at this critical and emotional juncture.

Col. Sorrell described the tactical situation at the time of their arrival as "appalling," with "[f]ugitives from the broken lines of the Third Corps … pouring back in disorder and it looked as if things were past mending."[25] Upon arriving near the front on the Orange Plank Road, from the ranks of the Texas Brigade, Joe Polley, Co. F, 4th Texas, described a "scene of utter, and apparently, irremediable confusion, such as we had never witnessed before in Lee's army. It was crowded with standing and moving wagons, horses and mules, and threading their way through this tangled mass, each with his face to the rear, were hundreds of the men of Wilcox's and Heth's divisions, which were being driven from their lines."[26] Following the passage of the fleeing troops, Gen. Kershaw said that, ... "[a]lmost immediately the enemy were upon us."[27] It was that close!

Col. Alexander saw it otherwise about the deportment of Hill's troops and he was eminently qualified to judge. Riding with Gen. Longstreet and his staff, he said they met "what seemed to be an orderly body of troops marching in the opposite direction, who parted, taking the woods on each side and giving us the road." They were soon followed by an excited staff officer who said, "They are running, d — n them."[28] Calmly, Longstreet surveyed the ground, took in with that glance the tactical situation and then shook his troops out in line of battle on either side of the road. Also there, Col. Sorrell thought that "in its entire splendid history the simple act of forming line in that dense undergrowth, under heavy fire and with the Third Corps pushing to the rear through the ranks, was perhaps its greatest performance for steadiness and inflexible courage and discipline."[29]

By chance, J. B. Minor's unit, the Richmond Howitzers, received the support of the 3rd Arkansas, in his battery's attempt to stem the Blue tide. In that interim, he had an opportunity to observe Lt. Col. Robert S. Taylor of the 3rd Arkansas during the melee. Minor's amusing tale may be apocryphal but it rings true. Before the action began, probably taking whatever opportunity presented itself, be it seconds or minutes, Col. Taylor was seen, frying pan in hand, to be hastily cooking his own breakfast. In that situation, if one was to get any breakfast, he had better cook fast and at the first chance afforded. Then, according to Minor, "without any warning, three [Federal] lines of battle with a terrific yell burst from the woods in our front." Minor's battery "showered canister upon them, but they kept coming, reached our breastworks, charged over them, and pinned to the ground with their bayonets several of the Third Arkansas.... Col. Taylor had his frying pan by the handle, and was swinging it round and round his head, scattering the hot gravy in every direction as he rallied his men, shouting, 'We must hold this position.'" Minor said "...the shouting, the shooting, the dead, and the dying made a lasting impression on [him]." However, "...nothing [was] more vivid in [his] memory of that morning than Col. Taylor in the midst of the melee, scattering hot gravy on all sides as he shook the frying pan over his head, rallying his men."[30]

When within 600 yards of the enemy front, M. V. Smith, Co. D, 4th Texas, said that to their right the woods were astream with hundreds of the wounded making for the rear. He asked of those nearest, "How is it going in front boys?" The reply was, "Too bad boys they are driving us." His reply, "Wait until we get there, we'll set em up." Two of his comrades, Shumate and Manning, cast him doleful looks as if to say, yes, but at what great cost?. Both were dead within a matter of minutes.[31]

Double-quicking to the sound of the firing, perhaps a mile, Joe Polley, Co. F, 4th Texas, said they were "called to a halt, [they] formed line of battle facing the north side of the road, loaded [their] guns, and by a right wheel brought itself into position fronting the enemy, on an open hill, the highest probably in the section, and immediately in rear of a battery said to have been Poague's."[32] O. T. Hanks,' Co. K, 1st Texas was given the order to "load and cap ... pieces," followed by the "jingle of the hundreds of iron ramrods up and down the line [denoting] that something horrible [was] soon to take place."[33]

Gen. Gregg, overseeing the deployment of the brigade, was joined by Gen. Lee and some of his staff. Being new to the Army of Northern Virginia, Gregg was not known to the commanding general. "General," said Lee, "what brigade is this?" "The Texas Brigade," was the proud answer. To which Gen. Lee replied, "I am glad to see it! When you go in there, I wish you to give those men the cold steel. They will stand and fire all day, and never move unless you charge them." "That is my experience," answered Gregg. At that moment, an aide from Longstreet arrived: 'Advance your command, General Gregg,' he said. Gregg drew in his breath and shouted: 'Attention, Texas Brigade! The eyes ... of General Lee ... are ... upon you! Forward ... march!' Lee lifted his hat and raised himself in his stirrup. There was anxiety in his brief answer: 'Texans always move them!'"[34] Those close enough to hear began to cheer and as Lee's words were spread through the ranks the cheering spread. "I would charge hell itself for that old man," cried one courier.[35]

In his private notebook, Col. C. M. Winkler, 4th Texas, wrote that they "went in with a yell, made a half wheel to the left, swept through the pines, and across the plank road, through heavy timber and dense undergrowth." There was a heavy flanking fire from their left resulting in a "heavy loss of men." He said Gen. Gregg's horse was killed, also.[36]

During this action, Lee's staff observed that their chief was "intensely excited," more so than they had ever seen him before. One Texan observed him and said later that "the fire of battle was in his eye, and his form quivered with emotions."[37] He seemed to be intent upon leading the Texans personally into battle. However, the Texans refused to allow him to place himself in a position of such personal danger. As many as twenty men tried to restrain him, Joe Polley, Co. F, 4th Texas, said. The cry, "Lee to the rear," resounded through the Texan ranks. Traveler's reins were taken by several Texans, one of whom was reported as saying, "If you lead the charge, we won't follow you, but if you'll go back, we'll drive them to h — l."[38] E. J. Parrent, Co. D, 4th Texas, claimed to be one of those around Gen. Lee. He said that "every man there would have gladly died to save one drop of his precious blood."[39]

One of Lee's staff officers appealed to Longstreet to do something to deter Lee. Longstreet spoke up with affectionate bluntness and said "that his line would be recovered in an hour if he would permit me to handle the troops, but if my services were not needed, I would like to ride to some place of safety, as it [is] not quite comfortable where we [are]."[40] According to Col. Charles Venable, one of Lee's aides, the general said, "Well then, I will go back."[41] Reluctantly, he and his staff moved down the Orange Plank Road a short distance toward the west and rear.

The men of Hill's Corps were jeered roundly by their First Corps comrades as the former streamed back through the latter's ranks, the most insulting epithet being, "You're worse than Bragg's men."[42] Longstreet had nothing but praise for the conduct of his own men. "Thrown suddenly ... into the presence of an advancing foe with their ranks broken each instant by

Lt. Col. Clinton M. Winkler, 4th Texas

bodies of our retreating men, they not only held their own, but formed their line."[43] Once the rout had run its course, Longstreet's veterans closed ranks and prepared to receive the onrushing Federal horde.

Hill's men, gradually regaining their composure and thanks to the efforts of their officers, began to reform in the rear of Longstreet's position. Actually, they had stubbornly retreated only several hundred yards, many of the more stalwart among them reloading and firing as they walked rearward. Gen. Lee, once they were reformed, deployed them on Longstreet's left to fill the gap existing between Ewell and Hill and now Longstreet. The Blue ranks, sensing victory, were not to be deterred and sent a hail of minie balls into the Gray ranks. Longstreet was everywhere at the front urging his men to stand fast.

Gradually, after a period of standup fighting, on the right side of the road, Kershaw began to move his troops forward. On the other side of the road, Field moved his men forward slowly. Gen. Gregg led the Texas Brigade. They encountered the enemy's skirmishers whose fire proved to be lethal, killing or wounding "many of our best and bravest before they had fired a shot," said Joe Polley, Co. F, 4th Texas.[44]

After moving, perhaps, 500 yards, they encountered the Federal troops of Gen. Alexander Webb's Brigade, Hancock's II Corps. "There was a terrible crash, mingled with wild yells, which settled down into a steady roar of musketry. In less than ten minutes one-half of that devoted eight hundred were lying upon the field dead or wounded."[45] Among the wounded, Col. Van H. Manning, 3rd Arkansas, with a severe wound to the thigh. Later, he was picked up on the field by the Federals and made a prisoner of war, to be confined at Ft. Delaware for the remainder of the war and even beyond.[46] Following, to the main line of the enemy's breastworks along the Brock Road, they were then forced to withdraw. Nonetheless, they had achieved their goal; they had driven the Federal host back and recovered the ground lost by Wilcox' and Heth's Divisions earlier.

In the 4th Texas, a color bearer had been shot down, he then handing the colors to A. A. Durfee, Co. B, 4th Texas. Durfee carried the flag to within 150 yards of the Federal breastworks, where he received a severe wound to the abdomen. The flag was then passed to regimental Sgt. Maj. Charles S. Brown. He, immediately shot down, passed it on to a fourth man who carried it the rest of the day. Durfee and Brown crawled to the same tree seeking shelter from the battle raging around them. Durfee faced the Confederate lines, Brown the Federal. According to Joe Polley, Austin Jones, Co. L, 1st Texas, crept out to them offering to carry Brown to a place of safety. Brown refused the offer, saying, "Durfee and I were wounded together and must leave the field together."[47] Returning ten minutes later with litter bearers, Jones found Durfee alive but, alas, Sgt. Maj. Brown was dead, shot in the head, he appearing to be sleeping peacefully.

In the advance, B. M. Aycock, Co. E, 4th Texas, said they reached the Federal breastworks thrown up along the Brock Road. Fortunately, for them, the Federal troops had fled on beyond the works. Aycock, a little ahead of the others, went to a forked tree near the works, firing a shot at the retreating enemy. Looking around, he saw, seeking shelter from the fire," five boys behind me at the tree, one was our Lieutenant Ed Tilley, another was Lieutenant Boyd of Company C. Another was a private of Company C, Cosgrove, the others I don't remember."[48] Their fragile cover proved inadequate. Aycock said all five were either killed or wounded.

Joe Polley observed that even in life or death situations, which the Wilderness fight certainly was, there was always a sense of humor lurking near the surface. Jim Summerville, Co. F, 4th Texas, was one of the first men wounded, albeit slightly; a ball struck his belt buckle resulting in a small, superficial wound. Nonetheless, in the excitement of the moment and the usual mortal results of a stomach wound, Summerville "dropped his gun, folded his arms across the front of his corporosity, and, whirling around a couple of times, gave vent to a long-drawn, emphatic groan with all the variations of the gamut in it." The regiment roared with laughter, attempting, according to Polley, to "extract a little comedy out of deadly tragedy."[49] Their Federal opponents must have been highly puzzled at the laughter in the midst of the death and destruction. To the rear, Gen. Lee helped in getting Law's Brigade formed, admonishing them to keep up with the Texans. Benning's Georgians moved behind Gregg.

By mid-morning the relative positions were about where they had started earlier, Hancock's men back behind their fortifications thrown up the night before. Seeking to exploit their momentary advantage, Longstreet sent out his engineering officers, including the chief engineering officer of the army, at that time, Gen. Martin L. Smith, a New Yorker, West Point, Class of 1838. An engineer's combat task was to observe the enemy line and the terrain for any signs of weakness or opportunity. Later in the morning, they returned with the heartening news that the Federal left along the Brock Road appeared to extend only a little south of its intersection with the Orange Plank Road. If so, it was ripe for a turning movement. Also, out there in the woods to the right they had located an unfinished railroad cut that did not appear on the maps along which an attack might be mounted. Railroad cuts had the advantage of having been cleared of trees, their stumps notwithstanding, and other obstacles, its thrown-up banks offering some concealment. A tantalizing opportunity beckoned!

As usual, matters were in a confused state with troop dispositions mingled: "The Texans [had] lost nearly two-thirds of their numbers and the other brigades suffered heavily."[50] Longstreet briefly conferred with Gen. Lee, who approved the flanking attack. Longstreet, calling his proven and trusted adjutant general, Lt. Col. Sorrell, to his side, ordered him to gather all the troops to the south together for the assault. "Colonel," he said, "hit them hard when you start, but don't start until you have everything ready. I shall be waiting for your gunfire, and be on hand for further advance"[51] This was an assignment that carried huge risks but equally huge rewards, if successful. In an hour, Sorrell, with the cooperation of various unit commanders, had put together a flanking force. Although there is some confusion as to who was in command, most likely it was Gen. William Mahone, the senior brigadier present.

To their left along the Orange Plank Road, Longstreet and his subordinates and their commands awaited the sound of musketry signaling the beginning of Sorrell's attack. At about 11:00 A.M., to their anxiously straining ears came the sound of skirmish line firing followed shortly thereafter by the crashing sound of volley fire. The flanking party was moving. Col. Sorrell said that "with ringing yells we were upon Hancock's exposed left, the brigades being ably commanded by their respective officers." Gen. Mahone termed the movement "a success — complete as it was brilliant."[52] The Federal troops in front began to give ground. The fortunes of war; after a looming disaster that morning, a Southern victory was in the making in the afternoon! In the ranks there was no doubt about it; the Federal left flank had been turned. Victory was in the air and the old spirit of the Army of Northern Virginia, reunited once more, was astir in the Confederate ranks.

Gen. Joseph Kershaw, the South Carolinian, now in command of what was formerly McLaws' Division, had ridden ahead to supervise the front. Following along, Gen. Longstreet was joined by Gen. Micah Jenkins at the head of his brigade that was to move forward in support of Kershaw. Spotted by the troops, a cheer rang out for Longstreet that, reverberating through the thick woods, momentarily drowned out the sound of the struggle in full tilt up ahead.

Moving to the front, Longstreet's entourage increased. Moxley Sorrell, on this occasion responsible for the rallying together of the flanking troops, joined the group. He was in an exultant mood as a result of the success of the improvised attack. Returning from the front, Joe Kershaw and William T. Wofford, the Georgian, with their attendant staffs rode up also. Instructing his commanders as to the continuing course of the attack, Longstreet then put spurs to his mount and moved farther forward, staff and others following.

Reaching the Confederate line of battle, then arrayed along the south side of the Orange Plank Road, the party was startled to come under a scattered fire of musketry first from their left on the north side of the road, some of Jenkins' troops as it turned out. That was followed shortly thereafter by an answering volley of musketry from Gen. Mahone's men known to occupy the woods on the south side of the road. It was yet another case of mistaken friendly fire. As the minies filled the air, "Longstreet did not follow the rule of caution. Instead of throwing himself from his horse on the opposite side, he instinctively turned the animal's head toward the fire and started to dash forward to stop it."[53]

At that moment, a heavy volley of musketry crashed forth obscuring the surrounding area in a heavy cloud of acrid gun smoke, filling the airspace with hundreds of heavy, whistling .58 caliber missiles. Some of them wreaked an immediate and heavy toll upon the leadership of the First Army Corps. Gen. Longstreet was struck by one of the random rounds that lifted him, literally, from his saddle. Falling back heavily into place he was able, instinctively, to keep his seat. Gen. Jenkins and two others, Captain Alfred E. Doby, Gen. Kershaw's aide-de-camp, and Orderly Marcus Baum, fell to the ground heavily, all three, as it turned out, mortally wounded.[54] As Kershaw rode forward shouting, "They are friends!" every musket was lowered, and the men dropped upon the ground to avoid the fire.[55] It was by his exhortations that there was narrowly averted a heavy exchange of musketry between Jenkins' troops on the left and Mahone's troops on the right. It was the latter that was the author of the mistaken but fatal volley that had wreaked so much havoc in the corps' command structure.

Aides rushed forward and Longstreet was eased from his mount and laid out on the ground. He was seriously wounded, a ball having entered near his throat and lodged in his right shoulder. The bleeding was severe but quickly staunched by the corps' medical director, Dr. Cullen, who was soon on the scene. Longstreet was a soldier in every sense of the word and through the bloody froth engulfing his lips issued orders for the continuation of the fight. Other commanders, hearing the news of Longstreet's wounding, were soon on the scene to offer any aid and assistance that might be required. Gen. Lee arrived, to whom Longstreet painfully recited his continuing plan of battle. As Longstreet's familiar form was carried to the rear, his soldiers were heard to say, "He is dead ... and they are telling us he is only wounded."[56]

Longstreet, hat over his face, could hear the despairing comments of his men as they gathered round. To reassure them that he had not been killed, he raised his hat and was greeted with a rousing cheer that rang through the forests all around. The preliminary medical prognosis was that Longstreet's wound, though serious, was not necessarily mortal. It would prove to be, however, serious enough to incapacitate him and keep him from his command until the following fall. In the meantime, Micah Jenkins, his protégé, died on the field within two hours, a minie ball through his brain.

Gen. Field was the senior officer present and was placed in corps command only to be superseded by the even more senior Gen. R. H. Anderson when he arrived on the scene. It was not until about 4:15 P.M. that matters could be sorted out and the attack renewed. By that time the Federal entrenchments along the Brock Road had been greatly strengthened. An opportunity with far-reaching implications had evaporated!

Meanwhile, to the north, along the Old Turnpike, Ewell's Corps had been dealing with its own problems. During the night before, Gen. Gordon, commanding a brigade in Early's Division, had sent forth scouts to discover anything they could about the disposition of the Federal troops in their front. When they returned toward daybreak, their reports seemed hardly plausible. They said they had found the enemy right to be not only in the air but considerably overlapped by Ewell's line. A second scouting party was sent forward, returning a few hours later confirming the report of the first party. Further, they said there were no supporting units within easy marching distance. Still unbelieving that such an opportunity was being presented, Gen. Gordon went forward himself to reconnoiter. Near the front, he dismounted and crept forward. Shown the end of the temporary earthworks that the Federals had thrown up, he observed that there were no supports guarding that end of the line. By that time it was about 9:00 A.M. as Gordon made his way to his corps' headquarters.

There, the intelligence that Gen. Ewell had was somewhat counter to that being brought by Gen. Gordon. Scouts sent out by Ewell's headquarters during the night had reported Federal troops between Gen. Ewell's command and the Rapidan. Another report indicated that Gen. Burnside's IX Corps had crossed the Rapidan and was in position behind the Federal right. At that time, these were unsubstantiated reports and Gen. Ewell had not yet sent staff officers immediately to verify their accuracy. In the event that the reports were true, he ordered Gen. Early to be on the lookout for the phantom units and to prevent them from getting in rear of the army.

Upon reaching headquarters, Gen. Gordon poured out his story and asked permission to attack. "Permission denied," was the response of Gen. Early. Gen. Ewell concurred, at least until he could order a further reconnaissance later in the day. A distraught Gordon even offered to take any blame that might result from a failed attack.

During this time frame small actions were occurring along Ewell's Corps' front but were nothing compared to what was going on to their right on A. P. Hill's and Longstreet's front along the Orange Plank Road. Gen. Lee arrived late in the afternoon to ask what Gen. Ewell might be able to do to relieve the pressure on the army on the right. Gen. Gordon happened to be on the scene and overheard the conversation. Unable to contain himself, he broke in and related to the commanding general what he had seen earlier that day. Gen. Lee knew Gen. Gordon and had confidence in him as a field commander. Why had the attack not been made as recommended by Gordon? Receiving no plausible explanation, he ordered the attack to be made as soon and as vigorously as possible. Once the decision had been made by Gen. Lee, Gens. Ewell and Early threw their support and cooperation behind the attack.

Even though it was very late in the day, the attack was a great success and a great surprise to the enemy. The Federal right flank, Sedgwick's VI Corps, was turned and then rolled up. About 600 prisoners were taken, including two brigadier generals. Only darkness and their coming under the fire of their comrades to the south stopped Gen. Gordon's continuing the rout. The casualties on each side were disproportionately in favor of the Confederate troops. Gen. Gordon said that "had the movement been made at an earlier hour and properly supported, each brigade being brought into action as its front was cleared, it would have resulted in a decided disaster to the whole right wing of General Grant's army, if not in its entire disorganization."[57]

As night descended, the cries of the dying and wounded filled the air. On the right, fires sparked during the day's fighting, fanned by the winds, flared to the treetops. Those in the area of the fires who were wounded in such ways that they could not escape the flames were burned to death in the hundreds. It had been a victory but at quite a cost. Among others, Micah Jenkins was dead and Longstreet was seriously wounded, his return, if ever, uncertain. Gen. A. P. Hill was seriously ill. Gen. Ewell's hesitation in supporting Gen. Gordon's call for action put his capability to command even further in question.

Late on May 6, Joe Polley, Co. F, 4th Texas, was taken ill and sent to the field hospital. He was to remain on the disabled list for quite a while, at the beginning of which he visited the scene of the recent violence that he described as "terrible and sickening." He observed that most of the Confederate dead had been buried but only a tenth of the Federal dead had been attended to. The stench was overpowering. He observed "acres of ground, the trees on which were riddled with bullets, and on several portions of the field where small timber and undergrowth only grew, the trees were actually cut in two, and the undergrowth topped at about the height of a man's head." The Texas Brigade dead, he said, had been gathered and buried in a mass grave on the north side of the Orange Plank Road. Carved on a large board, the words "Texas Dead" identified the occupants of that burial place.[58]

Describing the aftermath as "destruction beyond measure," O. T. Hanks, Co. K, 1st Texas, said that the "wounded and dead are lying scattered here and there. Guns, iron ramrods and various kinds of equipment used by soldiers. Every twig in the woods was cut by a bullet. Some trees the size of a man's body had 25 or 30 bullets in them, besides a good many iron ramrods. These ramrods were shot into the trees so deep that they could not be pulled out."[59]

What would be the next move of the Army of the Potomac with the commander of all the Federal armies, Gen. Grant, in attendance? The night of May 6–7, was spent on the Confederate right, this time, in entrenchment. An attack was anticipated for the next morning. But when dawn came and went with only scattered picket firing, uncertainty mounted as to the Federal intention. In front of Ewell's Corps to the north, Gen. Early reported that the Federal troops were gone. It was obvious that they were not retreating back across the Rapidan as earlier Federal armies had done. There were two likelihoods, east to Fredericksburg to secure a supply line or to Richmond by way of Spotsylvania Court House to the southeast. Gen. Lee knew where they were going. He told Gen. Gordon, "Grant is not going to retreat.... He will move his army to Spotsylvania."[60]

To gain time in the coming race for position somewhere around Spotsylvania, Gen. Lee ordered Gen. Pendleton to cut a shortcut through the woods along the course of the unfinished railroad on the right, no small task that, from the Orange Plank Road south to a point on the road leading to Spotsylvania. This would allow the Army of Northern Virginia to cut across and, perhaps, reach the now tactically important junction ahead of the Army of the Potomac. Longstreet's Corps, composing the right flank of the army and closest to the route of march, would lead the way.

The presence of Federal cavalry on the Spotsylvania Road and the observed departure of Federal artillery units in that direction confirmed to watchful eyes that the Army of the Potomac was moving on Spotsylvania as Gen. Lee had predicted. Orders were issued to Gen. Stuart to reconnoiter "the roads on our right, which it would be advisable or necessary for us to follow should the enemy continue his movement toward Spotsylvania Court

House."[61] Orders were issued also for the First Corps to withdraw under cover of darkness, allow the troops some time to rest and then move toward Spotsylvania at 3:00 A.M. on May 8, by way of either Todd's Tavern or Shady Grove Church. Ewell's and Hill's Corps were to follow in that order.

When the movement began the men in the ranks misinterpreted it to mean that Grant's army had given up on the overland route leading to Richmond. Cheering and rebel yells rang forth from one end of the army to the other. Gen. Anderson, once the movement was started at about 11:00 P.M., there being no suitable place to rest the troops, decided to push on. That decision proved to be fateful and fortunate as far as Southern arms was concerned.

CHAPTER 15

"[T]he most painful and excruciating scenes of suffering and death"[1]: Spotsylvania Court House to Cold Harbor, May 8–June 3, 1864

The men of Longstreet's Corps respected the South Carolinian Gen. R. H. Anderson from past experience. In the aftermath of Gen. Longstreet's wounding, Anderson came upon Jenkins' South Carolina Brigade by chance in the Wilderness shortly after the latter's mortal wounding. Recognizing him, the men gave Anderson a rousing cheer of welcome. Their cheers were quickly silenced by their commanders, however, due to the close proximity of the enemy. Not to be denied, the soldiers continued their accolade by tossing their caps and hats silently into the air. Clearly moved by this unexpected display of admiration, Gen. Anderson drew rein and, removing his hat addressed them, "My friends, your silent expression makes me grateful for your kind remembrance. I thank you sincerely."[2] It was only later that they learned that he had been chosen by the army commander to replace the disabled Longstreet, his 1842 West Point classmate.

Once the collective information was in and Gen. Lee knew without any doubt that the Federals were moving on Spotsylvania, he had to act quickly if he were to interpose his army between the enemy and Richmond. It was to be a race and one of vital importance to both armies. Longstreet's Corps formed the right flank of the army and, being the closest troops to the objective, was designated to lead the way south. Fortunately, Anderson's reputation for pursuit in past campaigns was good. In the current situation he proved to be just the man for which the moment called. He had to reach Spotsylvania first or the road to Richmond would be open to the enemy. The initial route was to be by way of the road cut through the heavy woods by troops under Gen. Pendleton's supervision. As mentioned earlier, Gen. Anderson's decision to begin the movement at 11:00 P.M., the night of May 7, rather than at the commanding general's suggested time of 3:00 A.M., May 8, proved crucial for the continuation of the struggle. Gen. Anderson's decision was made largely on pragmatic grounds rather than on perceived tactical necessity. The still burning woods and the poor condition of Pendleton's improvised road were the main factors. There was really no suitable place for the troops to rest. The roadway through the woods was narrow and still contained many obstacles in the form of protruding tree stumps and some uncut trees. The movement had to be made slowly and in the dark. Therefore, the sooner it could be gotten underway the better. As it was commenced, a rebel yell, the likes of which had never been heard before was raised from one end of the army to the other. "The First Corps needed that stimulus on the march they were then beginning."[3]

The usual marching routine of the army was followed with fifty minutes devoted to the march and a ten minute pause to rest each hour. At about daybreak, May 8, Kershaw's Division in the van, Field's following, their struggling march had taken them through the worst part of the woods and a pause was ordered for rest and breakfast, such as was available. As the men were falling out to the roadside, to their collective ears came the sound of gunfire in the near distance. It came from the left, rear, northeast, from up the Brock Road from whence the Blue host would be expected to be advancing. Since there were not supposed to be any Confederate infantry in that quarter, most likely it must be Gen. Stuart's cavalry engaging the enemy. Cavalry or infantry was a key question.

The answer was both. Gen. Fitz Lee was engaging the screening elements of the Federal cavalry followed up closely by Warren's V Corps infantry. Urgently, Lee dispatched a courier seeking the nearest Confederate troops in a position to come to his aid. Later in the morning, the message reached Gen. Anderson on the Shady Grove Church Road at a junction known locally as the Block House. Anderson responded by redirecting his march north up a road leading toward the sound of the guns, Kershaw's Division still in the lead. A short march brought them to a point near the Spindler farm where the route of march intersected the Brock Road. At that point, information was received that their support was needed desperately by the cavalry fighting a delaying action just up that road.

Kershaw's (Henagan's), Law's and Humphrey's brigades were rushed forward. As they advanced there came into view an improvised breastwork of rails that had been hastily thrown up across the road by the Gray cavalry. At about that time, a hard-riding Gray cavalryman cantered toward them shouting, "Run for our rail piles ... the Federal infantry will reach them first, if you don't run!"[4] Sensing the urgency and without waiting for orders, the troops rushed forward, the first elements reaching the cover of the breastwork mere seconds before the advancing Federals who were only a short distance away. That narrowly won race was another one of those pivotal events that would keep the armies of the Confederacy fighting in the field for another year.

Once again Gen. Lee had guessed correctly what Gen. Grant's next move would be. Admiringly, Moxley Sorrell said Gen. Lee "invariably penetrated his adversary's design and objective and was there — perhaps in a hurry and breathless, but there.[5] Also, his decision to assign First Corps command to Gen. Anderson had paid off. According to Freeman, "Anderson deserved high credit because he had started early and had pushed on vigorously. It was, perhaps, his greatest single service to the Confederate cause."[6]

It proved to be a banner day for the sometimes maligned Gray cavalry. Often disdained by their leg and caisson-borne comrades in the army, this day fully justified their place in the ranks of the Army of Northern Virginia. When the Army came to know of what the cavalry had done there was a general outburst of admiration. Everybody was satisfied the cavalry would do.

It was the advance elements of Gen. Warren's V Federal Corps that, thus losing the race, formed for an assault on the improvised strongpoint. Advancing gallantly, now under fire from arriving Confederate artillery batteries, the Blue line reached the breastwork where there was a rare resort to the bayonet. The assault was repulsed with losses on both sides. As this engagement was concluding, another courier arrived, this time bringing a cry for help from Gen. Thomas Rosser, of Stuart's cavalry division. Rosser was engaging a much superior Federal cavalry force at Spotsylvania Court House, that site being back down the road several miles in the opposite direction from Gen. Anderson's position at the Spindler farm. Without hesitation, Gen. Anderson dispatched Wofford's and Bryan's Brigades, both of Kershaw's Division. The First Corps was confronted front and rear!

As the remaining elements of Gen. Warren's V Corps in great numbers began arriving on the field, they began to entrench, extending their line westward opposite the Confederate left. As Gen. Field's Division, including the Texas Brigade, was coming up, part of that command was diverted to Spotsylvania. The remainder extended Gen. Anderson's rail breast-works farther westward to the left.

As this was happening, Gen. Warren launched an assault upon the entire length of the Confederate line. It was repulsed only to be followed up by another assault in which the Federals advanced to a point where they were able to begin entrenching opposite the Confederate right flank. The Confederates were heavily outnumbered but they did not know by how much. "A bold front, stern resistance by the infantry, the most stubborn artillery fire and about the hardest fighting ever done by the cavalry kept the enemy at a distance. He must be held there till the remainder of Lee's Army arrived."[7]

In the meantime, Gen. Rosser had been expelled from Spotsylvania by the superior Federal cavalry force. However, when news of the approaching force of Confederate infantry reached the Federal cavalry commander, the Blue cavalry was withdrawn hastily toward Fredericksburg. When news of the Federal cavalry withdrawal reached Gen. Anderson, he felt it safe to recall his two brigades where he needed them most, to extend both his flanks.

Gen. Lee, riding on ahead of Ewell's and Hill's Corps, arrived at about 2:30 P.M., May 8. As the sweltering afternoon wore on, intelligence reports indicated that Gen. Sedgwick's VI Federal Corps had arrived on the field. It appeared that the greatly reinforced Federal host were preparing for a combined assault. They were and it came in all its fury at about 5:00 P.M.

The blue-coated ranks broke from their cover and advanced in great numbers across the fields abuzz with insects and through the scattered woods toward the waiting Confederate line. By then, Col. Alexander's artillery was in place to sweep the field and the old First Corps was grimly confident that they could hold their position. Their confidence was rewarded in the form of an uneven attack; it was not pursued on a broad front.

Only on the Confederate right was there any hint of danger. There the Federal line overlapped somewhat and there was, momentarily, the fear that that flank might be turned. But, then, as was the case on so many occasions in the history of that great army, reinforce-ments arrived at the crucial moment. This time it took the form of Gen. Ewell's Second Corps arriving by way of the Shady Grove Road. The Federal attack was broken up and that day's fighting came to a close. That night, the Confederate line was strengthened with the Second Corps extending it to the right. The Third Corps, bringing up the army's rear, bivouacked near Todd's Tavern. "Anderson had won his battle. It was because he had started early."[8]

The loss of Gen. Longstreet and Gen. A. P. Hill, the latter too ill to sit up, placed an added burden on Gen. Lee. Although their replacements, Gens. Anderson and Early, respec-tively, were highly competent military leaders, neither had ever had the responsibility of a corps command. The most immediate concern was to construct a defensive line adequate to deal with the overwhelming manpower facing them across the fields and in the woods opposite. Gen. Lee began to deal with that on May 9, as his Third Corps began to arrive. His considerable engineering skills came in handy as he surveyed the terrain roundabout that he had to work with.

Physically, Spotsylvania Courthouse "lies on a ridge between the Po and Ny Rivers, two of the small streams that contribute their waters and their names to the Mattapony. This ridge is about three and a half miles wide at Spotsylvania and is a well-secured military position, because the rivers, though they are not wide, are deep…. To cover the courthouse and the three important roads that led southward from it, Lee drew a crude semicircle with the Po as its diameter. Several nights were spent in extending this front. When the line was completed the extreme right was a trifle more than three miles from the extreme left, and the whole position was compact and thoroughly defensible, except for a long salient on the left centre."[9] This position would become the army's home for the next several blood-besmirched weeks.

Anderson's First Corps held the left of the line, his left resting in the vicinity of the Po River. Ewell's Second Corps held the semicircular center. Hill's Third Corps, now commanded by Gen. Early, after its arrival on May 9, held the right stretching out to the south-east to the vicinity of the court house. The entire convoluted line was about three miles long. It was to be the scene of some of the most desperate fighting in a terrible war characterized by desperate fights. On May 9, there was a respite in the fighting as the exhausted armies faced each other. The usual sharpshooting continued unabated. Gen. John Sedgwick, commanding the Federal VI Corps, fell victim at that time to a Confederate marksman.

On the morning of May 10, a Federal column, three divisions of Hancock's II Corps, was detected on the south side of the Po River moving toward the left flank of the First Corps' position. Unknown to Gen. Lee, the movement had been initiated by Gen. Grant based upon an erroneous report from Burnside's IX Corps on the Spotsylvania–Fredericksburg Road that Gen. Lee was moving toward Fredericksburg. To counter, Grant ordered the movement against his adversary's other flank. Regardless of the accuracy of the initiating report, the movement threatened gravely the left flank of the Army of Northern Virginia. It also placed the army's wagon trains arrayed along the Spotsylvania–Louisa Courthouse Road at risk.

To counter, Gen. Lee moved troops from Ewell's Corps, Mahone's and Hill's (Early) Brigades, Heth's Division positioned on the right, to the left thereby extending that exposed flank. Heth's Division was sent to meet the troops advancing south of the Po. The latter movement occurred early on May 10. According to Nicholas Pomoroy, Co. A, 5th Texas, it was about noon that they were "assailed by a terrible fire of artillery, the shells breaking through our frail breastworks in many places, killing and wounding some of our men. One came through where my company was stationed the wind from it threw a few of us down."[10] After some heavy fighting around Waite's Shop, the Federals recrossed the Po ending the threat from that particular quarter.

Gen. Lee had an uncanny eye for picking favorable ground, either for offensive or defensive positions. However, there was one worrisome feature of his hastily crafted line northwest of Spotsylvania and that occurred where the right of Anderson's First Corps abutted the left of Gen. Ewell's Second Corps position. At that point, the higher ground opposite offered the possibility of artillery enfilade of the entire Confederate position should the Federal commanders choose to occupy it. The Confederate line had been stretched forward to include that high ground resulting in a northward pointing salient measuring about a half mile wide and one mile long. Because of its shape, it was dubbed immediately the "Mule Shoe" by the soldiers who served within its vulnerable confines.

Tactically, such a position is vulnerable and invites assault from all sides . So, Gen. Lee, the former engineer, knowing this, was desirous of a line of defense being established along its base should an abandonment of the protruded position be required later on. As things turned out, it was required — and urgently. According to Freeman, responsibility for establishing the new line rested with the army's chief engineer, Gen. M. L. Smith. However, the work was not done in a timely fashion as required by the situation, that, probably because of enfilading fire and exhausted troops.

During the day, May 10, several attacks were directed against Gen. Field's Division position on the First Corps' front. Joe Polley, Co. F, 4th Texas, described their position as running "along a high ridge, and the dense undergrowth in its front had been so cut down and trimmed as to give a tolerably unobstructed view for a hundred and fifty yards. Beyond this clearing forbiddingly frowned a forest of heavy timber and small growth, a dark and dangerous *terra incognita*, somewhere in whose depths the enemy was presumed to be concealed."[11]

It was from those foreboding depths, at about 3:00 P.M., that parts of their works were overrun momentarily. The attack was ultimately repelled with heavy losses dealt to the attackers. "Anticipating a renewal of the assaults, many of [the] men went out in front of their breastworks, and gathering up the muskets and cartridge-boxes of the dead and wounded, brought them in and distributed them along the line."[12] Having two or three extra muskets compensated somewhat for the lack of yet-unknown automatic weapons with which to cut down the massive Blue attacks.

Acquisition of these Federally-supplied items were sometimes not lacking a price tag. B. M. Aycock, Co. E, 4th Texas, said Dave Decherd of that company went out to "see what [he could] find." He returned with a pair of boots and "sat down to try them on — was in the act of trying them on right at [Aycock's] side. [Aycock] heard something strike, and Dave was opening his bosom. [Aycock] saw the blood and a ball had entered between his ribs, in less than a minute a brave boy was dead."[13] The act of acquiring those boots had attracted the attention of an alert Federal sharpshooter.

Later in the afternoon, about 4:00 P.M., an hour long bombardment of the western face of the "Mule Shoe" erupted followed by a brief lull. On the First Corps' front, another attack was launched against the line held by Gregg's Texans. Skirmishers were driven in and "heavy dark lines of attack came into view, one after another, first in quick time, then in a trot, and then with a rush toward the works."[14] According to Gen. Law these "gallant [Texas] fellows, now reduced to a mere handful by their losses in the Wilderness, stood manfully to their work."[15] Joe Polley, Co. F, 4th Texas, said that the 4th and 5th Texas and the 3rd Arkansas were successful in repelling the attacks on their fronts.

It was during one of these attacks that Sam Bailey, Co. A, 5th Texas, met his long and, up until then, narrowly avoided end. He had been wounded twice already, once at Gaines' Mill. He had been taken prisoner at Second Manassas and later exchanged. At Gettysburg he had received a second wound; his right thumb had been blown off thereby disqualifying him for further service. However, while in a hospital in Richmond awaiting transportation home to Texas, he learned that the Texas Brigade was back from Tennessee. He applied for reinstatement to his old regiment and his request was granted. He rejoined in time to take part in the Wilderness fight.

He was described as a "gallant and already scarred young fellow," by Joe Polley. Nicholas Pomeroy, also of Co. A, 5th Texas, observed that he did not have to be with the army: "When killed near me this brave and gallant hero had his discharge certificate in his pocket."[16] Under heavy Federal artillery fire and behind flimsy breastworks, he was "at his post of duty plying his Enfield rifle, fast and furious." With "the smoke of battle drifting in weird and fantastic shapes around his young, devoted head, an oblong ball from one of the enemy's rifle guns, pierced the frail work immediately in his front, passed through, severed the brave fellow's head from his shoulders, scattered his brains upon his nearest comrades, drove his rifle through his body, and bent it in shape of a hoop or ring."[17] Those nearby, although "accustomed and hardened to the most painful and excruciating scenes of suffering and death," were caused to "shudder" and "feel the shade of a mighty grief."

In that attack the line held by the 1st Texas was breached. For whatever reason, there had been a gap, about forty feet wide, left in their front between the 3rd Arkansas on the left and the 1st Texas and unprotected by breastworks. Although driven from their works, the 1st Texans continued to fight in the rear.

D. H. Hamilton, Co. M, 1st Texas, said his company killed nine Federals on their front. Inside the works, the Federals "killed one man and frightened a good many very badly, myself among the number."[18] Robert Campbell, Co. A, 5th Texas, said the first Federal officers to come over the breastworks were shouting, "No quarter." "A captain of the 1st [Texas] who [snapped] his pistol at them four times, having killed two before, told them he would surrender as soon as they had surrounded him. [They] said '*we don't want you damn your souls to hell, we come here to kill you.*'"[19] O. T. Hanks, Co. K, 1st Texas, said the enemy came over their breastworks saying, "Surrender, Surrender." "They bayoneted our [color] bearer [and] several others. We had no bayonets.... After a while they become alarmed from some cause I do not know what and begun to run [and] leave our works.... I saw two Yankees run at [Lt.] Duck Ardrey with their bayonets, he caught one in each of his hands parted them run [between] them and made his escape.... During the fight a big Yank come up on the works over where myself [and] a comrade named Lige Cooper were [squatted] behind the works. I had just fired my gun[,] Lige had his loaded. [H]e shot that fellow just barely from the [muzzle] of his gun shooting him almost straight up. The fellow swayed back [and] forth a time or two[.] [Finally] [he] fell backward and rolled down [and] outside the works."[20] Eventually, after more hard fighting, they were able to regain their works and restore their segment of the line.

It was the philosophically-inclined 4th Texan Joe Polley's observation that the 1st Texans were "a peculiar regiment in many respects." They were, he said, without doubt, brave and daring, remembering their conduct at Sharpsburg. But they were "never strong on dress, drill and discipline, as laid down in *Hardee's Tactics*." While in East Tennessee they had taken up the notion that their bayonets were an unnecessary weight for them to be carrying around. So, they discarded them, and as O. T. Hanks observed at Spotsylvania, when they really needed them, they were without. There, it was amply demonstrated that bayonets were not a bad thing to possess in hand-to-hand fights. So, at the first opportunity, they reequipped themselves from the plentiful supply made available by the Federal dead left in their front. Polley suggested that when that source proved insufficient they "borrowed" more from "an Alabama brigade in another division." In dress, he noted them not to be "dudes or dandies," but who was in that ragtag army? They were fond of card games and, as a result, the seats of their pants were well-worn. On one occasion, during the retreat from Maryland, an English guest of Gen. Lee noted their threadbare condition with some derision. Gen. Lee remonstrated, saying, "Never mind their raggedness, Colonel ... the enemy never sees the backs of my Texans."[21]

A little later, around 6:00 P.M., to the Texans' right, Dole's Georgia Brigade, Rodes' Division, Second Corps, saw from their vantage point behind their parapets a heart-racing scene developing before their eyes, death on the move! Emerging from the woods close by, maybe 200 yards away, four lines of cheering Federal infantry heading their way with violent intent. According to Col. Alexander, in his postwar memoir, the attacking force comprised three brigades, twelve regiments. Leading the assault was Col. Emory Upton, Wright's Division, VI Corps, whose idea it was for the boldly-launched attack. Only three years out of the U.S. Military Academy, Upton's plan decreed: "No commands were [to be] given while moving into position. All had bayonets fixed and guns loaded, but only the front line had them capped. On reaching [the Confederate works] the 1st line [was to] divide, half going to the right and half to the left, to sweep in each direction. The 2nd line would halt at the works and open fire to the front. The 3rd would lie down behind the 2nd , and the 4th would lie down at the edge of the wood, whence they charged, and [await] the result. In the charge, all officers would constantly repeat the shout 'forward,' and the men would rush forward with eyes on the ground they were traversing."[22]

The Georgians had time for only one volley before they were engulfed, as if by a human tsunami. The wild Federal assault breached the Confederate line. Hundreds of them stormed into the works and fierce hand-to-hand fighting occurred. The overwhelmed Georgians broke for the rear and many were captured on the spot. Gen. Lee attempted to go forward to direct the defense personally but was restrained from doing so.

Eventually, because of a stout defense and the failure of Mott's Division, Hancock's II Corps, to properly support the attack, the Federals were forced from the salient and the line was restored. It had been a particularly bloody affair. Gen. Ewell said the Federal attackers left 100 dead within the works and many more in front. He further estimated 650 Confederate casualties, 350 of whom were captured.[23] The Federal claims were over 1,000 captured.

During the night several more attacks were made against Gen. Field's Division. "[As] if to expiate the butchery, a Confederate band played, 'Nearer, My God, to Thee,' and a Union band answered with the 'Dead March' from 'Saul.'"[24] It was by now abundantly clear that the Army of Northern Virginia was faced with a far more determined adversary in Grant than they had ever faced before. He was not turning back as had his predecessors and resolutely informed his masters in Washington, D.C., that he proposed "to fight it out on this line if it takes all summer."

After the fighting had died down, it was necessary to establish a picket line in advance of the main line. From the Texas Brigade, two men from each company were detailed. From Co. F, 4th Texas, the "Veteran Morris" and "Pokue" were chosen. All were under the command of Capt. Matt Beasley, Co. I, 4th Texas. "Pokue" Joe Polley described as a fine physical specimen, six foot four, 200 pounds, and steady in most ordinary circumstances. However, fine specimen that he was, he was not known for valor. In an advance in line he did fine until the artillery opened. Once those screaming messengers of death and destruction began to rend the air, he completely lost his nerve and dropped "broadcast to Mother Earth." That is understandable, even common-sensical, but, while in an army, unacceptable behavior.

Moving out into no-man's land, the pickets crept forward in skirmish fashion. By then, darkness had fallen and the enemy's exact position was unknown. Stealth was important but that was lost when someone's half-cocked musket was discharged accidentally. Considering that the ball whistled down the line rather than coming from the front, one of the pickets panicked and let out the cry, "Flanked, boys, flanked!" At that cry of alarm, with the exception of Capt. Beasley and the Veteran Morris, all broke for the rear and the relative safety of the main line.

Standing their ground, both Beasley and the Veteran shouted "Halt," but it was to no avail. Then they, no other choice available, taking to their heels, followed their stampeded comrades, shouting "Halt," at the top of their lungs. The Veteran, being fast of foot, soon caught up, coming up behind Pokue. Pokue, thinking the command "Halt" to be coming from pursuing blue-clad enemy, imagined them over his shoulder, presumably, overtaking him. Just at the wrong moment, he caught his foot under a root and down he went!

"Rolling quickly over on his back and raising his hands in supplication, he cried, 'I surrender, Mr. Yankee! I surrender, sir.' And such was the poor fellow's confusion and fright that not until the light of a campfire shone upon [Morris'] smiling face did he realize that he had surrendered to one of his own company."[25] A humorous occurrence in what were otherwise grim circumstances.

The next day, May 11, a week since the Army of the Potomac began crossing the Rapidan, as if to cleanse away the blood, it began to rain heavily. From observers on the Confederate left and from the Gray cavalry operating behind the Federal left, conflicting intelligence arrived regarding the movements of the Army of the Potomac. Were they moving around south of the Po once more to the southwest in another flanking attempt, or, perhaps, east toward Fredericksburg? In the face of uncertainty as to his opponent's intentions, Gen. Lee was forced to make tactical decisions based on the spotty intelligence that was available. To Gen. Harry Heth, he confided, "My opinion is the enemy are preparing to retreat tonight to Fredericksburg."[26] Regardless of the eventual movement, he had to be prepared to move his army quickly in whatever direction it became necessary.

In preparation, during the night of May 11–12, because of the difficulty of extricating them from their deep-woods positions, he ordered most of his Second Corps' artillery in the "Mule Shoe" to be withdrawn before dark to the rear. Only two batteries, eight pieces, were left with Gen. Edward Johnson's Division located at the apex of the salient, the point most susceptible of attack. The withdrawn guns were to be parked in rear until events dictated the direction they were to take. E. Porter Alexander's First Corps artillery remained in place but with caissons loaded and ready to be instantly withdrawn.

At about 11:00 P.M., suspicions should have been aroused when the Federal bands across the way struck up and, in the dripping darkness of that night, played on for hours. A little after midnight, Gen. Edward Johnson, reported sounds that suggested the enemy was massing before him. He requested of Gen. Ewell that his artillery be returned to his front. The request reached Ewell at about 3:30 A.M. Within a short period of time, the guns were moving forward.

When the music ended finally, the blackness was just beginning to turn a fog-enshrouded gray on the morning of May 12. From the direction of the salient's apex the sound of musketry, increasing steadily in volume, could be heard. Then, from the northwest came the tramp, tramp, tramp of Hancock's II Corps infantry, 20,000 men, approaching accompanied by a mighty cheer. According to Gen. Johnson, they came on "in great disorder, with a narrow front, but extending back as far as [he] could see."[27] Joe Polley, Co. F, 4th Texas, noting how fast news traveled down the line, said news of the developing attack reached the Texas Brigade within three minutes of its commencement.

Col. Alexander observed later that had the withdrawn artillery been in place it would have been a slaughterhouse. "Nowhere else, in the whole history of the war, was such a target, so large, so dense, so vulnerable, ever presented to so large a force of artillery."[28] The awaiting Confederate infantry loosed a ragged volley their way. It was ineffective, however, because of wet powder in many of the muskets' chambers. Within the salient, men were seen to be fleeing their posts as officers tried to rally them and get them back into the line.

Gen. Lee, already up at his accustomed, bone-wearying 3:00 A.M., moved toward the firing, attempting to rally those he met fleeing but with little success. Shortly, he was met by an officer of Gen. Johnson's staff mounted on an artillery horse and was informed that the Federals had broken the front of his commander's line. Breaking through, the massed attackers had poured in as if a torrent, the line moving to the right and left. The withdrawn artillery had been rushed back, twenty-two pieces, all, save two, falling into the enemy's hands! Col. Alexander said the "two leading guns were in time to unlimber, and, between them, [fire] three rounds into the Federal masses before they were surrounded."[29] One battery was able to discharge only one round before a voice was heard from its rear ordering it to cease fire. The order came from an officer clad in blue backed up by many muskets borne by similarly clad men. They were already in and behind the Confederate positions in numbers. Gen. Johnson and one of his division commanders, Gen. George H. "Maryland" Steuart, and indeed, most of the division, 2,000–3,000 men, were captured! One of the units captured in almost its entirety was the famous Stonewall Brigade. Disaster impended once more as it frequently did for the Army of Northern Virginia.

In less than an hour, the Federal attack, joined by units from the VI Corps on the northwest and the IX Corps on the east, had swept over half of the salient. A force consisting of men from Early's Division commanded by Gen. John B. Gordon moved in skirmish line formation toward the breached section of the Confederate line. For the second time in a week, Gen. Lee moved forward to a position that indicated his intention of participating in the advance. Seeing this, Gen. Gordon said, "General Lee, this is no place for you. Go back, General; we will drive them back. These men are Virginians and Georgians. They have never failed. They never will. Will you, boys?"

"No, no," cried every man within hearing distance.

"General Lee to the rear; Lee to the rear!"[30]

Eventually, Gen. Lee was led to the rear, a sergeant of a Virginia regiment taking Traveler's reins in hand.

Gordon's command, joined by remnants of Gen. Johnson's Division, and Ramseur's Brigade of Gen. Robert Rodes' Division, moved forward, disappearing into the murky woodland scene. From the left, Anderson's First Corps divisions were drawn toward their right to help in sealing off the breach. Almost immediately, there arose the sounds of close combat which was to last throughout the day and late into the next night. As the daybreak advanced, Gordon's mélange was seen to be driving the enemy.

About mid-morning several violent attacks were directed against Gen. Field's First Corps front to the left of the salient. These attacks were beaten off successfully. Meanwhile, three brigades of the Third Corps, Perrin's Alabamians, Harris' Mississippians, McGowan's South Carolinians, entered the fray and, after horrific fighting, the salient was cleared of the enemy. In the aftermath, the "Mule Shoe" became more widely and appropriately known as the "Bloody Angle."

The enemy did not retreat entirely to their main line in the nearby woods. Some remained on the outer side of the Southern parapet, where taking refuge, they "threw bayoneted rifles over the parapet." "Sometimes, too, when a Confederate leaned out of the works, the Federals would grab him, pull him down and kill him or send him to the rear."[31] Even the most hardened veterans said afterwards that "the entire war had offered no scene to equal that fight at the apex of the salient."[32]

The Federal troops on the outside of the Confederate parapet had to be expelled! Examining his options, Gen. Lee found few available. However, one possibility presented itself. On the Third Corps' front to the right the fighting seemed to have lapsed into a lull. Near the center of that line an irregular bend in the defenses had created another, albeit smaller, salient than that at the Mule Shoe. Dubbed Heth's Salient due to the troops occupying it, it offered the possibility of a diversionary attack through a cloaking oak forest on the exposed left flank of the Army of the Potomac.

No other choice! From Gen. Cadmus Wilcox' Division, Gen. James H. Lane's North Carolinians, supported by Gen. William Mahone's Virginia Brigade of Anderson's Division, was fashioned into the attacking force. Moving forward into the oak woods on the right face of the salient, they were soon, undetected, in line and perpendicular to the left flank of the Federal army. At about that time, troops from Gen. Burnside's IX Federal Corps launched an attack on the left face of the salient. As the Confederate batteries opened on this force, Gen. Lane attacked them in flank. Burnside was repulsed and the Confederate right was secured. However, counter to the hoped-for result, the fighting at the "Bloody Angle" continued unabated supported by massive Federal artillery fire. To heighten the dreadful aspects of that terrible field, it commenced once more to rain in torrents.

At the parapet "the loss of life was staggering; some of the brigades, wet, bleeding, and decimated, were close to exhaustion.... Bayonets were thrust through the logs."[33] Gen. Lee considered another attempt at relief by another attack from Heth's Salient. However, since the earlier one, the Federal line had been strengthened making another attack impracticable. The fight at the Bloody Angle had to be continued until an effective secondary line could be established at the base of the salient.

As the long, terrible day came to an end and darkness began to blanket the scene, the fighting continued. "They had been fighting now for sixteen hours and more, with no rest, no food. The enemy, still two or three to one, fired ceaselessly through every opening in the parapet, or hurled bayoneted guns, like spears, down on the heads of the Confederates. The dead were so numerous that they filled the ditch and had to be piled behind it in a ghastly parados. The survivors waded in mud and gore, slipping now and then over the mangled bodies of their comrades."[34] Finally, at about midnight, the secondary line was completed and slowly, quietly, the troops were withdrawn unit by unit from that scene of unprecedented slaughter. Said Freeman of that day, "In all the bloody story of that mad, criminal war there had not been such a hideous ordeal."[35]

Casting a further pall upon that day, news reached the army that in a clash with Gen. Phil Sheridan's Federal cavalry near Yellow Tavern north of Richmond, the flamboyant Gen. J. E. B. Stuart had been mortally wounded the day before. Taken to Richmond, he had died later that evening. Grief stricken at the loss, Gen. Lee could only say of him, "He never brought me a piece of false information." One cannot imagine the depth of the despair he must have felt after witnessing the scenes enacted on that horrible day only then to learn of the death of another one of his trusted and beloved lieutenants.

As the rains continued heavily the next few days, it afforded a welcome respite from the close, deadly combat that came to characterize the last chapters of the war. News filtered through the army that the musketry had been so heavy in places that some large trees had been whittled down by the deluge of lead. Gen. Lee found this hard to believe until he was shown "an oak with a diameter of twenty-two inches, chipped away to an unsustaining splinter, as if beavers had gnawed it."[36]

The movements of the enemy across the way remained a mystery. On May 14, the continued presence of the enemy at the Mule Shoe ended as the troops were quietly withdrawn. On May 18, an attack by Hancock's II Federal Corps all along the line was easily repulsed thanks to twenty-nine pieces of well-placed Confederate artillery. Also, good news from the various other fronts served to bolster the spirits of the hard-pressed army. Gen. Benjamin Butler's two corps Federal army advancing upon Richmond from the south along the James had been effectively bottled up at Bermuda Hundred by Gen. Beauregard's Richmond garrison troops. For the time being, that ended that threat to the Confederate capital. A Federal army in the Shenandoah Valley had been driven back by forces commanded by Gen. Breckinridge, former vice president of the United States and, more recently, a leader in the Army of Tennessee. Supply lines severed by Federal cavalry had been restored and rations were, temporarily, adequate. The army would survive to continue the fight!

Bolstering spirits in the Southern ranks perhaps even more than the good news was the acquisition of coffee and sugar harvested from the vast crop of Federal dead littering the field of battle. "It may seem a small matter to the readers of war history," said Gen. Law, "but to the *makers* of it who were in the trenches, or on the march, or engaged in battle night and day for weeks without intermission, the supply of the one article of coffee furnished by the Army of the Potomac to the Army of Northern Virginia, was *not* a small matter, but did as much as any other material agency to sustain the spirits and bodily energies of the men, in a campaign that taxed both to their utmost limit." Newly acquired tin cups appeared among the troops who "at every rest on the march or interval of quiet on the lines could be seen gathered around small fires, preparing the coveted beverage."[37]

On May 15, Field's Division, First Corps, was shifted from the left to the right flank of the army to support an attack by Hill's Corps still under command of Gen. Early. During that time, the Confederate left was covered by Gen. Ewell's Second Corps, at least what was left of it, alone. On May 18, an attack was made by elements of the II and VI Federal Corps on Gen. Ewell's position. Col. Alexander said that the attack was made over the same ground as that of May 12, and that the stench from the unburied dead "was so sickening and terrible that many of the [Federal] officers and men were made deathly sick from it."[38] That, along with thirty pieces of well-laid artillery to sweep the field, easily repulsed the attack.

On May 19, amid reports that seemed to indicate the withdrawal of the Federal right, a reconnaissance by the Second Corps was ordered by Gen. Lee. The movement was mishandled and what was intended as a probe became a full-fledged fight. Heavy casualties, 900 men, were suffered and all just to find out that the enemy was still there in full force. This affair, as it turned out, ended the Spotsylvania phase of the campaign.

On May 20, further reports had a Federal movement south impending. The movement was sooner or later inevitable, and this time the reports made it seem more probable. The Texas Brigade was detached from the First Corps temporarily. This was for the purpose of defending some artillery positions placed south of the Po River for the purpose of covering the army's eventual crossing. By the next day, May 21, Gen. Lee was sure of Grant's movement south. Therefore, the army would fall back to the line of the North Anna River around Hanover Junction with Richmond only a little more than twenty miles in rear. There was no other viable choice in face of the overwhelming Federal superiority in men and materials. The three veteran Gray corps moved south and the great battle of Spotsylvania Court House was at an end.

Never again were those battle-scarred, bloodied environs to hear the clash of fratricidal arms.

The movement south had Anderson's First Corps following the Second Corps on Telegraph Road leading from Mud Tavern to Mt. Carmel thence to the North Anna crossings. Hill's Third Corps, Hill now recovered temporarily and back in command, moved by way of a road to the west of the road being followed by the other two corps. Even further west, the army's wagon trains rolled slowly southward through New Market, Chilesburg and Island Ford. One Texas Brigade soldier commented in a letter that since they had left Gordonsville they had not seen their wagons and "during that time [had] had no change of a single garment."[39]

Commenting on the more "slender" than usual rations received, Joe Polley, Co. F, 4th Texas, said they "grew less and less as the campaign progressed.... Flour became a luxury, corn-bread the staff of life. Hunger—incessant, never-satisfied hunger—prevailed, and the soldiers grew thin and gaunt. Still, on the pound of cornmeal to the man, and the less than half a pound of bacon, or as much beef which was occasionally issued, Lee's soldiery managed to live and retain the strength and the courage for almost continuous battle with a well-fed foe."[40]

Riding south in the wake of the First and Second Corps and with guides directing his way Gen. Lee saw a disheveled army but not a dispirited one. After dark, coming upon stragglers resting along the roadside he warned them of their impending capture by Federal forces if they did not move on, sooner better than later. Not recognizing him in the darkness, one replied, "Well you may order us to 'move on, move on' ... when you are mounted on a horse and have all the rations that the country can afford!" Gen. Lee made no reply but some of those nearer recognized him for who he was and set up the cry, "Marse Robert." "The effect was instantaneous. The soldiers got up as if they had never known weariness, and gave him a shout. 'Yes, Marse Robert, ... we'll move on and go anywhere you say, even to hell!"[41] And, as at other times and in other places, hell, or a reasonable facsimile thereof, was where they were headed once more.

Reaching the North Anna crossings at about noon, May 22, and before the Federal horde, Gen. Lee established his headquarters at Hanover Junction near the crossing point of the Central Railroad and the Richmond, Fredericksburg and Potomac Railroad. About a mile north of that point the Richmond, Fredericksburg and Potomac railroad bridge spanned the North Anna River. It and another bridge, referred to variously as the Fox, Chesterfield or Telegraph Road Bridge, both remained standing. Here, on the morning of May 22, Ewell's Second Corps crossed followed by Anderson's First Corps at about noon. The former took up a position on the right in reserve around Hanover Junction, the latter in front of the bridges. Here, two brigades of Pickett's long absent division from the Richmond defenses rejoined the army and were assigned temporarily to Hill's Corps. That corps arrived the next morning and was positioned to the west on the line of the Central Railroad around Hewlett's Station near the Ox Ford crossing of the North Anna.

The Gray cavalry, now under the South Carolinian Gen. Wade Hampton, reported the Federal advance. Hancock's II Corps was in the lead and observed to be widely separated from the rest of the Blue army. It was proceeding down the line of the Richmond, Fredericksburg and Potomac Railroad a short distance to the east. Actually, Grant was hoping to lure Lee into open country with the isolated II Corps acting as bait. In open country his manpower and artillery advantage would be telling. Gen. Lee did not rise to the bait. Actually, Col. Alexander said, without further explication, that Gen. Lee "never knew of the trap set for him."[42]

The probable point of the advance seemed to be Hanover Junction, most likely. If so, which proved indeed to be the case, the Army of Northern Virginia had won another critical race for position. Grant's blue-coated legions began to appear on the north bank of the river later in the afternoon. Almost immediately, artillery practice was begun by both sides. On upstream, large numbers of Federals were seen to be gathering opposite Ox Ford about two miles above the bridges. They were of Burnside's IX Corps. That proved to be only a feint.

However, about midafternoon, it was discovered that Federal troops of Warren's V Corps had crossed in force at Jericho Mills, about three miles northwest and upriver from Ox Ford. They were advancing southward through heavy woods. Gen. Hill ordered Gen. Wilcox's Division to attack them. In an unsuccessful and bungled affair, the division was withdrawn as night fell. Much to Gen. Lee's dismay and disdain for Gen. Hill's half-hearted effort, the Federal troops were across the river and entrenching along the south bank. They would be joined there by Wright's VI Corps on May 24.

Later in the evening, down river, a Federal attack was launched during a heavy thunderstorm against the troops holding the two bridges. Confederate positions north of the river were overrun and a number of defenders were captured. The survivors fled across the bridges and into the Confederate lines. Now, two wings of Gen. Grant's army were across the river. However, the two wings, Warren and Wright on the right, Hancock on the left were not connected. Later, an attempt to cross by Burnside's IX Corps in the center between Ox Ford and the lower bridges was quelled.

Uncertain as to Gen. Grant's exact intentions, Gen. Lee's approved a plan for an ingenious line of defense as suggested by the chief engineer of the army, Gen. Martin L. Smith. Around Ox Ford, several miles upriver from the bridges, there was favorable ground for defense, it being somewhat higher than that on the north bank. Although Gen. Lee, as army commander, is given credit, it was Gen. Smith who devised the ingenious position. "[Gen Lee] drew back Ewell and the right of Anderson to the southeast; he kept the left of Anderson opposite Ox Ford; and he directed that as soon as Hill's men were rested, they were to run a line from Ox Ford southwestward to Little River. Thus, Lee would have as his front a very wide inverted 'V' with its apex to the north and both flanks well secured — the left by Little River and the right by swampy ground east of Hanover Junction."[43]

In this arrangement, one of the most formidable that was devised during the entire course of the war, both flanks were secure. Any shifting of Gen. Lee's troops would be by interior lines and the two-faced front would require two separate and divided attacks by Federal assailants. An additional bonus, with the two wings of the Federal army across the river but not connected, was the fact that any Federal troop shifts from one front to the other would require two crossings of the river. The advantage they had in numbers was, thus, checkmated. However, the opportunity afforded by the army's favorable defensive position passed. Gen. Grant was too smart militarily to fall for the neatly baited Ox Ford trap and attack with his superior manpower divided, his advantage in numbers thereby neutralized.

By this time, with the campaign less than three weeks old, the Army of the Potomac had been reduced from about 120,000 to about 73,000. Adding to Gen. Lee's possibilities was the arrival of reinforcements, as mentioned earlier, Pickett's Division, Hoke's Brigade from the Richmond defenses and Gen. Breckinridge's troops from the Shenandoah Valley. Hoke's Brigade was assigned to Gen. Early's Division, Second Corps, from whence it originally came. Gen. Breckinridge's command of two brigades was kept independent and subject to orders from Gen. Lee. Altogether, the reinforcements numbered some 8,500 muskets bringing the Army of Northern Virginia to about 53,000.

On May 26, it appeared that Grant might be changing tactics and moving by his right against Richmond. However, on the next day, May 27, this was disproved when the Federal works on the south side of the North Anna were found to be abandoned. The Army of the Potomac was on the march down the north bank by their left. Cavalry reports had the enemy crossing the Pamunkey River around Hanovertown, far to the right and rear of the Confederate right flank. This development placed the Army of the Potomac only fifteen miles northeast of Richmond.

Once the Federal intention was established, no time was wasted in organizing the countermove. Ewell's Second Corps, holding the right, was put in motion during the morning of May 27, down the line of the Richmond, Fredericksburg and Potomac Railroad. Anderson's First Corps followed up. Hill's Corps on the left was designated the rear guard and moved out on the evening of May 27. The struggle was to continue, this time in the same environs along the Chickahominy as those of two years earlier.

* * *

The observed fact that Grant was once more moving by his left and crossing the Chickahominy farther down created multiple problems. What Gen. Lee feared mainly was being backed into a siege of the Confederate capital, a fight that he knew was not winnable. His only hope was in sustaining the maneuverability of his army. On May 31, Fitz Lee's cavalry reported the enemy advancing upon Old Cold Harbor beyond the Confederate right. The point of attack would be Old Cold Harbor for which the Army of Northern Virginia took up the march.

After the longest stretch of fighting since the war began over three year before, the stage was set for more of the savage fighting that had characterized the campaign thus far. On June 1, according to Joe Polley, Co. F, 4th Texas, they took up positions "on the identical ridge north of the Chickahominy, from which, in June 1862, it had helped drive Fitz-John Porter's command, of McClellan's army, to the south side of that stream."[44] The entire Confederate line consisted of A. P. Hill on the extreme left, then Breckinridge's command, Early (Ewell), Anderson (Longstreet) with Hoke's command anchoring the right end.

On the afternoon of June 2, heavy rains commenced and continued throughout the night, flooding much of the low-lying countryside around Cold Harbor including the shallow trenches dug hastily by the arriving troops. The Confederate line was lengthy having been extended periodically to counter the movements opposite by the Army of the Potomac. "The Federal breastworks were too close to those occupied by the Texas Brigade to permit a picket line, and ... an almost continuous exchange of rifle shots [was kept up] from the main line."[45]

During the night, the rain slacked off and "the men were no sooner awake than they commenced reading the morning papers, just out from Richmond, then but seven miles distant, breakfasting as they read on clammy corn-bread and raw bacon — the latter too precious then to be wasted by cooking.... Not a man dreamed that an attack would be made by the Union army; our position was too strong."[46] Nonetheless, as was the army's practice, as dawn approached the Confederate line stood to its positions. The men of the 3rd Arkansas had their cartridges "lined ... up on special declivities made for that purpose and poked their ramrods in the trench bank ready at hand. They had learned their lessons well in the Wilderness."[47] To their left, Kershaw's Division defended a salient, the weak point in the line and where the main thrust of the Federal attack was destined to fall. Between Kershaw and the Texas Brigade were Anderson's and Law's Brigades.

At 4:30 A.M., an all-out assault by the Federal army was begun all along the line beginning on the Confederate right. Col. Alexander said the battle "broke forth, mingled with vast cheering, in the stillness of early dawn, but it was no surprise."[48] Polley termed the charge "gallant enough to deserve success." It came "forward in four lines, about fifty yards apart." The sound of musketry was further punctuated by the sound of artillery firing in batteries. "Many excited and hurried Rebel riflemen fired ramrod and bullet into the Federal mass, forgetting to remove the ramrod in his haste to fire."[49] Citizens of Richmond lined the streets where the tumult of the battlefield was clearly audible. Volumes of smoke wreathed the countryside.

From the front, reports began to filter back to army headquarters. Heavy Federal attacks had created some breaches but these had been restored. "They fought bravely but could not enter our works," said O. T. Hanks, Co. K, 1st Texas, "and were mowed down almost like grain before the cradle."[50] "All along the line, the Federal dead and wounded were seen to be, literally, piling up. Gen. Anderson reported that his First Corps had experienced fourteen distinct assaults since 8:00 A.M. The Texas Brigade segment of the line did not come under direct attack, but they were able to deliver devastating musket fire on the left flank of the Federals attacking Kershaw's and Anderson's positions to their left. "The slaughter was terrible; in the fifteen minutes their struggle lasted, 10,000 Union soldiers were killed and wounded."[51] Across the line was heard the orders to advance again, but "not a man in the Union ranks moved forward, for not a man of them but knew it was suicidal to undertake the task ordered.... [T]he immobile lines pronounced a verdict, silent, yet emphatic, against further slaughter."[52]

By 1:00 P.M. it was, for all intents and purposes, over and the suicidal Federal assaults ceased. Lee's losses had been light, perhaps 1,200—1,500, while "more than 7000 of Grant's men crowded the field hospitals or lay, in every attitude of agony, on the open ground, in the ditches and among the slashed trees. Their agonized cries rose in a tragic chorus, but the sharpshooters were busy everywhere, and the suffering Northerners could not be relieved from the Confederate lines."[53] Given the news of the horrendous losses and suffering of his troops, Gen. Grant is said to have retired to his tent where he wept.

Grief-stricken or not, he could not bring himself to advance a flag of truce requesting permission to bury the dead and remove the wounded. Such would be an admission of defeat. Nor was there to be one until late on June 7, four days after the carnage, by which time, most of the wounded had died, all in agony. It was but another clear signal of the implacability of the Army of the Potomac's new leadership, in effect, no quarter! The battle of Cold Harbor proved to be the last great victory of the Army of Northern Virginia in the field even though the war would continue for another ten months.

The armies lay in place for the next ten days with "affairs quiet," mainly. The Texas Brigade remained in the same position until June 7, according to Joe Polley, Co. F, 4th Texas "the stench of the unburied, rotting corpses of the Federals slain on the 3rd constantly in our nostrils."[54] In the 3rd Arkansas, "[t]wenty-five percent [were] down, too sick to serve. Scurvy had broken out and was spreading at an alarming rate. The spectre of hunger was to be a permanent companion of the Confederate soldier from now until the end."[55] As if it had not been from the beginning.

On June 13, responding to Federal activities in the Shenandoah Valley, Gen. Lee detached the Second Corps, now under Early, Ewell worn out and reassigned. On June 13, it was discovered that the Army of the Potomac was, in keeping with its established pattern since crossing the Rapidan, absent in front. The Army of Northern Virginia, once more, as was its habit, took up the pursuit. On that same day, according to Joe Polley, Co. F, 4th Texas, Field's Division crossed "to the south side of the James River, crossing that stream on a pontoon bridge above Drewry's Bluff, and on the morning of the 16th, taking position in an old line of earthworks at Bermuda Hundred."[56] By then it was becoming evident that Grant's entire army had crossed the James River, thereby fulfilling Gen. Lee's worst fears. Earlier, he had stated to Gen. Early that if Grant reached the James "it will become a siege, and then it will be a mere question of time."

Thus began the final phase of the monumental struggle.

"No troops ... fought us with more bravery than did those negroes"[1]: James River to Forts Harrison and Gilmer, June–September 1864

In the aftermath of the Federal debacle of June 3, skirmishing continued along the lines in front of Cold Harbor, sometimes more deadly than at others. Due to battle fatigue, for which he was highly qualified, Gen. Ewell was relieved of Second Corps command. He was placed in command of the Department of Richmond, a supposedly less stressful position. Gen. Early was appointed in his stead as Second Corps commander. Gen. Kershaw was confirmed as the permanent commander of the former McLaws' Division, Longstreet's (Anderson's) Corps. As related before, Gen. Anderson had taken over command of the First Corps in the aftermath of Gen Longstreet's wounding in the Wilderness fight. Gens. Anderson and Early were promoted to lieutenant generalcies (temporary) commensurate with their greater command responsibilities.

Meanwhile, an aggressive advance up the Valley of Virginia by the Federal general David Hunter necessitated the detachment of Gen. Breckinridge's command from the Army of Northern Virginia on June 7 and its return to that theater from whence it had only recently come. By this time, Gen. Lee's outnumbered army of about 52,000 was facing a foe of more than 100,000 well-equipped soldiers.

Still in his lines around Cold Harbor, Gen. Lee was informed by Gen. Bragg from Richmond that a Federal attack had been made on June 9, upon the thinly defended lines before Petersburg, the important rail center south of Richmond. At first the precise origin of the attackers was unknown. They were either from Gen. Butler's Army of the James at Bermuda Hundred or from Gen. Grant's Army of the Potomac. At that time, the Army of the Potomac was occupying the lines across the way. No troop detachments had been detected and there were no reports of any units of Gen. Grant's army having crossed over to the south side of the James. Although possible, it seemed unlikely to Gen. Lee at that time that the aggressors came from that quarter.

The prime suspects, and the actual attackers it was later determined, were of Gen. Benjamin Butler's Army of the James, composed of Gen. Quincy A. Gillmore's X and Gen. William F. "Baldy" Smith's XVIII Corps. About 40,000 men strong, they had, beginning on May 5, 1864, in coordination with Gen. Grant's movement from the Rapidan, advanced from Fortress Monroe up the south bank of the James River toward Richmond. Landing at

Bermuda Hundred on May 5–6, by the latter date they had established a defensive position extending across the Bermuda Hundred neck.

The small force attacking Petersburg on June 9 was composed of three cavalry regiments led by Gen. August Kautz and two infantry brigades with a few pieces of artillery of Gen. Gillmore's X Corps, about 4,500 men total.[2] Hoping to take advantage of the weak defenses, their objective was "to capture the city and destroy the railroad bridge across the Appomattox."[3] Had that been accomplished, Richmond would have been further isolated from the rest of the Confederacy.

Narrowly failing in that attempt, on June 12, an advance on Richmond was begun. That thrust was thwarted, also, several days later by the Confederate forces occupying the fortifications at Drewry's Bluff on the James south of the Southern capital. Retreating, the troops rejoined their brethren within their Bermuda Hundred defenses, a position encapsulated by the vagaries of the river's twists and turns. It was a position chosen by a political general and one easily neutralized by an experienced and alert opponent. By establishing a line across the position's neck, the Army of the James was thus bottled up there by the Petersburg defenders.

The much-traveled and broadly experienced Gen. P. G. T. Beauregard was summoned from assignment in South Carolina and Georgia as the Federal forces attempted to close in on Richmond. Placed in command of the Department of North Carolina and Southern Virginia, his major responsibility was to defend Petersburg and Richmond. Acting with his customary energy, it was he who was able to put together the unlikely hodge-podge of older men and younger boys at Petersburg. It was they who, under Gen. Henry A. Wise, a former governor of Virginia, inspired by the martial music provided by a Negro band, and aided by an unnecessary delay in the Federal advance, who repelled the June 9 attack in truly heroic fashion.

Although their attacks failed, the attackers went away with first-hand information that the Confederate lines in front of Petersburg were very lightly defended and vulnerable. That fact was not likely to be lost on the Federal leadership councils. To the Confederate leadership, particularly to Gen. Beauregard, the troubling likelihood of Grant moving to the south bank of the James River lingered in everyone's thoughts. The key to the security of Richmond from the south was Petersburg.

Meanwhile, from the Shenandoah Valley came the disquieting news that the Federal army of Gen. David Hunter had occupied Lexington as of June 11. Effectively, that put the Valley under Federal control with the mountain passes open for incursions into central Virginia. Too much risk therein and to counter the threat, as mentioned earlier, the Second Corps, now Gen. Early's, some 8,000 muskets strong, was detached and began the march westward on June 13. "Coupled with the previous detachments ... [to the Valley], this meant that Lee was losing [twenty] per cent of his entire force or approximately one-fourth of his infantry at a time when his adversary was engaged in the most menacing maneuvers he had thus far undertaken."[4] The strain on available Confederate manpower was becoming more and more acute.

Simultaneous with Early's departure, Confederate skirmishers reported the Federal lines opposite at Cold Harbor to be vacant of its Blue inhabitants, all 100,000 and more of them — and, even more astounding, previously undetected! Nor was their presence found to be anywhere close beyond. Where had they gone? They had considerable room in rear down the Peninsula in which to maneuver. A cautious pursuit was immediately begun. With most of Gen. Wade Hampton's cavalry off chasing Gen. Sheridan's Federal cavalry, the eyes of the army were focused largely elsewhere.

Wasting no time, Gen. Anderson at the head of Longstreet's Corps began the pursuit of the missing Army of the Potomac, taking to the roads toward the Chickahominy River crossings at 11:00 A.M., June 13. On that march, the Texas Brigade, passing within sight of the Gaines' Mill fight of two summers earlier, had mixed emotions about their ordeal there. On one hand, they had great pride in being "the first to penetrate the line held by the foe, causing their whole line to break in confusion and flee from the field." On the other hand, they experienced "painful recollection" that "here we lost Colonel Marshall ... Lieutenant Colonel Warwick," and many others. Crossing the Chickahominy, the march continued over the York River Railroad, the battlefield of Seven Pines, the brigade bivouacking that night "a short distance north of Frazier's Farm and west of Malvern Hill."[5] There they remained awaiting further orders throughout the next several days, June 14–15. During their two days' respite, events were moving quickly nearby.

The unfolding evidence began to make it appear even more obvious that Grant was going to cross to the south bank of the James In fact, he had begun already to do so on the evening of June 12. Nonetheless, the days extending from then until the crossing was actually confirmed were attended by much uncertainty on the Confederate side of the military equation then under formulation. Until it was certain the whereabouts of the Federal army, Gen. Lee had to maintain his army's position on the north bank should there come an unexpected thrust toward the Confederate capital.

During this period of uncertainty, communications between Gen. Lee with the army north of the James and east of Richmond, Gen. Beauregard south of the James, and Gen. Bragg in Richmond were sporadic, often incomplete and frequently confusing. Some important messages requiring timely reply went unanswered for one reason or another. Some of the key communications did not include information needed in order to make timely tactical decisions. For four or five days, June 14–18, defective communications almost resulted in what could have spelled doom for the Confederate cause in Virginia and thus elsewhere.

On the evening of June 14, Gen. Smith's Federal XVIII Corps and Kautz's cavalry, about 16,000 in all, crossed the Appomattox River at Point of Rocks near Port Walthall and began to move on Petersburg. Gen. W. S. Hancock's II Federal Corps of the Army of the Potomac, having crossed to the south bank of the James thus far undetected, was nearby and moving into position to support the attack. According to Gen. Beauregard, the information on the Federal presence was conveyed to Gen. Lee but there was no reply received.

Receiving no reply, Gen. Beauregard sent an aide, Col. Samuel B. Paul, a pre-and postwar resident of Petersburg, directly to Gen. Lee to apprise him of his fears. When Paul arrived at Lee's headquarters on June 15, Gen. Lee was not impressed with the information he conveyed. He believed the reported Federal move on Petersburg was only a reconnaissance. Gen. Lee told Col. Paul that Gen. Beauregard "must be in error in believing the enemy had thrown a large force on the south side of the James; that the troops referred to ... could be but a few of [Gen. W. F.] Smith's [XVIII] corps [detached to Cold Harbor] going back to Butler's lines."[6] Gen. Beauregard later noted, ironically, that at that very moment Gen. Smith, with his entire corps, was attacking Petersburg. Early on June 15, Gen. Smith and Gen. Kautz had moved to the attack.

Even so, Gen. Lee, early on June 15, ordered Gen. Hoke's 6,000 man division then holding at the pontoon crossing of the James near Drewry's Bluff to reinforce the thinly defended Petersburg line. This was partly to assuage Gen. Beauregard's concerns and partly to hedge his position. Hoke's Division had been ordered earlier to discontinue an operation against New Berne on the North Carolina coast and had been brought only recently to the Virginia front.

Early on the morning of June 16, Gen. Lee received another enigmatic telegram from Gen. Beauregard. This missive advised that he had abandoned the Bermuda Neck, or Howlett Line, which was a most drastic measure given the circumstances as Gen. Lee understood them. Abandoning that line would leave the way open for Butler's Army of the James to spill forth from its encapsulation for whatever mischief it might wish to become involved in. Earlier that morning, Gen. Beauregard advised, he had moved the defenders, Gen. Bushrod Johnson's Division, to Petersburg. Why?

At Petersburg, the defense initially was by Gen. Wise's Virginia Brigade and some local militia units, about the same ones that had repelled the attack of June 9. Acting on his own authority, Gen. Beauregard had determined to reinforce Wise and concentrate his whole command at Petersburg. He knew he could not defend both fronts simultaneously. Within several hours of their vacating, as will be seen, the abandoned Confederate lines in front of Bermuda Hundred were partially reoccupied by Gray reinforcements from north of the river.

As it turned out, the force Gen. Beauregard was able to shift to Petersburg was a meager one. Although estimates vary, the total number of defenders must have been about 5,400. Later, Gen. Beauregard requested troops to retake and occupy his abandoned Bermuda Neck position. In his dispatch, inexplicably, Gen. Beauregard still made no specific mention as to the immediate and compelling reason for the withdrawal and concentration at Petersburg.[7] However, Gen. Lee, mindful of Gen. Beauregard's competence and experience, could only conclude that the vital rail hub was threatened in one way or another.

For the task at hand, Gen. Lee detached Pickett's and Field's First Corps divisions, Field to wait at the pontoon crossing of the James at Drewry's Bluff, to reoccupy the Bermuda Neck line. By 9:00 A.M., June 16, Pickett was south of the river via the pontoon bridge at Drewry's Bluff. Gen. Anderson was ordered to personally accompany Pickett's command and to take up the Bermuda Neck line. Later in the morning, Gen. Lee rode south of the river to try and see for himself what the situation was. No sooner had he arrived on the south bank than he was given a telegram from Gen. Beauregard at Petersburg.

This message told of heavy attacks and requested reinforcements. Still, there was no specific mention of whose army his opponents represented. As stated earlier, the attacking Federal force was Gen. Smith's XVIII Corps and allied units opposed by Beauregard's meager 5,400. Also in the area was Gen. Hancock's II Corps, some 28,000 strong although ordered not to become engaged until the arrival on the scene of Burnside's IX Corps. Once that occurred, there would be three Federal corps, 66,000 troops with which to contend. There were, maybe, 10,000 Confederate troops once Hoke arrived.

Long odds, indeed, and to become even longer when Gen. Warren's V and Wright's VI — the latter having replaced the slain Sedgwick — Federal Corps arrived, making the total about 90,000 muskets. However, Gen. Lee still lacked the specific information required for him to make a tactically sound decision. He could not strip the north bank of the James as long as he thought Gen. Grant's army, or any significant portion of it, posed a threat to Richmond from that quarter.

That afternoon, Gen. Lee received a dispatch from Gen. Anderson. It told of resistance being encountered along the Petersburg Pike. The pike, about twenty miles long connecting Richmond with Petersburg, passed just west of Drewry's Bluff; it continued south, passing just west of the Bermuda Neck lines, and then on south to Petersburg. At this news, to bolster Pickett's Division, Gen. Field's Division was ordered over the pontoon. As part of that movement, the Texas Brigade had marched from its bivouac near Frazier's Farm early on June 16 "crossed the James on pontoon bridges just below Drury' Bluff, took the south end of road from Manchester to Petersburg."[8] The other division of Longstreet's Corps, Kershaw's, was brought to the north end of the bridge to await orders.

Moving down the pike, Field's Division caught up with Pickett in line of battle behind the Bermuda Neck line. Once there, they were deployed on Pickett's right. M. V. Smith and his uninformed comrades in the ranks of Co. D, 4th Texas, "believed [the lines] to be filled with blue-coated Yankees, [and] we seriously expected to have another big killing before we got them."[9] Deploying skirmishers they "drove through the woods towards the [James] river some mile or so, and came upon a line of Beauregard's works [Bermuda Neck], but were disappointed in not finding them occupied by the enemy."[10] Scouts sent out found the next line likewise unoccupied. These two lines, being approached from the west, constituted Gen. Beauregard's secondary lines of defense. They were thereby reoccupied by late on June 16, early on June 17.

During the evening of June 16, Gen. Lee received yet another telegram from Gen. Beauregard. In it, Gen. Beauregard stated that he had no knowledge of Grant's having crossed the James. However, he did say that some of the troops captured on his front at Petersburg were of Hancock's II Corps. That body of troops Gen. Lee was intimately acquainted with. He had been fighting them for the last several years. They were of Grant's Army of the Potomac! Now, uncertainty deepened to anxiety.

On the afternoon of June 17, in possession of the secondary lines at Bermuda Hundred, Pickett, supported by Field, was ordered to mount an attack to restore the forward portions of the recently abandoned line. At the last minute, for tactical reasons, the attack was canceled. However, Pickett did not receive the message in time to stop his movement. As Pickett swept forward he requested Field's support. Always ready to oblige, Field joined in the assault. A member of the 4th Texas said that they "found only a line of skirmishers in possession, who mostly fled at our rapid advance. Some were taken prisoners, and a small number put hors-de-combat."[11]

Although it may be apocryphal, Joe Polley, Co. F, 4th Texas, had a different version of what transpired. According to Polley, as Pickett's troops swept past the enemy broke in front of their assault. At that moment an unidentified Texas private shouted, "Now's our time, boys!" Spontaneously, the entire brigade came to its collective feet and, without any given order to do so, leaped over the breastworks and joined in a wild, reckless charge up the slope of the hill on the enemy. "There was no alignment, no attempt at any, and such a yell as resounded was never before or since, heard between Richmond and Petersburg. Company, regimental and brigade officers, followed the lead of their men, and the other brigades of the division joined with a yell in the movement."[12] Polley said that Col. Winkler, "did manage to overtake them and cry 'Forward!' but it was a useless expenditure of breath; every man of the brigade was already running forward at the top of his speed."[13]

According to another account, upon reoccupying the main line, they came under a severe shelling from the Federal line opposite in which some casualties resulted. Then much to their chagrin, they were required to repair the damaged works, that carrying on into the night. Nonetheless, by 4:00 P.M., June 17, the Cross of St. Andrew was once more afloat above the restored Bermuda Neck line. The cork was back in the virtual bottle, although some of its leaked contents, mixing with the massive corps of the Army of the Potomac, were even then spilling over the Petersburg line.

As this affair was winding down, more dispatches were arriving at Gen. Lee's headquarters from Gen. Beauregard telling of continuing attacks on his Petersburg lines and repeating the call for reinforcements. In one dispatch he mentioned that a large number of Grant's army had crossed the river but again included no specifics. In the face of this, Gen. Lee could wait no longer; he had to act. Once more he was required to summon forth his innate audacity and vanquish any worries about the possibility of unanticipated consequences beyond his ability to control!

Later that evening, Hoke's Division trailed into the Petersburg lines in time to help stem what otherwise would have been a successful Federal attack. Gen. Lee ordered A. P. Hill with his Third Corps to move up to the north bank of the James River at Chaffin's Bluff while Kershaw's Division was ordered to cross the river and join the forces at Bermuda Neck. If Grant's army or any significant part of it lingered north of the river, now was their chance.

Gen. Lee's gamble paid off and his experiential judgement, as on many other occasions, proved sound. On the evening of June 17, a telegram from Gen. Beauregard reported, at last, that prisoners taken had identified themselves as belonging to the II, IX and XVIII Federal Corps. The first two were of the Army of the Potomac, the latter of Butler's Army of the James. Further, the prisoners reported the V and VI Federal Corps, Army of the Potomac, were coming up. The prisoners said that they had seen Gen. Grant on the south side of the James. Even though Gen. Lee was dubious of information yielded up by questionable sources, this did seem plausible enough to assume that the Army of the Potomac, or a large part of it, was over the river. Petersburg, the vital railroad hub, was its obvious and immediate objective. That captured, everyone could go home, the Blue, victors, the Gray, vanquished!

Actually, for a week following the Cold Harbor debacle, Gen. Grant was uncertain about what his next move should be. The most obvious move would have been to move up the north bank of the James from Malvern Hill toward Richmond. Instead, Gen. Grant determined to "cross the James at Wilcox Landing, 10 miles below City Point, and entirely out of Lee's observation, and to move thence directly upon Petersburg with his whole army. He would thus pass in rear of Butler and attack the extreme left flank of the Confederate line [at Petersburg], which, it is certain, would now be held by only a small force." Colonel Alexander admiringly described Grant's movement as "a feat of transportation which had never been equalled."[14] Moxley Sorrell was equally admiring, describing the move as a "narrow escape" for Confederate arms. The race for Petersburg was close and "Grant ... should have taken the place, notwithstanding Beauregard's boldness."[15]

Sometime that night Gen. Lee received the report that it had been ascertained that Grant and his entire army, less some units left to guard important points north of the river, had, indeed, crossed the James. The crossing had been accomplished by barge and via a remarkable pontoon bridge thrown across. The pontoon enthralled the engineer in Col. Alexander. He described the bridge as "the greatest bridge which the world had seen since the days of Xerxes."[16] Spanning the James at a point 2100 feet wide, it was completed within an eight hour time span. By midnight, June 16, the feat had been completed. Grant's army was across and finally, after five days of uncertainty, the disquieting truth was revealed fully.

On June 18, the Texas Brigade moved to Petersburg aboard the cars of the Richmond and Petersburg Railroad. There, said Col. Winkler, 4th Texas, they were greeted heartily by the citizens of Petersburg. "Everybody was either on the streets or at the doors and windows. Ladies, old and young, were out in the sun and dust, bare-headed, in many instances, numbers of them drawing and carrying water to the troops, and distributing it as they walked along. At two places were found large hogsheads of coffee."[17] Later that night "Field's

[D]ivision moved to the left, nearer the Appomattox, east of the city, and relieved other troops occupying the trenches near the point where the enemy gained his temporary advantage on Friday, the 17th."[18] According to Col. Simpson, the Texas Brigade was to remain in this line for thirty long, weary days.[19]

It did not take long, with the infusion of troops, for a new, expanded front to be established. When the troops were finally and fully deployed and in place before the city, the line was some twenty-six miles in length. The original line extended from "the ... outposts at White Oak Swamp ... to a point beyond the Jerusalem Plank Road."[20] The drawn lines were so close that, according to Moxley Sorrel "a biscuit could be thrown across, and conversations went on constantly between the fighters, who the next minute were firing at any head or arm that might be incautiously exposed."[21]

Affirming the closeness of the lines was Joe Polley, Co. F, 4th Texas. "The opposing lines [were] too close together to permit either side to send pickets to the front, the watching of each other and the guarding against surprise was done in and from the main lines, and lest the vigilance exercised there prove insufficient, each side maintained a rifle fire, which, although in the daytime somewhat scattering and perfunctory, was at night an unceasing volley.[22] According to Nicholas Pomeroy, Co. A, 5th Texas, "We were kept well supplied with ammunition; big boxes of it were placed along close to the works, and when empty were replaced by full ones."[23]

Col. Winkler, 4th Texas, observed that "it is not at all safe for one to raise his head above the works.... In our present position, we have lost in our regiment four killed, three wounded. When a shot takes effect, it is generally fatal. It is not considered ungallant for a man to take care of his upper story when lying in the trenches."[24] They manned the line "under a hot, almost blistering sun, and with only the shade made by blankets and tent-cloths, stretched across such rails and planks as could be brought long distances on the shoulders of its men through an incessant storm of bullets to protect them from its heat and glare. There was little breeze, scant rain, and much dust."[25]

There were five key rail lines traversing the area which, under the circumstances, made Petersburg's defense vital to the cause of the Confederacy. It was upon these rusty streaks that the Army of Northern Virginia relied for its sustenance and, therefore, its continued ability to keep the field. The most endangered line during these initial phases of the developing siege was the Petersburg and Weldon, lying just a few miles beyond the left flank of the Union Army's line opposite. It was only a matter of time, and Gen. Lee knew it, before this rail line wending its way up from the south would be in enemy hands.

During the weeks following, active operations were suspended while both sides labored in the torrid heat of a Southern summer to further improve and extend their respective lines. To the west in the Shenandoah Valley, Gen. Early's Second Corps was driving Gen. Hunter's Federal army out. There was hope in Confederate leadership circles that an advance down the Valley toward the Potomac might lead to a lessening of the pressure on the Petersburg front. Gen. Grant might be compelled to detach troops to the defense of Washington, D.C., if he felt the threat to be credible. It became credible by the first few days of July.

On the American nation's eighty-eighth birthday, Early, having advanced down the Valley, crossed the Potomac at Harper's Ferry. By July 9, he had marched to and crossed the Monocacy, defeating a Federal force under Gen. Lew Wallace, the aspiring novelist, sent to intercept him. Several days later, July 11, observed by President Lincoln personally, he was in front of the forts defending the capital on the north. He was not strong enough to mount a meaningful attack, however, and by July 14, was back on Virginia soil. There he would remain, too weak to venture abroad further. Grant did dispatch some units of the VI Corps to reinforce the capital defenses but it did not weaken significantly his Petersburg positions.

* * *

From this point onward, the art of wide-ranging military maneuver was no longer possible. The Army of Northern Virginia had been, after four terrible years, brought to bay! News from the other fronts, particularly in Georgia, were not encouraging. Before Petersburg, it was a siege. If Gen. Lee's worst fears were realized, and they were, "it would only be a matter of time."

As the fortifications and entrenchments grew, a daily routine developed along the Confederate defensive lines. In anticipation of the constant possibility of Grant's favorite tactic, an early morning attack, at an "hour before dawn every man was aroused and stood at arms to repel attack. After daylight, one man in two could sleep as best he might under summer sun. The other [50] percent of each command had to remain constantly on the alert, weapons in hand. Half an hour before dusk the whole of each regiment mounted the fire step and remained there until dark. Then those who had slept during the day went on duty."[26] In the Texas regiments it was reported that about a third of the officers and men were alert and on duty at any given time.

Col. Winkler, 4th Texas, described the developing Confederate defenses as "substantial." The "embankments of earth are sufficiently high to allow a man to stand erect without being exposed, if he is careful, and of sufficient thickness to resist the effect of their artillery, having a place to stand upon to fire over the works if necessary. There are obstructions of different kinds beyond calculated to tangle the enemy's legs and retard progress, should he have the temerity to attempt an assault. These works are filled with muskets and bayonets — the sameness relieved at proper intervals by menacing batteries."[27] With works such as these to contend with, he mused, the Federals had a greater chance of getting to heaven than they did of getting to Petersburg.

Referring to the trenches as "ditches," Joe Polley, Co. F, 4th Texas, said the ones about Richmond and Petersburg were "ready for occupancy" when they arrived. The trench systems became even more elaborate over time. "Leading back from the main 'ditch' at acute or obtuse angles, according to the nature of the ground and situation of the enemy's works, and with the dirt likewise thrown on the side nearest to the enemy, are small ditches, called traverses, in which the soldiers sleep and do their cooking, washing, starching, and ironing."[28]

Sometimes when traverses did not exist, the men would dig square holes in rear of the main ditch in order to have a place to sleep without getting stepped on in the dark. Joe Polley claimed a permanent scar on the side of his head was imprinted there by a hobnail of a booted soldier who stepped on him while passing down the main ditch in the dark, there being no traverses in that location.

While the square holes were effective in assuring that one would not be trodden upon by one's comrades while trying to sleep, they posed other dangers. Nicholas Pomoroy, Co. A, 5th Texas, had the following experience in which he and Capt. D. C. Farmer shared the same square hole. It was just big enough for them to lie down in. A piece of canvas was rigged so as to deflect the sun and the rain. Pomoroy said that one morning when he awakened he "noticed a bullet hole in the canvas roof close to where [his] head lay, and when [he] called the Captain's attention to it, he made little of it and said it was only a stray bullet. However next night [he] removed [his] blanket and slept closer to the breastworks. Early next morning on going to the pit or sleeping place [he] discovered two bullet holes on the lower edge of the canvas roof, where [his] head would have been, so that if [he] had slept there that night those two bullets would have passed through [his] head, so we moved our quarter after that."[29]

Adding to this unremitting routine of manning these works, the artillery thundered constantly along the line showering the trenches with hails of deadly shrapnel and dirt. The use of Coehorn mortars came into use by both sides. These ordnance pieces were thick-barreled, stubby tubes that hurled their missiles aloft in a towering arc. Their shells were usually of the fused, exploding type. The moment of detonation was determined by the length of the fuse attached. The idea was, generally, for the device to detonate above the trenches opposite, thereby showering the cowering occupants with shards of steel. With abundant practice available over the months, many artillerists became quite skillful at cutting fuses accurately.

Nighttime mortar barrages were particularly disconcerting to prospective recipients. Their burning fuses were clearly visible and traced their fiery arcs first up, then down. They were not always very accurate so their point of impact was always in doubt. O. T. Hanks, Co. K, 1st Texas, said of the mortars, "If you would hear a sound like a thud or ["pum"], over their way, look out its [coming]. [D]irectly you would [see] smoke[.] [D]irectly you would see a shell about the size of a peck [m]easure. It would come on upward [and] over [until] it would fall, into our works. [I]f dangerously near we would [skedaddle] into our [b]omb proofs which [were] holes dug in the ground [and] covered with logs [and] dirt thrown on them."[30]

While some accounts describe unceasing noise, others speak of times when the front was strangely quiet. According to Col. Winkler, 4th Texas, the cannonading and sharpshooting notwithstanding, given the closeness of the lines, "everything is remarkably quiet." O. T. Hanks, Co. K, 1st Texas, observed similarly that "[s]ometimes there would be a perfect quiet for a long spell."[31] That is, unless someone did something to stir up the boys in blue across the way. In one instance, it was Hanks himself who was the disturber of the peace.

During one long lull, Hanks noticed activity around several gaps near one of the Federal forts across the way. He decided he would do a little sniping of his own. His comrades begged him not to because of the hornet's nest he was sure to stir up. He had not fired on them more than three times, when "...of a [sudden] there was a [t]remendous [s]wish about [ten] feet directly over my head. I had made them [m]ad. [T]hey opened on me with a [sixty-four] pound [cannon] [firing] [three shots], each [s]hell going well into the rear[,] [n]ot doing one [particle] of damage. The boys [guyed] me, so ... I did not fire anymore."[32] His opposites, certain that they dispatched the annoyance, ceased fire.

The routine of the field messes, if there ever really was one, was disrupted. Col. Winkler, 4th Texas, said "We eat what we can get hold of, and prepared as it may be, every fellow for himself." Their bread was made from corn meal and was baked by a cooking detail who stayed in the rear of the lines for several days at a time. Two days' supply of bacon was issued and it was up to the recipients to cook it or eat it raw. A rare delicacy was "an issue of coffee and sugar, sometimes both at once. The coffee we parch in a frying pan, beat in a cloth, and boil in a tin cup, each one for himself, so we have a fine opportunity to suit our tastes as to whether it shall be strong or weak, as well as the time we drink it — having reference to the firing of cannon and sharp-shooters, as to when we go after water, etc."[33] On rare occasions they might get an issue of rice and cow peas.

Remembering it the same as Winkler, Polley, Co. F, 4th Texas, said that "coffee ... was a rarity" and that the quantity of rations was "disproportioned to the appetites and capacities of the recipients." In a letter to "Charming Nellie," he recounted how the commissary sergeant dispensed the alloted seven pounds of "rancid bacon." Trying to be as equitable as possible the sergeant, without accurate scales available, would "cut it up into as nearly equal shares as possible, and then, requesting a comrade to turn his head, call upon him to say who should get this or that pile.[34] Even though the rations remained meager, at least in their fixed positions, the commissaries knew where their troops were located and did not have to chase them down as was the case when they had been actively campaigning in the field.

The procurement of water posed a potentially deadly situation. Since there were no sources of water in the line, it had to be brought canteen by canteen from any nearby springs. In order for Joe Polley's company to secure water, a dangerous, open gap in the line subject to sniper fire had to be passed in order to reach a nearby spring. After several casualties, one mortal, they adopted the method of sending two men to the spring with all the canteens to be filled. One man would negotiate the dangerous gap, fill the canteens and then toss them one by one back to the second man waiting to receive them.

The uncertainty attending one's mortality resulted in some changed behaviors. In the 4th Texas, Col. Winkler said that the "monotony is frequently relieved by a group of a dozen or more engaged in singing religious songs, while others, in pairs, are quietly absorbed in an intricate game of chess, which amongst us, is fast superseding cards, which I think a decided improvement. Gambling, so far as my observation extends, is, I am glad to say, becoming unfashionable."[35] Danger and adversity have a way of fixing one's attention upon one's behavior.

Adding to the discomfiture imposed by the sharpshooters and artillery was the weather. "In hot weather the heat, the flies, and the stench of the [open pit] latrines made existence a torture. When a long June drought ended and thunderstorms became frequent, the water was often two-feet deep in the trenches."[36] It was a dread situation that had developed, discomfort, constant danger, instant death and the always present disease and resultant illnesses.

Eventually, after being relieved from the Petersburg line the butcher's bill was totaled up. In the 4th Texas, Col. Winkler reported casualties in his regiment as one killed, 3rd Arkansas, one killed and 5th Texas, three wounded. In the 3rd Arkansas, Capt. Samuel C. Harrell, acting regimental commander, was killed July 1 by a shell falling into the trenches. On July 19, Capt. T. J. Hadley, Co. A, 3rd Arkansas, received a head wound, compliments of a watchful Federal sniper, that placed him *hors de combat* for the remainder of the war.[37]

All of these were considered light losses, the credit going to "good fortifications and covered passageways leading in every direction the men have to go."[38] Life on this front for all concerned was one of "hours of boredom (and discomfort), moments of terror." Joe Polley, Co. F, 4th Texas, quoted Bill Calhoun, the philosopher of Co. C, 4th Texas, in calling it a "a rest between roasts' ... as the unrepentant are sometimes allowed in the next world."[39] And it lasted for a long time, until April 1865.

The men under arms were not the only sufferers. The citizens of Petersburg were not untouched by the developing drama. The city itself came under artillery fire. One observer said that "inhabitants, as a general thing, have left the shelled district. Many families are living in tents furnished by the quartermasters, out of reach of the enemy's cannon."[40]

According to Joe Polley, Co. F, 4th Texas, the brigade that was to relieve them on the line arrived on the morning of July 20. For the next few days they were held in reserve and rested "under the shade of trees, near a little stream of clear, running water, and sufficiently far from the firing line to dull the roar of guns, big and little."[41] On or about midnight,

July 28, the Texas Brigade and the other units of Field's Division marched through the darkened streets of Petersburg bound for the eastern end of the Confederate line. There they were to take part in an assault on a Federal fort opposite. For various reasons, the attack did not occur, although they came under a severe Federal bombardment.

In the meantime, on July 27, in response to Gen. Grant's transfer of Hancock's II Federal Corps and Sheridan's cavalry to the north side of the James, Gen. Lee sent Anderson's Corps, and the divisions of Wilcox and Heth from A. P. Hill's Third Corps to counter. On July 27 and 28, the first of the Confederate units across the river fought engagements with the enemy southeast of Richmond. On July 29, Field's Division and the cavalry of Fitz Hugh Lee followed. The Texas Brigade marched once more through Petersburg and at a depot on the Richmond and Petersburg Railroad they, less the 3rd Arkansas and Benning's Georgia Brigade that had gone on the day before, boarded the cars for Drewry's Bluff. Taking up the march from that point, they crossed the pontoon bridging the James, according to Col. Winkler, 4th Texas. They were to remain north of the river until the very last stage of the campaign.

Once back across the river, during the next several days they marched downstream and took up a position at Fussell's Mill near Deep Bottom. In the ranks the speculation was that Gen. Grant was making a move against Richmond from that quarter and they had been relocated to counter that threat. Whatever the cause, they were "rejoiced to get out of the trenches, and soldier-like, glad of a move of any kind.... All is mist before [our] eyes; cannot see an hour ahead."[42] As it turned out, the movement of Hancock and Sheridan was a feint, the feint being made to draw troops away from the Petersburg front, which it did. There, a dramatic event was planned that, if it worked, might break the Confederate lines protecting Petersburg.

As July had advanced, rumors began to spread up and down the line that the sounds of digging could be heard under some parts of the Confederate line in front of Petersburg. Countermining failed to discover any such activity, however. "The men in the ranks took the talk of a mine as something of a joke and told newcomers that Grant was trying to mine all the way under Petersburg, so as to take the army in reverse."[43] O. T. Hanks, Co. K, 1st Texas, said that their method of trying to locate the mining operation was to "drive a peg in the ground [and] hold it with our [t]eeth to get a [s]ound if [possible.]"[44] Sensing some advantage in a possible eruption, Joe Polley, Co. F, 4th Texas, said that if any such event were to occur on a segment of the line held by the Texas Brigade, it would send "us Texans farther heavenward than many of us ever expect to get otherwise, and certainly farther than any of us ever have been."[45]

By the wee hours of July 30, Gen. Lee, having studied dispatches decided that the movement involving Hancock's Federal II Corps was but a feint. The real attack would come against Petersburg. Then, just several hours later as a timely confirmation, around 4:45 A.M. "there came across the Appomattox ... the sound of a distant but mighty explosion, somewhere to the southeast of Petersburg."[46]

Across the James in the Texas Brigade, those that were awake at the time, heard the muffled roar of the distant explosion. As it turned out, the site of the mine explosion was very near that segment of the line that they had just vacated a few days earlier. Like everyone else, they thought that a mine detonation was somewhere in the offing. So, as the facts became widespread, there was rejoicing at their reprieve. Bill Calhoun, Co. B, 4th Texas, who always had a timely — and homely — comment, said, "Well, boys, hit's a d—d sight more comfortabler ter be stannin' here on good ole Virginny *terror firmer* than ter be danglin', heels up an' heads down, over that cussed mine, not knowin' whether you'd strike soft or hard groun' when you lit."⁴⁷

Hurrying to the front, Gen. Lee surveyed the scene. Joined by Gen. Beauregard, they viewed the huge crater made by the explosion. It had been detonated a little north of the Baxter Road that intersected with the Jerusalem Plank Road a little further north. The crater had destroyed the front line for a distance of 135 feet and had left a crater some thirty feet deep, with a breadth, from front to rear, of ninety seven feet.⁴⁸

As Gen. Lee viewed the dismaying scene before him, the shouldering crater teemed with Union blue, many of them U.S. Colored Troops. The Confederate troops, some of them hurled into the air by the blast, once they returned to the surface, recovered quickly. Manning the rim of the crater, they discharged volley fire into the mass of blue below. Some of the Confederate artillery, similarly become airborne, recovered and laid down a devastating fire into the pit. Several mortar batteries joined in.

At 1:00 P.M. the counterattack to recover the lost ground moved forward. "The artillery roared anew; the shells screamed over their heads like frightened birds. Soon all were in the open.... Directly up the incline they went, straight for the crater.... The melee was like a battle of despairing demons.... Bewildered by the onslaught, all the Federals who could do so fell back into a smaller pit, in front of which the explosion had raised an earthen barrier."⁴⁹ In this disorganized state, there were cries for mercy, often unheeded, and soon, capitulation. It had been a close call for the Confederate defenders but the battle of the Petersburg Crater was over. The next day, July 31, a truce was agreed upon in order to bury the dead and remove the wounded. It was a bungled attempt that was costly in terms of life in both the Blue and Gray ranks.

Following the Crater fight, Gen. Grant withdrew most of his troops from north of the James and into the Petersburg effort. Gen. Lee followed suit leaving only Gregg's Texans, Benning's Georgians, Gary's cavalry and Gen. Ewell's small defense force in front of Richmond. Gen. Grant, for the remainder of the campaign, transferred troops back and forth, always testing his opponent's alertness and looking for weak spots to be exploited.

During the subsequent eight months that the Texas Brigade remained north of the James, they were to occupy successive positions around Deep Bottom, Chaffin's Bluff, Darbytown Road, Charles City Road and the Williamsburg Road.⁵⁰ With but several exceptions, the situation at the front settled into the dangerous but predictable routine described earlier.

* * *

Several days later, it was observed that Gen. Grant was moving troops by barge down the James River. Gen. Lee's instinct and fear was that these troops were destined for deployment against Gen. Early's Second Corps and associated troops in the Valley of Virginia. In a conference with President Davis and First Corps commander Anderson in Richmond on August 6, it was decided to send Kershaw's Division of the First Corps and a cavalry force under Gen. Fitz Lee to bolster Early's command. Gen. Anderson would go to command in person. The movement began soon thereafter.

From the time they left Petersburg until August 13, the Texas Brigade had a rare but pleasant and well-deserved respite on the northside. "Peace and quiet reigned ... in shaded camp and with nothing to disturb its rest, the Texas command felt that its lines were cast in pleasant places. Vegetables were to be had in abundance from the Portuguese, negro and 'poor white trash' truck-farmers of the section, and having been recently paid off, the men fared as sumptuously as their wretchedly small allowance of bread and meat permitted."⁵¹ However, it did not last long.

On August 16, the Federals began an advance up the Charles City Road. Near Fussell's Mill, they were successful in breaching the Confederate line. For a time it looked like the way into Richmond lay open. Gen. Field's troops, veterans of many hard-fought battles, were shifted to their left to meet the Blue tide. Among them, the Texas Brigade had a key role, as Joe Polley, Co. F, 4th Texas, put it, "playing a game of hide and seek with the Federal cavalry. It was hard work as the "...sky was cloudless, the sun had a full head of steam on; not a breath of air was astir in the dense woodlands through which the infantry brigade marched and countermarched, and water was not to be had except at the slow-flowing wells of the few denizens of the section."[52] Federal attackers were driven back beyond White Oak Swamp. With the crisis surmounted, the Texas Brigade was returned to its former position on New Market Heights.

While in the Market Heights position, from that elevated point in the line the brigade could "look down with lofty scorn, and defiance upon the enemy in the open [James River] valley below." Several batteries were brought forward and began to shell the Federals below. Seated near the batteries with his back to the breastworks, Joe Polley, Co. F, 4th Texas, was at work on his journal. Being an old veteran, he felt "neither curiosity nor fear." Lt. Eli Park and Pat Penn, of Co. F, not being similarly occupied and curious, were standing and peeking carefully over the top of the breastworks.

Lt. Park was the original first corporal of the company. He had been promoted to the commissioned ranks just prior to the beginning of the Gettysburg campaign, effective April 8, 1863. Presently, he was awaiting word on a request for a transfer to Texas so that he could provide care for his widowed mother. Pat Penn had been promoted to fifth sergeant November 22, 1862, and to fourth sergeant May 20, 1863. Penn was close enough for Polley to touch him with Park just beyond.

The artillery barrage had continued for about ten minutes when Polley said Penn "stepped back, ejaculating, 'Oh, pshaw!' in such a peculiar tone as to attract my attention." Looking beyond Penn, he saw that Park's head had fallen forward and was resting on the top of the breastwork. From somewhere to their right, a vigilant Federal sharpshooter had drawn a bead and placed a musket ball through the lieutenant's head, " ending a vigorous and promising young life." Polley mused that although Park had "made but the one application, two transfers came 'approved' before the sun set — one from an earthly commander to Texas, the other from his God to another world — the last alas! first."[53]

This was not to be an uncommon occurrence along the defensive lines in front of Richmond and Petersburg in the long months stretching from June 1864 toward April 1865. During the trench warfare that developed, the "sharpshooters became so proficient on both sides that momentary exposure of the person was almost certain to result in a serious wound, if not in death."[54] Only the reckless or unthinking allowed any part of their anatomy to become visible to the Blue omnipresence across the way.

As for Pat Penn, a little more than a month later, on September 29, he was wounded in the shoulder, slightly, so he thought, at a place called Chaffin's Farm. "[A]lthough he walked back to the field hospital laughing, next day he was a corpse."[55]

Meanwhile, on the south side of the river, on August 20, the Weldon Railroad fell, effectively, under Federal control. "The defense of the capital and the subsistence of the Army of Northern Virginia had now to depend on the full employment of the Southside and of the Richmond and Danville Railroads."[56]

On August 21, the Texas Brigade was moved to a position near the Phillips house. There, the staff sharing the house with the owners, it remained for the next five weeks.

Their assignment was to "watch the movements of the negro brigades in Deep Bottom, and give notice of any attempt to reinforce them." Joe Polley, Co. F, 4th Texas, described their stay there as "not unenjoyable." "Many vegetables and fruits were in season, and high-priced as they were, they were bought as long as the last two months' pay lasted, all $22 Confederate dollars of it. Moreover, not only were the Richmond papers brought daily to camp, but the New York *Herald* and other Northern journals were easily to be had from negro pickets, in exchange for the tobacco which Commodore Dunn, our sutler, kept the brigade well supplied."[57]

After severe reverses at Winchester and Fisher's Hill suffered by Early's Corps in the Valley, in mid–September, Gen. Anderson was ordered to rejoin the army and to resume command of the First Corps. After his return, on September 28, he received orders to move his headquarters to the "north side of James River and take command of the troops and line of defense about Chaffin's Bluff, New Market, etc."[58]

In late September, in the Texas Brigade, at least some of the officers, had a brief respite and glimpse of almost forgotten sociability enjoyed in happier times before the war. Col. Winkler's wife was taking advantage of an unusual opportunity to visit the front. This was because she had relatives living in the immediate vicinity with whom she could stay. While there, she was afforded a chance to see life at the front as few other females were. Visiting the picket line within sight of the enemy the "sentinels were very much surprised to see a woman on the picket line, but showed us where we could get a glimpse of the blue coats, who were somewhat in the habit of popping away at the rebels when in sight."[59]

Later, she was persuaded to act as chaperone for a group of young ladies coming down from Richmond for a party. On September 28, with the camp "swept and garnished," everything was in readiness for their arrival. They arrived at the river landing nearby at 10:00 A.M. and there followed, at Maj. Littlefield's quarters "a day they all seemed to enjoy very much, dancing under the large tent, with music by string and brass band, conversing, resting on seats made quite comfortable, and partaking of the dinner.... At 5[:00 P.M.]... the boat arrived, and they returned to the city, expressing their pleasure and enjoyment of the occasion."[60] Later, Mrs. Winkler confided that it seemed an odd place for gaiety. In war, one must take gaiety wherever its available; God only knows when the opportunity might arise again, if ever.

The day after Gen. Anderson was ordered to the north side of the river, September 29, the Federals in that locale attacked Fort Harrison, a key position in the outer defenses of Richmond. Gen. Grant's immediate objective was to tie down Confederate troops there and prevent any further reinforcement of Gen. Early in the Valley. The Federal troops involved were of Gen. Butler's Army of the James, Gen. Birney's X Corps and the XVIII Corps, now commanded by Gen. E. O. C. Ord. There were about 15,000 infantry and Kautz' cavalry, numbering about 4,000 sabers.

These forces were withdrawn from the Petersburg line and moved across the James at several crossing points at Deep Bottom the day before. Gen. Ord's troops crossed on the night of September 28, and advanced up the Varina Road, its objective the defensive works at Chaffin's Bluff. Gen. Birney's Corps moved up the New Market and Darbytown Roads toward Richmond. Kautz' cavalry followed Birney's Corps to operate along the Darbytown Road.

The Confederate works north of the James defending Richmond were complex, some of them having been in place since earlier in the war. According to Col. Alexander the line of breastworks was about eleven miles long, stretching from Chaffin's Bluff on the James to the Chickahominy near New Bridge. Called the Exterior Line, the greater portion of it, from about seven miles north of the New Market road was the abandoned trenches of the campaign of 1862. It was in a state of neglect and ill-repair. Within was the interior line extending from the river below to the river above. On its perimeter was "about a dozen interior small forts on the edges of the city, which were built during the first year of the war." To protect the Chaffin Bluff batteries and the pontoon bridge, a spur line of trenches had been extended "south, from the Interior Line down to the Exterior Line, so as to embrace Chaffin's Bluff & the Osborne Pike, the principal road to it." There the Spur Line joined the exterior line at a point occupied by a work designated as Fort Harrison. About a mile north of that point on the line was a small fort designated Gilmer.[61]

Although extensive, much of the works was defective in at least one particular. None of the lines had abatis in front of them. That defensive device, if haste was required in establishing them, sometimes consisted of available trees felled in front of the line with their branches pointing toward the enemy's line of approach. In more permanent positions where there was time to fortify properly, abatis took the form of stakes sharpened to a point and driven in the ground. The sharpened logs were angled to point about chest-high at an assaulting force. Without abatis in place the defenders were at a disadvantage in trying to hold their positions against mass attacks by determined infantry.

At the time, the sole defenders of these lines were the infantry brigades of Benning, Law, Gregg and Fulton (of Bushrod Johnson's Division), numbering about 5,000 and Gary's cavalry, about 1,000.[62] Not mentioning Law's Brigade, Joe Polley, Co. F, 4th Texas, said that Fulton's Brigade was positioned on the river above Drewry's Bluff, Benning's Brigade was at New Market Heights, Gary's cavalry was guarding the Charles City Road and the Texas Brigade was at the Phillips house, "between Benning and Fulton." He placed the tactically important Fort Harrison halfway between the Texans and Fulton's command.

The morning of the attack to overwhelm Ft. Harrison was shrouded in "a dense, obscuring fog." As it became apparent that the route of the attack was to be up a "narrow creek valley," the Texas Brigade was moved into that position. The fog was so thick that visibility was limited to maybe a hundred feet. The brigade formed a single line with a space of about six feet between each man. They could "distinctly hear the Federal officers, as in loud tones they gave such commands as were needed to keep their men moving in line, but until the line approached within a hundred feet, could see nothing; even then, only a wavering dark line was visible. As it became so, and as was usual in those days, without waiting for orders, the Confederates sprang to the top of the low breastworks, and commenced firing—'shooting at shadows,' one of them said.[63]

The Federal troops advancing in that area were of Gen. Birney's X Corps. In front the order to charge was heard. The Federal troops advancing out in front against the Texas Brigade were U.S. Colored Troops, presumably Paine's 3rd Division. Joe Polley, Co. F, 4th Texas, writing disdainfully, said their rush, carried some of them "across the breastworks, and right among the First Texans. The latter, since Spottsylvania Court House well-provided with bayonets, were experts in the use of them, defensively and offensively, and in less than three minutes one-half of the assailants were shot down or bayoneted and the other half, prisoners."[64] He claimed that not a "dozen shots" were fired by the ranks of the Texas Brigade and not a man received a wound. The firing lasted only five minutes, he thought.

Actually, the Federal attack was a great success, overall. Afterwards, Gen. Paine in a note to Gen. Butler lauded his colored troops, particularly "the Thirty-sixth U.S. Colored Troops [who] behaved excellently in the assault of September 29.... [S]o did every regiment concerned (the First and Thirty-seventh were not engaged...).”[65] At least one member of the Texas Brigade admired their behavior that day. Although it took decades for him to say so, in a print article published nearly fifty years later, J. D. Pickens, Co. E, 3rd Arkansas, who received a wound in the hand in the action, spoke respectfully of the black troops' conduct. Of them he said, “No troops up to that time had fought us with more bravery than did those Negroes.”[66]

The attack, in which Gen. Ord was wounded and of which Gen. Grant was a spectator, succeeded in capturing Ft. Harrison, a key point in the outer defenses of Richmond. In the debacle that ensued, the Texas Brigade was forced to beat a hasty retreat, closely pursued by their opposite numbers, to the interior defenses near Ft. Gilmer. Once gaining those works, they turned on their pursuers, and, according to D. H. Hamilton, Co. M, 1st Texas, “killed or captured the whole bunch.... We were then charged by a line of white soldiers which we whipped out.”[67] It was a narrow escape for them; they were almost cut off from Richmond by the Federal advance.

In front of the 1st Texas' new position, there was a cornfield, the corn cut and shocked. The Federals established a skirmish line using the corn shocks from behind which they stationed their sharpshooters. In front of Co. M, was stationed a particularly annoying rifleman. Stepping out from behind his shock, he would fire and then jump back to his place of safety. One such time, he managed to kill Eb Eaves, he having been already wounded once at Sharpsburg two years earlier. This angered Eaves' comrades to the point that they “all got busy with [the killer].” “Several ... tried shots at him without effect.” Misjudging the distance, D. H. Hamilton's two shots fell short. Then L. M. McLendon, “raising his sights to three hundred yards, he waited for the Yankee to step out and, when he did, he fired and downed his man, whereupon there was much rejoicing in [the] company.”[68]

The next day, according to Hamilton, they were double-quicked to a fort in the line to their left. There they received a frontal assault, their attackers under the impression that the position was thinly manned. When they began their advance, they were surprised when “the batteries of twenty guns opened up on them with grape shot and in a short time [Co. M, 1st Texas] was ordered to fire, and fired three rounds before ... ordered to cease firing.” Smoke created by the volleys obscured the scene and, oddly enough, it had become perfectly quiet. It took about fifteen minutes for the smoke to dissipate, and when it did, to their astonishment, the Yankee force was nowhere to be seen! Then Ephriam Dial, “always a dare devil,” set out in front to seek their whereabouts. No one tried to stop him, and he “went down in the direction of where [they] had seen the Yankees approaching.... Out there he found “a squadron of them lying down in a depression and walked right up on them. We could see him making motions and directly he took his hat and waved it in the air and yelled, whereupon the Yankees all rose and waved their hats.” Ordering them to leave their rifles where they were, he marched them to the rear where he turned them over to the provost marshal troop, demanding a receipt for their delivery![69]

The loss of Ft. Harrison was a serious blow because its possession had enabled Gen. Lee “to confine the enemy on the north side of the valley of the James, below Drury's Bluff; losing it, he was compelled to withdraw his forces from the heights north of the James, and place them within a line of entrenchments encircling Richmond.... This gave the Federals outlet into the country north of Richmond.”[70] “As this was one of the most important positions on the outer line of Richmond, and was close to the fortifications of Chaffin's Bluff, its loss was serious in itself and might open the road to the capital.”[71] It had to be recovered!

Gen. Lee, on the field by the afternoon of September 29, ordered reinforcements from the south side. By the morning of September 30, there were ten brigades at Ft. Gilmer and everything was in place for a counterattack. Under the overall command of Gen. Anderson, it was not until afternoon, after an artillery preparation by Col. Alexander's guns, that the attack moved forward. The coordination of forces was incorrect and ultimately, after two assaults, in which the Texas Brigade did not participate, the attack failed. Fort Harrison remained in Federal hands.

For Gen. Lee, there was nothing else to do but reroute the Confederate lines to not include the lost bastion.

CHAPTER 17

"*The Texas Brigade is always ready*"[1]: Darbytown Road to Five Forks, October 7, 1864–March 30, 1865

In early October, the Texas Brigade remained on picket duty until there was an attempt mounted to recover a segment of the exterior line above Fort Harrison. Field's Division, along with several brigades of Hoke's Division, was a major player in the planned attack to be remembered as Darbytown Road. According to one source, at that time the entire Texas Brigade could muster only 425 muskets whereas a fully-manned brigade would have numbered in excess of 4,000 men.[2] On the morning of October 7, Gen. Lee was present to observe the opening of the attack. Inquiring of one of his staff officers if the troops were ready to move forward, the answer was, "None but the Texas Brigade General." "The Texas Brigade is always ready," Lee commented, half proudly, half sadly."[3] Some Texans overhearing the remark, said that, "'Marse Robert' was on the field and had his eye on [the Texas Brigade], and inspired by the consciousness of that fact, every man in it went forward with the resolve to do his level best."[4]

Joe Polley, Co. F, 4th Texas, whose long and faithful service in the Texas Brigade came to an end in the attack, said of it, that to him and the dead and wounded of the Texas Brigade "it was a desperate assault by a small force upon well-manned earthworks, approachable only through open ground, and protected by a *chevaux-de-frise* made of felled timber."[5] The Federal troops occupied a strongly fortified line of "well-constructed entrenchments, extending along the crest of a long ridge, in front of which much timber had been felled and fashioned into an abatis exceedingly difficult of passage."[6] A member of the 4th Texas said that the advantage lay "overwhelmingly with the Yankees." Their position was strong, and "every tree of the many lying on the ground over which we charged, pointed its sharpened branches at our eyes, faces, bodies and clothing. No sooner was a fellow out of the detaining clutch of one, than another presented itself, and taking hold of flesh or clothing, held him captive a while. There was no staying in line, and could be none."[7] It was every man for himself to surmount the abatis.

Moving forward with his company, Joe Polley's rifle was hit by a ball which struck between his left thumb and forefinger, burning both. Another ball passed through the lapel of his coat. A few minutes later, with others, he was forced to take cover from the overwhelming fire. Attempting to flee, he was hit in the foot but, although the wound was serious, he was able to make it back to the regiment on his own. He said he had often thought that if he were to be killed or wounded in battle he hoped it would be in a big one. "Wounded there, I could boast of it in this world; killed there, the fact might give me a standing in the other, superior to that which I can now hope will be accorded me."[8]

He was placed on a litter carried by four of his taller friends. In that elevated and exposed position, with his head toward the enemy and still under a heavy fire, he feared for his life as he was taken to the field hospital. Once there, he was examined by the much respected, ever-faithful regimental surgeon, Dr. John Curtis Jones, who kindly acceded to Polley's request for morphine. As with most wounds of that type, Dr. Jones was compelled to amputate the severely injured foot.

From the field hospital he was taken by field ambulance to the Howard Grove Hospital in Richmond and eventually to the private home of a friend where he was welcomed to recuperate. Alas, the Texas Brigade had lost a true and loyal soldier but it would gain, in the future, an equally loyal biographer.

Basil Brashear, Co. F, 5th Texas, participated in the attack that, he said, started with the "old Texas yell." His description of the enemy's rapid fire accorded with that of others. He said it "mowed us down like hay." He and another soldier took shelter hastily behind a pine stump where they found a dead comrade shot through the head. Soon thereafter, the other soldier received a wound in the arm whereby he decided to take his chances and broke for the rear. This left Brashear "very lonesome there with that poor dead brother comrade." Shortly, he was likewise wounded in the side, his second, the first being at Gaines' Mill several years earlier. Breaking for the rear, he "did not stop but had to go a good deal slower as the wound was hurting me very badly. When I got back to the ravine from whence we first started I found what was left of the command getting into line again. I had to have the ball cut out and it was two months before the wound got well."[9]

As the fighting continued, the advance was moving forward when, due to a misunderstanding or otherwise, Hoke's Division failed to join in on cue on the right. Gen. Field attacked again but was repelled by the strong Federal defense. They were forced to take refuge in a depression in front of the Federal line.

Moxley Sorrell said the enemy was armed with Spencer magazine rifles, and "such a fire had never before jarred and stunned us. We had to retire and resume our position."[10] Of the rapid fire, M. V. Smith, Co. D, 4th Texas, who was to become a prisoner of war in the aftermath, said the Federal ranks were arrayed in two lines of battle. They held their fire until "we were within [150] yards of them when two ranks arose and fired, as they went down the other two ranks arose and fired, [etc]."[11] O. T. Hanks, Co. K, 1st Texas, said of the fire "if the first [bullet] fired had remained in the air after it spent [and] the last one fired had remained at the [muzzle] of the gun there would have been a [s]olid [s]heet of [lead]." He estimated in their headlong withdrawal that "we run so fast I do not [suppose] we were [s]triking the ground only [about] every [t]en feet[,] the [bullets] pounding the [l]ogs [and] [s]tumps on every [s]ide."[12] Losses were heavy. Capt. A. C. Jones, commanding the 3rd Arkansas, reported fifteen dead and fifty missing with survivors numbering no more than eighty.[13]

In the failed assault, the Texas Brigade's Gen. John Gregg, leading up front, was pierced mortally through the neck by a Federal ball. It was thus that he achieved the dubious distinction of being the only commander of the brigade to be killed on the field of battle during the course of the war. Col. Winkler, 4th Texas, said the brigade took the loss of their general hard. They had driven the enemy back into their breastworks and were pursuing when Gregg fell. Forced to retire by the rapid fire of the Spencer-wielding Federals, Gregg's body was left behind about 100 yards in front of their line.

Capt. John Kerr of Gen. Gregg's staff came down the line and informed Col. Winkler, of the situation: "Gregg's killed." Returning a few moments later, he said "Bass, [1st Texas] is wounded; you must take command of brigade." Capt. Shotwell, also of Gregg's staff, volunteered to recover the body. With three men "in a rain of shot and shell, where it seemed nothing could live, they ran out, rolled the body on [a] blanket, and safely bore it to the rear."[14]

Later, Gen. Gregg's remains lay in state at the capitol in Richmond, his casket draped with Confederate and Texas flags. The Texas Brigade was allowed on this solemn occasion to attend the funeral. Other notables included President Davis and members of his cabinet and staff, among them Postmaster General John H. Reagan and Col. F. R. Lubbock, both Texans. Members of the Texas delegation acted as pallbearers. With reversed arms and a riderless horse, the brigade followed the hearse to the burial place in Hollywood Cemetery.[15]

In early October, Gen. Longstreet, reasonably recovered from his Wilderness wounds "was strong enough to ride horseback, and after a little practice, and having become weary of idle hours, took leave of wife and children and traveled back to Richmond."[16] With Longstreet's return, Gen. Anderson was reassigned to command Hoke's and Bushrod Johnson's divisions which were treated thereafter as akin to a fourth corps.

It was learned shortly afterward that on October 19, in the Valley, Gen. Early had launched an attack upon Gen. Sheridan's forces near Cedar Creek. The affair opened favorably. However, Sheridan, having been away from the field at the onset, arrived at a critical time. Seizing a flag, he had led personally a brilliant counterattack. Early's losses were substantial, including the loss of a large number of artillery pieces. He retreated up the Valley at the head of a broken army that never was to recover from the Cedar Creek debacle. The sun was slowly setting on Confederate hopes of victory throughout the South.

According to Joe Polley, Co. F, 4th Texas, following the unsuccessful attack in which Gen. Gregg was killed, the Texas Brigade marched to and took a position about four miles from Richmond. There, he said, they remained until the next spring, "practically undisturbed," a small fray on October 27 notwithstanding. In that minor action, one Texan, W. A. Traylor, Co. D, 5th Texas, exhibited that the old Texas spirit was still alive and well. Becoming impatient with a lull in the action, according to Capt. W. T. Hill, 5th Texas, Traylor leaped over the breastworks and began to advance alone against the enemy position opposite. He was pushing his luck, having been wounded at the Wilderness and again, more recently, on the Darbytown Road. Ignoring orders to return to the line, Traylor continued to advance. Inspired by his example, his comrades, also unordered, surmounted their breastworks and followed their comrade in his quest. Their impromptu charge was successful in capturing a number of the Federal infantry.[17] Following that action, O. T. Hanks, Co. K, 1st Texas, said of that time that hostilities had ceased "[n]ot a report of a gun to be heard for many days[.] [W]e [c]ook [and] eat our rations in quiet."[18]

As the year turned to November, the weather worsened heralding the coming of winter and winter quarters. The Confederate troops manning the defenses were in fairly good health considering their dire supply circumstances. They were receiving only a bacon ration, and it often rancid, irregularly along with a pint of corn meal per day. Col. Winkler's man, Pat, scoured the neighborhood for rations and generally came back with something besides, "dried peas and cornbread." Winkler said that they were, strange to say, "athletic and strong" and "accepted the scarcity of food as a feature of the times, and spent few hours grieving over the matter."[19] Later in the winter, individual soldiers were granted furloughs to visit nearby states. Sometimes they returned with rations procured elsewhere which they shared with their friends and comrades. However, there were other necessities not to be had, like soap, for example.

This fourth and final winter quarters of the war was spent in close proximity to the enemy in the siege lines before the Confederate capital, which O.T. Hanks, Co. K, 1st Texas, said were on the Charles City Pike, eight miles from Richmond. Unlike past years when huts were winter quarters, the soldiers of '64-'65 were oft-times ground dwellers. Holes dug in the ground, called by the soldiers "rat holes," were one form of shelter for the enlisted subsurface dweller. Hanks described what must have been a typical winter quarters, a small pen about a foot high, covered with small pine poles. On these were piled leaves and pine straw over which blankets were spread and a bed was created. From captured Federal stores, canvas tent cloth was raised over the bed and "we now have a real snug little nest for two fellows."[20]

For others, what sparse materials and few tools that could be acquired were put to the best uses possible. Joe Polley, Co. F, 4th Texas, gone from the field and minus a foot, years later wrote from descriptions related to him that "hovels were built which, when roofed with tents, blankets and like makeshifts, and provided with fireplaces and chimneys made of mud and sticks, proved desirable dwelling places for men so long inured to hardship. In them the soldiers cooked, ate and slept, played cards, checkers, cribbage and chess, laughed, talked, jested and joked, and, strange to say, were not altogether unhappy." There was, also, the monotony of picket duty as well as some opportunities for scouts beyond the enemy's lines, usually conducted at night. He went on to describe the winter spent thus as "pleasant."[21] There were occasional passes issued to go into town. Discipline was not relaxed and if one was caught without a properly issued pass, punishment could be severe depending upon circumstances.

Officers fared better. Col. Winkler, 4th Texas, was fortunate to share with others quite suitable quarters provided by Maj. Littlefield, the regimental quartermaster. The major had his large tent pitched adjacent to the chimney of a burned house. It consisted of "one very large room, one small room, and a camp kitchen made of logs half way, with a tent stretched above. The house was well daubed with mud, with a fly-tent stretched overhead. A carpet of bagging, a glass window, some chairs, a settee and tables, all of camp manufacture, with a cheerful fire in the chimney, built half of brick, the rest of sticks and mud, gave an air of comfort to the place."[22] They even hired a servant girl to keep the place clean. From Richmond, newspapers and books were available, Hugo's *Les Miserables* being the then current favorite. Off-duty hours were spent pleasantly in conversation and chess playing.

A log chapel was built for the conduct of religious services on Sundays. Ministers from Richmond usually conducted the services. Members of the Texas delegation to the C. S. A. Congress were frequently in attendance. Under the circumstances, the business conducted within the "primitive building" with its "rough seats, rude pulpit" was serious, indeed. "Every head was bowed in prayer, every eye fastened upon the speaker, and every ear drank in eagerly the word of life uttered with an earnestness only possible from a man who knew his hearers carried their lives daily in their hands."[23] Again, the presence of danger and adversity has a way of refocusing attention on the state of one's soul.

While the lot of some of the officers was better than that of others, the enlisted men, as stated before, did not fare as well. That, along with the lack of logistical support and a general dissatisfaction with the way the war was going, resulted in various displays of dissatisfaction. Desertion became a worrisome matter. Moxley Sorrell, Gen. Longstreet's chief of staff, was somewhat sympathetic in light of their physical plight, "No wonder they sometimes weakened to better themselves ... and stayed with the fat-jowled, well-clad, coddled up masses opposite them." At the same time, realizing it could not be allowed, he said, to discourage deserters "at night steady, continuous musketry firing was ordered, sweeping the glacis in front of our entrenchments."[24]

Desertion had always been a problem and became moreso as the war progressed toward its conclusion. In order to encourage deserters to return to their commands, amnesties were sometimes declared. Men returning under these amnesties were received back with no questions asked. However, when deserters were captured by the provost marshals or others and returned to their commands, the court-martials resulting often were concluded with the death penalty by firing squad being assessed.

On the north side of the James, Gen. Longstreet, saw the constant sniping across the lines as "an annoyance, and not a legitimate part of war to carry on the shooting of sentinels on guard duty."[25] Accordingly, he ordered it stopped to which the enemy across the way responded in kind. Taking advantage of the welcome opportunity, a barter in tobacco and coffee soon sprang up and an agreement was established to give ample warning before warlike intentions were recommenced. It must have helped in those last, hard months before the war came to its end. Why squander any more lives needlessly?

Dwindling manpower became Gen. Lee's major worry. Kershaw's Division was recalled from the Valley on November 14 as a partial attempt to shore up the numbers. By the end of November, the returns indicated a force, including the Richmond garrison, of about 66,000 troops.[26] It was with that number that Gen. Lee had to contend with Gen. Grant's army of almost twice that size — and it well-fed and equipped!

In the other theaters, matters had gone from bad to worse. In August, Gen. Hood, recovered from his Chickamauga wound and recalled to duty with the Army of Tennessee, was promoted commanding general of that army, replacing Gen. Johnston. As mentioned in passing earlier, quitting Atlanta, he harbored the hope that in threatening Gen. Sherman's supply line stretching back into Tennessee, it would force the latter to abandon Georgia. D. S. Freeman termed this as perhaps "the fatal military decision of the war."[27] Hood underestimated his adversary; Sherman did not bite. Instead, abandoning his base, he undertook his devastating march across Georgia to the sea at Savannah. Why not? Gen. Winfield Scott had done it successfully in Mexico. Hood continued with his campaign plan and went on to be soundly defeated first at Franklin, Tennessee, and then again in front of Nashville in mid–December. Although keeping the field until its end in North Carolina, the Army of Tennessee never recovered fully from the twin defeats. All grim news to be added to the grim news in the East.

In the meantime it was learned that the elements of the Federal VI Corps had returned from its detached duty against Early. To try and offset this Federal manpower advantage, Gen. Lee brought Gordon's and Early's II Corps Divisions from the Valley to the Petersburg front. No sooner than they had taken position on the right end of the line than a Federal raid down the Weldon Railroad was launched. Except for some miles of track torn up, the raid came to little. Other troops shifts occurred as well along the front. The Texas Brigade, Field's Division, remained north of the James.

In early December, struggling to bolster manpower and with the Valley enshrouded in snow, the Second Corps' last division, Rodes,' was returned to the main army. It came less its gallant commander, he having fallen on the field of Cedar Creek in October. In the meantime, Fort Fisher, guarding the maritime approaches to one of the last Confederate ports remaining open, Wilmington, North Carolina, was in danger of falling. It had been beleaguered for most of the war but was now threatened by a large Federal armada as never before. Even though it could be ill-afforded, Hoke's Division was detached to the defense of the important port. In the end, the Federal attack failed and Wilmington remained open, but realistically, how much longer could it hold out?

On December 20, "a bitter cold, gloomy day with murky clouds hung low," the Texas Brigade participated in a small-scale affair that, the retreat to Appomattox, notwithstanding, would be its last of the war. According to J. H. Cosgrove, Co. C, 4th Texas, the purpose of the "dash on the enemy's lines on the 'North Side,' was "not so much to achieve important direct results as to annoy the Yankees, keep them in the open, and disturb as much as possible their repose." Could have been, too, that the boys were just plain bored with winter quarters.

Cosgrove and some of his friends found themselves in a party of sixty to eighty men under the command of Maj. "Howdy" Martin. Crossing the New Market Road they encountered the enemy's picket line, and "with a rush and a yell, ran in on the reserves at the heels of the videttes." About noon they came to the James River's "second-bottom land, a plateau following that stream to the coastlands below." Pushing forward through the broken, brushy landscape, Cosgrove became separated from his companions. Pushing on, he unexpectedly came face to face with a Yankee skirmisher peering at him from behind a rotten log. Cosgrove, whose musket was at a "trail," fired from the hip. "I hit that log, and the rotten dust flew like a cloud. I knew my best chance was to charge him, and as there was no return fire I was sure I had my man. A step or two and I was at the log, but that Yankee had rolled down the hill and was clean gone. I never touched him; but he was at least worse scared than I was, and that was enough."[28]

Later in the day Cosgrove was reunited with his friends. Together they scouted forward and found what they concluded to be the enemy's main line along Deep Bottom. Finding Maj. Martin, also lost from the brigade, they suggested an attack on the enemy line. Said the ever colorful Martin, "I gad, boys, we'll do it, [yelling out] 'Charge 'em.... At 'em we went, shooting and yelling like H-alifax. They broke and fled and we followed across the snow-covered field, close on their heels. Major Martin cried out, 'Go into the breastworks with 'em,' and go we did!" And there they were, in possession of a section of the enemy's works with only about forty men and no idea where the rest of the brigade might be.

Shortly, the enemy returned in numbers and with artillery support. The Texans were expelled quickly, they returning at a run to the woods from whence they had so recently debouched. There they hung on, building fires against the cold. Later they were found and Gen. Field, surveying the scene, concluded that their earlier advantage had been lost by then. Maj. Martin was philosophical, remarking, "I gad, I couldn't whip the whole Yankee army with forty Texans, but I did carry their works and whip a whole lot of 'em, by gad."

Returning to their camps took them "through that dark and slush and cold, [and] was one of [Cosgrove's] most trying experiences but when [he] had warmed up, had supper and a smoke, and was cozy in [his] bunk, [he] heard the horsemen coming along the Charles City Pike, and remarked to [his] comrades: 'Well, at least I wouldn't be a cavalryman.'"[29]

By January 1865, the lines extended some thirty-five miles in front of Richmond, then to Petersburg and beyond on the Confederate far right. To the south, Savannah, Georgia, had fallen to Sherman's army in December. Preparations were observed to be underway there to continue the campaign elsewhere, probably toward Charleston. Further troop detachments were sent to South Carolina in expectation of the onslaught. In early January,

Fort Fisher once more came under severe attack. On January 15, the fort fell to Federal control thus closing the last Southern port remaining open to shipping. Among the Confederate losses, Gen. Whiting, the Texas Brigade's first divisional commander, was mortally wounded.

As the new year advanced, so did the suffering of the army for want of subsistence. In early February 1865, the widely disparaged and close friend of President Davis, Col. Lucian Northrup, was relieved of duty as head of the C.S.A. Commissary Department. His replacement, Brig. Gen. I. M. St. John, formerly of the Mining and Nitre Department, assumed the thankless task. Gen. St. John adopted the expedient of dealing directly with the sources of subsistence. From those sources the rations were then conveyed directly to the army. No central depots to snarl the process was the secret of success, even though momentary. In the end, it all came to naught.

According to Mrs. Winkler, sometime in January or early February a review of the troops occupying the lines north of the James was held. The reviewing officers included Pres. Davis and Gens. Longstreet and Field, among others. There is no mention of Gen. Lee being in attendance. If Gen. Field was in attendance, as stated, it would seem likely that his division, or units thereof, would have participated. There is no mention of the Texas Brigade's participating. An observer described it as a "most imposing military spectacle." The troops were as trim as the conditions allowed "their polished muskets glistening in the sunshine ... gallant officers riding along their front, handsomely accoutered, receiving the salutes of the men and ever and anon pausing to acknowledge a demonstration of respect, while the bands played their most inspiring and exhilarating airs."[30] The "brilliant pageant" would have made it difficult for anyone to realize that the participants were living on "the scantiest rations possible." While pomp and circumstance elevated spirits temporarily, as was its purpose, once the troops returned to their camps reality set in once more.

In the camps of the Texas Brigade, as the next campaign season approached, there were some privately stated expressions of anguish at what the future might hold. Maj. Littlefield, 4th Texas quartermaster, confided to his wife in a letter that"[w]e are dreading the coming campaign. It will be hotly contested.... All is night with us. We cannot fathom the future, and shrink from speculating on our fate or future locality; all depends on events now transpiring.... We have a pleasant camp and much company, but how I long for home. What would I not give to see you once more — everything but honor. We have our trials but not above measure."[31] The "events now transpiring" were in reference to Sherman's rampage then ongoing through South Carolina and threatening North Carolina.

On February 17, Columbia, South Carolina, fell to Sherman's torch-wielding army, forcing the city's evacuation. As February advanced into March, Gen. Lee's army had dwindled — through illness, capture, death in its many forms and, alas, desertion — to maybe 50,000. There were proposals to negotiate an end to the war, but nothing came of them. Gen. Grant's forces were strengthening while Sherman was devastating the Carolinas. They had no reason to negotiate unless the South was willing to accept unconditional surrender. Although that would be accepted at Appomattox several months later, it was not an alternative at the time.

On March 2, Gen. Sheridan's forces in the Valley vanquished for once and for all Gen. Early's skeleton force remaining in that locale. At Waynesboro, on that date, ended forevermore the four year reign the Confederacy had enjoyed in the Valley of Virginia. Sheridan's army was thereafter free to join Grant or be sent to any other place where needed. During a meeting with Gen. John B. Gordon, Gen. Lee reckoned, "Adding all the Union forces together, there would soon be in the seaboard states 280,000 Federal troops, to whom the Confederacy could oppose with only 65,000."[32]

There were various plans from various sources afloat as ways to deal with the worsening crisis. The only one that came to fruition involved Gen. Gordon's command. Gordon was ordered by Gen. Lee to observe the Federal center opposite Petersburg for any signs of weakness and the possibility of a successful attack to break the enemy line. Gordon, after careful observation, concluded that an attack was feasible and the probability of success reasonably good. The suggested point of attack was a Federal strongpoint named Fort Stedman. Gen. Lee thought that if the attack could be successfully executed, "one of two things would happen." "Either General Grant would have to abandon the left of his line, or, what was more likely, he would have to shorten his front."[33] If, indeed, the latter occurred, fewer men would be required to defend the contracted front. Troops could be detached to deal with Sherman's troops approaching from the southwest. That accomplished, the victors could return to Petersburg to deal with Grant.

Hope sprung eternal! Among many other things, the Confederate horses and mules were so weakened and spare from lack of proper forage that they did not have the strength necessary to move the army's artillery and wagons. That's to say nothing of the condition of the food- and quartermaster-deprived troops! However, what else was one to do in those desperate straits but plan and try to remain optimistic? The order for the attack on Ft. Stedman was issued on the evening of March 23.

Fort Stedman was located on the Federal line "on the high ground known as Hare's Hill, at the crossing of the Federal lines and the Prince George Courthouse Road, three quarters of a mile southeast of the Appomattox."[34] One reason for Gordon's choosing it as a point of attack was its relative nearness to the Confederate line opposite, maybe 150 yards or so. The plan was to move quickly upon the fort in the predawn darkness. Some troops were assigned the task of removing the defensive barriers while the others were to rush the fort. Having breached the line, the troops were then to move right and left behind the front. Cavalry was to follow and attack and disrupt communications. "Four and a half divisions of infantry and a division of cavalry — nearly half the army — concentrated close to the centre, around Colquitt's salient."[35]

At 4:00 A.M., March 25, the attack moved forward. The Federal line was breached successfully and the sound of fighting could be heard spreading left and right. But then, alas, word was passed back that some of the landmarks, keys to the attack's success, could not be found or identified in the cold, black darkness of the predawn. By 8:00 A.M. it was apparent to Gen. Lee, he observing from his own lines, that the continuation of the attack was futile. He ordered the attack abandoned and the troops withdrawn to the relative safety of their own lines. Some troops refused the return trip because the field over which they had recently advanced was swept by gales of Federal artillery fire. According to Gen. Longstreet, "Many Confederates got back to their lines in disordered flight, but 1949 prisoners and nine stands of colors were taken by the [Federal] Ninth Corps."[36]

A strong Federal counterattack followed almost immediately in order to take advantage of the confusion in the Confederate line. It encompassed almost the entire Confederate right. "In this counterstroke, they captured about 800 prisoners and held their ground against all attempts to drive them back to their main lines. The enemy was thus placed where he could advantageously launch a direct attack to break the Confederate front whenever he chose to do so."[37]

All things considered, Sherman's advance was proceeding through the Carolinas, little impeded by the shadow-like presence of the Army of Tennessee, once more commanded by Joe Johnston. The approach of Gen. Phil Sheridan's victorious cavalry from the Valley was imminent. The unthinkable now must be thought about — the abandonment of the capital and a retreat. To just where and how was debatable.

"The week beginning March 27, 1865, was one on which the survivors of the Army of Northern Virginia were loath to dwell, because it was to them, in memory, the first stage of a gruesome nightmare."[38] Gen. Grant was not long in following up the abortive attack on Ft. Stedman. His obvious move would be, predictably, to his left. If he could cross Hatcher's Run, reach Dinwiddie Court House on the lower Boydton Plank Road he would be beyond the right of thinly stretched Confederate line. Then, by striking north, if he moved fast enough he might be able to outflank his adversary somewhere in the vicinity of a five road intersection called, appropriately enough, Five Forks. Beyond Five Forks, one of the last arteries of Confederate survival, the Southside Railroad was open for capture and all that that meant. "The railroad, of course, was the prime objective of any attempt Grant might make on his left to drive Lee from Petersburg without a direct frontal assault."[39]

Even though Gen. Lee knew where the attack would surely proceed from, he had limited manpower options with which to oppose it. To begin, all of the cavalry north of the James, with the exception of Gary's, was started trotting toward the right end of the line. The only infantry troops available, quasi-reserves, was Pickett's Division. At that particular time, however, the immortalized division was very much mortal and suffered from the usual human weaknesses and was riddled by desertion.

The movement of this mobile force began on March 29, by way of the Southside to Sutherland Station, ten miles west of Petersburg. By then, it had been learned that Sheridan's fast-moving cavalry was in the vicinity of Dinwiddie Court House. Its next move was expected to be in the direction of Five Forks. The Southern Horse, under the overall command of Fitz Lee, was ordered to proceed there and break up any attempt to move past Five Forks against the Southside.

On the morning of March 30, Gen. Lee rode to Sutherland's Station where he learned that Fitz Lee was advancing toward Five Forks. Pickett was ordered to take his division down the same road. Once there, the two commands, cavalry and infantry, were to join and, then, attack the advancing Federal force in flank. Fitz Lee, arriving at Five Forks first, advanced down the road toward Dinwiddie where he encountered the Federal line. He was able to drive them back momentarily. Returning to Five Forks, he was greeted by Pickett. Discussing the tactical situation as they understood it, they decided to rest their hard-used troops. Operations would be resumed the next day, March 31.

Several brigades were deployed south of Five Forks. These troops "had, ominously enough, to drive back dismounted Federal cavalry who used repeating rifles and offered stiff resistance."[40] What they were actually facing west of Hatcher's Run was Sheridan's and Gregg's cavalry divisions, plus the V and parts of the II and VI Federal Corps. Other elements of the Army of the Potomac and the Army of the James were not far removed. Grant's strategy was on the verge of success. But not quite yet.

On the morning of March 31, Gen. Lee visited the line in the area where it crossed Hatcher's Run. There it was observed that the left of the Federal line opposite was in the air, unsupported. Of course, the combative Lee called for an immediate attack by the troops of Anderson's so-designated Fourth Corps in that area to roll up the Federal flank. As was so often the case, it had been raining for hours, the troops were miserable and the terrain doubly difficult to navigate. The attack proceeded, started prematurely by some overly zealous troops, and the Federal flank was turned. A pursuit was organized until, reaching the banks of a stream called Gravelly Run, the momentum was lost as a Federal counterattack blunted the drive. Across the stream and at the Boydton Plank Road and beyond were Federal forces in much superior numbers. The Confederate force was withdrawn to a position that was about where they had started the attack that morning.

Beyond the area of Anderson's attack, Pickett and Fitz Lee had advanced on Dinwiddie Court House, successfully driving the strong enemy force before them. Nightfall had found them only a short distance from the court house. The troops were reported to have performed admirably. At this point, Gen. Lee was less sanguine than usual. He realized that the enemy was on his flank and it was likely to be turned, sooner rather than later. Once that happened, the rail lines in his rear were forever lost.

Then, a field report from Gen. Pickett arrived stating that he had been forced to withdraw from in front of Dinwiddie Court House. The distance to the Southside Railroad from that point was a little over seven miles. Gen. Lee sent immediately a dispatch, "Hold Five Forks at all hazards. Protect road to Ford's Depot and prevent Union forces from striking the Southside Railroad."[41] North of the James, Gen. Field's Division was readied to move to the threatened area.

On the afternoon of April 1, the sound of battle was heard from the direction of Five Forks. Since Pickett's and Fitz Lee's mobile forces were operating beyond the end of the Confederate line, it was some time before news arrived informing Gen. Anderson of occurrences beyond his right flank. What had occurred was a strong Federal attack that had driven Pickett back on Five Forks. In his postwar memoir, Gen. Longstreet said Pickett had but 9,000 troops with which to contend against 26,000.[42]

Thinking the position secure and that another attack that day unlikely, Gens. Pickett and Fitz Lee had gone off to briefly enjoy a "shad bake." In their absence, about mid-afternoon, a strong Federal attack had broken and routed the Confederate line and a wild retreat to the Southside Railroad had followed. Upon receiving the news brought by a cavalry officer, Gen. Lee, as was oft his habit, matter-of-factly addressed the cavalryman, "Well, Captain, what shall we do?"[43] he asked. "[I]n two calamitous hours, the mobile force that Lee had established to protect his right flank was swept away and virtually ceased to be.... His most strategic position had been lost.... Five Forks was only one scene removed from the dread denouement."[44]

In the meantime, Field's Division, ordered south of the James, had marched during the night passing over the pontoon bridge near Drury's Bluff. By early morning, April 2, accompanied by Gen. Longstreet, they were nearing Petersburg by rail. Gen. Longstreet, going on ahead and seeking out Gen. Lee's headquarters found the army commander not well and still abed. Gen. Longstreet was conferring with Gen. Lee when a staff officer came in to announce that a general assault was in progress by Federal forces all along the line. The line in front of Gen. Lee's headquarters was reported to be broken. "Drawing his wrapper about him, [Gen. Lee] walked with [Longstreet] to the front door and saw, as far as the eye could cover the field, a line of skirmishers in quiet march towards [them]. It was hardly light enough to distinguish the blue from the gray."[45] As it turned out, they were mostly blue.

CHAPTER 18

"[F]rom first to last the most dependable brigade of the Army of Northern Virginia"[1]: Retreat to Appomattox, April 2–April 9, 1865

The general assault against the Confederate works in front of Petersburg ordered by Gen. Grant following Gen. Sheridan's victory at Five Forks was to begin at 4:00 A.M., April 2. In anticipation of the coming strenuous events, Federal officers, including the commanding general, attempted to get as much sleep as possible, much of it in the form of catnaps. When 4:00 A.M. proved too dark to launch the operation, the assault was delayed forty-five minutes. At that time "there was a streak of gray in the heavens which soon revealed another streak of gray formed by Confederate uniforms in the works opposite.... The thunder of hundreds of guns shook the ground like an earthquake and soon the troops were engaged all along the lines."[2]

Wright's VI Federal Corps' attack was on A. P. Hill's Third Corps' front and shattered Heth and Wilcox's divisions. "Still further to the left, Gordon's picket posts had been taken at 11:00 o'clock on the night of April 1–2.... Neither Gordon nor Lee, nor anyone else now believed that more could be accomplished at Petersburg than to occupy the breaking line until nightfall."[3]

As Gen. Lee watched the advancing Blue skirmishers from the front door of his head-quarters near Petersburg he must have known at that moment that the situation of his army had become hopeless. Nonetheless, he soldiered resolutely on, his remarkable character and sense of duty demanding it. He ordered Gen. Field's Division, including the Texans, to cross the James and march to the broken Confederate right. The movement was to be partly by rail and the troops were marched into Richmond where they boarded the cars. According to Capt. W. T. Hill, 5th Texas, the brigade then consisted of "the Third Arkansas Colonel R. S. Taylor; the First Texas Colonel F. S. Bass; the Fourth Texas Lieutenant-Colonel C. M. Winkler, and the Fifth Texas Captain W. T. Hill. Colonel R. M. Powell, of the Fifth Texas [returned from captivity], commanded the brigade."[4]

To accompany the division was their corps commander, Gen. Longstreet. "In the last struggle [Gen. Lee] wanted near him that lieutenant, who, for all his stubborn self-opinion, was the best corps commander he had left."[5] Since this would reduce the defensive lines

271

north of the James in front of Richmond, the citizenry was alerted to the possible dangers approaching. "Orders were dispatched to Mahone on the Howlett Line [Bermuda Hundred] and Ewell on the Richmond front to start their troops that evening by routes previously determined."[6]

Gen. Longstreet arrived in advance of Field's Division at about 4:00 A.M., April 2. After the war he recalled the trip as memorable, with "land and water batteries [lifting] their bombs over their lazy curves, screaming shells [coming] through the freighted night to light [their] ride, and signal sky-rockets [giving] momentary illumination.... A hundred guns and more added their lightning and thunder to the storm of war that carried consternation to thousands of long-apprehensive people."[7]

Shortly thereafter, the approach of the Federal skirmishers, as previously mentioned, was reported. Gen. A. P. Hill, by then arrived at headquarters, hurriedly took to his horse to reconnoiter. Gen. Lee shouted out a caution to his Third Corps commander, but it went unheard in the tumult of the moment. As that valiant and gallant figure rode from view, Gen. Lee knew not that it would be the last time he would see his fellow Virginian alive; Hill, shortly thereafter, fell to the marksmanship of two Federal skirmishers.

Later that morning, as the situation clarified, dispatches were sent to the War Department advising of the turn of events. News of the reversal was taken to President Davis, attending church that Sunday morning in Richmond. Having read the note conveyed to him, Davis quietly arose and left the church, much to the consternation of the congregation who knew that serious circumstances were abroad.

Later in the day, Gen. Lee and his staff abandoned their headquarters at the Turnbull House. As they rode away, the party was recognized by the pursuing Federals from whom they were fleeing. "Soon a shell exploded only a few feet behind, killed a horse and scattered fragments." Gen. Lee's face flushed, a sure sign his aides had come to recognize as barely-controlled anger. He wanted to charge his pursuers but, regaining control, he rode on. As he entered the relative safety of the inner defenses in front of Petersburg, he is said to have remarked to an aide "It has happened as I told them it would at Richmond. The line has been stretched until it has broken."[8]

Establishing his new headquarters at the McIlwaine House within the inner defenses of Petersburg, Gen. Lee called some of his commanders to that location. The plan of evacuation was explained "but so calm was the manner of the commanding General that none of those who participated in the conference left any record of it."[9] Although the plan was not announced immediately, there must have been few that did not expect marching orders soon.

Around noon, April 2, the first elements of Field's Division, Benning's Brigade, arrived on the north bank of the Appomattox and reported to Gen. Longstreet. According to one source the Texas Brigade did not cross the James until Sunday night, so it must have arrived late that night or early on April 3.[10] Even though Gen. Lee felt that things had stabilized to the point where the line could be held until at least that evening, he began to prepare for the retreat of his army. A contingency plan laying out the various routes to be used by the various commands had already been formulated by the army's engineers. This would be as one would expect of any army, especially of one besieged and of one commanded by an officer formerly a revered member of the Corps of Engineers.

The details of the plan were extensive but basically "[t]he [retrograde] march was to be directed to Burkeville, and the point of reconcentration was to be Amelia Court House, a village distant forty miles from Petersburg, on the railroad from Richmond to Danville."[11]

Amelia was chosen "because it was approximately equidistant from the major sectors and was on the railroad that would be the Army's principal supply line on any retreat to join the Confederate forces in North Carolina."[12]

The evacuation of Petersburg was scheduled to begin after dark on Sunday, April 2. Field's Division, upon reaching the Petersburg front, had been placed in line of battle along the banks of Indian Town Creek southwest of Petersburg with orders "to take position at the fords and crossing of the Appomattox, and prevent the passage of the enemy to its north bank."[13] From that point they were able to observe the successful Federal assault on Ft. Gregg. The fort's garrison had been encouraged by the promise that "'...Longstreet's coming. Hold for two hours and all will be well.'"[14] They came but were not committed. The fight for Gregg, although gallant, was hopeless. However, its defense provided the time needed by Gen. Lee to get his army away.

Soon after dark, the evacuation was begun. "The march was to the growl of the Federal guns on the lines and to the groan of heavily laden wagons. The different commands could not be distinguished in the blackness."[15] The Texas Brigade began its march at about "11 o'clock ... bringing up the rear of Lee's army.... [Fires burned all around lighting up the countryside.] Near where the 5th Texas was stationed on the Appomattox, a house stored with bacon was burned, and as [they] were without food and hungry, [they] felt it a hardship not to be allowed to fill [their] haversacks with bacon before it was destroyed."[16] As the evacuation was going forward, at 4:28 A.M., April 3, the city of Petersburg was officially surrendered. Later in the morning, word reached Gen. Grant that Richmond had been surrendered at 8:15 A.M.[17]

The Army of Northern Virginia retreating from Petersburg and Richmond on the night of April 2–3, 1865, was a far cry from the robust army of previous years. Numbering maybe 28,000, they were to be hounded in the week following by five powerful Federal corps consisting of overwhelming numbers with artillery and led out front by Sheridan's hard-riding cavalry. The general plan was to join, somewhere, Gen. Joe Johnston's frazzled army, that much-traveled leader summoned forth yet again, retreating before Gen. Sherman to the southwest in North Carolina.

Johnston's army was composed of the garrisons formerly defending Charleston and Savannah and the remaining fragments of the Army of Tennessee brought from Alabama and Georgia. Indeed, the joining of those two forces had been one of Gen. Grant's concerns since the beginning of the operations around Petersburg. He "had been sleeping with one eye open and one foot out of bed for many weeks, in the fear that Lee would thus give him the slip."[18] If the junction of the two armies was allowed to happen it would prolong the war for who knew how long. Grant could have saved himself the anxiety had his intelligence service been better. Said E. Porter Alexander of his own army's capabilities to maneuver, "Deficiencies in transportation were so great that no such movement was practicable."[19]

During the first day's march, the Federals did not appear to be vigorously pursuing as one would expect. Capt. W. T. Hill, 5th Texas, said that the Texas Brigade's "march that night and next day was uninterrupted by attack from the enemy."[20] There was a reason. When Ft. Gregg, the last bastion in the Confederate outer defenses fell on April 2, Gen. Grant was urged by some of his senior officers to mount an all-out attack on the city immediately. Not wishing to sacrifice any more lives needlessly, he opted to regroup before beginning a pursuit. He foresaw that "the city would undoubtedly be evacuated during the night, and he would dispose the troops for a parallel march westward, and try to head off the escaping enemy."[21] But, once the pursuit began in earnest, by early morning April 4 it "had

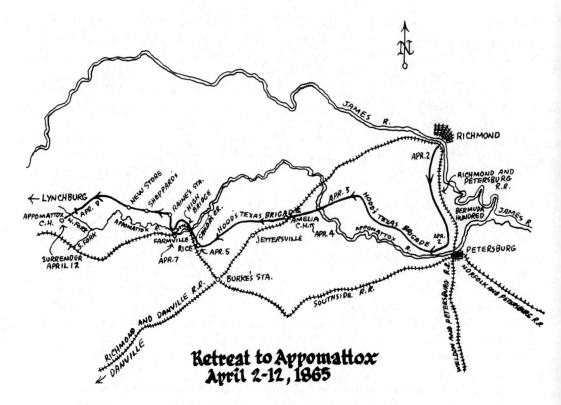

Retreat to Appomattox, April 2–9, 1865

... become unflagging, relentless. Grant put a spur to the heel of every dispatch he sent. "Sheridan 'the inevitable' as the [Confederates] had learned to call him, was in advance thundering along with his cavalry, followed by ... the rest of the Army of the Potomac.... [T]he troops found this campaign was to be won by legs, that the great walking-match had begun, and success would attend the army that could make the best distance record."[22]

A word about the general route of the Confederate retreat; in its first phase to Amelia it was west with some units north, some south of the Appomattox River. West of Petersburg, maybe three-quarters of the way to Amelia, the river begins to come out of a big, looping turn from the north and northwest. In that vicinity, there were four bridges spanning the river. The northernmost was the Genito Bridge, the middle Goode's and the southernmost was known as Bevill's. There was also an unplanked railroad bridge, which, under ordinary circumstances, was considered unsuitable for crossing troops. Over those bridges, units north of the river were to move to the south bank, where they would be reunited with those units of their army already following that route. The river crossings, although necessary as the most direct route to Amelia, placed the Confederate forces on the same side of the river as their dogged Federal pursuers. Also, once the army was reconcentrated during the course of the retreat the various units' positions in the column of march changed from time to time for tactical reasons.

As the retreat developed, the approaches to Bevill's Bridge were found to be flooded, forcing a change in plans. Longstreet's Corps and others that were to cross at Bevill's were rerouted upriver to cross at Goode's. Where hours were critical, all of this added to the time, congestion and confusion of the withdrawal. By late in the day, April 3, Longstreet's troops and others were across. These, including Field's Division, were entrenched on the farther bank to protect the crossing of the remaining units. Amelia Court House lay about eight miles to the west. By early morning, April 4, most of the command was across but was already beset by Federal cavalry. At about 7:30 A.M., Gen. Lee crossed over the river and joined the head of Longstreet's column.

Bringing up the rear, the Texas Brigade "engaged in skirmishes ... burned bridges over which they passed, and with the old spirit of determination, followed the fading fortunes of their leader.... The Texans were too far from their homes for the temptation of straggling from their ranks to be entertained, and foot-sore and weary, they marched on, believing the union would be effected with the Southern army, and the reverse yet changed into victory."[23] They had prevailed in circumstances similarly dire before; why not once again?

Further south those soon-to-be dogged pursuers that got underway on April 3–4 included Humphrey's II Corps, Griffin's V Corps, Warren having been relieved, Wright's VI Corps and Parke's IX Corps. About half of Gen. Ord's Army of the James formed the left of the pursuit along the line of the Southside Railroad, the other half was left to occupy Richmond. Sheridan's cavalry divisions led. All of these westward marching forces, Blue and Gray, were now on a parallel and collision course that should occur around Jetersville, southwest of Amelia on the line of the Richmond and Danville Railroad.

Thus it was that having gained a partial day's march on the pursuers, the first waypoint, Amelia Court House, was reached largely unopposed except for some cavalry harassment. However, once the army reached Amelia it would have to turn to the southwest, down the line of the Richmond and Danville Railroad, in order to reach its next waypoint, Burkeville by way of Jetersville. At that point, the advantage would pass to Gen. Grant, his army advancing south of the Appomattox River and on a shorter chord to Burkeville. Beyond that, "Lee's total distance to ... the nearest point where he could hope to meet Johnston, was 107 miles. Grant's was [eighty-eight]."[24] The odds were already stacking up against Gen. Lee's being able to reach Gen. Johnston in North Carolina.

At the very beginning of the final retreat, the troops and train of the Army of Northern Virginia resembled already Sir John Moore's English army at the end of its ghastly retreat across Galicia in northern Spain to the port city of Corunna during the Peninsular War in 1808–1809. The troops were ragged and hungry with some already beginning to fall, literally, by the wayside. The surviving animals upon which the army depended for its many transportation needs were starved and often too weak to pull their heavy burdens. The situation was grim and obviously hopeless, yet the army struggled on.

The need for the hasty withdrawal had caught the army somewhat unawares and the few rations that had been carried along were quickly consumed. D. H. Hamilton, Co. M, 1st Texas, said that when they commenced the march they had "only one cup of flour for each man and no meat."[25] However, experienced leadership had anticipated that possibility. Accordingly, the Commissary Department had been ordered to gather a reserve ration supply in Richmond. This was to be forwarded by way of the Richmond and Danville Railroad to Amelia. The idea was, once resupplied, to continue the retreat down the line of the railroad with Danville becoming the new base of supply. However, when early on April 4, the column reached Amelia it was found that while munitions of war had arrived there in plenty, there was no food. "More than 30,000 hungry men were moving on a village where there was not an army ration!"[26]

Nothing else could be done but request help from the local citizens and to deploy foragers across the landscape. Any available rations down the railroad line at Danville were ordered up. If there were rations available from Danville or below, it would require time. The loss of any time could be ill-afforded as the Federal pursuit gained momentum and threatened to cut the rail line to the south.

Even under these stressful, exhausting circumstances, the army remained in good spirits, generally. Not wasting any time, Gen. Lee ordered the army's artillery and supply wagons reduced to the minimum required. The excess was rerouted over the country roads to the west so as not to impede the army's retrograde progress. In the meantime, the other units of the army strung out behind began to arrive at Amelia. By late in the day, April 4, only the whereabouts of Gen. Ewell's troops from the Richmond defenses remained unknown.

The Federal cavalry was beginning to show up in ever greater numbers. That evening word arrived at last from Ewell. Due to circumstances, he was forced to cross the Appomattox via the railroad bridge. Even then, at the time the message was being composed, engineers were at work planking the span to accommodate the infantrymen. Ewell was sent orders as to the line of march he was to take up once across the river. Thus, the "reconcentration was [progressing], but it was bringing more men together where no food was available."[27]

By early the next morning, April 5, the foraging parties were returning to the army, most of them empty-handed. This was not due to a lack of desire to help by the locals. There was simply nothing to be had; the countryside had been stripped bare already by four years of war. Capt. W. T. Hill, 5th Texas, said the Texans "managed to secure a little meal, which the men made into gruel and ate without salt."[28] "It was worse than a disappointment; it was a catastrophe. Often the loyal old army had been hungry, but now starvation seemed a stark reality."[29] Later, in a report to President Davis, Gen. Lee defined the effect of the delay in the search for subsistence at Amelia as ultimately "fatal, and could not be retrieved."[30]

As the men were ordered to fall in to continue the retreat, they were slow in doing so. All were severely weakened by lack of rations and many were beginning to face the stark reality of their plight. Nonetheless, on April 5, the march down the Richmond and Danville Railroad to Danville began, with first Jetersville and then Burkeville intermediate. Field's Division led off behind a thinly-stretched cavalry screen. As the head of the column was leaving Amelia, Ewell's command was arriving in rear.

The inevitable rumors spread through the ranks that the rerouted artillery and wagon train to the west had come under Federal cavalry attack. If true, and it was, it took no great imagination to realize that the Federals had passed over the army's route of retreat to reach the train. In the meantime, Gen. Lee joined Gen. Longstreet in the early afternoon. Shortly thereafter, as the head of the column neared Jetersville, it came upon a Federal force in the process of entrenching across their line of retreat. The message that presence conveyed was stark; the Army of Northern Virginia had lost the race for Danville! Now what?

A reconnaissance of the Federal position indicated that the troops entrenching were of Gen. Sheridan's cavalry command. However, in close proximity was Federal infantry, the II and V Corps with the VI coming up. Gen. Ord's column was reported to be advancing on Burkeville. Gen. Lee, in carefully examining the enemy position, came to the painful but realistic conclusion that the line was unassailable in light of his army's physically weakened condition. The alternative plan that he was forced to adopt was, first, to abandon the line of supply afforded by the Richmond and Danville Railroad.

A little farther down that line, at Burkeville, the Southside Railroad crossed on its way west from Richmond toward Lynchburg. The second part of the plan was to bypass the Federal cavalry line, cut across country and join the line of the Southside around Farmville, a distance of about twenty miles. Third, supplies would be ordered down that railroad from Lynchburg. Once the army was reprovisioned at Farmville or thereabouts, and somewhat revitalized, the line of march to Danville would once more be resumed. The overall objective remained to reach Gen. Johnston's army in North Carolina. In order to execute the plan effectively time was of the essence, too much having already been lost. That meant a night march would be required of an army already beginning to drop in its tracks.

The alternative route selected to Farmville was to be over roads to the west, they being those whose current use was for passage of the extra artillery and wagon trains. As a result, "[t]he forced night march of April 5–6, now Lee's chief hope of escape, almost immediately became a slow stumble over crowded roads where confusion ruled and panic easily was spread."[31] Said Capt. W. T. Hill, 5th Texas, of the brigade's experience, "[t]he Federal infantry overtook the Texas Brigade, then the rear-guard of the rear-guard of our army, on the evening of the 5th [April] and the brigade skirmish line had a hot fight with them — so hot that it had to be heavily reinforced before it drove the enemy back."[32]

Later, captured Federal dispatches revealed to Gen. Lee the intelligence that Gen. Grant himself was nearby at Jetersville and Gen. Ord, of the Army of the James, was nearby also at Burkeville. It appeared that most likely the whole Federal force, Army of the Potomac and Army of the James, were on the ground nearby! The cost of the lost time at Amelia was coming due. The need for haste was even greater than thought a few hours earlier. The night march must be pursued with renewed vigor. "Longstreet was to remain in the van, and Lee determined to march with him in hope of expediting the retreat. Behind Longstreet were to come Anderson, Ewell and, in the rear, the alert, hard-hitting Gordon."[33]

In the meantime, early on the morning of April 6, the Confederate commissary general, now Col. St. John, reached Gen. Lee after having been forced to abandon Richmond earlier. During the interim, he had been attempting to urge the wagon trains forward. Once arrived, he was able to inform Gen. Lee as to the fate of the rations ordered for Amelia. However, there might be rations available that had been sent earlier from Lynchburg via the Southside Railroad before a segment of that road had fallen into Federal hands. Those 80,000 rations were then thought to be on railroad sidings at Farmville. In any event, Gen. Lee sent Col. St. John on ahead to prepare for distribution of the rations, if indeed they were there, once the army reached that station.

While all of this was going on, the retreat of the deteriorating army stumbled forward "soldiers, wagons, and guns mingled together, men and horses tottering in their weakness and their misery. Straggling was perceptibly worse."[34] On the morning of April 6, the head of the column had reached Rice's Station, about halfway between Burkeville and Farmville. Around mid-morning, it was reported to Gen. Lee that there was a widening gap in the trailing column.

As he was to learn later, the remnant of Pickett's Division heading up Anderson's small Corps that included also Bushrod Johnson's Division, had not closed up on Mahone's Division in rear of Longstreet's Corps as the order of march dictated. As a consequence, Sheridan's cavalry and Wright's VI Corps operating on the flanks of the column had been able to attack and set afire a number of wagons in that column. The column now exhibited vulnerable gaps in its conformation.

This set in motion an even graver chain of events. In the rising confusion, Gordon's trailing command took a wrong turn leading away and to the north of the planned route. This left Anderson and Ewell with their columns broken into disconnected segments, wagons trains intervening, the rear then open to attack. Additionally, the countryside in that vicinity was not at all suited for a retreating army beset by an unremitting pursuer. "There could hardly have been a stretch of Virginia countryside better suited for an attack by cavalry on an encumbered column of infantry.... Over nearly the whole of the landscape grew dark pine woods, broken by scattered plantations and a few small farms — just the setting for a military tragedy."[35] In his subsequent report, Gen. Andrew A. Humphreys, commanding the Federal II Corps concurred, describing the landscape as "a country where forests with dense undergrowth and swamps alternated with cultivated fields."[36]

In the afternoon Gen. Lee rode ahead to examine the ground in the vicinity of the point where Sayler's Creek runs into the Appomattox River. At that point "the road 'forks,' — one road to the High Bridge crossing of the Appomattox River, the other by Rice's Station to Farmville."[37] There he came upon a cavalry unit of his army commanded by Gen. William P. Roberts, who, at age twenty-four, was the youngest general officer in the Confederate Army.[38] The men of that command were watching with interest a scene being enacted to their north toward the river. A fight was in progress between what they were able to identify as Gordon's Corps and an unidentified Federal force, which, in fact was Sheridan's cavalry and elements of Wright's VI Corps. Now this posed a curious conundrum for the army commander who did not know yet of Gordon's misrouting. Gordon's Corps was the army's rear guard; where were the marching units intermediate — Anderson and Ewell? White-covered Federal wagons, which usually trailed a line of march, were visible on the field which meant a considerable enemy force was already up.

The only ready troops nearby were of Mahone's Division. Committing them to battle, Gen. Lee, along with Gen. Mahone, led them toward the scene of Gordon's fight. From a height overlooking the valley, General Lee surveyed what lay before him. To what must have been his horror, he saw "streaming out of the bottom and up the ridge to them ... teamsters with their wagons, soldiers without their guns, and shattered regiments without their officers, a routed wreck! My God! cried Lee, as if to himself; has the army been dissolved?"[39] Seizing a battle flag and holding it aloft he attempted to stem the tide of fleeing men.

Some were too terrified to be stopped by anyone. Others recognized the beloved leader and soon a knot began to form around him. Gen. Mahone led his troops forward but it soon became apparent that, although Gordon was still fighting, the absence of Ewell and Anderson suggested the likelihood of their surrender to the enemy. Quickly a new plan of action was patched together. At Mahone's suggestion, he would hold his present position while Longstreet continued to Farmville. Later, Mahone would withdraw under cover of darkness and follow. All the bridges over the Appomattox in that area were to be burned. Gordon could not be helped under the circumstances; he would have to fight his way out if he could. If anyone in the army could do it, he could.

Later that evening, the fate of Anderson's and Ewell's commands was learned. In the confusion of the day's events, they had been separated from the rest of the column. Beset on all sides by the enemy, "Anderson's troops were captured, except for Wise's Brigade and a few scattered individuals who escaped through the woods. Ewell's Corps was taken in front, in flank, and in rear, and after hand-to-hand fighting, where the bayonet was used, was forced to surrender."[40]

Gen. Horatio Wright, commanding the Federal VI Corps, expressed astonishment at the resistance he encountered from those troops of Ewell's command formerly of the Richmond defense forces. "These troops were surrounded.... Looking upon them as already our prisoners, I had ordered the artillery to cease firing as a dictate of humanity; my surprise therefore was extreme when this force charged upon our front; but the fire of our infantry ... the capture of their superior officers, already in our hands, the concentrated and murderous fire of six batteries of our artillery within effective range, brought them promptly to a surrender."[41]

Gen. Ewell, "with both of his division commanders, Kershaw and Custis Lee, and his brigadiers, were taken prisoner."[42] Ewell lost 2800 in this way, Anderson perhaps 1500."[43] It was a disaster; half of the army was gone! Of the debacle, in his postwar memoir, General Longstreet absolved his fellow commanders of any blame, saying, "General R. S. Ewell and General R. H. Anderson are barely known in the retreat, but their stand and fight on that trying march were among the most soldier-like of the many noble deeds of the war."[44]

Later, a note arrived from Gen. Gordon. He reported heavy fighting all day with "considerable" losses to his command and "very heavy" losses inflicted upon the enemy. Later, Gordon was attacked once more by troops of Gen. Sheridan's command and from Gen. Humphrey's II Corps and his division was broken by the overwhelming numbers. Those that could crossed to the west bank of Sayler's Creek and reformed. All in all, on that dreadful and confusing day, the Army of Northern Virginia lost to killed, wounded, captured and missing maybe as many as 8,000 men. It had lost at least half of its artillery. The Federals claimed the capture of "six general officers and about seven thousand men, and, [in General Sheridan's favorite phrase] 'smashing things' generally."[45] The Confederates were beset by four Federal corps numbering 80,000. They were well-equipped and well-fed troops, all with their blood up sensing the end of the awful war that had been in progress for nearly four years now. Even in the face of that disastrous event, the Army of Northern Virginia was not yet ready to call it a day.

Shortly after dark on April 6, Gen. Lee ordered Longstreet's Corps, including what survived of Heth's and Wilcox's Divisions, to begin a night march on Farmville and then Lynchburg. At Farmville, there were two bridges. Longstreet, who had been marching along south of the river, was to cross to the north bank. Once across, destroying the bridges behind, perhaps they could steal a few hours of repose. Mahone, and what remained of Gordon's, Anderson's and Ewell's Corps following the Sayler's Creek affair, were to cross over the Appomattox River via the High (Southside Railroad) Bridge, between Rice and Farmville. Once across to the north bank, they were to destroy the High Bridge and, like at Farmville, a wagon bridge nearby. When those tactically important tasks were accomplished, they were to rejoin Longstreet on the bank opposite Farmville. If the bridge demolitions were successful, the flowing waters of the upper Appomattox River would then separate the contending armies.

Meanwhile, to the front, Col. St. John, the commissary general, was in Farmville. Sent there the day before to secure rations, he had been smiled upon by good fortune. He had found the 80,000 rations thought to have been sent to the area from Lynchburg. Additionally, there were 40,000 rations of bread located. Additional grain had been procured and submitted to local mills for grinding immediately. All of this was turned over to the army's commissaries as they arrived for distribution to the troops, most of whom had received no rations for days. Assuming all the bridges spanning the Appomattox had been destroyed as ordered thereby denying passage to Federal troops, the army might even have time to eat first and then rest.

Alas, it was not to be! Although the High (Railroad) Bridge was successfully fired, a nearby wagon bridge was not. Federal troops were able to extinguish the tardily lit flames.[46] They, crossing to the north bank, were soon to be followed by many others and the chase resumed, as dogged as ever. "The failure to burn the wagon bridge below High Bridge [would cost the Army of Northern Virginia] dearly!"[47] Uncharacteristically, Gen. Lee, showing the strain of the last few days, if not years, was livid. "The last hope of the shattered army was being allowed to slip away!"[48] he said. Regaining his seldom-lost composure, he returned to the task at hand.

Consulting the maps, Gen. Lee dispatched artillery under Col. Alexander to the point ahead where he thought the pursuing Federals would next assail his column. The Texas Brigade, having marched to Farmville, passed over the wagon bridge there before it was fired. Moving into the hills north of the town, Capt. W. T. Hill, 5th Texas, sent a message back to Farmville requesting the purchase of all the bread in town for the relief of the 5th Texas. "But, alas, there was not a loaf of bread in the town, and the Fifth Texas had to remain hungry, for when, late in the afternoon [April 7], a little meat and corn-meal was issued to it along with the other regiments, its march was resumed before any cooking could be done."[49]

Later in the day, Federal cavalry was across the river at Farmville by way of a nearby ford. There they attacked the wagon train still lingering in the area. The attack was broken up in grand style, prisoners were taken including their commander, Brig. Gen. J. Irvin Gregg. The Texas Brigade, in position on the hills north of town, had grandstand seats for viewing these events laid out before them. Here they saw, belying other descriptions of the disarrayed state of the retreating Confederate army: "...Lee's men, moving rapidly but in the most admirable order, to the west ... Grant's, moving steadily in pursuit, his purpose, seemingly, to get around Lee's right flank.... Perched on a high and perfectly open hill as our brigade was, the enemy hidden in the dark at the foot of the hill, and his sharpshooters behind trees, they could see all we did."[50] To avoid the Federal sharpshooting, the men were forced to keep down and "crawl around like so many lizards."

Gen. Lee then ordered Mahone's Division forward in support of Alexander's artillery position near Cumberland Church and Price's farm. Also coming up, what remained of Gordon's Corps was sent forward to protect the wagon train. Later that afternoon, Federal infantry appeared in front of the position. A heavy attack was launched against Mahone's position which was beaten off but only narrowly.

Riding along for a while that day with Gen. Pendleton, the army's chief of artillery, E. P. Alexander, was told that "some of the leading generals had conferred, and decided that it would be well to represent to Lee that, in their opinion, the cause was now hopeless." Further, they felt that Gen. Longstreet was the man to make their opinion known to the army commander. Later, when approached, Gen. Longstreet, staunch to the end, was indignant. He said "that his duty was to help hold up Lee's hands, not to beat them down; that his corps could still whip twice its number and as long as that was the case he would never be the one to suggest a surrender."[51] So it was that later Gen. Pendleton took it upon himself to broach the suggestion. In this he was snubbed by Gen. Lee who noted there were still too many men in the field for them to give up without a fight.

By late evening, April 7, Gen. Lee had established his field headquarters in a house near Cumberland Church. Meanwhile, Gen. Grant was spending the night in Farmville. It was while in Farmville that Gen. Grant penned the famous dispatch stating his desire to shift responsibility for "any further effusion of blood..., [asked Gen. Lee to surrender] that portion of the C. S. Army known as the Army of Northern Virginia." The note was dispatched through the lines under a flag of truce. Gen. Lee was nearby and after reading the note, without comment, he handed it to Gen. Longstreet who was in attendance. Having read the note, Longstreet passed it back commenting in his characteristically laconic way, "Not yet."[52] In this, Gen. Lee concurred.

Taking up pen and paper, Gen. Lee replied, disagreeing that the Army of Northern Virginia was at the point of surrender but expressing his desire also to avoid further and needless bloodshed. He requested Gen. Grant's proposed terms of surrender. The Federal officer conveying Gen. Grant's note and awaiting the reply to be conveyed to his chief was Gen. Seth Williams. Gen. Williams had been a close friend of Gen. Lee before the war, his adjutant during Lee's superintendency at West Point in the early 1850s.[53]

The retreat continued on April 8, a pleasant spring day, unmolested. For the day's march, Longstreet's Corps was ordered from "forward to rear-guard," with the cavalry screening the rear. "The [Confederate] troops who still carried their muskets had hardly the appearance of soldiers as they wearily tramped along, their clothes all tattered and covered with mud, their eyes sunken and lustreless, and their faces pale and pinched from their ceaseless march."[54] Gen. Longstreet described their condition as "troubled and faint of heart." Men and animals were dropping by the roadside too broken down to continue.

With Gordon's remaining troops leading and Longstreet's Corps the rear guard of the much reduced army, they were closely hounded. The line of retreat along the north bank of the Appomattox River had offered a buffer, the unfired bridge, notwithstanding, between the main bodies of the two armies to this point. But now that defensive feature was coming to an end as the headwaters of the river was being reached. Studying his maps, Gen. Lee saw that maybe a dozen miles distant lay the city of Lynchburg on the banks of the James River. Most important, passing through that city was the Southside Railroad, it having paralleled the army's retreat albeit on the south side of the river. There were supplies and rations available somewhere on that line, they having been sent there as Farmville was abandoned and some having been ordered down the line from that point earlier. "The most convenient place to reach the trains was where the road of [the] march crossed the railway at a station called after the county and the river, Appomattox."[55]

In the meantime, Commissary General St. John, once again sent ahead of the army the day before, had located the stores from Farmville on the railroad about halfway between Farmville and Appomattox at a place called Pamplin's Station. Apparently not wishing to put all his eggs in one basket, Gen. Lee ordered those stores to be held there. The army would march ahead to claim the rations that were to have been sent eastward down the rail line from Lynchburg. If that did not work out, then the Farmville rations at Pamplin's could be sought.

With no cavalry screen ahead, what was left of that command bringing up the rear, there was no intelligence as to enemy troop composition or location available to the army commander. In fact, the army was closely hounded with the Federal II and VI Corps close behind the ragged, retreating column. On the south side of the river "the cavalry corps, the V, the XXIX and part of the XXV were hurrying forward, unencumbered by wagons and weak horses, in an effort to beat him to Appomattox Station."[56] The net was closing.

Later in the day another note arrived through the lines from Gen. Grant. In it the Federal commander provided an answer to Lee's earlier request for proposed terms of surrender. In the note, General Grant offered a simple and generous prescription for the surrender of the Army of Northern Virginia; "the only condition on which he would insist would be that the officers and men who were surrendered should be disqualified to bear arms until properly exchanged."[57] Gen. U. S. Grant's Civil War career to that point had been characterized by successful campaigns, finalized by the uncompromising terms "unconditional surrender," e.g., Ft. Donelson and Vicksburg. Thus, the sobriquet, "Unconditional Surrender" Grant. So, the generosity in terms must have come as quite a surprise to the Southern leadership, with, perhaps, the exception of James Longstreet, the close friend of happier times.

Even so, while some of his staff urged him not to even deign to answer, Gen. Lee knew that would never do. So, later that night he took up his pen to fashion a response. While disclaiming that in any way was he proposing the surrender of his army but only requesting terms, he proposed a meeting to discuss those and other matters at mid-morning the next day. Gen. Lee had only recently been appointed commanding general of all Confederate armies and the "other matters" in his note hinted at general peace terms. Then, the note was delivered across the lines. Gen. Grant received Gen. Lee's note at Curdsville at about midnight. He did not reply until the next morning.

Longstreet's Corps, Gen. Lee present, was behind Gordon and late on the evening of April 8 took to the adjacent fields for the night's bivouac. There was no camp equipment available, all of it lost somewhere in the jumbled wagon train scattered along the line of march. As the weary officers sat on the ground around a campfire, bereft of food or drink, at about 9:00 P.M., they were startled by a sudden booming of artillery up front. The meaning of this was immediately apparent to all those present; the Federal army was across their line of retreat. As the evening advanced, this was further emphasized by the twinkling of innumerable campfires surrounding the army, they casting their reflections on the low clouds overhead. After four long years of march and maneuver, the Army of Northern Virginia was finally brought to bay!

Summoning his top commanders surviving, Fitz Lee, Gordon, Longstreet, Gen. Lee conducted his last council of war. Recounting what he knew of the present tactical situation and reading Gen. Grant's notes to them, he requested that they state their respective views as to what they thought they should do. At that time, they advised a continuation of hostilities, one more attempt to break through. It was decided that an immediate attack would be mounted, this plan calmly and quietly arrived upon. Fitz Lee's cavalry was shifted from the rear to the fore.

The movement was to begin after midnight with an attack up front by Fitz Lee's cavalry. Gordon was to follow up with Longstreet marching closely behind. Parts of Ewell's, Anderson's and Pickett's commands not captured on the march were near and reported to Gen. Longstreet. As the council ended, orders were issued to the much reduced commands. "It was then about midnight, the beginning of one of the three or four most memorable dates in American history, April 9, 1865, Sunday, Palm Sunday."[58]

As the movement got underway there came softly wafting upon the spring air a bit of doggerel:

> The race is not to them that's got
> The longest legs to run
> Nor the battle to that people
> That shoots the biggest gun.

"The intonation was unmistakable, and the words were familiar in the army as part of the so-called 'Texas Bible.' The elocutionist who was reciting the lines for his solace must be a member of the famous old 'Hood's brigade' of the First Corps."[59] Longstreet's Corps was beginning its final advance.

All of the commands still in the field were mere shadows of their former numbers. At about daybreak, in the midst of a fog bank, the ghost commands launched their attack a little west of Appomattox Court House. It was to be the Army of Northern Virginia's last.

As Gen. Gordon led his command forward, passing through the village, he found just beyond, hastily thrown-up Federal entrenchments across the road and manned by Sheridan's dismounted cavalry. An attack was mounted immediately and the works were carried, the defenders, dismounted cavalrymen, fleeing beyond. As this action was ending "Gen. Ord's column came up. He had, besides his Army of the James, the Fifth Army Corps. These commands, with the cavalry, pushed the Confederates back a little, while the two corps, [the II and VI], of the Army of the Potomac were advancing against ... [Longstreet's] rear guard."[60] Gordon's Corps was in danger of being separated from the rest of the surviving army in the rear. It was as if a beehive had been disturbed and the angry bees were counterattacking from all directions.

Gordon, reporting "he had fought his Corps to a frazzle," requested of the army commander reinforcements. When informed, Gen. Lee at last recognized the utter futility of further efforts, saying, "Then there is nothing left me but to go and see Gen. Grant, and I would rather die a thousand deaths."[61]

Summoning Longstreet to his side, he laid out the state of affairs: "Gordon blocked, no food at hand [Sheridan having captured the rations from Lynchburg waiting at Appomattox Station], and the rearguard facing a large part of Meade's army, and he ended with the statement that he did not think it was possible to get on."[62] After a brief discussion, Longstreet asked "if the bloody sacrifice of his army could in any way help the cause in other quarters. [Gen. Lee] thought not. Then, [Longstreet] said, your situation speaks for itself."[63] Consulted, Gen. Mahone concurred; Col Alexander suggested what amounted to continuation of the conflict as a "guerrilla war." "'What would you hope to accomplish by that?' Lee queried." He then went on to explain all of the ramifications of such a course as he saw it, much to Alexander's embarrassment. Said Alexander later, "I had not a single word to say in reply.... He had answered my suggestion from a place so far above it, that I was ashamed of having made it."[64] Gen. Lee would go to Gen. Grant seeking specific terms.

In the meantime, the Texas Brigade had completed its last march. Having reached a point within a mile of Appomattox and threatened on all sides, they did what any experienced infantry unit would do in similar circumstances: they began to entrench. Capt. W. T. Hill, 5th Texas, remembered his regiment "appropriating a rail fence for the purpose.... Premonition of the inevitable swept through air, and a death-like stillness prevailed. Work ceased, hunger stayed its gnawing ... faces grew grave and serious, and men when they talked at all spoke in whispers."[65]

On that line, Capt. A. C. Jones (3rd Arkansas) and his men were surprised to see Gen. Lee passing through their lines at about 8:00 A.M. Of him, Jones said, "He looked about as usual except that he wore a bright, new uniform." They were even more surprised later in the morning when a group of Federal cavalrymen bearing a white flag rode by, one of their officers overheard to say, "Those men had as well quit work."[66]

"The prospect of having a conference between commanding officers occur outside of his lines was disturbing to Longstreet. Nothing had been said about authorizing a truce. All indications were that the Federals in the rear were preparing to attack also."[67] Eventually, word was sent to Gen. Gordon requiring him to arrange a truce in front, which was accomplished with some difficulty.[68]

Accompanied by his aides, Cols. Taylor and Marshall, and Gen. A. P. Hill's courier, Sgt. Tucker, Gen. Lee mounted Traveler at about 8:30 A.M., April 9, and together they rode to the suggested meeting place, "on the old state road, between the picket lines." Expecting to meet Gen. Grant there, Gen. Lee was disappointed when that proved not to be. Various notes were exchanged while the Southern leadership waited there in an apple orchard between the lines.

Gen. Lee confided to Gen. Longstreet, who had joined the party, that he feared that Gen. Grant would change the generous terms offered the day before since, in effect, they had been rejected. "Lee did not say so, but his dread was that his men would be marched off to Federal prisons."[69] Gen. Longsteet, knowing Grant, reassured his chief that that would be out of character for the man. However, the last thing said before the Federal messenger returned was by Gen. Longstreet: "General [Lee], unless he offers us honorable terms, come back and let us fight it out."[70]

Shortly after noon, a messenger in the person of Col. Orville E. Babcock, aide-de-camp to Gen. Grant, arrived with a note from his chief. The Federal commander was nearby and ready to meet at any time and place of Gen. Lee's choosing. Then, Gen. Lee, after sending his military secretary, Col. Marshall, to seek out a satisfactory place for the meeting, waited. Shortly, Gen. Lee was advised that a house had been located that would suffice; it was the home of Maj. Wilmer McLean at Appomattox Court House.

Arriving at the site, Gen. Lee was ushered into the front parlor. There, he seated himself at a small table to await the arrival of Gen. Grant. At about 1:30 P.M., there was a clatter of hooves heralding the arrival of a large party of horsemen. Shortly, there entered the room a "man of middle height, slightly stooped and heavily bearded."[71] Gen. Grant, plainly dressed, appeared disheveled, as he often did, his clothing and boots laden with mud. Arising, Gen. Lee advanced to meet him and they shook hands.

Seating themselves at different tables, they waited as a group of Federal officers, including Gens. Sheridan and Ord, were ushered into the room to stand behind Gen. Grant. Gen. Grant opened the conversation by observing that he had once met Gen. Lee in Mexico during that war when the latter was serving on Gen. Scott's staff. To which Lee replied, "'Yes ... I know I met you on that occasion, and I have often thought of it and tried to recollect how you looked, but I have never been able to recall a single feature.'"[72]

Then, ending the casual conversation in what must have been an uneasy situation for all present, Gen. Lee asked for the terms his army could expect if they were to surrender. Gen. Grant replied that, essentially, Lee's army would be paroled to their homes, never to take up arms against the United States again. All arms and ammunition would be delivered up. Officers were to be allowed to retain their sidearms and horses. All of this was committed to paper, when Gen. Lee had an afterthought. Unlike the Federal army, all of his troops who had animals were their personal owners. Could not these men, most of whom in more peaceful times were farmers, retain their animals in order to be able to plant and work their spring crops upon their return to their homes. Gen. Grant said that although this provision was not a part of the surrender terms committed to paper, he would, nonetheless, instruct his paroling officers to allow the requested retention. Expressing "relief and appreciation," Gen. Lee replied, "This will have the best possible effect upon the men ... it will be very gratifying and will do much toward conciliating our people."[73]

While the final draft document was being committed formally to paper, Gen. Grant took the opportunity to introduce Gen. Lee to some of his staff. Receiving each politely, Gen. Lee spoke only to his former friend and adjutant at West Point, Gen. Seth Williams. Then, as the meeting was concluding the subject of rations, or, in the case of the Southern army, the lack thereof, came up. Gen. Grant, further extending his already remarkable generosity, said he was sending over 25,000 rations to relieve the plight of the Southern soldiers. Appreciatively, Gen. Lee said "[I]t will be a great relief, I assure you."[74]

After all had been transferred to paper and signed, about two and a half hours had elapsed. The surrender was completed. Leaving the room, Gen Lee exited onto the porch where "he drew on his gauntlets, and absently smote his hands together several times as he looked into space — across the valley to the hillside where his faithful little army lay. Summoning his orderly to bring Traveler, he mounted, the vanquished hero of the then and forever lost Southern cause. As he prepared to ride away, Gen. Grant, stepping down from the front porch of the McLean house and in salute "took off his hat, but did not speak. The other Federals followed the courteous example of their chief. Lee raised his hat, without a word, turned his horse and rode away."[75]

The Texas Brigade, in rear of Longstreet's corps, did not receive the news of the surrender immediately. Even though the surrender had been completed, some of them were engaged still in throwing up defensive fortifications. When orders reached them to cease their labors, one questioned the messenger: "What for...? We had our orders to throw up this line."

"Yes, but now it is useless. General Lee has surrendered."

Disbelieving, the soldier replied: "I don't believe that yarn. You can't come any such stuff over me."

"Well, it's true, nevertheless. General Lee had no other alternative. Grant's army is surrounding us, and he thought it better to surrender than to try and cut our way through."

Remaining loyal to the revered leader to the end, the soldier replied: "I'd rather have died than surrender, but if 'Marse Bob' thinks that is best, then all I've got to say is, that 'Marse Bob' is bound to be right, as usual."[76]

There was much emotion displayed throughout the thinned ranks. Capt. A. C. Jones, then commanding the 3rd Arkansas, described that moment as a "mental shock," as if the world had come to an end. He "fell face down in the dust and wept."[77] Said he later, "I went almost into a state of unconsciousness."[78] Such was the reaction in the ranks of Hood's Texas Brigade and Longstreet's Corps to the loss of a cause dearly fought for four long, grueling years..

To the Army, Gen. Lee issued his final general order:

> Headquarters, Army of Northern Virginia, April 10th 1865.
> After four years of arduous service, marked by unsurpassed courage and fortitude, the Army of Northern Virginia has been compelled to yield to overwhelming numbers and resources. I need not tell the survivors of so many hard-fought battles, who have remained steadfast to the last, that I have consented to this result from no distrust of them, but, feeling that valor and devotion could accomplish nothing that could compensate for the loss that would have attended the continuation of the contest, I have determined to avoid the useless sacrifice of those whose past services have endeared them to their countrymen.
> By the terms of the agreement, officers and men can return to their homes, and remain there until exchanged. You will take with you the satisfaction that proceeds from the consciousness of duty faithfully performed; and I earnestly pray that a merciful God will extend to you his blessing and protection.
> With an increasing admiration of your constancy and devotion to your country, and a grateful remembrance of your kind and generous consideration of myself, I bid you an affectionate farewell.
> R. E. Lee, General[79]

CHAPTER 19

"[T]he Texas Brigade ... the most renowned of all"[1]: Advance into Legend, April 12, 1865, and Beyond

Morning, April 12, 1865, dawned chill, gray and depressing to Gen. Joshua Lawrence Chamberlain as he waited for the proceedings to begin. He, in command of the 20th Maine Infantry at Gettysburg on Little Round Top, was a Union hero of that great battle. Since that day in July 1863, the college professor turned soldier had further proved his military mettle on numerous occasions, suffering six grievous wounds in the process. Having risen to the rank of brigadier general in command of a brigade in the V Army Corps, he was appointed by Gen. Grant, above all others of equal or greater rank, to receive the surrender of the Army of Northern Virginia on that memorable day. It was an honor of signal significance.

Just east of Appomattox, with his veteran troops lining both sides of the Richmond to Lynchburg Stage Road upon which the surrendering army would tread, he viewed the slopes where his opposite numbers were "breaking camp for the last time, taking down their little shelter-tents and folding them carefully as precious things, then slowly forming ranks as for the unwelcome duty." Then, as he watched, the "dusky swarms forge[d] forward into gray columns of march. On they [came], with the old swinging route step and swaying battle-flags. In the van, the proud Confederate ensign — the great field of white with canton of star-strewn cross of blue on a field of red, the regimental battle flags, with the same escutcheon following on, crowded so thick, by thinning out of men, that the whole column seemed crowned with red."[2] The Army of Northern Virginia was making its last march.

Chamberlain, a man possessed of a large degree of sensitivity, was aware of the "momentous meaning" of the occasion and determined that he would "mark it by some token of recognition." That token, he decided, would be by means of a "salute of arms," one military organization's way of expressing respect for another military organization. The decision was his alone and he knew that he would be criticized afterwards by those bent upon revenge both in and out of the army. He knew also that before him would stand "the embodiment of manhood: men whom neither toils and sufferings, nor the fact of death, nor disaster, nor hopelessness could bend from their resolve; standing before us now, thin, worn, and famished, but erect and with eyes looking level into ours, waking memories that bound us together as no other bond;— was not such manhood to be welcomed back into a Union so tested and assured?"[3]

286

As the surrendering column drew abreast, blue-clad buglers sounded a command that brought the whole Federal line, "regiment by regiment in succession," to attention and then from "order arms" to "carry arms," the marching salute. It was a dramatic moment and a gallant gesture by the victorious to the vanquished. Chosen to lead the Confederate column on its final march, a heavy-spirited Gen. John B. Gordon, like his opposite not a professional soldier but a proven and valiant one on many a field, was startled, not expecting to hear the crash of ceremonial arms. Then, he mounted, "taking the meaning, wheel[ed] superbly, making himself and his horse one uplifted figure, with profound salutation as he drop[ped] the point of his sword to [his] boot toe; then facing to his own command, [gave] word for his successive brigades to pass ... with the same position of the manual, — honor answering honor." In the "awed stillness" there was not "a sound of trumpet ... nor roll of drum; not a cheer, nor word nor whisper.... [It was] as if it were the passing of the dead."[4] And thus it was to be, by order of Gen. Grant, in the days following. "Let um' up easy," had been President Lincoln's advice.

Each surrendering division, all mere skeletons of more robust times, "dress their lines," "each captain taking pains for the good appearance of his company, worn and half-starved as they were.... They fix bayonets, stack arms; then ... remove cartridge-boxes and lay them down. Lastly, — reluctantly, with agony of expression, — they tenderly fold their flags, battle-worn and torn, blood-stained, heart-holding colors, and lay them down."[5]

All day, Chamberlain and his men watched the passing of an army, "the men of Antietam ... the men who swept away the Eleventh Corps at Chancellorsville; who left six thousand of their companions around the bases of Culp's Hill and Cemetery Hill at Gettysburg; these survivors of the terrible Wilderness, the Bloody Angle at Spottsylvania, the slaughter pen of Cold Harbor.... [And once again, the rear guard of the army, the place of military honor], Longstreet and his men! ... Now comes the sinewy remnant of fierce Hood's Division.... Ah, is this Pickett's Division?"[6]

Longstreet's Corps was last and the last of it was brought up by Gen. Field leading Hood's old Division, the Texas Brigade among the ranks. Of the Texas Brigade at the surrender, D. S. Freeman had this to say: "The Texas Brigade itself, perhaps the most renowned of all, 476 officers and men marched up the road, and stacked the rifles that had been heard in all the Army's great battles except Chancellorsville. For absence from that action, they had made atonement at Chickamauga and in Tennessee. Their name, their deeds, with which the old Third Arkansas was associated, already had become a part of the tradition of their State. Defeat, at the end of their military career, could not dim their record. 'I rely upon [the Texans] in all tight places,' Lee had said."[7]

With the surrender completed, paroles in hand, it was time to consider, for most, going home. For one unnamed member of the Texas Brigade, there was one last duty to be performed before setting out on the long journey leading to the Lone Star State.

Col. Clement Sullivane served as adjutant general on the staff of Gen. G. W. C. (Custis) Lee for the latter half of the war. After the surrender at Appomattox, Col. Sullivane was paroled, that parole limiting his presence to the city of Richmond. During that time, Gen. R. E. Lee, also returned from Appomattox, resumed residence with his family in a small house on Franklin Street in that same city. Custis Lee was in residence there with his family.

For a time the Lees were besieged by visitors seeking an audience with the vanquished but venerated former commander of the Army of Northern Virginia. Visitors included throngs of former army officers and common soldiers, all anxious to see their beloved leader one more time before returning to their respective homes throughout the South and else-where. There were Southern politicians as well as the always present just plain curious. It fell to Custis Lee's responsibility the management of these sometimes considerable throngs. Additionally, there were bundles of correspondence requiring attention and this duty was taken up also by Custis Lee. To help deal with the considerable matters at hand, it became Col. Sullivane's custom each morning to go to the Franklin Street address to help in admin-istering the work. While there he had the unique opportunity to observe the comings and goings.

On one particular morning, Custis Lee was turning away all visitors, "generals and statesmen, high and low alike," no exceptions. The reason being given was that Gen. Lee had matters of correspondence that had to be attended to that day. Col. Sullivane, seated in the parlor, was in a position from which place he could see and hear all that transpired. By and by, he saw coming up the steps "a tall, ragged Confederate soldier, with his left arm in a sling." He was met at the door by Custis Lee who was asked by the ragged apparition to see Gen. Lee. Custis Lee was in the process of explaining why the General was unavailable when the old soldier mentioned the fact that he was — had been — a member of Hood's Texas Brigade. He went on to say that he had followed Gen. Lee for four years and was about to leave Virginia and walk home to Texas. He wanted to shake his commander's hand and tell him goodbye for one last time. However, said he, if that was not possible, it was not possible.

As he turned to leave, Custis Lee hesitated briefly and then called the man back, telling him to wait; he would see if Gen. Lee might be available. Ushered into the parlor, the Texan was offered a seat by Col. Sullivane and a brief conversation ensued. Presently, Col. Sullivane heard the general's footsteps descending the stairway. Entering the room, the always courtly Lee bowed to Col. Sullivane and with extended hand approached the Texan. Grasping his general's hand and looking him in the eye, the "poor fellow" tried to speak but was overcome by emotion. Bursting into tears, he covered his face and turning, walked out of the room and the house. General Lee gazed after him, his own eyes "suffused and darkened with emotion." Bowing once again to Col. Sullivane, he left the room. "Not a single word was spoken during the meeting by any one of the three participants," said Col. Sullivane.

"[To Col. Sullivane], as General Lee gazed after the departing soldier and I gazed at him, it seemed probable to me that all the glories of the Seven Days, Antietam, Fredericks-burg, Chancellorsville, Manassas, Cold Harbor, etc, and all the disasters of his bloody defeat at Malvern Hill, Gettysburg, the terrible nine months in the trenches at Petersburg, and the crowning ruin of Appomattox were flashing through that capacious mind, conjured up by the appearance before him of this wounded soldier of the famous Texas Brigade, from first to last the most dependable brigade of the Army of Northern Virginia."[8]

After that memorable moment, Col. Sullivane recalled, he never again saw Gen. Lee. Nor is it likely that the emotionally-stricken Texan ever did either.

There were a number of ways of getting home, none of them quick or easy even for men inured of the terrible hardships of serving with ill-prepared armies in the field. Accord-ing to Nicholas Pomoroy, Co. A, 5th Texas, one term of the surrender agreement was that the Federal government would provide free railroad transportation for infantrymen to the station nearest their homes. However, since maintenance of the railroads throughout the South had been seriously neglected during the war, they were in bad shape and subject to interruption. They were scarce to non-existent beyond the Mississippi River. Since Con-federate cavalrymen and artillerymen furnished their own horses, they were expected to use them for their journey home or elsewhere.[9] Most, if not all of those surviving animals, must have been in poor condition to make such a journey. Sufficient forage along the way was problematic, also. So, for the Texans, the long road home was to be hard, they coming from the farthest corner of the now former Confederate States of America.

The Arkansans' route was somewhat less arduous, railroads being available, by way of Chattanooga, to Memphis, Arkansas being just across the Mississippi River from that point. Generally, Texans chose to either stay on in other Southern states or elsewhere, to take trains bound eventually for New Orleans, to return via U.S. government steamers leaving from Yorktown bound by various courses for Galveston or to join groups formed together for mutual security in getting home to Texas overland. So, after bidding a final farewell to their comrades of the 3rd Arkansas on April 13, they individually or in groups set out on their final trek to Texas. There is no record of how many completed the journey.

One large group of Texans choosing to return together formed up and began the march to their first waypoint. That was Danville, Virginia, on the line of the Richmond and Danville Railroad, one of their unrealized destinations on the retreat from Petersburg. Leading the group, by popular consent, were Maj. "Howdy" Martin, 4th Texas, and Capt. W. T. Hill, 5th Texas. It only took a day or two to realize the problems inherent in traveling in large numbers at that time. In a country devoid of enough rations to sustain a large group, many began to drop off. With no accurate maps available, the remaining column often lost its way. After reaching Danville, it took several days for those remaining with the strung-out column to catch up.

Alas, at Danville, they discovered that there was no transportation to be had. Further south in North Carolina, Sherman's marauding army had destroyed the railroads to such an extent that they were useless to the wayfaring Texans. So, nothing to do but push on and walk to Greensboro, North Carolina. There they were joined up by many of the Texans who had served in Gen. Joe Johnston's army, which had surrendered recently to Sherman in North Carolina.

With organization pretty much gone, what was left then walked to Montgomery, Alabama; there is no mention of how long that lengthy route took, most certainly weeks, perhaps months. There, after reporting to the local Federal provost marshal, they were billeted in a "large two-story building ... near the artesian well." They remained there awaiting the next available means of transportation capable of carrying them further west.

According to Capt. Hill, after

Capt. James T. Hunter, Co. H, 4th Texas

about a week, a steamboat arrived laden with cargo. The local provost marshal made them a bargain; unload the vessel and he would allow them passage on its return voyage to Mobile. "[T]he Texans went to work with such energy as, in six hours, to unload and place in piles on the wharf, a mass of freight." Next morning, they embarked on the next leg of their odyssey. It was not destined to go smoothly. At Selma, Alabama, their boat was halted. Much to their dismay, they were invited to disembark in order that a black military unit could embark. Things had changed in their world.

However, as it turned out, they did not have long to wait. The next day another steamboat took them onboard and transported them to Mobile. There, Capt. Hill said, they "were assigned comfortable quarters, furnished with rations, and had ... paroles again inspected." They were there, in what sounds like pleasant surrounding for six days, then going by steamboat to New Orleans. There, they enjoyed another apparently pleasant stay.

Although billeted in a large cotton shed, it surely beat those years in which they had spent a goodly amount of their time under the sun and stars without benefit of any cover. While there, Capt. Hill said that the better classes of citizens treated them "with kindness and courtesy; [while] from people in the lower classes only came incivility.... The Irish ladies of the city could not do too much for us. They visited us at our quarters, and not only insisted on having our cooking done for us, but on our coming to their homes and taking our meals there. In addition, they furnished every one of us with a suit of good clothes." Hurray for the Irish! must have been in their hearts and on their lips.

On their last night in the great port city, a party for the men was given by one Col. Henry. An elegant supper was served them at the colonel's house. A Dr. Greenleaf hosted a similar party for the officers. Going back to their less-than-elegant quarters, they were all anxious for the morrow to dawn because with it came their departure for Galveston.

Next morning, they boarded their steamer, the *Hudson*, only to be disembarked at midmorning to help fight a fire in the neighborhood of Colonel Henry's residence. The Texans, more than gladly, rushed to the rescue. They removed all the valuables from the colonel's house and placed a guard over it while the nearby fire was fought and extinguished. They then returned the valuables to the colonel's house, all without damage. That task completed, at about 4:00 P.M., they returned to the steamship just in time for its departure.

Although they were then on the last leg of their journey, they were not destined to be home free. Traveling down the Mississippi River, near its mouth, the steamer went aground. Two tugs were unable to dislodge the vessel from the mud. Much to their relief, on the third day with their vessel still hard aground, an outbound steamer for Galveston took them onboard.

They were awakened the next morning by the sound of the anchor being let go. As they hurried on deck they were greeted by the nearby presence of the Federal blockading fleet swinging to its anchors. In quarantine until midday, they were then cleared to dock. Capt. Hill noted that they "lost no time in getting ashore."

The citizenry of Galveston, having sponsored one company in the brigade, Co. L, 1st Texas, were anxious to help in any way they could to get their returning heroes to their homes as soon as possible. With transportation by boat up Buffalo Bayou to Houston arranged, there they were to be feted by the citizens of that city. It was not to be; the Federal official in charge in Texas, Gen. E. J. Davis, a Southerner but staunch Unionist, would not allow the passage: "Rebels, he said were entitled to no courtesies."

So, the only way to get to Houston was by rail, that having fallen into disrepair during the war. But, once again, it was the citizens of Galveston to the rescue. They patched up an old locomotive that proved able to make the fifty mile run. Once again it was Irish ladies who, when seatless flat cars proved to be the only thing available in way of passenger transport, cleaned them up for that purpose.

Departing about sunset, by midnight they were in Houston. There, never mind the late hour, they enjoyed a banquet prepared for them by the citizens of that great city. The next day, "rejoicing that [they] had been spared to again set [their] feet on Texas soil, and feeling that [they] had done [their] duty, [their] whole duty, and nothing but [their] duty, [they] separated, each of us going home."[10]

It must have seemed a suddenly altered world these veterans found themselves in. For most of them, the last four years had been lived in close proximity to hosts of men. Close bonds of comradeship had been formed. Now, in a glimmering, they found themselves on their way home, alone or in small groups at the most. For most, it would probably be years, if ever, before they would meet their comrades of the war years again.

Capt. A. C. Jones, (3rd Arkansas), who commanded that regiment for the last phases of the war, led a group of Arkansans on their homeward trek. Traveling through miles of Federal encampments they passed unhindered. Said Jones of their former antagonists: "We have no cause to complain of the conduct of those men, as they treated us with the utmost respect and courtesy." Stories abound of Federal soldiers sharing their campfires, their rations and their war yarns with their recent enemies.

Their Federally-issued rations went fast and it did not take Jones long to realize that their fraternal travel plans were not going to be workable. A foraging foray yielded no food but valuable information about a possible corn cache at a nearby mill. Once located, the miller who had been deferred from field service because of his essential trade, was not interested at all in aiding his former defenders. First denying possession of any corn, once the cache had been uncovered, he retreated to his secondary line of defense; the mill was inoperative. Not so, said one of Jones' men, "Captain, there is nothing the matter with the mill. I am a miller; I can run the mill if you wish it."[11] Thus, thanks to the talent on hand, they were able to grind enough corn to last them a few days. After that was expended it was decided to break up into smaller groups in order to better deal with the shortages of rations along the way. Although Jones' account does not proceed beyond that point, presumably, most or all of the band finally reached their Arkansas homes to resume their lives in peace, if not in prosperity.

Another band of indeterminate numbers, led by D. H. Hamilton, Co. M, 1st Texas, joined the ranks, initially, of the group led by Maj. Martin and Capt. Hill, it also of indeterminate numbers. The 1st Texans were "without rations and without a cent of money." On their first day's march, foraging parties found a farmer whose barn housed about a hundred bushels of corn. The farmer agreed to supply two roasting ears per man and Hamilton was detailed to supervise the transfer. He confessed to "being so hungry I could have eaten a piece of a rubber boot," and he appropriated an extra half dozen ears for himself. Going into camp that night they were so famished that they roasted and ate all that ration at one time.

The next day, fortune smiled upon them once more when they located a mill from which they procured a supply of flour. However, without other ingredients, they discovered they could not do anything useful or edible with the flour alone. Their dilemma did not last long as they scattered throughout the neighborhood, enlisting the aid of their most loyal supporters in their former country, its Southern women! In no time, Hamilton said, those women had "made us the finest biscuits I ever ate in all my life." They ate them all, and then lying down on the ground, went to sleep.

At 3:00 A.M. they were awakened by a cold rain. Holding a conference of four, Hamilton and the other three decided it best that they strike out on their own, subsistence being easier to obtain in small amounts. Revived somewhat by the corn and biscuits they set out with a renewed vitality. At Griffin, Georgia, in a skirmish with former Confederate quartermasters following orders to secure their stores, they replenished their supplies and headed next for Selma, Alabama. Traveling only in the early morning and at night to take advantage of the cooler conditions, they reached Selma a week later. Their next way-point was Jackson, Mississippi, which they said "took [them] quite a while to reach."

By the time they reached Jackson, their Griffin, Georgia-acquired rations were expended. Acquiring more, they rested "two or three days" before setting out for Vicksburg. Having walked the entire distance from Virginia, at Vicksburg, they were able to hitch their first ride, this on a river transport. That part of the trip took them from Vicksburg, down the Mississippi to the Red River, up that waterway to Wilson's Landing, some twenty miles downriver from Alexandria, Louisiana.

Once again, forced to resort to "brogan transportation," they walked the remaining 225 miles home. "We lost no time on the last lap of our journey. Being in good condition we walked day and night."[12] Presumably, they lived, if not happily, at least more securely and better-fed than they had during the days of their Confederate service. They left no record of how long their walk had taken them to complete.

Nicholas Pomoroy (Co. A, 5th Texas) was ill at the time of the surrender and did not take part in the final formalities, apparently. Receiving his parole, rations and free transportation, he and two comrades set out to reach Texas. Although he does not mention any details of how they found transportation, they went by train to Jackson, Mississippi, and then "walked from there all the way to Texas." They crossed the mighty Mississippi in a "small row boat." Reaching the other side of the river, they found the bottom land flooded for great distances beyond the river. By wading and swimming "shoving a little raft of sticks with [their] clothes on it," they finally reached dry land.

Stopping at a planter's house, they were supplied with rations, but declined an offer of lodging because they had become accustomed to camping out. Movement westward went well until their path was complicated by encounter with the pine woods that dominated western Louisiana and eastern Texas. Traversing that thick tangle took several days during which the roads were all but non-existent as were any sources of food and water. Claiming too much space would be required to detail the remainder of the trip to Houston, he arrived in that bayou city "none the worse for my four years campaigning in old Virginia."

Since Houston was where his company, Co. A, the Bayou City Guards was raised, initially, he had many friends there to welcome him home. He advised his family of his whereabouts but remained in Houston, jobs being available, for about two years after the war ended. Until he notified his family, they had thought him dead, killed or dead of disease in Virginia. When he finally did go home at his mother's urging, he was too late to ever see his brother, Robert, again. He had died several weeks earlier of unspecified causes.

Brother Robert's will left all of his worldly goods to Nicholas, the "old homestead and lands." Really wishing to return to Houston with its lure of opportunity, he was compelled by the same sense of duty that had stood him in good stead as a soldier to remain instead. "My mother begging me not to leave her and my father in their old age, I remained."[13]

Thus, some of the last soldiering experiences, still fraught with great difficulty, of these men of Hood's Texas Brigade who had served so long, so well and so conspicuously in one of their country's most momentous and terrible times.

> Not for fame or reward, not for place or
> for rank, Not lured by ambition or goaded
> by necessity, But in simple obedience to
> duty as they understood it These men suf-
> fered all, sacrificed all, endured all ... and
> died.[14]

That war is terrible and that among American wars, the War of the Rebellion was the worst is an accepted fact. Just how terrible can only be realized by those that have actually borne arms and experienced armed combat. Gerald Linderman cites the feelings of some Civil War–era combatants that must mirror the feelings of all. One Wisconsin officer, speaking for himself and his comrades said that "once at home, they wished only to forget the war.... The glitter of gun barrel and sword, the red carnage of the field, the terrible echoes of ... artillery, were yet close realities.... I do not for a moment delude myself with the idea that this epoch was the most important in my life. It was not." Another, a New Englander, was ... "'reluctant to reminisce about his army days' and was unwilling to publish his war journals." Future president William McKinley, a Union non-commissioned officer serving in an Ohio regiment commanded by another future president, Rutherford B. Hayes, "would rarely speak of the war. He preferred to forget the trying days and nights, the hunger and personal discomfort, the danger, and above all, the agony for which the war stood." Future associate justice of the U.S. Supreme Court Oliver Wendell Holmes, Jr., whose "heart was touched by fire" as a result of his war experiences "did not read of the war or observe the anniversaries of its battles." No less a personage than Robert E. Lee, assuming the helm of Washington College in Lexington, Virginia, after the war "did not read books on the war and seldom even read newspapers." "'I do not wish to awaken memories of the past,'" said Lee.[15] It is said that on any occasion when martial music was played in his presence, he purposefully strived to walk along unmilitarily out of step. In his later life as college president, he thought that his choice of a military career had been a mistake. It took a long time, decades for most, for the unpleasant memories of the war to be ameliorated by age and the passage of time and for nostalgia to take over.

As a result, early attempts to form veterans fraternal and commemorative organizations met with very little success. The first, the Federal Grand Army of the Republic, the G. A. R., first appeared in 1866 but failed of any significant membership. It was not until the late 1870s that its memberships rolls began to fill. "In 1890—at 428,000—it touched its crest."[16] In the South it was much the same. "In 1870 Generals Pickett and Early founded the Society of the Army of Northern Virginia; most of its chapters soon became skeletons."[17] It was not until 1889 that the United Confederate Veterans organization made its appearance, its successor organization, the Sons of Confederate Veterans continuing to this day.

The veterans of Hood's Texas Brigade do not appear to have shared a war reticence to the same extent as that exhibited by their former Gray comrades or their Blue contenders in the years following the war. The Hood's Texas Brigade Association was organized within seven years of the war's conclusion. It continued unabated, with several exceptions, for sixty-one years. With sixty-five attendees, it was founded at the Hutchins House in Houston on May 24, 1872. Among that initial throng there was none other than Gen. John B. Hood. As a result of a motion put forth by Gen. Jerome B. Robertson, Hood's successor as brigade commander, Hood presided over the organizational meeting. The names of the first officers elected at that meeting to lead the fledgling organization have a familiar ring: president, Col. C. M. Winkler; vice president, Gen. J. B. Robertson; and secretary-treasurer, Maj. J. H.

Littleton. The organization's object was established to be "for the purpose of friendly and social reunion of the survivors of the brigade, and to collect all data for rolls and history and to perpetuate all anecdotes, incidents and many things connected therewith and to succor the needy among its members."[18]

The association held reunions from that time through 1933, with the exception of the war years 1898 and 1918. Altogether sixty regular reunions and three special reunions were held in twenty-eight different Texas towns. The special reunion held on September 13, 1879, was for the purpose of finding a way to aid Gen. Hood's children following the death of their parents earlier in that year. The only reunion scheduled to be held outside of Texas was to be that of 1898 at Malvern, Arkansas. Alas for the Arkansans, the declaration of war with Spain resulted in that reunion's cancellation. The majority of the reunions, seventeen, were held in Bryan, Texas, usually over a two day period. Traditionally, the reunion centered around June 27, the anniversary of the brigade's first big victory at Gaines' Mill in 1862.

The reunions were always attended by a great deal of fanfare by the sponsoring city and the veterans, particularly as they grew older, loved the adulation heaped upon them by an admiring public. Although each reunion must have held varying degrees of significance for individual veterans, the thirty-ninth, that of 1910, must have been particularly special for them all. In that year the reunion was held in Austin.[19]

On that date there gathered "the majority of the 200 surviving veterans of Hood's Texas Brigade, tottering old men, come from the four corners of the State — and some of them from beyond its borders — they and their wives, daughters and sons, drawn by the common impulse of love and sentiment. Old and young, man and woman, entered into the spirit of the occasion, for all honored the cause and admired the heroism of the men who fought for it."[20] They had come, on that occasion, to take part in the unveiling and dedication ceremonies of the Texas Brigade Monument on the capitol grounds.

The efforts to erect a monument and elect a historian to write the brigade history had been launched three years earlier at the 1907 reunion held that year on June 27–28, in Navasota, Texas. At that time, Edward K. Goree ,Co. H, 5th Texas, who had lost a leg to amputation at the Wilderness, served as president of the association. A resolution to appoint a historian and select a monument committee was offered by Frank B. Chilton, Co. H, 4th Texas, on Thursday, June 27, the forty-fifth anniversary of the Gaines' Mill fight. Noting that other states of the former Confederacy had erected monuments to their honored veterans, he said it was the duty of the state of Texas to do the same. In part, his resolution called for the election of "a President who shall preside over a Hood's Texas Brigade monument committee until a suitable and creditable monument adorns the capitol grounds at Austin."[21] Quickly, Chilton the proposer became Chilton the disposer. Nominated by President Goree, he was elected unanimously. To assist in the effort, a committee composed of one former member each of the 1st, 4th, 5th Texas, 18th Georgia and 3rd Arkansas was named. Acting immediately upon his new authority, Chairman Chilton raised $448.75 on the spot. The monument would eventually come in at a cost of $15,000. It was a good beginning.

In the matter of a written history and a historian to write it, it was Frank Chilton once more who raised the issue. Speaking of the need to correct the "many mistakes and errors of [the] present brigade history," Mrs. Winkler's, he stressed the urgency "before it proved too late for the living to do the justice to the noble dead of the brigade." His resolution called for selection of a brigade historian "whose duty it [would] be to collect all data from every available source and give to the world a fair and impartial history of Hood's Texas

Brigade from first to last."[22] It was to include the exploits of the 1st, 4th, 5th Texas, 3rd Arkansas, 18th Georgia and Hampton's Legion in its pages. By a unanimous vote, Joe Polley, Co. F, 4th Texas, was elected to accomplish the task. In recent years, Polley had been writing articles for the *Confederate Veteran* and his *Letters to Charming Nellie* had been recently published. His *Hood's Texas Brigade: Its Marches, Its Battles, Its Achievements* was the eventual outcome. Although there are errors in Polley's book, it is a valuable contribution to the literature of the brigade. Joe Polley was there at the front first to nearly the last, wounded twice, the last time losing a foot on the Darbytown Road thus ending his military career. He knew first-hand of which he wrote.

So it came to be that over a three year period funds had been raised, and thanks to the generous largess of the McNeel Marble Company of Marietta, Georgia, the Hood's Texas Brigade Monument was erected on the capitol grounds in Austin. The two McNeels were native Texans. In honor of their nativity and in memory of the 18th Georgia they had donated $5,000 of their work in order to complete the $15,000 project.[23] There remained only to unveil and dedicate the monument. Amidst the flowery oratory characteristic of that day and the air resounding with the strains of martial music of a Confederate flavor, "Dixie" and "The Bonnie Blue Flag," the aging veterans and their kin in caravan made their way to the capitol grounds. The crowd was swelled by the presence of thousands of school children, Austinites and other interested Texans. It was the second day of the reunion, the afternoon of Thursday, October 27, 1910.[24]

The parade was one of the largest that the city of Austin had ever seen. It was over a mile long, the front having reached the capitol grounds before the end had taken up the route. The parade route was thronged with a crowd estimated to be as many as 10,000. Above the parade column the cross of St. Andrew, side by side with the Stars and Stripes, billowed forth to the breeze. At the capitol grounds, the 200 or so brigade survivors dismounted from their automobiles, fell into line and marched to the place of dedication. According to one account, they displayed "the same spirit that they had displayed in the '60s when they were young men and some of them mere boys."

There was much oratory in the style and spirit of the day. The first was delivered by the then brigade president, "Gen." William R. Hamby, Co. B, 4th Texas. In the course of his speech, he read a letter from the late Gen. Stephen D. Lee of what the latter had seen at Sharpsburg from his artillery position near the Dunker Church. This is the man who had coined the phrase associated ever-after with Sharpsburg as "artillery hell." Speaking of the Texans, Georgians and Carolinians: " I saw them sweep the enemy from their front. I saw them almost annihilated, and even then I saw them contribute the greater part to the repulse of Hooker's corps, then of Mansfield's corps.... I saw them hold off Sumner's corps until reinforcements came. I saw them pursue the enemy. I saw them broken, shattered and falling back before overwhelming numbers; the few who were left giving the rebel yell with more spirit than the hurrahs of the Union troops advancing upon them."[25]

The Honorable John H. Kirby of Houston, four years old at war's end and an honorary member of the association, made the presentation address. Quoting from an unnamed source, Kirby spoke of the men of Hood's Brigade as "the pick and flower of the young men of Texas ... the knightliest, gamest, freest ... that ever faced a foe.... It will not be many decades until the last of them will have heard the order to bivouac with their immortal commanders and comrades upon the other shore." Upon completing his presentation speech, he addressed the governor of Texas, Thomas M. Campbell, "Through you, sir, we commit this monument into the keeping of the people of this incomparable State in memory of the grandest body of citizen- soldiers that ever enriched the history or immortalized the manhood of any country on earth."

In reply, Gov. Campbell accepted the monument: "In behalf of the great State of Texas, I, as the Governor of the state accept into her care this monument, this tribute to the memory of patriotism of our fathers, which will never die, and whose deeds will live long after this beautiful monument has crumbled into ashes and mouldered in dust."[26]

Above the resounding applause of the crowd, the strains of "Dixie" could be heard, loudly played.

* * *

Completing his narrative of wartime experiences some forty years after the fact, J. M. Polk, Co. I, 4th Texas, expressed the hope that it would be sufficient "to show to the young men and women of our country and future generations what a horrible thing war is."[27]

> We led the charge on many a field,
> Were first in many a fray;
> And turned the bloody battle tide
> On many a glorious day.

In 1966, after a thirty-three year hiatus, the Hood's Texas Brigade Association, Reorganized, was established. It holds biennial reunions at Hillsboro, Texas, or elsewhere.

Epilogue — "*Home at last*"[1]:
Captain Ike N. M. Turner, Co. K,
5th Texas, Comes Home to Texas, 1995

As the dirt was carefully loosened and shoveled aside, the men peering down into the 131 year old grave could begin to make out the outline of a coffin. Or more accurately, what had once been a coffin. Rows of glass buttons reflected the long-absent rays of the sun. All else had long since crumbled into dust or did so at the time when touched.[2]

The date was May 11, 1994; the place was the former Turnwold Plantation near Eaton-ton, Georgia, and the Texans conducting the exhumation were members of the Ike Turner Camp 1275, Sons of Confederate Veterans (S.C.V.) of Livingston, Texas. Led by their camp commander, Col. Mack Neal, they had been on a long quest to locate the burial place of their chapter's namesake, Capt. Isaac N. M. Turner, Co. K, 5th Texas Volunteer Infantry. The location of the grave was to be only the first step in an odyssey that would see Capt. Turner's remains returned to his prewar Texas home for re-interment.

It had been Capt. Turner's last request. Shortly before his final breath, it is said he asked one of his brothers, also of Co. K, "If you can, please take me home to my mother, for I fear that she will worry so about me."[3]

* * *

Ike Turner was a native Georgian. He was born April 3, 1839, on the Turnwold Plan-tation in Putnam County. He was barely twenty-four years old at the time of his untimely death on April 15, 1863. His parents were Martha Eveline Hubert Turner and Joseph Alger-non Sydney Turner. In addition to three brothers, all of whom served in Co. K, he had two sisters.[4] The family had a military history prior to the Civil War. In 1846, Joseph A. S. Turner raised a company of Georgians and served as their captain in the Mexican War.

Young Ike completed the schools of Americus, Georgia. Upon graduation, he entered the Georgia Military Institute located at Marietta. Just before his senior year and at the age of nineteen, his father dispatched him to Polk County, Texas, to oversee and prepare some land he had purchased there some years earlier. By 1859, Ike had the place ready for the family's habitation. They all came, the Turners and the Huberts. Then, in 1861, there came the devastating, fratricidal war.

In the euphoria of the times, there were several attempts by the Turners and the Huberts to raise local companies of varying types for Confederate service. Finally succeeding, on September 3, 1861, with about eighty men comprising the company, known locally as the

Polk County Flying Artillery, they set off for the front in Virginia, by way of Camp Van Dorn. Capt. Ike Turner was already in command. When they reached Virginia they were more prosaically designated as Co. K, 5th Texas Volunteer Infantry. From that point, their war experience was also the Texas Brigade's experience.[5]

After Capt. Turner's mortal wounding in front of Suffolk on April 14, 1863, and his death the next day, there was much anguish at his passing. Reading of his exploits and leadership, one can but come to the conclusion that he was a charismatic, natural-born leader. Gen. Hood deplored his loss in a report to Gen. Lee. A fellow officer, Lt. James Cobb, Co. F, 5th Texas, described his comrade's death as "casting a gloom over the whole reg't." "In his death we have suffered a heavy, almost irreparable loss."[6] The death of one thus admired, respected and, theretofore considered invincible could not but have been a serious blow to the morale of all of those of lesser stature hoping just to survive the war.

Although the record is not complete, some evidence suggests that Captain Ike's interment in Georgia was meant to be but a temporary expedient until the war was over. However, it was not until that mission was taken up by the Livingston Sons that the plan was finally carried forth to completion.

What eventually became a plan to bring Capt. "Ike," home first came up during the chapter's formative period in the early 1990s. In the process of organizing, the membership was casting about for projects that would "appeal to and benefit the community." Among a number of suggestions, the question was raised, believe it or not, "Who was Ike Turner and where was he buried?" They did not have a clue; the name had simply been passed

down. It was the name of a predecessor camp established in Livingston by the United Confederate Veterans in the 1890s. When that organization faded away, the origin of many camp titles faded with it. "But at this time, in 1992, none knew much about who Turner was." Gradually, the cause was joined and bits and pieces of the Ike Turner puzzle began to come together.

S.C.V. camp meetings usually occur monthly, at which time there is a business meeting accompanied by refreshments and usually, a guest speaker. At one such meeting, soon after the camp's charter, the speaker was a local historian, Ruth Peebles, who revealed all about Ike Turner's identity. She had, in fact, gone to Georgia in search of the grave. She had been unsuccessful in her quest, but unknown to her until later, she had come within a quarter mile of the site.

The next step in the quest came as a result of an article that appeared in the official publication of the S.C.V., the *Confederate Veteran* magazine. The Houston-based publication dispatched a reporter to Livingston to gather information on the new camp for an

Capt. Ike N. M. Turner, Co. K, 5th Texas, last member of the Texas Brigade to return to Texas, 1995.

article for a later edition. When the article appeared in the magazine, it included mention of the camp's search for Capt. Turner's grave site.

The article was read with interest and captured the imagination of Richard H. Joslyn, a resident of Sparta, Georgia, which is nearby the site of the former Turnwold Plantation. An excursion to the area by Joslyn failed to turn up the sought-after site. However, on a second trip, he chanced upon a farmer who told him of the location of an old, overgrown and abandoned cemetery nearby. Following the directions given him by the fortuitously-placed farmer, he found the elusive cemetery. Entering the gate, nearby in plain sight "was the tombstone of Capt. I. N. M. Turner."[7] After his discovery, Joslyn contacted the Livingston S.C.V. chapter, also providing them with a photograph of the gravesite. After that, things began to move quickly.

With the help and assistance provided by the Old Capitol Camp, 688, S.C.V. of Milledgeville, Georgia, several legal obstacles, mainly related to exhumations, were overcome. Then came the May 11, 1994, date, when with witnesses aplenty and video cameras recording, Capt. Ike's remains were removed from their domain of 131 years standing. From there the remains were removed to the Old Capital Museum in Milledgeville where they lay in state for several months."[8] Draping the simple pine coffin were the Confederate battle flag and the first national flag of the C. S. A. Nearby, a spray of yellow roses of Texas and a photograph of Capt. Ike added to the scene.[9]

On September 24, 1994, an elaborate ceremony was held after the remains were transferred to the St. Stephen's Episcopal Church in Milledgeville. A funeral cortege, including a period horse-drawn hearse, accompanied by over 100 gray-clad Civil War reenactors, wended its way to the church. A twenty-musket salute rattled forth as the casket was transferred inside. A sizeable throng, over 150 by one count, occupied the church pews.

The funeral service itself, interspersed by period hymns and Confederate marches, evoked emotion and tears were in evidence. To Col. Neal, "It was a very emotional upwelling, like I had accomplished something that I had set out to do and that was going to make a difference in the future of the history of the Confederacy and our Southern heritage." The conclusion of the service was the transfer of Capt. Ike's remains to the custody of the Texas S.C.V. s.[10]

The re-interment in Texas soil was scheduled for the 132nd anniversary of Capt. Ike's demise. With several thousand people in attendance, the ceremonies got under way on the morning of April 15, 1995. All during the day prior, Turner's body had lain in state in the Polk County Courthouse in Livingston. The next morning, a funeral procession similar to the one that had occurred in Milledgeville the year prior, made its way through the crowd-lined streets of Livingston to the Old Methodist Church. There, at 11:00 A.M., a funeral service was conducted once more. Presiding over the service was the Rev. Presley Hutchins of Shepherd, Texas. Delivering the eulogy was Dr. B. D. Patterson, Director, Confederate Research Center, Hill College, Hillsboro, Texas.

Following the services, the remains were removed to the J. A. S. Turner Cemetery, nestling among the pines east of Livingston. There, accompanied by Confederate reenactors, infantry, cavalry, military bands, and many interested spectators — among them, this writer — Capt. Turner's remains were recommitted to the earth, presumably for the last time. Said Col. Neal at the time, "These proceedings are being dedicated to the mother of Capt. Ike, Mrs. Martha Eveline Hubert Turner, and to all the mothers of the South whose sons never returned home."[11]

Capt. Ike N. M. Turner, formerly of Co. K, 5th Texas, at his mother's side, was home again at last.

Appendices

A. Companies in Hood's Texas Brigade, A.N.V., Including Local Designations, Original Captains and Where Raised[1]

1st Texas Infantry Regiment

Company A (Marion Rifles)—Capt. Harvey H. Black, Jefferson, Marion County
Company B (Livingston Guards)—Capt. D.D. Moore, Livingston, Polk County
Company C (Palmer Guards)—Capt. A.G. Dickerson, Houston, Harris County
Company D (Star Rifles)—Capt. Albert G. Clopton, Jefferson, Marion County
Company E (Marshall Guards)—Capt. Frederick S. Bass, Marshall, Harrison County
Company F (Woodville Rifles)—Capt. Philip A. Work, Woodville, Tyler County
Company G (Reagan Guards)—Capt. John R. Woodward, Palestine, Anderson County
Company H (Texas Guards)—Capt. Alex. T. Rainey, Palestine, Anderson County
Company I (Crockett Southrons)—Capt. Edwin Currie, Crockett, Houston County
Company K (Texas Invincibles)—Capt. Benjamin F. Benton, St. Augustine, St. Augustine County
Company L (Lone Star Rifles)—Capt. Alfred C. McKeen, Galveston, Galveston County
Company M (Sumpter Light Infantry)—Capt. Howard Ballenger, Sumpter, Trinity County

4th Texas Infantry Regiment

Company A (Hardeman Rifles)—Capt.John C.G. Key, Goliad, Goliad County
Company B (Tom Green Rifles)—Capt. Benjamin F. Carter, Austin, Travis County
Company C (Robertson Five Shooters)—Capt. William P. Townsend, Owensville, Robertson County
Company D (Guadalupe Rangers/Knights of Guadalupe County)—Capt. John P. Bane, Seguin, Guadalupe County
Company E (Lone Star Guards)—Capt. Edw. D. Ryan, Waco, McLennan County
Company F (Mustang Grays)—Capt. Ed. H. Cunningham, San Antonio, Bexar County
Company G (Grimes County Greys)—Capt. John W. Hutcheson, Anderson, Grimes County
Company H (Porter Guards)—Capt. Proctor P. Porter, Huntsville, Walker County
Company I (Navarro Rifles)—Capt. Clinton M. Winkler, Corsicana, Navarro County
Company K (Sandy Point Mounted Rifles)—Capt. William H. Martin, Athens, Henderson County

5th Texas Infantry Regiment

Company A (Bayou City Guards)—Capt. W.B. Botts, Houston, Harris County
Company B (No local designation)—Capt. John C. Upton, Colorado County
Company C (Leon Hunters)—Captain D.M. Whaley, Centerville, Leon County
Company D (Waverly Confederates)—Capt. Robert M. Powell, Walker, Montgomery Counties
Company E (Dixie Blues)—Capt. John D. Rogers, Washington County

Company F (Company Invincibles) — Capt. King Bryan, Washington, Jefferson, Liberty Counties
Company G (Milam County Greys) — Capt. Jefferson C. Rogers, Cameron, Milam County
Company H (Texas Polk Rifles) — Capt. John C. Cleveland, Coldspring; Polk, Liberty Counties
Company I (Texas Aides) — Capt. Jerome B. Robertson, Independence, Washington County
Company K (Polk County Flying Artillery) — Capt. Ike N. M. Turner, Livingston; Polk County

18th Georgia Infantry Regiment

Company A (Acworth Rifles) — Capt. J. B. O'Neill, Cobb County
Company B (Newton Rifles) — Capt. Jos. A. Stuart (or Stewart), Newton County
Company C (Jackson County Volunteers) — Capt. D. L. Jarrett, Jackson County
Company D (Davis Invincibles) — Capt. Samuel D. Irvin, Doutherty County
Company E (Stephens Infantry) — Capt. E. L. Starr, Gordon County
Company F (Davis Guards) — Capt. Joel C. Roper, Sr., Bartow County
Company G (Lewis Volunteers) — Capt. Joh. C. Maddox, Bartow County
Company H (Rowland Highlanders) — Capt. Frank M. Ford, Bartow County
Company I (Dooly Light Infantry) — Capt. Jos. Armsrong, Dooly County
Company K (Rowland Infantry) — Capt. John A. Crawford, Bartow County

Hampton's South Carolina Legion — Infantry Battalion

Company A (Washington Light Infantry Volunteers) — unknown, Charleston
Company B (Watson Guards) — Capt. Martin W. Gary, Charleston
Company C (Manning Guards) — unknown, Columbia
Company D (Gist Rifles) — Capt. Henry J. Smith, Columbia
Company E (Bozeman Guards) — unknown, Columbia
Company F (Davis Guards) — Capt. James S. Austin, Columbia
Company G (Claremont Rifles) — unknown, Columbia
Company H (South Carolina Zouave Volunteers) — Capt. L. Cheves McCord, Charleston

3rd Arkansas Infantry Regiment

Company A (No local name) — Capt. William H. Tebbs, Ashley County
Company B (No local name) — Capt. James H. Capers, Ashley County
Company C (No local name) — Capt. Thomas M. Whittington, Drew County
Company D (No local name) — Capt. Robert S. Taylor, Drew County
Company E (No local name) — Capt. Thomas F. Nolan, Union County
Company F (Hot Springs Hornets) — Capt. Daniel A. Newman, Hot Springs County
Company G (No local name) — Capt. John W. Reedy, Union County
Company H (No local name) — Capt. Samuel V. Reid, Drew County
Company I (Tulip Rifles) — Capt. George D. Alexander, Dallas County
Company K (Arkansas Travelers) — Capt. Van H. Maning, Ashley County
Company L (Rust Guards) — No officers listed, Ashley County

B. "Oh! This is a dreadful war"[1]: Representative Mortality Figures

In her recent book, *This Republic of Suffering*, Drew Gilpin Faust quotes information that places total Union deaths 1861–1865 at 360,222. Because of a dearth of records, Confederate dead have only been estimated at about 285,000, a very rough guess at best. To place Texas Brigade losses in perspective, the estimated total Confederate losses in the battles selected by Col. Simpson are cited from

Frederick Phisterer, *Statistical Record of the Armies of the United States, Campaigns of the Civil War, 1881–1883*, 213–219.

In this book the representative figures relative to Texas Brigade battle losses in six of its major engagements were compiled by Col. Harold Simpson in his *Compendium*, cited frequently in foregoing chapters. One exception is the inclusion of the figures of Surgeon Lafayette Guild, Medical Director of the Army of Northern Virginia, from his after-action report of Sharpsburg found in the *Official Records*. Col. Simpson does not cite the source of his figures. He may have used some of the figures given in the "Opposing Forces" articles contained in the four volume, *Battles and Leaders of the Civil War*. His own extensive research at the National Archives that yielded up the individual information contained in the *Compendium* would, perhaps, have included such information. There is scant information on deaths and injuries suffered during the "bad, dull times" intervening between the big engagements.

So, any attempt to establish exact figures is doomed from the beginning. The following figures from Phisterer and the *Compendium* are cited subject to the foregoing caveats.

Gaines' Mill

The figure quoted from Phisterer of total Confederate losses during the Seven Days Campaign, June 26 through July 1, 1862, is 17,583.[2] At Gaines' Mill, the casualty figures according to Simpson for the 4th Texas were seventy-nine killed, 190 wounded for a total of 269. The 18th Georgia lost twenty-seven killed, 131 wounded, one POW for a total 159 casualties. Casualty figures for the 1st Texas were twenty-one killed, sixty-three wounded, one POW for a total of eighty-five; 5th Texas, twenty-two killed, fifty-five wounded for a total of seventy-seven, Hampton's Legion, three killed, seventeen wounded, one POW for a total of twenty-one. Altogether the Brigade lost at Gaines' Mill 152 men killed, 456 wounded, three POWs, a total of 611 casualties.[3]

Second Manassas

At Groveton, Gainesville and Second Manassas, Phisterer places losses at 10,700.[4] Texas Brigade losses at Second Manassas are placed at 143 killed, 377 wounded, fifty-eight POWs, a total of 578 casualties. A further breakdown shows how the 5th Texas earned its "Bloody 5th " title. Of the 578 total casualties suffered by the Texas Brigade, almost half, or 214, were attributed to the 5th Texas; fifty-four killed, 143 wounded, 17 POWs. The 18th Georgia ran a somewhat distant second with 151 total casualties; third, the 4th Texas with a total of 112 casualties, Hampton's Legion was fourth with seventy total casualties and the 1st Texas was fifth with thirty-one total casualties.[5] It was a costly claim to fame for the Texas Brigade in general and the 5th Texas in particular. In the decimated ranks of the 5th New York Zouaves one private lamented, "I hardly expect to survive another such engagement .... Oh! This is a dreadful war."[6]

Sharpsburg

Phisterer places Confederate losses at Antietam at 25,899.[7] Surgeon Lafayette Guild was the medical director of the Army of Northern Virginia. His report in the aftermath of Sharpsburg listed a total of 1,567 killed, 8,724 wounded for a total of 10,291. The losses of the Texas Brigade in order of severity are listed as: 1st Texas, forty-five killed, 141 wounded, a total of 186; 4th Texas, ten killed, ninety-seven wounded, a total of 107; 18th Georgia; thirteen killed, seventy-two wounded, a total of eighty-five; 5th Texas, five killed, seventy-seven wounded, a total of eighty-two; Hampton's Legion, six killed, forty-seven wounded, a total of fifty-three; Reilly's battery, two killed, eight wounded, a total of ten.[8]

Col. Simpson's figures show a total of 137 killed, 361 wounded, 99 P.O.W.s for a total of 597. In the 1st Texas, fifty-seven are listed as killed, 130 wounded, twenty-three P.O.W.s, a total of 210; in the 4th Texas, thirty-two are listed as killed, eighty-three wounded, thirty-nine P.O.W.s; a total of 154; in the 5th Texas, twenty-one are listed as killed, forty-six wounded, nineteen P.O.W.s for a total of eighty-six lost. In the 18th Georgia sixteen are listed killed, fifty-seven wounded, twelve

P.O.W.s, for a total of eighty-five. In Hampton's Legion, eleven were killed, forty-five wounded, six P.O.W.s, for a total of sixty-two.[9]

Fredericksburg

Phisterer lists 4,576 Confederate casualties.[10] Col. Simpson does not list any figures for this battle in which the Texas Brigade was not engaged. However, in *B&L*, Brigade losses, reflecting their reserve status, are placed at one killed, four wounded.[11]

Gettysburg

Phisterer places Confederate losses at 31,621.[12] By this time, the 18th Georgia and Hampton's Legion had been detached from the Texas Brigade and the 3rd Arkansas had joined. Simpson places Texas Brigade losses at, 1st Texas, thirty killed, fifty wounded, forty-five P.O.W.s, total 125; 4th Texas, twenty-five killed, fifty-seven wounded, fifty-eight P.O.W.s, total 140. 5th Texas: thirty-seven killed, 102 wounded, 115 P.O.W.s, total 254; and, 3rd Arkansas: thirty-three killed, seventy-one wounded, eighty-three P.O.W.s, total 187. The brigade aggregate totaled 706 killed, wounded or prisoners-of-war.[13]

Chickamauga

Phisterer places Confederate losses at 17,804.[14] Casualties for the Texas Brigade on September 19–20, 1863, were heavy. The 1st Texas lost thirty-nine killed, 122 wounded and nine P.O.W.s, for a total of 170. The 4th Texas lost thirty-four killed, forty wounded, and three P.O.W.s, for a total of seventy-seven. The 5th Texas lost twenty-two killed, sixty-six wounded, and eight P.O.W.s, for a total of ninety-six. The 3rd Arkansas lost 5 killed, fifty-two wounded, and ten P.O.W.s, for a total of sixty-seven. Combined casualty figures for the brigade was 100 killed, 280 wounded and thirty P.O.W.s, for a total of 410.[15]

The Wilderness

Phisterer places Confederate losses, at 11,400.[16] In the Texas Brigade, Simpson lists eighty-five killed, 331 wounded, twenty-four prisoners-of-war for a total of 440.[17] In the 3rd Arkansas alone "[e]very officer save two ... was dead or wounded.... The total number of unwounded men was ninety.... They had left nearly sixty-five percent of their men in the tangled thickets of the Wilderness."[18] For an 800 man brigade, that was over a fifty percent casualty rate.

Although Phisterer estimates Confederate loss figures until the end of the war, Confederate records are so lacking that it is not possible to establish those losses with any degree of accuracy. Col. Simpson does not list casualty figures beyond this point.

Surrender at Appomattox

Col. Simpson estimated that about 5,300 men had enlisted during the course of the war in the four regiments comprising the brigade at the end. At variance somewhat with Freeman's figures, Simpson said that at Appomattox, 617 were paroled. "Thus, some 4,700 members of the old Brigade had been killed in battle, had died of disease, had been invalided home due to sickness or crippling wounds, or had been discharged for being either over or under age—but few had deserted." Col. Robert M. Powell, with five staff officers, commanded the brigade at the end, Col. Frederick S. Bass, with sixteen officers and 153 enlisted commanded the 1st Texas, Lt. Col. Clinton M. Winkler, with fifteen officers and 143 enlisted, commanded the 4th Texas, Col. William T. Hill, with thirteen officers and 148 enlisted, commanded the 5th Texas and Lt. Col. Robert S. Taylor, with fifteen officers and 129 enlisted, commanded the 3rd Arkansas.[19]

C. Deaths by Disease in the Texas Regiments

Col. Simpson lists regimentally deaths attributable to disease. The diseases he lists include, typhoid fever, respiratory diseases, measles, digestive and intestinal diseases, smallpox, neurological diseases, other diseases (venereal disease, typhus, malaria, heart attack, cholera, rheumatism and old age) and, leading the pack, unknown. In the 1st Texas, 189 deaths attributable to disease, a 12 percent casualty rate. In the 4th Texas, eighty-seven deaths listed, 11.9 percent casualty rate. In the 5th Texas, 293 deaths by disease, a 14.8 percent casualty rate.[1]

Chapter Notes

Preface

1. W. D. Pritchard (Co. I, 1st Texas), unpublished typescript of a series of newspaper articles that appeared in the Crockett, Texas, *Courier,* circa 1898 or 1899, No. 2, Texas Brigade file, Antietam National Battlefield Park, Sharpsburg, MD. Hereinafter cited according to the article number appearing on the typescript.

2. http://www.nytimes.com/2012/04/03/science/civil-war-toll-up-by-20-percent-in-new-estimate.html?_r=1&pagewanted=all

3. J. M. Polk (Co. I, 1st Texas), *The North and South American Review* (Austin: Von Boeckmann-Jones, 1912), 15.

Introduction

1. Quoted from a letter written by Gen. Robert E. Lee to Senator Louis T. Wigfall in Harold B. Simpson, "Hood's Texas Brigade: A Biographical Sketch." Address delivered before the Texas Sesquicentennial Civil War Symposium on Hood's Texas Brigade, Fort Worth, TX, May 31, 1986. Confederate Research Center, Hill College, Hillsboro, TX, Hood's Texas Brigade File 8–2, 7. Hereafter referred to as C.R.C., H.C., H.T.B. files. This introductory chapter appeared, in part, in the Summer 1996 edition of *Heritage Magazine,* published by the Texas Historical Foundation, Austin, TX.

2. Ibid., 12–13.

3. Harold B. Simpson, *Hood's Texas Brigade: Lee's Grenadier Guard* (Waco, TX: Texian Press, 1970), 9.

4. Cooper K. Ragan, "Tyler County Goes to War: Company F, First Texas Regiment, C.S.A." Tyler County Dogwood Festival, Woodville, TX, Saturday, March 25, 1961, n.p.

5. Frank B. Chilton, comp. (Co. H, 4th Texas), *Unveiling and Dedication of Monument to Hood's Texas Brigade and Minutes of the Thirty-ninth Annual Reunion of Hood's Texas Brigade Association* (Houston: Chilton, 1911), n.p.

6. Harold B. Simpson, *Hood's Texas Brigade in Reunion and Memory* (Hillsboro, TX: Hill Junior College Press, 1974), xii.

7. Chilton, *Unveiling and Dedication of Monument to Hood's Texas Brigade,* 29.

8. Joseph B. Polley (Co. F, 4th Texas), *Hood's Texas Brigade: Its Marches, Its Battles, Its Achievements* (1910, reprint, Gaithersburg, MD: Butternut Press, 1984), 287. Hood's Texas Brigade Association was reactivated in 1966 for descendants of the original members. It meets every other year.

9. Simpson, *Hood's Texas Brigade,* title page.

Chapter 1—Texas Leaves the Federal Union

1. J. K. F. Blackburn, "Reminiscences of the Terry's Rangers," *Southwestern Historical Quarterly* 22 (July 1918): 39. Hereinafter, *S.W.H.Q.*

2. Caroline Baldwin Darrow, "Recollections of the Twiggs Surrender," in *Battles and Leaders of the Civil War,* Robert U. Johnson and Clarence C. Buel, eds. (New York: Yoseloff, 1956), I:33–39. Hereafter referred to as *B&L.*

3. Douglas S. Freeman, *Robert E. Lee: A Biography.* Vol. 1 (New York: Charles Scribner's Sons, 1934), 437.

4. Darrow, "Recollections of the Twiggs Surrender," in *B&L,* I:33.

5. Dudley G. Wootan, "The Texas Ordinance of Secession," in B.P. Gallaway, ed., *Texas: The Dark Corner of the Confederacy* (Lincoln: University of Nebraska Press, 1994), 75.

6. Simpson, *Hood's Texas Brigade,* 1.

7. Anna I. Sandbo, "The First Session of the Secession Convention in Texas," in Eugene C. Barker, ed., *History of Dallas* (Dallas: Southwest Press, 1929), quoted in Simpson, *Hood's Texas Brigade,* 2.

8. Wootan, "The Texas Ordinance of Secession," 77.

9. William C. Davis, *Jefferson Davis: The Man and His Hour* (New York: Harper Collins, 1991), 308.

10. J. J. Bowden, *Exodus of Federal Forces in Texas* (Austin: Eakin Press, 1986), 3.

11. Frederick L. Olmstead, "San Antonio Before the War," in *Texas: The Dark Corner of the Confederacy,* 26–28, 31–32.

12. George Ballentine, *Autobiography of an English Soldier in the United States Army,* William H. Goetzmann, ed. (Chicago: Lakeside Press, 1986), 150.

13. Freeman, *Robert E. Lee*, I: 417.

14. Jean T. Heidler, "Embarrassing Situation: David E. Twiggs and the Surrender of United States Forces in Texas, 1861," in Ralph A. Wooster, ed., *Lone Star Blue and Gray: Essays on Texas in the Civil War* (Austin: Texas State Historical Association, 1995), 31–32. Hereafter, *Lone Star Blue and Gray*.

15. Ibid.

16. Ibid., 37.

17. U.S. War Department, comp., *The War of the Rebellion: A Compilation of the Official Records of the Union and Confederate Armies*, Ser. 1, Vol. I, 506. Hereinafter, O.R.

18. Ibid., 507.

19. O.R., Ser. 1, Vol. 1, 509.

20. Ibid.

21. Russell K. Brown, "An Old Woman with a Broomstick," *Military Affairs* (April 1984): 58–59.

22. Ibid., 59.

23. James P. Newcomb, *Sketch of Secession Times in Texas* (San Francisco: n.p., 1863), 6.

24. Darrow, "Recollections of the Twiggs Surrender," *B&L*, I:35.

25. "Report of Lieut. Col. Wm. Hoffman, Eighth U.S. Infantry…," O.R., Ser. 1, Vol. 1, 517.

26. Ibid., "Report of Bvt. Maj. Larkin Smith, Eighth U.S. Infantry…," 519–520.

27. J. K. P. Blackburn, "Reminiscences of the Terry Rangers," *Southwestern Historical Quarterly* 22 (July 1918): 39.

28. Heidler, "Embarrassing Situation," 39–40.

29. San Antonio *Triweekly Alamo Express*, "A Sad Day to San Antonio, Evacuation of the U.S. Troops, Feeling of the People," Monday, February 19, 1861.

30. Ibid., "Birthday of Washington," Saturday, February 23, 1861. In May 1861, the *Triweekly Alamo Express* building was burned and its presses destroyed by some rangers and Knights of the Golden Circle. See Newcomb, *Sketch of Secession Times in Texas,* 10.

31. Darrow, "Recollections of the Twiggs Surrender," I, 33.

32. Simpson, *Hood's Texas Brigade,* 2.

33. John W. Thomason, *Lone Star Preacher* (Fort Worth: Texas Christian University Press, 1992), 55–57.

34. "Surrender of United States Property by General Twiggs," *Harper's Weekly,* 9 March 1861.

35. Brown, "An Old Woman with a Broomstick," 60.

36. Thomas W. Cutrer, *Ben McCulloch and the American Frontier Tradition* (Chapel Hill: University of North Carolina Press, 1993), 304.

Chapter 2 — On to Richmond, Texas-Style

1. John W. Stevens (Co. K, 5th Texas), *Reminiscences of the Civil War* (Hillsboro, Texas: Hillsboro Mirror Print, 1902), 8.

2. Oscar J. Downs (Co. E, 4th Texas), unpublished diary, 1, C.R.C., H.C., H.T.B. file 2–10.

3. Harold B. Simpson, *Hood's Texas Brigade: A Compendium* (1977; reprint, Fort Worth: Landmark, 1999), 124.

4. Pritchard (Co. I, 1st Texas), No. 2, A.N.B.P.

5. Ibid.

6. See Simpson, *Compendium,* 249. Stevens is shown as enlisting March 9, 1862, but his memoirs indicate he was there from the beginning in the summer of 1861.

7. Stevens (Co. K, 5th Texas), *Reminiscences,* 11.

8. Ibid.

9. Stevens (Co. K, 5th Texas), *Reminiscences,* 12.

10. Calvin L. Collier, *They'll Do To Tie To* (Little Rock, AK: Pioneer Press, 1959), 10.

11. Ibid., 11.

12. D. H. Hamilton (Co. M, 1st Texas), *History of Company M, First Texas Volunteer Infantry, Hood's Texas Brigade* (Waco, TX: Morrison, 1962), 17–18.

13. Harold B. Simpson, "The Recruiting, Training, and Camp Life of a Company of Hood's Brigade in Texas, 1861," *Texas Military History* 2 (August 1962): 186.

14. Bruce Catton, "Hayfoot, Strawfoot," *American Heritage* 8 (April 1957): 31–32.

15. Donald E. Everett, ed., *Chaplain Davis and Hood's Texas Brigade* (Baton Rouge: Louisiana State University Press, 1962), 34.

16. Downs (Co. E, 4th Texas), unpublished diary, 3. C.R.C., H.C., H.T.B. file 2–10.

17. Campbell Wood (Co. D, 5th Texas), typescript of unpublished papers, C.R.C., H.C., H.T.B. file 3–32.

18. Downs (Co. E, 4th Texas), unpublished diary, 4. C.R.C., H.C., H.T.B. file 2–10.

19. Ibid.

20. Wood (Co. D, 5th Texas), typescript of unpublished papers, C.R.C., H.C., H.T.B. file 3–32.

21. Basil C. Brashear (Co. F, 5th Texas), typescript of unpublished manuscript, C.R.C., H.C., H.T.B. file 3–6.

22. Decimus et Ultimus Barziza (Co. C, 4th Texas), *Adventures of a P.O.W.*, R. Henderson Shuffler, ed. (Austin: University of Texas Press, 1964), 21.

23. Miles V. Smith (Co. D, 4th Texas), *Reminiscences of the Civil War*, photocopied booklet Civil War Miscellaneous Collection, U.S. Army Military History Institute, Carlisle Barracks, PA, 4.

24. "From Texas," Richmond *Enquirer*, Sunday, October 5, 1861.

25. Wood (Co. D, 5th Texas), unpublished typescript, C.R.C., H.C., H.T.B. file 3–32.

26. Ibid.

27. Wood (Co. D, 5th Texas), unpublished typescript, C.R.C., H.C., H.T.B. file 3–32.

28. Mark J. Smither (Co. D, 5th Texas), to his mother, September 12, 1861, Richmond, Virginia, 1. C.R.C., H.C., H.T.B., file 3–29.

29. Virginius Dabney, *Richmond: The Story of a City* (New York: Doubleday, 1976), 163.

30. Ibid., 159.

31. Dabney, *Richmond,* 162.

32. O. T. Hanks (Co. K, 1st Texas), *History of Captain B.F. Benton's Company, 1861–1865,* unpublished typescript, 2–3. C.R.C., H.C., H.T.B. file 1–9.

33. Val C. Giles (Co. B, 4th Texas), *Rags and Hope,* Mary Lasswell, ed. and comp., (New York: Coward-McCann, 1961), 23.

34. Pritchard (Co. I, 1st Texas), No. 6, A.N.B.P.

35. Ibid.

36. George T. Todd (Co. A, 1st Texas), *First Texas Regiment* (Waco, TX: Texian Press, 1963), 3.

37. From "General Orders," unit file, Co. D, 18th Georgia, July 20, 1861, Georgia Department of Archives & History. Hereinafter, G.D.A.H.

38. Pritchard (Co. I, 1st Texas), No. 7.

39. Stevens (Co. F, 5th Texas), *Reminiscences,* 15.

40. Ibid., 16.

41. Smith (Co. D, 4th Texas), *Reminiscences,* 5.

42. Everett, *Chaplain Davis ,* 44.

Chapter 3 — An Anatomy of the Brigade

1. Hamilton (Co. M, 1st Texas), *History,* 30.

2. Lloyd Lewis, *Sherman: Fighting Prophet* (1932; reprint, New York: Konecky and Konecky, 1993), 138.

3. Simpson, *Compendium,* 540. Without explication, J. S. W. Cooke is listed as the only member of the brigade to be conscripted, he into Co. B, 4th Texas. Simpson records that as having happened at Culpepper Court House, Virginia, on June 6, 1862.

4. See Harold B. Simpson, ed., "'Whip the Devil and His Hosts': The Civil War Letters of Eugene O. Perry," *Chronicles of Smith County,* Fall 1967, 11.

5. Although the Perry letters were edited by Col. Simpson, he does not include George F. Perry in his *Compendium.* He does list Sidney Franklin Perry (Bose) who enlisted on the same day and at the same place as the other three Perry brothers. Presumably, this is the fourth brother. See Simpson, *Compendium,* 42.

6. Simpson, "Whip the Devil and His Hosts," 11.

7. Cooper K. Ragan, "Tyler County Goes to War," *Texas Military History* 1, no. 3 (November 1961), republished from Tyler County Dogwood Festival brochure, "Gone Are the Days," Saturday, March 25, 1961.

8. Harold B. Simpson, "The Navarro Rifles," *Navarro County Scroll* (Corsicana, TX: Navarro County Historical Society, 1965), n.p.

9. William A. Fletcher (Co. F, 5th Texas), *Rebel Private, Front and Rear* (1908. Reprint, Washington, DC: Zenger, 1954), 6–7.

10. See Simpson, *Compendium,* 167.

11. Ibid., 210–217.

12. Ibid., 213.

13. See Gerard A. Patterson, *Rebels From West Point* (New York: Doubleday, 1987), 160. Lt. Col. McLeod graduated fifty-sixth in the fifty-six member class of 1835.

14. See Robert K. Krick, *Lee's Colonels: A Biographical Register of Field Officers of the Army of*

Northern Virginia (Dayton, OH: Morningside Press, 1992), 255–256.

15. "In Memory of the Late Col. Hugh McLeod of the 1st Texas Regiment," *The State Gazette,* Austin, TX, February 1, 1862.

16. James H. Hendricks (Co. E, 1st Texas), to his mother, March 13, 1863, in Hugh I. Powers, "A Texan at War: Letters of Private James Hendrick A. N. V.," Texas Brigade files, A.N.B.P. Also, C.R.C., H.C., H.T.B. file 1–10.

17. Gen. Hood received a similar gift from the 4th Texas while in command of that regiment.

18. Robert V. Foster (Co. C, 4th Texas), to Lida, March 18, 1862, Fredericksburg, Virginia, C.R.C., H.C., H.T.B. file 2–13.

19. W. S. Oldham, "Colonel John Marshall," *S.W.H.Q.,* 20: October 1916, 136–137.

20. Ibid., 137.

21. For biographical sketches of the 4th Texas leadership, see Everett, *Chaplain Davis,* 148- 173.

22. Simpson, *Hood's Texas Brigade,* 120.

23. Giles (Co. B, 4th Texas), *Rags and Hope,* ed. and comp., Lasswell, 176–177.

24. See "Brig. Gen. James J. Archer," *Confederate Veteran* 8, no. 2 (February 1900): 65–67.

25. Tacitus T. Clay (Co. I, 5th Texas), to Bettie Clay, October 6, 1861, Richmond, Virginia, "War Letters of Captain Tacitus Clay, C.S.A.," 2, ed. Judy and Nath Winfield, in Miscellaneous Confederate Files, Vol. 131, Fredericksburg National Military Park, Fredericksburg, Virginia. Hereinafter, F.N.B.P.M.C.F.

26. Watson Dugat Williams (Co. F, 5th Texas), to Laura, October 7, 1861, C.R.C., H.C., H.T.B. file 3–31.

27. James J. Archer (5th Texas), to his brother, Robert, December 18, 1861, Dumfries, Virginia, C.R.C., H.C., H.T.B. file 3–2.

28. James J. Archer (5th Texas), to his brother, Robert, January 8, 1862, in C. A. Porter Hopkins, ed., "The James J. Archer Letters," *Maryland Historical Magazine* 52, no. 2 (June 1961): 125.

29. Ibid., 126.

30. James J. Archer (5th Texas), to his brother, Robert, May 8, 1862, New Kent Courthouse, Virginia, in Hopkins, "The James J. Archer Letters," *Maryland Historical Magazine,* 133.

31. Ibid., to his brother, Robert, May 13, 1862, New Kent Courthouse, Virginia., 134.

32. Rufus K. Felder (Co. E, 5th Texas), to his mother, March 3, 1862, Richmond, Virginia, C.R.C., H.C., H.T.B. file 3–13.

33. Nicholas Pomeroy (Co. A, 5th Texas), *Reminiscences of the American War, 1861—1865,* in the Barker Center for American History University of Texas, Austin, Texas, unpublished, no date. Pomeroy was wounded at Gettysburg, held as a prisoner of war at Fort McHenry, Maryland. He was exchanged and returned to the brigade at Chattanooga. He survived the war. Both Capt. Farmer and Lt. Fuller, although receiving wounds, seem to have survived the war. See Simpson, *Compendium,* 174–175.

34. Val C. Giles (Co. B, 4th Texas), "Capt. J. D.

Roberdeau," *Confederate Veteran* 18, no. 9 (September 1910): 439.

35. Ibid., 440.

36. See Simpson, *Compendium*, 243.

37. Gen. Hood to Gen. Lee, April 29, 1863, Suffolk, Virginia, in Charles Venable Papers, University of North Carolina, Chapel Hill. Hereinafter U.N.C.C.H., S.H.C.

38. J. A. Howard (Co. B, 5th Texas), to his father, April 15, 1863, Suffolk, Virginia, in Howard Family Papers, U.N.C.C.H., S.H.C.

39. James E. Cobb (Co. F, 5th Texas), Diary, in the Cobb-Hunter Family Papers, U.N.C.C.H., S.H.C.

40. The seven counties included Bartow, Cobb, Dooley, Dougherty, Gordon, Jackson and Newton. See Simpson, *Compendium*, 323.

41. Krick, *Lee's Colonels*, 328.

42. Ibid., 209–210.

43. *Spirit of '61*, 18th Georgia regimental newspaper in Woodruff Library, Emory University, Atlanta.

44. Pritchard (Co. I, 1st Texas), No. 10.

45. Joseph H. Crute, Jr., *Units of the Confederate States Army* (Gaithersburg, MD: Olde Soldier Books, 1987), 96–97.

46. Simpson, *Compendium*, 397.

47. John Cox (Co. F, Hampton's South Carolina Legion), "Wade Hampton," *Confederate Veteran* 30, no. 12 (December 1922): 460.

48. Gerard A. Patterson, *Rebels from West Point* (New York: Doubleday, 1987), ix.

49. See Krick, *Lee's Colonels*, 255–256, 312.

50. Frank E. Vandiver, *Rebel Brass: The Confederate Command System* (Baton Rouge: Louisiana State University Press, 1984), 12.

51. See Simpson, *Compendium*, 3–4.

52. W. C. Nunn, ed., *Ten Texans in Gray* (Hillsboro, TX: Hill Junior College Press, 1968), 181.

53. Joseph B. Polley (Co. F, 4th Texas), *A Soldier's Letters to Charming Nellie* (1908. Reprint, Gaithersburg, MD: Butternut Press; 1984), 17–18.

54. Robert Gaston (Co. H, 1st Texas), to his sister, July 23, 1861, C.R.C., H.C., H.T.B., file 1–7B.

55. Hendrick (Co. E, 1st Texas), to his mother, in Hugh I. Powers, Jr., Texas Brigade file, A.N.B.P. and C.R.C., H.C., H.T.B. file 1–10.

56. See Ezra Warner, *Generals in Gray* (Baton Rouge: Louisiana State University Press, 1959), 11.

57. After recuperating from the loss of his right leg as a result of a wound received at Chickamauga in September 1863, Hood was appointed a corps commander in Gen. Joseph E. Johnston's Army of Tennessee. In the opposing Federal army, commanded by Gen. William T. Sherman, were Hood's former classmates, Schofield and McPherson. Also, serving in the Federal army was Gen. George H. Thomas, with whom Hood had served in the U.S. 2nd Cavalry just prior to the war. Hood's reverses in Georgia and Tennessee are sometimes attributed, in part, to his former friends' knowledge of his personality and tendency to recklessness.

58. J. T. Hunter (Co. H, 4th Texas), "Lieut. Gen. John B. Hood," *Confederate Veteran* 24, no. 2 (June 1916): 257.

59. Mrs. A. V. Winkler, *The Confederate Capital and Hood's Texas Brigade* (1894; reprint, Baltimore: Butternut and Blue, 1991), 295.

60. Ibid., 74–75.

61. Polk (Co. I, 4th Texas), *The North and South American Review*, 32.

62. Polley (Co. F, 4th Texas), *Hood's Texas Brigade*, 204.

63. Todd (Co. A, 1st Texas), *First Texas Regiment*, 18.

64. See Warner, *Generals in Gray*, 343–344.

65. See Harold B. Simpson, ed., *Touched with Valor: Civil War Papers and Casualty Reports of Hood's Texas Brigade* (Hillsboro, TX: Hill Junior College Press, 1964).

66. Polley (Co. F, 4th Texas), *Hood's Texas Brigade*, 142.

67. Ibid., 142–143.

68. B. I. Franklin (Co. I, 5th Texas), to his wife, Mary, August 8, 1863, Fredericksburg, Virginia, C.R.C., H.C., H.T.B. file 3–15.

69. Ibid., to his wife, Mary, October 2, 1863, Chattanooga, Tennessee.

70. See, "Charges and Specifications Against Brig. Gen. J. B. Robertson," in Garnett Andrews Papers, U.N.C.C.H., S.H.C.

71. See Warner, *Generals in Gray*, 118–119.

72. Harry McCorry Henderson, *Texas in the Confederacy* (San Antonio: Naylor, 1955), 39.

73. A. C. Jones (3rd Arkansas), "Brig. Gen. John Gregg," *Confederate Veteran* 17, no. 6 (June 1909): 269.

74. "Death of Gen. Gregg," Marshall, Texas, *Republican*, January 13, 1865. Some sources give Gen. Gregg's place of death as having been on the Charles City Road.

75. See Krick, *Lee's Colonels*, 48, and Simpson, *Compendium*, 2.

76. See, Krick, *Lee's Colonels*, 308–309, and Simpson, *Compendium*, 4.

77. See, Warner, *Generals in Gray*, 334–335.

78. Ibid., 87–88.

79. See Warner, *Generals in Gray*, 192–193.

80. John M. Smither (Co. D, 5th Texas), to his mother, May 12, 1863, Frederick Hall, Virginia, C.R.C., H.C., H.T.B. file, 3–29.

81. Edward Porter Alexander, *Military Memoirs of a Confederate* (1907. Reprint, New York: Da Capo Press, 1993), 110–111.

82. Ibid., 111.

83. Stevens (Co. K, 5th Texas), *Reminiscences*, 63.

84. William A. Kenyon (Co. A, Hampton's Legion), to his brother, Bob, January 22, 1862, Moses W. Kenyon Papers, Perkins Library, Duke University, Winston-Salem, NC. Hereafter referred to as D.U.P.L.

85. Robert H. Gaston (Co. H, 1st Texas), to his parents, July 30, 1861, Richmond, Virginia, C.R.C., H.C., H.T.B. file 1–7B.

86. Ralph A. Wooster and Robert Wooster, "'Rarin' for a Fight': Texans in the Confederate Army," *S.W.H.Q.* 84 (April 1981): 54.

87. A. C. Jones (3rd Arkansas), "A Veteran's Refutation of the 'Dense Ignorance' Charge," *Confederate Veteran* 17, no. 3 (March 1909): 108.

88. Bell I. Wiley, *The Life of Johnny Reb* (New York: Bobbs-Merrill, 1943), 335.

89. James I. Robertson, *Soldiers Blue and Gray* (Columbia: University of South Carolina Press, 1988),122.

90. Giles (Co. B, 4th Texas) *Rags and Hope*, 119–120.

91. Stevens (Co. K, 5th Texas), *Reminiscences,* 17.

92. Randolph H. McKim, "Glimpses of the Confederate Army," *American Review of Reviews* 43 (April 1911): 434.

93. Hamilton, *History of Co. M,* 30.

Chapter 4 — From the Potomac to the Peninsula, July 1861–June 1862

1. Judith N. McArthur and Orville V. Burton, eds., *A Gentleman and an Officer* (New York: Oxford University Press, 1996), 144.

2. Thomason, *Lone Star Preacher,* 93.

3. Pritchard (Co. I, 1st Texas), No. 11, A.N.B.P.

4. W. C. Collins to the Marshall, Texas, *Republican,* Saturday, October 26, 1861. Rev. Collins was discharged as "non-conscripted clergy," in August 1862.

5. Mark J. Smither (Co. D, 5th Texas), to an aunt, January 17, 1862, Camp Neabsco near Potomac, Prince William County, Virginia, C.R.C, H. ., H.T.B. file 3–29.

6. Smith (Co. D, 4th Texas), *Reminiscences,* 5.

7. Robert H. Gaston (Co. H, 1st Texas), to his sister, Priscilla, November 5, 1861, Camp Quantico, Virginia, C.R.C., H.C., H.T.B. file 1–7b.

8. Pritchard (Co. I, 1st Texas), No. 12, A.N.B.P.

9. Polley (Co. F, 4th Texas), *A Soldier's Letters,* 16

10. Pomoroy (Co. A, 5th Texas), *Reminiscences,* 9.

11. Harold B. Simpson, *Gaines' Mill to Appomattox* (Waco, TX: Texian Press, 1988), 55.

12. Pritchard (Co. I, 1st Texas), unpublished typescript, No. 7, A.N.B.P.

13. Ibid. Simpson's *Compendium* lists an Elisha B. Andrews as a member of Co. I. He was wounded at Gaines' Mill and eventually captured on the retreat to Appomattox on April 4, 1865.

14. J. M. T. to Mr. Loughery in the Marshall, Texas, *Republican,* Saturday, November 9, 1861.

15. Robert V. Foster (Co. C, 4th Texas), to his sister, Eliza, January 17, 1862, C.R.C., H.C., H.T.B. file 2–13.

16. "J. M. T." (Co. E, 1st Texas), "Letter from the Marshall Guards," Marshall *Republican,* October 8, 1861, Camp McLeod, Virginia.

17. John Coxe (Hampton's Legion), "Bloody Night Affair at Colchester, Va.," *Confederate Veteran* 23, no. 4 (April 1915), 168.

18. For information on the 37th New York, see Frederick Phisterer, comp., *New York in the War of the Rebellion* (Albany: Weed, Parsons, 1890), 400–401.

19. McArthur and Burton, *A Gentleman and an Officer,* 144.

20. "The Brave Texans Scouts — Gen. Whiting's Special Order," Richmond *Dispatch,* Thursday, February 6, 1862.

21. David Donald, "The Confederate as a Fighting Man," *Journal of Southern History* 25, no. 2 (May 1959): 181

22. Pritchard (Co. I, 1st Texas), No. 25, A.N.B.P.

23. Ibid., No. 15, A.N.B.P.

24. R. H. Gaston (Co. H, 1st Texas), to his mother and father, April 26, 1862, Richmond, Virginia, C.R.C., H.C., H.T.B. file 1–7b

25. Ibid.

26. John F. McKee (Co. K, 5th Texas), to his sister, Vashti, April 27, 1862, Yorktown, Virginia, C.R.C., H.C., H.T.B. file 3–24. This letter was one among several that appeared under the title "Old Letters Tell Appealing Story of Texas Lad Who Died for the South," by Hubert Mitchell, Houston *Chronicle,* Sunday, May 30, 1937.

27. William J. Hardee, *Rifle and Light Infantry Tactics* (New York: Kane, 1862), 22–25. Quick-time is defined as 165–180 steps per minute. At 189 steps per minute, 4,000 yards could be covered in about twenty-five minutes. Burdened troops can not keep that pace for very long.

28. A. A. Congleton (Co. I, 1st Texas), to his brother, March 22, 1862, Fredericksburg, Virginia, Texas Brigade File, A.N.B.P.

29. Robert H. Gaston (Co. H, 1st Texas), to his parents, April 26, 1862, Richmond, Virginia, C.R.C., H.C., H.T.B. file 1–7 b

30. Congleton (Co. I, 1st Texas), to unspecified recipient, April 6, 1862, Fredericksburg, Virginia, Texas Brigade file, A.N.B.P.

31. Ibid.

32. Winkler, *The Confederate Capital,* 50.

33. Ibid.

34. Winkler, *The Confederate Capital,* 51.

35. Pritchard (Co. I, 1st Texas), No. 18, A.N.B.P.

36. J. H. L., "Hood Feeling the Enemy," *B&L,* Vol. 2, 276

37. Pritchard (Co. I, 1st Texas), No. 19, A.N.B.P.

38. Ibid., No. 19.

39. Smith (Co. D, 4th Texas), *Reminiscences,* U.S. A.M.H.I.M.C., 9.

40. Pritchard (Co. I, 1st Texas), unpublished typescript, No. 17, A.N.B.P.

41. Robert H. Gaston (Co. H, 1st Texas), to his parents, May 19, 1862, Richmond, Virginia, C.R.C., H.C., H.T.B. file 1–7b.

42. Pomoroy (Co. A, 5th Texas), *Reminiscences,* 24–25.

43. Polley (Co. F, 4th Texas), *Hood's Texas Brigade,* 33.

44. Fletcher (Co. F, 5th Texas), *Rebel Private,* 1954.

45. Pritchard (Co. I, 1st Texas), No. 21, A.N.B.P.

46. William P. Powell (Co. D, 5th Texas), to his parents, July 19, 1862, C.R.C., H.C., H.T.B. file 3–26.

47. Pritchard (Co. I, 1st Texas), No. 21, A.N.B.P.

Chapter 5—The 4th Texas and 18th Georgia at Gaines' Mill, Virginia, June 27, 1862

1. Smith (Co. D, 4th Texas), *Reminiscences*, 13.
2. See, D.H. Hill, "Lee's Attack North of the Chickahominy," *B&L*, Vol. 2, 347–348.
3. Polley (Co. F, 4th Texas), *Hood's Texas Brigade*, 38.
4. Polley (Co. F, 4th Texas), *A Soldier's Letters*, 52–53.
5. William R. Hamby, "Fourth Texas in Battle of Gaines' Mill," *Confederate Veteran* 14, no. 4 (April 1906): 183.
6. Smith (Co. D, 4th Texas), *Reminiscences*, 14.
7. Stevens (Co. K, 5th Texas), *Reminiscences*, 25.
8. For Gen. A. P. Hill's after-action report, see, O.R., Ser. 1, Vol. 11, 834–836.
9. Ibid., "Reports of Gen. Robert E. Lee," 491–493.
10. "Reports of Maj. Gen. Ambrose P. Hill," O.R., Ser. 1, Vol. 11, 836–837.
11. Barziza (Co. C, 4th Texas), *Adventures*, 26–28.
12. Polley (Co. F, 4th Texas), *Hood's Texas Brigade*, 41.
13. Ibid., 40.
14. Hamby (Co. B, 4th Texas), "Fourth Texas in Battle of Gaines' Mill," *Confederate Veteran* 14, no. 4 (April 1906): 184–185.
15. Granville Crozier (Co. B, 4th Texas), "A Private with General Hood," *Confederate Veteran* 25, no. 12 (December 1917): 556–557.
16. Polley (Co. F, 4th Texas), "Brave Texans in the Virginia Army," *Confederate Veteran* 5, no. 5 (May 1896): 158–159.
17. Leonidas Holliday (Co. E, 5th Texas), to his father, July 1, 1862, in "Another Account of the Great Battle of the 27th," Galveston *Tri-Weekly News*, Tuesday, July 29, 1862. Col. Simpson's *Compendium* lists an R. W. Pearson in that unit as being killed at Gaines' Mill.
18. Polley (Co. F, 4th Texas), "Brave Texans in the Virginia Army," *Confederate Veteran* 5, no. 5 (May 1896): 158–159.
19. Crozier (Co. B, 4th Texas), "A Private with General Hood," *Confederate Veteran* 25, no. 12 (December 1917): 556–557.
20. See Giles (Co. B, 4th Texas), *Rags and Hope*, 110–112.
21. Campbell (Co. A, 5th Texas), "A Lone Star in Virginia," *Civil War Times Illustrated*, December 2000, 88. Hereinafter, *C.W.T.I.*
22. Chickahominie, "The Eighteenth Georgia Regiment," Richmond *Whig*, Thursday, July 10, 1862.
23. Pritchard (Co. I, 1st Texas), No. 24, A.N.B.P.
24. Crozier (Co. B, 4th Texas), "A Private with General Hood," *Confederate Veteran* 25, no. 12 (December 1917): 556–557.
25. Everett, *Chaplain Davis*, 86.
26. Polley (Co. F, 4th Texas), "Brave Texans in the Virginia Army," *Confederate Veteran* 5, no. 5 (May 1896): 158–159.
27. Simpson, *Compendium*, 137.

28. Campbell (Co. A, 5th Texas), "A Lone Star in Virginia," *Civil War Times Illustrated,* December 2000, 88, 90.
29. Barziza (Co. C, 4th Texas), *Adventures*, 28.
30. "Chickahominie, the Eighteenth Georgia Regiment," Richmond *Whig*, Thursday, July 10, 1862.
31. Ibid.
32. "Report of Col. James H. Simpson," O.R., Ser. 1, Vol. 11, pt. 2, 444–446.
33. Polley (Co. F, 4th Texas), "Brave Texans in the Virginia Army," *Confederate Veteran* 5, no. 5 (May 1896): 158–159. Simpson's *Compendium* does not list a John Ferris in Co. B, 5ᵗʰ Texas but does list a John Farris of Co. C, 5th Texas.
34. Arthur Edey (Co. A, 5th Texas), to Houston *Tri-Weekly Telegraph,* dated June 30, 1862, in Friday, July 25, 1862, edition.
35. Campbell (Co. A, 5th Texas), to his father, in Houston *Tri-Weekly Telegraph*, Friday, August 22, 1862.
36. Everett, *Chaplain Davis,* 92–93.
37. Hanks (Co. K, 1st Texas), *History*, C.R.C., H.C., H.T.B. File 1–9, 8.
38. John Bell Hood, *Advance and Retreat* (1880. Reprint, New York: Da Capo Press, 1993), 28.
39. Campbell (Co. A, 5th Texas), "A Lone Star in Virginia," *C.W.T.I.*, December 2000, 90, 92.
40. Hamby (Co. B, 4th Texas), "Fourth Texas at Battle of Gaines' Mill," *Confederate Veteran* 14, no. 4 (April 1906): 184–185.
41. Smith (Co. D, 4th Texas), *Reminiscences*, 13.
42. Hood, *Advance and Retreat*, 28.
43. "Report of Gen. James Longstreet," O.R., Ser. 1, Vol. 11, pt. 2, 756–757.
44. Pomoroy (Co. A, 5th Texas), *Reminiscences*, 25.
45. "Col. John Marshall," Houston *Tri-Weekly Telegraph*, Monday, July 14, 1862.

Chapter 6—The 5th Texas at Second Manassas, Virginia, August 29–30, 1862

1. Penfield Doll, "Facts, Incidents and Casualties of the Late Battle," Richmond *Enquirer*, Friday, November 4, 1862.
2. See John Pope, "The Second Battle of Bull Run," *B&L*, Vol. 2, 451.
3. Polley (Co. F, 4th Texas), *Hood's Texas Brigade*, 72–73
4. Pomoroy (Co. A, 5th Texas), *Reminiscences*, 44.
5. Pritchard (Co. I, 1st Texas), No. 25, A.N.B.P.
6. Everett, *Chaplain Davis*, 174–175.
7. Ibid., 108–109.
8. Robert G. Holloway, unpublished diary, Museum of the Confederacy, Richmond, VA, 23. Fragmentary observations of daily events into 1863, even though Holloway served to Appomattox.
9. Stevens (Co. K, 5th Texas), *Reminiscences*, 51–52.
10. Pritchard (Co. I, 1st Texas), No. 26, A.N.B.P.
11. Everett, *Chaplain Davis*, 109.

12. Freeman, *Robert E. Lee*, Vol. 2, 300.

13. See John Pope, "The Second Battle of Bull Run," *B&L*, Vol. 2, 461.

14. Pritchard (Co. I, 1st Texas), No. 27, A.N.B.P.

15. Hood, *Advance and Retreat*, 32–33.

16. Ibid., 33.

17. Doll (chaplain, 18th Georgia), "Facts, Incidents and Casualties of the Late Battle," Richmond *Enquirer*, Friday, November 4, 1862.

18. Edward J. Stackpole, *From Cedar Mountain to Antietam* (Harrisburg, PA: Stackpole Books, 1993), 173.

19. Ibid., 174.

20. Stevens (Co. K, 5th Texas), *Reminiscences*, 57.

21. Pritchard (Co. I, 1st Texas), No. 27, A.N.B.P.

22. Ibid.

23. Todd (Co. A, 1st Texas), *First Texas Regiment*, 9.

24. Pritchard (Co. I, 1st Texas), Nos. 27–28, A.N.B.P.

25. "Reports of Lieut. Col. P. A. Work, 1st Texas Infantry," O.R., Ser. 1, Vol. 26, 611–612.

26. "Reports of Col. William T. Wofford, 18th Georgia Infantry," O.R., Ser. 1, Vol. 26, 608–609.

27. J. J. O'Neill (Co. A, 18th Georgia), "Membership Record of Miss Leni L. O'Neill, being a Brief History of the Military Career Her Father, J. J. O'Neill, 18th Georgia Infantry, Co. A. C.R.C,H., H.T.B. file 5–2.

28. R. H. Leonard (Co. E, 4th Texas), "The Texians at Manassas," Houston *Tri-Weekly Telegraph*, Friday, November 28, 1862.

29. Stevens (Co. K, 5th Texas), *Reminiscences*, 58.

30. Longstreet, "Our March Against Pope," *B&L*, Vol. 2, 520.

31. Hood, *Advance and Retreat*, 35.

32. Polley (Co. F, 4th Texas), *Hood's Texas Brigade*, 92.

33. Crozier (Co. B, 4th Texas), "A Private with General Hood," *Confederate Veteran* 25, no. 12 (December 1917): 557.

34. M. V. Smith (Co. D, 4th Texas), *Reminiscences*, 16.

35. Crozier (Co. B, 4th Texas), "A Private with General Hood," *Confederate Veteran* 25, no. 12 (December 1917): 557 .

36. Ibid.

37. Polley (Co. F, 4th Texas), *Hood's Texas Brigade*, 93–94.

38. Brian C. Pohanka, "'The Very Vortex of Hell,'" *America's Civil War*, September 2002, 49.

39. "Reports of Col. William T. Wofford, 18th Georgia Infantry," O.R., Ser. 1, Vol. 16, 609–610.

40. Polley (Co. F, 4th Texas), *Hood's Texas Brigade*, 103.

41. Pohanka, "'The Very Vortex of Hell,'" 50.

42. Stevens (Co. K, 5th Texas), *Reminiscences*, 59.

43. Pohanka, "'The Very Vortex of Hell,'" 52.

44. Ibid., 53.

45. "Sidney Virgil Patrick," (Co. E, 5th Texas), *Confederate Veteran* 15, no. 7 (July 1907): 322.

46. "Reports of Col. J. B. Robertson, 5th Texas Infantry," O.R., Ser. 1, Vol. 16, 617.

47. Hood, *Advance and Retreat*, 36.

48. Polley (Co. F, 4th Texas), *Hood's Texas Brigade*, 89.

49. Rufus K. Felder (Co. E, 5th Texas), to his sister, October 1, 1862, camp near Winchester, Virginia, C.R.C., H.C., H.T.B. file 3–13.

50. See, Simpson, *Compendium*, 199.

51. Pomoroy (Co. A, 5th Texas), *Reminiscences*, 32.

52. H. H. Cunningham, *Doctors in Gray* (Gloucester, MA: Smith, 1958), 221–222.

53. Stevens (Co. K, 5th Texas), *Reminiscences*, 60.

54. Smith (Co. D, 4th Texas), *Reminiscences*, 17–18.

55. Pomoroy (Co. A, 5th Texas), *Reminiscences*, 35–36.

Chapter 7—The 1st Texas at Sharpsburg, Maryland, September 16–17, 1862

1. "Report of Lieut. Col. P. A. Work, First Texas Infantry," O.R., Ser. 1, Vol. 19, 933.

2. Stevens (Co. K, 5th Texas), *Reminiscences*, 65–66.

3. Galveston *Tri-Weekly News*, October 9, 1862, letter from A. N. Erskine (Co. D, 4th Texas) September 9, 1862, near Frederick, Maryland.

4. Felder (Co. E, 5th Texas), to his sister, October 1, 1862, camp near Winchester, Virginia, C.R.C., H.C., H.T.B. file 3–13.

5. Hanks (Co. K, 1st Texas), *History*, 20.

6. Galveston *Tri-Weekly News*, October 9, 1862, letter from A. N. Erskine (Co. D, 4th Texas), September 9, 1862, near Frederick, Maryland.

7. Stevens (Co. K, 5th Texas), *Reminiscences*, 66–67.

8. Galveston *Tri-Weekly News*, October 9, 1862, letter from A. N. Erskine (Co. D, 4th Texas), September 9, 1862, near Frederick, Maryland.

9. Stevens (Co. K, 5th Texas), *Reminiscences*, 65–68.

10. D. H. Hill, "The Battle of South Mountain or Boonesboro," *B&L*, Vol. 2, 564

11. Hood, *Advance and Retreat*, 39–40.

12. Ibid., 46.

13. Polley (Co. F, 4th Texas), *Hood's Texas Brigade*, 114–115.

14. Stevens (Co. K, 5th Texas), *Reminiscences*, 70.

15. "Report of Col. W. T. Wofford, Eighteenth Georgia Infantry," O.R., Ser. 1, Vol. 19, 927.

16. Ibid., "Report of Col. E. M. Law, Fourth Alabama Infantry," 937.

17. P.A. Work (1st Texas), "The 1st Texas Regiment of the Texas Brigade of the Army of Northern Virginia at the Battles of Boonesboro Pass or Gap and Sharpsburg or Antietam, MD. In September 1862." C.R.C., H.C., H.T.B. file 1–18, 1–2.

18. "Report of Col. W. T. Wofford, Eighteenth Georgia Infantry," O.R., Ser. 1, Vol. 19, 927.

19. Ibid., "Report of Lieut. Col S. Z. Ruff, Eighteenth Georgia Infantry," 930.

20. James Longstreet, *From Manassas to Appomattox*, (no date; reprint, Secaucus, New Jersey: Blue and Gray Press, 1988), 241.

21. Winkler, *The Confederate Capital*, 106.

22. Stevens (Co. K, 5th Texas), *Reminiscences*, 74.

23. Polk (Co. I, 4th Texas), *The North and South American Review*, 14–15.

24. "Report of Lieut. Col. M. W. Gary, Hampton Legion," O.R., Ser. 1, Vol. 19, 931.

25. Ibid., "Report of Lieut. Col. B. F. Carter, Fourth Texas Infantry, 935.

26. Polk (Co. I, 4th Texas), *The North and South American Review*, 15.

27. Member of the 4th Texas, "The Texans at Sharpsburg," *Confederate Veteran* 22, no. 12, (December 1914): 555.

28. "Report of Lieut. Col. B. F. Carter, Fourth Texas Infantry," O.R., Ser. 1, Vol. 19, 935.

29. Ibid., "Report of Col. S. Z. Ruff, Eighteenth Georgia Infantry," 930.

30. "Report of Lieut. Col. M. W. Gary, Hampton Legion," O.R., Ser. 1, Vol. 19, 931. The first three color bearers Lt. Col. Gary named were Herod Wilson, Co. F, James Estes, Co. E, and C. P. Poppenhem, Co. A.

31. Samuel M. Priest, ed., *Stephen Elliott Welch and the Hampton Legion* (Shippenburg, PA: Burd Street Press, 1994), 6–7.

32. "Report of Lieut. Col. P. A. Work, First Texas Infantry," O.R., Ser. 1, Vol. 19, 932.

33. Hanks (Co. K, 1st Texas), *History*, 21–22.

34. Rufus R. Dawes, *A Full Blown Yankee of the Iron Brigade: Service with the Sixth Wisconsin Volunteers* (1894. Reprint, Lincoln: University of Nebraska Press, 1999), 95.

35. Work (1st Texas), "The 1st Texas Regiment of the Texas Brigade of the Army of Northern Virginia at the Battles of Boonesboro Pass or Gap and Sharpsburg or Antietam, Maryland, in September 1862," C.R.C., H.C., H.T.B. file 1–18, 3.

36. Ibid., 4.

37. "Report of Lieut. Col. P. A. Work, First Texas Infantry," O.R., Ser. 1, Vol. 19, 933. Lt. Col. Work identified John Hanson, Co. L, James Day, Co. M, Charles H. Kingsley, Co. L, and James K. Malone, Co. A.

38. Ibid.

39. Work (1st Texas), "The 1st Texas Regiment of the Texas Brigade of the Army of Northern Virginia at the Battles of Boonesboro Pass of Gap and Sharpsburg or Antietam, Maryland in September 1862," C.R.C., H.C., H.T.B. file 1–18, 4.

40. James J. and Patience P. Barnes, eds., "'What I Thought at Antietam,'" *Civil War Times*, 45, no. 7 (September 2006): 54.

41. "Report of Lieut. Col. B. F. Carter, Fourth Texas Infantry," O.R., Ser. 1, Vol. 19, 935.

42. Stevens (Co. K, 5th Texas), *Reminiscences*, 74–76.

43. Pomeroy (Co. A, 5th Texas), *Reminiscences*, 41–42.

44. Simpson, *Hood's Texas Brigade* , 174.

45. Hood, *Advance and Retreat*, 44.

46. "Report of Lieut. Col. P. A. Work, First Texas Infantry," O.R., Ser. 1, Vol. 19, 933

47. Freeman, *Robert E. Lee*, Vol. 2, 392.

48. Ibid., 400–401.

49. James I. Robertson, *General A. P. Hill: The Story*

of a Confederate Warrior (New York: Random House, 1987), 143.

50 Ibid., 148; Quoted from Henry Kyd Douglas, *I Rode with Stonewall: The War Experiences of the Youngest Member of Jackson's Staff* (Chapel Hill: University of North Carolina Press, 1980).

51. "Report of Lieut. Gen. James Longstreet, C.S.A. Army," O.R., Ser. 1, Vol. 19, 841.

52. Hamilton (Co. M, 1st Texas), *History*, 24.

53. Polk (Co. I, 4th Texas), *The North and South American Review*, 15.

54. Stevens (Co. K, 5th Texas), *Reminiscences*, 76–77.

55. Pomeroy (Co. A, 5th Texas), *Reminiscences*, 43.

56. Daffan (Co. G, 4th Texas), unpublished typescript, C.R.C., H.C., H.T.B. File 2–8, 7.

57. Polley (Co. F, 4th Texas), *A Soldier's Letters*, 85–86.

58. "Report of Lieut. Gen. James Longstreet, C.S.A. Army," O.R., Ser. 1, Vol. 19, 841.

59. Longstreet, *From Manassas to Appomattox*, 266.

60. Polk (Co. I, 4th Texas), *North and South American Review*, 18.

61. Simpson, *Compendium*, 157.

62. Pomeroy (Co. A, 5th Texas), *Reminiscences*, 43.

63. Robertson, *Soldiers Blue and Gray*, 122.

Chapter 8 — Fredericksburg, Virginia, December 13, 1862

1. Giles (Co. B, 4th Texas), *Rags and Hope*, 151.

2. Ibid., 134.

3.. "Letter from Virginia," Houston *Tri-Weekly Telegraph*, November 10, 1862.

4. Polley (Co. F, 4th Texas), *Hood's Texas Brigade*, 137.

5. Freeman, *Robert E. Lee*, Vol. 2, 418.

6. Stevens (Co. K, 5th Texas), *Reminiscences*, 82–83.

7. "Letter from Gen. J. B. Robertson," Houston *Tri-Weekly Telegraph*, Monday, December 22, 1862.

8. Polley (Co. F, 4th Texas), *Hood's Texas Brigade*, 138.

9. "Wanderer," Camp Near Fredericksburg," Houston *Tri-Weekly Telegraph*, Monday, December 29, 1862.

10. Stevens (Co. K, 5th Texas), *Reminiscences*, 84.

11. Stevens (Co. K, 5th Texas), *Reminiscences*, 86. This does not sound like the habitually courtly and courteous Lee and is probably apocryphal.

12. Collier, *They'll Do To Tie To*, 105–106.

13. Fletcher (Co. F, 5th Texas), *Rebel Private*, 48.

14. Ibid., 49.

15. Pomeroy (Co. A, 5th Texas), *Reminiscences*, 46.

16. Hood, *Advance and Retreat*, 49.

17. Stevens (Co. K, 5th Texas), *Reminiscences*, 89.

18. Giles (Co. B, 4th Texas), *Rags and Hope*, 150.

19. Stevens (Co. K, 5th Texas, *Reminiscences*, 88.

20. Giles (Co. B, 4th Texas), *Rags and Hope*, 151.

21. Polley (Co. F, 4th Texas), *Hood's Texas Brigade*, 139.

22. Longstreet, "The Battle of Fredericksburg," *B&L*, Vol. 3, 81.

23. Fletcher (Co. F, 5th Texas), *Rebel Private*, 50.

24. Polley (Co. F, 4th Texas), *A Soldier's Letters*, 92.

25. Stevens (Co. K, 5th Texas), *Reminiscences*, 89–90.

26. A. C. Jones (Co. G, 3rd Arkansas), "Inaugurating the Picket Exchange," *Confederate Veteran* 26, no. 4 (April 1906): 154–156.

27. Longstreet, *From Manassas to Appomattox*, 309.

Chapter 9 — Campaigners and Commissaries on the Nansemond, Spring 1863

1. Stevens (Co. K, 5th Texas), *Reminiscences*, 99.

2. Todd (Co. A, 1st Texas), *First Texas Regiment*, 12–13.

3. Stevens (Co. K, 5th Texas), *Reminiscences*, 93.

4. Ibid., 94.

5. Stevens (Co. K, 5th Texas), *Reminiscences*, 94. One knowledgeable source identifies Stevens as the model for John W. Thomason's "Lone Star" preacher, Praxiteles Swan.

6. See Polley (Co. F, 4th Texas), *Hood's Texas Brigade*, 139–140.

7. Giles (Co. B, 4th Texas), *Rags and Hope*, 168–170.

8. See "Abstract from 'Record of Events in Department of Virginia, April 11–May 4,'" O.R., Ser. 1, Vol. 28, 271.

9. A. B. Hood (Co. I, 5th Texas), to his cousin, Jennie, March 2, 1863, near Richmond, Virginia, C.R.C., H.C., H.T.B. file 3–20.

10. Ibid.

11. See Arthur Edey (Co. A, 5th Texas), "Letter from Virginia," Galveston *Tri-Weekly News,* Thursday, March 26, 1863.

12. Polk (Co. I, 4th Texas), *North and South American Review*, 21.

13. John B. Jones, *A Rebel War Clerk's Diary* (1958; reprint; Baton Rouge: Louisiana State University Press, 1993), 167.

14. See Polley (Co. F, 4th Texas), *Hood's Texas Brigade,* 140–141. Polley's commendable history of the Texas Brigade is not without error. Other accounts place this incident earlier in the war when the first eight companies of the 1st Texas were still encamped in the Richmond area prior to their departure for Manassas. Of course, this type of occurrence could have happened more than once in that spirited organization.

15. James H. Hendricks (Co. E, 1st Texas), to his mother, March 13, 1863, camp near Richmond, in Powers, *Texan at War*, 20. Snuff was a powdered tobacco product that could be inhaled through the nose, chewed or rubbed on the gums.

16. Mary Boykin Chesnut, *A Diary From Dixie* (1949; reprint, Boston: Harvard University Press, 1980), 297. "Buck" Preston was Sally Buchanan Campbell Preston. She was described by Mrs. Chesnut as being "the very sweetest woman I ever knew, had a knack of being fallen in love with at sight, and of never being fallen out of love with. But there seemed a spell upon her

lovers; so many were killed or died." While Hood was smitten with her, she was not smitten with him and their relationship eventually faded away.

17. "Confederate Correspondence, Orders, Returns..., #8, Gen Longstreet to Gen Lee, March 24, 1863," O.R., Ser. 1, Vol. 28, 942. At Gettysburg, several months later, Gen. Longstreet expressed a similar reluctance to start the attack on the second day because all of his troops had not yet reached the front. In his words, he said he did not like to go into battle "with one boot off."

18. Gen. Lee to Gen. Longstreet, March 27, 1863, O.R., Ser. 1, Vol. 28, 943.

19. Stevens (Co. K, 5th Texas), *Reminiscences*, 97–98.

20. See *Official Military Atlas of the Civil War* (1891; #17.48, reprint, New York: Gramercy Books, 1983), Plate 26, "Military Map of Suffolk and Vicinity."

21. "Reports of Maj. Gen. John Peck, U.S. Army, Commanding at Suffolk," O.R., Ser. 1, Vol. 28, 283.

22. Longstreet, *From Manassas to Appomattox*, 325–326.

23. "Report of Capt. Robert M. Stribling, Fauquier Artillery," O.R. Ser. 1, Vol. 28, 336.

24. Ibid., "Report of Col. John E. Ward, Eighth Connecticut Infantry," 314.

25. Longstreet, *From Manassas to Appomattox*, 325.

26. Polk (Co. I, 4th Texas), *North and South American Review*, 21.

27. Ibid., 22.

28. Hendricks (Co. E, 1st Texas), to his mother, April 18, 1863, Camp Suffolk, in Powers, *Texan at War,* 21.

29. Stevens (Co. K, 5th Texas), *Reminiscences*, 99.

30. Isaac A. Howard (Co. B, 5th Texas), to his mother, April 22, 1863, camp near Suffolk, in Howard Papers, U.N.C.C.H., S.H.C.

31. Longstreet, *From Manassas to Appomattox*, 326.

32. Henderson, *Texas in the Confederacy* 28–29

33. Smith (Co. D, 4th Texas), *Reminiscences,* U.S. A.M.H.I.M.C., 34

34. Hood, *Advance and Retreat*, 52.

Chapter 10 — The Pennsylvania Campaign, June–July 1863

1. Jones (3rd Arkansas), "Longstreet at Gettysburg," *Confederate Veteran* 23, no. 12 (December 1915): 551.

2. See Clark B. Hall, "The Army Is Moving: Lee's March to the Potomac, 1863," *Blue and Gray Magazine* 21, no. 3 (Spring 2004). According to Hall, there were three cavalry reviews conducted on May 22, June 5 and 8, respectively. He says that Hood's division is erroneously placed at the June 8 review whereas it actually attended the one on June 5.

3. Champ Clark, *Gettysburg: The Confederate High Tide* (Alexandria, VA: Time-Life Books, 1985), 10.

4. W. W. Blackford, *War Years with Jeb Stuart* (New York: Charles Scribner's Sons, 1946), 212–213.

5. Ibid., 212.

6. "Report of Lieut. Gen. James Longstreet," O.R. Ser. 1, Vol. 27, Pt. 2, 357.

7. John C. West (Co. E, 4th Texas), *A Texan in Search of a Fight* (1901; reprint, Baltimore: Butternut and Blue, 1994), 76–77. In those days before weather forecasting and reporting, this could have been the remnants of a hurricane.

8. Stevens (Co. K, 5th Texas), *Reminiscences,* 103–104.

9. Albert Sims Co. F, 1st Texas), Jasper *Newsboy,* May 17, 1911, 7, in R. H. and W. H. Gaston file, C.R.C., H.C., H.T.B. File 7B.

10. Barziza (Co. C, 4th Texas), *Adventures,* 40.

11. Stevens (Co. K, 5th Texas), *Reminiscences,* 105.

12. Smith (Co. D, 4th Texas), *Reminiscences,* 35.

13. West (Co. E, 4th Texas), *A Texan in Search of a Fight,* 70–71.

14. Giles (Co. B, 4th Texas), *Rags and Hope,* 177.

15. R. M. Powell, *Recollections of a Texas Colonel at Gettysburg,* Gregory A. Coco, ed. (Gettysburg, PA: Thomas, 1990), 8.

16. "Report of Lieut. Gen. James Longstreet," O.R., Ser. 1, Vol. 27, Pt. 2, 358.

17. See Freeman, *Robert E. Lee,* Vol. 3, 57.

18. Smither (Co. D, 5th Texas), to his mother, June 28, 1863, C.R.C., H.C., H.T.B. file 3–29.

19. James H. Hendrick (Co. E, 1st Texas), to his mother, June 28, 1863, in Power, "A Texan at War," C.R. C., H. C., H. T.B. file 1–10, 25.

20. Polk (Co. I, 4th Texas), *North and South American Review,* 23.

21. Arthur J. L. Fremantle, *Three Months in the Southern States* (1864; reprint, Lincoln: University of Nebraska Press, 1991), 250.

22. G. Moxley Sorrell, *Recollections of a Confederate Staff Officer* (New York: Konecky & Konecky, 1994), 164.

23. Freeman, *Robert E. Lee,* Vol. 3, 65.

24. Freeman, *Lee's Lieutenants,* Vol. 3, 78.

25. Longstreet, "Lee in Pennsylvania," *The Annals of the Civil War,* ed. Alexander K. McClure (1878; reprint, New York: Da Capo Press, 1994), 421.

26. Sims (Co. F, 1st Texas), "Hood's Texas Brigade, Co. F, 1st Texas Infantry Regiment," Jasper *Newsboy,* May 17, 1911, C.R.C., H.C., H.T.B. file 1–7B, 9.

27. Jones (3rd Arkansas), "Longstreet at Gettysburg," *Confederate Veteran* 22, no. 12 (December 1915): 551.

28. West (Co. E, 4th Texas), *A Texan in Search of a Fight,* 84.

29. Sims (Co. F, 1st Texas), "Hood's Texas Brigade, Co. F, 1st Texas Infantry Regiment," Jasper *Newsboy,* 9.

30. Longstreet, *From Manassas to Appomattox,* 365.

31. Sorrell, *Recollections,* 167.

32. Giles (Co. B, 4th Texas), *Rags and Hope,* 178.

33. See Harry Pfanz, *Gettysburg—The Second Day* (Chapel Hill: University of North Carolina Press, 1987), 161. The author identifies the scouts as members of the 1st Texas. Simpson's *Compendium* identifies two as being members of the 4th Texas.

34. E. M. Law, "The Struggle for Round Top," *B&L,*

Vol. 3, 321.

35. Polk (Co. I, 4th Texas), *North and South American Review,* 37. There is no evidence that Hood spoke directly to Gen. Lee.

36. A. W. Greely, "The Signal Corps in the Civil War," *Review of Reviews,* 1911, 61.

37. Longstreet, *From Manassas to Appomattox,* 367.

38. Law, "The Struggle for Round Top," *B&L,* Vol. 3, 320.

39. See "Report of Gen. J. B. Robertson," O.R., Ser. 1, Vol. 27, Pt. 2, 404–407.

40. Work (1st Texas), to Tom Langley, May 28, 1908, Kountze, Texas, C.R.C., H.C., H.T.B. file 1–18, 4.

41. Fremantle, *Three Months in the Southern States,* 261.

42. Collier, *They'll Do To Tie To,* 139.

43. See Sims (Co. F, 1st Texas), "Hood's Texas Brigade, Co. F, 1st Texas Infantry Regiment," Jasper *Newsboy,* C.R.C., H.C., H.T.B. file 1–7b, 10.

44. Polley (Co. F, 4th Texas), *Hood's Texas Brigade,* 172.

45. "Report of Lieut. Col. P. A. Work, First Texas Infantry," O.R., Ser. 1, Vol. 27, Pt. 2, 410.

46. Simpson, *Compendium,* 79.

47. "Report of Lieut. Col. P. A. Work, First Texas Infantry," O.R., Ser. 1, Vol. 27, Pt. 2, 409. According to Lt. Col. Work, Gen Robertson sent him to take command of the 3rd Arkansas. Upon arriving there, he said he found the regiment "doing its duty nobly and well."

48. Polk (Co. I, 4th Texas), *North and South American Review,* 24.

49. Ibid., 24–25.

50. West (Co. E, 4th Texas), *A Texan in Search of a Fight,* 85.

51. Barziza (Co. C, 4th Texas), *Adventures,* 46.

52. Ibid., 45.

53. Giles (Co. B, 4th Texas), *Rags and Hope,* 180.

54. Ibid., 186.

55. Giles (Co. B, 4th Texas), *Rags and Hope,* 180.

56. West (Co. E, 4th Texas), *A Texan in Search of a Fight,* 94.

57. Giles (Co. B, 4th Texas), *Rags and Hope,* 181.

58. Ibid., 182.

59. "Report of Maj. John P. Bane, Fourth Texas Infantry," O.R., Ser. 1, Vol. 27, Pt. 2, 410–411.

60. Caddell (Co. I, 4th Texas), to his sister, July 22, 1863, Richmond, Virginia, C.R.C., H.C., H.T.B. file 2–4. Also see Simpson, *Compendium ,* 94. Caddell is listed as a commissary–subsistence sergeant ,appointed thus in October 1863. Although a Gettysburg wound is not listed, his appointment might indicate some disability. He is listed as being killed at Petersburg the following summer.

61. Pomeroy (Co. A, 5th Texas), *Reminiscences,* 53–54. Also see Simpson, *Compendium,* 170, 178. Fitzgerald was taken prisoner of war, paroled, and returned only to be wounded again at Cold Harbor the next year. Morris was wounded twice more, at Chickamauga and at Petersburg. He was taken prisoner of war in Richmond on April 13, 1865, at which time the war was over.

62. Stevens (Co. K, 5th Texas), *Reminiscences,* 114–116.

63. Fletcher (Co. F, 5th Texas), *Rebel Private*, 60.

64. Smither (Co. D, 5th Texas), to his mother, July 29, 1863, Culpeper Court House, Virginia. Typescript in Robert L. Blake Collection, U.S. A.M.H.., Carlisle Barracks, Pennsylvania. Also see Simpson, *Compendium*, 204. Lt. Harper must have been R. Thomas Harper, Co. E, 5th Texas. He was wounded in the thigh and shoulder, taken prisoner of war and spent the remainder of the war in captivity, apparently.

65. See Law, "The Struggle for Round Top," *B&L*, Vol. 3, 326. Gen. Law incorrectly pronounced Col. Powell dead. Actually, he was captured, recovered from his wound and exchanged later. He was to be the last commander of the Texas Brigade. Law says that his Federal captors thought him, for a time, to be Gen. Longstreet, they looking somewhat alike.

66. "Report of Maj. J. C. Rogers, Fifth Texas Infantry," O.R., Ser. 1, Vol. 27, Pt. 2, 413.

67. Fletcher (Co. F, 5th Texas), *Rebel Private*, 62.

68. Powell (5th Texas), *Recollections of a Texas Colonel at Gettysburg*, 16.

69. "Report of Maj. J. C. Rogers, Fifth Texas Infantry," O.R., Ser. 1, Vol. 27, Pt. 2, 413–414.

70. Jones (3rd Arkansas), "Longstreet at Gettysburg," *Confederate Veteran* 23, no. 12 (December 1915): 551.

71. "Report of Lieut. Gen. James Longstreet," O.R., Ser. 1, Vol. 27, Pt. 2, 358.

72. Ibid., "Report of Lieut. Col. P. A. Work, First Texas Infantry," 409.

73. Sims (Co. F, 1st Texas), "Hood's Texas Brigade, Co. F, 1st Texas Infantry Regiment," Jasper *Newsboy*, May 17, 1911, 9. C.R.C., H.C., H.T.B. file 1–7b, 12–13.

74. James Longstreet, "Lee in Pennsylvania," in *The Annals of the Civil War* (1884–1887; C.M. of S. (13) #17.48, reprint, New York: Da Capo Press, 1994), 424.

75. Ibid., 429.

76. Alexander, *Military Memoirs*, 419. During the course of the battle, 220 pieces of Federal artillery were brought to bear.

77. Fletcher (Co. F, 5th Texas), *Rebel Private*, 61.

78. Freeman, *Robert E. Lee*, III, 129.

79. W. T. White (Co. K, 1st Texas), "First Texas Regiment at Gettysburg," *Confederate Veteran* 30, no. 5 (May 1922): 185. About White, see Simpson, *Compendium*, 77.

80. Todd (Co. A, 1st Texas), *First Texas Regiment*, 16.

81. White (Co. K, 1st Texas), "First Texas Regiment at Gettysburg," *Confederate Veteran* 30, no. 5 (May 1922): 185.

82. Todd (Co. A, 1st Texas), *First Texas Regiment*, 16.

Chapter 11— "Westward Ho" to Chickamauga, September 1863

1. Giles (Co. B, 4th Texas), *Rags and Hope*, 203. See also, Roy Morris Jr., "Ambrose Bierce's Civil War," *Military History Quarterly* 27, no. 2 (Winter 2005): 22. Morris says that Chickamauga was romanticized as the "river of death" whereas its literal meaning is "bad water." Hereinafter, *M.H.Q.*

2. U.S. Department of the Interior, *Chickamauga and Chattanooga Battlefields*, prepared for the National Park Service by James R. Sullivan (Washington, DC: U.S. Government Printing Office, 1956), 2.

3. See Edward B. Williams, "Reinforcements by Rail to Chickamauga," *America's Civil War*, January 1996, 48.

4. Longstreet, *From Manassas to Appomattox*, 436.

5. Collier, *They'll Do to Tie To*, 153.

6. Sorrel, *Recollections*, 189.

7. Chesnut, *A Diary from Dixie*, 308.

8. Augustus Dickert, *History of Kershaw's Brigade* (1899; reprint, Dayton, OH: Morningside Press, 1976), 263–264.

9. Hanks (Co. K, 1st Texas), *Account*, 12–13.

10. Simpson, *Gaines' Mill to Appomattox*, 153–154.

11. Ibid., 154.

12. See "Report of Brig. Gen. Bushrod R. Johnson...," O.R., Ser. 1, Vol. 30, Pt. 2, 451.

13. In *Hood's Texas Brigade*, Col. Simpson has Hood arriving at Ringgold Station on September 17 and bivouacking there that night. In *Advance and Retreat*, p. 16, Gen. Hood has them arriving the afternoon of September 18. The latter is used in this account.

14. Polley (Co. F, 4th Texas), *Hood's Texas Brigade*, 199.

15. West (Co. E, 4th Texas), *A Texan in Search of a Fight*, 111–112.

16. "The Battle of Chickamauga," Houston *Tri-Weekly Telegraph*, Thursday, November 5, 1863.

17. Polk (Co. I, 4th Texas), *North and South American Review*, 28.

18. Hood, *Advance and Retreat*, 62.

19. Simpson, *Gaines' Mill to Appomattox*, 157.

20. Giles (Co. B, 4th Texas), *Rags and Hope*, 199.

21. Polk (Co. I, 4th Texas), *North and South American Review*, 28.

22. Polley (Co. F, 4th Texas), *Hood's Texas Brigade*, 206.

23. Ibid., 207–208.

24. Polk (Co. I, 4th Texas), *North and South American Review*, 28.

25. Ibid., 28, 30.

26. Polley (Co. F, 4th Texas), *Hood's Texas Brigade*, 209.

27. Ibid.

28. "Report of Brig. Gen. Bushrod R. Johnson, C.S. Army," O.R., Ser. 1, Vol. 30, Pt. 2, 454–455.

29. West (Co. E, 4th Texas), *A Texan in Search of a Fight*, 114–115.

30. Hamilton (Co. M, 1st Texas), *History*, 31.

31. Ibid., 32–33.

32. Giles (Co. B, 4th Texas), *Rags and Hope*, 204–205.

33. Ibid., 208.

34. Fletcher (Co. F, 5th Texas), *Rebel Private*, 73–75.

35. "The Battle of Chickamauga," Houston *Tri-Weekly Telegraph*, Thursday, November 5, 1863.

36. Polley (Co. F, 4th Texas), *Hood's Texas Brigade*, 211–212.

37. Ibid., 205.

38. Polk (Co. I, 4th Texas), *North and South American Review*, 30.

39. Ibid., 32.

40. William G. Piston, *Lee's Tarnished Lieutenant* (Athens: University of Georgia Press, 1987), 69.

41. Polk (Co. I, 4th Texas), *North and South American Review*, 32.

42. "Report of Lieut. Gen. James Longstreet, C.S. Army," O.R., Ser. 1, Vol. 30, Pt. 2, 288.

43. Giles (Co. B, 4th Texas), *Rags and Hope*, 201.

44. Polk (Co. I, 4th Texas), *North and South American Review*, 32–33.

45. Longstreet, *From Manassas to Appomattox*, 447.

46. In, Morris, "Ambrose Bierce's Civil War," *Military History Quarterly* 27, no. 2 (Winter 2005): 22.

47. Ibid.

48. Daffan (Co. G, 4th Texas), unpublished typescript, C.R.C., H.C., H.T.B. file 2–8, 3. See also Todd (Co. A, 1st Texas), *First Texas Regiment*, 17. Todd says new uniforms were issued when the brigade passed through Richmond bound for Georgia. The blue trousers "caused us to be mistaken for the enemy later on the field of Chickamauga."

49. See Robertson (5th Texas), "Report of General J. B. Robertson," *Southern Historical Society Papers* 13, 386.

50. See "Report of Capt. R. J. Harding, First Texas Infantry," O.R., Ser. 1, Vol. 30, Pt. 2, 513–514.

51. Todd (Co. A, 1st Texas), *First Texas Regiment*, 18.

52. Polley (Co. F, 4th Texas), *Hood's Texas Brigade*, 204.

53. Hood, *Advance and Retreat*, 65. Later, the members of the Texas Brigade raised $5,000 for the purchase of a prosthetic leg for their beloved commander.

54. J. T. Hunter, "Hard Fighting of Fourth Texas," *Confederate Veteran* 14, no. 1 (January 1906): 22.

55. Giles (Co. B, 4th Texas), *Rags and Hope*, 202–203.

56. "Report of Brig. Gen. Bushrod R. Johnson, C.S. Army," O.R., Ser. 1, Vol. 30, Pt. 2, 457–458.

57. Longstreet, *From Manassas to Appomattox*, 451.

58. Ibid., 452.

59. Ibid., 456.

60. Sorrell, *Recollections*, 196.

61. Morris, "Ambrose Bierce's Civil War," *Military History Quarterly* 27, no. 2 (Winter 2005): 23.

62. Giles (Co. B, 4th Texas), *Rags and Hope*, 205–206.

63. Ibid., 200–201.

Chapter 12 — Chattanooga to Knoxville, September–December 1863

1. Smith (Co. D, 4th Texas), *Reminiscences*, 44.

2. Longstreet, *From Manassas to Appomattox*, 462.

3. Edward Porter Alexander, "Personal Recollections of the Knoxville Campaign." *Alexander Papers, 1854–1865*, M.D., L.O.C., unnumbered.

4. Longstreet, *From Manassas to Appomattox*, 463.

5. Ibid.

6. Polley (Co. F, 4th Texas), *A Soldier's Letters*, 146–147.

7. William G. Le Duc, "The Little Boat That Opened the Cracker Line." *B&L*, Vol. 3, 678.

8. "Report of Lieut. Gen. James Longstreet, C.S. Army," O.R., Ser. 1, Vol. 31, Pt. 1, 217.

9. Longstreet, *From Manassas to Appomattox*, 474.

10. "Report of Lieut. Gen. James Longstreet, C.S. Army," O.R., Ser. 1, Vol. 31, Pt. 1, 218.

11. See Judith Lee Hallock, *Braxton Bragg and Confederate Defeat*, Vol. 2, 122–123. According to Hallock, Gen. Longstreet was grossly negligent in carrying out his duties and self-serving and inaccurate in his memories of that time.

12. Polley (Co. F, 4th Texas), *Hood's Texas Brigade*, 213–214.

13. Ibid., 215.

14. "Report of Brig. Gen. E. McIver Law, C.S. Army," O.R., Ser. 1, Vol. 31, Pt. 1, 226.

15. Giles (Co. B, 4th Texas), *Rags and Hope*, 214.

16. Polley (Co. F, 4th Texas), *Hood's Texas Brigade*, 216. This alignment does not square with other accounts which have the 3rd Arkansas adjoining the Alabamians, thence the 1st Texas and then the 4th Texas on the far right.

17. "Report of Col. James Wood, Jr., 136th New York Infantry," O.R., Ser. 1, Vol. 31, Pt. 1, 106.

18. Polley (Co. F, 4th Texas), *Hood's Texas Brigade*, 216.

19. "Report of Col. James Wood, Jr., 136th New York Infantry," O.R., Ser. 1, Vol. 31, Pt. 1, 106.

20. Polley (Co. F, 4th Texas), *Hood's Texas Brigade*, 217.

21. Ibid.

22. Polley (Co. F, 4th Texas), *Hood's Texas Brigade*, 219–220. Val Giles, Co. B, 4th Texas, identified the human bridge as "Old Man Reece." The only Reece listed in Simpson's *Compendium* is a W.R. Reece Co. C, 4th Texas. Giles said he was, indeed, an old man, recruited where he did not know.

23. "Report of Col. James Wood, Jr., 136th New York Infantry," O.R., Ser. 1, Vol. 31, Pt. 1, 107.

24. Smith (Co. D, 4th Texas), *Reminiscences*, 43.

25. "Report of Brig Gen. E. McIver Law, C.S. Army," O.R., Ser. 2, Vol. 31, Pt. 1, 228.

26. Ibid., "Report of Brig. Gen. Jerome Robertson C.S. Army," O.R., Ser. 2, Vol. 31, Pt. 1, 234.

27. Longstreet, *From Manassas to Appomattox*, 477.

28. "Report of Capt. Frank Potts, Assistant Quartermaster, C.S. Army," O.R., Ser. 1, Vol. 31, Pt. 1, 476.

29. Ibid., See "Report of Maj. R. Z. Moses, Commissary of Subsistence," 477.

30. Longstreet, *From Manassas to Appomattox*, 486.

31. Polley (Co. F, 4th Texas), *A Soldier's Letters*, 175.

32. West (Co. E, 4th Texas), *A Texan in Search of a Fight*, 131.

33. Polley (Co. F, 4th Texas), *A Soldier's Letters*, 176.

34. Ibid., 176–177.

35. Sorrell, *Recollections*, 211–212.

36. See Ezra Warner, *Generals in Blue* (Baton Rouge: Louisiana State University Press, 1992), 419–420. Fort Sanders was named after Gen. William P. Sanders, mortally wounded on November 18, 1863, in the preliminary skirmishing before Knoxville. He was born in Kentucky but moved to Mississippi with his family at age seven. His father was a prominent lawyer. Ironically, in the early 1850s when he was about to be dismissed from West Point because of a "deficiency in languages," Senator Jefferson Davis interceded on his behalf and he went on to graduate with the Class of 1856. At Knoxville, unknown to Gen. Sanders, in the skirmish in which he was mortally wounded, the artillery opposite was commanded by an old West Point comrade and friend, Col. Edward Porter Alexander. They had last met in San Francisco in 1861 when they bade each other farewell prior to the beginning of hostilities.

37. Alexander, "Personal Recollections of the Knoxville Campaign," n.p.

38. Polley (Co. F, 4th Texas), *Hood's Texas Brigade*, 222.

39. Polley (Co. F, 4th Texas), *A Soldier's Letters*, 178.

40. West, *A Texan in Search of a Fight*, 132.

41. Polley (Co. F, 4th Texas), *A Soldier's Letters*, 179. Col. Simpson lists James Mayfield as being wounded in the thigh on September 15, 1863, and no other records are available. In this case, the action took place in November.

42. William Marvel, *Burnside* (Chapel Hill: University of North Carolina Press; 1991), 326. The author mentions "Burnside's special orders," however, the writer could not locate any further mention of those orders and their content.

43. In the military age of fortresses, attackers routinely carried ladders for the purpose of surmounting walls. Fascines are bundles of sticks tied together to fill or reinforce trenches.

44. See "Report of Maj. Gen. Lafayette McLaws, C.S. Army," O.R., Ser. 1, Vol. 31, Pt. 1, 491. After the attack, one of Gen. Longstreet's surgeons, Dr. Cullen, was in the ditch attending the wounded. He estimated it to be on the west side from twelve to thirteen feet deep, on the north front an average of ten feet deep and about ten feet wide all around the work. On the northwest bastion where the attack was made he estimated it be four to four and a half feet deep. He estimated the height from the bottom of the ditch to the top of the parapet to be at least twenty feet.

45. Orlando M. Poe, "The Defense of Knoxville," *B&L*, Vol. 3, 741.

46. Alexander, "Personal Recollections of the Knoxville Campaign," n.p.

47. Marvel, *Burnside*, 327.

48. Freeman, *Lee's Lieutenants*, Vol. 3, 293.

49. Poe, "The Defense of Knoxville," 741.

50. Alexander, "Personal Recollections of the Knoxville Campaign," n.p.

51. Marvel, *Burnside*, 328.

52. Poe, "The Defense of Knoxville," 741.

53. Ibid., 743.

54. Alexander, "Personal Recollections of the Knoxville Campaign," n.p.

55. Marvel, *Burnside*, 328.

56. Ibid.

57. Alexander, "Personal Recollections of the Knoxville Campaign," n.p.

58. Polley (Co. F, 4th Texas), *A Soldier's Letters*, 180.

59. Poe, "The Defense of Knoxville," 743.

60. Longstreet, *From Manassas to Appomattox*, 505.

61. Polley (Co. F, 4th Texas), *A Soldier's Letters*, 181. According to Col. Simpson, 1st Sgt. Henry Martin was killed at Second Manassas, and 3rd Lt. Robert B. Martin was killed at Knoxville. Polley's accounts are sometimes inaccurate in the details. See Simpson, *Compendium*, 161.

62. Smith (Co. D, 4th Texas), *Reminiscences*, 44.

Chapter 13 — The Brigade's Tortuous Road Home, December 1863 – April 1864

1. Polley (Co. F, 4th Texas), *Hood's Texas Brigade*, 223.

2. Ibid.

3. Collier, *They'll Do To Tie To*," 168.

4. Smith (Co. D, 4th Texas), *Reminiscences*, 45–46

5. Longstreet, *From Manassas to Appomattox*, 513. See Polley, *Hood's Texas Brigade*, 224. Polley, known for some inaccuracy, places the brigade at Rogersville on December 8, departing on December 9 for Bean's Station in support of Wheeler's cavalry against a pursuing Federal force. He has them staying at Bean's Station until December 19, at which time it marched to Morristown, arriving there on December 22.

6. Freeman, *Lee's Lieutenants*, Vol. 3, 315.

7. Longstreet, *From Manassas to Appomattox*, 515.

8. Ibid., 519.

9. Longstreet, *From Manassas to Appomattox*, 515.

10. West, *A Texan in Search of a Fight*, 140–141.

11. Polley, *Hood's Texas Brigade*, 224.

12. See, Hamilton (Co. M, 1st Texas), *History*, 39–45.

13. Longstreet, *From Manassas to Appomattox*, 521.

14. Ibid., 517.

15. "Synopsis of the Tennessee Campaign by Longstreet, September 1863 to May 4, 1864," T. L. McCarty Collection, Center for American History, University of Texas, Austin. 5.

16. Freeman, *Lee's Lieutenants*, Vol. 3, 301.

17. Susan Leigh Blackford, comp., Charles Minor Blackford, annot., and Charles Minor Blackford, III, ed., *Letters from Lee's Army* (New York: Charles Scribner's Sons, 1947), 231. Hereinafter, Blackford, *Letters*.

18. Polley, *Hood's Texas Brigade*, 225.

19. Ibid., 226–227.

20. Alexander, "Longstreet at Knoxville," *B&L*, Vol. 3, 750–751.

21. Longstreet, *From Manassas to Appomattox*, 521.

22. Alexander, "Longstreet at Knoxville," *B&L*, Vol. 3, 750.
23. Longstreet, *From Manassas to Appomattox*, 525.
24. Ibid., 521.
25. Sorrel, *Recollections*, 218.
26. See Longstreet, *From Manassas to Appomattox*, 525.
27. Sorrel, *Recollections*, 219.
28. Longstreet, *From Manassas to Appomattox*, 527.
29. Sorrell, *Recollections*, 220.
30. Ibid., 220–221.
31. Fletcher (Co. F, 5th Texas), *Rebel Private*, 81. The term jayhawker is not listed in the author's dictionary. However, it is thought to be a term originally assigned to the pro–Union guerilla-type forces in Bleeding Kansas engaged with the pro-slavery forces over that state's eventual status as free or slave.
32. Polley (Co. F, 4th Texas), *Hood's Texas Brigade*, 226.
33. Longstreet, *From Manassas to Appomattox*, 550.
34. Winkler, *The Confederate Capital*, 152.
35. Ibid., 153–154.
36. Pomoroy (Co. A, 5th Texas), *Reminiscences*, 70–71.
37. Winkler, *The Confederate Capital*, 154.
38. Ibid.
39. Winkler, *The Confederate Capital*, 155.

Chapter 14 — The Wilderness, May 5–6, 1864

1. Freeman, *Lee's Lieutenants*, Vol. 3, 357.
2. Edward Porter Alexander, *Fighting for the Confederacy: The Personal Recollections of General Edward Porter Alexander*, Gary Gallagher, ed. (Chapel Hill: University of North Carolina Press, 1984), 345.
3. Dickert, *A History of Kershaw's Brigade*, 340, in Freeman, *Lee's Lieutenants*, Vol. 3, 342.
4. Alexander, *Fighting for the Confederacy*, 346.
5. Ibid.
6. Ibid.
7. Longstreet, *From Manassas to Appomattox*, 554.
8. Polley (Co. F, 4th Texas), *Hood's Texas Brigade*, 228.
9. Sorrel, *Recollections*, 236.
10. Freeman, *Robert E. Lee*, Vol. 3, 264.
11. E. M. Law, "From the Wilderness to Cold Harbor," *B&L*, Vol. 4, 118–119.
12. Polley (Co. F, 4th Texas), *Hood's Texas Brigade*, 229.
13. Mark Mayo Boatner III, *The Civil War Dictionary* (New York: McKay, 1987), 919.
14. "G. M. Sorrell to Maj. Gen. C. W. Field, Commanding Division, 11:00 A.M., Headquarters First Army Corps," O.R., Ser. 1, Vol. 36, Pt. 2, 947.
15. Winkler, *The Confederate Capital*, 164.
16. Freeman, *Lee's Lieutenants*, Vol. 3, 350
17. Law, "From the Wilderness to Cold Harbor," *B&L*, Vol. 4, 122–123.

18. Alexander, *Military Memoirs*, 501.
19. Freeman, *Lee's Lieutenants*, Vol. 3, 354.
20. Ibid.
21. "Reports of General Robert E. Lee, C.S. Army," O.R., Ser. 1, Vol. 36, Pt. 1, 1028.
22. Alexander, *Military Memoirs*, 503
23. Collier, *They'll Do To Tie To*, 172–173.
24. Law, "From the Wilderness to Cold Harbor," *B&L*, Vol. 4, 124.
25. Sorrel, *Recollections*, 240.
26. Polley (Co. F, 4th Texas), *Hood's Texas Brigade*, 230–231.
27. "Report of Brig. Gen. Joseph B. Kershaw, C.S. Army," O.R., Ser. 1, Vol. 36, 1061.
28. Alexander, *Military Memoirs*, 503.
29. Sorrel, *Recollections*, 240
30. J. B. Minor, "Rallying with a Frying Pan," *Confederate Veteran* 13, no. 2 (February 1905), 72–73.
31. Smith (Co. D, 4th Texas), *Reminiscences*, 49
32. Polley (Co. F, 4th Texas), *Hood's Texas Brigade*, 231.
33. Hanks (Co. K, 1st Texas), *History*, 16.
34. Freeman, *Lee's Lieutenants*, Vol. 3, 357.
35. Ibid.
36. Winkler, *The Confederate Capital*, 164.
37. Ibid., 167.
38. Winkler, *The Confederate Capital*, 165. Capt. James Harding, 1st Texas, is identified as one of the men grabbing Traveler's reins.
39. E. J. Parrent (Co. D, 4th Texas), "General Lee to the Rear," *Confederate Veteran* 2, no. 1 (January 1894): 14–15
40. Longstreet, *From Manassas to Appomattox*, 560–561.
41. Charles Venable to Gen. James Longstreet, October 21, 1877, James Longstreet Papers, 1875–1904, U.N.C.C.H., S.H.C.
42. Freeman, *Lee's Lieutenants*, III, 358.
43. "Report of Lieut. Gen. James Longstreet, C.S. Army," O.R., Ser. 1, Vol. 36, Pt. 1, 1055.
44. Polley (Co. F, 4th Texas), *Hood's Texas Brigade*, 232.
45. Law, "From the Wilderness to Cold Harbor," *B&L*, Vol. 4, 125.
46. See Krick, *Lee's Colonels*, 262.
47. Polley (Co. F, 4th Texas), *A Soldier's Letters*, 233–234.
48. Aycock (Co. E, 4th Texas), *A Sketch of the Lone Star Guards*, 13.
49. Polley (Co. F, 4th Texas), *A Soldier's Letters*, 234.
50. Freeman, *Robert E. Lee*, Vol. 3, 290.
51. Sorrel, *Recollections*, 241–242.
52. "Report of Brig. Gen. William Mahone, C.S." O.R., Ser. 1, Vol. 36, Pt. 1, 1091.
53. Mary C. Moffett, ed., *Letters of General James Connor, C.S.A.* (Columbia, SC: n.p., 1933), 133.
54. "Report of Brig. Gen. Joseph B. Kershaw, C.S. Army," O.R., Ser. 1, Vol. 36, Pt. 1, 1061.
55. Law, "From the Wilderness to Cold Harbor," *B&L*, Vol. 4, 126.
56. Freeman, *Lee's Lieutenants*, Vol. 3, 366.

57. "Report of Brig. Gen. John B. Gordon, C.S. Army," O.R., Ser. 1, Vol. 36, Pt. 1, 1078.

58. Polley (Co. F, 4th Texas), *Hood's Texas Brigade*, 233–234.

59. Hanks (Co. K, 1st Texas), *History*, 38.

60. Freeman, *Robert E. Lee*, Vol. 3, 302

61. W. H. Taylor to Maj. Gen. Stuart, Headquarters Army of Northern Virginia, May 7, 1864, O.R., Ser. 1, Vol. 36, Pt. 2, 970.

Chapter 15 — Spotsylvania Court House to Cold Harbor, May 8–June 3, 1864

1. Winkler, *The Confederate Capital*, 172.

2. Freeman, *Lee's Lieutenants*, Vol. 3, 375.

3. Ibid., 380.

4. Dickert, *History of Kershaw's Brigade*, 357–358, in Freeman, *Lee's Lieutenants*, Vol. 3, 382.

5. Sorrel, *Recollections*, 252.

6. Freeman, *Robert E. Lee*, Vol. 3, 306.

7. Freeman, *Lee's Lieutenants*, Vol. 3, 385.

8. Ibid., 387.

9. Freeman, *Robert E. Lee*, Vol. 3, 309.

10. Pomoroy (Co. A, 5th Texas), *Reminiscences*, 78.

11. Polley (Co. F, 4th Texas), *A Soldier's Letters*, 237.

12. Law, "From the Wilderness to Cold Harbor," *B&L*, Vol. 4, 129.

13. Aycock (Co. E, 4th Texas), "A Sketch—Lone Star Guards," 14. Presumably, Aycock was referring to David M. Deckerd, listed in Simpson's *Compendium*, 126, as being killed at Spotsylvania.

14. Law, "From the Wilderness to Cold Harbor," *B&L*, Vol. 4, 129.

15. Ibid.

16. Pomeroy ("A," 5th Texas), *Reminiscences*, 78. Pomeroy said that Bailey's musket killed another man, John Bell, also of Co. A.

17. Winkler, *The Confederate Capital*, 172.

18. Hamilton (Co. M, 1st Texas), *History of Company M*, 58.

19. Robert Campbell (Co. A, 5th Texas), "Letter from the Virginia Army," Galveston *Tri-Weekly News*, Wednesday, July 20, 1864.

20. Hanks (Co. K, 1st Texas), *History*, 19–20.

21. Polley (Co. F, 4th Texas), *Hood's Texas Brigade*, 239.

22. Alexander, *Military Memoirs*, 516.

23. "Report of Lieut. Gen. Richard S. Ewell, C.S. Army," O.R., Ser. 1, Vol. 36, Pt. 1, 1072.

24. Henry W. Thomas, *History of the Doles-Cooke Brigade* (Atlanta: n.p., 1903), 479.

25. Polley (Co. F, 4th Texas), *A Soldier's Letters*, 238–239. See Simpson's *Compendium*. Presumably, the "Veteran Morris," was William Morris who had been wounded at Gaines' Mill and again in the Wilderness, several days earlier, apparently not seriously. "Pokue" was, presumably, Levi S. Pogue, who, while lacking in courage at times was not lacking in perseverance. He is listed as being wounded later on the Darbytown Road

and being paroled at Appomattox Court House.

26. Freeman, *Lee's Lieutenant's*, Vol. 3, 398.

27. Law, "From the Wilderness to Cold Harbor," *B&L*, Vol. 4, 130.

28. Alexander, *Military Memoirs*, 520.

29. Ibid.

30. Freeman, *Robert E. Lee*, Vol. 3, 318.

31. Freeman, *Lee's Lieutenants*, Vol. 3, 407–408.

32. Ibid., 408.

33. Freeman, *Robert E. Lee*, Vol. 3, 324.

34. Ibid., 325.

35. Freeman, *Robert E. Lee*, Vol. 3, 325.

36. Ibid., 329. The trunk of one of these trees is on display at the Smithsonian in Washington, DC.

37. Law, "From the Wilderness to Cold Harbor," *B&L*, Vol. 4, 134.

38. Alexander, *Military Memoirs*, 527.

39. Winkler, *The Confederate Capital*, 172.

40. Polley (Co. F, 4th Texas), *Hood's Texas Brigade*, 237.

41. Freeman, *Robert E. Lee*, Vol. 3, 347.

42. Alexander, *Military Memoirs*, 529.

43. Freeman, *Robert E. Lee*, Vol. 3, 356.

44. Polley (Co. F, 4th Texas), *Hood's Texas Brigade*, 241.

45. Ibid.

46. Polley (Co. F, 4th Texas), *Hood's Texas Brigade*, 242.

47. Collier, *They'll Do To Tie To*, 190.

48. Alexander, *Military Memoirs*, 540.

49. Collier, *They'll Do To Tie To*, 191.

50. Hanks (Co. K, 1st Texas), *History*, 41.

51. Collier, *They'll Do To Tie To*, 191.

52. Polley (Co. F, 4th Texas), *Hood's Texas Brigade*, 242–243.

53. Freeman, *Robert E. Lee*, Vol. 3, 391.

54. Polley (Co. F, 4th Texas), *Hood's Texas Brigade*, 243.

55. Collier, *They'll Do To Tie To*, 192.

56. Polley (Co. F, 4th Texas), *Hood's Texas Brigade*, 243.

Chapter 16 — James River to Forts Harrison and Gilmer, June–September 1864

1. James D. Pickens (Co. E, 3rd Arkansas)," "Fort Harrison," *Confederate Veteran* 21, no. 10 (October 1913): 484.

2. See Boatner, *Civil War Dictionary*, 644

3. Andrew A. Humphreys, *The Virginia Campaign of '64 and '65: The Army of the Potomac and the Army of the James* (1881–1882; reprint, New York: Charles Scribner's Sons, 1992), 196.

4. Freeman, *Robert E. Lee*, Vol. 3, 401.

5. Winkler, *The Confederate Capital*, 178.

6. P. G. T. Beauregard, "Four Days of Battle at Petersburg," *B&L*, Vol. 4, 540.

7. Actually, early on June 15, Gen. Smith's Federal

XVIII Corps and Kautz' cavalry, about 16,000 strong, crossed the Appomattox to attack Petersburg. Hancock's II Federal Corps was to cross the James that day and move in support of the attack. The initial assaults by Smith and Kautz were successful in capturing a portion of the Confederate line. However, due to various errors and miscues, when Hancock's II Corps came up, the attack was not pressed further. It was a missed opportunity of great proportions for Federal arms. See Boatner, *Civil War Dictionary*, 644–645.

8. Winkler, *The Confederate Capital*, 179.

9. Smith (Co. D, 4th Texas), *Reminiscences*, 55

10. Winkler, *The Confederate Capital*, 179

11. Ibid.

12. Polley (Co. F, 4th Texas), *Hood's Texas Brigade*, 244.

13. Polley (Co. F, 4th Texas), *A Soldier's Letters*, 248.

14. Alexander, *Military Memoirs*, 546.

15. Sorrell, *Recollections*, 262.

16. Alexander, *Military Memoirs*, 549.

17. Winkler, *The Confederate Capital*, 182.

18. Ibid., 180.

19. According to Col. Simpson, after their greeting by the citizens of Petersburg, the Texans and Arkansans moved "to the trenches east of the city and south of the Appomattox River," and "mid-way between the Norfolk and Petersburg Railroad and the Jerusalem Plank road and one and one-half miles east of the Blandford Cemetery." See Simpson, *Hood's Texas Brigade*, 424.

20. Freeman, *Robert E. Lee*, Vol. 3, 448.

21. Sorrell, *Recollections*, 263.

22. Polley (Co. F, 4th Texas), *Hood's Texas Brigade*, 245.

23. Pomeroy (Co. A, 5th Texas), *Reminiscences*, 83.

24. Winkler, *The Confederate Capital*, 180.

25. Polley (Co. F, 4th Texas), *Hood's Texas Brigade*, 245.

26. Johnson Hagood, *Memoirs of the War of Secession*, (1910; reprint, Camden, SC: J. J. Fox, n.d.), 283–284.

27. Winkler, *The Confederate Capital*, 181.

28. Polley (Co. F, 4th Texas), *A Soldier's Letters*, 244. Polley is obviously joking.

29. Pomeroy (Co. A, 5th Texas), *Reminiscences*, 83.

30. Hanks (Co. K, 1st Texas), *History*, 21.

31. Ibid.

32. Hanks (Co. K, 1st Texas), *History*, 22–23.

33. Winkler, *The Confederate Capital*, 181.

34. Polley (Co. F, 4th Texas), *A Soldier's Letters*, 250.

35. Winkler, *The Confederate Capital*, 183.

36. Freeman, *Robert E. Lee*, Vol. 3, 463.

37. Collier, *They'll Do To Tie To*, 197. According to Col. Simpson, Hadley, Co. K, was, while still a lieutenant, wounded on July 16, 1864, promoted captain during the winter of 1864–1865 and became a prisoner of war at Richmond on April 3, 1865. See *Compendium*, 313.

38. Winkler, *The Confederate Capital*, 182.

39. Polley (Co. F, 4th Texas), *A Soldier's Letters*, 230. See Simpson, *Compendium*, 105. William Calhoun, Co. B, 4th Texas, is listed as being taken prisoner in East Tennessee. There is no further information included. Polley's reference to him must indicate that he was later exchanged or somehow released otherwise.

40. Winkler, *The Confederate Capital*, 183.

41. Polley (Co. F, 4th Texas), *Hood's Texas Brigade*, 247.

42. Winkler, *The Confederate Capital*, 184–185.

43. Freeman, *Robert E. Lee*, Vol. 3, 464.

44. Hanks (Co. K, 1st Texas), *History*, 21.

45. Polly (Co. F, 4th Texas), *A Soldier's Letters*, 230–231.

46. Freeman, *Robert E. Lee*, Vol. 3, 467.

47. Polley (Co. F, 4th Texas), *Hood's Texas Brigade*, 248.

48. "The Richmond, Virginia Campaign, #302 Reports of Maj. Gen. Bushrod R. Johnson, C.S. Army," O.R., Ser. 1, Vol. 40, Pt. 1, 788.

49. Ibid., 476–477.

50. Simpson, *Hood's Texas Brigade*, 431.

51. Polley (Co. F, 4th Texas), *Hood's Texas Brigade*, 249.

52. Ibid., 250.

53. Polley (Co. F, 4th Texas), *A Soldier's Letters*, 254–255.

54. Freeman, *Robert E. Lee*, Vol. 3, 463.

55. Polley (Co. F, 4th Texas), *A Soldier's Letters*, 264.

56. Freeman, *Robert E. Lee*, Vol. 3, 487.

57. Polley (Co. F, 4th Texas), *Hood's Texas Brigade*, 252.

58. Freeman, *Robert E. Lee*, Vol. 3, 500

59. Winkler, *The Confederate Capital*, 190.

60. Ibid., 192.

61. Alexander, *Fighting for the Confederacy*, 474–475.

62. Ibid., 475.

63. Polley (Co. F, 4th Texas), *Hood's Texas Brigade*, 253.

64. Ibid.

65. "Brig. Gen. Chas. J. Paine to Maj. Gen. B. F. Butler, Headquarters, Third Division, Eighteenth Corps, October 6, 1864," O.R., Ser. 1, Vol. 42, Pt. 3, 100–101.

66. James D. Pickens (Co. E, 3rd Arkansas)," "Fort Harrison," *Confederate Veteran* 21, no. 10 (October 1913): 484.

67. Hamilton (Co. M, 1st Texas), *History of Company M*, 62–63.

68. Ibid.

69. Ibid., 65.

70. Polley (Co. F, 4th Texas), *Hood's Texas Brigade*, 256

71. Ibid.

Chapter 17 — "Darbytown Road to Five Forks, October 1864–March 30, 1865

1. Polley, *Hood's Texas Brigade*, 257.

2. Collier, *They'll Do To Tie To*, 203.

3. Freeman, *Robert E. Lee*, Vol. 3, 508, in Polley, *Hood's Texas Brigade*, 257.

4. Polley (Co. F, 4th Texas), *Hood's Texas Brigade*, 258.

5. Polley (Co. F, 4th Texas), *A Soldier's Letters*, 264.

6. Polley (Co. F, 4th Texas), *Hood's Texas Brigade*, 257.

7. Ibid., 258.

8. Polley (Co. F, 4th Texas), *A Soldier's Letters*, 266.

9. Basil Brashear (Co. F, 5th Texas), unpublished typescript, March 5, 1911, Gregory, Texas, C.R.C., H.C., H.T.B. file 3–6.

10. Sorrell, *Recollections*, 267.

11. Smith (Co. D, 4th Texas), *Reminiscences*, 58.

12. Hanks (Co. K, 1st Texas), *History*, 23.

13. Collier, *They'll Do To Tie To*, 206.

14. Winkler, *The Confederate Capital*, 195.

15. Ibid., 196. Mrs. Gregg was unable to attend because she was within Federal lines at the time. Later, she had his body removed to Aberdeen, Mississippi.

16. Longstreet, *From Manassas to Appomattox*, 573.

17. Polley (Co. F, 4th Texas), *Hood's Texas Brigade*, 260.

18. Hanks (Co. K, 1st Texas), *History*, 23.

19. Winkler, *The Confederate Capital*, 202.

20. Hanks (Co. K, 1st Texas), *History*, 152.

21. Polley (Co. F, 4th Texas), *Hood's Texas Brigade*, 262–263.

22. Winkler, *The Confederate Capital*, 202–203.

23. Ibid., 204.

24. Sorrel, *Recollections*, 272.

25. Longstreet, *From Manassas to Appomattox*, 581.

26. Freeman, *Robert E. Lee*, Vol. 3, 518.

27. Ibid., 519.

28. Polley (Co. F, 4th Texas), *Hood's Texas Brigade*, 263–265.

29. Ibid., 267–268.

30. Winkler, *The Confederate Capital*, 240.

31. Ibid., 239–240.

32. Freeman, *Robert E. Lee*, Vol. 4, 8.

33. Ibid., 12.

34. Freeman, *Robert E. Lee*, Vol. 4, 14.

35. Ibid., 16.

36. Longstreet, *From Manassas to Appomattox*, 595.

37. Freeman, *Robert E. Lee*, Vol. 4, 19.

38. Ibid., 22.

39. Freeman, *Robert E. Lee*, Vol. 4, 22.

40. Ibid., 31–32.

41. Freeman, *Robert E. Lee*, Vol. 4, 36.

42. Longstreet, *From Manassas to Appomattox*, 601–602.

43. Freeman, *Robert E. Lee*, Vol. 4, 41.

44. Ibid., 40.

45. Freeman, *Robert E. Lee*, Vol. 4, 44–45.

Chapter 18—Retreat to Appomattox, April 2–April 9, 1865

1. Col. Clement Sullivane, "Last Meeting with Gen. R. E. Lee," *Confederate Veteran* 28, no. 12 (December 1920): 459.

2. Horace Porter, "Five Forks and the Pursuit of Lee," *B&L*, Vol. 4, 716.

3. Freeman, *Lee's Lieutenants*, Vol. 3, 680.

4. Polley (Co. F, 4th Texas), *Hood's Texas Brigade*, 274.

5. Freeman, *Robert E. Lee*, IV, 41.

6. Freeman, *Lee's Lieutenants*, Vol. 3, 680.

7. Longstreet, *From Manassas to Appomattox*, 603.

8. Freeman, *Robert E. Lee*, Vol. 4, 51.

9. Freeman, *Lee's Lieutenants*, Vol. 3, 683.

10. Winkler, *The Confederate Capital*, 248.

11. Freeman, *Robert E. Lee*, Vol. 4, 53.

12. Freeman, *Lee's Lieutenants*, Vol. 3, 681.

13. Polley (Co. F, 4th Texas), *Hood's Texas Brigade*, 274.

14. Alexander, *Military Memoirs*, 593.

15. Freeman, *Robert E. Lee*, Vol. 4, 57.

16. Polley (Co. F, 4th Texas), *Hood's Texas Brigade*, 275.

17. Porter, "Five Forks and the Pursuit of Lee," *B&L*, Vol. 4, 718.

18. Ibid., 708.

19. Alexander, *Military Memoirs*, 590.

20. Polley (Co. F, 4th Texas), *Hood's Texas Brigade*, 275.

21. Porter, "Five Forks and the Pursuit of Lee," *B&L*, 718.

22. Ibid., 719. Gen. Sheridan, in his report, said that the cavalry took up the pursuit on the morning of April 3. See "Report of Maj. Gen. Philip H. Sheridan, U.S. Army," O.R., Ser. 1, Vol. 46, Pt. 1, 95, 1106.

23. Winkler, *The Confederate Capital*, 258.

24. Freeman, *Robert E. Lee*, Vol. 4, 60.

25. Hamilton (Co. M, 1st Texas), *History*, 68.

26. Freeman, *Robert E. Lee*, Vol. 4, 66.

27. Ibid., 71.

28. Polley (Co. F, 4th Texas), *Hood's Texas Brigade*, 275.

29. Freeman, *Robert E. Lee*, Vol. 4, 71.

30. "Lee's Report of the Surrender at Appomattox," *B&L, Vol. 4*, 724.

31. Freeman, *Robert E. Lee*, Vol. 4, 77.

32. Polley (Co. F, 4th Texas), *Hood's Texas Brigade*, 275

33. Freeman, *Robert E. Lee*, Vol. 4, 80.

34. Ibid., 81.

35 Freeman, *Robert E. Lee*, Vol. 4, 83.

36. "Report of Maj. Gen. Andrew A. Humphreys, U.S. Army," O.R., Ser. 1, Vol. 46, Pt. 1, 95, 674.

37. Longstreet, *From Manassas to Appomattox*, 611.

38. See Warner, *Generals in Gray*, 258–259.

39. Freeman, *Robert E. Lee*, Vol. 4, 84.

40. Ibid., 91.

41. "Report of Maj. Gen. Horation G. Wright, U.S. Army," O.R., Ser. 1, Vol. 46, Pt. 1, 905- 906.

42. "Lee's Report of the Surrender at Appomattox," *B&L*, Vol. 4, 724.

43. Freeman, *Robert E. Lee*, Vol. 4, 91.

44. Longstreet, *From Manassas to Appomattox*, 614.

45. Porter, "Five Forks and the Pursuit of Lee," *B&L*, Vol. 4, 720.

46. "Report of Maj. Gen. Andrew A. Humphreys, U.S. Army," O.R., Ser. 1, Vol. 46, Pt. 1, 95, 674. In his report, Gen. Humphreys said the troops of his 2nd Division, II Corps, Gen. Barlow commanding, on the morning of April 7, found both the bridges afire. However, he goes on to say that Barlow's troops were able to save both bridges, the High Bridge with "great difficulty."

47. Freeman, *Robert E. Lee*, Vol. 4, 102.

48. Ibid., 99.

49. Polley (Co. F, 4th Texas), *Hood's Texas Brigade*, 276.

50. Ibid., 276–277.

51. Alexander, *Military Memoirs*, 600.

52. Longstreet, *From Manassas to Appomattox*, 619.

53. See Freeman, *Robert E. Lee*, Vol. 4, 106.

54. Ibid.

55. Freeman, *Robert E. Lee*, Vol. 4, 107.

56. Ibid., 109.

57. Freeman, *Robert E. Lee*, Vol. 4, 112.

58. Ibid., 116.

59. Col. Charles Marshall, "Occurrences at Lee's Surrender," *Confederate Veteran* 7, no. 2 (February 1894): 44.

60. Longstreet, *From Manassas to Appomattox*, 623–624.

61. Alexander, *Military Memoirs*, 603.

62. Freeman, *Robert E. Lee*, Vol. 4, 121.

63. Longstreet, *From Manassas to Appomattox*, 625.

64. Alexander, *Military Memoirs*, 605.

65. Polley (Co. F, 4th Texas), *Hood's Texas Brigade*, 277.

66. A. C. Jones, "Third Arkansas Regiment at Appomattox," *Confederate Veteran* 23, no. 7 (July 1915): 313.

67. Freeman, *Lee's Lieutenants*, Vol. 3, 731.

68. Ibid., 733–736. The first Federal officer entering Gordon's lines demanded immediate surrender. He was an outrageously dressed twenty-five-year-old brevet major general named George A. Custer. After speaking with Gen. Gordon, he requested to speak to Gen. Longstreet. His request was granted and after he left, Gen. Sheridan arrived and held a conference with Gen. Gordon. Reaching Longstreet, Custer made the same demand for immediate surrender. In the exchange he managed to make the usually taciturn lieutenant general angry—very. Custer was dismissed by Longstreet's remonstrance: "'I suppose you know no better and have violated the decencies of military procedure because you know no better, but it will not save you if you do so again. Now, go and act as you and Sheridan choose and I will teach you a lesson you won't forget! Now go!'—and he raised both hand and voice."

69. Freeman, *Lee's Lieutenants*, Vol. 3, 738.

70. Alexander, *Military Memoirs*, 609.

71. Freeman, *Robert E. Lee*, Vol. 4, 135.

72. Ibid., 136.

73. Freeman, *Robert E. Lee*, Vol. 4, 138–139.

74. Ibid., 141.

75. Freeman, *Robert E. Lee*, Vol. 4, 143.

76. Winkler, *The Confederate Capital*, 268.

77. Collier, *They'll Do To Tie To*, 219.

78.. Jones, "Third Arkansas Regiment at Appomattox," *Confederate Veteran* 23, no. 7 (July 1915): 314.

79. Freeman, *Robert E. Lee*, Vol. 4, 154–155.

Chapter 19—Advance into Legend, April 12, 1865, and Beyond

1. Freeman, *Lee's Lieutenants*, Vol. 3, 751.

2. Joshua L. Chamberlain, *The Passing of the Armies* (1915; reprint, New York: Bantam Books, 1993), 195.

3. Ibid.

4. Chamberlain, *The Passing of the Armies*, 196.

5. Ibid.

6. Chamberlain, *The Passing of the Armies*, 198–200.

7. Freeman, *Lee's Lieutenants*, Vol. 3, 751.

8. Clement Sullivane, "Last Meeting with Gen. R. E. Lee," *Confederate Veteran* 27, no. 12 (December 1920): 459.

9. Pomoroy (Co. A, 5th Texas), *Reminiscences*, 86. The writer has not seen these specific options in print elsewhere. Where there is mention of transportation for paroled Confederates, it is usually specified as free transportation by U.S. military rail and water-borne vessels.

10. Polley (Co. F, 4th Texas), *Hood's Texas Brigade*, 279–282.

11. Jones (3rd Arkansas), "Third Arkansas Regiment at Appomattox," *Confederate Veteran* 23, no. 7 (July 1915): 314–315.

12. See, Hamilton (Co. M, 1st Texas), *History of Company M*, 69–74.

13. Pomoroy (Co. A, 5th Texas), *Reminiscences*, 87–89.

14. Simpson, "Hood's Texas Brigade at Appomattox," in Wooster, *Lone Star Blue and Gray*, from the Confederate Memorial, Arlington National Cemetery, 347.

15. Gerald F. Linderman, *Embattled Courage: The Experience of Combat in the American Civil War* (New York: The Free Press, 1987), 269.

16. Ibid., 275.

17. Linderman, *Embattled Courage*, 272.

18. Frank B. Chilton, "Formation of Hood's Texas Brigade Association," *Unveiling and Dedication of Monument to Hood's Texas Brigade* (Houston: Chilton; 1911), 79.

19. See pages xi–xiv in the Preface to Simpson, *Hood's Texas Brigade in Reunion and Memory*. This is in Volume 3 of his four-volume history of the brigade. This writer is here acknowledging the summarized use of the extensive information on the basic facts of the history of the brigade association gathered by Col. Simpson; he did his research thoroughly and further delving would be unlikely to turn up any new information.

20. Frank B. Chilton, *Unveiling and Dedication of Monument to Hood's Texas Brigade* (Houston: Chilton; 1911), 16.

21. Chilton, "First Successful Move to Build a Mon-

ument, and How It Began at Navasota Reunion," *Unveiling and Dedication of Monument*, 87.

22. Ibid., 86.

23. "Monument to Hood's Texas Brigade," *Confederate Veteran* 22, no. 12 (December 1909): 582.

24. The writer found no mention of why the monument dedication reunion was held in October instead of its usual June date. One explanation might be that the age of the surviving attendees suggested a cooler time of the year. However, now, almost 100 years later, October in Texas can be just about as hot as it is in June.

25. Chilton, "Statue Presented to the State," *Unveiling and Dedication of Monument to Hood's Texas Brigade*, 33.

26. Ibid., 39–40.

27. Polk (Co. I, 4th Texas), *North and South American Review*, 36.

Epilogue: Captain Ike N. M. Turner, Co. K, 5th Texas, Comes Home to Texas, 1995

1. "Capt. Ike Comes Home," Supplement, Polk County *Enterprise*, April 9, 1995, 1C.

2. See, Kevin Moran, "The Homecoming," Houston *Chronicle*, Sunday, November 6, 1994, *Texas Magazine*, 6–10.

3. Paul McKay, "Confederate Hero Finally to Be Buried in Texas Soil," Houston *Chronicle*, Saturday, April 15, 1995, 1A, 10A.

4. According to a biographical sketch by Dr. B. D. Patterson, one-time director of the Confederate Research Center at Hill College in Hillsboro, Texas, Capt. Turner had three brothers in Co. K. See Simpson's *Compendium*, in which there are listed 3rd Lt. Joseph Turner, 244, who is the most likely candidate to have heard his dying brother's last words. C. H. Turner is listed, 250, as being recruited on March 21, 1863, in Livingston County. If he were the one, he would have had to make an unusually fast trip to Virginia to have been at his brother's side. And its Polk, not Livingston County and is probably a typographical error. W. H. Turner is listed, 250, but had already been discharged from the company in August 1862.

5. "Capt. Ike Comes Home," "Ike Turner — A Born Leader on the Field," Supplement, Polk County *Enterprise*, April 9, 1995, 7C.

6. Diary, Lt. James E. Cobb, Co. F, 5th Texas, entry of April 14, 1863, Cobb — Hunter Family Papers, U.N.C.C.H., S.H.C.

7. "Capt. Ike Comes Home," "Death Wish to Reality," Supplement, Polk County *Enterprise*, April 9, 1995, 4C.

8. Ibid., 4C–5C.

9. "The Homecoming," Houston *Chronicle*, *Texas Magazine*, 6.

10. Ibid., 6–7.

11. "Confederate Hero," 10A.

Appendix A: Companies in Hood's Texas Brigade, A.N.V.

1. See A. V. Winkler, *The Confederate Capitol*, ix, and Simpson, *Compendium*, 15–250.

Appendix B: Representative Mortality Figures

1. Pohanka, "The Very Vortex of Hell," 72.

2. Frederick Phisterer, *Statistical Record of the Armies of the United States, Campaigns of the Civil War* (1881–1883; reprint, Harrisburg, PA: The Archive Society, 1992), 214.

3. Simpson, "Casualties for Six Major Battles," *Compendium*, 535.

4. Phisterer, *Statistical Record*, 214.

5. Simpson, *Compendium*, 535.

6. Pohanka, "The Very Vortex of Hell," 72.

7. Phisterer, *Statistical Record*, 214.

8. "Report of Surg. Lafayette Guild, C.S. Army, Medical Director of the Army of Northern Virginia," O.R., Ser. 1, Vol. 19, 811–812.

9. Simpson, *Compendium*, 535.

10. Phisterer, *Statistical Record*, 215.

11. "The Opposing Forces at Fredericksburg, Va.," *B&L*, Vol. 3, 146–147.

12. Phisterer, *Statistical Record*, 215.

13. Simpson, *Compendium*, 535.

14. Phisterer, *Statistical Record*, 215.

15. Simpson, *Compendium*, 535.

16. Phisterer, *Statistical Record*, 216.

17. Simpson, *Compendium*, 535

18. Collier, "*They'll Do To Tie To*," 178–179

19. Simpson, "Hood's Texas Brigade at Appomattox," in Wooster, *Lone Star Blue and Gray*, 344–345.

Appendix C: Deaths by Disease in the Texas Regiments

1. Simpson, *Compendium*, 536.

Bibliography

Primary Sources

MANUSCRIPTS, DIARIES, PERSONAL PAPERS AND LETTERS

Alexander, Edward Porter. *Papers, 1854–1865.* "Personal Recollections of the Knoxville Campaign." Manuscript Division, Library of Congress, Washington, DC.

Andrews, Garnett. Papers. Southern Historical Collection, University of North Carolina, Chapel Hill.

Archer, James J. Letters. Hood's Texas Brigade Files, Confederate Research Center, Hill College, Hillsboro, TX.

Aycock, B.M. *"A Sketch—The Lone Star Guards."* Miscellaneous Confederate Files, Vol. 28, Fredericksburg National Military Park, Fredericksburg, VA.

Brake, Robert L. Collection. Texas Brigade miscellany. U. S. Army Military History Institute, Carlisle Barracks, PA.

Brashear, Basil C. Unpublished typescript. Hood's Texas Brigade Files, Confederate Research Center, Hill College, Hillsboro, TX.

Caddell, Jeremiah. Letters. Hood's Texas Brigade Files, Confederate Research Center, Hill College, Hillsboro, TX.

Clay, Tacitus T. Letters. Miscellaneous Confederate Files, Vol. 131, Fredericksburg National Military Park, Fredericksburg, VA.

Cobb, James E. Cobb–Hunter Family Papers. Southern Historical Collection, University of North Carolina, Chapel Hill.

Congleton, Andrew A. Letters. Hood's Texas Brigade File, Antietam National Battlefield Park, Sharpsburg, MD.

Daffan, L.A. Typescript. Hood's Texas Brigade Files, Confederate Research Center, Hill College, Hillsboro, TX.

Downs, Oscar J. Diary. Hood's Texas Brigade Files, Confederate Research Center, Hill College, Hillsboro, TX.

Felder, Rufus K. Letters. Hood's Texas Brigade Files, Confederate Research Center, Hill College, Hillsboro, TX.

Foster, Robert V. Letters. Hood's Texas Brigade Files, Confederate Research Center, Hill College, Hillsboro, TX.

Franklin, B. I. Letters. Hood's Texas Brigade Files, Confederate Research Center, Hill College, Hillsboro, TX.

Gaston, Robert, and W.H. Gaston. Letters. Hood's Texas Brigade Files, Confederate Research Center, Hill College, Hillsboro, TX.

Hanks, O.T. *History of Captain B. F. Benson's Company, 1861–1865.* Confederate Research Center, Hill College, Hillsboro, TX.

Holloway, Robert G. Diary. Museum of the Confederacy, Richmond, Virginia.

Hood, A.B. Letters. Hood's Texas Brigade Files, Confederate Research Center, Hill College, Hillsboro, TX.

Howard, J. A. Howard Family Papers. Southern Historical Collection. University of North Carolina, Chapel Hill.

Kenyon, Moses Warren. Papers. Perkins Library, Duke University, Durham, NC.

Longstreet, James. Papers, 1874–1905. Southern Historical Collection, University of North Carolina, Chapel Hill.

McCarty, T. L. "Synopsis of the Tennessee Campaign by Longstreet, September 1863 to May 4, 1864." T. L. McCarty Collection. Center for American History, University of Texas, Austin.

Northrop, Lucian B. Papers. South Caroliniana Library, University of South Carolina, Columbia.

Pomeroy, Nicholas. *Reminiscences of the American War, 1861–1865.* Unpublished manuscript, no date. Center for American History, University of Texas, Austin.

Power, Hugh Irvin. Jr., ed. "A Texan at War: Letters of Private James Hendricks, Army of Northern Virginia." Unpublished typescript. Hood's Texas Brigade Files, Confederate Research Center, Hill College, Hillsboro, TX.

Pritchard, W. D. Typescript of newspaper articles from an unpublished manuscript. Texas Brigade File, Antietam National Battlefield Park, Sharpsburg, MD.

Roberts, Albert S. *Reminiscences.* Center for American History, University of Texas, Austin.

Schiwetz, Mrs. E. M. Papers. Center for American History, University of Texas, Austin.

Shockley, W. S. Papers. Perkins Library, Duke University, Durham, NC.

Sims, Albert C. In Jasper *Newsboy,* May 17, 1911, 20–21. Hood's Texas Brigade Files, Confederate Research Center, Hill College, Hillsboro, TX.

Smith, Miles V. *Reminiscences of the Civil War,* Civil War Miscellaneous Collection, U.S. Army Military History Institute, Carlisle Barracks, PA.

Smither, John, and Mark Smither. Unpublished typescript. Hood's Texas Brigade Files, Confederate Research Center, Hill College, Hillsboro, TX.

"*Spirit of '61.*" Regimental newspaper, 18th Georgia Infantry Regiment. Woodruff Library, Emory University, Atlanta, GA.

Townsend, William P. Papers. Hood's Texas Brigade Files, Confederate Research Center, Hill College, Hillsboro, TX.

Venable, Charles. Papers. Southern Historical Collection, University of North Carolina, Chapel Hill.

Wigfall, Louis T. Family Papers. Manuscript Division, Library of Congress, Washington, DC.

Williams, Watson Dugat. Letters. Hood's Texas Brigade Files, Confederate Research Center, Hill College, Hillsboro, TX.

Wood, Campbell. Papers. Hood's Texas Brigade Files, Confederate Research Center, Hill College, Hillsboro, TX.

PUBLISHED RECORDS OF THE CONFEDERATE STATES GOVERNMENT

Confederate States War Department. *Regulations for the Army of the Confederate States: 1863.* 1863. Reprint. Harrisburg, Pennsylvania: National Historical Society, 1980.

PUBLISHED RECORDS OF THE UNITED STATES GOVERNMENT

United States War Department. *The War of the Rebellion: Official Records of the Union and Confederate Armies.* Washington, DC: Government Printing Office, 1880–1901.

United States Department of the Interior. *Chickamauga and Chattanooga Battlefields.* Washington DC: Government Printing Office, 1961.

PUBLISHED BOOKS AND MEMOIRS

Alexander, Edward Porter. *Fighting for the Confederacy: The Personal Recollections of General Edward Porter Alexander.* Edited by Gary W. Gallagher. Chapel Hill: University of North Carolina Press, 1989.

_____. *Military Memoirs of a Confederate.* 1907. Reprint. New York: Da Capo Press, 1993.

Ballentine, George. *Autobiography of an English Soldier in the United States Army.* Edited by William H. Goetzmann. Chicago: Lakeside Press, 1986.

Barziza, D. U. *The Adventures of a Prisoner of War and Life and Scenes in Federal Prisons: Johnson's Island, Fort Delaware, and Point Lookout.* Edited by R. Henderson Shuffler. Reprint. 1865. Austin: University of Texas Press, 1964.

Blackford, Charles Minor, III, ed., Susan L. Blackford, comp., Charles Minor Blackford, annot. *Letters From Lee's Army: Memoirs of Life in and Out of the Army of Northern Virginia During the War Between the States.* New York: Charles Scribner's Sons, 1947.

Blackford, W. W. *War Years with Jeb Stuart.* New York: Charles Scribner's Sons, 1946.

Chamberlain, Joshua L. *The Passing of the Armies.* 1915. Reprint. New York: Bantam Books, 1993.

Chesnut, Mary Boykin. *A Diary From Dixie.* 1949. Reprint. Boston: Harvard University Press, 1980.

Commager, Henry Steele, and Erik Bruun, eds. *Living History: The Civil War.* 1950. Reprint. New York: Tess Press, 2000.

Cooke, John Esten. *The Wearing of the Gray.* Reprint. 1867. Baton Rouge: Louisiana State University Press, 1997.

Dame, William M. *From the Rapidan to Richmond and the Spotsylvania Campaign.* Baltimore: 1920.

Davis, Maj. George B., Leslie J. Perry, Joseph W. Kirkley and Capt. Calvin D. Cowles. *Official Military Atlas of the Civil War.* 1891. Reprint. New York: Gramercy Books, 1983.

Dawes, Rufus R. *A Full-Blown Yankee of the Iron Brigade: Service with the Sixth Wisconsin Volunteers.* 1894. Reprint. Lincoln: University of Nebraska Press; 1999.

Douglas, Robert Kyd. *I Rode with Stonewall: The Youngest Member of Jackson's Staff.* Chapel Hill: University of North Carolina Press, 1980.

Everett, Donald E., ed. *Chaplain Davis and Hood's Texas Brigade.* Baton Rouge: Louisiana State University Press, 1962.

Fletcher, William A. *Rebel Private Front and Rear.* Reprint. 1908. Washington, DC: Zengler, 1954.

Freemantle, Lt. Col. Arthur J. L. *Three Months in the Southern States: April–June, 1863.* 1864. Reprint. Lincoln: University of Nebraska Press, 1991.

Gallaway, B. P., ed. *Texas: The Dark Corner of the Confederacy.* Lincoln: University of Nebraska Press, 1994.

Giles, Val C. *Rags and Hope: The Memoirs of Val C. Giles, Four Years with Hood's Brigade, Fourth Texas Infantry, 1861–1865.* Edited and compiled by Mary Lasswell. New York: Coward-McCann, 1961.

Grant, U. S. *Personal Memoirs of U. S. Grant.* Edited by E. B. Long. Cleveland and New York: World, 1952.

Hagood, Johnson. *Memoirs of the War of Secession.* Columbia, SC: n.p., 1910

Hamilton, D.H. *History of Company M, First Texas Volunteer Infantry, Hood's Brigade.* 1925. Reprint. Waco, TX: Morrison, 1962.

Hardee, William J. *Hardee's Rifle and Light Infantry Tactics.* New York: Kane, 1862.

Hood, John Bell. *Advance and Retreat.* 1880. Reprint. Edison, NJ: Blue and Gray Press, 1985.

Houston, Sam. *Writings (1813–1863).* In Marshal De Bruhl, *Sword of San Jacinto: A Life of Sam Houston.* New York: Random House, 1993.

Humphreys, Andrew A., *The Virginia Campaign of '64 and '65: The Army of the Potomac and the Army of the James.* 1881–1882. Reprint. New York: Charles Scribner's Sons, 1992.

Johnson, Robert U., and Clarence C. Buel, eds. *Battles and Leaders of the Civil War.* 4 vols. New York: Yoseloff, 1956.

Jones, John B. *A Rebel War Clerk's Diary.* 1958. Reprint. Baton Rouge: Louisiana State University Press, 1993.

Longstreet, James. *From Manassas to Appomattox.* No date. Reprint. Secaucus, NJ: Blue and Gray Press, 1988.

McArthur, Judith N., and Orville V. Burton, eds. *A Gentleman and an Officer: A Military and Social History of James B. Griffin's Civil War.* New York: Oxford University Press, 1996.

McClure, Alexander K., ed. *Annals of the Civil War.* 1878. Reprint. New York: Da Capo Press, 1994.

Moffett, Mary C., ed. *Letters of General James Connor, C. S. A.* Columbia, SC: n.p., 1933.

Myers, William S., ed. *The Mexican War Diary of George B. McClellan.* Princeton: Princeton University Press, 1917.

Newcomb, James P. *Sketch of Secession Times in Texas.* San Francisco: n. p., 1863.

Oates, William C. *The War Between the Union and the Confederacy.* 1905. Reprint. Dayton, OH: Morningside Bookshop, 1985.

Polk, J. M. *The North and South American Review.* Austin, TX: Von Boeckmann-Jones, 1912.

Polley, Joseph B. *A Soldier's Letters to Charming Nellie.* 1908. Reprint. Gaithersburg, MD: Butternut Press, 1984.

_____. *Hood's Texas Brigade: Its Marches, Its Battles, Its Achievements.* 1910. Reprint. Dayton, OH: Morningside Bookshop, 1988.

Powell, Robert M. *Recollections of a Texas Colonel at Gettysburg.* Edited by Gregory A. Coco. Gettysburg, PA: Thomas, 1990.

Priest, John M., ed. *Stephen Elliott Welch of the Hampton Legion.* Shippensburg, PA: Burd Street Press, 1994.

Putnam, Sallie Brock. *Richmond During the War.* 1867. Reprint. Lincoln: University of Nebraska Press, 1996.

Sorrell, G. Moxley. *Recollections of a Confederate Staff Officer.* New York: Konecky & Konecky, 1994.

Stevens, John W. *Reminiscences of the Civil War.* Hillsboro, TX: Hillsboro Mirror Print, 1902.

Taylor, Walter H. *Four Years with General Lee.* Bloomington: Indiana University Press, 1996.

_____. *General Lee: His Campaigns in Virginia, 1861–1865, With Personal Reminiscences.* 1906. Reprint. Lincoln: University of Nebraska Press, 1994.

Todd, George T. *First Texas Regiment.* Waco, TX: Texian Press, 1963.

West, John C. *A Texan in Search of a Fight.* 1901. Reprint. Baltimore: Butternut and Blue Press, 1994.

Winkler, Mrs. A.V. *The Confederate Capital and Hood's Texas Brigade.* 1894. Reprint. Baltimore: Butternut and Blue Press, 1991.

NEWSPAPERS

Austin State Gazette. 1861–1862.
Galveston Tri-Weekly News. 1861–1865.
Houston Chronicle.

Houston Tri-Weekly Telegraph. 1861–1865.
Marshall Texas Republican. 1861–1865.
Polk County Enterprise.
Richmond Enquirer. 1861–1865.
Richmond Whig. 1861–1865.
San Antonio Tri-weekly Alamo Express. 1861.

ARTICLES

Alexander, Edward Porter. "Confederate Artillery Service," *Southern Historical Society Papers* 11, 104.
_____. "Longstreet at Knoxville." In Robert U. Johnson and Clarence A. Buel, eds. *Battles and Leaders of the Civil War.* Vol. 3. New York: Yoseloff, 1956, 745–751.
"Anecdotes of the Peninsular Campaign." J. H. L., "Hood Feeling the Enemy." In Robert U. Johnson and Clarence A. Buel, eds. *Battles and Leaders of the Civil War.* Vol. 2. New York: Yoseloff, 1956, 275–277.
Barnes, James J., and Patience P. Barnes, eds. "'What I Thought at Antietam.'" *Civil War Times* 40, no. 7 (September 2006): 15–19, 54.
Beauregard, P. G. T. "Four Days of Battle at Petersburg." In Robert U. Johnson and Clarence A. Buel, eds. *Battles and Leaders of the Civil War.* Vol. 2. New York: Yoseloff, 1956. 540–544.
Blackburn, J. K. P. "Reminiscences of the Terry Rangers." *Southwestern Historical Quarterly* 22 (July 1918): 39.
"Brig. Gen. James J. Archer." *Confederate Veteran* 8, no. 2 (February 1900): 65–67.
Burrage, Henry S. "Burnside Holds Out at Knoxville." In *Living History: The Civil War.* Edited by Henry Steele Commager and Erik Bruun. 1950. Reprint. New York: Tess Press, 2000, 691–694.
Campbell, Robert. "A Lone Star in Virginia." *Civil War Times Illustrated* 39, no. 6 (2000): 34–40, 86, 88, 90, 92, 94, 96, 98–99.
Cox, John. "Wade Hampton." *Confederate Veteran* 30, no. 12 (December 1922): 460–462.
Coxe, John. "Bloody Night Affair at Colchester, VA." *Confederate Veteran* 23, no. 4 (April 1915): 168–169.
Crozier, Granville. "A Private with General Hood." *Confederate Veteran* 25, no. 12 (December 1917): 556–558.
Darrow, Caroline Baldwin. "Recollections of the Twigg Surrender." In Robert U. Johnson and Clarence C. Buel, eds. *Battles and Leaders of the Civil War.* Vol. 1. New York: Yoseloff, 1956, 33–39.
"Dr. J. C. Jones." *Confederate Veteran* 12, no. 5 (May, 1904): 237–238.
Fullerton, J. C. "Reinforcing Thomas at Chickamauga." In Robert U. Johnson and Clarence C. Buel, eds. *Battles and Leaders of the Civil War.* Vol. 3. New York: Yoseloff, 1956, 665–667.
Giles, Val C. "Capt. J. D. Roberdeau." *Confederate Veteran* 18, no. 9 (September 1910): 439–440.
Hamby, William R. "Fourth Texas in Battle of Gaines' Mill." *Confederate Veteran* 14, no. 4 (April 1906): 183–184.
Harris, F. S. "General James J. Archer." *Confederate Veteran* 3, no. 1 (January 1895): 18–19.
Hill, Daniel H. "McClellan's Change of Base and Malvern Hill." In Robert U. Johnson and Clarence C. Buel, eds. *Battles and Leaders of the Civil War.* Vol. 2. New York: Yoseloff, 1956, 383–395.
_____. "The Battle of South Mountain." In Robert U. Johnson and Clarence C. Buel, eds. *Battles and Leaders of the Civil War.* Vol. 2. New York: Yoseloff, 1956, 559–581.
_____. "Chickamauga — The Great Battle of the West." In Robert U. Johnson and Clarence C. Buel, eds. *Battles and Leaders of the Civil War.* Vol. 3. New York: Yoseloff, 1956, 638–662.
_____. "Lee Attacks North of the Chickahominy." In Robert U. Johnson and Clarence C. Buel, eds. *Battles and Leaders of the Civil War.* Vol. 2. New York: Yoseloff, 1956, 347–362.
Hitchcock, W. H. "Recollections of a Participant in the Charge." In Robert U. Johnson and Clarence C. Buel, eds. *Battles and Leaders of the Civil War.* Vol. 2. New York: Yoseloff, 1956, 346.
Hopkins, C. A. Porter, ed. "The James J. Archer Letters: A Marylander in the Civil War, Part I." *Maryland Historical Magazine* 56, no. 1 (March 1961): 72–93.
_____. "The James J. Archer Letters: A Marylander in the Civil War, Part I." *Maryland Historical Magazine* 56, no. 2 (June 1961): 125–135.
Hunter, J. T. "Lieut. Gen. John B. Hood." *Confederate Veteran* 24, no. 2. (June 1916): 257.
_____. "Hard Fighting of Fourth Texas." *Confederate Veteran* 14, no. 1 (January 1906), 22.
Jones, Alexander C. "Brig. Gen. John Gregg." *Confederate Veteran* 17, no. 6. (June 1909): 269.
_____. "A Veteran's Refutation of the 'Dense Ignorance' Charge." *Confederate Veteran* 17, no. 3 (March 1909): 108–109.
_____. "Arkansas Soldiers in Virginia." *Confederate Veteran* 20, no. 10 (October 1912): 464.
_____. "Inaugurating the Picket Exchange." *Confederate Veteran* 26, no. 4 (April 1918), 154–156.
_____. "Longstreet at Gettysburg." *Confederate Veteran* 23, no. 12 (December 1915): 551–552.
_____. "Third Arkansas Regiment at Appomattox." *Confederate Veteran* 23, no. 7 (July 1915), 313–315.

Law, Evander M. "The Struggle for 'Round Top.'" In Robert U. Johnson and Clarence C. Buel, eds. *Battles and Leaders of the Civil War*. Vol. 3. New York: Yoseloff, 1956, 318–330.

_____. "From the Wilderness to Cold Harbor." In Robert U. Johnson and Clarence C. Buel, (eds.). *Battles and Leaders of the Civil War*. 4 Vols. New York: Yoseloff, 1956. IV, 118–144.

"Lawrence Aylett Daffan." *Confederate Veteran* 25, no. 4 (April 1907).

Le Duc, William G. "The Little Boat that Opened the Cracker Line." In Robert U. Johnson and Clarence C. Buel, (eds.). *Battles and Leaders of the Civil War*. Vol. 3. New York: Yoseloff, 1956, 676–678.

"Lee's Report of the Surrender at Appomattox." In Robert U. Johnson and Clarence C. Buel, eds *Battles and Leaders of the Civil War*. Vol. 4. New York: Yoseloff, 1956, 724.

Longstreet, James. "Our March Against Pope." In Robert U. Johnson and Clarence C. Buel, (eds.) *Battles and Leaders of the Civil War*. Vol. 2. New York: Yoseloff, 1956, 512–526.

_____. "The Battle of Fredericksburg." In Robert U. Johnson and Clarence C. Buel, (eds.). *Battles and Leaders of the Civil War*. Vol. 3. New York: Yoseloff, 1956, 70–85.

_____. "The Invasion of Maryland." In Robert U. Johnson and Clarence C. Buel, (eds.). *Battles and Leaders of the Civil War*. Vol. 2. New York: Yoseloff, 1956, 663–674.

_____. "Lee in Pennsylvania." In *Annals of the Civil War*. Edited by Alexander K. McClure. 1878. Reprint. New York: Da Capo Press, 1994, 414–446.

Marshall, Charles. "Occurrences at Lee's Surrender." *Confederate Veteran* 7, no. 2, (February 1894).

McKim, Randolph H. "Glimpses of the Confederate Army." *American Review of Reviews* 43 (April 1911): 431–437.

Member of the 4th Texas. "The Texans at Sharpsburg." *Confederate Veteran* 22, no. 12, (December 1915).

Minor, J. B. "Rallying with a Frying Pan." *Confederate Veteran* 13, no. 2 (1905) 72–73.

Mitchell, Mary Bedinger. "A Woman's Recollections of Antietam." In Robert U. Johnson and Clarence C. Buel, (eds.). *Battles and Leaders of the Civil War*. Vol. 2. New York: Yoseloff, 1956, 686–695.

"Monument to Hood's Texas Brigade." *Confederate Veteran* 27, no. 12 (December 1909): 582.

Oates, William C. "Grant Hurls His Men to Death at Cold Harbor." *Living History of the Civil War*. Edited by Henry Steele Commager and Eric Bruun. New York: Tess Press, 2000, 740–741.

Olmstead, Frederick L. "San Antonio Before the War." In *Texas: The Dark Corner of the Confederacy*. Edited by B. P. Gallaway. Lincoln: University of Nebraska Press, 1994.

"The Opposing Forces at Chickamauga, GA." In Robert U. Johnson and Clarence C. Buel, eds. *Battles and Leaders of the Civil War*. Vol. 3. New York: Yoseloff, 1956, 672–675.

"The Opposing Forces at Fredericksburg." In Robert U. Johnson and Clerence C. Buel, eds. *Battles and Leaders of the Civil War*. Vol. 3. New York: Yoseloff, 1956, 145–147.

"The Opposing Forces at Gettysburg." In Robert U. Johnson and Clarence C. Buel (eds.). *Battles and Leaders of the Civil War*. Vol. 3. New York: Yoseloff, 1956, 434–440.

"The Opposing Forces at Knoxville." In Robert U. Johnson and Clarence C. Buel (eds). *Battles and Leaders of the Civil War*. Vol. 3. New York: Yoseloff, 1956, 751–752.

"The Opposing Forces in the Maryland Campaign." In Robert U. Johnson and Clarence C. Buel, eds. *Battles and Leaders of the Civil War*. Vol. 2. New York: Yoseloff, 1956, 598–603.

"The Opposing Forces at the Second Bull Run." In Robert U. Johnson and Clarence C. Buel, eds. *Battles and Leaders of the Civil War*. Vol. 2. New York: Yoseloff, 1956, 497.

"The Opposing Forces in the Seven Day's Battles." In Robert U. Johnson and Clarence C. Buel, eds. *Battles and Leaders of the Civil War*. Vol. 2. New York: Yoseloff, 1956, 313–317.

Ould, Robert. "The Exchange of Prisoners." *Annals of the Civil War*. Alexander K. McClure, ed. 1878. Reprint. New York: Da Capo Press, 1994. 32–59.

Parrent, E. J. "General Lee to the Rear." *Confederate Veteran* 2, no. 1 (1894): 14–15.

Pickens, James D. "Fort Harrison." *Confederate Veteran* 21, no. 10 (1913): 484.

Poe, Orlando M. "The Defense of Knoxville." In Robert U. Johnson and Clarence C. Buel, eds. *Battles and Leaders of the Civil War*. Vol. 3. New York: Yoseloff, 1956, 731–745.

Polley, Joseph. "Brave Texans in the Virginia Army." *Confederate Veteran* 5, no. 5 (1896): 158–159.

_____."Hood's Texans in Pennsylvania." *Confederate Veteran* 4, no. 11 (1896): 377.

Pope, John. "The Second Battle of Bull Run." In Robert U. Johnson and Clarence C. Buel, (eds.). *Battles and Leaders of the Civil War*. Vol. 2. New York: Yoseloff, 1956, 449–494.

Porter, Fitz-John. "Hanover Court House and Gaines' Mill." In Robert U. Johnson and Clarence C. Buel, eds. *Battles and Leaders of the Civil War*. Vol. 2. New York: Yoseloff, 1956, 319–343.

Porter, Horace. "Five Forks and the Pursuit of Lee." In Robert U. Johnson and Clarence C. Buel, eds. *Battles and Leaders of the Civil War*. Vol. 4. New York: Yoseloff, 1956, 708–722.

Randolph, Mrs. Janet H. W. "James K. P. Harris of Fifth Texas Infantry." *Confederate Veteran* 13, no. 9 (September 1905).

"R. H. Skinner." *Confederate Veteran* 22, no. 1 (January 1914), 35.

Robertson, Jerome B. "Report of General J. B. Robertson." *Southern Historical Society Papers.* Vol. 13, 1907: 384–386.

"Sidney Virgil Patrick." *Confederate Veteran* 15, no. 7 (July 1907), 322.

Simpson, Harold B., ed. "'Whip the Devil and His Hosts:' The Civil War Letters of Eugene O. Perry of Hood's Brigade." In *Chronicles of Smith County* 6 (Fall 1967): 10–49.

Sims, Albert C. Jasper. "Recollections of the Civil War." In the Jasper, Texas, *Newsboy*, May 17, 1911. C.R.C., H.C., H.T.B. file 1–7b.

Sullivane, Clement. "Last Meeting with Gen. R. E. Lee." *Confederate Veteran* 28, no. 12 (December 1920): 459–460.

Todd, George. "Gaines' Mill — Pickett and Hood." *Confederate Veteran* 6, no. 12 (December 1898).

Weaver, Janet H. "James K. P. Harris, of Fifth Texas Infantry." *Confederate Veteran* 13, no. 9 (September 1905).

White, W. T. "First Texas Regiment at Gettysburg." *Confederate Veteran* 30, no. 9 (1922): 185, 197.

Wight, Willard E., ed. "Some Letters of Lucius Bellinger Northrup, 1860–1865." *Virginia Magazine of History and Biography* 68, no. 4 (October 1960): 456–477.

Work, P. A. "The 1st Texas Regiment of the Texas Brigade of the Army of Northern Virginia at the Battles of Boonesboro Pass or Gap and Sharpsburg, Maryland, in September, 1862." Hood's Texas Brigade Files, Confederate Research Center, Hill College, Hillsboro, TX.

OTHER

Chilton, Frank B. *Unveiling and Dedication of the Monument to Hood's Texas Brigade and Minutes of the Thirty-ninth Annual Reunion of Hood's Texas Brigade Association.* Houston: F.B. Chilton, 1911.

Secondary Sources

BOOKS

Bill, Alfred H. *The Beleaguered City: Richmond 1861–1865.* New York: Knopf, 1946.

Black, Robert C. *Railroads of the Confederacy.* Wilmington, NC: Broadfoot, 1987.

Boatner, Mark M. *The Civil War Dictionary.* New York: McKay, 1987.

Bowden, J. J. *Exodus of the Federal Forces in Texas.* Austin, TX: Eakin Press, 1986.

Clark, Champ. *Gettysburg: The Confederate High Tide.* Alexandria, VA: Time-Life Books, 1985.

Clark, Walter, ed. *Histories of the Several Regiments and Battalions from North Carolina in the Great War, 1861–1865.* 5 Vols. Raleigh, NC: N. p., 1901.

Coddington, Edwin B. *The Gettysburg Campaign: A Study in Command.* New York: Charles Scribner's Sons, 1968.

Collier, Calvin L. *"They'll Do to Tie To": The Story of the Third Regiment, Arkansas Infantry, C.S.A.* Little Rock: Pioneer Press, 1959.

Cunningham, H.H. *Doctors in Gray.* Gloucester, MA: Smith, 1970.

Crute, Joseph H., Jr. *Units of the Confederate States Army.* Gaithersburg, MD: Olde Soldiers Books, 1987.

Cutrer, Thomas W. *Ben McCulloch and the American Frontier Tradition.* Chapel Hill: University of North Carolina Press, 1993.

Dabney, Virginius. *Richmond: The Story of a City.* New York: Doubleday, 1976.

Davis, William C. *Jefferson Davis: The Man and His Hour.* New York: Harper Collins, 1991.

De Bruhl, Marshal. *Sword of San Jacinto: A Life of Sam Houston.* New York: Random House, 1993.

Dickert, Augustus. *History of Kershaw's Brigade.* 1899. Reprint. Dayton, OH: Morningside Press, 1976.

Dupuy, R. Ernest, and Trevor N. Dupuy. *The Harper Encyclopedia of Military History.* 4th ed. New York: Harper Collins, 1993.

Faust, Drew Gilpin. *This Republic of Suffering: Death and the American Civil War.* New York: Knopf, 2008.

Faulk, J. J. *History of Henderson County, Texas.* Athens, TX: n.p., 1929.

Fox, William F. *Regimental Losses in the American Civil War, 1861–1865.* Albany, NY: Randow, 1889.

Freeman, Douglas S. *Robert E. Lee: A Biography.* 4 Vols. New York: Charles Scribner's Sons, 1934–35.

_____. *Lee's Lieutenants: A Study in Command.* 3 Vols. New York: Charles Scribner's Sons, 1942–46.

Gallaway, B.P., ed. *Texas: The Dark Corner of the Confederacy.* Lincoln: University of Nebraska Press, 1994.

Goff, Richard D. *Confederate Supply.* Durham, NC: Duke University Press, 1969.

Griffith, Paddy. *Battle Tactics of the Civil War.* New Haven, CT: Yale University Press, 2001.

Hattaway, Herman. *General Stephen D. Lee.* Jackson: University of Mississippi Press, 1976.

Henderson, Harry McCorry. *Texas in the Confederacy.* San Antonio: Naylor, 1955.

Hood, R. Maurice, M.D., ed. *Early Texas Physicians, 1830–1915.* Austin: State House Press, 1999.

Horn, Stanley. *The Army of Tennessee.* Norman: University of Oklahoma Press, 1954.

Johnson, Curt, and Richard C. Anderson. *Artillery Hell: The Employment of Artillery at Antietam.* College Station: Texas A & M University Press, 1995.

Krick, Robert K. *Lee's Colonels: A Biographical Register of Field Officers in the Army of Northern Virginia.* Dayton, OH: Morningside Press, 1992.

Lewis, Lloyd, *Sherman: Fighting Prophet.* 1932. Reprint. New York: Konecky and Konecky, 1993.

Linderman, Gerald F. *Embattled Courage: The Experience of Combat in the American Civil War.* New York: The Free Press, 1987.

Lonn, Ella. *Desertion During the Civil War.* Gloucester, MA: Smith, 1966.

Martin, Samuel J. *The Road to Glory: Confederate General Richard S. Ewell.* Indianapolis: Guild Press of Indiana, 1991.

Marvel, William. *Burnside.* Chapel Hill: University of North Carolina Press, 1991.

McDonald, Archie P., ed. *Make Me a Map of the Valley.* Dallas: Southern Methodist University Press, 1973.

McWhiney, Grady, and Judith L. Hallock. *Braxton Bragg and Confederate Defeat.* 2 Vols. Tuscaloosa: University of Alabama Press, 1991.

Naisawald, L. Van Loan. *Grape and Canister: The Story of the Field Artillery of the Army of the Potomac, 1861–1865.* Undated. Reprint. Oxford: Oxford University Press, 1960.

Nunn, W.C., ed. *Ten Texans in Gray.* Hillsboro, TX: Hill Junior College Press, 1968.

Patterson, Gerard A. *Rebels from West Point.* New York: Doubleday, 1987.

Pfanz, Harry W. *Gettysburg: The Second Day.* Chapel Hill and London: University of North Carolina Press, 1987.

Phisterer, Frederick. *New York in the War of the Rebellion.* Albany: Weed, Parsons, 1890.

_____. *Statistical Record of the Armies of the United States Campaigns of the Civil War.* 1881–1883. Reprint. Harrisburg, PA: The Archive Society, 1992.

Piston, William G. *Lee's Tarnished Lieutenant.* Athens: University of Georgia Press, 1987.

Radley, Kenneth. *Rebel Watchdog: The Confederate States Army Provost Guard.* Baton Rouge: Louisiana State University Press, 1989.

Robertson, James I., Jr. *General A. P. Hill: The Story of a Confederate Warrior.* New York: Random House, 1987.

_____. *Soldiers Blue and Gray.* Columbia: University of South Carolina Press, 1988.

Sears, Stephen W. *George B. McClellan: The Young Napoleon.* New York: Ticknor and Fields, 1988.

Simpson, Harold B. *Gaines' Mill to Appomattox.* Waco, TX: Texian Press, 1988.

_____. *Hood's Texas Brigade: A Compendium.* 1977. Reprint. Fort Worth, TX: Landmark, 1999.

_____. *Hood's Texas Brigade: Lee's Grenadier Guard.* Waco, Texas: Texian Press,1970.

_____. *Hood's Texas Brigade in Reunion and Memory.* Hillsboro, TX: Hill Junior College Press, 1974.

_____. *Touched with Valor: Civil War Papers and Casualty Reports of Hood's Texas Brigade.* Hillsboro, TX: Hill Junior College Press, 1964.

Speer, Lonnie. *Portals to Hell: Military Prisons of the Civil War.* Mechanicsville, PA: Stackpole Books, 1997.

Spencer, John W. *From Corsicana to Appomattox.* Corsicana, TX: The Texas Press, 1984.

Stackpole, Edward J. *From Cedar Mountain to Antietam.* Harrisburg, PA: Stackpole Books, 1993.

Thomas, Henry W. *History of the Doles Cooke Brigade.* Atlanta: N.p., 1903.

Thomason, John W. *Jeb Stuart.* 1930. Reprint. New York: Smithmark, 1994.

_____. *Lone Star Preacher.* 1941. Reprint. Fort Worth: Texas Christian University Press, 1992.

Tucker, Glenn. *Chickamauga: Bloody Battle in the West.* Indianapolis: Bobbs-Merrill, 1961.

Vandiver, Frank E. *Rebel Brass: The Confederate Command System.* Baton Rouge: Louisiana State University Press, 1959.

Warner, Ezra J. *Generals in Gray.* Baton Rouge: Louisiana State University Press, 1959.

_____. *Generals in Blue.* Baton Rouge: Louisiana State University Press, 1964.

Wiley, Bell I. *The Life of Johnny Reb.* New York: Bobbs-Merrill, 1943.

Wise, Jennings Cropper. *The Long Arm of Lee.* 2 Vols. 1915. Reprint. Lincoln: University of Nebraska Press, 1991.

Wooster, Ralph A., ed. *Lone Star Blue and Gray: Essays on Texas in the Civil War.* Austin: Texas State Historical Association, 1995.

ARTICLES

Adams, George W. "Confederate Medicine." *Journal of Southern History* 6, no. 2 (May 1940): 151–166.
Brown, Russell K. "An Old Woman with a Broomstick." *Military Affairs* (April 1984): 58–59.
Catton, Bruce. "Hayfoot, Strawfoot." *American Heritage* 8 (April 1957): 31–32.
_____. "Prison Camps of the Civil War." *American Heritage* 10, no. 5 (August 1959): 4–9, 96–97.
Donald, David. "The Confederate as a Fighting Man." *Journal of Southern History* 25, no. 2 (May 1959).
Fuer, A.B. "John McGrady and the Confederate Prisoners at Camp Morton." *Civil War Quarterly*, September 1987.
Greely, A. W. "The Signal Corps in the Civil War." *Review of Reviews* (July 1911): 55–63.
Hall, Clark B. "The Army Is Moving: Lee's March to the Potomac, 1863." *Blue and Gray* Magazine 21, no. 3 (Spring 2004): 6–20;-52
Hay, Thomas R. "Lucius B. Northrop: Commissary General of the Confederacy." *Civil War History* 9, no. 1 (March 1963): 5–23.
Heidler, Jean T. "Embarrassing Situation: David E. Twiggs and the Surrender of United States Forces in Texas in 1861." In *Lone Star Blue and Gray: Essays on Texas in the Civil War*. Edited by Ralph A. Wooster. Austin: Texas State Historical Association, 1995.
Iekel, John. "Civil War Weather in Virginia." *Weatherwise* 42, no. 5 (October 1989): 268–273.
Mallett, J. W. "Work of the Ordnance Bureau," *Southern Historical Society Papers* 37 (January–December 1909): 1–20
Morris, Roy, Jr. "Ambrose Bierce's Civil War." *Military History Quarterly* 17 (Winter 2005): 16–25.
Oldham, W. S. "Colonel John Marshall." *Southwestern Historical Quarterly* 20 (October 1916): 132–138.
Ottot, George. "The 1st Texas Volunteer Infantry in the Maryland Campaign." *Civil War Regiments* 5, no. 3 (1997).
Patterson, Gerard A. "Rebels from West Point." *American History Illustrated* 20 (April 1985).
Pohanka, Brian C. "The Very Vortex of Hell." *America's Civil War*, September 2002: 46–53, 72.
Sandbo, Anna I. "The First Session of the Secession Convention in Texas." In Eugene C. Barker, ed. *History of Texas*. Dallas: Southwest Press, 1929.
Simpson, Harold B. "The Recruiting, Training, and Camp Life of a Company of Hood's Brigade in Texas, 1861." *Texas Military History* 2 (August 1962): 186.
"Surrender of United States Property by General Twiggs." *Harper's Weekly*, March 9, 1861.
Tunis, Edwin. "Weapons of the Civil War." *Popular Science* 178, no. 5 (May 1961).
_____. " Weapons of the Civil War." *Popular Science* 178, no. 6 (June 1961).
Williams, Edward B. "Reinforcements by Rail to Chickamauga." *America's Civil War*, January 1996: 46–53.
Williams, Roy. "Many Doctors Were Not School Trained." In "Medicine and Surgery in the Civil War." *Science Digest*, October 1961: 26–33.
Wooster, Ralph A., and Robert Wooster. "Rarin' for a Fight: Texans in the Confederate Army." *Southwestern Historical Quarterly* 84 (April 1981): 387–426.
Wootan, Dudley G. "The Texas Ordinance of Secession." In B. P. Gallaway, ed. *Texas: The Dark Corner of the Confederacy*. Lincoln: University of Nebraska Press, 1994.

OTHER

Howerton, Bryan. "A Study of the 3rd Arkansas." Typescript. In Hood's Texas Brigade Files, Confederate Research Center, Hill College, Hillsboro, TX.
O'Neill, J. J. "Membership Record of Miss Leni L. O'Neill being a Brief History of the Career of Her Father, J. J. O'Neill, 18th Georgia Infantry, Co. A. Hood's Texas Brigade Files, Confederate Research Center, Hill College, Hillsboro, TX.
Ragan, Cooper K. "Tyler County Goes to War: Company F, First Texas Regiment, C.S.A. *Tyler County Dogwood Festival*. Woodville, Texas, Saturday, March 26, 1961, mimeographed.
Simpson, Harold B. "Hood's Texas Brigade: A Biographical Sketch." Address delivered before the Sesquicentennial Civil War Symposium on Hood's Texas Brigade, Fort Worth, Texas, May 31, 1986.
"The Navarro Rifles." *Navarro County Scroll*. Corsicana, TX: Navarro County Historical Society, 1965. In Hood's Texas Brigade Files, Confederate Research Center, Hill College, Hillsboro, TX.
Wilkerson, John A. "An Arkansan at Gettysburg": The Experience on the Battlefield of John A. Wilkerson, of Alexander, Pulaski County, Arkansas." Typescript. Arkansas History Commission.

Index